A Study of Modern Confucian Philosophy

www.royalcollins.com

A Study of Modern Confucian Philosophy

CHEN LAI

Books Beyond Boundaries

ROYAL COLLINS

A Study of Modern Confucian Philosophy

By Chen Lai

First published in 2024 by Royal Collins Publishing Group Inc.
Groupe Publication Royal Collins Inc.
550-555 boul. René-Lévesque O Montréal (Québec) H2Z1B1 Canada

10 9 8 7 6 5 4 3 2 1

ISBN: 978-1-4878-1202-7

To find out more about our publications, please visit www.royalcollins.com.

Contents

Chapter 1 The Concept of Philosophy in Modern Neo-Confucianism / 1

Chapter 2 Xiong Shili's *A Treatise on Substance and Function* and Its Cosmology / 17

Chapter 3 Xiong Shili's Theory of *Mingxin* in "The *Mingxin* Section" / 35

Chapter 4 The Theory of Principles, Vital Energy, Substance, and Function in Ma Yifu's Philosophy / 57

Chapter 5 The Theory of Mind and Matter in Ma Yifu's Philosophy / 73

Chapter 6 Liang Shuming's Cultural Pluralism and *Eastern and Western Cultures and Their Philosophies* / 97

Chapter 7 Liang Shuming's Discourse on Chinese Culture / 127

Chapter 8 Liang Shuming's *Human Nature and Human Life*: An Exploration of the Theory of the Human Nature / 151

Chapter 9 Liang Shuming's Views on Confucian Ethics / 177

Chapter 10 Self-Cultivation and Progress in Liang Shuming's Thought / 197

Chapter 11 Liang Shuming and Esoteric Buddhism / 217

Chapter 12 Metaphysics in Feng Youlan's *New Neo-Confucianism* / 249

Chapter 13 Feng Youlan's Cultural Views in *A New Treatise on Practical Affairs* / 261

Chapter 14 Feng Youlan's Philosophy of Life in *A New Treatise on the Way of Life* / 289

Chapter 15 Mysticism in the Philosophy of Feng Youlan / 309

Chapter 16 Feng Youlan on Emotion and Non-emotion in Chinese Philosophy / 325

Chapter 17 Feng Youlan's Ethics of Realm in *New Origins of Humanity* / 341

Afterword to the *Collected Works of Chen Lai* in the *Boya Yinghua* Series / 385

CHAPTER 1

The Concept of Philosophy in Modern Neo-Confucianism

The "modern Neo-Confucianism" discussed in this chapter refers to the first generation of Neo-Confucianism that emerged after the May 4th Movement, which is different from what is known as "contemporary Neo-Confucianism." This chapter focuses on the work of Xiong Shili (1885–1968) and compares the concepts of Confucianism and philosophy he developed alongside Liang Shuming (1893–1988) and Ma Yifu (1883–1967), with the aim of reviewing some basic issues that arose in the construction of Chinese philosophy in the 20th century.

I

In 20th-century Chinese culture, one of the key ways the inheritance and development of classical Chinese philosophy came about was through the work of philosophical reconstruction, which involved comparing and absorbing the theories, concepts, and methods of Western philosophy. Through its reconstruction, Chinese philosophy became a philosophical system that bore the marks of modernity, while also retaining the ontology and cosmology of the Chinese philosophical tradition, allowing it to occupy a place in the ranks of world philosophy. In this respect, compared with scholars who aspired to promote other ancient schools of thought, the achievements of modern Neo-Confucianism can be described as outstanding. But of course, every neo-Confucian thinker had a different understanding of Confucian thought (or Confucianism), which determined the different directions they took, which in turn meant that the systems they constructed were also different. In terms of its inheritance and development of Chinese philosophy, Xiong Shili's philosophical theory—substance and function—was recognized by his contemporaries as the most distinctive, most successful system.

The most prominent feature of Xiong's philosophy was his onto-cosmology.[1] However, Xiong's "philosophical" activities were not without their critics. The most severe criticism came from Liang Shuming, another prominent figure in modern Neo-Confucianism and the one who had the closest relationship with Xiong. Liang's criticism focused on the idea of philosophy in Xiong's work. From his criticisms, the differences between the various concepts of philosophy within modern Neo-Confucianism are evident.

In 1950, Xiong Shili wrote to Liang Shuming:

> The meaning of "philosophy" is not merely "the love of wisdom," and there are many schools of philosophy. The definitions offered by academics are precisely what you don't want. Philosophy cannot leave out rational thinking or debate; in fact, it should not be limited to the realm of rational thinking and debate. Discussion of this issue is very complicated. Though Chinese learning has a long history, Confucianism, Daoism, and other survivors cannot be said to be non-philosophical, because their thought is not religion or art, but is reasoning. However, their attainments are not limited to rational thinking and deliberation, which are the hallmarks of philosophical authenticity. If you write off Chinese philosophy and all things Chinese, isn't that like destroying yourself? Why resort to such self-abuse?[2]

Western philosophy believes that philosophy is merely the study of wisdom, which is also how Liang Shuming regarded it. In contrast, Xiong Shili believes that philosophy has many forms and is not limited to the study of wisdom. The love of wisdom embodies the intellectual speculative aspect of philosophy, but philosophy is not limited to the intellectual speculative aspect. It is evident from the outset that Xiong Shili does not understand the concept of philosophy from the perspective of the Western philosophical tradition, but from that of the world's diverse philosophical traditions. In his view, Confucianism, Daoism, and other schools of thought in Chinese philosophical tradition are characterized not only by rational speculation, but also by aspects beyond it. Xiong does not explain what he means by what is beyond rational speculation, but it appears to refer to internal physical evidence. He holds that only the sort of philosophy that is rational but not limited to rational speculation should be regarded as authentic philosophy. Rational speculation alone, or inner experience alone, is an incomplete form of philosophy. It is Xiong's view that philosophy should not be understood as a theoretical activity in the sense of the Greek pursuit of wisdom, but that it should also include other intellectual activities besides rational speculation, indicating that he does not blindly accept a Eurocentric philosophy, but instead views philosophy from a universalist standpoint.

In 1951, in another letter to Liang Shuming, he wrote:

> You called Chinese academics non-philosophical, or what we might as well call dogma, ideology, and art. I cannot agree with this. Philosophy refers to the well-founded, systematic thought that is neither utopian nor fantasy, which is why it can be said to

> be well-founded, and seeking truth from facts, analyzing thoroughly, and rehashing all kinds of questions from an initial question—there are many sorts of issues, and to find a way to understand them, we must go back to the source—which is why it can be said to be systematic. Grand, precise thinking is like this is what is called philosophy [...] Ideologues thoroughly integrate their entire thought system, or they religiously follow their own thinking, and in order to make it clear to others, they make a doctrine of it. Who can discuss ideology without achieving scholarship? Art ultimately resides in the realm of sentiment, not merely attained through the depth of interpretative ability (the ability to explain is called wisdom, and the content being explained is called principle).[3]

Of course, saying that Chinese scholarship is not philosophical is not the same as saying it has no philosophy. Looking at Liang Shuming's meaning, it seems he holds that Chinese Confucianism and Daoism were not philosophical. Xiong Shili holds a different view. His belief that Chinese Confucianism and Daoism are philosophies is not merely the result of some sense of nationalism or loyalty to his culture, but a natural outgrowth of his understanding of philosophy. In the passage above, Xiong outlines his definition of philosophy, saying it is well-founded, systematic thinking characterized by grandeur and precision, and it is capable of reaching rationality from the intellect. Based on this view, he expressly disagrees with Liang Shuming's opposition to the application of philosophical methods to Chinese scholarship.

This sort of discussion does not arise out of thin air, but is instead Xiong's defense of his own theoretical approach. A few years later, he again discussed the topic with Liang Shuming, saying:

> I like to use old Western philosophy's cosmology, ontology, and other theories to show that the ancients in the East are especially useful for physical and mental life. If you say that you do not agree, you are not the only one. Ouyang Jingwu and Ma Yifu have always likewise disagreed. I am fond of using it, and yet none of you understand my deepest thoughts behind it.
>
> In the extant books of ancient philosophy, there is no real cosmological theory... My book aims at establishing a cosmology in a philosophical way. Once it is established, it is easy to talk about the practical skills of physical and mental life. I suspect you think this unnecessary, as Ma Yifu has thought from the beginning, but he does not object to me taking this approach. You have a good deal of the aliment of subjectivity, and you don't observe everything. I have always felt that the influential schools of Chinese thought do not recognize the great learning of Chinese scholarship. They disdain terms such as body, mind, and life, and they cannot be coaxed to work on such topics. This is my own intention, so I concentrate on diving in, and I aim to establish a theory.[4]

Xiong Shili acknowledges directly that he likes talking about ontology and cosmology. Still, according to the statement above, the focus of his thinking, like Liang and Ma, is physical and mental life, implying that cosmology is not his primary concern. For him, on the one hand, cosmology offers a way to explain his theory of physical and mental life, while on the other, it is only a logical, theoretical premise of the theory of physical and mental life. In terms of motivation, the reason he constructed a systematic cosmology, put negatively, was so that it could be recognized by philosophical circles in Chinese schools. Put more positively, it aims to guide philosophers in Chinese schools to work on the theory of physical and mental life. In fact, though there is some tension between Chinese philosophers outside the modern university, such as Xiong Shili and Liang Shuming (although both taught at Peking University in the early days), and the university professors trained in Western philosophy, this new consciousness-only philosophy cannot be written with the university professors in mind as the main object of debate. In this respect, then, rather than offering guidance for philosophy professors in the university context, Xiong's appreciation of Western philosophy's ontology leads him to the conscious response of establishing a type of ontological philosophy for Confucianism that can be recognized by Western philosophy without departing from its Confucian roots.[5] Thus, this philosophy does not aim to induce academic philosophers, but to respond to Western philosophy. Such a modern reconstruction of "continued dialogue" not only reveals the ontological dimension of Confucianism, but also persuades philosophers influenced by Eurocentric thought to recognize Confucianism as a philosophy.

He noted in the same letter:

> As a result, I elaborated on the unity of substance and function, confident that I could forever avoid confusion. Unfortunately, I was unable to use scientific materials, but as I started, I hoped there would be others who would later continue to pursue the concept of form and function, as it is only when this concept is established that we can discuss physical and mental life... There are distinctions to be made by reason and good sense, and I believe ontology and cosmology are good distinctions to make. But in Western rhetorical discourse, there is often a division between human life and the universe, which is not right. Bergson talked about life without making such divisions, but unfortunately, he did not reach real life. The meaning of the universe in the *Book of Changes* is indeed the integration of the universe and life. I use these ideas to discuss cosmology.[6]

Xiong Shili believes that only when ontology and cosmology are established is it possible to discuss physical and mental life, but he does not explain why it is necessary to discuss cosmology before discussing a theory of life. Though ancient Chinese philosophers argue from cause to effect, considering the psychological characteristics of Xiong's thought, he seems to be influenced by Western philosophical thought at this point, believing that cosmology is a prerequisite for a theory of life. In his view, philosophy as a system of thought has different parts, and the way these parts are divided does not need to adhere to ancient Chinese methods of classification. He believes that Western philosophy does well to distinguish between ontology and cosmology, and this distinction should be adopted and absorbed. At the same time, he also points out that Western philosophy quite prominently distinguishes ontology and cosmology from other parts of philosophy, expounding and developing them vigorously, which is a positive move. However, this means it also separates ontology and cosmology from a theory of life. Xiong holds that it is undesirable to separate human life from the existence of all things. In his philosophy, he speaks of the mutual development of cosmology, with *yang* governing *yin*, while in his theory of human life, he speaks of the mind governing things. This is the sense in which he seeks to bridge the two disciplines, integrating cosmology and a theory of human life. Cosmology explains the theory of life as "integrating the universe and human life, which is unlike what Western scholars mean."[7] Thus, he believes that while there is nothing wrong with the discussion of cosmology, it is a mistake to sever cosmology from human life, as if they have nothing to do with one another.

In a letter to Lin Zaiping (1878–1961) on the same day, he said, "Ancient Eastern scholarship has no roots, but it has heart. Like scientific philosophy, the origin of the mind and the material is the object. Ancient learning cuts off the roots, making wisdom and morals the source. Such self-cultivation is meritorious, and it cannot be shaken ... My current draft only focuses on the word 'intentional.'"[8] The draft he mentions here is "The *Mingxin* Section." (Explaining the Mind). The term "intentional" is a reference to his response to Liang Shuming, written the same day, which says, "In the four studies in Yan Yuan's teaching, I emphasize the first, which I believe to be the heart, on which all the others depend for their own existence. All ancient scholarship collapses without it."[9] It is evident that, while he works hard to establish an ontology and cosmology, Xiong also emphasizes that the theory of the mind is the root and foundation of all Eastern scholarship.

II

While this view acknowledges the positive significance of philosophy, Xiong Shili's view seems to be expressed in a traditional way, holding that cosmology comes first in the order of establishing theory, while the study of human life ranks first in significance. In the theory of the relationship between nature and humans, the universe and human life must be unified throughout. This view is consistently espoused by Xiong.

According to Xiong's thinking, the primary importance of the theory of human life does not only mean that within a theoretical philosophical system, the theory about physical and mental life is more important than the cosmological theory, but also that the practice of physical and mental life is the basis by which one comes to the truth.[10] The first part of *Essential Sayings of Xiong Shili* and a letter to Zhang Jitong both record, "Eastern scholarship returns to origins, and Mencius' phrase 'practical form and perfect nature' are the ultimate rule."[11] Another letter states, "The sages of this land are impoverished in cosmology and theories of human life. It must be entered between the practice of the body and mind, but it disdains to become a theory. Although knowledge has not been abandoned, it is required to return to the extreme, to experience truth, and to be one with it."[12] In other words, the purpose of Chinese philosophy is to experience the truth and to be united with it in spirit and life. Thus, the importance of the theory of life is not only the goal, but also the method.

In Xiong Shili's view, reflexive practice is the key to studying the reality of human life and the universe, precisely because the essence of the universe is the essence of human life. This is why he says, "Although cosmology, the theory of human life, and epistemology are distinct from one another in Western philosophy, it seems they are too tightly bound in Chinese philosophy. The essence of my mind is the noumenon of the universe, and human lives and the universe are analyzed as two pieces in the pursuit of knowledge. The ultimate goal is to reverse the pursuit of assumed knowledge. This is different from Western epistemology."[13] On the one hand, he points out that Western epistemology excels in the development of science, while on the other, he emphasizes that Chinese philosophy's focus on knowledge is beneficial for the sake of more thoroughly understanding the universe and human life and for the personal witness of the essence of a thing. It is evident that Xiong's philosophical view predetermines his philosophical prepositions, which is to say that he holds that the essence of the universe is the essence of the individual's mind, which means that self-knowledge is proof of the thing-in-itself.

On numerous occasions, Xiong discusses the issues of Chinese and Western philosophies and cultures with Zhang Dongsun (1886–1973). He notes, "This belief [of mine] is based on the philosophy of the East, though contemporary scholars may not see it this way. However, my philosophy has only ontology as its duty. Aside from this, its internal matters are mostly theoretical sciences. The current analytical school is only a kind of knowledge based on logic, which is definitely required by scholars, but it is not true philosophy. The contemporary scholars despised ontology, and I thought it goes to the very core of things, and hence the origin of learning… Seeing the essence is part of the study of Eastern learning."[14] This indicates that Xiong understood the anti-metaphysical, anti-ontological trends of world philosophy at the beginning of the 20th century, but he insisted that philosophy should be based on ontology, focused on theory, and investigating the foundation of the universe. He determined that China's Eastern philosophy was the most capable of seeing the essence (seeing the root of the thing-in-itself), so Eastern learning was not only undoubtedly philosophy, but also authentic philosophy; that is to say, it represented the correct direction in philosophy. He went on to say:

> Yesterday, Lin Zaiping said that the term "philosophy" used by Westerners originally referred to knowledge, while I took Chinese learning as philosophy and advocated consistency between knowledge and cultivation, which is avoided by Western philosophy, so it might be advisable not to use the term philosophy… I firmly advocate dividing the fields of science and philosophy. Science assumes that the outside world exists alone, so reason lies in the external object, and thorough reasoning must use purely objective methods, so it is a learning rooted in knowledge. Philosophy unifies the universe, human life, truth, and knowledge; there is no inside or outside of its essence. Therefore, the way is in self-cultivation, a knowledge that grows out of actual practice. In this sense, there is no need to establish a category of the non-philosophical and non-religious outside of philosophy… I think that the realm of philosophy is delineated; that

> is, ontology is its domain. However, Chinese and Western philosophy have different methods and techniques for studying ontology in different contexts. Because of their different achievements, these phenomena are consistent, and they will not be hindered from reaching their goal simply because they approach it via different paths.[15]

According to Lin Zaiping, Western philosophy, including metaphysics, concerns itself with the realm of knowledge, having nothing to do with the physical and mental cultivation of people, while Chinese scholarship emphasizes such cultivation and advocates consistency between the mind and cultivation. From the perspective of Western philosophy, Chinese scholarship is not easily recognized as philosophy at all, so it is not necessary to use the term "philosophy" to refer to Chinese or Eastern thought. Zhang Dongsun argues that in addition to religion and philosophy, there is a non-philosophical, non-religious scholarship with the nature of philosophy and religion, and Chinese scholarship seems to be worthy of such a label. Xiong Shili holds a different view. He believes that there are only two types of scholarship, science and philosophy, and there is no need to establish a non-philosophical, non-religious category outside of philosophy. In the face of the Western philosophical trend of turning toward epistemology, Xiong insists that philosophy should be based on ontology. He points out that Western philosophy seeks ontology through knowledge, while Chinese scholarship seeks ontology through self-cultivation. He thus holds that both Western and Chinese thought can be generally referred to as philosophy. Obviously, he does not understand "philosophy" to be based on the traditions of Western philosophy. Rather, he regards Western and Chinese thought as different paths, and "philosophy" is the general term that refers to both Western and Chinese thought.

In his response to a long note from the Italian thinker Magrini, Xiong wrote:

> Truth is nothing but the reason why we live and why the universe was formed. Thus, as far as truth is concerned, our life, nature, and even the entire universe, are mutually integrated and cannot be separated for the same reasons as the manifestation of this truth... It is the job of the philosopher to explore the origin of all things, to understand the principles and their extremes, but it must be between the practice of the body and mind and in the secret examination of solitary, hidden spaces... It should be noted that philosophical research is governed by truth, and truth must be practiced before it becomes apparent. Truth cannot be regarded as something outside the mind but depends on our knowledge and understanding. That is to say, we must cultivate the inner self until it becomes clear, by which I mean until the truth is revealed. In this way alone, it is possible to see that there are not two truths in a clear consciousness. This is the only thing that Chinese philosophy demonstrates.[16]

For this reason, Xiong emphasizes, "Philosophy is the study of the fundamental principles of all things, in other words, the reason we live and why the universe was formed. The reason we exist and the reason the universe was formed are not two separate things, so this reason is not objective and not external. Only when the work of inner cultivation is deep and pure can this theory be revealed and reach a state of self-understanding and self-evidence. This is what is known as the knowledge of the body. Thus, philosophy is not a study of knowledge, but a study of self-awareness."[17] These statements indicate that Xiong regards self-cultivation as philosophy, but not out of an emphasis on overall spiritual development. The underlying reason is his belief that only cultivation can provide positive evidence for ontology. In this sense, cultivation is not a moral practice unrelated to ontology but an important aspect of it.

Of course, what is involved here is not only Xiong's understanding of philosophical concepts, but also his own philosophical inclinations. Though he believes that there are both Eastern and Western philosophies, he also believes they have different characteristics, and he holds that Eastern philosophy is more authentic. From the standpoint of its equal emphasis on knowledge and accomplishment, he believes that "the spirit of exploring ontology seen in Western scholars is admirable, but their ontology is probably lacking in its ability to contribute to the genuine improvement of the mind."[18] He also notes, "In recent years in the West, those who talk about ontology are all theoretical, thinking about structure, but they always look outward, so they are like blind men touching an elephant. *A New Treatise on Consciousness-Only* looks at the West without repeating its mistakes, beginning with discernment and ending with self-reflection."[19] In short, in establishing his cosmology and ontology, he emphasizes that one's personal life is cosmic life, and only through inner cultivation can the truth be revealed in the mind. Philosophy, then, is not a pure knowledge, but it is a clear knowledge.

III

Liang Shuming and Xiong Shili hold different views on the question of philosophy. In the *Complete Works of Liang Shuming*, there is a "Letter to Mr. XX," which reads:

> Philosophy is a Western construct, and speculations about the fundamental questions in the universe are all based on the work of a sort of the sixth consciousness. It is inevitable that saints and Buddhas will fall into this path. However, the ancient Buddhas advocated personal experience apart from words, so the matter of turning knowledge into wisdom or seeing according to the sixth consciousness is nothing more than a spectacle. There is a huge gap between the two. How can there be a comparison? In your letter, you mentioned the comparisons, and I think it is a mistake.[20]

According to this view, philosophy is just a theory, simply "insight," not "wisdom." True wisdom is "personal experience apart from words," a theory that appeals to personal experience and leaves behind the renowned sayings of past ages. Liang suggests that it is fundamentally wrong to compare Eastern wisdom with philosophy.

In commenting on the strengths and weaknesses of Xiong Shili's writings, the fifth part of Liang Shuming's "Notes on Reading Xiong's Works" in *Records of the Readings at Mianren Residence* notes that Confucianism cannot be equated with philosophy. He writes:

> As for Confucianism, the study of mind, body, and life cannot be equated with what people today call "philosophy," which Mr. Xiong is not aware of, but he has gone along with the common practice of calling it philosophy. Intentionally or unintentionally, this has blurred the characteristics of Confucianism, and it falls short of the original Confucian task. He does not clarify the scholarly connotation from the root, thoroughly correcting the superficial deficiencies embraced by Western academic culture since ancient times. Though he has pointed out the proper place of the learning of the ancient peoples of the East in the academic world, he occasionally emphasizes that "philosophy should be studying this or that," which is sorely inadequate... He has followed the common practice of attributing Confucianism to what is called Western philosophy, by which it loses its own position. Yet, he insists that philosophers give up their general studies and put effort into self-cultivation. Why is this so?[21]

In Liang Shuming's view, the basic feature of Confucianism is the study of mental and physical life. Confucianism cannot be categorized as a philosophy. If it is classed as a philosophy, then its characteristics will be blurred. He believes that Xiong Shili understands this principle, but Xiong's strategy is to call both Western philosophy and Eastern scholarship philosophy, treating them as different concrete manifestations of philosophy and thus proposing that philosophy should be based on Eastern thought as the more authentic form, placing equal emphasis on knowledge and achievement. Liang Shuming believes that this approach is completely inadequate. He believes that, on the one hand, people view Confucianism as a general philosophy and fail to understand the fundamental characteristics of Confucianism as the study of mental and physical life. In his view, it is also unrealistic and inappropriate for those who argue for reason to turn to the study of mind and body. Liang sums up Xiong's strategy as "mixing first, then dragging over," by which he means mixing Confucianism into philosophy and then drawing ordinary philosophers to the study of mind and body. It is evident that Liang's view of "philosophy" limited it completely to Western intellectual traditions. With this understanding, he invited Xiong to tidy up the academic classification to adapt to the Western academic climate. This seems to be an error and a contradiction.

From here, Liang offers several criticisms of Xiong's learning. He especially criticizes Xiong's "trick of fetishizing philosophy." He said:

> Mr. Xiong certainly emphasizes that it has a supra-intellectual, non-theoretical aspect, and he strongly denounces the errors of knowledge and opinion, imagining and constructing, and seeking everything from the outside, which represents Eastern theory. But at the same time, he affirms that it is based on thinking. He says that it is extremely valuable

> to pursue metaphysical thought, by which he intends to absorb the entire length of Western philosophy in order to establish his ontology, cosmology, and so forth, claiming that "internal evidence is free from words" and that "the body's divine unpredictability between human nature and daily use" is the aim of philosophy. In fact, he is not engaged in the practice of self-cultivation at all, being fond only of intellectual trickery.
>
> Philosophy—the study of the love of wisdom—was originally advanced by the ancient Greeks and later developed by Westerners. The ancient people of the East were different in that they did not have a single fully-fledged field of study to pursue. If they had a philosophy, it was only an unintentional byproduct of the religious life in India and of the moral life in China, nothing more.[22]

This suggests that, while Liang Shuming affirms Xiong Shili's Eastern theory of mind and body, he is also dissatisfied with and objects to the speculation and metaphysics, absorption of the strengths of Western philosophy, and the need to establish an ontology and cosmology. In his view, within Confucian thought, speculation and metaphysics are merely the byproduct of its moral life. Compared with Xiong's stance that equal attention should be paid to knowledge and cultivation while striving to absorb Western philosophy, Liang is obviously more conservative and has a certain anti-intellectual tendency.

Therefore, in the seventh part of his article, which Liang titled "The Serious Failure of His Ontology and Cosmology," he accused Xiong Shili of being "low on religion but high on philosophy. His so-called philosophy is particularly concerned with ontology. His book often says this clearly, but he does not realize that ontology is dead, unless he combines it with religion."[23] Without going into great detail about the differences between the two men's views in regard to religion, Liang is completely opposed to Xiong's ontology and cosmology. In his view, Xiong's construction of a cosmology and ontology is not only unnecessary but also a "serious failure." Digging deeper into his meaning, Xiong's ontology seems to deviate from the ancient philosophy of "personal experience apart from words" in the interpretation of these theories. In fact, in a work from his later years, *Human Mind and Life,* Liang himself not only discusses the psychological history of science, but also explains that individual life is the ontology and cosmology of cosmic life, which indicates that he is unable to hold onto the goal of "personal experience apart from words."

Liang also points out, "Ontology is prevalent among Western thinkers who have always had a strong desire for knowledge. This is a further step toward seeking knowledge of everything. This is a further conception of the matter and the pursuit of knowledge, and it is inherently linked with the ontology of all things, without realizing that seeking knowledge from the outside is to be already trapped between what can be treated, which has long been irrelevant to ontology."[24] Similar to the views of Lin Zaiping, Zhang Dongsun, Ouyang Jingwu (1871–1943), and others,[25] Liang Shuming believes that ontology originated from the desire for knowledge, and Westerners had a strong desire for knowledge and a demand for specific things. The ontological vision arose from the demand to seek an ontology of all things, in addition to a knowledge of concrete things. He believes that this search for ontology from the perspective of knowledge is wrong, because ontology is not an external object to be treated by the mind. This obviously means that while ontology exists, it is not a thing that can be sought by this epistemological approach. The ontology of the mind and body cannot be handled by the mind and body, and the ontology of the original mind is no different. In fact, these statements are all consistent with Xiong's Shili's view. According to these statements, the logical conclusion should be a change in the epistemological method of the Western pursuit of ontology and the establishment of a way that would be close to ontology, not an elimination of it.

Liang Shuming believes that Confucianism is "simply the practice of the form and the nature," and ancient Eastern learning "returned to one's own life, and its work is to deepen the mind."[26] He believes that Confucius and Confucianism are not interested in the study of knowledge nor philosophical mysteries, but in "the study of the practice of life."[27] His statement is obviously not a complete view of Confucianism. Although "the study of physical and mental life" is certainly a very visible part of Confucian thought, in this statement, it is not only the political, social, ethical, intellectual, and transcendental aspects of Confucianism that are obscured, but the development of the ontology and cosmology of Confucianism is in fact so obscured that the difference between Confucianism, Buddhism, and celestialism cannot even be discerned. The only thing that stands out is the "physical and mental life." This emphasis on understanding Confucianism as a religion of the mind is not compatible with Liang Shuming's own neo-Confucian rural reconstruction and local governance, which focused on social transformation.

IV

As Xiong Shili notes, Ma Yifu disagreed with his efforts to establish an ontological cosmology. "Learning" is the most important feature in Ma's works. In his reply to Yang Shoujing (1839–1915), he writes, "If a man learns to achieve virtue, but the virtue is not achieved, where did the learning go? You believe one learns by gaining knowledge through seeing and hearing. Does this mean learning has nothing to do with action?[28] He continues, "In *Hongfan* (*The Great Plan*), the various schools of thought often engage in the not very beneficial practice of looking for a certain kind of explanation. In fact, if you fail to rigorously examine yourself, what gains will there be to speak of?"[29] He refutes the notion of "learning" as mere knowledge and understanding, instead viewing virtue as the goal of all learning. Ma Yifu points out that the literati in both ancient and modern times "take one learns as an object," which has nothing to do with reason or good sense, so that, "in recent years, the self-proclaimed experts in learning have dedicated themselves to the objectification of learning, elevating it to the level of reason and good sense, embellishing everything in flowery language only in the hope that their own work will passed down to future generations, and without regard for anything else."[30] He criticized the tendency to separate academic pursuits from self-cultivation in the strongest terms.

Following the Fuxing Academy's rules of study, he made clear that the academy advocated learning "to ensure that scholars have a good mental foundation, so that, if they apply themselves, they can follow the teachings and live a model life," and "it will help him be virtuous and reform his life, to improve oneself spontaneously."[31] He says in a letter, "As the academy has taught us, we should first seek to cultivate ourselves, then learn more," and "focus on knowledge and understanding—such learning is not enough. Attention to upholding the teachings is also needed for one who hopes to be virtuous. Lectures can only do so much; one must apply oneself if they are to be of any use."[32] These ideas are all opposed to the focus on knowledge and understanding alone and emphasize the self-reflection and nurturing Confucianism advocates, putting knowledge and understanding opposite to self-cultivation, which is consistent with Liang Shuming's statement.

Ma Yifu expresses dissatisfaction with the approach to the study of Confucianism that employs "the methods and critical attitudes which approximate those of philosophy," believing that "philosophers of the Central Plains shared what they had gained from their experience; they had no cosmology or theory of the mind as a starting point." He notes, "Preferring the words of righteousness and the principles over the teachings of Western philosophy seems somewhat excessive in terms of wisdom and virtue."[33] Though this statement is not directed at Xiong Shili, it does show that he, like Liang Shuming and others, does not approve of using cosmology or other aspects of Western philosophy to study the ideas of ancient Chinese philosophers. He specifically mentions the difference between learning from the academy and that of philosophy, saying, "The lecturers at the academy must invent the basic principles of the essential self based on the original teachings, which is not at all like what is taught by today's philosophers. The wisdom of the virtuous still governs philosophy, but if you consider the wisdom of past eras and judge it with the general objective manner of today's philosophers, it may not be of much benefit." And, "scholars are advised to temporarily set aside these philosophical mindsets and focus exclusively on the writings of the ancient sages and the Confucian works of thinkers from times past." They should "really take their time to cultivate and understand their own minds and uprightness."[34] In his view, philosophy is external and objective, while Confucianism is introspective and restrained.

He calls the nature of learning in academics "sacred learning." He explicitly states that "scholars learn in order to become sages. The scholar's responsibility is to go to the very bottom of things and seek to understand, and to understand his own nature." And, "If one abandons the pursuit of principles and understanding his own nature in favor of other types of learning, what is the point of his studies?"[35] He notes, "This must be personally experienced and understood. This sort of sudden breakthrough is only achieved over a long period of time. Merely dabbling in various subjects is like skimming over them; they have no impact on one's mind or body that way."[36] He further points out:

> The methods of science and philosophy in modern times generally involve analyzing and observing things based on empirical inference. Though they may vary in depth and breadth, they all rely on comparison for understanding. Some engage in intense thinking

> and exploration, like a mole searching for the meat of a wild cow, while others are influenced by shadows, like apes capturing the reflection of the moon in water. The more successful ones have well-organized theories and notable insights, but they rely on forced logic and lack inherent understanding. Compared to the comprehensive, systematic knowledge pursued by the sages of the Central Plains, they are far from adequate. The discernment of categories and the understanding of things must rely on profound enlightenment, and the exploration of divine spirit and knowledge of transformation is rooted in sacred verification, which cannot be acquired by mere imitation. One may read extensively from the works of contemporary authors and gather knowledge from various sources, but it is a waste if they do not devote themselves to the study of the original teachings of Confucianism and fail to make gains through personal effort.[37]

Liang Shuming regards philosophy as the study of the sixth consciousness, while Ma Yifu sees philosophy as the pursuit of knowledge. In Ma's view, Confucianism is "self-attained" learning or an experiential understanding of one's own mind and nature. Confucian sacred learning is thus a type of profound enlightenment and personal verification, rather than a thing achieved through knowledge and external observations. The profound enlightenment discussed here does not refer to speculations on essence, but rather on an internal realization.

This view of Ma Yifu is related to his concept of the Six Arts. He believes that "all academic endeavors are encompassed by the Six Arts," including Western academia. All aspects of human life fall within the scope of the Six Arts. He says specifically, "Therefore, the desire to promote the path of the Six Arts is not merely about preserving national heritage in a narrow sense or expressing the spirit of one's people alone. It is rather about making this sort of culture universally applicable to all of humanity."[38]

Compared to the perspectives on the philosophy of Xiong Shili and the modern Neo-Confucianist, Liang Shuming seems to hold to a form of fundamentalism, adhering to the school of Confucian learning and considering philosophy to be nothing more than a unique tradition of Western culture. At the same time, Liang Shuming's perspective appears to have a form of particularism rather than universalism. He believes that Eastern sacred learning is a study of body and mind, while Western philosophy is a study of knowledge, and each is suited to its own cultural traditions. According to Liang, they are different and do not require a unified form. He completely overlooks how these two forms of learning might be integrated into modern academic fields. This seemed consistent with multiculturalism, but it could easily lend itself to relativism. This simplistic view made it difficult to imagine the various ways in which Confucian learning could exist and develop in modern times, such as developing the philosophical aspects of Confucian learning within the framework of modern academic education, coexisting with other traditional forms of Confucian learning, such as lecture-based cultivation in academics. Compared to Liang Shuming, Ma Yifu's theory of the Six Arts represents a China-centric form of universalism. He asserts that the Six Arts encompassed all academics and that they are a universally applicable category that extends to every corner of the world. He believes that all academic developments that have emerged in modern Western society should be categorized under the Six Arts, suggesting that the ancient Chinese system of the Six Arts is more universal than the academic systems that developed in the West in modern times.

In terms of their actual implications, both Liang and Ma's perspectives are relatively conservative and difficult to adapt to global cultural development. Compared to them, Xiong Shili's proposition is undoubtedly more reasonable. Xiong Shili incorporates the strengths of Western philosophy in such a way as to compensate for the shortcomings of Chinese philosophy. He also understands philosophy as having a meaning beyond Western intellectualism, incorporating the academic significance of Eastern and Chinese traditions into philosophical concepts, aiming to expand the universality of philosophy. Although his understanding of Chinese philosophy is colored by his own theory of the mind proposition, this view aligns with the values of multiculturalism, affirming unity while acknowledging differences. Furthermore, Xiong Shili actually established his own ontology-cosmology system, a significant contribution to 20th-century Chinese and world philosophy.

In the development of modern Western philosophy, the shift in focus to epistemology marked the diminishing status of ontology. After Kant and Hegel, ontology gradually declined, and Marx's subversion of metaphysics led to a transformation of philosophy, bringing about an anti-metaphysical trend. In the early 20th century, a "philosophical revolution" emerged, with a linguistic turn that aimed to dissolve the traditional significance of ontology. By the end of the century, the notion of the "end of philosophy" had appeared. In light of this development, the significance of ontology and cosmology, which were so highly valued in ancient times, seemed difficult to establish in the modern context. But with the reflection on the Western philosophical tradition in the 20th century, there was also a revival of ontology. From the perspective of logical thinking on topics including human existence and understanding, fundamental contemplation ultimately arose from the inner demands of the mind and served as the foundation for the unity of the world and the basis for the existence and change of things. It preceded specific philosophical investigations. The development of modern science brought forth new cosmological perspectives, challenging the ideas of fundamental elements in matter and the extension of time, with these concepts gradually being negated, to be replaced by a dynamic, ever-changing cosmological landscape experienced as an active, holistic universe.[39] The ontology and cosmology of Xiong Shili's philosophy hold great significance in this context.

In the 20th century, it was not only Chinese philosophy that faced powerful disruptive forces; the Western philosophical tradition also underwent fundamental changes. In these circumstances, it was important to re-evaluate and reshape the philosophical traditions of both East and West through interpretation and development, while affirming breakthroughs and transcendence in even ancient philosophies. Xiong Shili understood the overall trend of modern philosophical development, and he recognized that ontology was a favorite topic of Western philosophy, but one which had been neglected in modern times. He insisted on the foundational significance of ontology to philosophy and sought to develop a modernized ontology-cosmology that reflected the spirit of Chinese philosophy. In his philosophical construction, he synthesized the foundations of Chinese philosophy and incorporated the notions of Western materialism and idealism, striving to respond to the challenges Western philosophy posed to Eastern philosophy. In this way, he successfully established his distinctive philosophical system. The profundity, uniqueness, and grandeur of this system make his philosophy an indisputable model for modern Chinese philosophy's entry into the world.

Source: *Collected Readings on Academic Discussions: Xiong Shili and the Theory of Traditional Chinese Culture,* (Hubei Education Publishing House, 2003).

Notes

1. Guo Qiyong points out, "Xiong's cosmology is not a general cosmology, but is a onto-cosmology." See Guo Qiyong, *The Thought of Xiong Shili* (Tianjin People's Publishing House, 1993), 52.
2. Xiong Shili, "To Liang Shuming (1950)," in *Correspondence of Xiong Shili,* ed. Jing Haifeng (Institute of Chinese Studies, Shenzhen University, November 1985), 17.
3. Xiong Shili, "To Liang Shuming (May 24, 1951)," in *Correspondence of Xiong Shili,* ed. Jing Haifeng (Institute of Chinese Studies, Shenzhen University, November 1985), 25.
4. Xiong Shili, "To Liang Shuming (June 25, 1957)," in *Correspondence of Xiong Shili,* ed. Jing Haifeng (Institute of Chinese Studies, Shenzhen University, November 1985), 36.
5. In his response to Tang Junyi, Xiong Shili wrote in *A New Treatise on Consciousness-Only,* "It both aims at Western philosophical thought and completes the form and appearance of Eastern philosophy." Xiong Shili, *Essential Sayings of Xiong Shili* (Zhonghua Book Company, 1996), 125.
6. Xiong Shili, *Essential Sayings of Xiong Shili,* 37.
7. Xiong Shili, "To Liang Shuming (June 25, 1957)," in *Correspondence of Xiong Shili,* 38.
8. Xiong Shili, "To Lin Zaiping (June 25, 1975)," in *Essential Sayings of Xiong Shili,* 34–35.
9. Xiong Shili, "To Liang Shuming (June 25, 1957)," in *Correspondence of Xiong Shili,* 37.
10. Regarding the meaning of "truth," Xiong Shili proposes that there are three meanings of truth in metaphysics, and the main meaning is essential truth. There are six meanings of truth in the sciences, the main being objective laws. See his letter "Reply to Tang Junyi," in *Essential Sayings of Xiong Shili,* 135–137.
11. Xiong Shili, "To Zhang Jitong," in *Essential Sayings of Xiong Shili,* 2.
12. Xiong Shili, "To Zhang Jun," in *Essential Sayings of Xiong Shili,* 3.
13. Xiong Shili, "Reply to Xie Shilin," in *Essential Sayings of Xiong Shili,* 61.
14. Xiong Shili, "To Zhang Dongsun," in *Essential Sayings of Xiong Shili,* 71.
15. Ibid., 72.
16. Xiong Shili, "Reply to Magrini," in *Essential Sayings of Xiong Shili,* 142, 144.
17. Xiong Shili, *Essential Sayings of Xiong Shili,* 145.
18. Xiong Shili, "Reply to Tang Junyi," in *Essential Sayings of Xiong Shili,* 140.
19. Xiong Shili, "Reply to Hu Sheng," in *Essential Sayings of Xiong Shili,* 278.
20. Liang Shuming, *Complete Works of Liang Shuming,* vol. 8 (Shandong People's Publishing House, 1987), 315.
21. Liang Shuming, *Complete Works of Liang Shuming,* vol. 7, 755.
22. Ibid., 757.
23. Ibid., 759.

24. Ibid., 762.
25. Ouyang Jingwu's own words have not yet been found, but Lü Cheng's letter to Xiong Shili's says, "Metaphysics, ontology, cosmology, and other such things, though Western scholars embrace them, according to my judgment, are beyond the scope of where scholarship can exist. We push the words of Confucius and Buddha into this trap, and this approach is also wrong." (Quoted in Guo Qiyong, *The Thought of Xiong Shili*, 36)
26. Liang Shuming, "Reading Ma Yifu's Miscellaneous Writings," in *Complete Works of Liang Shuming*, vol. 7, 849.
27. Liang Shuming, "An Overview of Eastern Scholarship," in *Complete Works of Liang Shuming*, 332.
28. "A Reply to Yang Shuojing 3," in *Responses to Inquiries at Erya Tai*, vol. 1 of *Collected Works of Ma Yifu*, 498.
29. "A Reply to Yang Shoujing 4," 499.
30. "A Reply to Yang Xiafeng," in *Collected Works of Ma Yifu*, vol. 1, p. 499.
31. "A Reply to the Fuxing Academy Rules of Study," in *Fuxing Academy Recorded Lectures*, vol. 1 of *Collected Works of Ma Yifu*, 105.
32. "A Reply to Cheng Depu 1, 2," in *Responses to Inquiries at Erya Tai*, vol. 1 of *Collected Works of Ma Yifu*, 503–504.
33. Ibid., 503.
34. "A Reply to Mr. Xu," in *Responses to Inquiries at Erya Tai*, vol. 1 of *Collected Works of Ma Yifu*, 527.
35. "A Reply to Mr. Wu," 510.
36. "A Reply to Mr. Chi," 511.
37. "A Reply to Mr. Zhang," 519.
38. "Conversations in Taihe and Yishan," in *Collected Works of Ma Yifu*, vol. 1, 23.
39. Zhang Rulun, *Heidegger and Modern Philosophy* (Fudan University Press, 1995), 96.

CHAPTER 2

Xiong Shili's *A Treatise on Substance and Function* and Its Cosmology

Xiong Shili (1885–1968) was a modern philosopher from Huanggang, Hebei, China, who served as a professor of philosophy at Peking University. He took part in the Revolution of 1911 in his early years and later devoted himself to the study of philosophy, leaving behind a considerable body of writing. Xiong's academic pursuits, mainly focused on the comparison and integration of Confucianism and Buddhism, were influenced by some ideas drawn from modern Western philosophy. Today, scholars both in and outside China unanimously acknowledge that Xiong Shili's ideas hold an important position in modern and contemporary Chinese philosophy.

Xiong's philosophy began with "the two schools of emptiness" in Mahayana Buddhism, but he ultimately returned to the Confucian *Book of Changes*, from which he developed the concept of "the unity of substance and function." In his later years, he moved away from Buddhist studies and focused on the *Book of Changes*, authoring such works as *A Treatise on Substance and Function* and *On Change*. He established his own philosophical school based on the concept of "the unity of substance and function" in the *Book of Changes*, which is both refined and profound. This chapter focuses on *A Treatise on Substance and Function*[1] in an exploration of Xiong Shili's philosophy of "universal substance and function," leaving aside his earlier work, *A New Treatise on Consciousness-Only*.

I. Introduction to the Theory of Emptiness and Existence

Xiong Shili states, "The term 'substance and function' has been used very loosely by scholars. This work discusses the concept in the context of the universe, giving it unique significance."[2] According to Xiong Shili's definition, "Substance refers to the material reality of the universe, while function refers to the various phenomena that arise from the changes of substance. Universe here refers to the general term for both material and spiritual phenomena,"[3] indicating that Xiong's philosophy of substance and function focuses on the relationship between the material reality of the universe and its various phenomena. In his view, the relationship between substance and function (phenomena) in the universe is "a fundamental philosophical problem that has always been difficult to solve."[4]

Xiong Shili pays special attention to the relationship between the universe itself and its myriad phenomena. He puts forward the idea of "the non-duality of substance and function" (体用不二), which is closely linked to Mahayana Buddhism. He writes, "When I was young, I sought to explore theories of the universe, but I found nothing from the Confucianism of the Song and Ming dynasties. I took delight in Daoist philosophy for its vastness, but it lacked the stimulation of speculative thought. I briefly examined the Six Classics, but at that time, I was unable to discern the correct from the chaotic. I glanced at the hexagrams of the *Book of Changes*, but I couldn't grasp their profound meaning. So I focused my attention on Mahayana Buddhism, contemplating the concepts of Emptiness and Existence."[5] He goes on to say, "The aspect of Buddhism that I dedicated my efforts to lay in the Mahayana teachings of Emptiness and Existence," and, "the area I particularly explored and sought after lay in the theory of its nature and characteristics (i.e., the Buddhist discussion of nature and characteristics, similar to my discussion of substance and function)."[6] He says, "The principle of my theory of the universe lies in the unity of substance and function, as I do not simply accept the tenets of Buddhism."[7] In discussing his own doubts, he says, "I later turned inward and had an epiphany from the *Book of Changes*. The meaning of substance and function, when thoroughly examined, is undoubtedly beneficial, and I came to know where it belongs. My thoughts were indeed influenced by the inspiration of Emptiness and Existence found in Mahayana Buddhism. If I had not approached the question from that angle, I would not have understood the concept of self-will and how to comprehend the *Book of Changes*."[8] The *Book of Changes* here refers to the *I Ching*. Xiong's point is that in his early years, he focused on the discussions on nature and characteristics that are found in Buddhism, which led him to study the question of substance and function. Later, because of his doubts about Buddhism, he realized for himself the proposition of "the non-duality of substance and function." He believed that this proposition aligned perfectly with the aims of the *Book of Changes*.

According to Xiong Shili's understanding, Mahayana Buddhism places particular emphasis on the debate between nature and characteristics. He believed that in Mahayana Buddhism, "*faxing* (法性, dharma nature) refers to the true essence of all phenomena, which is also called *zhenru* (真如, suchness) or ultimate reality," and "*faxiang* (法相, dharma characters) is another term used to refer collectively to the various manifestations of all things and actions."[9] *zhuxing* (诸行, various manifestations) or *xianxing* (现行, current manifestations) is another term to describe ever-changing phenomena that do not abide. In other words, in Buddhism, *faxing* refers to the underlying nature of the universe, while *faxiang* refers to the phenomena of both the spiritual and material realms. Xiong states, "The term *faxing* in Mahayana Buddhism is equivalent to the term substance in my theory. The term *faxiang* in Mahayana Buddhism is equivalent to the term function in my theory."[10]

Xiong Shili's contemplation on the concept of substance and function is influenced on a fundamental level by the debate on nature and characteristics that are found in Mahayana Buddhism. However, Xiong's theory does not simply follow the Buddhist's explanations of nature and characteristics, but rather extends and develops them. When Xiong delved into the study of Buddhism, he had doubts about the Buddhist view of substance and function. He states, "Initially, when I studied Buddhism, I started with the Yogācāra school of thought, and according to its perspective on nature and characteristics, the true nature is referred to as *faxing*, which is described as non-arising, non-ceasing dharma, while current phenomena are referred to as *faxiang*, which is described as arising, ceasing dharma." He notes, "The arising, ceasing dharma and the non-arising, non-ceasing dharma are completely separate realms that do not interact with one another. I strongly disagree with this… After some time, when I thoroughly studied *Middle Treatise*, I came to understand the distinction between arising, ceasing dharma and non-arising, non-ceasing dharma, which was already elucidated in the Madhayamaka school."[11] Xiong holds that the Emptiness school of Mahayana Buddhism primarily aims to break through appearances (characteristics) and reveal the true nature (essence) of things by negating their utility (*faxiang*) and proclaiming that as "emptiness." As a result, substance (*faxing*) likewise became empty. The Existence school emerged as a correction to the extremism of the Emptiness school, emphasizing the reality of *faxing*. However, in the Existence school, the *zhenru*, *zhongzi* (种子, seeds), and *faxiang* are still divided into two worlds: one world of constant arising and ceasing, with ever-changing phenomena, and another of the non-arising and non-ceasing, representing the eternal and true. It is evident that Xiong Shili's basic starting point in contemporary substance and function is to oppose the idea of regarding substance and function as two distinct, unrelated worlds. It is from this point that the notion of "the non-duality of substance and function" and "co-existing substance and function" (即体即用) developed. This chapter explores the original intent behind Xiong's proposition of "the non-duality of substance and function" and "co-existing substance and function."

II. On Substance and Function

There are several key points in Xiong Shili's theory of substance and function. They are outlined here.

1. The Reality of Substance and Function

Though Xiong Shili's theory of substance and function is deeply rooted in the Buddhist concept of the appearance and nature of things, there is a fundamental difference between his theory and Buddhist ideas. While Buddhism considers the universe and all phenomena to be illusory, Xiong affirms the reality of the universe and all things. Xiong states, "The prijñā (wisdom) school perceives the universe as empty and detached. Our Confucian school perceives the universe as vibrant, lively, and defined by substantiality, without stagnation but not endless."[12] He goes on, "I have thought deeply, contemplating the teachings of Confucius, which emphasize sincerity and truthfulness. The concept of sincerity holds infinite significance. It represents genuine reality, and the universe and human existence are real in the truest sense. When one delves into this contemplation and establishes oneself in this truth, it prevents the rise of forms of delusion and falsehood."[13]

In other words, Xiong holds that all phenomena in the universe are real and dynamic. He asserts that any false teaching or misguided action arises from the denial of the reality of the universe. He says, "I believe that the universe, with its myriad transformations, changes, creatures, and events, is truly real and abundantly vibrant."[14] He sees the Buddhist notion of the illusory nature of phenomena as contrary to the principles of human life and thus believes they are detrimental to the universe. He argues that the belief in the illusory nature of things undermines the natural order and human life. He says, "Because the notion of illusion goes against the principles of nature and undermines human abilities, I am forced as a Confucianist to uphold the truth."[15] His abandonment of Buddhism and turn to Confucianism, viewing the latter as the fundamental, essentially came about because he took the affirmation of the real, dynamic existence of the universe as the cornerstone of his philosophy.

2. Substance Is Not the Ultimate Cause

Xiong writes, "Confucius directly affirms that all things are the ultimate existence, without suggesting that substance is the primary cause of all things... Claiming that substance is the primary cause of all things is like placing a lead above all else, even if it causes all things to lose their own essence and leads to a negative perception of the real world."[16] In Western philosophy, there is a concept of God as the entity and supreme being who initiated all things. Among Chinese philosophers, some advocate that the ultimate root lies before all things. These perspectives consider substance as the primary cause and regard function as something derived from substance. According to Xiong, there is no priority between substance and function. He refers to the notion of the primary cause as the "idea of transcending all things through substance." He criticizes the view that claims that "substance is independent, and function arises from substance," stating that "if this were true, then substance would be no different from the Creator, leading to absurdity."[17] Indeed, he holds that the idea that a primary cause is the root of all absurd superstitions.

3. Substance Is Not Separate from Function

Xiong Shili emphasizes that substance and function are not two separate realms. He advocates that function is inseparable from substance and cannot be sought outside it. He states, "I have previously mentioned that substance and function are not two separate realms; this is the root cause of everything."[18] He believes that separating substance and function into two separate realms has been a major flaw in philosophy throughout history. "In their understanding of the universe, scholars in both ancient and modern times rarely consider phenomena as rising out of thin air. They believe there must be some unknown entity beyond and detached from the phenomena that serve as the root cause of the phenomena… This unknown entity, detached from phenomena, creates a separation between the two worlds, rendering them mutually inaccessible."[19] He believes that affirming the existence of a root cause of phenomena is correct, but opposing the phenomena and the root is a mistake. Buddhism presents "the non-arising, non-ceasing, non-doing, as one realm, and the arising, ceasing, doing, as another."[20] He goes on to say that "Western philosophy considers phenomena as changeable and the uncanny reality as true; this is a flaw similar to Buddhist philosophy."[21] He says, "I firmly believe that the world of phenomena must have a root, but this root is not something beyond phenomena, separate and unknowable. The root is not another realm."[22]

In Xiong's view, the way to correct the errors brought only by ontological philosophy throughout history is to emphasize the non-duality of substance and function. He says, "Outside of function, there is no substance." And, "If one thoroughly comprehends the non-duality of substance and function, one should believe that substance is inseparable from function."[23] In other words, substance is not external to phenomena. He states, "This treatise (*A Treatise on Substance and Function*) establishes the principle of the non-duality of substance and function. Scholars should not seek beyond the breadth of function. I personally believe this is a settled matter that cannot be shaken."[24] He later adds, "If one fails to comprehend this, they will seek substance outside of function, which is like seeking the vast ocean waters beyond the multitude of waves."[25] He says that substance is like the vast ocean, and function is like the numerous ripples on it. Seeking substance beyond function is like seeking the ocean beyond the ripples. He says, "Substance is never hidden behind the universe, nor is it constant and separate from things."[26] He goes on to say, "What is called substance is not above and beyond the realm of the mind and phenomena, and it is not hidden behind them. It should be understood that substance is the very essence of all things and phenomena, just as the vast ocean waters are the essence of the numerous ripples upon them."[27] Viewed from this perspective, Xiong's concept of the non-duality of substance and function has three characteristics in its negation: substance is not something transcendent beyond all things (like God), substance is not another world co-existing with phenomena but separate from them (like Plato's world of ideas), and substance is not hidden behind phenomena.

From this, it is evident that Xiong's theory of substance and function is based on Buddhism's denial of the reality of phenomena and Western philosophy's separation of ontology from phenomena, opposing both views. However, as stated previously, the concept that substance is inseparable from function and that function is devoid of substance, as well as the idea that substance and function do not have a sequential relationship in terms of generation, can also be found in traditional Chinese ontological philosophical theories, such as Cheng Yi's concept of the unity of substance and function. Xiong states, "*The Great Commentary on the Book of Changes* says, 'Manifest the benevolent and conceal the function.' In one phrase, the non-duality of substance and function is shown to be profoundly significant. What does it mean to manifest benevolence? It means the ceaseless generation of life, which is the function of the supreme ultimate. And what does it mean to conceal function? It means that the benevolence mentioned before—the ceaseless generation of life—is not separate from its function."[28]

Tracing the idea of substance and function back to the "Appended Remarks" in the *Book of Changes,* the notion of "revealing benevolence and concealing function" indicates that the debate on substance and function had already begun in the early Qing Dynasty, with Gu Yanwu (1613–1682) and Li Erqu (1627–1705). Further, from the Song to the Ming dynasties, Daoist scholars such as Zhu Xi (1130–1200) and Cheng Yi (1033–1107) emphasized that *taiji* (太极, supreme ultimate) exists within *yin-yang* (阴阳, two complementary forces that make up all aspects and phenomena of life), not outside of it. It is worth asking whether Xiong Shili's idea of "the non-duality of substance and function" is the same as the Cheng-Zhu school's concept of "the singular source of substance and function." According to Cheng-Zhu Neo-Confucianism, though substance and function are unified and substance is inseparable from function, the relationship between the two is one of "non-separation and non-mixture," similar to that seen between *taiji* and *yin-yang.* In his *Explanation of the Supreme Ultimate,* Zhu Xi states, "*Taiji* is the fundamental essence that gives rise to movement and tranquility, and to activity and passivity, but it is not separate from *yin-yang.* It points to the fundamental essence that is not mixed with *yin-yang.*"[29]

It is evident that Cheng Yi and Zhu Xi's concept of the unity of substance and function affirms that substance exists within function, without either separation or mixture. Substance is an abstract entity that is inherent in and inseparable from function. Xiong Shili states, "Reading the *Book of Changes,* I was deeply impressed by the phrase 'conceal the function,' which conveys the idea that substance is not external to function, which is why it can be said that it conceals function. The term 'conceal' merely describes the non-duality of substance and function and should not be misunderstood as something being hidden in something else. Substance and function are in no sense separated."[30] In Cheng-Zhu Neo-Confucianism, the concept of substance and function distinguishes between "this" and "that," asserting that reason (substance) is present in everything. Zhu Xi says, "*Li* (principles) and *qi* (vital energy) are two separate entities, but when we observe them in things, they are intermingled and cannot be separated into distinct parts. However, this does not mean that they consume one another or that they are not each an individual entity."[31] In the context of Neo-Confucianism, *li* (substance) is something that converges with "the essence of the Two and the Five" (the *yin-yang* and the Five Elements), leading Cheng and Zhu to emphasize that people should recognize that "the fundamental essence has never departed from this, and it has never mixed." The phrase "never been mixed" suggests that it exists as a separate entity within function. This differs greatly from Xiong Shili's emphasis on substance being like the vast ocean and function being like its countless waves. It is evident that Xiong's proposition of the non-duality of substance and function and the absence of substance outside of function has a specific meaning that is distinct from Cheng and Zhu's concept of the unity of substance and function. To further illustrate this point, it is necessary to delve into Xiong's specific comments regarding the concept of the non-duality of substance and function.

III. Substance Is Function, Function Is Substance

Several propositions in Xiong Shili's discourse on his theory of substance and function deserve special attention. Those propositions are explored here.

1. Substance Is the Essence of Function

Xiong Shili emphasizes that "substance is the essence of function, just as the vast ocean is the essence of its numerous waves."[32] He further notes that "substance is the essence of everything, just as the vast ocean is the essence of its numerous waves. If scholars recognized this essence, they would see that the absolute and relative aspects are inherently non-dual."[33] He repeatedly emphasizes his deep understanding and firm belief that "the substance of everything is the essence of everything."[34] Viewed from this perspective, function (the waves) is the manifestation of essential substance (the ocean), and substance is the inherent existence of phenomenal function.

2. The Non-Duality of Substance and Function

In comparing his own theory of the non-duality of substance and function with the Buddhist concept of suchness as the embodiment of myriad dharmas, Xiong observes, "I have studied the scriptures of the Mahayana Sect, which indeed proclaim that the suchness is the essence of myriad dharmas, though they expressly forbid stating that suchness changes into myriad dharmas. These two expressions are different, and their relationship is of great significance."[35] This means that although the Emptiness school of Mahayana Buddhism acknowledges the existence (essence) of all phenomena (myriad dharmas), the Emptiness school's claim that "the suchness is the essence of myriad dharmas, like the Cheng-Zhu theory of "the unity of substance and function," only recognizes that suchness is the essence of myriad dharmas, while failing to acknowledge that myriad dharmas are transformed from suchness. Xiong Shili states that the key to his theory of the non-duality of substance and function lies in its emphasis on "the transformation of essence into function."[36] He says, "Only the *Book of Changes* clearly establishes the non-duality of essence and function, affirming function and not seeking essence outside of function, as essence has already transformed into function."[37] This indicates that his assertion that "there is no substance outside of function," is based on the view that function arises from the transformation of substance.

According to Xiong's explanation, function arises from the transformation of substance, meaning that function is the manifestation or transformed form of substance. It is important to note several points here. First, there is no substance that has not transformed into function. It cannot be said that there was a period in which the universe had a substance that had not yet transformed into function. In *On Change*, we read, "When there is no change in substance, there is no moment when it does not become function or phenomenon."[38] Substance always exists in the form of function. Second, the transformation of essence into function is not like a mother giving birth to a child. Xiong states, "It is not that another world, known as the world of phenomena, is created from the transformation of essence."[39] He also notes that one should not "regard it as the function of essence itself to initiate outward action," because in this case, "substance would be like a creator and not inherently one with function."[40] In other words, it is not substance that produces function, but rather, essence itself transforms into function. This leads to the third point, which is that the transformation of substance into function means that substance fully and completely transforms into function. Xiong says, "One should understand that substance completely and fully transforms into vast, diverse function, and there is no separate substance outside of the circulation of functions."[41] He further explains, "Substance indeed transforms completely into all things or phenomena. Outside of all things, there is no separate existence of substance. For example, the vast waters of the ocean completely transform into countless waves. Outside of these waves, there is no separate existence of the vast ocean waters."[42] He specifically emphasizes that the term "transform into" has profound significance. "The term 'transform into' clearly indicates that substance undergoes transformation, completely and fully transforming into diverse functions. For example, when the ocean water undergoes transformation, it completely transforms into turbulent waves. It is with this transformation that the unity of substance and function is realized."[43] According to this explanation, when essence transforms into function, it is similar to water transforming into ice. It cannot be said that there is water beyond the ice, because the water itself has completely transformed into ice. Therefore, it is precisely because function is the substance's transformation that substance is referred to as the "essence" of function, just as water is the "essence" of ice.

3. Substance Is Function, Function Is Substance

Based on this discussion, it is not difficult to further explore the meaning of Xiong's concept of the unity of substance and function. In his philosophy, the notion of the unity or non-duality of substance and function, also expressed as "substance is function, function is substance," provides a key to understanding his overall thought.

Xiong states, "It should be understood that while substance and function can be distinguished, they are, in practice, inseparable. What can be distinguished is the undifferentiated substance (like the vast ocean water, which is all-encompassing), while function is diverse (like the countless waves, which manifest as distinct entities). What is inseparable in reality is that substance is function, and function is substance (as the vast ocean waters completely become the countless waves), and outside of function, there is no substance (just as, without waves, there are no ocean waters). Function brings about the existence of substance (as the countless waves from the ocean waters), and function is brought into being by substance (as the ocean water does not exist independently beyond the countless waves). Wang Yangming (1472–1529) has said, 'When speaking from the perspective of the substance, function is contained within substance, but when speaking from the perspective of function, substance is contained within function.' This is an explanation of the true situation."[44] He goes on to say, "For instance, each individual wave regards the ocean as its own self. The self of one wave is the ocean water, and the self of the next wave is the ocean water, and so on for countless waves. From this, we can understand the idea that substance is function. 'Substance is function' means that function is the body itself, just as each wave is the ocean water itself." And, "The transformation of substance into inexhaustible functions, like the vast ocean waters transforming into leaping waves, allows us to understand the principle that substance is function."[45] From this discussion, it is evident that in Xiong's philosophy, the idea that substance is function refers to the transformation of substance into function (and in this sense, substance is function). "Function is substance" means that the essence of function itself is the substance (and thus, function is substance). The former emphasizes substance, while the latter emphasizes function.

The expression 即甲即乙 ("A is B") as a mode of discourse is common in religious and philosophical discourse from the Tang Dynasty (AD 618–907) onwards, but its usage and significance can vary. The interpretation of Xiong's expression "substance is function" thus requires closer analysis. In Chinese, the grammatical structure uses the character 即 twice, with the first instance meaning "in terms of" or "regarding," as in Wang Yangming's phrase 即...而言, and though the second use of the character in Chinese can be loosely interpreted as "is," it does not, in the original, connote an absolute equivalence, as seen in the phrase 孔丘即是仲尼 ("Confucius is Zhongni"). For instance, Xiong Shili argues, "According to my view, the unity of substance and function means that substance is function (like the ocean water is the waves), and function is substance (as outside of the waves, there is no ocean water)."[46] He criticizes the idea that "substance is not the same as function, and the body is not the same as manifestation." On the other hand, he states, "What is called function is essentially a unified flow of spirit and material force. Substance is not the same as function (in other words, the body is not the same as the unified flow of spirit and material force). For example, the ocean water is not the same as the waves (the ocean water symbolizes substance, and the waves symbolize function, or the unified flow of spirit and material force). However, outside of function, or the unified flow of spirit and material force, there is no substance. For instance, outside of the waves, there is no ocean water."[47] This indicates that in Xiong's thought, substance and function are not synonymous. Otherwise, there would be no need to affirm the existence of substance beyond the phenomenal realm. Therefore, substance is function, in the sense that there is no substance beyond function, and yet substance is not an exact equivalent to function. The idea that substance is function does not imply a straightforward equation between substance and function. The first 即 in the original phrase refers to a standpoint or perspective, while the second indicates a relationship of dependence and interplay between substance and function. The understanding of this concept requires careful analysis of Xiong's specific philosophical framework and his nuanced treatment of the relationship between substance and function.

To grasp the true meaning of Xiong's concept of the unity of substance and function and his idea that substance is the totality of all phenomena, it is necessary to determine whether he considered the term substance to refer to the entirety of the universe. In examining the familiar Buddhist terms frequently used by Xiong, it is important to first clarify whether the term substance in his philosophy refers to the totality of myriad dharmas (phenomena) or to their dharma nature (essential nature). A closer examination of his works makes clear that substance does not refer to the totality of phenomena, but to their essential nature. Xiong frequently equates the term substance with the Mahayana Buddhist concept of dharma nature, rather than the totality of phenomena. To assume that when he says, "Substance is the totality of phenomena," he means that substance refers to the overall appearance of the universe could be a misinterpretation.

To understand Xiong's philosophy, it is important to discuss the metaphors that recur in his discourse. In works like *A Treatise on Substance and Function*, Xiong often used the analogy of the ocean and its waves to illustrate the relationship between substance and function. He states, "The unity of substance and function is accurately illustrated by the analogy of the ocean and its waves."[48] He goes on, "The substance of all things is their very self, just as the ocean is the self of the waves. This analogy is most fitting, and it would be difficult to explain this theory otherwise."[49] However, in reality, the analogy of the ocean and its waves in Xiong's philosophy is not entirely precise. While there are indeed waves on the surface of the oceans, there are none in the depths. The waves are merely a layer on the surface of the ocean, a part of the ocean as a whole. In this sense, the analogy fails to fully demonstrate "the complete transformation of substance into function." However, for Xiong, this metaphor still holds certain advantages over others, which is why he gives it priority in his discourse.

From this perspective, in order to understand Xiong's concept of the unity of substance and function, it is important to take note of the supplementary metaphor of ice and water, which complements Xiong's metaphor of the sea and its waves. In discussing the philosophical method of "absorbing function through substance," or going from function into substance, Xiong uses the example of perceiving water through the observation of ice. He states, "By perceiving ice without holding on to its icy form, one directly enters water and only water. Similarly, in the study of the universe, when we speak of absorbing function through substance, we mean observing the various actions of mind and matter and directly entering their essence."[50] This indicates that philosophical understanding should be like recognizing water through the observation of ice, which is to say, recognizing substance through function. It is evident that in Xiong's philosophy, the relationship between water and ice also applies to his understanding of the relationship between substance and function. When discussing the recognition of substance through function, he notes that "ice is formed from water, but ice is not water."[51] And in emphasizing that the nature of function is equivalent to the nature of substance, he says, "Ice appears from water and does not lose the wetness of water. This is what is meant by absorbing function through substance."[52]

From this, it is clear that in his philosophy, Xiong does not merely affirm the existence of the universe as a whole. The fundamental premise of A Treatise on Substance and Function is that he first affirms the existence of the essence of the universe. For Xiong, the relationship between the essence of the universe and its totality is, to some extent, similar to the relationship between water and ice. Xiong's notion of the absorption of substance through function can only be understood through the mutual relationship of water being the self of ice, through water being ice's true substance, through the transformation of water into ice, and through ice being derived from water. It is also in this sense that one can understand the difference between the ideas of the non-duality of substance and function and the unity of substance and function, as well as the difference between the transformation of suchness into myriad dharmas and suchness being the true nature of myriad dharmas.

As mentioned above, the functions and purposes of the ice-water and the ocean-waves metaphors are consistent, in that they aim to explain the concept stated as "substance is function" and "function is substance." However, the overarching reason for Xiong's emphasis on the ocean-waves metaphor is that it can express how function arises from the changes within the substance itself (i.e., the formation of the waves depends on the movement of the ocean) and how function is impermanent (i.e., the waves rise and then cease in an instant). However, it is crucial to note that just because Xiong uses the metaphors of the ocean and waves or water and ice, this does not mean that he understands essence to be a material entity, a point that deserves further discussion.

Based on this discussion, it is evident that the concept of substance in Xiong's philosophy is essentially the notion of an entity or essence in traditional metaphysics. The relationship between substance and function that he raises is, in fact, an exploration of the relationship between the entity and phenomena of metaphysics using the categories of traditional Chinese philosophy. In this regard, he is clearly influenced by Western philosophical modes of thought. In traditional metaphysics, it is believed that all things have an absolute entity as their ultimate source or foundation. The multitude of phenomena is merely a manifestation of the entity or essence, and the entity is not a directly perceptible existence. According to Xiong's understanding, this entity or essence is not outside of the multitude of phenomena, nor is it hidden within it. Rather, it manifests itself in a multitude of phenomena. This is akin to water transforming into ice, where the essence serves as the foundation or substrate for the myriad manifestations of mind and matter.

This is to affirm, then, that a non-sensory substance exists beyond the multitude of functions, which was originally a product of abstract metaphysical thinking. However, Xiong argues, "It is a great fallacy to despise the notion of substance. It is absolutely untenable to suggest that the universe and human life have neither roots nor foundation. In the *Book of Changes*, Confucius affirms the existence of substance, but this substance is the true self of all things, not to be indulged in empty speculation or fantasies, nor to be considered as existing outside the selfhood of the multitude of functions."[53] He goes on to say, "Many philosophers acknowledge the objective existence of the universe and its functions, but deny the existence of substance. They even disdain the study of ontology. This is as shallow as the ancient Indian nihilists. I believe that the universe has a true source, and everything did not just rise suddenly. If one only acknowledges the reality of the universe and its functions without recognizing the existence of substance, he is like a child standing on the shore and recognizing only the multitude of waves while remaining unaware that they arise from the transformation of the vast ocean."[54] Xiong holds that the myriad manifestations of mind and matter did not appear out of thin air, and thus, a failure to acknowledge the existence of substance would reduce all functions to mere fabrications. A denial of substance would imply the lack of an inherent source for the movement within the multitude of functions.

It is plain that Xiong's concept of "substance is function" is based on the fundamental premise of affirming the existence of the cosmic entity. Without this premise, there could be no notion of "substance is function."

The above explanation illustrates what is meant by "the essence is the self of the universe," where the term self is referred to as both *zishen* (自身) and *ziti* (自体). *On Change* frequently emphasizes that substance is the "true self" of function, as when it states that "substance is, in essence, the true self of functions."[55] The substance is also referred to as "the one ultimate," which points to the true self of cosmic functions.[56] It further states, "Since Confucius advocated the unity of substance and function, he clearly regarded substance as the true self of functions."[57] The concept of true selfhood refers to the "suchness" or the inherent, unified existence of cosmic phenomena. Understanding the concept of true selfhood offers further insight into Xiong Shili's thoughts on substance.

IV. Nature and Virtue

There are questions surrounding the meanings of certain terms and concepts in Xiong Shili's philosophy, such as substance, or spiritual and material. Conversely, one may ask, is the mind a substance? Or is matter substance? Xiong explicitly states that substance is neither spiritual nor material, but rather encompasses both spirituality and materiality. Mind and matter are both functions and phenomena of substance. He says that "the mind is the function of substance. It is ever-changing and unstable. Similarly, matter is the function of substance, and it is ever-changing and unstable. Mind and matter are simply two aspects of function and cannot be separated."[58] The term "separated" here refers to treating one aspect of mind and matter as source and substance. Xiong notes, "In my philosophy, I explain the meaning of the Great Function of Heaven and Earth, stating that mind and matter are two aspects of the Great Function, not two separate entities."[59]

Xiong believes that substance undergoes changes to manifest the Great Function, which manifests as the unity of two fundamental aspects, *xi* (翕) and *bi* (辟). This indicates that there are two basic forces in the universe. *Xi* represents the tendency and action of materialization, through the power of cohesion, which solidifies the universe into fixed, unchanging matter. *Bi* represents the tendency and action of spiritualization, resisting the solidification of the universe into fixed, unchanging matter, and actively promoting the ascension, progress, and development of the world. Xiong is here borrowing the notion that "*xi* gathers substance, and *bi* disperses force" from Thomas Henry Huxley's book *Evolution and Ethics* (天演论, *Tian Yan Lun*), which was introduced as part of the Western academic influence during the Qing Dynasty. In essence, the text discusses the relationship between mind and matter. Xiong explicitly states, "In terms of the Great Function, *bi* represents the vigorous, progressive developmental force that we call spirit. *Xi* represents the tendency of cohesion, gathering, closure, and solidity, which is what we call matter."[60] He goes on, "Function has both aspects, *xi* and *bi*. *Bi* represents spirit, and *xi* represents matter. What we call function, then, is essentially the great flow in which spirit and matter merge into one."[61] Xiong holds that in the relationship between mind and matter, mind is active, guiding the transformation and progress of matter through different forms within matter itself, thereby realizing the infinite process of cosmic development. The continuous development of the entire universe occurs precisely because of the active role of mind. In *On Change*, Xiong emphasizes *qian* as *bi*, representing life and consciousness and highlighting the important role of life and will as forms of spirit.

Xiong believes that the movement and development of the universe are due to the interaction of *xi* and *bi*, as opposing forces, in the process of development. He refers to this process as "the transformation of xi and bi," which he considers to be the fundamental principle of cosmic development, unity in opposition. He says, "The flow of great transformation does not arise from either opposition or lack of change. Without complexity, how could there be development?"[62] This means that the flow of the Great Function in the universe is in fact a result of the unity of spirit and matter in opposition, which leads to development and change. The unity of opposition in the flow of the Great Function fundamentally originates from the internal unity of substance. Xiong believes that substance has properties that are complex, not singular. The unity of opposition within the complex properties of substance is the decisive source of change and development. He points out that "substance undergoes changes to become the Great Function, and one can only understand the nature of substance through its functions. It is important to realize that function has properties, such as spiritual and material power, which are the properties of substance. The reason this is so is that substance is the self of function, just as the wet and wavy properties of water are properties of the ocean. The ocean is the self of waves."[63] This indicates that the nature of function is the nature of substance, and understanding the properties of function means understanding the properties substance possesses. Function has both spirituality and materiality, and the same is true of substance. He goes on, "The two aspects of spirituality and materiality are the two opposite poles in substance. It is through their opposition that they complement each other, and it is through substance that they are transformed into the Great Function."[64] And, "Spirituality and materiality are both inherent in substance."[65] He further notes that "when it comes to change, there must be opposition. In simple terms, it is because the universe's substance contains several opposite ends that change can occur and development can follow."[66] Xiong's ideas about the unity of opposition, which determines and propels change and development, embody a distinct dialectical perspective.

Xiong Shili not only uses the concept of substance with its two opposite aspects of spirituality and materiality to explain cosmic changes; he also proposes that the inherent source of the universe's ongoing development is due to the fact that substance itself is alive, active, and dynamic, rather than being constant and static. It is for this reason that he emphasizes the metaphor of the ocean and waves, as the multitude of waves and their surge originate from the movements of the vast ocean. Xiong believes that from the perspective of the unchanging nature of substance amid cosmic changes, it can be said that the nature of substance was that it might be constant. However, overall, the fundamental nature of substance is that it is alive (living). He argues that if substance is perceived as silent, lifeless, and devoid of activity, then its "unending vitality and ceaseless change" would be cut off. He thus criticizes the Buddhist and Daoist philosophies, which emphasize emptiness and stillness, advocating instead for an emphasis on the "living," "dynamic" nature of substance. He criticizes both the emptiness view and the substantialist view for believing that "all phenomena lack vitality, movement, and change."[67] He believes that substance itself is vibrant, flowing, and endlessly vigorous. He says, "According to my view of the unity of substance and function, substance is function, and function is substance. The rising and ceasing of function is precisely the rising and ceasing of substance. The constant flux of function is precisely the constant flux of substance."[68] He holds that treating function as dynamic and substance as unchanging is a mistake that divides substance and function, placing them in two separate realms. In his view, acknowledging the dynamic nature of substance is essential to truly explain all creative activities and the ultimate source of a vibrant existence.

It is for this reason that Xiong states in *A Treatise on Substance and Function* that "substance is the essence of the Great Function,"[69] while in *On Change*, he repeatedly uses the term "inherent source" to define substance. He writes, "The entity is the inherent source that all things possess and share."[70] He goes on, "The sages regard all things as the principal, but substance is the inherent source of all things."[71] He notes, "The Confucian idea of the Great Change affirms that *qian-kun*, or all things, are real and encompass the substance within all things. In simple terms, substance is the inherent source of *qian-kun* or all things."[72] He argues that his advocacy of the unity of substance and function is equivalent to tracing the dynamic source of change within things. He rejects the Buddhist notion that negates function and only acknowledges unchanging substance, which he calls "the absorption of all function into substance." He refers to his own philosophy as "the absorption of all substance into function." He says, "The absorption of substance into function is fundamentally a rejection of philosophers' fantasies of transcending phenomena and existing independently as entities. It correctly elucidates that substance is the true self of function. In other words, substance is the inherent source of all things, the origin, the birth, and the ever-developing, though not by external forces. The absorption of substance into function means that all things have inherent sources, which are real and not illusory, and that they undergo constant change and variation. This is why all things never tire of creating."[73] The absorption of substance into function is thus the search for the genuine dynamic source of cosmic change within all things.

The philosophy of Xiong Shili clearly exhibits idealistic tendencies in its discussion of the relationship between spiritual and material substances. Its proposition on the cosmic principle of life was greatly influenced by Schopenhauer and Bergson, and while Xiong uses the traditional Chinese philosophical concepts of substance and function to describe the relationship between the two, as well as the Buddhist concepts of nature and appearance, it can be said that his theoretical approach bears marks of the influence of Western philosophical discourse on ontology and phenomenology. It should also be noted that his idea that "substance is the self of everything" bears similarities to Spinoza's concept of "substance (God) as nature" in many aspects. Descartes advocates the existence of spiritual and material substances which interact with each other, while Spinoza affirms the existence of only one substance, which serves as the foundation for all material and spiritual phenomena and is manifested through them. According to Spinoza, the world lacks any external transcendent cause, and substance exists "within the world" as the immanent foundation of the universe. In other words, the world is in substance, and substance is in the world. Substance is the source of all existing things, and substance and the world are both one in two and two in one. Substance is the "external entity, substrate, or original" within things, the "original or source of all real flow." Spinoza holds that spirit and matter, or thought and extension, are "different attributes of the latent substance." Spirit and matter are "different manifestations of the same universal reality," and "neither is the cause or effect of the other."[74] He asserts that all things and all phenomena in the natural world are "modifications," "aspects," or "modes" of the universal substance. These ideas in Spinoza's philosophy bear resemblances or affinities to many of the fundamental views in Xiong's theory on substance and function. While it is not certain whether Xiong personally studied Spinoza's philosophy, there are clear, notable similarities between their basic viewpoints.

In terms of fundamental ideas, Xiong's insistence that substance is not separate from function, his affirmation of the dominance of the spiritual over the material, and his recognition that substance itself is dynamic and ever-changing are clearly based on his adherence to the Confucian worldview. For this reason, his theory of substance and function can be seen as an ontological foundation for Confucian values such as robustness, moral cultivation, and engagement with the world. It is in this aspect that it differs from Buddhism or the philosophy of Spinoza.

Xiong Shili is a particularly unique figure in Chinese philosophical circles after the May Fourth Movement. His philosophical ideas, the historical context in which they emerged, and their significance and influence are all highly complex and warrant further in-depth research and analysis. Only through a thorough examination of these issues can we accurately evaluate the philosophical system he proposed.

Notes

1. Xiong Shili stated in *A Treatise on Substance and Function* that although the text was revised from the earlier work *A New Treatise on Consciousness-Only,* its principles are mainly based on the *Book of Changes.* He says, "In terms of the Buddhist Yogācāra, there is no fundamental similarity between the *New Treatise* and the Yogācāra school. The *New Treatise* is thus not necessary." See *A Treatise on Substance and Function* (Shanghai Longmen Press, 1958), 4. The ideas presented in *A Treatise on Substance and Function* differ greatly from the ideas in the *New Treatise,* which regarded the mind as the main substance of the universe.
2. *A Treatise on Substance and Function,* 31.
3. Ibid., 1.
4. Ibid., 108.
5. Ibid., 80.
6. Ibid., 30.
7. Ibid.
8. Ibid., 4.
9. Ibid., 33.
10. Ibid.
11. Ibid., 98.
12. Ibid., 119.
13. Ibid.

14. Ibid., 107.
15. Ibid.
16. *On Change*, vol. 2 (China Science Academy Printing Press, 1961), 26.
17. Ibid., 124.
18. Ibid., 11.
19. Ibid., 12.
20. Ibid., 43.
21. Ibid., 169.
22. Ibid., 12.
23. *A Treatise on Substance and Function*, 3.
24. Ibid., 32.
25. Ibid., 125.
26. Ibid., 150.
27. Ibid., 112.
28. Ibid., 109.
29. "Explanation of the Supreme Ultimate," in *Collected Works of Zhou Dunyi*, vol. 1, 1.
30. *A Treatise on Substance and Function*, 111.
31. "Reply to Liu Shiwen," in *Collected Works of Zhu Xi*, vol. 46.
32. *A Treatise on Substance and Function*, 149.
33. Ibid., 147.
34. Ibid., 150.
35. Ibid., 45.
36. Ibid., 3.
37. *On Change*, vol. 2, 4.
38. Ibid., 4.
39. Ibid., 11.
40. Ibid., 128.
41. Ibid., 6.
42. *On Change*, vol. 2, 40.
43. *A Treatise on Substance and Function*, 128.
44. Ibid., 53.
45. Ibid., 110.
46. Ibid., 148.
47. Ibid., 163.
48. Ibid.,158.
49. Ibid., 150.
50. Ibid., 11.
51. Ibid., 8.
52. Ibid., 10.
53. *On Change*, vol. 2, 26.
54. *A Treatise on Substance and Function*, 5.
55. *On Change*, vol. 2, 12.
56. Ibid., 36.

57. Ibid., 37.
58. Ibid., 110.
59. *A Treatise on Substance and Function*, 111.
60. Ibid., 113.
61. Ibid., 164.
62. Ibid., 128.
63. Ibid., 3.
64. Ibid., 16.
65. Ibid., 15.
66. Ibid., 6.
67. Ibid., 62.
68. Ibid., 148.
69. Ibid., 26.
70. *On Change*, vol. 2, 26.
71. Ibid., 27.
72. Ibid., 121.
73. Ibid., 38.
74. Frank Thilly, *A History of Philosophy*, vol. 2 (The Commercial Press, 1979).

CHAPTER 3

Xiong Shili's Theory of *Mingxin* in "The *Mingxin* Section"

Xiong Shili's philosophical thought is strongly rooted in the tradition of the May Fourth Movement, as evidenced in the general textual form, which ranges from *A New Treatise on Consciousness-Only* to the classical Chinese text *On Change,* as well as in the main categories and conceptual paradigms he employs. Though he was influenced and driven by modern Western philosophy to a degree, his system of thought also demonstrates its direct connections with traditional Chinese philosophy, including Buddhism, in terms of both intellectual resources and ideological orientation. In the process of studying Xiong's philosophy, then, it is necessary to further highlight these connections and clarify how he adjusted and transformed tradition as he adapted it to the modern world, in order to better understand certain characteristics that constitute the "new" in the Neo-Confucianism of the modern era.

The theory of substance and function and the theory of *mingxin* constitute the main components of Xiong's philosophical system. The theory of substance and function establishes a distinctive cosmology with the principle of the non-duality of substance and function. The theory of *mingxin* focuses on the distinction between innate and acquired nature and proclaims itself to be "philosophical psychology." In the relationship between these two cornerstones of Xiong's thought, the theory of substance and function serves as the cosmological foundation for the theory of *mingxin,* and the theory of *mingxin* is the manifestation of the theory of substance and function in human mental activity. This unified structure and the correlation between the two are evident even in Xiong's early work, *A New Treatise on Consciousness-Only.*

In *A Treatise on Substance and Function,* written in Xiong's later years, he states, "Now that I have completed this book, the *New Treatise* should be abandoned," indicating that *A Treatise on Substance and Function* was intended to replace his earlier work, and it marks the completion of the reconstitution of his philosophical system in his later years. However, when *A Treatise on*

Substance and Function was published in 1958, only four chapters were complete: "Manifestation and Transformation," "Buddhist Teaching, Part 1." "Buddhist Teachings, Part 2," and "The Formation of Phenomena." The fifth chapter, "The *Mingxin* Section," was not included. As a result, *A Treatise on Substance and Function* only accomplished the construction of a new cosmological system, but did not completely replace *A New Treatise on Consciousness-Only.* It was only the following year, when the "The *Mingxin* Section" was published, that the overall construction of the system was completed.

A New Treatise on Consciousness-Only originally consisted of two chapters, the first and second part of the *Mingxin*. Just as *A Treatise on Substance and Function* served as a replacement for *A New Treatise on Consciousness-Only* in terms of cosmology, the "The *Mingxin* Section" was Xiong's late work that was meant to replace his earlier theory of *mingxin*. This theory, which Xiong referred to as "philosophical psychology," differed from scientific psychology. It inherited the tradition of the analysis of consciousness from the Yogàcàra school and the Confucian concept of mind and nature, encompassing both epistemological and practical (or ethical) significance. Essentially, it corresponds to the mind-nature theory and the theory of investigating principles in Song-Ming era Neo-Confucianism. Unlike the cosmological focus of the rest of *A Treatise on Substance and Function*, "The *Mingxin* Section" is a discourse on human life. The main themes of the theory of *mingxin*, viewed from the perspective of mind and nature, revolve around the question of the nature and cultivation of the mind, while from the perspective of investigative principles, it addresses the issue of wisdom and knowledge. Overall, it is concerned with the issue of mind and matter, though the term "mind and matter" here should not be understood to refer to the relationship between subject and object in the epistemological sense, or to the relationship between spirit and matter in the ontological sense. Rather, its ultimate focus is on the relationship between the development of the spiritual life (turning inward) and the pursuit and study of the material world (engaging with the world). This chapter serves as an examination and study of Xiong Shili's theory of *mingxin* based on the analysis of his existing theory of substance and function.[1]

I. Theory of Habituation

Xiong pointed out that the theory of *mingxin* aims to draw from the tradition of Confucius and Mencius' "learning to exhaust the mind." Its essence lies in the investigation of the fundamental distinction between the original mind (本心, *benxin*) and the habitual mind (习心, *xixin*).[2] This section begins with a discussion of the issues of habituation and acquired tendencies.

1. The Root and Structure of Habituation

In his "Preface" to "The *Mingxin* Section," Xiong offers a general overview of his theory of habituation. He writes, "Humans are born with a spiritual nature and endowed with vital energy, which constitutes independent individuals capable of exerting their own effort in performing both virtuous and non-virtuous actions. Every action spans a vast duration from its inception to its completion and constantly undergoes changes and transformations without even a brief cessation. Viewed from another perspective, although actions do not remain fixed, the residual force of their subsequent movements continues to generate and reside within certain aspects of our being, constantly fluctuating even when they are latent. For instance, if I performed a certain action in the past, I can still recall the pleasure, pain, gains, and losses associated with it. This attests to the fact that while the event has passed, the residual force has not been severed."[3] Xiong uses two terms in connection with this theory: 余 (*yu*), referring to the consequences of past actions, and 势 (*shi*), referring to a kind of influence or force. Together, the term *yushi* refers to the impact of individual activities that lingers within the subconscious structure, or residual force. Xiong further states, "This unceasing residual force is called habituation (习, *xi*). When there is habituation, it enters into the realm of consciousness to participate in new activities, which is called the habitual mind. From birth, every person possesses an original mind, and upon becoming an independent individual, they also possess a habitual mind. Acquired habits arise from minor indulgences of the self, while virtuous habits stem from the original mind. Once a person becomes an independent individual, they have autonomy, making it easier for acquired habits to exert their influence. However, the original mind cannot be completely extinguished, and virtuous habits persist against one's own resistance. The key to human life lies in preserving the clarity of the original mind and constantly cultivating new virtuous habits to transform old impurities and bad habits; in doing so, the inherent goodness of the original mind expands and magnifies, constituting the foundation of humane conduct and laying the foundation for human character."[4] This passage succinctly expresses the overall purpose of "The *Mingxin* Section" and provides a concise explanation of habituation, its roots, and its effects.

The term "independent individual" used by Xiong refers to the physical body of an individual, equivalent to "the small self," mentioned by Mencius, a concept focused on the individual as a sensory, material entity. At the same time, there is the operation of the "original mind," which also plays a role in forming the independent individual. From the perspective of the individual, the original mind, as a category of cognitive consciousness, can be used as a tool for cognition and interaction. As a material subject, the independent individual is a subject of sensibility and experience, with its own specific needs, directions, and tendencies in its actions, which Xiong refers to as capabilities. The independent individual often utilizes the original mind's thinking capacity to pursue and develop its capabilities in order to satisfy its needs. The capabilities Xiong mentions clearly refer to sensual desires.

According to Xiong, the original state of consciousness is like white silk, and every subsequent conscious or practical activity in life will leave a stain on the white silk, leaving behind traces in the consciousness that are more than just passive memories. They continuously participate in conscious activities and influence the conscious subject. Xiong refers to this power, which is the residue of past activities that continues to operate in the consciousness, as residual force. He holds that each ideational activity or behavior leaves behind residual force in the consciousness, which is stored within the human body as a latent stream of consciousness. In terms of past experiences, these residual forces are referred to as habituation or habits, while their latent presence in the consciousness is called seeds of habituation, or seeds, and their continuous emergence and participation in conscious activities is referred to as the habitual mind. The habitual mind, then, is consciousness formed by various past experiences. However, it should be noted that the consciousness formed by experiences does not here refer to the essential or systematic understanding derived from the general concept of rationality through the synthesis and abstraction of experiences. For Xiong, past experiences are stored and have an immediate impact. For instance, a virtuous conscious activity will generate a virtuous residual force, continuously influencing subsequent activities of the subject, and the same is true for negative actions. Thus, the habitual mind is not just a repository of past experiences, but is instead a consciousness formed by the accumulation of past experiences, and Xiong's understanding of it is more direct and concrete. This concept of the continuous influence of past activities is clearly related to Buddhist concepts such as karma, seeds, and habitual tendencies. Xiong removes the religious implications of these concepts and focuses on the broader category of habituation as a specific phenomenon that encompasses conscious activities and psychological experiences.

From an ethical perspective, human conscious activities and practical behaviors can be virtuous or negative, and the residual force or habits resulting from these activities also draw a distinction between virtue and negativity, i.e., between "virtuous habits" and "habituation to defilements." According to Xiong, virtuous habits originate from the fundamental mind (macrocosm), while habituation to defilements stems from the individual self (microcosm). Since the habitual mind is the result of various activities in the psychological realm (though it also participates as a motive for subsequent actions), it is undoubtedly empirical rather than innate. The negative habits within the habitual mind arise from the residual force caused by past negative conscious activities and practical behaviors. Once formed, these negative habits can manifest in current conscious activities, motivating new negative actions. The root of these initial negative thoughts or actions lies in the self as a sentient, material entity. Xiong's ideas still maintain that humans are both rational beings (macrocosm) and sentient beings (microcosm). Considering his concept of humans as "endowed with spirit and vitality" and his comparison of the fundamental mind to the "mind of *Way*" and the "nature-based mind," and the habitual mind to the "human mind" and the "dependent mind," these ideas have direct connections with the dualistic perspectives on the mind in traditional Chinese Buddhism and the dualistic perspectives on human nature in Neo-Confucianism.

2. The Categories and Functions of the Habitual Mind

Xiong's theory of the habitual mind is not limited to its ethical significance. In fact, in writing "The *Mingxin* Section" in his later years, he seemed to pay more attention to epistemological issues when drawing the distinction between inherent and acquired knowledge.

Xiong states that "upon being born, individuals become dependent entities with tangible form and practical lives. As such, these independent entities possess their own capabilities. The inherent mind, then, operates within the independent entity, allowing it to actively govern its current activities through the natural clarity of the mind [...] When the independent entity utilizes this innate clarity as a tool to engage with the external world, there will be habituation. Habituation is not devoid of potentiality. Its latent presence within us is referred to as seeds, which manifest as habitual tendencies in the realm of consciousness. This is what is meant by the term habitual mind."[5]

Here, the reference to the independent entity utilizing innate clarity is related to the individual's cognitive ability and interaction with the external world. From an epistemological perspective, the inherent mind is often referred to as innate clarity, denoting its inherent cognitive capacity, while habituation refers to memories formed through experiences within consciousness. Or, as Xiong states, "All past experiences are habituations, and the residual forces of all habituations lie dormant in the storehouse of habits, becoming seeds that emerge from the storehouse as memories."[6]

In terms of general conscious activities, the combined effect of innate clarity and habituation serves as the fundamental condition for the occurrence of cognitive activities. Xiong states, "When thinking takes effect, it is the motion of innate clarity, yet the residual forces of habituation lie dormant and spring forth from the storehouse of habits, blending with the motion of innate clarity." He goes on, "When thinking takes effect, without memory, there is no basis for inference and no foundation for imagination."[7]

Since cognitive activities are realized through the combined action of innate thinking and memories formed through experiences, habituation in this context differs from its purely negative connotation in ethical terms. In the realm of cognition, habituation is regarded as positive and indispensable. This does not pose a contradiction for Xiong himself. Although habituation is fundamentally a sensory category, in ethical terms, it refers to sensory desires, while in cognitive terms, it refers to sensory experiences. The evaluation of habituation may vary in different domains and does not require uniformity.

Based on the aforementioned stance, Xiong Shili categorizes habituation into two types: the first type is "cognitive habituations," and the second type is "emotional habituations." Emotional habituations refer to "personal desires for fame, profit, and authority, as commonly understood in the world." The seeds created by these habituations, when they give rise to habitual thoughts, "have the most detrimental effects," hence these types of habituations "must be eradicated completely." Cognitive habituations refer to memory and the like, and also include prejudices formed by narrow experiences. Although the latter can also obscure the inherent clarity of thinking abilities, overall, cognitive habituations "should be carefully guarded against but cannot be eradicated."[8]

From this, it is evident that in Xiong's philosophy, the theory of habituation does not focus on the innate role of temperament in terms of understanding. Instead, it emphasizes the significance of experience as a condition for the formation of knowledge. He points out, "If there is no habituation, can there be knowledge? If someone brings you a cup of soup, without deliberation, you know it's soup, and you immediately begin to eat it. In reality, you have the latent habituation seeds from countless past soups. When the old habituation seeds emerge simultaneously with the arrival of the new soup, you know that this new soup is edible. If you deny habituation, could you have the knowledge of the soup at that moment?"[9] He believes that if all experiences immediately disappeared after occurring, knowledge could not be formed at all. The term habit as the seeds of habituation refers to the ability to store experience in the structure of consciousness to serve as the basis for further understanding. Thus, "the function of memory always combines with the movement of clarity, constantly evoking all past experiences, assisting and initiating clarity, and providing a basis for solving many known things through new encounters."[10]

In terms of the direction of mental activity, the two types of habituations mentioned above, when understood in terms of the mind-matter question, both refer to the pursuit of materiality and the discrimination of material objects. Just as a distinction is needed for habituation, when speaking of pursuing, discriminating, and clinging to material objects, a distinction should also be made. "From the perspective of life," he notes that seeking and clinging to material objects out of self-centeredness is considered evil, but "from the perspective of knowledge, the relentless pursuit, attachment, and discrimination of material objects are essential qualities of scholars who study rigorously."[11] He continues, "Otherwise, how can we exhaust the principles of all things? Therefore, all habituations of scrutinizing, pursuing, and discriminating material objects are extremely valuable accumulated experiences."[12] Xiong's full affirmation of habituation in epistemology contrasts sharply with his strict attitude toward habituation in ethics.

A significant difference between Xiong's theory of habituation and the traditional Confucian theories of temperament or habitual tendencies is that his theory of habituation is not only a discussion of ethics, but also explicitly includes elements of epistemology. Although he still employs categories from traditional philosophy, he distinguishes them in terms of their different meanings in epistemology and ethics. While his fundamental standpoint continues to emphasize morality and values, his conscious differentiation hits precisely at the weakness of traditional philosophy. One reason for this is that within the tradition of consciousness analysis in Yogācāra Buddhism, there is an inherent theory explaining the process of cognition, and Xiong was greatly influenced by Yogācāra Buddhism. Furthermore, it is closely related to the significant progress in modern Western science and the development of epistemology in modern philosophical discourse. Xiong recognizes that "philosophical psychology," which focuses on consciousness and psychological phenomena, must encompass cognitive activities and give them an important position.

Strictly speaking, there are some aspects in Xiong's theory of habituation that remain unclear. From an ethical perspective, does habituation include the five desires or the five cravings (i.e., for self-indulgence, for future indulgence, for continuation, for sex, and for material possessions)? According to Xiong's logic, the five cravings should be included in habituation, in terms of emotion and sentiment. However, Xiong holds that the five cravings cannot be completely eliminated. In this sense, it cannot be said that habituation in terms of emotion and sentiment "must be eliminated and exhausted." Further, though virtuous habits originate from the inherent nature of the individual, they are still a form of habituation. If all habituations, aside from habituations in terms of knowledge and perception, are considered habituation in terms of emotion or sentiment, then virtuous habits should also be included within habituation in terms of emotion and sentiment. In this sense too, it cannot be said that habituation "must be eliminated or exhausted." Additionally, the negativity of habituation in an ethical sense and all forms of inherent evil in reality, according to Xiong's philosophy, are primarily the results of individual self-activity, neglecting the influence of the external world. This can be seen as a limitation on the scope of a modern philosophical system.

Regarding the mechanism of formation and the structure of habituation, Xiong holds that "the formation of habituation is derived from the interaction between external objects and the responsive mind. It is through material objects that the mind penetrates all their inner and outer aspects, and the mind and objects transform each other, forming habituation and experience. When the mind interacts with objects, it moves and changes in sync with them, without cessation. It is at that moment that the mind experiences a residual force from the habituation formed by the objects. It does not perish along with the mind and objects. All habituations have a residual force, countless intricacies that cannot be explored exhaustively, all hidden within the storehouse of habituation, which is called seeds. When the seeds of habituation encounter the appropriate conditions in the realm of consciousness, they manifest as memory. This is a general outline of my theory of habituation."[13]

From the perspective of the progress of cognition, conscious responses, contact, and the investigation of external objects lead to the formation of habituation, in terms of knowledge and perception, which is experience. After each cognitive activity is completed, the experience is not extinguished but stored as information, ready to be retrieved as memory and participate in new cognitive activities. In terms of ethical significance, various seeds of habituation are formed during the process of the mind's interaction with external objects. It is necessary for individuals to govern their conscious activity with their inherent nature, discerning between good and evil, to ensure that habituation becomes virtuous seeds, thus making the habitual mind a component of wisdom.

II. Theory of Original Mind

According to Xiong Shili, "the distinction between original mind and habitual mind is an extremely important issue in ancient Chinese *philosophy*."[14] Original mind is a concept highly valued in the Confucian tradition, from Mencius to Lu-Wang,[15] and it is commonly seen in Zen Buddhism as well. If the concept of habituation has mainly been derived and adapted from Buddhist thought, then the concept of the original mind mainly incorporates the ideas of Mencius and Wang Yangming. Depending on the specific discussion, the concept of the original mind is also referred to as innate knowledge (良知, *liangzhi*), clear understanding (明几, *mingji*), benevolent mind (仁心, *renxin*), celestial illumination (天明, *tianming*), wisdom (智, *zhi*), and other similar terms. The concept of the original mind forms the foundation of Xiong's theory of clarifying the mind.

Xiong often uses the term *mingji* to refer to the manifestation of the original mind. He says, "*Ming* refers to the bright and spiritually clear, while *ji* refers to subtle movements. The movement of spiritual brightness is called *mingji*, and the activation of innate knowledge is *mingji*."[16] Spiritual brightness is also known as *tianming*, encompassing both the inherent cognitive ability of humans and their innate moral rationality. *Ji* indicates the initial state of mental activity and operation; thus, Xiong explicitly affirms that, in the ethical sense, *mingji* is equivalent to Wang Yangming's notion of *liangzhi*. He therefore regards "knowing what is right and what is wrong" as the fundamental characteristic of *mingji*.

Original mind is humans' innate perceptual ability, distinct from the "subsequently arising" habitual mind. It "intrinsically exists," and Xiong asserts that "there is no person who lacks original mind in their nature," and "original mind is that which is intrinsically existing, not subsequently arising, hence the name original mind."[17] Because of its inherent nature, original mind is also referred to as original illumination (本明, *benming*) or, in the context of epistemology, celestial illumination (天明, *tianming*).

Unlike the habitual mind theory, which emphasizes discussing habituation's structure and mechanism of formation, Xiong's original mind theory not only emphasizes the a priori nature of the mind in the general sense, but also emphasizes the cosmological root of this a priori nature. He states in the preface to "The *Mingxin* Section," "*Mingji* arises from the spiritual nature." This does not imply that humans have another "nature" outside of the original mind. Instead, spiritual nature here refers to the cosmological root of the original mind.

In his theory of substance and function, Xiong affirms the existence of cosmic entities and asserts the idea that these entities are "neither purely material nor purely spiritual," but rather "contain both material and spiritual aspects." He further suggests that the self-manifestation of entities results in the Great Function, which is manifested as the unity of opposition between *xi* and *bi*. *Xi* represents the material aspect, while *bi* represents the spiritual aspect. Xiong sometimes uses the concepts of *qian* and *kun* to express the ideas of *bi* and *xi*, believing that within the Great Function, *kun* or *xi* represents the tendency toward materialization and solidification, while *qian* or *bi* represents the tendency toward strength and progress, with *qian* (*bi*) being the dominant aspect. It is precisely through the guidance and developmental function of *qian* that the continuous development of the universe is realized. In this sense, Xiong essentially regards *qian* as the inherent nature of the universe.

As the spiritual aspect of the Great Function, *qian* is also known as the "life-mind" or "spirit of life." It represents the vital force, the capacity for thinking, and the dynamic source of progress for the entire universe. In Xiong's philosophy, the life-mind cannot be regarded as separate entities. He states, "The life-mind should not be thought of as two separate things. It is called life due to its unpredictable vitality, and it is called mind because it serves as the principle of moral wisdom, intellectual abilities, and other functions."[18] He further explains, "There is almost no essential difference between life and mind. Life cannot manifest its grandeur as mind unless it develops to an advanced stage."[19] The foundation of the concept of life undoubtedly lies in the phenomena of life in the natural world. In Xiong's philosophy, it refers to the attribute and tendency of all things in the universe to continuously generate and progress. From this perspective, even before the emergence of living beings, the vitality of life exists in a latent form. Once living beings appear, the vitality of life operates and manifests in all organisms. Mind, on the other hand, is the highest form of the life force that has developed in humans through the process of biological evolution. Life and mind are thus inherently inseparable, representing different manifestations of the same life force or spiritual force (*qian*). The life force is a universal characteristic that exists in all things in the universe. The universe itself can be considered a great life entity. The point of convergence between the theory of substance and function and the theory of *mingxin* lies in the understanding that at the root of the original mind is the life force, the *qian* and *bi* nature of cosmic entities.

The life force operates within the myriad of things in the universe, forming a great flow of life. Although the cosmic functions have the aspects of *bi* and *xi*, the mind actually dominates over the matter, and thus manages it. Xiong holds that the entire evolutionary process of the universe demonstrates the dominance of the spiritual over the material. Of course, in his later work, Xiong's cosmology states that substance is neither mind nor matter, but instead undergoes a transformation from potentiality to actuality. The relationship between substance and function is summed up in the notion of "the unity of substance and function." Function is divided into mind and matter, with the mind not being confined by material constraints and thus guiding the advancement of matter. Xiong's cosmology can thus be seen as a form of idealism based on function, rather than a materialistic idealism. Based on this idealism of function, humans are understood to be inherently connected to the great flow of life in the universe, and the *qian* and *bi* nature of the universe is manifested in humans as the original mind. The original mind's various virtues and its characteristic of breaking free from material constraints are determined by the entire cosmic entity.

In his exploration of how the *qian* nature of the universe is manifested as the original mind in humans, Xiong adopts the traditional concepts of receiving and the unity of all things. He believes that the individual's life-mind receives the great life of the universe, though this does not mean that the individual only receives a part of the universal life. In his view, the relationship between the great life of the cosmic flow and the life (mind) possessed by individuals is similar to the Buddhist concept of "the moon reflected in a thousand rivers" or the Neo-Confucian concept of "the one actually manifesting in the myriad phenomena." He says, "The individual lives of all things are the great life of the universe, and the great life of the universe is the individual life of all things."[20] This indicates that, in terms of individual life, the individual's original mind receives the entirety of the great life of the universe, while in terms of universal life, the great life is not separate from all things, and there is no great life outside of all things. In other words, there is also a reciprocal relationship between the great life of the universe and the individual's original mind. It is in this sense that he agrees with the concept of "the unity of all things in the universe." He says, "The grand current of the great life of the universe is called the great life. But the great life does not exist independently of all things. Just as Object A receives the grand current of the great life to live, then the great life is indeed the life of Object A. Object B also receives the grand current of the great life to live, then the great life is the life of Object B as well. The same is true for countless objects."[21] When Xiong speaks of "the unity of all things in the universe," the foundation of its unity is not *qi* or *li*, but life. He points out, "In terms of physical form, humans and all things are distinct, but in terms of life, they are fundamentally one. The original mind of humans is often not confined by selfish desires and intentions, and it is in harmony with all things.[22] Again, the concept of life here differs from its general usage, referring to the mind or consciousness of humans.

Since the individual's life is the received life of the universe, humans' original life possesses the same nature as the universal life. For this reason, Xiong says, "The life-mind inherently possesses the virtues of vitality, smoothness, clarity, strength, and progress. Characteristically, it silently operates within matter, breaking through constraints."[23] In the ethical sense, the life manifested in the individual is the original mind, which is also known as the benevolent mind. In terms of cosmology, *qian* dominates *kun*, and in humans, it manifests as the mind governing the body, not confined by desires or external objects. Xiong says, "The benevolent mind is the discovery of the life force. Life is vast and boundless. In the *Book of Changes*, it is called *qian*, while in my theory of substance and function, I refer to it as *bi*. *Bi* is the dominant force, silently operating within the body and the material universe surrounding the body. It is the one that governs. Before the appearance of living organisms, the tendency of *bi* remained hidden in the material realm, not being revealed. When living organisms first appeared, life force was only manifested as vital functions, and the phenomena of the mind had not yet emerged. From higher animals to humans, the mind began to manifest prominently with the completion of bodily organization, displaying its ability to overcome selfish desires. This is what we call the benevolent mind."[24] This suggests that the root of the original mind lies in the tendency toward *bi* as the cosmic life force, and its basic characteristics include clarity, strength, smoothness, and progress. Its primary function is to restrain the selfish desires of the individual entity. Thus, a person is like a microcosm, being both substance and function. The independent entity represents matter, while the original mind represents spirit. The original mind governs the individual, and efforts to realize the inherent characteristics of the life-mind are deeply rooted in cosmology.

Unlike the emphasis on the "later born" theory of habituation, the theory of original mind focuses on its cosmological significance of "original existence." However, according to Xiong's cosmology, the cosmic entity is unified, and the unified entity inherently possesses the qualities of both *qian* and *kun*. Logically speaking, then, *qian* and *kun* should both have their manifestations in human nature. In other words, since *qian* and *kun* are dual characteristics inherent in the entity, they should also be present as dual aspects in humans. Xiong does not, though, consider himself to be promoting a dualism of good and evil. He states, "There is darkness in *kun*, and all things receive it to take shape. There is light in *qian*, and all things receive it to establish their nature. Nature commands substance, which is the great righteousness of principles. When form burdens nature, things become deformed."[25]

However, he does not believe that *kun* can constitute a contrasting nature to *qian*. *Kun*'s function is to form the body and possess material abilities, while the function of *qian* is to be nature itself, the life-mind. Some of Xiong's students questioned this, asking, "Your teachings are based on the *Book of Changes*, where *qian* represents the mind, light, and strength, without any evil, and *kun* represents matter, darkness, and confusion, inherently lacking good. Does your theory imply a dualism of good and evil, following the coexistence of *qian* and *kun*?"[26] To this, Xiong responds, "Your interpretation seems accurate, but it is not entirely so. *Qian* and *kun* are both aspects of the same unified entity, like the numerous rivers flowing into the vast ocean, and they cannot be regarded as dual elements. Although *qian* and *kun* have opposing natures, *qian* effectively governs *kun*, and it is precisely through their opposition that they complement each other. This is the marvelous aspect of the universal flow."[27] He further states, "Substance cannot possess only the qualities of brightness and clarity without the qualities of darkness and confusion. Substance inherently contains internal contradictions. Otherwise, it would not be capable of transforming and manifesting its functions. As Laozi said, 'Reversal is the movement of the Way.' This understanding is evident in the *Book of Changes*. *Qian* ultimately governs *kun*, and brightness governs darkness, and the contradiction is resolved, leading to the harmony of *qian* and *kun*."[28] He goes on, "Good and evil contradict each other, originating from the opposition between the brightness of *qian* and the darkness of *kun*. When brightness governs darkness, the contradiction is resolved, and *qian* and *kun* merge into one. As for human life, it receives the light to form nature and receives the darkness to shape form. Nature governs form, establishing the path of humanity and expanding the path of the heavens."[29] Based on these statements, Xiong's thought can be summarized as follows: (1) If the entire universe is observed separately, there appear to be two opposing attributes, but when viewed as a whole, *qian* governs *kun*, and *kun* follows *qian*. Therefore, the overall nature of the universe is one of goodness, rather than a duality of opposing nature. (2) Since Xiong defines the entity as unified, the opposing attributes are manifested at the functional level, so it cannot be considered a dualistic theory in terms of entity. (3) Within the universal flow of manifestation, *qian* and *kun* are relatively opposite, representing contradiction, but ultimately, the contradiction is resolved when one aspect submits to the other. This represents complementarity. Since humans are integral to the universal manifestation, the nature of humans also belongs to the goodness of *qian* governing *kun*.

Xiong clearly faces a dilemma here, in that, if the contradiction between *qian* and *kun* is ultimately resolved, the dynamic of "Reversal is the movement of the Way" as further development will be obstructed. However, if the contradiction between *qian* and *kun* is not resolved, there is a possibility of falling into the dualism of good and evil that he seeks to avoid. Therefore, an appropriate interpretation must be given to Xiong's notion of "resolution," i.e., that the resolution of contradiction is not structural but functional. Structurally, the entity always possesses both qualities, light and darkness. However, functionally, they maintain a balance in which light governs darkness. According to Xiong's understanding, functional balance is not merely a result of a power struggle but also of actual harmony. Under the dominance of *qian*, *kun* not only has a contradiction with *qian*, but also cooperates and complements *qian*'s function, mutually realizing the process of cosmic advancement. In his view, opposition does not mean enmity, and endless enmity cannot truly provide a dynamic source for development. It is precisely the harmonious, unobstructed universal manifestation that can be achieved.

From the perspective of the history of dialectics, Xiong's thought offers a unique understanding of the unity of contradictions.

In the ethical sense, original mind refers to conscience and the moral sense, which is consistent with traditional Confucianism. Xiong holds that within human consciousness, there exists both the activating force of benevolence and the selfish desires of the individual. It is incumbent upon individuals to return to themselves and recognize the inherent benevolence within, restraining their selfish desires. Regarding the relationship between original mind and habitual mind, original mind represents the innate self, while the habitual mind represents the experiential self. Original mind is associated with reason (including intuition), while the habitual mind is associated with sensibility. The realization of human life's value lies in the expansion and development of benevolence. The fundamental approach is to preserve one's original mind, expand the virtuous qualities, transform harmful habits, and cultivate virtuous habits.

III. The Theory of Knowledge and Wisdom

In a sense, Xiong's entire theory of *mingxin* aims to demonstrate that traditional ethical cultivation has a foundation in cosmology and anthropology, giving it eternal and universal significance. In another, it attempts to establish a relationship between ethical cultivation and empirical investigation that is consistent with Confucian traditions and adaptable to social development. The "ethical cultivation" he refers to pertains to the cultivation of the spirit and moral character, while "empirical investigation" refers to scientific research. Ethical cultivation aims to expand one's innate moral nature, subdue impurities, and fully realize "wisdom." Empirical investigation, on the other hand, emphasizes clarity of mind, values empirical experience, and seeks "knowledge." Ethical cultivation emphasizes introspection and intuitive understanding, while empirical investigation emphasizes empirical verification and analysis. Ethical cultivation is seen as the Way, while empirical investigation is seen as learning. Xiong holds that the correct approach to these two aspects is to "revere wisdom without belittling knowledge" and to achieve a unity of knowledge and wisdom, giving primacy to moral conscience. Only in this way can the healthy overall development of the spiritual life be ensured.

Ethical cultivation and empirical investigation are both human spiritual activities, but their orientations are different. Ethical cultivation focuses on the self-cultivation of the subject, while empirical investigation involves the study of the external world. According to Xiong's view, this difference lies in the understanding of the relationship between mind and matter. Ancient studies of inner cultivation "only recognized the matters of the mind, while ignoring the external objects," and empirical investigation "only recognized the existence of objects, while ignoring the mind."[30] From Xiong's ontological standpoint, mind and matter are inseparable; thus, any neglect of mind or matter in one's spiritual life is one-sided. When referring to a lack of recognition of the mind in empirical investigation, he points specifically to the original mind. He holds that scientific empirical investigation starts from external things, with subjectivity subordinated to objectivity, aiming to align thinking with the inherent laws of things to form knowledge. Thus, it is characteristic of scientific activity that "knowledge is derived from things." On the other hand, ancient studies of the mind emphasize nurturing the original mind, rejecting the pursuit of external objects, and focusing on self-reflection and transformation to achieve the value of human life. It is therefore characteristic of ethical cultivation that "knowledge is derived from the mind." Xiong holds that both the study of the mind and science have their own rationality, but science neglects the mind in pursuit of external objects, while the study of the mind neglects knowledge and desires. Both, then, are one-sided. Xiong's "philosophical psychology" aims to reconcile the two, providing what he considers to be a comprehensive interactive model between philosophy and science, and between morality and knowledge.

As a modern philosopher, Xiong fully affirms science and scientific methods. He states, "Since the advent of science, its methods have been rigorous, meticulous, thorough, and accurate. The constant advancement of the tools that assist the senses is a great strength. Its achievements accumulate the discoveries and explorations of generations, accumulating steadily and growing continuously. They will continue infinitely, along with boundless nature, and this too is a great strength. Its efficacy conquers nature, utilizes nature, transforms and shapes all things, and even encompasses the entire universe. It is truly impressive."[31] He wholeheartedly acknowledges the effectiveness, systematic nature, and rigor of scientific methods in their pursuit of an understanding of the objective world. He recognizes that the observational tools and experimental means employed in scientific development greatly enhance humanity's ability to perceive the world. He praises the tremendous power of science in understanding the world, transforming the world, and generating wealth. The progress and power of science are key driving factors for Xiong's full affirmation of the status of knowledge and his push to distinguish himself from traditional anti-intellectualism.

On the other hand, Xiong points out that science is only one aspect of human intellectual activity. Scientific methods have both their applicability and their limitations. In his view, the characteristics of scientific methods are "empirical measurement as the foundation and analysis as the essence."[32] These methods cannot be used to apprehend the cosmic ontology or create the original mind. The method of apprehending the cosmic entity is the "technique of contemplation," which involves using the intuitive clarity of the original mind to perceive deeply. Through continuous apprehension, one naturally comprehends and utilizes what is comprehended. The method of creating the original mind is the "introspective recognition" or the "silent knowing method." It involves realizing the innate benevolent mind of human life and discovering the supervisor of inner life. These methods are distinct from scientific methods or psychological methods in philosophy. From the perspective of Xiong's philosophical methods, the technique of contemplation refers to an "outward intuition," while the silent knowing method of introspective recognition is an "inward intuition." It is evident from this that Xiong's philosophy generally emphasizes intuition.

The limitation of science, apart from its inability to serve as a method in philosophy, is that its role as an active force in transforming the natural world does not spontaneously enhance moral realms and moral life. Xiong holds that Zhuangzi's criticism of Hui Shi (also Huizi), calling him "strong in tangible things, but weak in virtue," is equally applicable to science. It correctly highlights the role and limitations of science in the development of material and spiritual civilization. These viewpoints of Xiong evidently aim to resist the spread of scientism. "Strong in tangible things" refers to the effective conquest of nature, while "weak in virtue" implies the inability to establish human values and elevate moral consciousness. This standpoint aligns with the Mystical school in the ongoing debates between science and the philosophy of life.

If, in his later years, Xiong merely repeated the views of the Mystical school from the 1920s, his argument would have lacked any new advancement in the field. The difference between his theory of *mingxin* in "The *Mingxin* Section" and in *A New Treatise on Consciousness-Only* is that, in his later years, Xiong proposed the theory of the unity of wisdom and knowledge. Wisdom refers to sagacity, while knowledge refers primarily to scientific knowledge, encompassing cognitive reason, practical reason, and existential wisdom. Since Xiong pointed out that the role of science is not unlimited and that the progress of scientific knowledge does not necessarily lead to the enhancement of philosophical insight and moral wisdom, it inevitably raises the question of the distinction between wisdom and knowledge.

1. Investigating Things as the Basis of Acquiring Knowledge

Xiong holds that the distinction between wisdom and knowledge is an important issue in ancient philosophy. Daoism advocates returning to profound, transcendent knowledge, while Buddhism emphasizes the emptiness of knowledge. Although they have their biases, distinguishing between wisdom and knowledge is a matter of practical observation. In Xiong's philosophy, wisdom refers to the function of the inherent mind, which has four characteristics. The first characteristic is that it is "concentrated, not scattered" and "clear, not confused." The second is that it is "ignorance and omnipotence." Ignorance here refers to the inherent nature of wisdom without false thoughts, while omnipotence refers to wisdom in perceiving things and being able to clearly illuminate the physical world. The third characteristic is that wisdom serves as the guiding force of ethical consciousness, known as "conscience," enabling wisdom to dominate and eliminate bad habits. The fourth is that wisdom is not static knowledge, but an active subject. It serves as the fundamental condition for the formation of knowledge, playing an important role in intellectual activities.

In Buddhism, there is the concept of transforming consciousness into wisdom, and in the study of the mind, a distinction is likewise drawn between conscience and knowledge. Regarding the first three characteristics of wisdom, its proposition obviously inherits the distinction between wisdom and knowledge in Buddhism, as well as the differentiation between knowledge based on moral virtues and knowledge based on sensory perception in Neo-Confucianism. The difference between Xiong's theory of knowledge and wisdom and the concepts found in Buddhism and Neo-Confucianism lies in his emphasis on the significance of wisdom as a cognitive subject. On the one hand, he points out, "Knowledge is indeed a reflection of the objective reality of the world, but the formation of knowledge ultimately requires an inherent driving force that delves into and distinguishes things, and this driving force is the inherent clarity of our own minds, which is what wisdom is."[33] This indicates the agency of the cognitive subject in the formation of knowledge. On the other hand, his description of the clarity and the omnipotence of wisdom both imply the intuitive nature of wisdom itself, thus emphasizing the important role of wisdom's intuition in knowledge. He states, "I believe that all major academic discoveries arise from the sudden movement of the celestial mechanism. This celestial mechanism is the sudden opening of a single point of clarity," and "this single point of clarity is naturally inherent in our minds." He continues. "For anyone engaged in the study of investigating things, when solving major problems, they must first start with assumptions, and when making assumptions, they rely solely on the internal clarity of the mind and are immediately inspired." He adds, "Purely objective methods are particularly important after assumptions are made, but the process of making assumptions relies on a single point of clarity in the mind, in other words, the matter of wisdom."[34] In other words, intuition is the unique attribute of wisdom, and it is argued that the acquisition of knowledge depends on wisdom and the cultivation of the wise subject in order to generate intuition.

Xiong refers to the cultivation of the wise subject and the full utilization of its functions as "attaining wisdom." He summarizes the viewpoint that acquiring knowledge depends on the wise subject and its cultivation as "investigating things based on attaining knowledge (wisdom)." Here, he clearly implies a certain model of Wang Yangming's theory of attaining knowledge. However, he believes the knowledge that is "attained" actually refers to wisdom, and he criticizes Wang Yangming for considering consciousness as a core entity rather than as a function. Nevertheless, he acknowledges that Wang Yangming's theory of attaining knowledge had a significant influence on him. Similar to Wang Yangming's explanation of "attaining," attaining wisdom means nurturing, expanding, developing, and utilizing one's inherent innate "wisdom." Based on the four fundamental characteristics of wisdom mentioned earlier, four specific approaches to attaining wisdom can be derived: self-reflection, emptiness and tranquility, abandoning selfishness, and utilizing objects. Self-reflection involves introspection and experiential verification of the inherent clarity of one's own mind. Abandoning selfishness means restraining various unwholesome habits and transforming them into wholesome ones. Emptiness and tranquility refer to a cultivation practice that aims to enhance the capacity for heightened intuition through a state of emptiness and tranquility. Utilizing objects implies that the attainment of conscience must manifest in and be expressed through activities that involve understanding and transforming the world. The aspects of self-reflection, emptiness and tranquility, and abandoning selfishness suggest that attaining wisdom is a subjective method that differs from the objective method of investigating things (science). It consistently focuses on the cultivation of the subject and the expression of its inherent moral and cognitive functions. In these aspects, we can observe an inheritance from the Song-Ming Confucian statement that "investigating things pertains to the world, and attaining knowledge pertains to the mind."[35]

2. Investigating Things as the Beginning of Attaining Knowledge

Where Xiong's theory of attaining wisdom particularly differs from Wang Yangming's theory of attaining knowledge is in the aspect of "utilizing objects." Xiong says, "Wang Yangming opposes investigating things, which means rejecting knowledge."[36] He adds, "*Great Learning* investigates things, and Zhu Xi's commentary supplements it. It does not deviate from the intention of the sages, but Lu-Wang misunderstood it."[37] He holds that Wang Yangming's theory of attaining knowledge through investigating things only focuses on self-reflection, while neglecting the utilization of objects. He advocates that attaining wisdom must be realized through attaining knowledge. He states, "Wisdom should not be stagnant in emptiness or succumb to annihilation," but, "it must be applied to all things, originated in all knowledge, in order to witness wonderful transformations and the subtlety of changes."[38] Wang Yangming's theory of attaining knowledge also emphasizes "learning through engagement with things." It states that attaining knowledge "must be based on real matters" and "should not be the mere empty pursuit of knowledge, but knowledge should be applied to practical matters." There is, though, a subtle yet significant difference between Xiong's insistence on utilizing objects in attaining wisdom and Wang's approach. While Xiong's explanation of attaining knowledge is similar to Wang Yangming's, his interpretation of investigating things differs. Xiong understands investigating things as the study of various phenomena to acquire knowledge, and science is understood to be the primary form of investigating things. He says, "It is necessary to expand the inherent clarity of our own minds and apply it to all external objects, exhaustively study the laws and essence of things, and adapt and transform them to fully utilize their nature. Thus, we gain knowledge that enables us to experience, delve into, control, create, and utilize things. It can be said that the key to attaining knowledge lies in investigating things."[39] He adds, "I believe that the inherent clarity of the mind is a natural phenomenon. We must strive to use this inherent clarity to pursue, distinguish, govern, and utilize things in order to obtain accurate knowledge."[40] It is clear that "utilizing objects" refers to investigating things and acquiring scientific knowledge. In Wang Yangming's philosophy, investigating things is understood as a specific form of attaining a moral conscience, which is to employ specific actions or employ the principle of Heaven in concrete matters to transcend personal desires. It does not affirm the independent, rational status of attaining knowledge, such as resolving disputes by upholding the principle of Heaven while listening to litigation or upholding the principle of Heaven while reading. Although Xiong's formulation follows the expression, "attaining knowledge through investigating things," his interpretation differs from that of Zhu Xi and Wang Yangming. He provides a modern interpretation of the text of the *Great Learning* by stating that "conscience must be applied to practical matters and developed into knowledge."[41] In this interpretation, scientific research is considered an essential part of attaining wisdom. Science and knowledge attainment are no longer regarded solely as a form of moral practice. As a part of the pursuit of wisdom, science includes the need to develop knowledge and overcome nature. In this interpretation, science undoubtedly gains a considerable degree of independence compared to previous understandings.

3. The Prevalence of Moral Conscience as a Guide for the Application of Knowledge

As mentioned earlier, the affirmation of scientific knowledge is just one aspect of Xiong's philosophy. In fact, it is the emphasis on life and values that forms the central theme of the entire theory of *mingxin*. The distinction between wisdom and knowledge is precisely to emphasize the guidance of wisdom in light of the acknowledged role of science. In terms of the relationship between moral conscience and knowledge, the cultivation of wisdom requires the utilization of moral conscience in engaging with the world and expanding into knowledge. At the same time, the process of applying knowledge must be guided by moral conscience. Xiong states, "If moral conscience remains in control and selfish desires are unable to exploit opportunities for personal gain, then the utilization of all knowledge will undoubtedly follow the prevalence of moral conscience."[42] He goes on, "Moral conscience is ever-present in daily life. When it governs, one interacts with and discerns all things, shaping and transforming them in accordance with moral conscience."[43] In other words, the path of cultivating wisdom requires the integration of moral conscience into knowledge attainment, and knowledge must be attained and prevalent in accordance with moral conscience. The combination of these two aspects constitutes the concept of "the unity of wisdom and knowledge," which means that wisdom cannot be separated from knowledge, and knowledge cannot be separated from wisdom. In terms of the Confucian tradition, these ideas espoused by Xiong are inherited from the School of Mind. Wang Yangming, for instance, states, "If one's thoughts and mind are exclusively dedicated to the realization of moral conscience, then the accumulation of knowledge and experience in daily life is nothing other than the conscience."[44] Wang Longxi (1498–1583) likewise emphasizes the distinction between wisdom and knowledge, stating, "If one genuinely believes in moral conscience and acts accordingly, then all knowledge will serve the purpose of moral conscience."[45] These ideas had a profound influence on Xiong Shili.

In Xiong's theory of the unity of wisdom and knowledge, the proposition, *investigating things as the basis of acquiring knowledge, investigating things as the beginning of attaining knowledge*, and *the prevalence of moral conscience as a guide for the application of knowledge*, summarize the dominant view expressed in "The *Mingxin* Section." In this model, cultivating wisdom entails both cognitive and ethical functions, asserting that wisdom must unfold into cognitive activities. At the same time, it still insists on the priority of wisdom over knowledge, thereby failing to fully realize the independence of knowledge. Ultimately, the issue addressed in the entire theory of *mingxin* revolves around the relationship among morality, values, science, and technology. This problem can be traced back to the debates on virtue and learning in the medieval period and remains a central topic of contention between the rationality of science and the morality of worldview after the spread of Western learning in the East. In fact, Max Weber notes that the process of modernization involves a conflict between value rationality and instrumental rationality. In this sense, Xiong's theory of *mingxin* not only inherits the classical spiritual tradition, but also faces the crisis of values that emerged alongside the great development of the modern world and instrumental rationality. He points out, "In recent times, humans have been inclined toward the development of knowledge. Once knowledge becomes established, it becomes power. Power is something that is exercised upon the external world. Laozi and Zhuangzi rejected knowledge, not without reason... Rejecting knowledge is not taking a middle path. If one pursues knowledge, loses one's spiritual essence, and sacrifices life for material things, then one cannot disregard the purpose of Daoism. At the same time, Daoism rejects desires and discards material possessions, sacrificing life for material things results in a fall and the loss of meaning and value in human life. This is lamentable."[46] According to Xiong, science and knowledge themselves are not irrational. Still, if the subject employing knowledge lacks the constraints of moral values, knowledge can become an accomplice to tyranny and oppression. On the national level, imperialism utilizes science and technology to oppress less developed countries and peoples, exemplifying knowledge detached from the guidance of wisdom. This is the knowledge-power relationship he refers to. On an individual level, those with knowledge who lack ethical guidance often commit greater evil than the ignorant. Therefore, although the knowledge system itself is neither good nor evil, when understanding knowledge from a practical perspective, one cannot unconditionally affirm the neutrality of knowledge's value. In social life, knowledge that actively operates takes on a specific practical form. For example, lawyers use legal knowledge to handle litigation, and doctors utilize medical knowledge to treat patients. Though the process of using knowledge to achieve certain goals is not identical to knowledge itself, knowledge is undoubtedly an important factor in this process, and this process cannot be completely detached from the significance of values. In ethical terms, the unity of wisdom and knowledge refers to the fact that the process of applying knowledge should not deviate from the constraints of moral conscience. Positively speaking, the process of applying knowledge should simultaneously be a process of the prevalence of moral conscience. Xiong believes that this model of the unity of wisdom and knowledge is also the appropriate relationship between philosophy and science in modern society. "If wisdom is the master of knowledge, knowledge will not be used for evil purposes. Philosophy relies on science without becoming abstract, while science relies on philosophy and has its overall framework. The paths are different, but converge into the same channel."[47] Wisdom must unfold into knowledge and dominate it, while philosophy relies on knowledge and governs it. However, it should be noted that when Xiong speaks of philosophy, he is referring to systems that have traditionally had the function of nurturing the mind and purifying the heart.

The fundamental ideas contained in Xiong's theory of the unity of wisdom and knowledge are clear, but upon closer examination, the argumentation and conceptual elaboration still lack rigor, and they tend to remain in the realm of generalities within traditional philosophy. For instance, in terms of the statement "the investigation of things is based on attaining knowledge," attaining wisdom is meaningful from the perspective of the cognitive subject, but the concept of attaining knowledge lacks clarity of meaning when considering the statement, "Attaining knowledge lies in the investigation of things." While the demand for integrating conscience into knowledge attainment represents progress compared to Neo-Confucianism, the justification for why moral knowledge should be developed into intellectual knowledge is not well established.

In the notion of the unity of wisdom and knowledge, the term knowledge primarily refers to the application of knowledge. However, using the general term knowledge can easily blur the distinction between the system of knowledge and practical knowledge, between the pursuit and the utilization of knowledge, and between epistemology and ethics. As the study of knowledge, epistemology is unrelated to moral considerations such as the origin, occurrence, and development of knowledge. The acquisition of knowledge also has its independent mechanisms that do not rely on moral awareness or require its involvement. Advocating a general unity of wisdom and knowledge can lead to misunderstandings that moral awareness must be involved in all cognitive activities, blurring the boundaries between the fields of epistemology and ethics.

Xiong's theory of *mingxin* aims to "preserve the original mind, transform habitual tendencies, and prioritize wisdom over knowledge." In terms of its relationship with traditional Confucianism, it bears many characteristics of the School of Mind, though Xiong exhibits some noticeable differences from the traditional Lu-Wang School of Mind. Xiong's distinction between the original mind and the habitual mind is based on his own philosophy of the non-duality of substance and function, regardless of whether this philosophy is inherent in the original ideas of the *Book of Changes*. This point is clearly distinct from the views of Lu-Wang. Additionally, Xiong's differentiation between the original mind and habitual mind is influenced by the Yogācāra school of Buddhism, from which he draws several ideas and transforms them.

Regarding Xiong's theory of mind and matter, while he considers the original mind and moral awareness as the transcendental principles of knowing right from wrong, he clearly expresses his disagreement with the notion that there is no reason outside of the mind and opposes the theory of no external existence. He emphasizes that there is reason and substance beyond the mind, thus necessitating scientific investigation. Although he still regards rationality as a unified entity and emphasizes the unity of morality and knowledge within the same subject (original mind, wisdom, natural clarity, moral awareness), he explicitly distinguishes between the domains of moral and intellectual functions. He no longer adheres to the School of Mind's traditional opposition between knowledge derived from moral character and that obtained through sensory experience. Instead, he affirms the positive significance of knowledge acquired through perception and experience. His pursuit of knowledge is no longer solely focused on ethical self-cultivation, as it has been endowed with the function of cognition.

In particular, unlike the School of Mind's vehement opposition to Zhu Xi, Xiong affirms Zhu Xi's theory of investigating things, while criticizing Wang Yangming's theory of investigating things. This does not imply that he does not confine himself to the intentions of the Lu-Wang tradition. In fact, Xiong's theories of investigation and intellectual comprehension incorporate elements from both Zhu Xi and Wang Yangming, providing evidence for each. His advocacy for the extension of moral awareness incorporates Wang's theory of attaining knowledge, but he simultaneously rejects the purely introspective aspects and seeks to develop moral awareness into knowledge. His adoption of scientific investigation draws from Zhu Xi's theory of investigating things, but unlike Zhu Xi, he does not attempt to enhance moral character through exhaustively comprehending principles. Instead, he acknowledges the independent significance of science and considers investigating things to be an indispensable part of manifesting the full power of wisdom. This makes his assertions, "investigating things as the basis of acquiring knowledge" and "investigating things as the beginning of attaining knowledge," distinct from both Zhu Xi and Wang Yangming.

From the perspective of "The *Mingxin* Section," the biggest difference between Xiong and traditional Confucianism lies in their attitudes toward knowledge. Although he still adopts a value-oriented position, his system dissolves the tension between value and knowledge in the traditional sense, achieving a certain degree of balance and rejecting the anti-intellectualism demonstrated by traditional Confucianism through criticism of "fragmentation and external searching." This reflects an effort to accommodate science and the status of knowledge to the greatest extent, while adhering to the priority of Confucian values and rationality. In other aspects, such as the affirmation of desire based on the ontology of life and criticism of traditional philosophy's idea of sacrificing desire, as well as the emphasis on "vigorous progress" based on the principle of *qian* / *bi* dominance and criticism of the traditional philosophical emphasis on static cultivation, it also demonstrates his conscious efforts to overcome the shortcomings of traditional Confucianism.

Even so, Xiong still shows a tendency toward pursuing a unifying skill. The goal of the unity of wisdom and knowledge as an ideal personality undoubtedly provides a direction for human life in modern society. If, like traditional Neo-Confucianism, one believes that there can be a unified approach to learning, whether it is through the investigation of things and the exhaustion of principles or the cultivation of the ultimate good of moral knowledge, aiming for the perfection of human development, then the inherent shortcomings of traditional Confucianism have not been completely overcome. It is unable to truly transform Confucianism into a theoretical form that is adaptable to modern society. In other words, unity of wisdom and knowledge cannot be regarded as a unifying skill. The principle of the unity of wisdom and knowledge must be clearly defined to not involve epistemology because the social application of knowledge does not belong to the realm of epistemology. The process of cognition and education have their independent laws, and because of this, we can completely avoid the various negative effects of moralistic doctrine. It should be acknowledged that in these aspects, the resolution in "The *Mingxin* Section" must be considered imperfect.

From the perspective of daily life and the hierarchy of needs, moral demands receive a higher evaluation than knowledge. While the development and achievements of cognition have been the main driving force behind historical progress in modern times, viewed from the perspective of the Confucian emphasis on value-oriented rationality, it is always a meaningful issue to establish an appropriate relationship between the two. It should be pointed out that many contemporary critics have criticized the notion of "combining democracy and science" in contemporary Neo-Confucianism. In fact, the notion of "combination" does not mean that democracy and science can only be achieved based on Confucian thought. It simply means that contemporary

Confucianism consciously seeks the integration of traditional values and scientific democracy in modern society. This integration, as reflected in the theory of Neo-Confucianism, still needs to be established on the basis of value-oriented rationality. Otherwise, this theory would not be "Confucian" in any form. Only in this sense can we avoid the shallow criticism of the notion of "combination" and delve into the essence of "modernity" as a fundamental issue.

Notes

1. Chen Lai, "A Study on the Theory of Substance and Function in Xiong Shili's Philosophy," *Philosophy Research*, no. 1 (1986).
2. *The* Mingxin *Section* (Shanghai Longmont Publishing, 1959), 1.
3. "Preface," in *The* Mingxin *Section*.
4. *The* Mingxin *Section*, 1
5. Ibid., 147.
6. Ibid., 118.
7. Ibid.
8. Ibid., 120.
9. Ibid., 148.
10. Ibid., 123.
11. Ibid., 121.
12. Ibid., 121.
13. Ibid., 122.
14. Ibid., 149.
15. The concept of the habitual mind is also seen in classical Confucianism, as Liu Zongzhou also discusses both the original mind and the habitual mind. Editor's note: Lu-Wang means Lu Jiuyuan and Wang Yangming.
16. *The* Mingxin *Section*, 3.
17. Ibid., 1.
18. Ibid., 2.
19. Ibid., 8.
20. Ibid.
21. Ibid., 154.
22. Ibid., 198.
23. Ibid., 5.
24. Ibid., 90.
25. Ibid., 153.
26. Ibid., 158.
27. Ibid.
28. Ibid., 169.
29. Ibid., 177.
30. Ibid., 22.
31. Ibid., 101.

32. Ibid., 205.
33. Ibid., 124.
34. Ibid., 129.
35. *Zhuzi Yulei*, vol. 15.
36. *The* Mingxin *Section*, 137.
37. Ibid., 33.
38. Ibid., 123.
39. Ibid., 117.
40. Ibid., 180.
41. Ibid., 133.
42. Ibid., 175.
43. Ibid., 135.
44. "Response to Quyang Chongyi," in *The Collected Works of Wang Yangming*, vol. 2.
45. "Response to Wu Wuzhai," in *The Collected Works of Wang Longxi*, vol. 10.
46. *The* Mingxin *Section*, 134.
47. Ibid., 203.

CHAPTER 4

The Theory of Principles, Vital Energy, Substance, and Function in Ma Yifu's Philosophy

Ma Yifu (1883–1967), formerly known as Ma Fu, was a famous scholar in modern times. He ranked first at the county examinations in Shaoxing in the Wuxu year during the reign of Emperor Guangxu (1898). Other well-known candidates who took the examination at the same time include Zhou Shuren, known by his pen name Lu Xun, and his younger brother Zhou Zuoren. Following the Reform Movement of 1898, Ma Yifu planned to revitalize China through academics with Xie Wuliang and Ma Junwu, and they founded the *Translation World of the Twentieth Century*. Ma Yifu later pursued Western Literature and History in the United States in 1903 and subsequently Western Philosophy in Japan in 1907. In the sixth year of the Republic of China (1917), Cai Yuanpei was appointed Education Minister, and he recruited Ma Yifu as the Secretary-General, but the latter resigned in March due to differences in views. Ma Yifu later retired to Guanghua Temple by West Lake and devoted his time to the study of the *Complete Library of the Four Treasuries*. He also delved into both Confucianism and Buddhism, with a particular interest in the study of righteousness. In 1918, Cai Yuanpei invited Ma Yifu to be the Dean of the Faculty of Arts at Peking University, but Ma declined, citing the urgency of his commitments.

While residing in the countryside, Ma Yifu forged friendships far and wide. In 1938, he sought refuge from the war in Taihe, Jiangxi. He accepted the invitation from Zhu Kezhen, the President of Zhejiang University, to deliver lectures while on the move to Zhejiang University. In the same year, he relocated to Yishan, Guangxi, and continued teaching at the new campus of Zhejiang University. In 1939, Ma taught at the Fuxing Academy in Leshan, Sichuan, where he emphasized the importance of discussing engraved books in the context of Confucianism. In

1953, he was appointed Director of the Zhejiang Museum of Culture and History. He suffered from eye ailments in his later years, but it was during that period of time when he penned the poem "Riding the winds of transformation, I find peace in adaptability—Embracing the boundless, where form and spirit freely roam—Gathering and dispersing, a harmonious dance unfolds—Sight and sound dissolve into a tranquil state—Effortlessly merging with the vast sea, extinguishing the self—Blossoms unfold, adorning every branch in full bloom—Standing on the precipice, I wave my hand in farewell—As the setting sun descends beyond the distant hills."[1] Scholars hold Ma Yifu in high regard in the context of the intellectual history of 20th-century China. In the 1940s, He Lin once lauded him as "the last gem of traditional Chinese culture," and Taiwan and Hong Kong-based Neo-Confucian philosopher Xu Fuguan regarded Ma Yifu, Xiong Shili, Liang Shuming, and Zhang Junmai as "the Four Contemporary Confucians." This chapter delves into the theory of principles, vital energy, substance, and function in Ma Yifu's philosophy and, in so doing, explores his attitude towards traditional discourse and its significance.

I. Function Begins with Substance

The theory of *li* (principles) and *qi* (vital energy) is the primary concern in Ma Yifu's philosophy, as it is in Neo-Confucianism. Ma Yifu's perspective of principles and vital energy was deeply influenced by the Cheng-Zhu school of thought. He believes that:

> Both principles and vital energy originated from Confucius' idea that "whatever is metaphysical is Way, whatever physical is tools." In other words, what is said with constant principle is Way, while the condensation of vital energy is tools. In *Qian Zao Du* (On Chiseling Open the Regularity of Heaven), it is said, "The *taiyi* (Great Change) has yet seen *qi*; the *taichu* (Great Inchoate) is the beginning of *qi*; the *taisu* (Great Purity) is the beginning of substance; the *taishi* (Great Extreme) is the beginning of form." This statement suggests that where there is form, there must be substance; where there is substance, there must be vital energy; and where there is vital energy, there must be principles. The concept of "unseen *qi*" is akin to principles, much like what Chengzi* calls "boundless and without form." Without differentiating principles, it can be said to be pure principles, but vital energy is not absent. The latter is merely yet to be visible. Thus, Chengzi also says, "Everything is already in place and exists for a reason." Principles are inherently silent, and it is only with movement that vital energy becomes apparent, which explains the term "the beginning of *qi*." *Qi* begins with movement, and it is through movement that *qi* becomes visible. Movement progresses from slight to coarse, from minute to substantial, and therefore transitions from vital energy to substance and from

* An honorific title for Neo-Confucianists Cheng Hao and Cheng Yi in the Song Dynasty.

> substance to form. The movement of the metaphysical involves gradually advancing segment by segment, from coarse to slight, from visible to invisible. It is then understood that when vital energy is yet to be visible, only pure principles exist. When vital energy becomes visible, principles operate within it. Thus, it is said, "All substances originate from a single source, unified without separation." They did not emerge as two distinct entities from the primordial beginning.[2]

Ma Yifu concurs with the key categories outlined in *Yi Wei* that distinguish the main stages of cosmic evolution. He also embraces certain ideas in Neo-Confucianism about the origin of the universe. He believes that *taiyi* corresponds to the state or stage that Cheng Yi describes as "boundless and without form, and everything is already in place and exists for a reason." According to traditional interpretations of Neo-Confucianism, "boundless and without a form" refers to the purely metaphysical realm of principles. Ma Yifu thus also uses the phrase "purely of principles" to denote this stage. According to Ma, everything is considered a "form," and form is made of substance, which is composed of vital energy. The relationship of vital energy—substance—form not only represents different constitutive levels in a synchronic sense, but also constitutes the evolutionary process of cosmic development. In Ma Yifu's view, *qi* is not the representative state of the beginning of the universe, as asserted by proponents of the primordial *qi* theory. There exists a more fundamental stage before the prevalent activity of *qi*, known as unseen *qi*. At the stage of unseen *qi*, *qi* is not absent; it is purely made up of principles, which explains the saying, "When *qi* is yet to be visible, only pure principles exist." At the stage of visible *qi*, it is not that principles disappear. Rather, "When *qi* becomes visible, principles operate within it." Similarly, when form and substance are present, principles operate within all things.

However, acknowledging the presence of the stage of unseen *qi* and recognizing that "when *qi* is yet to be visible, only pure principles exist" does not imply that Ma naturally subscribes to the belief that vital energy is generated from principles, or that principles precede vital energy. He says:

> "The positions of heaven and earth" and "the formation of *qian* and *kun*" were in place only after *qi* became visible. As for "changes occurring within" and "the position within," those refer to principles. "There is no way to perceive changes when *qian* and *kun* are destroyed," which implies that there is no way to perceive principles without vital energy. We read, "If changes cannot be observed, *qian* and *kun* could almost cease to exist," which implies that vital energy would not exist without this principle either. Changes involve *taiji* (the supreme ultimate), which gives rise to the two principles. The two principles give rise to the four phenomena, and the four phenomena give rise to the eight trigrams. This explains the saying, "The generation of life is known as changes." The reason for generation is infinite. Before the *taiji* took form, it was boundless and without form. It can be said that *qi* was within *li*. After the *taiji* took form, everything became diverse and varied. It can be said that *li* was within *qi*. Seasons change, beings come to live, and time

> passes like the river flow, going on day and night. The great transformations of heaven and earth move silently, unending. This is what is meant by "changes occur within."[3]

Ma Yifu asserts that without *qi*, there is no way to perceive *li*; without *li*, *qi* would not exist. Thus, the term *taiji* here refers to primordial *qi*. "Before the *taiji* took form" can also be said to be a state of unseen *qi*, not an absence of *qi*. It can be said that "*qi* was within *li*" at this stage. "After the *taiji* took form" can be said to be the state after *qi* became visible, or that *li* was within *qi*. As Cheng Yi puts it, "Boundless and without form, everything is already in place and exists for a reason," and the pure realm of principles encompasses everything that exists. "Exists" includes the existence of *qi*. While Ma Yifu's theory was derived from Cheng Yi's, there is a difference.

Qi is in the physical form, while *li* is in the metaphysical form. It is difficult to justify assertions that *qi* "is" or "exists" in *li*, even within the system of Neo-Confucianism. We need not explore how Ma's *qi* exists within *li*. In fact, Ma's statement simply suggests that at the stage of *taiyi*, *qi* is not truly non-existent, only unseen. It is "purely in principle, but vital energy is not absent." The saying "*qi* is within *li*" also suggests that while *qi* is unseen, it still exists and is not absent. In other words, the primordial state of the universe is a special state where both *li* and *qi* exist.

Ma Yifu further points out:

> Shao Yong* says, "Flow is *qi*, while mastery is *li*." Those who are not adept tend to dichotomize *li* and *qi*, unaware that there is no clear divide between motion and stillness, and no beginning to *yin* and *yang*. *Li* and *qi* coexist in no particular order, only when verbalized.[4] *Qi* refers to the functional manifestation, while *li* refers to the substrate of manifestation. Manifestation is evident, but the substrate is subtle. While they can be separated by words, they cannot be divided in reality.[5]

This goes to show that in reality, *li* and *qi* are inseparable. In philosophical utterance, *li* is an abstraction of principles in reality, which can be separated from things in thought. This is a separation by logic. In philosophy, the categories of *li* and *qi* are discussed separately, but in reality, *li* and *qi* are inseparable. Therefore, in reality, *li* and *qi* coexist in no particular order. In theory, the analysis and correlation of *li* and *qi* are only the result of logical analysis, as *li* serves as the basis and premise of *qi* logically. Thus, the order that arises from verbal expression is merely a logical sequence in analytical terms and does not indicate an actual sequence. In reality, there is no clear divide between motion and stillness, and no beginning to *yin* and *yang*. *Li* and *qi* coexist in no particular order.

Ma also largely inherited the analyses of Neo-Confucianism in other aspects of the theory of principles and vital energy. For instance, he says, "The existence of one *yin* and one *yang* inherently

---

* Shao Yong (1011–1077), courtesy name Yaofu, named Shao Kangjie, was a Chinese cosmologist, historian, philosopher, and poet who greatly influenced the development of Neo-Confucianism across China during the Song Dynasty.

has a reason, and this is Way,"[6] and, "The terms congeal and gather in Wang Yangming's School of Mind are inappropriate to begin with, ... both congeal and gather pertain to the aspect of *qi*. *Li* operates within *qi*. It is not correct to say that *li* congeals within *qi*."[7] He also says, "Heaven, Earth, humans, and objects fundamentally share the same nature. In other words, they share the same principles and vital energy. Principles are undifferentiated, while vital energy has differences."[8] Ma's theory of principles and vital energy is significantly influenced by Zhu Xi.

Ma Yifu particularly opposes interpreting the classical philosophical view of principles and vital energy as a form of dualism. Indeed, in the history of Western philosophy, typical dualism reduces the universe to two completely different independent entities that cannot be determined or derived from each other. In this sense, the theory of principles and vital energy, whereby flow is vital energy and mastery is principles, does not consider principles and vital energy as two independent entities. In Chinese philosophy, vital energy is the functional manifestation of flow, while principles are the substrate of manifestation. The two share a common source, intimately connected at a microscopic level, "not emerging as two distinct entities from the primordial beginning."

II. Returning Function to Substance

The philosophical analysis of principles and vital energy in Neo-Confucianism is not confined to the scope of ontology. A typical example is the Four-Seven Debate by Zhu Xi in Korean Confucianism during the Joseon period, which integrates the theory of principles and vital energy into the theory of mind and nature, whereby emotions are regarded as vital energy, while nature is regarded as principles. Broadly speaking, the theory of principles and vital energy not only has ontological significance, but also carries the theory of mind and nature. Ma Yifu also inherited this tradition.

Ma states:

> It is important to make a clear distinction when using the terms *li* and *qi*, and Way and tools. At times, without careful consideration of the text, a lack of understanding may result in generalization. Now, let me illustrate with the simplest example: the ears, eyes, mouth, and body are tools. Those capable of seeing, hearing, speaking, and moving embody *qi*. To see, hear, speak, and move is part of *li*. Seeing, hearing, speaking, and moving should be considered *li* and constitute Way.[9]

Here, he states that the physiological body and organs of a person are tools, the functional activities of the organs are *qi*, the norms of the organ activities are *li*, and sensory physiological activities in accordance with principles are Way. Ma believes that there is a subtle distinction between *li* and Way, in which he says, "Speaking of *li* and Way, there is a slight difference. *Li* is inherently silent, only perceptible through deep understanding; Way is explicit and observable, evident in its manifestation."[10] *Li* refers to the profound and subtle principles of the universe, while Way is the rational state manifested in specific entities. He further states:

> It must be understood that perception, observations, and movement are all manifestations of *qi*. The reason they are perceived, moved, seen, and heard is attributed to *li*. *Li* operates within *qi*, so how can *li* exist when separated from perception, observations, and movement? However, ordinary people regard perception and observations as the result of *qi*, while *li* remains concealed and inactive. … Perception and observations still exist only within the realm of *qi*, without the presence of *li*. It is important to note that the learning of sages involves the entirety of *qi* being *li*, and the entirety of *li* being *qi*. One cannot speak of *qi* without reference to *li*, nor can one discuss *li* without considering *qi*. Therefore, to align with principles and guide this vital energy, the key lies solely in the virtue of reverence. This approach is remarkably concise, unlike the elaborate methods of various external paths.[11]

The activities of the body, as well as perceptions, emotions, and thoughts, all fall under the realm of vital energy. Principles, on the other hand, refer to the inherent guidelines of these activities. From an ontological perspective, *taiji* takes the form of *qi*, with *li* existing within *qi*. There are inherent principles in the activities of *qi*. However, *li* and *qi* in the human body differ from those in the heavens and earth. In the cosmos, the movement of *qi* is natural, and what is necessary invariably permeates within it all the time. Yet, within the human body, there is a distinction between the action and inaction of the principles of perception, observations, and movement. Perception and movement are entirely governed by sensory nature. Although *li* is present within them and not apart, it remains "concealed and inactive." Only by allowing rationality to adhere to guidelines to govern sensory movements can one truly embody *li* within the realm of *qi*. Ma further states:

> The mind controls nature, emotions, principles, and vital energy. Principles operate within the realm of vital energy, while nature operates within the realm of emotions. However, there are times when there is an imbalance of energy, a failure in principles, when emotions are in excess, or when true nature is concealed. This is why it is said that when the mind is synonymous with principles, there is no place for emotions.[12]

In other words, the saying, "The mind controls nature and emotions," encompasses both the aspects of principles (nature) and vital energy (emotions). If we say, "The mind is synonymous with principles," it can only encompass principles, while the status of vital energy (emotions) is lost. Therefore, with regard to the theory of mind and nature, Ma Yifu advocates following the teachings of Zhang Zai and Zhu Xi rather than those of Lu Jiuyuan and Wang Yangming. There, he emphasizes considering the mind as the encompassing framework for all conscious activities, which covers both aspects of principles and vital energy. If perceptual movement is subject to the influence of vital energy without restraint, the imbalance of the vital energy's rigidity, flexibility, goodness, and evil will manifest as the loss of emotions. The outcome would be "a failure in principles." In this case, it cannot be said that the mind is synonymous with principles. The function of vital energy is to make sight, hearing, speech, and movement possible, while the function of principles is to provide rational guidelines for sight, hearing, speech, and movement. Therefore, in the field of ethics, vital energy represents all sensory activities, while principles represent the rational guidelines that sensory activities should adhere to. Moral conduct thus involves aligning the mind to "follow principles and be guided by vital energy." If examined strictly, the "principles" to be followed are not those inherently present in this mind or detached from perceptual movement. Instead, they manifest as something embodied in specific principles. He further states, "Sight, hearing, speech, and movement are related to vital energy, form, appearance, and manifestation. Ritual embodies principles, aligns with natural disposition, and fulfills the body. Inappropriate manifestation is impropriety, going against one's nature, and a lack of ritual results in incomplete use. Appropriate manifestation is propriety, aligning with one's nature, and conforming to ritual leads to prepared use. For this reason, considering sight, hearing, speech, and movement as rituals is the embodiment of shaping one's conduct. By aligning with principles and being guided by vital energy, these four aspects manifest the flow of heavenly principles and display benevolence."[13] Here, aligning with principles and being guided by vital energy does not refer to a pre-existing state, but rather, the effort of the heart and the mind. It does not mean that principles naturally guide and govern perceptual movement through the inherent reason of every individual. Instead, sensory activities are led by the acknowledgment of specific principles through rational activities, though Ma himself has not clearly articulated this distinction.

III. The Whole Substance Is Function, the Whole Function Is Substance

Ma Yifu's philosophy of substance and function, like Xiong Shili's, is significantly influenced by Chinese Buddhist tradition's discourse on substance and function. He builds upon this and develops a theory of substance and function that represents his worldview to a considerable extent. This theory serves as a paradigm for his method, evident in analysis and construction across various specific domains. Further research into his theory of substance and function will give us more comprehensive insights into Ma Yifu's philosophy.

Ma's theory of substance and function can be simplified as a process of "affirmation, negation, synthesis," or function beginning from substance, function returning to substance, the whole substance as a function, and the whole function as a substance. Such a model is not the same as Hegel's diachronic logical structure. Instead, it is a synchronic comprehensive analysis that originated from Buddhism. The propositions of function beginning from substance and function returning to substance are common in Chinese Buddhist literature, especially the Huayan school.

It not only serves as a method of analysis but also holds practical significance. Ma uses this form to articulate the relationships within Neo-Confucianism, such as the interplay between principles and vital energy, nature and emotions, nature and cultivation, and their overall connections, presenting a distinctive and characteristic theory of substance and function.

Conversations in Taihe records:

> Question: If it is said that vital energy begins with movement, why is it said that there is no clear divide between motion and stillness, and no beginning to *yin* and *yang*?
>
> Answer: It is said that a beginning is present when function begins from substance, while a beginning is absent when function returns to substance. Consultation of Zhu Zi's commentary on the *Taiji Diagram Explanation* will bring clarity to this point.[14]

In terms of the logical relationship between substance and function, substance is primary, while function is derivative. Substance gives rise to function, which is the process of function beginning from substance. In this sense, the derived function is said to have a beginning. On the other hand, it is also said, "The Five Elements established will govern all things under heaven, with no exception. The Five Elements are attributed to *yin* and *yang*, two energies are one, and one vital energy is one principle."[15] Tracing back from function to substance, all things can be attributed to one vital energy, and this vital energy can be traced back to one principle. This principle is substance, and it, itself, is the origin. Therefore, substance has no beginning. If we were to assert that substance has a beginning, it would be substance built upon substance.

Ma Yifu states, "Function derived from substance is the manifestation of the hidden, while function returning to substance is the deduction from the apparent to the hidden."[16] This means that the method of returning function to substance refers to deducing the inherent substance (hidden) from phenomena (visible). Phenomena is the apparent manifestation and is prevalent, while the inherent substance is subtle and hidden. Function beginning from substance involves deriving phenomena from the inherent substance. In the former, it is function that is directly presented and acquired, while in the latter, it is substance that is directly acquired and proposed. In Buddhism, deriving function from substance is also known as "expressing appearance based on nature," and returning function to substance is known as "integrating appearance back to nature." To Ma Yifu, deriving function from substance, expressing appearance based on nature, returning function to substance, and integrating appearance back to nature are not only modes of exposition and analysis, but also propositions of existence. They also serve as methods of practice.

This theory of substance and function is, first and foremost, an ontology. Ma discusses the threefold meanings of the *yi* (changes) in this context:

> The *yi* (changes) has three meanings: change, constancy, and simplicity. Scholars should be aware that vital energy is change, principles are constant, the totality of vital energy is principles, and the totality of principles is vital energy, which is also simplicity. Only understanding change leads to a fixation on nihilism, while only understanding

constancy results in a fixation on eternalism. It should be known that change originates from constancy, and even the constant changes. To be free from nihilism and eternalism is the right understanding, and this is simplicity.[17]

The concept of nihilism and eternalism originated from Buddhism. In Buddhism, nihilism refers to the insistence that the universe is discontinuous, with individual bodies and minds experiencing cessation and not continuing, while eternalism refers to the insistence that the universe is continuous, with individual bodies and minds persisting without interruption. Ma believes that only understanding change and not recognizing the enduring aspect within change is a form of nihilism. Similarly, only understanding constancy and not recognizing the constant aspect within change is a form of eternalism. Change is associated with function, and constancy is associated with substance. The statement, "Change originates from constancy," signifies that function is substance, and "The constant changes" signifies that substance is function. Neo-Confucianism advocates the theory of simplicity, which overcomes the dichotomy of nihilism and eternalism. Ma once explained the *General Book* using the concept of changes:

> *Cheng* (sincerity) is a concept of constancy, while "the beginning of all things" and "the transformation of the *qian* hexagram" are clearly manifestations of change, deriving function from substance and expressing appearance based on nature. It is said that the origin of sincerity and its establishment are the fundamental principles of simplicity and constancy, emphasizing that the reason for change lies in its nature of constancy.[18]

In other words, only understanding change means that one does not comprehend the integration of appearance back to nature and the return of function to substance. Likewise, solely grasping constancy means that one does not understand the concept of expressing appearance based on nature and deriving function from substance. A true understanding of the study of simplicity in the *Book of Changes* lies in recognizing that complete utility of the whole substance is only achieved when function is substance, and substance is function.

Such a theory of substance and function also signifies a particular methodological approach and worldview. Ma emphasized that "to separate essence and application is absolutely impermissible. Constancy is only its substance, simplicity is only its function, and change is only its manifestation. Without substance, there is no function; without nature, there is no manifestation. But appearance can be integrated back into nature, and function can be returned to substance. How, then, can one unite substance and separate from it?"[19] He further states, "The display of benevolence is a function derived from substance, while concealing utility is the return of function to substance. To manifest is to reveal substance within function, while to conceal is to reveal function within substance."[20] Again, he explains the Doctrine of the Mean using the concept of changes, in which he states, "Not deviating is a display of one's true self, while hiding one's motive is an act of concealment. Even the slightest change can be revealed, which leads to an understanding of substance, and only when nothing is concealed can one truly understand its function. There is hardly a distinction between manifestation and subtle changes, and substance and function originate from the same source. Thus, there would be no deviation and no need for concealment."[21] In such a theory of substance and function, the two are not mutually independent, opposed binaries with no causal relationship. Instead, they constitute an interactive, closely related, and inseparable unity with two sides. Thus, when discussing what is termed as the convergence of substance and function in the Huayan school of Buddhism, Ma points out, "Convergence suggests that substance is the function, and integration is the return of function to substance. Overall, substance and function are inseparable and have no distinction."[22] Beyond substance, there is no function; beyond function, there is no substance. Such a perspective of the non-duality of substance and function acknowledges the intrinsic interconnectedness of the world.

This theory of substance and function holds even greater significance in the context of the cultivation of the mind and nature. Ma says:

> His [Mencius'] discourse on knowledge and ability originated from the essence of Confucius' teachings in the *Book of Changes*. What is referred to as simplicity in the *Book of Changes* is termed goodness by Mencius. When discussing inherent principles, it should be called goodness. When discussing the unity of principles and vital energy, it should be termed simplicity. Mencius' discourse, then, is a direct indication, while Confucius' discourse is all-encompassing. What I mean by all-encompassing is that it comprehensively and thoroughly considers substance and function, the beginning and the end, the concealed and the revealed, and the internal and the external. Indeed, merely emphasizing direct indication without delving into thoughtful learning and lacking the ability to integrate results in adherence to one's nature at the expense of neglecting cultivation. To be all-encompassing means to elucidate that nature and cultivation are inseparable. Cultivation arises completely from nature, while complete cultivation is one's nature. Such is the teaching of simplicity. The inseparability of nature and cultivation is a concept found in Buddhist teachings, and it is drawn upon because it aligns with the idea of the unity of principle and vital energy. Nature is expressed through principles, while cultivation is expressed through vital energy. Knowledge originates from nature, and the ability to act arises from cultivation. Nature is purely based on principles, and cultivation is the execution of deeds. Therefore, the unity of knowledge and action is equivalent to the inseparability of nature and cultivation. It is also the fusion of principles and deeds, as well as the complete alignment of principles with vital energy and vice versa.[23]

This suggests that in the cosmological aspect, change represents vital energy, phenomena, and function; constancy represents principles, the fundamental nature, and substance; simplicity represents the unity of principles and vital energy, and the non-duality of substance and function. Emphasizing either change alone or constancy alone leads to a dichotomy of nihilism and eternalism. The unity of principles and vital energy is an all-encompassing perspective, and to be all-encompassing means to provide a comprehensive definition or expression. As such, it is evident that the proposition of the unity of principles and vital energy represents the overall stance of Ma Yifu's philosophy. The proposition of the unity of principles and vital energy in his theory suggests that the universe can be viewed in two aspects: principles and vital energy. Principles and vital energy are not mutually exclusive dual entities. Analogous to the concept of inseparability of nature and cultivation, it can also be said that principles and vital energy are inseparable. The universe is a vast circulation, where principles constitute the regularity of this circulation, and vital energy is the dynamic force behind it. Principles cannot be separated from vital energy, and vital energy cannot be separated from principles.

Ma Yifu particularly emphasized that the inherent entirety of cosmological expansion is the unity of principles and vital energy. This unity is expressed as, "All principles make vital energy, and all vital energy makes principles." Ma advocates the model of *All of A is B, and all of B is A* in Buddhism. In the context of the theory of substance and function, "all principles make vital energy" is equivalent to function being derived from substance, while "all vital energy makes principles" is equivalent to the return of function to substance. The combination of these two aspects results in the unity of principles and vital energy. "All vital energy makes principles" means that vital energy completely embodies principles, while "all principles make vital energy" indicates that principles are fully expressed as (in) vital energy. Building on the previous example, "all vital energy makes principles" corresponds to "change originates from constancy," and "all principles make vital energy" corresponds to "even the constant changes." The combination of "all vital energy makes principles" and "all principles make vital energy" lends itself to simplicity.

As mentioned above, according to Ma Yifu, in the cosmological context, "All vital energy makes principles, and all principles make vital energy" is inherent and natural. In the philosophy of human life, the notion that "all vital energy makes principles, all principles make vital energy" represents an ideal state that individuals should strive to achieve. In other words, the unity of principles and vital energy is inherent in the universe, but achieving this unity in the philosophy of human life requires effort and cultivation. He states:

> The mind does not serve external objects. Instead, it adheres to principles. When the mind is aligned, vital energy flows harmoniously, allowing human nature to be nurtured. Speaking of nature and emotions, when emotions align with nature, function returns to substance, substance is fully expressed in function, the entirety of emotions constitutes nature, and all vital energy makes principles. ... However, when emotions dictate nature and nature follows emotions, reality becomes entangled with illusion, and the entire being falls into confusion. This occurs when actions are driven solely by vital energy, and the principles of the heavens are not adhered to.[24]

In the philosophy of human life, cultivation is aimed at transforming one's disposition, achieving the state where all vital energy embodies principles and ensuring that vital energy aligns with principles. Ma Yifu views both the book of Mencius and Zhang Zai's Doctrine of

Moral Triumph as ways to attain the state where all vital energy embodies principles. He says, "Sight, hearing, speech, and movement are all expressions of vital energy, while ritual is the manifestation of principles within vital energy. … When all four are in accordance with ritual, then all vital energy embodies principles, and the entirety of emotions constitutes nature."[25] "'Whatever metaphysical is Way' is a principle. 'Whatever physical' is also a principle. Observing principles within vital energy means that all vital energy is principles. Observing Way within tools means that without Way, there is no vital energy."[26]

Function beginning from substance and function returning to substance are two different narrative approaches to the analysis of primordiality. Substance is metaphysical, while function is physical. Substance is primary, while function is derivative. Substance is the essence, while function is the phenomena. Thus, in the metaphysical sense, function derived from substance is a top-down (from metaphysical to physical) narrative approach, which explains the logical sequence from substance to function. On the other hand, function returning to substance is a bottom-up (from physical to metaphysical) narrative approach, illustrating the logic of "identifying principles in the midst of vital energy, seeing constancy in change, and seeing the essence in the midst of phenomena."[27] Using the commonly employed metaphor of ocean and waves in Buddhism, water is substance, and waves are function. When the sea water moves and creates waves, that is the substance expressing its function. "All waves are ultimately one water" signifies the return of function to substance. In the theory of principle and vital energy, the assertion that the original state of the universe is without visible *qi* is an expression of the standpoint of the function being derived from substance. On the other hand, the assertion of adhering to principles and regulating vital energy in the theory of mind and nature reflects the mode of returning from function to substance.

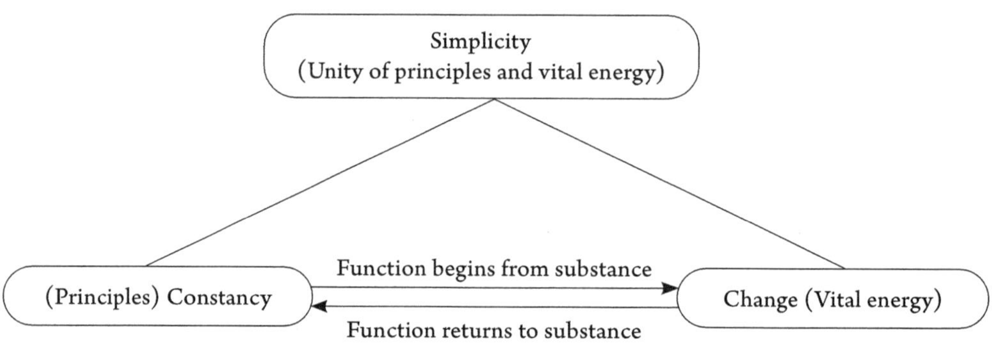

"Function begins from substance" means speaking from the perspective of substance and implementing it in function, while "function returning to substance" is, on the other hand, speaking from the perspective of function but culminating in substance. Both are narrative approaches affirmed by Ma Yifu as "single emphasis."

However, in achieving a comprehensive understanding of the whole, it is necessary to integrate both affirmation and negation to achieve harmony, that is, the "comprehensive function of the whole," which also means the entirety of substance turns to function, and the entirety of the function is substance. The concept of "all vital energy makes principles, and all principles make vital energy" in Ma Yifu's ontology clearly reflects a stark difference in construction and understanding from the dualism present in Western philosophical traditions. In his theory, principles and vital energy exist like essence and phenomena in a seamlessly blended, inseparable "mutual completeness." The concepts of function beginning from substance, the entirety of the function is substance, all principles make vital energy, and all vital energy makes principles in Ma Yifu's philosophy are not only descriptive, grasping of the natural state of the universe, but also an ideal realm of life. His theory of principle, vital energy, substance, and function is not just a statement of existence, but also a mode of practice and an analytical method. All of his theories, such as the inseparability of nature and cultivation, the unity of knowledge and action, and the harmonization of principles and affairs, must be interpreted in this sort of all-encompassing context. In fact, every aspect of his ideology can be understood through the unity of function beginning from substance and function returning to substance.

It should be noted that the proposition, *function is substance, and substance is function* in Ma Yifu's philosophy is very similar to Xiong Shili's notion. However, in terms of cosmology, Ma insists that principles and vital energy are the essential elements for explaining and grasping the world. This differs from Xiong's view. At the fundamental stance, Ma's assertion that all principles make vital energy and all vital energy makes principles is still within the framework of Neo-Confucianism. This concept is far from Xiong's theory of substance and function, which focuses on "substance itself transforming into Great Function." Ma emphasizes returning function to substance, whereas Xiong proposes "function returning to substance," which has a larger impact in terms of breakthrough. Although Ma achieved "the entirety of substance is function, and the entirety of function is substance," conceptually, his understanding still adheres to the Neo-Confucianism theories of substance and function originating from the same source and there being hardly a distinction between manifestation and subtle changes. In comparison, Xiong's philosophy truly achieved the status of "the comprehensive function of the whole." This is certainly not a difference in intellectual capacity, but a difference in perspectives. In other words, the problematic nature (in principle and vital energy) of Ma's philosophy lies within Neo-Confucian traditions and does not address the issue of actual entities.

The theory of principle and vital energy is the primary form of ontology in Neo-Confucianism. It reflects the distinctive contemplation of fundamental philosophical issues by Chinese philosophers. While the theory of principle and vital energy advocated by Cheng Yi and Zhu Xi has a different standpoint from that emphasized by Luo Qinshun and Wang Fuzhi to begin with, they are inherently part of the same discourse. They share a common premise in acknowledging the significance of this discourse. In recent times, under the influence of Western civilization and a significant shift toward the dominance of modern vernacular language in all writing, traditional philosophical discourse that embodies the problematic nature of Chinese philosophy in the form of classical Chinese has almost become a thing of the past. Chinese philosophers of the 20th century made great efforts to draw lessons from Western philosophy, resulting in a complete departure from tradition. This has led to the absolute dominance of Western philosophical domains and problematics over modern Chinese philosophical thinking. However, there are still a few notable philosophers who tenaciously adhere to the traditional discourse of classical Chinese philosophy, in both content and form, and their works are worth noting and researching. Ma Yifu, who received his education in the West, maintained an intriguing indifference towards the dominance of Western philosophy that was backed by the expansion of modern instrumental rationality in the 20th century. This is not due to a disappointment in Western civilization, as felt by figures like Liang Qichao after the First World War. It was also different from the challenges posed to Western cultural hegemony in recent postcolonial discourse. It seems like his attitude stemmed from a profound cultural confidence in the sense of purpose and identity, developed through immersion in Chinese culture (Confucianism and Buddhism) over a long period of time. As a result, the world of classical philosophical discourse was still meaningful to him. This suggests that our understanding of philosophy may not need to be solely based on a Western-centric perspective. Rather, it should be developed according to the diverse needs of the people of different cultures.

Notes

1. Ma Jingquan, *Chronology of Ma Yifu.*
2. *Conversations in Taihe* (Taiwan Guangwen Shuju, 1976), 45.
3. *Conversations in Taihe,* 45.
4. Note: The two schools cannot be mouthed simultaneously.
5. *Conversations in Taihe,* 44.
6. *Supplement to Responses to Inquiries at Erya Tai,* vol. 2 (Taiwan Guangwen Shuju, 1976), 28.
7. Ibid., 24.
8. *Fu Xing College Records of Lectures,* vol. 5 (Taiwan Guangwen Shuju, 1976), 173.
9. "Remarks from Observing Phenomena, Part 8," in *Fu Xing College Records of Lectures* (Taiwan Guangwen Shuju, 1976), vol. 6, 222.
10. "Remarks from Observing Phenomena, Part 8," in *Fu Xing College Records of Lectures,* vol. 6, 18.
11. *Responses to Inquiries at Erya Tai,* vol. 1 (Taiwan Guangwen Shuju, 1976), 32.
12. *Supplement to Responses to Inquiries at Erya Tai,* vol. 4, 18.
13. *Conversations in Yishan* (Taiwan Guangwen Shuju, 1976), 24.
14. *Conversations in Taihe,* 45.
15. "Essence of the Great Plan, Part 2," in *Fu Xing College Records of Lectures,* vol. 5, 136.
16. "Remarks from Observing Phenomena, Part 1," in *Fu Xing College Records of Lectures,* vol. 6, 190.
17. *Conversations in Taihe,* 43.
18. *Supplement to Responses to Inquiries at Erya Tai,* vol. 1, 15.
19. *Supplement to Responses to Inquiries at Erya Tai,* vol. 1, 16.
20. *Supplement to Responses to Inquiries at Erya Tai,* vol. 4, 6.
21. *Supplement to Responses to Inquiries at Erya Tai,* vol. 2, 40.
22. Ibid., 46.
23. *Conversations in Taihe,* 47.

24. *Conversations in Yishan*, 14.
25. "Essence of the Great Plan, Part 3," in *Fu Xing College Records of Lectures*, vol. 5, 143.
26. "Essence of the Great Plan Part 2," 136.
27. *Conversations in Yishan*, 23.

CHAPTER 5

The Theory of Mind and Matter in Ma Yifu's Philosophy

Ma Yifu is regarded as a master in modern Chinese studies, with his distinctive philosophy of "dualism in Confucianism and Buddhism." His philosophical theories can be said to be one of the most traditional systems in Chinese philosophy in the 20th century. He is also the most accomplished and knowledgeable scholar of the Chinese classical cultural system in the 20th century, rising to the level of excellence in Confucianism, Buddhism, Daoism, classical literature (poetry), and art (calligraphy). Early representatives of Neo-Confucianism, such as Xiong Shili and Liang Shuming, often sought his guidance and hailed him a master of his generation.

Ma Yifu's philosophy, particularly the theory of principles and vital energy, utilizes the contextual framework and style of expression of the Huayan school of Buddhism to expound on the view of principles and vital energy. It can be said that Confucianism is the substance, while the Huayan school of Buddhism serves as the function. Another focal point of his philosophical thought is the theory of mind and matter. Unlike his theory of principles and vital energy, his theory of mind and matter inherits the traditions of the School of Mind from Confucianism and Buddhism.

It is worth noting that, if Ma's theory of principles and vital energy is said to inherit the perspective of principles and vital energy from the Cheng-Zhu school of thought and the theoretical thinking of the Huayan school of Buddhism, then his theory of mind and matter may be said to have inherited Lu Jiuyuan and Wang Yangming's theory of idealism, as well as the complete idealist tradition in Buddhism, including Chan school. In this sense, his theory of mind and matter can be seen as a synthesis of Chinese traditional philosophical "mind-only" theories.

I. Nothing beyond the Mind

There are a few different forms of expression for Ma's theory of mind and matter. While these expressions may differ in topic, all of them reflect the fundamental stance of his theory of mind and matter, which is that there is "nothing beyond the mind." We will elaborate further on the expressions developed from the different scenarios below.

1. The Universe as Part of Nature

Ma Yifu particularly advocates Lu Jiuyuan's thought of regarding everything in the universe as part of one's nature. He says:

> Those who do not understand *fen* (duty) do not understand *xing* (nature) to begin with. Duty is human nature. How can there be duty without nature? People today only seek matters beyond their duty, oblivious to their own, which explains why they are unable to find peace. Ultimately, this is because they fail to fully comprehend and acknowledge their own nature. One will understand duty when one understands nature. Without yet comprehending nature, what use is it to discuss about duty? Even if the words are spoken, there is no meaning.[1]

In other words, modern people pursue matters completely beyond their duties, while disregarding their obligations. This stems from not understanding one's duties, which is a result of not knowing one's nature. Here, *fen* refers to one's duties, which encompass one's actions and pursuits. Ma Yifu believes that only by achieving a "wholehearted understanding of one's nature" and fully comprehending one's own nature can one establish one's duties and align his or her actions and pursuits with nature, thereby fulfilling one's obligations. He also says:

> [Lu] Jiuyuan said, *Matters within the universe are part of the duty of my nature, and matters that are part of the duty of my nature are matters within the universe.* This statement is concise, yet profound. When one does not understand his or her duty and nature, but merely relies on observations, then with a myriad of changes unfolding before one's eyes, one would be overwhelmed by perplexing feelings, which would affect one's understanding and judgment of matters. Those who claim to be able to unravel the secrets of Heaven, Earth, and all things, but remain narrow-minded, only spiral deeper but do not see the truth.[2]

In line with this statement, the correct understanding of one's nature and duty is to recognize that "all matters within the universe are part of the duty of my nature, and matters that are part of the duty of my nature are matters within the universe." This emphasizes the unified nature of the universe, as well as one's nature and duty. It is thus evident that, for Ma Yifu, such an expression is not only an ontological statement, but a critique of the theories of methodology, time, and practice of "merely relying on observations." We will elaborate on this point later.

Ma particularly emphasizes the notion that "all matters within the universe are part of the duty of my nature." This proposition has two key meanings for him. On the one hand, it emphasizes that the myriad phenomena of the universe exist in one's mind. As he puts it:

> The benevolent person delves into the heart and finds it easy to comprehend signs... The sages of the Central Plains all consider the universe as part of the duty of their nature. The signs indicate this, and the hexagrams follow suit. It does not mean that there is a separate world beyond the mind, which is vastly different from the Western philosophical research methods upheld by contemporary philosophers. If one seeks to use such methods, there is bound to be misinterpretations and a loss of the original meaning.[3]

It is evident that Ma believes that "all matters within the universe are part of the duty of my nature," a proposition opposed to "a separate world beyond the mind." To say there is "a separate world beyond the mind" is to acknowledge that there are matters external to the mind. In contrast, "all matters within the universe are part of the duty of my nature" implies the stand that there is nothing beyond the mind.

On the other hand, considering matters within the universe as part of the duty of one's nature represents an ethical proposal, just like "the benevolent regards the universe as one entity," as advocated by Neo-Confucian scholars. As Ma notes:

> What is termed matters today is received from others, as if there is nothing inherent in oneself. What was termed matters in the past was spoken from one's own perspective, where one regards everything in the universe as matters of one's own. Therefore, it is said that there is nothing beyond the self, the sage has no personal matters, and everything is part of one's duty. All matters within the universe are part of the duty of one's nature, and all those who speak of matters are speaking of their own. Nature is synonymous with principle, and principle and matters are inseparable. There are no matters beyond principle. Likewise, there are no matters beyond nature.[4]

He also says:

> People today are unaware of their inherent nature, which also means they do not recognize the existence of the Way of Heaven. They perceive all things in the universe as unrelated to themselves, resulting in people harming one another, showing disrespect for the five constant virtues, and bringing calamity upon the natural order. As a result, Heaven and Earth lose their positions, and all things cease to flourish. Therefore, it is said that Heaven, Earth, and all things are of the same nature, which is the essence of *The Great Plan*.[5]

This means that everything—from the individual's body and mind to all affairs in the world—is related to oneself and is within one's responsibility. Therefore, all matters within the universe are part of the duty of one's nature. In this sense, there is "nothing beyond oneself," and all the harm that people do unto one another ultimately stems from the perspective that "everything in the world is not related to oneself."

In this way, Ma directly deduces that there is "nothing beyond oneself" from the proposition that "all matters within the universe are part of the duty of one's nature." He writes:

> The phrase "the great man aligns his virtue with Heaven and Earth," means he embodies Heaven and Earth. "Illuminating virtue throughout the world" implies that the world is synonymous with one's body. How, then, can there be a distinction between self and others? I have always asserted that exhausting oneself is equivalent to exhausting all things, for there is nothing beyond oneself. Understanding one's nature is understanding Heaven, for there is no Heaven beyond one's nature. The sage has no personal matters, and everything is part of one's duty. Therefore, Heaven, Earth and all things are one. This is the true principle. Without realizing this truth, one may succumb to selfishness, may remain confined to the mundane, and is thus unable to enter the realm of the sages.[6]

Exhausting oneself allows one to fully execute all things, while fully apprehending one's own nature allows one to apprehend Heaven. Strictly speaking, "oneself" and "nature" here refer to the individual's own mind and nature, while "things" and "Heaven" exist beyond oneself and one's nature, in a sense. However, in the Chinese philosophical tradition of the School of Mind, and as perceived by Ma Yifu, the relationship between oneself and things, and nature and Heaven, is one of "one body" and "one nature," implying a fundamental unity. Consequently, apprehending one's own nature allows one to apprehend Heaven, and exhausting oneself allows the execution of all things. In this sense, "nothing beyond oneself" signifies the oneness of Heaven and man and the unity of all things. The main reason Ma Yifu and the School of Mind use the assertive tone of expression, "nothing beyond self," is to urge individuals to work hard and seek experiential understanding. It is essential to grasp the assertive proposition within the School of Mind in a concrete manner, rather than getting a superficial interpretation based on text. In fact, the interpretation of most texts in Chinese philosophy that are characterized by "poetic philosophy" requires a primary focus on "understanding the intention against the will" and "knowing the mind," which is a significant difference in the history of philosophy between China and the West.

2. Nothing beyond the Mind

The sayings "all matters within the universe are part of the duty of one's nature" and "nothing beyond oneself" can be understood as expressions of Ma's theory of mind and matter, though they do not directly juxtapose mind and matter. Ma has many other arguments that discuss the relationship between mind and matter directly, which can be laid out in two parts.

First, drawing on materials from traditional Confucian thought, Ma Yifu clearly declares, "nothing beyond the mind." He says:

> *Taiji* symbolizes a unified mind, while the Eight Trigrams symbolize all things. With nothing beyond the mind, it is said that *yin* and *yang* are one *taiji*.[7]

He goes on:

> Isn't the mind the most profound and dynamic essence in the world? There is nothing beyond the mind. All intricate movements of things are orchestrated by the mind. The mind is fundamentally like *taiji* in its tranquility, singular principle, and absence of form. When it stirs, it differentiates into *yin* and *yang* and is referred to as *qi* (vital energy) in the realm of fate, where *li* (principles) operates within it. It is thus called the Way of one *yin* and one *yang*, and as a result, Heaven, Earth, and all things achieve stability.[8]

Ma believes that the relationship between *taiji* and the Eight Trigrams in the *Book of Changes* symbolizes the relationship between the mind and all things, which is characterized by the notion of "nothing beyond the mind." Ma similarly acknowledges that having "nothing beyond the mind" does not mean asserting that nothing other than the mind exists in the universe. As noted in the phrase, "all intricate movements of things are orchestrated by the mind," he does not completely deny the movement of entities. In this line of thought, having "nothing beyond the mind" is more accurately interpreted as an expression of the viewpoints of "entities inseparable from the mind" and "nothing exists without the mind," which also means that there are no entities independent of the mind.

On the other hand, Ma also extensively employs the Buddhist idealist thought to expound his theory of nothing beyond the mind, as he explains in his interpretation of *Shuogua* (*Explaining the Hexagrams*):

> "The emperor emerges from *zhen* (excitation)" ... and "all things arise from *zhen*." Why is this so? The emperor is the mind, while things are the fundamental laws. When the emperor arises, so do all things, just as fundamental laws are formed when the mind does. At the mention of the mind, things will follow. There is nothing beyond the mind. This is clear once the distinction is made.[9]

He interprets "all things arise from *zhen*" as all things arising from the mind. He equates this with the Buddhist saying, "The mind engenders myriad dharmas," which leads to the conclusion that there is "nothing beyond the mind." Ma takes the same perspective when explaining the theory of fortunes and misfortunes in *Book of Documents*, whereby he says:

> The "five matters" are the mind, and the "five virtues" are *qi* (vital energy). All fortunes and misfortunes reside in a single mind, and the five *qi* follow suit. *Qi* is the manifestation of thought, also called "thought in action." The theory of fortunes and misfortunes is spoken of as the creation of virtues, in which "it is deemed a fortune when the mind is at rest," "remain cautious from the beginning to the end," and "avoid misfortunes." All of these are expressed in terms of the mind, while all calamities and blessings are expressed in terms of external circumstances. It is only through the mind that one can understand external circumstances. There are no circumstances without the mind. Thus, instead of calamities and blessings, one only speaks of fortunes and misfortunes.[10]

He goes on:

> All blessings and tragedies are sought by oneself. Thus, it is clear that fortunes and misfortunes lie within the self, not external things. They are within the mind, not dependent on external circumstances.[11]

Ma advocates that the origin of blessings and tragedies lies within oneself and not in external things. This is clear, based on general knowledge. He further categorizes all blessings and tragedies as "external circumstances," which aligns with Buddhist concepts such as "understanding circumstances only through the mind, and no circumstances exist beyond the mind." This reflects his general stance on the issue of the mind and circumstances.

Ma once commented on Zhuangzi and Shao Yong's theories of the relationship between humans and things, saying:

> Shao's statement originates from Zhuangzi's maxim, "utilize things but do not be driven by them," suggesting that one should entrust oneself to things, but not be at their mercy. There is nothing wrong with Zhuangzi's statement, but the same cannot be said of Shao's. The flaw lies in the concept that "I am a human among things, a thing among things." This way, humans and things need to be treated as a whole, and it is to be acknowledged that there is nothing beyond the mind. "The inner mind comes from within. It is not formed by illusionary means." This means that the saying, "things serve humans, and humans serve things," goes against the principle of the treatment of humans and things. Shitou* says, "Engage one another time and again, not dwelling in fixed positions." Humans reside in the position for humans, while things reside in the position for things. How does one acquire the other, when the two do not overlap? Mencius asserts that those who put in deep thought will receive. Chengzi upholds the same belief. Humans return to other humans, while things return to other things. There is no need to discuss which is the subject and which is the object. That is why such explanations are unnecessary.[12]

* Shitou Xiqian (700–790) was an 8th-century Chinese Chán (Zen) Buddhist teacher and author.

Shao Yong asserts that "if things can be utilized, then I am a human among things. If things cannot be utilized, then I am a thing among things." Ma comments that such a saying is flawed, as it separates human from things, but in reality, there is nothing beyond the mind. To set up a dichotomy between humans and things and to divide them into subject and object is merely a result of misguided thought. Neo-Confucian philosophers Cheng Hao and Cheng Yi once criticized Shao Yong's statement as well, saying, "This is unnecessary. Humans are humans, and things are things. The principles are very clear." Ma's affirmation of the Cheng brothers' perspective does not necessarily show that he believes there is nothing beyond an individual's body and mind. It is only clear that he opposes the idea of treating humans and things as mutually exclusive subjects and objects.

Ma further employs the principle of Three Changes, which he frequently uses in the theory of principles and vital energy as grounds for argument to explain the relationship between mind and matter. He writes:

> People are often deluded into thinking that matter exists beyond the mind, and thus, they see matters but fail to see the mind. They are ignorant of the fact that matters emerge from the mind and are projections of the mind. Without the mind, how can there be matters? Some might argue that when a person dies, knowledge ceases, and the mind dissolves, yet objects still exist. People holding such a belief have misunderstood the concept of nihilism and eternalism. The dissolution of the mind is nihilism, while the retention of objects is eternalism. They do not understand that the mind itself is inherently impermanent, and so are objects. Even with the cessation of old thoughts, new thoughts will arise, and with death comes life. Would they stand by in anticipation of the cessation of life? Their deluded minds have, in fact, arbitrarily created their own births and deaths.
>
> The wise would observe that all phenomena arise from conditions, thus are impermanent, and are termed "changes." However, your true mind can reflect all conditions without arising from conditions. It can shine with spiritual radiance, transcending sensory dust. It does not arise from conditions and does not extinguish with the cessation of conditions. All impermanent phenomena manifest within it, like a clear mirror that displays a reflection before an object and retains its presence even when the object is taken away. This is termed "constancy." There are no other objects that are constantly changing beyond this mind of constancy. This is analogous to the absence of reflections without a mirror. With change, there is no eternalism, and with constancy, the argument for nihilism does not stand. To break free from nihilism and eternalism would be to adhere to simplicity.[13]

Ma insists that without the mind, there is no matter. In response to this, opponents point out that one's mind dissolves when dead, but objects remain. This suggests that objects exist independently of the mind. Ma Yifu points out that the belief that the mind can cease to exist is nihilism, while the thought that objects will remain in perpetuity is eternalism. The mind is impermanent to begin with. Even the consciousness of a living person is a continuous cycle of past thoughts flashing through and subsequent thoughts being generated. The mind does not achieve the state of impermanence only at the end of life. Objects do not exist permanently, either. All phenomena arise from the interplay of causes and conditions. They come into existence when the conditions are right, and they cease to exist when the conditions are absent. Therefore, both thoughts and objects are impermanent. This also reflects the profound meaning of changes in the *Book of Changes.*

On the other hand, our true mind does not arise due to the right conditions, nor does it cease with the absence of conditions. It is like a clear mirror that displays a reflection in the face of an object and retains its presence even when the object is taken away. Things like true minds that exist independently of other conditions reflect the meaning of constancy in the *Book of Changes.* The various changing and impermanent appearances are merely reflections in the mirror. They do not have physical bodies and only exist because of the mirror. Therefore, without the constant true mind, there will be no manifestation of changes, just as there will be no reflections without a mirror. Change negates eternalism, while constancy negates nihilism. The reality of the universe is neither eternal nor discontinuous, thus embodying the nature of simplicity. Clearly, Ma's thought is largely derived from Buddhist discussions on mind and matter. He even proposes that the Buddhist theory (dharma) of mind and matter is a common stand that sages share throughout history, of which he says:

> "There are no phenomena beyond the mind that can be connected with the mind." This is because all phenomena are the mind. The mind can produce all phenomena, encompass all phenomena, and is, in fact, all phenomena. The sages may have lengthy explanations, but they all mean to clarify this. Speaking of the principle of life reveals the fundamental nature of the mind. Speaking of the way of the three realms demonstrates the great utility of the mind. Therefore, it can be said that the aim of writing the *Book of Changes* and imparting of teachings is to allow one to recognize the mind. Without understanding the principles of nature and life, the essence of the mind will remain concealed. This means that one merely follows habitual tendencies in everyday activities and lacks true autonomy. This is also known as losing one's true mind.[14]

The mind nature, which we often speak about, is the essence of this mind, while the myriad phenomena and events in the universe constitute the extensive utility of this mind. This mind is both the source from which all phenomena arise and the entity that encompasses all things and events. Simply put, the mind is all phenomena. It is just that the true essence of the human mind is veiled by habits, and its inherent nature cannot be fully realized unless one understands the principle of nature and life, governing form and energy. The reason sages impart teachings is to help people recognize this mind.

II. All Phenomena Originate from the Mind

Centering on "nothing beyond the mind," Ma Yifu's theory of mind and matter is directly inherited from the tradition of idealism in ancient Chinese philosophical theories. In *Awakening of Faith in the Mahāyāna*, it is highly regarded in the tradition of idealism in Chinese Buddhism. Although various sutras and treatises contain idealistic thought as well, *Awakening of Faith in the Mahāyāna* has exerted a profound influence on all schools of Chinese Buddhism since it introduced the concepts of "one mind with two doors," and the nature of the "true mind" in terms of "constancy" and "leaving things to fate."

According to the system in *Awakening of Faith in the Mahāyāna*, the true form of all dharmas in the universe is suchness, also known as "one mind." This shows that *Awakening of Faith in the Mahāyāna* does not establish a cosmic source like typical metaphysical philosophies. Since *Awakening of Faith in the Mahāyāna* regards this true form as the mind, it implies that such a mind has close connections with the individual minds of sentient beings and possesses distinctive qualities of a mind. It is said in *Awakening of Faith in the Mahāyāna* that:

> According to the One Mind Dharma, there are two doors. Which two? One is the mind of suchness, while the other is the mind of birth and extinction. Both aspects fully encompass all dharmas. This is precisely because the two doors are inseparable. The mind of suchness represents the essential nature of the entire dharma realm, wherein the nature of the mind is neither born nor extinguished. Differences in dharmas originate from deluded thoughts. Without mental attachment, there will be no distinction between realms. Therefore, all dharmas originate from one's inherent nature, are free from names and forms, and transcend mental associations. They are ultimately equal, unchanging, and indestructible. They are solely one mind and are thus named suchness.[15]

A mind of suchness refers to the source from which all dharmas arise and change. Suchness itself is tranquil and constant to begin with. However, as suchness is synonymous with the mind, when it does not abide by its own nature, thoughts arise. These thoughts constitute the mind of birth and extinction, giving rise to the myriad transformations of birth and extinction as a result of attachment to deluded thoughts. Therefore, even though all dharmas arise from the ignorance born of thoughts in a direct sense, and ignorance and thoughts come about due to suchness and are a function of suchness, ignorance does not have its own inherent nature. It can thus be said that suchness is the ultimate source of all dharmas. Such an ontology in Buddhist philosophy is different from those in general philosophies, as all dharmas in Buddhist philosophy do not have absolute true forms. This ontology serves to explain that such dharmas without absolute true forms arise in accordance with conditions, and *Awakening of Faith in the Mahāyāna* asserts that the ultimate source of this is the "one mind."

This sort of thought has become one of the important theoretical forms of idealism in the Buddhist tradition. The *Awakening of Faith in the Mahāyāna* says, "All dharmas originally concern only the mind and are non-existent in thought. In deluded minds, thoughts manifest without awareness and result in various perceptions, thus termed ignorance."[16]

Because all thoughts lack inherent reality, they are called deluded thoughts, also termed ignorance. It also says: "All colors and dharmas originate from the mind; they do not exist in external reality. In other words, without physical existence, there is no appearance of emptiness. The myriad circumstances arise solely from the delusions of the mind. When the mind is free from delusions, all boundaries cease to exist, leaving only the true, impartial mind."[17]

Buddhist scriptures state, "The awakening of the mind creates various dharmas, while the quelling of the mind extinguishes all dharmas." This explains various sayings in the Buddhist philosophy of mind and matter, such as "no dharmas beyond the mind" and "no color beyond the mind." From the perspective of practice, Buddhism idealism advocates keeping the human mind away from delusions, while from the ontological perspective, it asserts that the mind is real and dharmas are imaginary. This philosophy has a clear influence on Ma's theory of mind and matter. The *Awakening of Faith in the Mahāyāna* notes:

> All dharmas arise from delusions of the mind. All distinctions arise from the mind. When the mind does not see the mind, there is no appearance. One should understand that all circumstances in the world are upheld by the ignorance and deluded minds of sentient beings. Therefore, all dharmas are like reflections in the mirror: they have no physical bodies and remain imaginary in the mind. The awakening of the mind creates various dharmas, while the quelling of the mind extinguishes all dharmas.[18]

This matches Ma's thought in the previous section, whereby he uses the analogy of the mirror to illustrate change and constancy and proves the absence of external entities beyond the mind by demonstrating the creation and cessation of deluded thoughts.

The theory of idealism in the *Awakening of Faith in the Mahāyāna* differs from the idealism in Western philosophy that affirms the reality of objects. In such an idealism, the true mind is a universality beyond individuality, while the awakening and quelling of the mind often refer to individual consciousness displaying specific thoughts. Therefore, the essence of the *Awakening of Faith in the Mahāyāna* is closer to Western philosophical objective idealism. In Buddhist philosophy, the mind often possesses such dual natures simultaneously, and different schools of thought have different emphases. The Huayan school in the Tang Dynasty developed such an objective idealism, while the Chan school emphasized subjective idealism.

"No dharmas beyond the mind" is a traditional saying in Buddhism, taking the forms of "there is no other dharma apart from the mind" in the *Nirvana Sutra*, "there are no boundaries and no dust, only illusions beyond the mind" in the *Lankavatara Sutra*, and "the three realms are illusionary, only the mind is at work" in the *Ten Stages Sutra*. However, different Buddhist sects have different interpretations of the mind. The *Mahāyānasaṃgraha* interprets it as the ālayavijñāna, the *Ten Stages Sutra* interprets it as "the true mind of the first principle," and the *Awakening of Faith in the Mahāyāna* emphasizes the Tathagatagarbha, discussing the dependence between and harmonization of reality and illusion. The Huayan school emphasizes the dharma realm, in which the dharma realm is the substance and dependence the function. Where function originates from substance, the dharma realm is also interpreted as the true mind.

Early wisdom, such as the philosophy of Zhiyan,* also says, "There are no separate circumstances beyond the mind, thus the saying 'mind only.'"[19] Similarly, Fazang† says, "All dharmas in the three realms are created by one mind. No dharma can be achieved beyond the mind, thus the saying 'return to the mind.' All distinctions arise solely from one's own mind. There has never been any circumstance beyond the mind that could relate to the mind. Why is this so? The external realm is empty to begin with, when the mind is not awakened."[20] He further explains, "Ultimately, there is no dharma beyond the mind that can relate to the mind… Dust does not relate to itself; it must depend on the mind. The mind does not relate to itself; it must depend on conditions."[21]

The mind, as discussed in the Huayan school, inherits the theory of "one mind with two doors" from the *Awakening of Faith in the Mahāyāna*. It primarily refers to the ultimate truth of all dharmas, but also often denotes individual consciousness. In Indian Buddhist philosophy, there is a significant emphasis on the concept of vijñāna or consciousness, as it is viewed as another name for the mind. Consciousness is highly valued for its discriminative function for objects. Subsequently, various Buddhist schools adopt the interpretation of consciousness and use it to refer to the mind.

The Buddhist discourse on consciousness takes various forms, such as two consciousnesses, three consciousnesses, six consciousnesses, eight consciousnesses, and more. The Yogācāra school, in particular, emphasizes the doctrine of the eight consciousnesses, and its theory of consciousness has had a significant influence. The name of the eighth consciousness, the ālayavijñāna, is also present in texts like the *Lankavatara Sutra* and the *Awakening of Faith in the Mahāyāna*. These teachings were later absorbed into various Buddhist traditions, including Chan school.

Hongren's‡ philosophy emphasizes that "consciousness originates from the inherent mind, while perception arises from inherent nature." It asserts that "without recognizing the inherent mind, the study of dharma is futile. When one recognizes the inherent mind and perceives based on inherent nature, one is then called a great teacher, a teacher of celestial and human beings, and a Buddha."[22]

Later, when the Chan lineage was passed down to Huineng,§ he did not emphasize philosophical arguments about dharmas arising from illusions. Instead, he stresses that "one

* Zhiyan (602–668) was considered the second patriarch of the Huayan school.

† Fazang (643–712) was the third patriarch of the Huayan school.

‡ Hongren (602–675) was the fifth patriarch of Chan school.

§ Huineng (638–713) was the sixth patriarch of Chan school.

should observe one's own mind and realize one's inherent nature," "uninterrupted mindfulness," and "freedom in movement." Before Huineng passed away, he instructed his disciples, "Your own mind is Buddha. Do not doubt this. Dharmas can be established without reliance on any external objects because they originate from the mind. This is why the sutra states that "the awakening of the mind creates various dharmas, while the quelling of the mind extinguishes all dharmas."[23] Yet, based on *The Platform Sutra of the Sixth Patriarch*, it can be observed that when Huineng speaks of one's own mind, he mainly refers to the individual, which differs in emphasis from the teachings of the *Awakening of Faith in the Mahāyāna* and the Huayan school. Such a perspective of the mind in the Chan school was also later absorbed by Ma Yifu.

Due to the diverse interpretations of the concept of mind in various Buddhist traditions, Zongmi's* analysis is quoted below to provide a general overview. Zongmi integrates the perspectives of the *Awakening of Faith in the Mahāyāna* and the Yogācāra school of thought, asserting that sentient beings possess true nature to begin with, though they are not consciously aware of it, which is called the Buddha-nature. Buddha-nature has one mind with two doors: the true mind that neither awakens nor ceases is integrated with illusions that are created and ceased. This is also known as the eighth consciousness, the ālayavijñāna. The ālayavijñāna functions without awareness, which gives rise to karma. This thought does not exist to begin with, but transforms to visible cognitions and perceived realms. Zongmi believes that, ultimately, all dharmas can be reduced to *qi* (vital energy). At the same time, he states:

> Truth be told, all dharmas beyond the mind are nothing but manifestations of the mind. The six *qi* also originate from the transformations of the mind, and they represent the stage where knowledge is transformed into reality. These are governed by the eighth consciousness that arises from a thought of karma to two states of mind. As the mind's thoughts progress from subtle to coarse, it engages in various delusions, ultimately leading to the creation of karma. Similarly, the circumstances progress from minor to significant and, through various transformations, extend to the vastness of the heavens and the earth.[24]

In the *Origin of Human*, Zongmi criticizes those who engage in Buddhist practices without understanding their true meaning. He critiques the teachings that consider the heart of flesh as the true mind, condemns the Hīnayāna teaching that equates thinking with the mind, criticizes the Mahāyāna school of Existence that only recognizes consciousness without acknowledging the existence of the true mind, and disapproves of the Mahāyāna school of Emptiness which posits that both the mind and its objects are empty. Zongmi's arguments revolve around his views on the concept of the mind in Buddhist scriptures. Thus, he approves of the teaching that "one Vehicle that reveals nature," which acknowledges the existence of a true mind, where it states, "On recognizing the true mind, one realizes that everything is an illusion." When discussing

* Zongmi (780–841) was the fifth patriarch of the Huayan school.

the Huayan school's common reference to the nature of gold as constant and the artisan as the condition to explain the doctrine of constancy yet adjusting to conditions, he points out:

> If someone asks, "What object remains constant? What object adjusts to conditions?" It is only fitting to answer, "Gold."
>
> If someone asks, "Which dharma remains constant? Which dharma adjusts to conditions?" It is only fitting to answer, "The mind."
>
> Constancy is the nature, while adjusting to suit conditions is the manifestation. It should be understood that nature and manifestation are both part of the ultimate meaning of one mind. Those who disregard either nature or manifestation are simply ignorant of the true mind. On hearing the word mind, one may relate to the eighth consciousness, but the eighth consciousness is simply a manifestation of the true mind. This is why Aśvaghoṣa Bodhisattva regards the one mind as dharma and the dual aspects of birth and extinction of suchness as the meaning.[25]

Zongmi is well-known for his Huayan-Chan teachings, which are rooted in the doctrine of the true mind adjusting to conditions, as presented in the *Awakening of Faith in the Mahāyāna.* What is particularly noteworthy is his detailed analysis and commentary on the concept of the mind within the traditional framework of Buddhism. He says:

> Various sutras either condemn the mind as a thief, prescribing its elimination, or praise the mind as Buddha, urging its cultivation. They describe the mind as virtuous or wicked, pure or impure, greedy or angry, compassionate or benevolent. Some posit that the mind awakens depending on external conditions, while others assert that the mind gives rise to conditions. Some proclaim the cessation and extinction as the mind, while others identify mental activity and contemplation as the mind. These diverse perspectives seem contradictory. If not presented in the context of different schools, how can the reader discern them? Are there truly multiple minds, or are they fundamentally one and the same? Now, let's briefly outline their names and natures. When it comes to the term mind, there are generally four aspects, each expressed differently in Sanskrit and various translations.[26]

He points out that in Buddhist scriptures and commentaries, the term mind primarily holds four meanings. First, it refers to the heart of flesh, one of the five organs within the body. Second, it denotes the conditioned and discriminatory mind, also known as the eight consciousness, often associated with cognitive functions. Third, it signifies the mind of comprehensive awareness, pointing to the eighth consciousness, the ālayavijñāna, which has the capacity to give rise to all dharmas. Fourth, it represents the firm, substantial mind, which is the true mind, also known as suchness, or the inherently pure, tranquil mind of Tathāgatagarbha.

In the Nature school, as demonstrated in the *Awakening of Faith in the Mahāyāna*, suchness or the true mind is considered the true nature of all dharmas. On the other hand, the Characteristics school, such as the Yogācāra school, asserts that the creation and cessation of all dharmas are not related to suchness, but are merely manifestations of the eighth consciousness. Although both perspectives can be said to be aligned with idealism, they differ in their understanding of the nature of mind. The mind in the Yogācāra school refers to an individual's mind, while that in the Nature school refers to the cosmic mind. Both perspectives have a level of influence on Ma's philosophy. Zongmi quotes the *Śūraṅgama Sūtra* in the *Preface to the Collection of Writings on the Source of Chan*, "The inner mind comes from within; it is not formed by illusionary means," to demonstrate that suchness is not an external condition and cannot be validated by appearance. Ma quotes the same line to prove that there is nothing beyond the mind.

The connection between the traditional Confucian philosophy of the mind and Ma's theory of mind and matter is even more apparent. Lu Jiuyuan says, "Matters within the universe are part of the duty of my nature, and matters that are part of the duty of my nature are matters within the universe."[27] Wang Yangming also frequently proclaims, "There is nothing beyond the mind." These propositions are reiterated in statements in Ma's theory of mind and matter, and they have become the keynote of the theory. This goes to show that Ma has fully inherited the legacy of ancient Chinese thought of the mind in the aspect of mind and matter.

III. No Circumstances Exist Independent of the Mind

To understand Ma Yifu's theory of mind and matter, it is necessary to compare it with contemporary scholar Xiong Shili's theory of mind and matter. In the early 30s, Ma penned high praise for Xiong Shili's book *A New Treatise on Consciousness-Only*, stating:

> With the complete collection of sacred evidence, everything achieves utmost reality, whereby all things are exhausted when the self is exhausted. Nothing exists beyond the self. By apprehending nature, one apprehends Heaven, and no Heaven exists without nature. This is the fundamental life of all things and the great origin of change.[28]

This goes to show that the two philosophers share a similar stance on the concepts of "nothing beyond the self" and "no Heaven exists without nature." Ma lacks clarity in organizing his thoughts in a systematic manner as he relied on recorded quotes, while Xiong provides clear, articulate arguments in his comprehensive works. Therefore, understanding Xiong's work can aid in comprehending Ma's discourse.

The opening of *A New Treatise on Consciousness-Only*, "The Mingzong Section," states that the creation of this work "aims to clarify that the true substance is not an external circumstance separated from one's own mind, nor is it the circumstance traversed by knowledge. Instead, it is a seeking of concrete evidence and corresponding reasons."[29] It mainly discusses two major issues:

(1) that substance is not external to one's own mind, and (2) that substance is not the object of knowledge and understanding can only be achieved when concrete evidence is sought. Ma and Xiong basically share the same views on these two major issues. The difference lies in the fact that Ma does not discuss substance, focusing only on the mind and matter, while Xiong appears in the guise of discussing philosophy.

Xiong believes that when people mention substance, they "generally seek outward," but in reality, "the only way to encompass all things without missing any, is solely through the mind. Seeing the mind is tantamount to seeing substance."[30] He provides his own explanation, saying, "On the mention of encompassing all things, this mind is designated as the substantial essence of all things, and there is not a single thing left that can be constituted as a separate entity. It is thus expressed as such."[31] This indicates that the mind is the essence of the universe, and it is also this mind, which means that it is not a separate entity unrelated to individual conscious minds. While it is this mind, it pervades as the substantial essence of all things. In an explanation of this point in the original text, he says:

> Substance is not something external to my mind, because the entirety (notably referred to as *daquan*, meaning substance) does not obstruct the manifestation as individual parts, and each part is itself the entirety. For instance, in the case of Zhang, there was an entirety to begin with, but Zhang could not be separated from his own mind to seek the entirety externally. Similarly, Li, who also had an entirety to begin with, could not be separated from his own mind to seek the entirety externally. Each person's universe is the direct manifestation of the entirety as a whole.[32]

This shows that Xiong believes the essence of the universe is the mind, which is a grand mind that is fully manifested within each of our individual minds. This is evidently a connection drawn from the unique logic of classical Buddhism, such as "one is all, and all is one" and the concept of "the moon reflected in every drop of water." However, this assertion is a progression when compared to the often-confusing conflation of the universal mind and individual minds, as seen in the *Awakening of Faith in the Mahāyāna* and Huayan literature. Xiong further points out:

> People often doubt how my own mind (referred to as the essential mind in the original text) can encompass all things. How does this analogy work? The answer is that those who fail to understand this discriminate the mind according to habitual and illusionary ways. They only see the small self and are thus unable to perceive nature (here, the essential mind is synonymous with nature but named differently according to the context. It is called the mind, where it pertains to the individual, while it is called nature, where it pertains to the principle of our existence).
>
> When overly focused on the small self, one diverges between self and others and discerns between internal and external, thus casting doubt on how my mind can encompass all things. However, when one expansively forgets oneself, one would comprehend that

> profound tranquility is non-empty. Giving birth yet not possessing and the principle of ultimate sincerity with no end are inherent principles shared by myself and all things, and they are the true nature that we encompass. This true nature resides in my body, consistently pure and clear, and is referred to as the essential mind when it governs my body. Thus, when speaking of the mind, it is not something privately owned by my body, but the true nature shared harmoniously with all things. Therefore, in reverse, my mind has encompassed all things.[33]

The true essence of the universe being manifested in the human body as the essential mind is why the essential mind and the true essence of the universe are identical. Therefore, it can be said that the mind is the entity of the universe. Taking this perspective, the mind is not exclusive to the individual body. Such a mind "truly pervades the entire universe without exception."[34] Everyone possesses such a mind, and everything is inseparable from such a mind. In summary, the entity of the universe is none other than the one mind. This argument by Xiong is a robust discourse on the mind in the context of Zongmi's commentary.

In *A New Treatise on Consciousness-Only*, there is a chapter dedicated to consciousness-only, which challenges "the notion of an external reality independent of the mind." Xiong advocates against the existence of a circumstance detached from consciousness. Taking a bottle as an example, he says that the bottle is merely a collection of attributes such as hardness and whiteness. On one hand, such attributes are merely sensations of various consciousnesses, while on the other, even if one acknowledges hardness and whiteness as independent external entities, the complete perception of the bottle arises only through the comprehensive function of consciousness. This argument, like Gongsun Long's* theory of hardness and whiteness, employs a discussion of perception and the synthesizing function of consciousness. However, there is a difference, as Gongsun Long acknowledges the independent existence of attributes like hardness and whiteness, while Xiong denies the existence of all entities independent of consciousness.

Xiong also emphasizes that opposing the notion of circumstances independent of the mind does not fundamentally deny the existence of a circumstance. He says:

> The appearance of attributes like hardness and whiteness in the mind implies the existence of a circumstance, and this interpretation is acceptable. However, this causal circumstance is not independent of the mind. When discussed from the standpoint of deluded emotions, there is an external reality independent of the mind, but when adhering to true principles, the circumstance and the mind are two distinct aspects of a unified whole.[35]

---

* Gongsun Long (c. 320–250 BC), was a member of the School of Names (Logicians) of ancient Chinese philosophy.

Here, the mind refers to consciousness. This argument is centered around mental activities that have a dependency on others. Both circumstances and consciousness are manifestations of different functions of the universe, and yet, they are inseparable. He goes on:

> Summarizing what has been said before, it is not a denial of the existence of circumstances, but rather a rejection of the idea of circumstances that exist independently of the mind. As the term mind is only used in reference to circumstances, it is said that the mind exists, and thus, there are circumstances. Without circumstances, the designation of the mind would not stand. In reality, the mind and circumstances are an internally contradictory and developing whole. … We only acknowledge that the mind and circumstances are two distinct aspects of a unified whole. We cannot accept that circumstances exist independently of the mind. We must understand that from my body to the sun, stars, earth, and even other minds. Everything is a circumstance. The circumstances of my body exist without separation from my mind, and this is something that no one would deny. As for the circumstances of the sun, stars, earth, and other minds, they are all encompassed by my mind, and they are all flowing through my mind, with no distinction between inside and outside.[36]

The distinguishing feature of Xiong's new consciousness-only school of thought from the old consciousness-only school, then, lies in the fact that while it agrees with the general proposition of the old consciousness-only school that there are no circumstances beyond consciousness, it does not consider consciousness as an ultimately real entity. Instead, it views both consciousness and circumstances as different manifestations of the entity of the universe. On the other hand, the new consciousness-only school of thought does not assert that circumstances are non-existent. "The consciousness-only doctrine rejects the delusion of external circumstances but does not claim that circumstances are non-existent, as they do not exist independent of the mind. Therefore, it is termed 'consciousness-only,' with the term 'only' having a specific meaning, not simply implying absolute singularity."[37] Xiong's new study of the mind employs both the theory of the true mind and the theory of consciousness-only in its argument. In this regard, it aligns with traditional Buddhist teachings.

Looking at this discussion, it is evident that Xiong's assertion of "no circumstances without consciousness" aligns fundamentally with Ma's ideas that "nothing exists beyond the mind." Further, Xiong's new consciousness-only theory can help us understand the specific meaning of Ma's notion of "understanding circumstances only through the mind, and no circumstances exist beyond the mind." It is evident from these discussions that Ma's idea that "all phenomena arise from conditions" and "a true mind can illuminate all conditions without being conditioned by them" lean more toward what Zongmi calls the "one Vehicle that reveals nature" or "the manifestation of the true mind as the teaching of nature," emphasizing the intrinsic true mind without delving into the consciousness that differentiates conditions and circumstances. Ma's thought is more aligned with the *Awakening of Faith in the Mahāyāna* and Huayan school, with the consciousness-only philosophy playing a less prominent role in his thinking. Emphasizing inner cultivation of the mind, however, is a fundamental stance shared by various Buddhist schools, as well as Xiong and Ma.

IV. Immanent and Transcendent

Ma's theory of mind and matter highlights the relationship between traditional Chinese ideas of idealism and the Western concept of philosophy. Despite his alignment with Confucianism and adherence to the Six Classics, Ma particularly emphasizes the ontological perspective of the inseparability of mind and matter and the methodological approach of understanding nature through clear perception of the mind. Such a philosophical stance differs from Western emphasis on the analysis of cognitive functions and subject-object distinctions. Consequently, Ma makes a point to distinguish traditional "learnings from the sages" from philosophy. Such a distinction, in our view, does not imply an exclusion from the realm of philosophy for analysis. Rather, it signifies his inherited perspective on learning and presuppositions about ontology, which presents distinct characteristics from traditional Western philosophy.

At the time, a scholar advocated for the use of scientific methods to study Confucianism. When consulted about this, Ma did not agree. He says:

> Today, the methods of science and philosophy generally rely on empirical reasoning, observation of phenomena, and subsequent analysis. Although the depth, breadth, and width of these approaches vary, they share a commonality in seeking knowledge through comparison. Some pour effort into thinking and seek knowledge like a field mouse searching for large prey as food, while others engage in speculative endeavors akin to a monkey trying to scoop the moon's reflection in the water. Those who excel in such pursuits may present compelling theories and well-organized ideas, but rely on contrived arrangements rather than innate understanding. For the sage in the Central Plains who begins and ends with order, though the analogy may fall short, the classification and discernment of phenomena must draw upon profound insight. The exploration of divine knowledge and transformation is rooted in sacred evidence, and cannot be acquired through mere imitation.[38]

In his view, the methods developed in science and philosophy in the West pursue matters external to the mind through emotional understanding and the discriminating mind. The relentless pursuit of wonder and knowledge cannot rely on sensory experiences and rational thinking. Instead, it must rely on internal realization and verification. The reason he advocates the ideas of "nothing beyond the mind" and that "matters within the universe are part of my duty" is that he wants people to work on the cultivation of their own minds. He believes the nature and direction of such knowledge are different from what is known as philosophy in the West, in that "the sages of the Central Plains consider matters within the universe as part of the duty of their nature and do not believe that there is another world beyond the mind. This is rather different from the research methods of Western philosophy by contemporary scholars."[39] He believes that Western philosophy and science are "built upon observations." Such knowledge is based on the separation of mind and matter. In contrast, the learning of the sages in the Central Plains does not separate things from the mind, but instead emphasizes the complete understanding of the mind and nature.

Another scholar, seeking to establish philosophy for humanity, asked Ma for guidance. Ma replied:

> Those who taught at the academies had to delve into the original scriptures and create the inherent principles of self-nature. They cannot be spoken of in the same breath as today's philosophers. The virtue of the wise lies in the pursuit of philosophical governance. If one takes the objective attitude held by contemporary philosophers today to study what is now the philosophy of the past era, it may not yield profound benefits.[40]

He points out that the so-called philosophical methods generally emphasize "the study of knowledge through a certain method. Speaking from the perspective of the teachings of the sages in the Central Plains, such a method is unattainable, because its pursuit lies externally. Regardless of how it is arranged, organized, justified, and articulated with reasons, it has no interference with self-nature." Finally, he advised this gentleman to "temporarily set aside such philosophical thoughts" and "to keep an open mind. First, thoroughly understand literature and its meaning, make an effort to cultivate your understanding, recognize the principles of your own nature, and do not be misguided by such miscellaneous thoughts. Only then can you truly grasp the principles."[41] This implies that the characteristics of Western philosophy are firstly analytical and discriminating and, secondly, focused on understanding external objects. In contrast, Chinese academic thought is characterized firstly by introspective cultivation and secondly by the creation of self-nature. Western philosophy is analytical and outward-focused, while Chinese thought is holistic and inwardly insightful.

Ma's rejection of philosophy differs from other early 20th-century Neo-Confucian scholars. For instance, Xiong Shili also strongly advocates "seeking evidence as justification" and "looking introspectively," opposing the use of rationality of discrimination to "seek principles externally" and "observe things." However, Xiong believes that the mistake in using wisdom to seek externally lies not in seeking it through philosophy, but in the failure of philosophy to truly understand "substance." People mistakenly believe in the independent existence of the external world, so they direct all their mental energy outward, pursuing and objectifying the external world. Only through the theoretical explanation of the new consciousness-only theory can one understand that circumstances belong to the mind, and the mind can distinguish, transform, and dominate circumstances. Only then can the mind be independent and free from objectification.[42] On the other hand, Feng Youlan considers Western philosophy the direction for the modernization of philosophy, emphasizing logical analysis and aiming to reach the highest realms of life through logical analysis.

In comparison, Ma Yifu leans more towards Chan school and the School of Mind in his practice and methods. He strongly advocates the approach of seeking evidence and places less emphasis on theoretical analysis. This stands in contrast to Xiong Shili, who was trained in Yogācāra Buddhism, or the consciousness-only school of thought, and Feng Youlan, who was trained in logic, both of whom emphasize theoretical discernment.

In contemporary academic terms, these characteristics of Ma Yifu and Xiong Shili's thoughts fall under the category of internal transcendence. There have been many schools of thought that have emerged in the long history of Chinese Confucian tradition, and not all can be categorized as internal transcendence. For instance, classical Confucianism (in the pre-Qin period) still retains the religious concept of Heaven to a certain extent. Although the understanding of Heaven has been rationalized to a considerable extent in the Song Dynasty and later periods, it is still regarded as the highest domain with ontological significance. Therefore, it would be inaccurate to solely categorize Confucianism as internal transcendence, as there is still an aspect of external transcendence in it.

The term internal transcendence, as commonly used within contemporary academic circles, is often used in contrast to the Christian concept of external transcendence, with the former mostly referring to the branch of Neo-Confucianism. In the School of Mind, the term internal transcendence does not capture the complete essence and requires further elaboration. This can be further examined in accordance with the categories of substance and cultivation in Ming Dynasty Neo-Confucianism.

In the aspect of substance, as mentioned in the second and third sections of this chapter, the form and structure of consciousness-only thinking in the *Awakening of Faith in the Mahāyāna*, Huayan school, and Chan school manifest in a characteristic of being "both transcendent and immanent." That is, on one hand, it advocates the existence of suchness as a substance, and on the other hand, it considers suchness as both manifesting and existing within individual minds. The connection between suchness as a substance and the suchness within individual minds is constructed by special formulations of logic such as "one is all, and all is one" and "the moon reflected in every drop of water," thus allowing the suchness in individual minds to possess the same completeness as the suchness in the form of a substance.

In the aspect of cultivation, since suchness as a substance both fully manifests and exists within everyone's minds, the pursuit of completeness and perfection only requires dedicated introspection and cultivation of the inner self. Chan school takes this internal aspect to the extreme. *The Platform Sutra of the Sixth Patriarch*, attributed to Huineng, advocates the concept of Buddha's three bodies, Dharmakāya (body of essence), Sambhogakāya (body of enjoyment), and Nirmāṇakāya (body of transformation), residing within one's own nature. Individuals only need to seek Buddha within their own nature. There is no need to seek externally.

From Lu Jiuyuan and Wang Yangming to Ma Yifu and Xiong Shili, Confucian studies of the mind in modern times have consciously or unconsciously absorbed or been influenced by

Buddhist studies of the mind. They believe that the mind is the essence of the universe, which manifests and exists within every individual's mind. Through introspection and cultivation from within, individuals can unite with their essence and achieve a state of perfection. It is thus evident that in the tradition of the study of the mind in Confucian philosophy, it is "both transcendent and immanent" when viewed from the perspective of essence and "transcending from within" when viewed from the perspective of cultivation. Representative propositions for the former include "both substance and function are one," while representative propositions for the latter include "putting in the utmost effort to apprehend one's nature allows one to apprehend Heaven."

Strictly speaking, due to assertions in the study of the mind such as "Heaven and humanity are not separate in the first place; there is thus no need to speak of their unity," "Wholeheartedness is Heaven," and "Three matters realized simultaneously," internal realization is synonymous with knowing and harmonizing with Heaven. This does not imply that a separate process is required to connect and transcend. Therefore, according to its inherent definition, it is more accurately described as "simultaneously immanent and transcendent." The substance-cultivation structure in the study of the mind cannot be adequately and accurately expressed with a simple phrase like internal transcendence.

External transcendence is not something that can be understood with intellect and reason. Similarly, in this regard, internal transcendence also cannot be understood with intellect and reason. While the ontology of the simultaneously transcendent and immanent tradition of the study of the mind can be expressed through a certain intellect structure, true verification requires self-verification and self-realization by cultivation. Therefore, whether it is the wake-up call by the Chan master or the admonition of the master of mind studies, it presupposes that internal completeness requires an unreasonable method of self-verification and self-realization to verify. Certainly, the term unreasonable here is not pejorative but simply indicates that such knowledge has a different characteristic from the philosophy derived from Greek traditions. From a sympathetic understanding perspective, while such a realization is not verified through logical analysis and theoretical thinking, from the standpoint of the School of Mind, it is the only self-evident method of verification that stands without the need for explanation. This is why Ma Yifu emphasizes a sacred verification method that is different from Western philosophy. Evidently, this thought is based on a unique understanding of the relationship between mind and matter, or a philosophy that is both immanent and transcendent.

The significance of such a type of sacred verification that is different from Western philosophy, as emphasized by Ma (as well as Liang Shuming), in modern society and the academic realm is worthy of further exploration. The structure and demands of modern Chinese society are fundamentally different from those of traditional Chinese society, and the development of philosophical thought is unlikely to detach from theoretical discourse. Moreover, philosophical practitioners often engage in the profession of academic teaching. In such a society, knowledge that is both transcendent and immanent, if supported by external organizations such as Buddhism, can still play a positive role in a cultural setting that values material pursuits over spiritual ones.

However, while inner sagehood in the Confucian philosophical system may be embraced by individuals as it remains relevant in emphasizing the importance of individuals' inner lives in modern industrial society, it may find itself in a precarious position in contemporary society, which has abandoned the ideals of attaining sagehood and moral excellence. After the thorough deconstruction brought about by the May Fourth Movement, and in the face of strong rising trends of materialism and vulgarization in modern Chinese society, breaking free of such a predicament may be a fundamental question for the Confucian tradition, especially for the School of Mind that focuses on the immanent and transcendent nature.

Notes

1. *Responses to Inquiries at Erya Tai*, vol. 1, 22.
2. Ibid., 24.
3. *Responses to Inquiries at Erya Tai*, vol. 1, 29.
4. "Essence of the Great Plan, Part 3," in *Fu Xing College Records of Lectures*, vol. 5, 141.
5. "Essence of the Great Plan, Part 5," 152.
6. *Responses to Inquiries at Erya Tai*, vol. 1, 2.
7. "Remarks from Observing Phenomena, Part 1," in *Fu Xing College Records of Lectures*, vol. 6, 189.
8. "Remarks from Observing Phenomena, Part 2," 192.
9. "Remarks from Observing Phenomena, Part 3," 198.
10. "Essence of the Great Plan, Part 9," in *Fu Xing College Records of Lectures*, vol. 5, 171.
11. Ibid., 174.
12. *Responses to Inquiries at Erya Tai*, vol. 2, 7.
13. "Remarks from Observing Phenomena, Part 2," in *Fu Xing College Records of Lectures*, vol. 6, 194.
14. "Remarks from Observing Phenomena, Part 8," 223.
15. *Collation and Annotation of the Awakening of Faith in the Mahāyāna* (Zhonghua Book Company, 1992), 17.
16. Ibid., 104.
17. Ibid., 121.
18. *Collation and Annotation of the Awakening of Faith in the Mahāyāna* (Zhonghua Book Company, 1992), 59.
19. *Huayan's One Vehicle, Ten Philosophic Ideas.*
20. *The Concept of Returning to the Source by Practising the Huayan Philosophy.*
21. *Various Entrances to the Sea of Meanings of Avatamsaka.*
22. "Action and Intention," chap. 1 in *The Platform Sutra of the Sixth Patriarch.*
23. "Final Instructions," chap. 10 in *The Platform Sutra of the Sixth Patriarch.*
24. "Meeting of the Roots and Branches,"chap. 4 in *Huayan Sutra's the Origin of Human.*
25. *Preface to the Collection of Writings on the Source of Chan.*
26. Ibid.
27. *Collected Works of Lu Jiuyuan*, 483.
28. *A New Treatise on Consciousness-Only* (Zhonghua Book Company, 1985), 39.
29. Ibid., 43.
30. Ibid., 44.
31. Ibid.

32. *A New Treatise on Consciousness-Only* (Zhonghua Book Company, 1985), 247.
33. Ibid., 252.
34. Ibid., 43.
35. *A New Treatise on Consciousness-Only* (Zhonghua Book Company, 1985), 260.
36. Ibid., 271.
37. Ibid.
38. *Responses to Inquiries at Erya Tai,* vol. 1, 25.
39. Ibid., 29.
40. "A Reply to Mr. Xu," in *Responses to Inquiries at Erya Tai.*
41. *Responses to Inquiries at Erya Tai,* vol. 1, 33.
42. *A New Treatise on Consciousness-Only,* 257.

CHAPTER 6

Liang Shuming's Cultural Pluralism and *Eastern and Western Cultures and Their Philosophies*

Regardless of whether one agrees with Liang Shuming's cultural philosophy, it is impossible to deny that his work *Eastern and Western Cultures and Their Philosophies* is one of the classics of 20th-century Chinese intellectual and academic discourse. Any discussion of modernity in 20th-century China, especially the ideas of intellectuals during the May Fourth Movement, must consider Liang Shuming, alongside Chen Duxiu and Hu Shi.

At the time of its publication, *Eastern and Western Cultures and Their Philosophies* became the most influential work since the New Culture Movement, although much of its influence stemmed from the criticism it provoked. Within a year of its publication, the book sparked nearly a hundred articles and discussions, along with another ten or twenty pamphlets on the topic of Eastern and Western Cultures. It was translated into twelve languages soon after its publication in Chinese. Such an impact was unprecedented for any work since the publication of the *La Jeunesse* (*New Youth*) magazine in 1915. It is no wonder that people at the time referred to it as a groundbreaking work, observing that it "stirred up scholars from both the Eastern and Western hemispheres, so that there was not a single peaceful day."[1] Even in the 1930s, it was said that Liang was the only Chinese philosopher recognized by Westerners.[2]

Yet, there seems to be a significant disparity between the perception of *Eastern and Western Cultures and Their Philosophies* in the minds of the general public and the original aims of Liang's work. At the time, Liang was seen as a leading figure who opposed Westernization. As late as the 1930s, Guo Zhanbo regarded him as a symbol of resistance against Western culture in his book *A History of Chinese Thought in the Past Fifty Years*. He writes:

> Starting in 1919, the New Culture Movement emerged during a period of Western industrial and capitalist ideological influence. It aimed to resist China's traditional agricultural, feudalistic ideology and its customs, morals, habits, and ethics. The leading intellectuals of this time included Chen Duxiu, Hu Shi, Li Dazhao, and Wu Zhihui, among others. Amidst this surge of Western ideas and new cultural movements, there arose a reactionary line of thought that opposed Western culture and advocated for the reverence of China's indigenous culture. Liang Shuming was one of the proponents of this line of thought.[3]

Guo Zhanbo even argued that Liang "opposed science and democratic politics" and that his ideas "still represented China's agricultural feudalistic ideology."[4]

Guo took this position from the perspective of the New Culture Movement, a view commonly held among the majority of New Culture proponents. Liang himself denied these claims. In the two years following the publication of *Eastern and Western Cultures and Their Philosophies*, he did not respond to most of the criticism. It was only after the last wave of criticism, particularly Hu Shi's article, was published months later that Liang wrote a lengthy response in which he explicitly refuted the accusations of being conservative and reactionary. He writes, "If so, then am I an obstacle? Am I hindering their intellectual reform movement? How can I bear that responsibility? It's not something I wish for. It makes me very sad. I don't believe that I am against their movement. I don't consider myself their enemy… I have no enemies!"[5]

Liang acknowledged that his cultural views differed from those of Chen and Hu, but he strongly refused to be seen as an obstacle to the intellectual reform movement. In fact, he was always open about his stance and viewpoints, and his expressions by no means aimed to guise his position. China's experiences since Reform and Opening Up have served as a reminder that in an era of profound social and cultural changes, there are often self-proclaimed reformers who readily label people with different cultural views as "opponents of reform." However, in reality, this mostly reflects the simplistic thinking of the critics and their inability to grasp the diversity and depth of the positions held by those criticized.

A profound yet complex work often eludes an immediate understanding of its intricate structure. By contrast, people tend toward superficial comprehension or a reductionist attitude, focusing only on one aspect and simplifying its treatment. If such a book emerges during a period of cultural debate and happens to tie outside the mainstream view, it becomes even more challenging for the public to examine it calmly and thoroughly. Liang's *Eastern and Western Cultures and Their Philosophies* can be regarded as such a work.

Having experienced the volatility of the 20th century, perhaps it is only today that readers can calmly and objectively grasp the true essence of Liang's complex cultural perspective more thoroughly. This chapter will focus on his views on Eastern and Western cultures. Examination of the issues related to Indian culture falls outside the purview of this chapter.

I. Europeanization and Globalization

In the three years before the 1918 publication of *Eastern and Western Cultures and Their Philosophies* and after publishing "Seeking the Research of Oriental Scholars" in the *Peking University Daily*, Liang was generally viewed as an opponent of Europeanization. Regarding this, he writes, "Some see me as an opponent of Europeanization, but Europeanization is synonymous with globalization, and the East cannot be excluded from it. However, the East also has its own contributions that make it indispensable to globalization, and Europe and other Western countries cannot do without it."[6]

In Liang's view, Europeanization was synonymous with globalization, and modern Western culture was not limited to a particular nationality, but rather a universal and universalizable culture that constituted an inevitable trend in global development. The phrase "Europeanization is synonymous with globalization" is a clear indicator that he did not oppose Europeanization. From a positive perspective, his position affirmed that Eastern culture similarly contained cultural elements that were universal and could be universally applicable while supporting globalization. From this perspective, it is evident that his stance was not against Western culture, but against the counteraction to Eastern culture. When he arrived at Peking University in early October 1917, he told Cai Yuanpei and Chen Duxiu that he had come to speak up for Shakyamuni and Confucius, reflecting his stance against the relegation of Eastern culture rather than opposing Western culture. From today's perspective, the statement that "the East also has its own contributions that make it indispensable to globalization, and Europe and other Western countries cannot do without it" is more easily recognizable as an assertion of multiculturalism.

In the summer of 1919, Liang wrote two chapters of *Eastern and Western Cultures and Their Philosophies* as a preface to *Explanation of Consciousness-Only*. In the autumn of 1920, he began delivering lectures on the issue of Eastern and Western culture at Peking University. The content of these lectures was serialized in the *Peking University Daily* from October to December in fifteen installments. In the summer of 1921, he was invited to Jinan to deliver lectures on Eastern and Western culture over a span of forty days. The records of these two sets of lectures in the autumn of 1920 and the summer of 1921 were published as the book *Eastern and Western Cultures and Their Philosophies* in October 1921. By October 1922, just one year later, the book went through five editions.

Eastern and Western Cultures and Their Philosophies begins with the following description of Western culture:

> What we see is a world that is almost completely Westernized. It goes without saying that countries like Europe and America are entirely Westernized. Even in Eastern countries, only those who can receive and embrace Westernization and make use of it can stand their ground as a nation or country. Those who fail to receive and embrace Westernization are occupied by the strong influence of Westernization. [...] China is also oppressed

> by Westernization. Westernization has been encroaching for several decades, forcing the Chinese people, who have long held Eastern values, to change their way of life and adopt Westernization. Almost every aspect of our lives, be it spiritual, social, or material, is filled with Westernization—a point that cannot be denied. The current situation, then, is not a battle between Easternization and Westernization, but an absolute victory of Westernization over Easternization, an absolute domination.[7]

It is important to clarify that when Liang Shuming used the terms Westernization and Easternization, he was mainly referring to Eastern and Western cultures. It is evident from the passage above that he understood that Westernization was the current trend in the world, and those who followed it prospered, while those who resisted it perished. People all over the world needed to adopt Westernization in order to survive. Furthermore, he acknowledged that the lives of the Chinese people were already filled with Westernization. Since he was well aware that not embracing Western culture leads to downfall, it is certain that he did not oppose Western culture.

Liang states that culture can be understood as various aspects of a nation's life, which can be categorized into three areas: spiritual life, social life, and material life. Comparing Eastern and Western cultures in these three areas, he points out that in terms of spiritual life, "Indeed, Westerners have made more progress than us," and "comparing the Western people, it is clear that we are still in an undeveloped state." In terms of social life, "The progress of the West is more apparent than that of China." As for material life, "It goes without saying that the East is far behind the West." After making these three comparisons, he concludes that:

> From this perspective, it appears that culture encompasses only these three aspects, and in all three aspects, Eastern culture falls short of Western culture. Thus, Eastern culture is clearly an underdeveloped culture, while Western culture is already developed. If an underdeveloped culture exists, there is no need to reference it; we can simply adopt the already-developed culture. I recall that Chang Naide once said that Eastern and Western cultures cannot be compared. Eastern culture is of the past, while Western culture is of the present; one is outdated, while the other is advanced. Based on the observations we have made from these three aspects, his argument seems valid. When we examine Eastern culture and philosophy, they remain unchanged and enduring throughout the ages. The cultural and philosophical beliefs of thousands of years ago are still the same today.[8]

Using the language of others in this passage, Liang presents views that he acknowledges. From this perspective, Eastern culture is synonymous with antiquity and Western culture represents modernity. Eastern culture is seen as underdeveloped, while Western culture is considered advanced. Liang openly acknowledges these views. In light of this, it is worth considering that he was not likely to be against Western culture, since he accepted these premises.

According to Liang's account, during the early stages of the New Culture Movement, many Chinese people were influenced by the contrasting views of Eastern and Western cultures. The prevailing belief was that Westerners sought to conquer nature, while Easterners sought harmony with nature. He cited examples of people who hold this viewpoint, such as Kaneko Umaji, John Dewey, and Kita Reikichi. Liang, however, did not agree with this perspective. He believed that although this viewpoint held some truth, it "greatly neglects the essence of Westernization and does not rise to our expectations to provide an answer." He says, "Let us take the most noticeable distinctive color of Western society, such as the so-called 'freedom' and 'equality'—the tendency towards 'democracy'—can these also be included in the conquest of nature? If we only look at its material splendor and disregard the aspects of social life, how is this different in terms of superiority or inferiority from the view of 'strong armor and sharp weapons' during the Tongzhi and Guangxu periods?"[9]

Liang's own views on the comparison between Eastern and Western cultures originated from his discussion with Zhang Shenfu in 1918. He writes, "At that time, I expressed my opinion, which is that I observed two distinctive features of Westernization, and all the strengths of Westernization can be summarized in these two aspects. I fully acknowledge these two aspects, which is why my advocacy of Easternization is different from rejecting Westernization from the perspective of an old mindset."[10]

It is important to note that he explicitly states that while he advocates Eastern culture, he is not rejecting Western culture, let alone opposing it. Concerning the two distinctive features of Western culture that he fully acknowledges, he says, "One is the scientific method, and the other is the development of individuality and sociality. The former is a unique spirit in Western academia, and the latter is a unique spirit in Western society. Zhang Shenfu seems to pay little attention to it, but I am confident and even feel that it is an exclusive insight."[11] This statement by Liang may not appear remarkable to people today, who are familiar with the slogan, Science and Democracy. However, as Liang states, he presented these two points before Chen Duxiu's summary. After finishing his previous statement, he goes on to say, "In the ninth year of the Republic of China, when I saw the first issue of the sixth volume of *La Jeunesse* in Chen Duxiu's 'Statement In Defense of Our Magazine's Crimes,' he said that all our crimes were merely supporting democracy and science."[12] This suggests that as early as 1918, Liang had already recognized the important characteristics of Western culture, and his views were consistent with the New Youth faction, especially when he says, "I fully acknowledge these two things," expressing complete support for science and democracy. It is no wonder that Ai Kai held that, compared to the cultural integration faction and the complete Westernization faction, "Liang Shuming's cultural perspective is more consistent with Chen Duxiu's position."[13]

II. Science and Democracy

Liang drew comparisons between Eastern and Western cultures in the aspects of science and democracy. Through his comparisons, we can understand his perspective on Eastern culture.

He points out that Eastern culture lags behind the science of Western culture, saying, "Though we also engage in blacksmithing, steelmaking, manufacturing gunpowder, carpentry, stonework, construction of buildings and bridges, and various production projects, our production techniques rely on the craftsmanship passed down by artisans. In the West, everything is based on science: using a method to organize fragmented experiences and incomplete knowledge into systematic knowledge, advancing exploration, completely separating from craftsmanship, and relying on science to handle and solve everything. Perhaps in the West, art is also scientific, while in the East, science is artistic."[14] This is a full affirmation of the scientific spirit of the West.

Liang further points out that "science seeks universal principles that everyone can collectively recognize through verification. Therefore, what previous generations have achieved is accessible to present generations. The value lies in new inventions and systematic progress, a steady forward movement, so that the present naturally surpasses the past. Art, on the other hand, relies on genius and skill, which are individual attainments. The achievements of the past are often seen as unattainable by later generations. The value lies in ancestral secrets, and naturally, there is a lament that the present falls short of the past."[15] He adds that the principles and thoughts emphasized in China "are practical in nature, more like techniques than scholarly learning. Much of China's knowledge is technical rather than academic, or one could say that there is no clear distinction between scholarship and practical skills."[16] This is a criticism of the lack of scientific spirit in Chinese culture.

It is useful here to examine the differences between China's political consciousness and Western democratic ideals. Liang states that in the Chinese mindset, it is strange to think that a country can exist without an emperor. He believed that there must always be someone in charge in order to be maintained. He writes, "Without someone in charge, how can there not be chaos? Who would be able to manage that chaos? It is inconceivable that there could be no chaos without someone in charge. The idea that chaos could be avoided without the need for a person to govern is beyond imagination."[17] There is no trace here of admiration for China's inherent culture.

According to Liang, "Chinese people are greatly astonished when they see Western methods that do not involve having one person in charge. They are also surprised to see that individuals of various stature are treated equally without any distinction of rank or hierarchy. For thousands of years, what has maintained social order in China is the concept of hierarchy and rank, making the absence of hierarchy and rank in society astonishing and unprecedented."[18] He further points out, "Following the path China had taken results in inequality among people and a lack of individual freedom. Although the original intention may have been to have one person make decisions and lead everyone forward together, it inevitably leads to that person dictating the private lives of individuals, rather than allowing each individual to make their own decisions. Not only are public affairs entrusted to that one person, but we also have no right to question their authority. Nor do we have the right to handle our personal speech and actions. We lose the freedom to handle things ourselves. This is a lack of freedom. Although in reality, we may still have a certain degree of freedom, it is because that person hasn't taken control, not because we have the right to it."[19] Liang thus summarizes China's political life as "limitless power for those in power and limitless powerlessness for those without power." He summarizes the principles of Western political life as "the right for everyone to participate and have a say in public affairs" and "the right for no one to interfere in personal matters."[20] These expressions reflect his genuine praise and wholehearted affirmation of the Western democratic spirit.

Based on this perspective, Liang believed that it was extremely urgent to transform the traditional political consciousness of the Chinese people. He pointed out that since the establishment of the Republic of China in the Revolution of 1911, the root cause of political problems was that "the Chinese people, under this Westernized political system, still maintain an attitude rooted in Eastern political systems. The Eastern attitude fundamentally contradicts Westernization. Unless this attitude is changed, a Westernized political system will never be successfully implemented."[21]

Based on the above, it is evident that the notion that Liang opposed science and democracy is either a fundamental misunderstanding of his ideas or an attempt to gain a political advantage by overpowering an opponent in debate. This attitude was common among cultural radicals in the 20th century and gave rise to many pointless arguments. In fact, Liang not only fully acknowledged the scientific and democratic aspects of Western culture, but also strongly advocated for freedom, equality, and rights. It is clear that the criticisms of Chinese culture by proponents of Westernization and Liang Shuming are fundamentally consistent. Liang expressed a positive view of Western cultural ethical concepts. For example, he states, "The ethical and moral concepts of Westerners are very different from ours. The most notable differences are, firstly, that Westerners place great emphasis on social morality, that is, public ethics, while Chinese culture focuses more on individual ethics, that is, private ethics… and secondly, that Chinese ethics revolve around the idea of serving and obeying a person as a moral duty."[22]

Liang's understanding of Western culture is summarized in his statement, "The academic and intellectual thought of the West, when examined closely, reveals a distinct color, completely different from ours, known as the spirit of science,"[23] and, "The social life of Westerners, when observed closely, also exhibits a distinct color, completely different from ours, known as the democratic spirit."[24] In connection with his admiration for Western thought and politics, we can clearly see Liang's explicit criticisms of the traditional academic and political shortcomings of Chinese culture.

III. Appearance and Orientation

Turning to his understanding of the characteristics of Western culture, we read, "How do we define Westernization? Most people would have a difficult time answering this question immediately. They might list various Western political systems, social customs, academic ideas, and so on. However, it is difficult to create such a comprehensive list, and even if it were, the more items listed, the less clear or accurate the concept of Westernization becomes. The question we ask requires condensing the vast, indescribable aspects of Westernization into one or two sentences that can express it. Only when all these things become something intriguing and vivid in our minds can we consider our question answered correctly."[25]

Like many intellectuals of that time, Liang liked to simplify the comparison between Eastern and Western cultures into a sentence or two. From today's perspective, this approach will inevitably appear one-sided, but for those who were eager to find a solution to cultural issues at that time, it was a necessary step.

Liang states, "The emphasis on science and democracy as the characteristics and strengths of Western culture is something everyone can see. It is not a unique insight of my own. In recent years, new thinkers have repeatedly discussed and emphasized this point, so it is not something I am only mentioning today."[26] As we have mentioned earlier, describing Liang's grasp of Western culture not only gives us insight into his profound understanding of it, but also shows that his stance is not fundamentally against Western culture. However, this is not the distinctive feature of Liang's cultural perspective.

With this understanding of the strengths of Western culture lying in science and democracy, it becomes clearer that the difference between Liang and other cultural factions lies in the fact that his thinking did not stop there. In his subsequent reflections, he noted that while people are aware of science and democracy as characteristics of Westernization, no one further asked, "How did Westernization become successful in this way?... How did science and democracy come to influence it?... Why couldn't China produce such things?"[27]

The primary reason he is not satisfied with using science and democracy as a generalization of Western culture is that, in his view, the phrase science and democracy fails to capture the characteristic of Western culture in conquering nature, which he sees as a shortcoming.[28] Further, driven by his one-sentence mode of thinking, he aimed to consolidate science and democracy into one spirit rather than two distinct, ambiguous spirits.[29] But more importantly, he points out that while Chinese people were focused on importing science and democracy, he believed that there was something more fundamental behind these two aspects. He states:

> We must understand that this is only the appearance that Westernization has gradually developed, and it is not the path that they have taken. If we want to learn from them, we may not necessarily follow their exact path, but we must follow the same direction. Otherwise, we won't truly grasp their essence by merely imitating their outward appearance. Furthermore, we should recognize that the essence of Westernization lies in that (the direction), not in this (the appearance). We should not consider this appearance as Westernization, but instead consider the direction they have taken as Westernization.[30]

This suggests that science and democracy still belong to the appearance of Western culture rather than its direction. "This" refers to the appearance, while "that" refers to the direction. He emphasizes that the essence of Western culture as Western culture does not lie in its appearance but in its direction. This direction is the fundamental essence of Western culture.

Liang proposed this idea because, in his view, using science and democracy to summarize Western culture was actually "extracting their common, distinct colors from various Western cultural artifacts." On the other hand, the method he adopted was "to seek out the source of its distinct colors." This method of seeking the source of a culture focused on identifying the direction or intention of that particular culture,[31] demonstrating that Liang's cultural perspective is a profound one. What he pursues is not an external, inducible pattern that can be deduced from culture, but rather an internal and experiential intention. It is from this standpoint that his cultural philosophy emerges. In explaining his approach to cultural research, he writes:

> I believe there is a method for us to seek the foundation or source of a culture. Let us consider what culture is. It is nothing more than the patterns of life of a particular ethnic group. And what is life? Life is the inexhaustible will… the constant cycle of satisfaction and dissatisfaction. Whether it is a nation or an individual life, why does the manifested pattern of life in the West appear as distinct, diverse colors? It is simply because the original inherent will of their respective patterns of life has diverged in different directions, resulting in the emergence of distinct manifestations. If you want to seek the foundation or source of a culture, you only need to look at the primal will underlying it and observe how its direction differs from that of another culture. To understand how these directions diverge, you can easily trace back to their respective starting points based on the known distinct colors, and it will become clear at a glance.[32]

The foundation or source of a culture refers to the direction of cultural will. It is from this direction of will that the patterns of life emerge, and different patterns of life exhibit distinct colors. Liang ultimately arrived at an answer to the question, *what is Western culture?* According to him, Westernization is rooted in the spirit of a forward-seeking will, or in other words, Westernization is a culture that is characterized by the emergence of the two remarkable aspects of science and democracy driven by the spirit of a forward-seeking will.[33]

IV. Three Directions Theory

Up to this point, Liang's cultural perspective has not only not been opposed to Western culture but, in a certain sense, it can still be said that he is very Westernized. He hoped that the Chinese people would not only learn science and democracy but also learn the direction from which science and democracy originated. He believed that failing to do so would make it impossible to truly grasp science and democracy. In this sense, he can be considered thoroughly Westernized, inside and out.

Liang not only believed that Eastern culture had not progressed, but also considered Western culture to have taken a big step forward compared to Eastern culture. He put forth the idea that without the infiltration of the West into the East, the East would not naturally progress to resemble the West. He states:

> I dare say that if the Eurasian trade routes had not been opened, the Chinese mentality would have remained unchanged for thousands of years, and there would have been no significant transformation in the economic phenomena of Chinese society. The Industrial Revolution in Europe would have never occurred. And if the Turkic people had not invaded India, allowing the Indians to pursue their own spiritual life, can we imagine how their economic phenomena would have progressed?[34]

This passage suggests that Liang believed that the progress of China and India was too slow. Up to this point, what we see in him is not much different from the Westernization faction. However, it is here that he begins to present his groundbreaking ideas:

> Let's first compare the appearance of Westernization with the appearance of Sinicization. The first aspect is the conquest of nature in material life, which China lacks and is inferior to Westernization. The second aspect is the scientific method in academic and intellectual thinking, which China also lacks. The third aspect is democracy in social life, which China does not possess. In these three aspects, China appears to be lacking and exhibits a predominantly negative image, making it difficult to find positive aspects.
>
> Therefore, we must ask: is the fundamental direction of Chinese culture the same as Westernization, but progressing at a slower pace without achieving the accomplishments of the West? Or is it a different path altogether, with its own achievements and positive aspects, beyond the realm of the negative image we currently perceive? Some people—most people— believe that China is simply inferior to the West, that Westerners have evolved faster and traveled further on the path, while the Chinese are slow and stagnant, having missed out on much of the journey. I initially thought the same way when I first looked at it... but the reality is different.[35]

Chen Duxiu and other advocates of Westernization listed all the maladies of Chinese culture, which Liang acknowledged. Liang endorsed all the proposals put forth by the advocates of Westernization regarding the study of Western culture. However, there is one aspect in which he differs from the advocates of Westernization: he cannot accept that Chinese culture is completely devoid of value, which is something he disagrees with both intellectually and emotionally. What he held in his heart was the idea of leaving a positive space for Eastern culture while studying Western culture.

His method for achieving this was to first acknowledge all the cultural propositions of the advocates of Westernization and then take a different approach. His first step was to differentiate between the three cultures of China, the West, and India, each having its own direction. He writes:

> Human culture can be seen as a journey, where Westerners have traveled about eighty or ninety miles, while the Chinese have only traveled about twenty or thirty miles. This may seem apparent, but it is not entirely true. I can assert that if we had no contact with Westernization, if China remained completely isolated from the outside world, even if we continued for three hundred, five hundred, or a thousand years, we would never have developed these ships, trains, and airplanes, the scientific method, or the spirit of democracy. This statement implies that the Chinese people are not following the same path as Westerners, and it is because they are progressing slowly that they are lagging behind by dozens of miles. If they were on the same path but just lagging behind, eventually they would catch up through gradual progress. However, if they each take different routes, heading in different directions, no matter how long they walk, they will never reach the same destination as the Westerners. In reality, China indeed falls into the latter category. In essence, the Chinese people have a different orientation and attitude toward their own path compared to Westerners.[36]

From this perspective, one could still arrive at the conclusion of Westernization, which suggests that the Chinese people initially took the wrong path and should quickly adopt the Western path. In other words, even at this point, proponents of Westernization can find support in Liang's arguments.

The divergence begins with the fact that while in the early stages of the New Culture Movement, Liang largely agreed with the cultural analysis and political proposals of the advocates of Westernization, the one thing he could not accept was the notion that Chinese culture was completely devoid of value. However, in the later stages of the New Culture Movement, he began to focus more on criticizing the shortcomings of Western culture. From this, he boldly predicted the future trend of world culture, stating that Western culture would undergo changes, while Eastern culture would experience a revival. To put it simply, the main difference between Liang and the advocates of Westernization lies not in their understanding of the past or their choices in the present, but in their different predictions regarding future development.

From here, it is useful to discuss the core of Liang's early cultural view, the Three Directions Theory. He believed that there are three fundamental approaches to problem-solving and ways of life, which he notes as:

> The first approach is to confront problems head-on, striving to transform the situation through active engagement and effort.
>
> The second approach is to accept circumstances as they come, without striving for change, but seeking personal contentment and satisfaction.
>
> The third approach is to try to eliminate problems and desires altogether, seeking a state of tranquility and liberation.[37]

Liang believed that Western, Chinese, and Indian cultures exemplify these three different attitudes toward life. He states:

> Western culture follows the first attitude, which is rooted in the spirit of aspiring and striving for progress.
>
> Chinese culture follows the second attitude, which is rooted in the spirit of seeking personal satisfaction, harmony, and moderation.
>
> Indian culture follows the third attitude, which is rooted in the spirit of seeking the elimination of problems and desires through introspection and backward reflection.[38]

This distinction can be clearly seen from a personal perspective. Some individuals are driven by a relentless pursuit of progress and advancement, always striving forward. Others adopt a harmonious, balanced approach, content with adapting to circumstances as they come. And there are those who maintain a negative attitude toward life, rejecting its various aspects.

As mentioned earlier, even proponents of Westernization can agree with the concept of these three orientations. From these three perspectives, one can derive the conclusion of thorough Westernization based on the idea of progress. It suggests that for countries to survive and modernize, they must adopt the first orientation, which emphasizes economic development, political democracy, and personal growth. In fact, Liang also supported the urgency of pursuing the first orientation for China in his time.

If this were the only aspect, he would appear to be no different from proponents of Westernization. However, there were differences between him and the proponents of Westernization, because he developed a unique cultural perspective based on the concept of the three orientations. He presented a cultural viewpoint that could affirm all three orientations, which set him apart from the advocates of Westernization. In essence, Liang affirmed Western culture in his time, while envisioning the affirmation of Chinese and Indian cultures in the future. Simply put, he believed that world culture was undergoing significant changes. The current trend was for the world to learn from the West and follow the first orientation. In the near future, the world would shift toward the second orientation, which embodied the essence of Chinese culture. In the distant future, the world would transition to the third orientation, reflecting the characteristics of Indian culture. In this temporal dimension, Liang ensured that the value of Chinese and Indian cultures continued to be recognized. Unlike the advocates of Westernization who sought to relegate Chinese and Indian cultures to the museums of history within the tide of Westernization, Liang affirmed their cultural worth. Additionally, apart from this temporal perspective, he employed a spatial approach to establish the position of Chinese culture. Like the advocates of Westernization, he criticized and rejected the backwardness of ancient China in terms of civilization, such as artifacts, systems, and academia. However, he did not consider the attitude toward life in Chinese culture as backward, as he believed that the attitude toward life was neither progressive nor backward in nature. Indeed, when he talked about the revival of Chinese culture in the future, he was not primarily referring to artifacts, systems, or academia. His focus was solely on the attitude toward life in terms of its orientation or direction.

V. Socialism

Liang's viewpoint is unique in that, while many acknowledge the historical value of Chinese and Indian cultures, they often consider these cultures to have lost their significance in the process of modernization. Liang's perspective is precisely the opposite. He believes that Chinese and Indian cultures are precocious, by which he means that they were not able to fulfill the needs and address the challenges faced by these nations in their respective historical contexts. He argues that the ideas and attitudes present in Chinese and Indian cultures were what the future of all nations required, and they would contribute to resolving the challenges faced by the development of world culture in the future.

Liang's evaluation and estimation were influenced not only by his affirmation of the inherent value of Eastern culture, but also by the awareness among intellectuals during that period of the drawbacks of Western capitalist culture and the strong influence of Western socialist ideology. These factors directly contributed to his perspective. He explains, "When we talk about future culture, we are not advocating that the world should adopt a certain culture, but rather pointing out the current trend. It is purely based on objective observations... From our objective observations, we can see that Western culture, which has been guiding the world, has undergone significant changes, and it seems that the future of world culture is not difficult to predict."[39] This theory, based on empirical facts, is approached methodologically by discussing actual trends, considering the actual as reasonable and regarding the inevitable as reasonable. It reflects the mindset of modern intellectuals who are influenced by world history and have a fear of lagging behind history. It also indicates that Liang's theory is not based on subjective preferences, but rather on the changing trends of world culture, or more specifically, Western culture.

Liang pointed out that the changes that have emerged in the West since the Middle Ages include the transition from small-scale production to large-scale production. This transformation was primarily attributed to two main factors: the invention of machines, which led to the concentration of capital and labor and resulted in a significant expansion of production scale, and the principle of free competition, in which society does not intervene in industry, and individuals compete for their own interests. He believed that this development had led to numerous problems and sharp contradictions. The progress of large-scale capitalist production resulted in the division of society into two major classes: the bourgeoisie and the proletariat. Capitalists oppressed workers, while workers constantly faced the threat of unemployment. On the one hand, unplanned production led to overproduction, and on the other hand, overproduction resulted in unemployment among workers. He observes, "The current approach is simply unacceptable, and such an economy is completely irrational. This unreasonable situation cannot continue indefinitely. It goes against the true nature of human beings, and naturally, there is a demand for correction and a return to rationality, which entails shifting from an individual-centered, production-centered economy to a society-centered, distribution-centered economy. This demand for correction aligns with the principles of socialism. The transformation of Western culture began to emerge from this point."[40] The significant influence socialist ideas had on Liang is clearly evident in this context.

This suggests that in Liang's view, the emergence of socialism brought about a transformation in Western culture. He notes here:

> Although we cannot determine the exact steps by which the economy will be corrected, there is no doubt that it must be corrected, and it is not some distant matter. As for what successful correction will look like, we should not speculate arbitrarily. It must necessarily return to reason, with society as the basis and distribution as the focus. This will lead to a fundamental transformation in human culture: a change from the first approach to the second approach, that is, from a Western attitude to a Chinese attitude. It must be this way simply because it facilitates a transition from dealing with the first type of problem to addressing the second type.[41]

Liang believed that Western culture, which represented world culture, would shift toward socialism, and the shift toward socialism implied a transformation of world culture from the first approach to the second. In other words, in his view, the cultural orientation of socialism aligned with Chinese culture, particularly Confucian philosophy, as they were the same kind of approach. The first type of problem refers to the relationship between humans and nature, while the second type of problem refers to the relationship between humans themselves. Both Chinese culture and socialist culture focus on adjusting and improving the relationships between people. They emphasize the importance of harmonious interpersonal relationships, social justice, and collective well-being.

Liang thus points out that "in recent times, the Western way of life has been characterized by this attitude; from this attitude arises their economic competition... This kind of life attitude will gradually fade away with the resolution of survival issues. Since adopting this attitude, Westerners have persistently sought to transform the external environment in order to fulfill their desires. They seek fulfillment externally, disregarding internal introspection and personal reflection. They focus on transforming nature when faced with it and transforming society when faced with it. As a result, they conquer nature, overcome authority, and constantly innovate in terms of tools and systems. They engage in continuous transformations, relentlessly pursuing progress. Ultimately, they have reached a point in which society has undergone a major transformation, and the ideal world has emerged. This path has reached its end."[42]

He goes on to say, "For humanity, there will be a transition from the era of humans dealing with material concerns to the era of humans dealing with interpersonal relations. With the attitude of treating others as objects, humans gradually become unable to bear this approach.

As society is transformed through economic corrections and evolves from a state of material conformity, it must progress toward a state of emotional and interpersonal harmony—there must be genuine harmony between individuals... It can also be said that in the past, humanity was in an era of material dissatisfaction, and in the future, it will transition into an era of spiritual unrest. All these factors contribute to the shift from the first orientation, the Western attitude, to the second orientation."[43] Liang's views on the future of modern capitalism were similar to those of the socialists of his time. However, his arguments were somewhat confused, as he sometimes described the second orientation represented by Chinese culture as being about contentment and self-adjustment, while also labeling socialism as the second orientation. In reality, it is difficult to characterize socialism in such a simplistic manner, but Liang did offer some valuable insights on the matter, as there are indeed similarities between Confucianism and socialism.

From this perspective, it can be seen that the term Chinese culture, as used by Liang, has two meanings. First, it refers to the overall culture created by the Chinese nation, with Confucianism at its core. Second, it refers to a spirit and direction of culture manifested in the Chinese historical and cultural context. In the latter sense, Chinese culture does not possess a distinct Chinese characteristic, but represents a cultural direction and spirit that emphasizes harmony, equality, and human nature. It is universalizable. For Liang, the idea that world culture would transform into Chinese culture did not imply that all ethnicities in the world would speak Chinese or read Chinese books in the Chinese language. Nor did it mean that China's traditional material culture, political system, and academic framework would become globalized. Rather, it suggested that cultures of various ethnicities around the world were moving toward socialism, and the attitude toward life embodied in socialist ideology and movements was what he understood as the attitude advocated by ancient Chinese Confucianism. It was precisely in this sense that he argued that Chinese culture had the potential to become universal, while European and Western cultures could not. For this reason, it is not inappropriate to describe Liang as "socialism with Confucian characteristics." When he speaks of the future revival of Chinese culture, he is referring to the combination of the Confucian attitude toward life and the political-economic system of socialism.

Based on the above, it is evident that the difference between Liang and the Westernization faction lay in their social ideologies. While both Liang and the Westernization faction advocated democracy, science, industrial revolution, and personal development, Liang also emphasized the importance of socialism. In terms of advocating for social-political-economic transformation, his views aligned with the Westernization faction in the first half, but in the latter half, he diverged by emphasizing socialism. It is incorrect, then, to label Liang as conservative, anti-modernization, or anti-science and democracy. From a socio-political ideological perspective, he can be considered fundamentally socialist. From a holistic perspective on culture, he sought both Westernization and socialism, as well as a combination of Confucianism and Eastern culture. Although he did not clearly explain the relationship between these three elements, it can be said that he advocated constitutionalism in politics, socialism in economics, and pluralism in culture. This complex cultural structure is difficult to comprehend if approached with a simplistic mindset.

VI. Global Context

Alongside Liang's profound recognition of the valuable elements in Eastern culture, the influence of global changes was an important factor in his espousal of these views. This raises the important question of the global context of Chinese cultural development. The development of Chinese modernity was shaped within the framework of global modernity and influenced by the development of world politics, economy, and culture. The simplistic explanatory model of radical-conservative is not sufficient to fully explain the transformations in modern Chinese culture. Conservatism is not necessarily a direct response to radicalism, but rather emerges from complex interactions within the global political and cultural processes. With the increasing exchanges between China and the West in the 20th century, China's understanding of the West not only greatly advanced, but also became more relevant to its times. The new developments in Western society and thought quickly drew attention in China. In particular, in considering the future of Eastern and Western cultures and human civilization, the trends in Western intellectual and cultural spheres were closely observed, and Chinese individuals were particularly sensitive to them.

As a result, the internal tensions and disagreements within the New Culture Movement, as well as its changes and developments, did not solely originate and develop independently within the Chinese cultural context. It is not accurate to suggest, as Guo Zhanbo has claimed, that figures like Chen Duxiu advocated Western culture, and then Liang Shuming suddenly emerged with reactionary ideas. Instead, the understanding of the drawbacks of Western culture by Chinese intellectuals and their critical discourse are not solely rooted in the domestic social changes in China. To a large extent, they were directly related to the social conditions in the Western world, the criticisms of Western culture by Western intellectuals, and the emergence of socialist ideologies and practices. In this sense, the criticism of Western culture by Chinese intellectuals was also influenced by Western culture itself.

Indeed, the First World War and the October Revolution in Russia were significant global events preceding the May Fourth Movement in 1919. These events marked the beginning of a new era in world history and had a profound impact not only on the historical processes in Europe, but also on various Asian countries. The First World War indeed marked the intensification and outbreak of inherent contradictions within capitalism. It led to a reevaluation and reflection on modern Western capitalism globally. The individuals advocating for the reconciliation or reevaluation of Eastern and Western civilizations after the October Revolution differed significantly from the conservatives of the late Qing Dynasty and early Republican era. One notable difference is that they had a deep understanding of Western civilization and a clear awareness of the drawbacks of capitalist society. Their exposure to modern Western capitalism led them to expose and criticize its shortcomings, influenced by thinkers such as Karl Marx and other Western intellectuals. They often pinpointed its flaws effectively. Later, those who failed to acknowledge the crisis within capitalist civilization and disregarded the inherent value of Chinese culture continued to defend the contradictions and shortcomings fully exposed by

Western capitalist systems. They even portrayed modern Western culture as flawless, which went against the global trend. This approach of defending Western capitalist civilization while ignoring its flaws was out of step with the rest of the world.[44] For Chinese intellectuals who were eager to study modern Western civilization, this global cultural environment posed a paradoxical dilemma. It was nothing short of a conflicting destiny.

In 1919, Liang Qichao traveled to Europe for a year and witnessed the post-war devastation and decline of Europe, which deeply shocked him. During his time there, he also engaged in discussions with Western intellectuals and received valuable advice. After careful observation and contemplation, he returned to China and wrote "Record of Thoughts during the European Journey." From March to August 1920, the series was serialized in the newspaper *Chenbao*, sparking widespread discussion.

Liang Qichao conveyed to his fellow countrymen that Europe was filled with a sense of doomsday and the extinction of civilization at that time. He writes:

> Since our arrival in Europe, we have indeed constantly been hearing such pessimistic views. I remember having a casual conversation with a well-known American journalist, Frank Herbert Simonds (1978–1936, his war history is recognized as the first good one). He asked me, "What will you do when you return to China? Are you planning to bring some Western civilization back with you?" I replied, "Naturally." He sighed and said, "Ah, pity. Western civilization has already gone bankrupt." I asked him, "What will you do when you return to the United States?" He replied, "I will go back and lock the door, waiting for you to bring Chinese civilization to rescue and uplift us." At first, when we heard such words, we thought he was intentionally mocking us. But later, as we heard it repeatedly from many enlightened individuals, we realized that they harbored boundless concerns and dangers. They felt that their material civilization was the seed of social peril and that the idyllic China still held the solution. This reflects a glimpse into the mentality of many people in Europe.[45]

He went on:

> I once met the great philosopher Émile Boutroux (1845–1921, teacher of Henri Bergson) in Paris, and he told me, "The most important thing for a nation is to promote and enhance its own culture, much like inheriting the legacy from ancestors, preserving it, and allowing it to serve a purpose. Even if a civilization is shallow, when it is brought forth and expressed, it is good because it always has its own characteristics. When its characteristics combine with the characteristics of others, a third and even better set of characteristics naturally emerges. You in China are truly admirable and lovely. While our ancestors were still hunting in the wild with a stone knife wrapped in deer skin, you had already produced numerous philosophers. Recently, I have been reading some translated Chinese philosophical books, and I always feel that they are profound and vast. It is a

> pity that I am old and cannot learn the Chinese language. I hope that the Chinese people will never lose this treasure." As I listened to his words, I felt as if an immediate weight of hundreds of pounds was placed upon my shoulders.
>
> Another time, I had a casual conversation with several prominent members of the Socialist Party. I brought up Confucius' teachings that "all men are brothers within the four seas" and "the concern is not about being few, but about being unequal." Following that, I discussed the system of communal land ownership and also mentioned some of Mozi's ideas, such as universal love and forbearance in war. They all jumped up and exclaimed, "If you have these treasures in your house, why are you keeping them hidden instead of sharing them with us? That's unfair!" I think we are not even worthy of apologizing to outsiders; we should first apologize to our ancestors. In recent years, many Western scholars have become interested in incorporating some Eastern civilization into their thought to bring about a balance for themselves.[46]

Liang Qichao had gone to Europe for investigation and learning, but after the Great War in Europe, the European thinkers and intellectuals he encountered were interested in incorporating Eastern civilization. This understanding of the interaction between Eastern and Western civilizations differed significantly from the absolute Westernization advocated by Chen Duxiu and others during the early period of the New Culture Movement. The situation in the West inevitably had an impact on progressive Chinese intellectuals who were dedicated to studying Western culture.

During this period, it was not only Chinese thinkers who traveled to Europe and heard these expressions of dissatisfaction and loss of confidence in Western civilization. Some renowned Western thinkers also came to China and expressed similar viewpoints. Liang Shuming was undoubtedly influenced by these views, and his work *Eastern and Western Cultures and Their Philosophies* begins with a discussion of John Dewey's visit to China in 1919. He writes:

> When Dewey arrived in Beijing, he often advocated for the harmonization of Eastern and Western cultures. He expressed similar sentiments during his encouraging remarks at Peking University. Later, Bertrand Russell came from Europe to China, and because he had a strong aversion to Western culture, it was inevitable for him to speak favorably about Chinese culture. … Later, after Liang Qichao returned from Europe, he too encountered Westerners' aversion to Western culture, along with a certain admiration for Chinese culture that he could not quite comprehend.[47]

As world renowned intellectuals, Dewey and Russell each noted positive aspects in their assessment of Chinese culture, leading them to believe in the need for harmony between Eastern and Western cultures. With the most influential, first rate intellectuals in Europe often expressing severe criticism of Western culture, their words, especially when they came to China and speak to Chinese intellectuals, undoubtedly had a significant impact.

Not only were top intellectuals in the West expressing such thoughts, but the situation in the East was also quite different from what it had been in the 19th century. In fact, during China's reform movement, Leo Tolstoy wrote a letter to the Chinese people, advising them against reform. Renowned Indian writer Rabindranath Tagore, whom Feng Youlan at the time referred to as an "outstanding figure in the East," expressed his views on the question of Eastern and Western cultures. He stated that the difference between Eastern and Western cultures was not a difference in hierarchy but a difference in nature. He said, "The Western concept of life is centered around activity, while the Eastern concept of life is centered around realization or fulfillment. The West emphasizes progress through action, without a fixed goal in mind. On the other hand, the East can provide wisdom to the West, while the West can contribute its dynamism to the East."[48] He believed that truth had two aspects, and Eastern and Western cultures each emphasized one aspect, and Eastern and Western cultures could thus be reconciled and harmonized.

Not all Western thinkers held this view, but the criticisms of Western civilization and the call for a harmonization of Eastern and Western cultures by these leading Western thinkers represented a certain trend within Western culture at the time. Their ideas undoubtedly had an impact on the cultural discussions in China and provided an important backdrop for the emergence of thinkers like Liang Shuming in the early 1920s.

During this global transformation, intellectual and academic circles in China gradually underwent a shift away from the absolute Eurocentrism of the early New Culture Movement. In 1920, at the heart of the movement at Peking University, Cai Yuanpei went to Europe for investigation. Liang Shuming reports that "farewell banquets were held by the Peking University community, and during the banquet speeches, most expressed a belief that Mr. Cai's journey would have a significant impact on the communication between Eastern and Western cultures and a hope that Mr. Cai could introduce the superior elements of Chinese culture to the West and bring back the superior elements of Western culture to China."[49] At this time, the advocacy for the fusion of Eastern and Western cultures had become the stance of the majority at Peking University.

VII. Bearing the Whole Responsibility and Fundamental Transformation

It is useful here to examine Liang Shuming's views on the path China needed to take at that time. In the final section of his book titled "The Attitude We Should Adopt Now," he presents three points:

(1) Reject any inclination toward Indian culture; there should be no tolerance for it whatsoever.

(2) Fully embrace Western culture while fundamentally reforming our attitude toward it. In other words, we should reassess our stance toward Western culture and make the necessary changes.
(3) Critique and reintroduce China's original attitudes.[50]

Liang's opinion on the attitude that the Chinese people should adopt at that time is clear: they should learn from the West and strive forward. He writes:

> At this moment, whether for the purpose of ensuring the security of life, property, and individual rights in the face of immediate needs, or of promoting the development of future world culture and achieving a rational life, it is necessary to adopt the first attitude. We must strive forward together. However, if we do not fundamentally integrate it into the framework of the second attitude in our lives, we will be unable to prevent its dangers, avoid its mistakes, and adapt to the transitional era between the first and second paths in the present world.[51]

He adds, "What we urgently need at the moment is to calm the chaos within our country, to secure our lives, property, and other individual rights. But how can we achieve this, from what attitude?" He says that it must come from the first attitude, because:

> The political system we currently use is adopted from the West and was developed based on their forward-seeking attitude. However, the majority of our citizens still adhere to the old attitudes that have persisted for thousands of years. They show little interest in politics and do not demand individual rights, which is fundamentally incompatible with this system. Hence, when a few individuals engage in competitive plunder and control, the political situation is constantly overturned, and turmoil follows. Therefore, today's problem lies not in the struggle for power and personal gain, but rather in the fact that people are not proactive enough in pursuing power and personal gain. Only when the majority of the people rise up and contend with the minority can this political system be established… In this regard, adopting the Western attitude is imperative. A submissive, self-effacing attitude is not suitable, let alone a mindset that solely promotes contentment and discourages striving for progress, as advocated by Buddhism.[52]

The submissive and self-effacing attitude mentioned here refers to the second attitude, while contentment and discouraging progress refers to the third attitude. According to Liang, both of these attitudes were not acceptable in his historical context. Based on this view, he criticized those from the old school for their inability to fully embrace science and democracy. He states:

> These two spirits (i.e., science and democracy) are completely right and can only be unconditionally acknowledged. This is what I mean by wholeheartedly embracing

> Westernization. Introducing these two spirits is truly the urgent task of the present time. Otherwise, we will forever be unworthy of discussing human character, and we will forever be unworthy of discussing academia. If you carefully examine the suffering and afflictions we have endured, you will understand that my words are not meant to be provocative. I lament that, while Dewey and Russell came to China in these past two years, Bergson and Rudolf Eucken did not. It is a great fortune for our academic and intellectual circle. If Dewey and Russell had not come, and instead Bergson and Eucken had come first, I ask you to imagine whether they would have effectively addressed the chronic issues that have plagued us.[53]

Indeed, it is clear from these statements that Liang advocated not a rejection of Western culture, but rather the complete assimilation of science and democracy and the adoption of a proactive, forward-looking attitude in life.

Unlike the Eurocentric faction, Liang recognized the profound crises and escalating contradictions of capitalism at that time, as well as the growing strength of the socialist movement. He therefore advocated a modified assimilation of Western culture, taking into account the need for adjustments and adaptations to suit the specific conditions and challenges faced by China. He writes, "The life attitude of Westerners has revealed many drawbacks and has been heavily criticized up to now, yet they (i.e., Chen Duxiu) still tend to indiscriminately adopt it without discernment or selection. Although this attitude causes even greater suffering for Westerners today, it can be a remedy for the inherent biases of traditional Chinese people. However, it must be revised and modified to be beneficial."[54] Although the first attitude faced criticism in the West, it was still necessary to adopt this attitude in China, albeit with certain modifications. Liang says, "It is important to learn from the drawbacks of Westernization and be prepared to promote the realization of a second direction for world culture."[55] These comments demonstrate that Liang's study of the West was steadfast, and the modifications he proposed were prudent.

In discussing how to make modifications while absorbing, he says, "My intention is merely to advocate a spirit of striving forward while rejecting the decadent trend of pursuing external possessions," which he believed was what Confucius referred to as strength.[56] Striving forward represented the first path, while simultaneously rejecting the pursuit of external possessions served as a limitation and modification to the advocacy of striving forward. It was not solely the first path. He says, "Now, we must first fundamentally inspire a certain kind of life that transcends personal selfishness, material desires, constant calculations, and actions driven by self-interest... Only through such forward action can we make up for the shortcomings of the Chinese people in the past, alleviate their current suffering, avoid the drawbacks of the West, meet the needs of the world, and fully align with our study and evaluation of the three cultures throughout history. This is what I mean by the attitude of strength, the suitable path of life."[57] There is no shadow of opposition to Western culture in these statements.

Liang Shuming's proposition can be seen as a combination of contemporary Westernization and future Easternization. His approach is not based on the cultural specificity of a particular nation, but rather on the universality of culture and the challenges faced by humanity as a whole. The notion of future Easternization, in his perspective, does not entail a nostalgic dream of returning to the past, but instead represents a rational anticipation of the challenges that humanity will face in the future. It reflects his understanding of the issues and offers insights into the potential solutions that lie ahead. His ideal vision of life is rooted in Confucius's philosophy, but it does not imply a desire to revert to the past in terms of politics, economy, or academia. His notion of the future involves the revival of Chinese culture, and it does not hinder his advocacy for the comprehensive acceptance of Western influences in the present. Liang's advocacy for the first path in the present and his concerns about the drawbacks of capitalism do not contradict his support for future socialist practices. In fact, when examining the influence of socialist ideology and practice on his thinking, it can be seen that his ideas are more accurately described as progressive rather than conservative.

VIII. Cultural Pluralism

Returning to the discussion of the three orientations in culture, Liang observes that these three orientations arise from three fundamental questions encountered in life: the pursuit of material satisfaction, the pursuit of communication and understanding with others, and the pursuit of enduring life.[58]

According to Liang, each culture represents a certain attitude or orientation toward life. Each culture thus tends to lean toward a particular direction, and as a result, every culture has its positive and negative aspects. It is incorrect to make a unilateral judgment by categorizing a culture as either good or bad. Furthermore, although we cannot categorize cultures as inherently good or bad, there are differences in how cultures address the problems faced by humanity.[59] This can be called an attitude of cultural pluralism, recognizing the diversity and suitability of various cultures in addressing human issues. From my perspective, based on Liang's standpoint, his assertion would be that as a product, civilizations can be compared in terms of their superiority or inferiority, but as attitudes, cultures do not possess a notion of good or bad.

In Liang's view, the problems faced by humanity are both universal and evolving. He holds that the first stage of human development is characterized by a focus on the first problem, and during this period, the first cultural orientation is deemed suitable. After the resolution of the first problem, humanity faces a period dominated by the second problem, during which the second cultural orientation becomes more suitable. Once the second problem is resolved, humanity enters a period primarily focused on the third problem, and the third cultural orientation becomes the most appropriate. In his view, regardless of the ethnic group, all cultures will encounter these three major problems, and these problems will unfold in a sequential and historical manner: the relationship between humans and the material world, the relationship between humans and other humans, and the meaning of life and death. If the culture of a particular ethnic group develops a cultural orientation of the second or third stage during the first stage and becomes dominated by it, then that ethnic group will not be able to effectively address the first problem and may even fail. However, the value of this culture will be manifested in the second or third stage, and it will be suitable for addressing the human problems of the second or third stage.

Liang believed that there are only three fundamental attitudes in human life, and these three fundamental attitudes give rise to the three major cultural systems in the world. He argues that "these three attitudes are necessary while at times inapplicable in response to the three major issues in human life." Greece, China, and India "have all made significant contributions to humanity, and from the perspective of their achievements, it is not a matter of which one is better or worse. However, from the perspective of their attitudes, the question of suitability may arise. The Greek attitude is more relevant because humanity was originally dealing with the first issue. The attitudes of the Chinese and Indian people may be considered premature, because the relevant problems have not yet arisen. The victory of Western culture lies in its adaptation to the current issues faced by humanity, while the perceived failure of Chinese and Indian cultures today is not inherently a matter of good or bad, but rather a result of being out of sync with the times. At the beginning of human culture, all civilizations must embark on the first path, and the Chinese people are no exception. However, instead of completing this path, they deviated midway and turned to the second path. They prematurely embarked on what should have been taken later, becoming precocious in human culture. But if the first problem has not been resolved, if the first path must be traversed, how can one smoothly transition to the second path?… And not only that, but it also hinders the progress of the first path. The world under the first problem shows significant failures due to this deviation."[60] So, in essence, "our Eastern culture itself cannot be judged as good or bad, or as inferior to the West. All the shortcomings and deficiencies lie in the disorderly progression, maturing too early, and lack of suitability. It is not that the attitude itself is wrong, but rather that it was presented too early. This is the only mistake we have made."[61] Indeed, this viewpoint aligns with the widely influential concept of cultural relativism in the contemporary postcolonial era. Liang's cultural perspective can be seen as a form of multiculturalism, which stands in contrast to the notion of linear development in human culture and the perception of Western culture as the ultimate achievement of this linear development. Indeed, the notion of linear cultural evolution is often intertwined with Western cultural centrism, which views Eastern culture as a primitive stage in human development. On the other hand, Liang's cultural perspective does not hinder his full acceptance of Western culture in the political and economic spheres. Rather, it enables him to critically examine his own culture while maintaining cultural confidence and achieving a sense of cultural equilibrium in his psychological outlook.

Liang's ideas are clear, but his statements also have some contradictions and inconsistencies. For example, he writes, "The origin of Western culture today, as everyone knows, can be traced back to the Renaissance, and the Renaissance has no other explanation but that it was when Westerners adopted what we call the first orientation. Originally, the way of life for Westerners during the ancient Greek and Roman eras could be said to have followed the first orientation. However, they shifted to the third orientation for over a thousand years during the Middle Ages.

It was only during the Renaissance that they consciously returned to the first orientation, carrying forward the achievements of their predecessors and giving rise to modern Western civilization."[62]

The primary question here is why Western culture would shift spontaneously from the first direction to the third direction, and then spontaneously return to the first direction, while China and India have always followed a single direction. Liang believed that China and India, if not influenced by the West, would have inevitably continued along a single direction without change. This is inconsistent with his observation that Westerners' direction can undergo multiple changes. In fact, any culture has the ability to make choices at each stage in response to the problems it faces.

Further, the underdevelopment of instrumental rationality in a culture in terms of conquering nature does not imply that the culture lacks value, as it may have developed value rationality or wisdom concerning life and death. In this regard, Liang is correct. However, the notion of being premature is a perspective that is detached from history. If ancient India had favorable natural conditions and the contradiction between humans and nature was not prominent, its culture, which was not predominantly oriented toward the first direction, was indeed suitable for the historical context in which it existed, and it cannot be said to be unsuitable.

Furthermore, the value of Eastern culture is not limited to situations where the second or third problem becomes the main concern. Even when the second and third problems are not predominant, Eastern culture still holds its own value. Moreover, within a larger culture, there are often several different subsystems that deal with different directions of problems. Liang's characterization of Western culture solely as striving forward is a form of reductionism.

In Liang's book *Eastern and Western Cultures and Their Philosophies*, it should be noted that the concept of modern or modernization is not explicitly mentioned. The term modern is relative to the concepts of ancient or traditional, and Liang encompassed pre-capitalist history (including capitalism) as a historical stage in which humanity confronts the first kind of problem. As a result, he did not believe that the task facing Eastern nations was a transition of culture from ancient to modern. Instead, he argued that the transformation of Eastern culture involved a shift from a premature orientation to a normal orientation. In other words, the essence of ancient Eastern culture was not archaic, but rather future oriented. In this sense, the fundamental issue with Eastern culture was not that it was too backward, but rather that it was too advanced. Although Liang's unique perspective on culture and history differed from the mainstream discourse of modern culture, it did not prevent him from advocating similar positions to Westernization or socialism in practical political and economic choices.

IX. Progress and Conservatism

To conclude this chapter, a brief discussion of the psychological background proposed by Liang Shuming in his early cultural views is in order. Liang was born in 1893 and received a modern education during his youth. He never studied the Four Books and Five Classics, and during his high school years, he secretly joined revolutionary organizations. In his early adulthood, he held radical thoughts, which he once described saying, "I was a constitutionalist during the late Qing Dynasty, and later I transformed into a proponent of revolution,"[63] and, "I used to greatly admire the modern Western political systems and believed that they were highly rational and ingeniously effective." He further recalls, "At that time, I always dreamed of how to bring the Western political systems to China and implement them. From the age of fifteen until my early twenties, this was constantly on my mind."[64] His father had doubts about the republican system, and Liang Shuming often clashed with him. He writes, "My father deeply resented the parliamentarians and doubted their system, while I staunchly supported the National Assembly. Our conversations invariably led to discord, and there were countless disagreements of various kinds." Liang passionately defended the republican system despite his father's opposition, which resulted in constant disputes between them.[65] In contrast to his political stance of republican democracy, in terms of culture (life attitude), he was a follower of Buddhism throughout the entire 1910s. However, these two aspects were not contradictory for him. Unfortunately, cultural radicals often seemed unable to understand this.

In his later account, he states, "In the sixth year of the Republic of China, I was invited by Cai Yuanpei, the president of Peking University, to join the faculty. At that time, the liberal arts professors at the university included Chen Duxiu, Hu Shi, Li Dazhao, Gao Yihan, and Tao Menghe. Chen served as the head of the liberal arts department. At that time, these individuals, including Mr. Chen, were known as the New Youth faction, all of whom advocated Western ideas and opposed Eastern culture. I spent my days and nights with them, constantly feeling the weight of their oppression... It was necessary to find a way to resolve this situation."[66] In another instance, he says, "At that time, the new intellectual trends advocated both Western modern ideas (science and democracy) and various socialist doctrines. Though I personally did not oppose the new intellectual trends, I felt a significant pressure from the prevailing atmosphere that implicitly dismissed Eastern philosophy. It was under this pressure that I wrote my book *Eastern and Western Cultures and Their Philosophies*."[67] This statement could not be any clearer. Liang did not oppose the new intellectual trends, as he stated that he did not go against them intellectually. That was one aspect of his thinking. At the same time, as someone who specialized in Eastern philosophy, he felt the pressure against Eastern culture at that time. The purpose of his writings was to combine his personal appreciation of the new intellectual trends with the recognition of the value of Eastern life attitudes. From a personal perspective, this effort was aimed at resolving his cultural psychological confusion and imbalance, while from a historical standpoint, it reflected the self-adjustment of a significant number of intellectuals during an era of cultural transformation. This further confirms what was mentioned earlier: Liang's early cultural views cannot be simply characterized as reactionary or conservative as used by the New Youth faction and other new schools at that time. On the contrary, his approach to cultural issues was one of the diverse progressive manifestations among intellectuals at that time.

The conversation between Liang and Guy Alitto in his later years is also of interest. The latter seemed to be a critic of modernization and a cultural conservative, so he frequently asked

Liang questions. Liang's cultural views can be considered, to some extent, cultural conservatism. Still, in his responses, it is difficult to see a resonance with Guy Alitto's anti-modernization and cultural conservative claims. As a result, at least to some extent, Guy Alitto found that the Liang Shuming he conversed with in person did not align with the conservative intellectual portrait he had depicted in his book. We read:

> Liang: I believe that development is always good.
>
> Alitto: "Development is always good." You are truly the opposite of conservatism.[68]
>
> Alitto: The term conservatism is sometimes difficult to define, and I have discussed this issue in the earlier part of my book. Some Chinese and foreign individuals have labeled you as a conservative or associated conservatism with him. Are you willing to accept that? Or do you oppose it?
>
> Liang: Of course not. I am not conservative. As you can tell from our conversation just now, I am not conservative.[69]

Based on this exchange, it is clear that in terms of his early cultural views, Liang was not fundamentally opposed to Western culture, but rather opposed to the rejection of Eastern culture. He was not against science and democracy, but consistently praised Mr. Democracy and Mr. Science. He did not represent agriculturalism, feudalism, or patriarchal ideology, but advocated socialist ideas of socializing production. His views on Eastern culture can be better described as cultural pluralism rather than cultural conservatism. His ideology does not stand in opposition to modernization by clinging to the past, but rather seeks to "rectify" capitalism from a standpoint oriented toward the future. His early cultural views not only demonstrated profound insights into cultural issues, but also served as a grounding for intellectuals immersed in millennia-old traditional culture to maintain cultural confidence. At the same time, these views also embodied a reflection of the experience of modernity on a global scale.

By examining the case of Liang Shuming and reviewing the history of the New Culture Movement of the previous decade, we can understand that the debates surrounding Chinese and Western cultures did not arise from a clash between the demands for science and democracy. Instead, they stemmed from a comprehensive struggle between anti-traditionalism and the reactionary responses it provoked. During the transformative era of the May Fourth Movement, intellectuals generally shared similar political and social demands. However, the cultural contradictions arising from this transformation carried different meanings for specific individuals. Each person required a different approach to address these contradictions, as there was not a one-size-fits-all solution. Alongside the varying levels of appreciation for cultural values, one obvious fact is that some individuals could convince themselves to engage in social activities simply by disregarding historical and cultural traditions. On the other hand, some individuals required a more complex settlement with cultural traditions to participate in the tide of progress with a clear conscience. However, they were united in their commitment to advancing progress in China. This demonstrated that managing cultural identity issues appropriately remained a significant challenge for non-Western countries in the process of modernization. From the perspective of the broader historical context of the entire century, it can be said that the social and cultural transformation in 20th-century China was not only a process of modernization but also a process of continuity and change in Chinese culture. Indeed, from the latter perspective, this process entailed both preserving cultural identity and dedicating efforts to cultural transformation and innovation. Therefore, the various factions involved in the debates of the New Culture Movement were actually participants and promoters of progress in 20th-century China. Each of them, from different perspectives and to varying degrees, contributed to this process.

The May Fourth spirit aimed to encompass the sense of mission of the intellectual generation in engaging with the world and the spirit of national self-strengthening.[70] It was not meant to be limited to the notion that continuing to oppose tradition was the only way to inherit the May Fourth spirit. Yin Haiguang is considered to be a representative of the inheritance of the May Fourth spirit in the Chinese Taiwan region. However, his attitude toward Chinese traditional culture underwent significant changes in the last few years of his life. In regard to this matter, Lin Yusheng points out, "This represents the glorious development of the intense anti-traditional thought in the later stage of the May Fourth Movement. At the same time, it symbolizes the approaching end of the May Fourth era and the arrival of a new era that inherits the May Fourth liberal tradition without being confined by the anti-traditional thought of the May Fourth Movement."[71] This holds true not only for liberalism. If we cannot break free from the notion that continuing to oppose tradition is the only way to inherit the May Fourth spirit, we will never be able to usher in a new era of cultural development. It is heartening to see that, more than eighty years after the end of the May Fourth Movement, we are finally starting to glimpse the arrival of this new era in China's intellectual realm.

Notes

1. Li Shicen, "A Review of *Eastern and Western Cultures and Their Philosophies*," *Mind and Dowry* 3, no. 3 (1922).
2. Sun Daosheng, "Anatomy of the Modern Chinese Philosophical Community," *National News Weekly* 12, no. 45 (1935).
3. Guo Zhanbo, *A History of Chinese Thought in the Past Fifty Years* (Shandong People's Publishing House, 1997), 135.
4. Ibid., 138.
5. *Complete Works of Liang Shuming*, vol. 4 (Shandong People's Publishing House, 1990), 738.
6. Liang Shuming, "Notice," *Peking University Daily*, October 31, 1918, qtd. in *Complete Works of Liang Shuming*, vol. 4, 547.
7. *Complete Works of Liang Shuming*, vol. 1, 332–333.
8. Ibid., 340.
9. Ibid., 347.
10. Ibid., 349.
11. Ibid.
12. Ibid., 350.

13. Guy Alitto, *The Last Confucian* (Jiangsu People's Publishing House, 1993), 80.
14. *Complete Works of Liang Shuming*, vol. 1, 354–355.
15. Ibid., 355.
16. Ibid., 356.
17. Ibid., 362.
18. Ibid., 363.
19. Ibid., 364.
20. Ibid., 365.
21. Ibid., 337.
22. Ibid., 369.
23. Ibid., 362.
24. Ibid., 370.
25. Ibid., 345.
26. Ibid., 370.
27. Ibid.
28. Ibid., 350.
29. Ibid., 351.
30. Ibid., 371.
31. Ibid., 353.
32. Ibid., 352.
33. Ibid., 353.
34. Ibid., 375.
35. Ibid., 391–392.
36. Ibid., 392.
37. Ibid., 381–382.
38. Ibid., 383.
39. Ibid., 488.
40. Ibid., 491.
41. Ibid., 493.
42. Ibid., 494.
43. Ibid., 495.
44. Luo Rongqu, "The Evolution of Modern Thought in China in the Past Century," preface to *From Westernization to Modernization* (Peking University Press, 1990).
45. Chen Song, ed., *Selected Works on the Cultural Debate between East and West Before and After May Fourth* (China Social Sciences Press, 1985), 349.
46. Ibid., 371–372.
47. Liang Shuming, "Eastern and Western Cultures and Their Philosophies," in *Complete Works of Liang Shuming*, vol. 1, 331.
48. *Collected Works of Sansongtang*, 12–13.
49. *Complete Works of Liang Shuming*, vol. 2, 12.
50. *Complete Works of Liang Shuming*, vol. 1, 523.
51. Ibid., 537.
52. *Complete Works of Liang Shuming*, vol. 1, 534–535.

53. Ibid., 532–533.
54. Ibid., 531.
55. Ibid.
56. Ibid., 537–538.
57. Ibid., 538–539.
58. Ibid., 379–381.
59. Ibid., 525.
60. Ibid., 526.
61. Ibid., 529.
62. Ibid., 383.
63. Ibid., 19.
64. Ibid., 18.
65. Ibid., 17.
66. *Complete Works of Liang Shuming*, vol. 2, 11–12.
67. Ibid., 697–698.
68. *Complete Works of Liang Shuming*, vol 8, 1168.
69. Ibid., 1175.
70. Lin Yusheng, *Passion and Calm* (Shanghai Literature and Art Publishing House, 1998), 119.
71. Lin Yusheng, *The Creative Transformation of Chinese Tradition* (Sanlian Bookstore, 1988), 313.

CHAPTER 7

Liang Shuming's Discourse on Chinese Culture

In the summer of 1920, Max Weber passed away suddenly. That same autumn, the *Peking University Daily* began serializing the lecture transcripts of Liang Shuming's *Eastern and Western Cultures and Their Philosophies.*[1] These two events were not related, and there is no evidence of any mutual influence between their thoughts. Still, these two scholars' perspectives on China's historical and cultural development from the standpoint of modern society have been representative in 20th-century academic circles in both China and the West. The issues they discussed also have many close connections.

Max Weber's work *The Religion of China: Confucianism and Taoism,* published in 1916, and Liang Shuming's *Essence of Chinese Culture,* published in 1949, were not given much attention in mainland China for many years. It was only in the mid-1980s that they gained recognition and sparked the interest of the domestic intellectual community, thanks to discussions initiated by overseas scholars. In 20th-century Western academic circles, Weber's views on Chinese culture held an important position in the field of Chinese studies. It was rare to find a scholar engaged in recent Chinese research who did not take Weber as a starting point. In 20th-century China, Liang's views on Chinese culture also held a special position. While his views may not have represented the majority of scholars, their depth and significance were no less profound than those of Weber. Since the publication of *Eastern and Western Cultures and Their Philosophies,* Liang has been widely known as a cultural philosopher in academic circles. His works are rarely seen as social science writings. Indeed, the pinnacle of his mature thought, represented by *Essence of Chinese Culture,* a specialized work that examines the social structure and value orientation of ancient China,[2] is closely related to sociology and cultural anthropology. His discussions and perspectives often align closely with Weber's, particularly in terms of his accurate, profound understanding of Chinese culture, which surpasses Weber in many aspects. When studying Liang

Shuming, it is meaningful to compare *Essence of Chinese Culture* as a social science work with *The Religion of China: Confucianism and Taoism* in order to gain a fresh understanding of the significance and contributions of Liang's views on Chinese culture.

I. Characteristics of Chinese Culture

In *Essence of Chinese Culture*, Liang first proposes that Chinese culture has seven characteristics, which are: (1) original creation, (2) independent system, (3) long-lasting existence, (4) strong assimilation ability, (5) greatest ethnic integration, (6) no progress in the last 2,000 years of cultural maturity, and (7) far-reaching influence on surrounding areas.[3] He listed fourteen commonly mentioned unique features of Chinese culture:

(1) Vast territory and numerous people
(2) Assimilation and integration of a large ethnic group
(3) Long-standing history that is unparalleled in the world
(4) Great strength of Chinese culture, yet its essence is elusive
(5) Social stability over a long period, but cultural stagnation
(6) Life without religion
(7) The family system holds an important position within the culture
(8) Academic progress does not prioritize scientific advancement
(9) Lack of demand and institutional framework for democracy, freedom, and equality
(10) Strong moral atmosphere
(11) Unlike a nation
(12) Culture without a military
(13) Culture of filial piety
(14) Culture of recluses or hermit scholars[4]

These fourteen characteristics can be divided into three groups. The first group consists of the external characteristics of Chinese culture and the Chinese nation, such as its vast territory and numerous people, long-standing history, and cultural stagnation. The second group includes the positive aspects of Chinese culture, such as the prominent family system and a strong moral atmosphere. The third group encompasses the negative aspects of Chinese culture, including the lack of religion, scientific progress, and democracy, and not being like a nation. The characteristics in the first group align with the previously mentioned seven characteristics and focus on cultural phenomena. In contrast, the characteristics in the second and third groups point to the structural features of social culture, representing more intrinsic elements of Chinese culture. The listing of these characteristics is clearly related to the frame of reference of the observing subject. The notions of cultural stagnation and the various perceived deficiencies in cultural structure are conclusions drawn in comparison to Western culture. At the same time, it should be noted that the individuality and characteristics of Chinese culture are not unique discoveries of Liang Shuming, but rather have been repeatedly mentioned by scholars in various disciplines since the early years of the Republic of China. These scholars critically examined Chinese culture in their respective fields of study.[5] Liang's unique insight lies in his explanations of the origins of all these characteristics.

Feng Youlan similarly sought to provide a consistent explanation for the various characteristics of traditional Chinese culture, using the concept of domestication of production to explain these features. However, Liang's explanations are much more complex. He held that:

> The unique importance of the family in Chinese culture is indeed one of the expressions of its strong underlying characteristics, rather than being solely a result of the domestication of production. It is also not a universal feature of a society characterized by the domestication of production, as suggested by Mr. Feng's concept of commonalities.[6]

Liang believed that the Chinese family was unique. He disagreed with Feng's view that it was a common phenomenon or a general feature before the Industrial Revolution. According to Liang, this characterization was incorrect. He points out that Feng's perspective was derived from a materialistic view of history, which focused on changes and progress in the mode of production. However, this approach could not fully explain the characteristics of Chinese culture. Liang placed greater emphasis on social structure, stating:

> The social structure of a specific time and place is, in fact, the backbone of the entire culture of that time and place. Everything else is merely superficial adornments attached to the backbone. If the social structures are similar, their cultures are likely to be similar. Conversely, if the social structures are different, other aspects will inevitably be different. This does not mean that everything else is determined, but it highlights the importance of cultural foundations.[7]

This clearly suggests that Feng's argument can only explain the differences between the past and the present, but it cannot account for the differences between the East and the West. It is precisely the difference in these viewpoints that leads to the overall divergence in their cultural perspectives. According to Liang's view, from the perspectives of cultural studies and the study of historical development, it is only by explaining the differences between East and West and understanding the reasons behind these differences that we can comprehend why the West has progressed toward the modern while the East has remained rooted in the ancient. He believed that the differences between Chinese and Western cultures are determined by their respective social structures, which today is referred to as social organization or social structure. In pointing to differences in social structure, he does not solely refer to the differences between modern Chinese and Western societies, but encompasses the differences between traditional Chinese and Western social structures as well.

Liang further argues that the differences between traditional Chinese and Western social structures can be traced back to the divergent evolution of religions in what we now refer to as the Axial Age. He writes:

> From my perspective, the question of religion is indeed a watershed between Chinese and Western cultures. Ancient Chinese society and ancient Greek and Roman societies were originally not far apart. Still, subsequent cultural development in the West centered around the great religion of Christianity, while China-centered its development around the non-religious teachings of Confucianism. From that point onward, the divergence in the evolution of social structures between the two sides can be attributed to this fundamental difference.[8]

Liang's particular emphasis on religion and social structure easily brings to mind Max Weber. It is worth examining Liang's analysis of Chinese culture and society through the interplay and mutual influence of religious culture and social structure.

II. Ethics-Based Perspective and Group-Based Perspective

Liang's views on the social structure of China were derived through comparisons with Western history. He believed that, from a social construction perspective, there were several forms of social organization, such as family-oriented society, individual-oriented society, society-oriented society, and ethics-oriented society. He notes, "Modern Western society is an individual-oriented society, exemplified by England and America, whereas the recent trend in the West is towards a society-oriented society, exemplified by the Soviet Union." From this perspective, China was an ethics-oriented society. The term "family-oriented society" was not appropriate, nor was it sufficient to explain the situation. Only a feudal society could be described as family-oriented, a view supported by Edward Jenks's *A History of Politics*. However, China today was already many years removed from a feudal society.[9] Feng argued that in ancient societies, the social system was based on the family as the primary unit, a view that applies to both Eastern and Western contexts. In contrast, he considered modern Western society to be society-oriented, with society as a whole taking precedence. Liang, by contrast, believed that in modern society, England and America represented an individual-oriented society, while the Soviet Union represented a society-oriented society. In ancient societies, neither China nor the West could be considered family-oriented societies. The concept of a family-oriented society only applies to the ancient eras of both the East and the West (prior to the Zhou Dynasty in China and the ancient Greek and Roman periods in the West). According to Liang's perspective, if we describe the ancient feudal society as a family-oriented society, modern Western capitalist society as an individual-oriented society, the socialist society of the Soviet Union as a society-oriented society, and ancient China as an ethics-oriented society, then ancient Western society can be seen as a group-oriented society that transcends the family as the primary unit. While Liang did not explicitly use the term group-oriented society, it can be inferred from his emphasis on group life in the West that ancient Western society can indeed be regarded as a group-oriented society.

	China	The West
Remote Antiquity	Family-oriented (Feudal society)	Family-oriented
Ancient Times	Ethics-oriented	Group-oriented
Modern times	Ethics-oriented	Individual-oriented, society-oriented

Liang believed that, Western society had been characterized by group life since ancient Greece and Rome. Group life refers to the existence of an organization rather than just a set of relationships. In addition, it extends beyond the family and is not based solely on the family as its organizing principle. And, within this scope, every individual feels certain constraints.[10] Liang points out, "Since the feudal system was broken, whenever we speak of a group, it means going beyond the family. Only an organization that goes beyond the family is worthy of being called a group."[11]

Based on the historical works available to him at the time, Liang believed that the feudal system had already disintegrated during the ancient Greek and Roman eras, but large-scale group life had not yet emerged. He writes, "We must understand that ancient Greek and Roman societies generally had a characteristic of group life. Although they had the family as the core, they also had (1) a large number of dependents, (2) class distinctions, (3) patriarchal authority, and (4) various forms of communal ownership of property. Considering these aspects, their way of life can be described as group-oriented. However, due to their shallow intellect and narrow consciousness, they were incapable of forming a large group. A large group does not revolve around individual families or lineages. It required the emergence of Christianity and Islam before it could be formed."[12]

In discussing how the spirit of Christianity could lead to the formation of large group organizations that go beyond the family, Liang noted that the spirit of Christianity could be summarized in three points: (1) In the past, there were as many gods as there were city-states, but now, there was only one absolute God who reigns above the world. (2) Everyone considered God as their Father, and they regarded each other as brothers, eliminating the distinction between those within and outside their own clans. (3) Transcending the secular realm, the spiritual realm became distinct from politics, allowing for the independence of the state and government. He says, "The collapse of the feudal system and the emergence of organizations beyond the family are primarily driven by this new spirit."[13] On the other hand, he says, "We should not misunderstand that the formation of large group life among Westerners was solely based on the conscious demands of religious leaders. The existence of group life among Westerners is a matter of fact, not just an idea."[14] However, these facts are particularly related to Christianity. According to Liang, spiritual elements are merely necessary conditions in the historical process.

Christianity, in particular, broke down small groups of families and the class system, organizing a supra-familial group, the church, where everyone was regarded as a brother. Through group life, a sense of collective consciousness gradually developed. Additionally, with Christianity's exclusivity in reference to other religions and the bloodshed caused by religious wars, this group spirit was further strengthened.

During the medieval period and beyond, there were other historical conditions that contributed to the consolidation of group life in the West. Politically, the decline and disintegration of great empires provided opportunities for local powers to emerge. This compelled weaker entities to seek alliances and dependencies in order to survive. As a result, numerous feudal groups were formed. Liang notes, "Economically, this was due to the Islamic conquest cutting off major trade routes in the Mediterranean, leading to the decline of cities. Western Europe as a whole transitioned from a commercial society to a primarily agricultural society during the late 8th century. … Under those feudal systems, the self-sufficient economic units of various sizes did inadvertently form a group-oriented way of life."[15] Liang cited the arguments of many historians to support the assertion that "Westerners were indeed characterized by group life during the medieval agricultural era."[16] Naturally, he also provided evidence from various sources to illustrate the group life within medieval urban guilds. All of these arguments aimed to highlight the emphasis on the group nature of Western medieval society, revealing its social structure and cultural characteristics.

In group life, the relationship between individuals and the group differs from the relationship between individuals and the family. Liang notes, "Firstly, in this context, individuals recognize their subordination to the group, with the group exercising direct authority over individuals," and "within this context, it is universally recognized that every individual within the group is equal."[17] Through the lessons and experiences of group life, several qualities are cultivated: "first, a sense of public consciousness; second, discipline and habits; third, organizational skills; and fourth, the spirit of the rule of law. These aspects can be summarized under the term 'public virtue.'"[18]

In discussing the differences between the structure of Chinese and Western society, Liang noted that the key lay in the fact that ancient Chinese society was not a group-oriented society. At the same time, he believed that considering traditional Chinese society as a family-oriented society, while a common view, was not quite appropriate. He believed that traditional Chinese society was an ethics-oriented society.

In describing an ethics-oriented society, Liang writes:

> When a person is born, they are immediately connected to other people (such as parents and siblings). Throughout life, they exist and live within these social connections (never separate from society). This leads us to understand that human life exists in various relationships. These relationships are precisely the various ethical connections. Familial relationships and social companionship refer to the mutual interactions between people, specifically indicating how individuals relate to one another. Relationships are formed through interactions. The natural, fundamental relationship is that of family, specifically

> the relationship between parents and children. Therefore, ethics is of great importance to the family. Parents are always the first relationship, followed by siblings. As one grows older, there are spouses and children. Thus, local communities and broader social groups are also formed as a result. Once one enters society, they encounter different relationships: in education, there are teachers and students; in the economy, there are business partners; in politics, there are rulers, officials, and citizens. With regular interactions and mutual support, one develops friendships with neighbors and acquaintances. As people grow older and their life unfolds, they gradually develop a multitude of relationships from various directions, some close and some distant. All these relationships are part of ethics. Ethics begins within the family, but extends beyond it.[19]

Liang's definition of ethics is not quite precise enough. If every relationship between individuals is considered ethical, then any society that consists of some form of interpersonal relationships could be called an ethical society. Indeed, it is evident that Liang's concept of ethical relationships refers specifically to familial and quasi-familial relationships. His notion of an ethical society can be understood as a society in which all social relationships are structured in a familial manner. He points out that the characteristic of ethical relationships is the presence of emotional bonds and moral obligations between individuals within these relationships. He says, "Ethical relationships are essentially relationships of emotional and moral connection."[20] Within these relationships, there is a regulation based on obligations and duties. Therefore, in this sense, family, kinship, and all relationships based on the regulation of obligations and duties can be considered ethical relationships. He points out:

> We should extend the concept of family to encompass all relationships within society, aiming to cultivate a sense of kinship and prioritize moral obligations within these relationships. Therefore, it is necessary for every individual in this society to bear corresponding responsibilities in their ethical relationships with people from all directions. At the same time, the individuals who have ethical relationships with them from all directions also have their respective obligations toward them. Every member of society, without planning, becomes interconnected and intertwined with one another, forming an intangible form of organization.[21]

Such a society is referred to as an ethics-oriented society. The guiding principle of an ethics-oriented society is based on emotions and reason, rather than solely on laws. For example, "within a family, the specific circumstances of different individuals, such as the young and old, the respected and subordinate, males and females, and the strong and weak, are clearly visible. Since there is no need to deal with the complexities of dealing with a large number of people, one can discuss and address matters based on their specific needs and circumstances. Furthermore, when living closely together, all the subtle intricacies and nuances become known to one another, making it difficult to ignore or overlook them. People are as close as blood relatives, and their mutual needs are like that of siblings. Thus, they naturally seek to be considerate and understanding of each other to maintain harmonious relationships and smooth lives. In this context, there is no need for strict legal enforcement, as the bonds formed by ethical relationships are beyond the scope of what laws can regulate.[22]

The starting point of an ethics-oriented society is the family or kinship. Due to the lack of historical conditions in China for the development of Western-style group life that extends beyond family in both spiritual and material aspects, there was a lack of group living and the habits developed through such group living. This led to a heavy reliance on family and kinship life, as well as the formation of corresponding customs and biases stemming from this reliance. Economy and politics were also influenced by this social structure. With the emphasis on emotional bonds and mutual dependency in an ethics-oriented society, regulated by obligations, the concept of rights was not developed significantly in either the political or economic domains. In the political sphere, the ruler was regarded as the patriarch, and local officials were referred to as parents, treating the entire nation as one large family. Therefore, it was said that filial piety was the basis for serving the ruler, sibling respect was the basis for respecting elders, and compassion was the basis for governing the people. When it came to governance, the focus was on nurturing and protecting the people as if they were one's own children. This tradition was passed down from ancient times over two or three thousand years. As a result, the people were well aware of the ethical obligations between rulers, officials, and citizens, but may not have fully understood the relationship between the people and the nation as a collective entity. Liang notes, "Not only is the entire political structure encompassed within ethical relationships, but the ideals and methods of politics likewise stem from and return to ethics."[23]

III. Occupational Paths and Class Contradictions

Liang believed that ancient Chinese society had two major characteristics in its social structure: one was its ethics-oriented nature, and the other was the divergence of occupations. The ethics orientation was in contrast to the Western emphasis on group-oriented or individual-oriented values, while the divergence of occupations was in contrast to the class differentiation in Western societies. He writes:

> The concept of an ethics-oriented society only describes one aspect of the structure of Chinese society; there is another aspect to consider. In Western society, during the medieval period, there was a class opposition between the aristocratic landowners and the serfs, while in the modern period, there was class opposition between capitalists and laborers. China's society is different in this regard. If Western society can be characterized as a society with class opposition, then China can be seen as a society with occupational differentiation.[24]

Liang admits that, in a broad sense, the differences in social status, wealth, and poverty among people can be regarded as social classes. However, his understanding of social classes is based on the example of medieval Western society. When he says that there are no social classes in China, he also means that there are no class conflicts similar to those in Western societies. Apart from cultural beliefs, Liang's perspective was largely based on his understanding of land distribution in rural areas of northern China, particularly in Dingxian County and Zouping County. He believed that traditional agricultural society in China did not have social classes, and his reasoning behind this was:

> First, everyone has the freedom to buy and sell land.
>
> Second, there is no significant concentration or monopoly of land. It is generally estimated that the majority of people own land.[25]

Although Liang acknowledged that the rural development work in Zouping and the social survey in Dingxian were universally applicable, he considered them random samples. He also took into account the relatively high number of sharecroppers in the southern regions as a middle ground. Therefore, the two points mentioned above still hold true, and he notes, "Based on this situation, regarding those who have land but do not engage in cultivation and those who cultivate but do not own land, the concept of a class society is far-fetched."[26]

In Liang's view, Chinese society lacked class conflicts in the economic realm, and the absence of class conflicts in the political sphere was even more apparent. He argues that "from the Warring States period onward, whether at the central or local level, all those in power were officials. The key distinction between officials and aristocrats was that officials no longer ruled for their own benefit. While they did indeed hold positions of authority, these positions were neither hereditary nor lifelong. Instead, they occupied the position of temporary agents for a limited period of time... To rule for one's own benefit is characteristic of a ruling class, while the fact that they were temporary agents indicates that they were not part of such a class. Moreover, the opportunity to become an official was originally open to anyone."[27] Therefore, in Chinese history, before the Warring States period, there was a class society consisting of nobles, high-ranking officials, and commoners. However, after the Warring States period, the ruling class shifted to educated individuals and professional officials. Like farmers, workers, and merchants, they, too, had their specific roles and responsibilities in the social structure, making them an indispensable component of society. This is what Liang meant by the term occupational differentiation.[28] Liang's views aligned closely with the sociological analysis of social stratification and social mobility.

To summarize, the nonexistence of social classes in China since the Qin and Han dynasties was a unique characteristic of medieval Chinese history. This phenomenon was based on (1) the widespread existence of independent producers, (2) land and capital being both relatively decentralized and not highly concentrated, and thus often undergoing fluidity and transformation, and (3) openness in political opportunities.[29]

Due to the absence of class conflicts in Chinese society, China exhibited characteristics that were unlike those of a nation, such as the lack of essential functions of a state and a politically passive, inactive approach. The relationship between the people and the government was primarily centered around the payment of taxes and tribute. China lacked international conflicts and was often seen as neglectful in terms of national defense, having unclear household registration systems, and placing more emphasis on scholarly pursuits rather than martial ones, among other things. Especially due to the lack of a strong sense of national identity among the Chinese people, they tended to use the term "all under heaven" to refer to the collective concept of the realm or world, rather than a specific nation. In the consciousness and daily life of Westerners, the individual and the group were the most important, while in the consciousness of Chinese people, the family and the heaven were the most important.

Liang argues that since China did not exist and develop in the world as a nation, in practical terms, there was only society in China and no state. More accurately, China could be described as the dissolution of the state within society, with the state being integrated into society. It was seen as only society and did not resemble a typical nation. In this sense, society was considered the essence of the state.[30] In Liang's view, a nation was constituted by class rule, but China lacked class divisions and did not have a dominant entity that exercised force.

The concept of society as a nation was determined by the specific characteristics of China's historical feudal disintegration. According to Liang, feudalism was characterized by the coercive and non-economic exploitation imposed by landowners on those who cultivated the land. This exploitation was accompanied by economic subordination, political fragmentation, and the influence of religious superstitions in terms of ideology. During the period of feudal disintegration in China, influenced by the rationality inspired by the teachings of Mencius and Confucius, law was based on rituals and moral principles. Politics served as ethics, and professional roles represented social classes. Moreover, moral values took the place of religious beliefs, integrating the class-based state into an ethical society. Therefore, Liang notes, "For the past three thousand years, our consistent spirit has been directed toward society rather than the state."[31]

IV. Social Progress and Capitalism

The major question Liang's analysis of Chinese history and culture aims to address is that of identifying the cultural and structural reasons behind China's historical stagnation and the failure of capitalism to emerge. He points out that it is particularly puzzling that after the disintegration of feudalism in China, there was no establishment of centralized power for more than two thousand years, and the economy remained stagnant for a long time. He considers these two factors most inexplicable. He states, "According to the arguments of those who hold such views, the two thousand years from the Qin and Han dynasties onward are an enigmatic era. To discuss the social history of China without a rational, satisfactory explanation for these issues would be to talk in vain. Ignoring and erasing them would be even more ridiculous."[32]

In ancient Chinese society, family inheritance in the patrilineal system was not solely inherited by the eldest son but rather divided among all sons. Liang notes, "This practice, in which inheritance is shared among the sons, is a distinctive feature of China's ethics-oriented society. It is uncommon in the Western and Japanese contexts but has been practiced in China for two thousand years. Indeed, in China's ethics-oriented society, the economic aspect is based on ethical principles. Property and wealth are commonly shared among family members, particularly between husbands and wives and between parents and children. Furthermore, they are shared among all individuals who are part of the ethical relationships within society. As a result, wealth is divided among brothers, and relatives and friends share wealth with one another. Within the kinship system, efforts are made to nurture and benefit shared wealth among the extended family. The larger one's wealth, the broader one's responsibility and obligation to assist others. This practice significantly reduces the tendency toward economic concentration and promotes a more decentralized approach. It also hinders the expansion of capitalism's mode of production and tends toward a focus on consumption rather than accumulation… Some argue that the core of feudal society lies in its system of primogeniture, where the eldest son inherits the majority of wealth and power. They suggest that it was precisely through this system of primogeniture that British society was able to generate capitalism, as it concentrated economic power early on."[33]

Based on this ethics-oriented society, there is no need for a property-based law system, like Roman law, which seeks to protect individual rights and promote self-interest and free competition. Therefore, "It can be understood that in this ethics-oriented social organization, not only does it become a significant burden for an individual to make economic progress, but it is not fundamentally conducive to the emergence of such an enterprising spirit… There is no doubt that an ethics-based ethical society is not conducive to the growth and development of capitalism on this land."[34]

Because an ethics-oriented society is not based on group living, it naturally lacks the laws and democracy that are required for group living. The strong emphasis on moral values and inward focus created by an ethics-oriented society make it difficult for science to flourish. Moreover, as occupational differentiation replaces class conflict and the absence of a distinct class structure, political progress becomes difficult to achieve, unlike in a nation. All of these factors made it difficult for China to follow the path that Western history took.

According to Liang's perspective, China's failure to develop science and democracy, and an industrial revolution was not due to slower progress, but because China initially embarked on a different path from the West. He says, "If you want to reach a destination, you can do so by walking slowly, and eventually, you will get there. But if you take a different path, you will never reach that destination. China is an example of the latter… It is not that China has not yet entered the realm of science, but rather, it has reached a point where it cannot progress in the field of science. China is not in a state where it is not yet entering capitalism, but rather in a state where it is unable to progress toward capitalism. China is not in a state where it is not yet entering democracy, but rather in a state where it is unable to progress toward democracy. China has taken a different path from the West, and on this path, it has been unable to break free and has become trapped in a state of stagnation."[35]

Feng Youlan believed that the differences between China and the West were actually differences between the medieval and modern periods. Liang, on the other hand, believed that China's problem was not merely a slow progression toward the medieval period on the sole path of human evolution, but rather that from the beginning, China embarked on a path that diverged from the West in a different direction. He said, "This difference is actually a difference in the cultural paths of China and the West. Seen solely from the perspective of the rise of modern industry, the loss of importance in family life, as well as the prominence of individual independence and freedom after the modern ideological trends, led to the idea that individuals could disappear within the family and that the weight of family life remained stagnant, similar to the cultural stagnation in China, reminiscent of the medieval period in the West. As a result, it is conjectured that this difference in the evolution of society before and after can be attributed to the distinction in social classes.[36] Those who perceive the difference between China and the West as a distinction between ancient and modern times consciously or unconsciously hold a perspective of linear evolution in history. Liang goes on, "They fail to recognize the possibility of divergent paths between China and the West, stubbornly adhering to the idea that social evolution can only progress along a single line, and that there is a superstitious belief that history always progresses systematically, without considering the uncertainty of whether progress will occur or not. In reality, there is no predetermined path for historical development."[37]

V. Rationality and Premature Culture

In both the mentality and institutional aspects, an ethics-oriented society fails to provide conditions favorable to capitalism. In this sense, the role of social structure is crucial and decisive. However, the reason Chinese history formed such a social structure instead of developing a Western-style one, and the reason it took a different path—the path of an ethics-oriented society—from Western development is closely related to its own cultural development during the Axial Age. From this perspective, the orientation of ancient religious thought played a fundamental role.

Western culture leans toward group living, while Chinese culture leans toward family life, leading to the development of two contrasting cultures. Tracing back to its origin, Liang notes that "the Western path is rooted in Christianity, while the Chinese path stems from the teachings of Mencius and Confucius."[38] He goes on, "China has embarked on this path, not without the arrangement of ancient sages, though it is not a result of the natural evolution of a patriarchal society. This means that in organizing a society based on ethics, China initially had individuals with a vision who recognized the genuine, benevolent feelings of humanity, which originated and were nurtured within the family. He not only promotes these values but also constantly reminds people of their importance, emphasizing filial piety, sibling respect, kindness, love, and respectful friendship. On the other hand, he derives principles from the structure of the family to construct the structure of society."[39] This is what Liang means by an ethics-oriented society. The most insightful individuals in this regard are the Duke of Zhou and Confucius.

Liang believed that an ethical society originated from an ancient patriarchal society, just as the ritual and music systems originated from ancient religion. He says, "The degeneration of ancient religion into rituals and music, as well as the degeneration of ancient patriarchal society into ethics, clearly went through a process of transformation."[40] He believed that in the early history of Chinese cultural development, rituals and music were largely influenced by the Duke of Zhou, while ethics were greatly influenced by Confucius. According to Liang, the establishment of the ethics-oriented social order in China could be dated to around the Western Han Dynasty. However, when tracing back to its roots, credit must be given to the Duke of Zhou and Confucius. He summarized the achievements of the Duke of Zhou and Confucius, saying:

> First, they inspired human rationality, challenging all traditional customs and beliefs, making them subject to doubt and open discussion. They advocated for the use of reason and principles to weigh and evaluate matters, rather than blindly accepting them… Second, they earnestly emphasized filial piety and sibling respect, emphasizing the deep bond between family members, particularly between parents and children. They advocated for extending these virtues to all relationships, cultivating a society built upon the foundation of emotional connections and mutual care.[41]

As a result, by appealing to human emotions and rationality, they sought to eliminate the unnatural aspects of the feudal order and ultimately replace it with ethics. Through ethics, they aimed to organize society based on principles of morality and virtue rather than rigid hierarchical structures.

The rationality mentioned by Liang refers to the emotional and rational aspects of the human heart. It differs from the conventional understanding, as it does not specifically refer to the capacity and function of thinking and cognition. In Liang's terminology, the capacity and function of thinking and cognition are referred to as reason or intellect. He states, "Reason and rationality are the two aspects of the mind's functioning: the cognitive aspect is called reason, and the emotional aspect is called rationality."[42] He even goes so far as to say, "Are you willing to recognize where rationality lies? You can observe others or reflect on yourself. When your mind is calm, free from distractions, and receptive to others' words, and when conversation flows smoothly and understanding is easily reached, that is when a person possesses rationality. In other words, rationality refers to nothing more than the tranquil, receptive state of our own minds."[43] From this perspective, Liang's notion of rationality seems to be closely aligned with Jürgen Habermas' concept of communicative rationality. That is to say, if we consider that in the West, the transcendence of the family and clan spirit, which was initiated by Christianity, ultimately led to the emergence of a society centered around groups or collectives, then in China, it can be argued that the inspiration of Duke of Zhou and Confucius in cultivating human emotions and rationality ultimately led to the development of a society centered around ethics.

As mentioned earlier, the teachings of the Duke of Zhou and Confucius inspired human rationality, which encompasses the ability to assess and weigh all matters based on emotions and principles. Just as the West and Japan practiced the system of primogeniture, ancient China also had a similar system in place. However, after the disintegration of feudalism, China implemented the principle of equal inheritance. Liang pointed out that "this is not a trivial matter, nor is it a coincidence. It is a natural outcome of appealing to human emotions and rationality, removing the unnatural aspects of the feudal order."[44] The replacement of feudalism with ethics is exemplified by this significant aspect. After the disintegration of feudalism, China did not follow the path of a class-based state but instead embarked on the path of an ethical society precisely because rationality was awakened early on. Liang's notion of Chinese culture maturing too early refers to this idea.

Liang's perspective on the early awakening of rationality and the early maturity of Chinese culture involves a dual assessment of history, encompassing both the scale of historical development and the scale of values. His fundamental view on Chinese social history is that after the disintegration of feudalism, China transformed classes into professions and organized society based on ethics. However, he recognizes that these two aspects have a dual nature or dual significance. In other words, on the one hand, these two aspects are in line with rationality, but on the other hand, they emerged too early in Chinese history. In essence, to say that various characteristics of Chinese culture are "reasonable" or "in line with reason"[45] means using a value scale as a standard. On the other hand, to say that China progressed "too early" or "deviated from the trend of progress" is to use a historical scale as a standard. There are, then, two notions of progress, one based on values and the other based on history. The characteristics of Chinese culture and the ideals inherent in it are in line with the ideals of humanity. However, their true realization requires certain historical conditions, such as integrating the state with society and transforming classes into professions. These ideals should be pursued on the basis of a highly developed civilization. If these ideals emerge too early, their inherent rationality may make them difficult to change, hindering the necessary progress in history. From an ethical perspective, goodness (rationality) is both progressive and rational. However, from a historical perspective, the presence of evil (irrationality) is necessary and can be considered rational in the context of historical development. Indeed, in a certain sense, these two forms of rationality align with what Max Weber referred to as value rationality and instrumental rationality. Indeed, from Liang's cultural standpoint, there is a clear presence of the contradiction and entanglement between these two forms of rationality.

VI. Weber's View on Chinese Culture

It is helpful here to examine Weber's understanding of the structure and institutions of Chinese society.

1. The Corvée and Patrimonial Systems

In Weber's view, the corvée system was the primary means of obtaining finances in traditional Chinese states. Various public burdens, such as irrigation, military expenses, grain supply, and the national treasury, were provided through the corvée system.[46] Certainly, the central government also directly engaged in productive activities as part of its fiscal operations. Due to the limited control exerted by the central government over local areas throughout various dynasties, the corvée burdens borne by local regions often, after a period of time, became entrenched as quotas due to the perpetuation of traditional practices.[47] With the development of monetary circulation, the quotas for corvée and taxes were transformed into monetary payments. The combination of a monetary economy and official salaries created special opportunities for the ruling class, strengthening their mentality of safeguarding vested interests.[48] The solid structure formed by the combination of the property or patrimonial systemand the salary structure could only be undermined by successful military or religious revolutions.[49]

The patrimonial system was a system in which rulers utilized political power as a useful adjunct to their private property.[50] Weber defined China as a patrimonial bureaucracy state, where rulers viewed the state as their personal property and employed bureaucratic administrative management. The patrimonial system emerged as a replacement for the feudal order. While it still maintained a hierarchical structure and emphasized social status, its fundamental principle was to open official positions to all members of society based on merit and educational qualifications.[51] Originally, officials were paid in kind by the state as remuneration. Later on, this practice was replaced by monetary salaries. In practice, officials were unable to rely solely on their salaries for their livelihood, nor could they cover their administrative expenses with their salaries alone. As a result, administrative leaders at various levels acted like landlords or governors. They would submit a certain amount of taxes to the provincial or central authorities, while using the taxes collected for their own administrative expenses and keeping the remaining balance for themselves. In this way, the patrimonial system became the underlying principle permeating the entire bureaucratic structure. Weber notes, "Characteristic of the patrimonial system is that officials consider the income they receive from their administrative jurisdiction as their salary, which is essentially indistinguishable from private income… The principle commonly observed in the patrimonial system is that officials not only have to cover the expenses of civil and judicial affairs within their administrative jurisdiction from their own income but also have to personally pay the salaries of their administrative staff."[52]

2. Clan Society and Village Autonomy

Weber believed that the family or clan was the most autonomous organization in traditional Chinese society and one of the few forces capable of resisting the authority of the patrimonial regime. The family not only held power over its members who went beyond legal boundaries, but also possessed the power to resist the law.[53] The strength of its cohesion far surpassed that of Western Europe and even India. From the shared burden of corvée obligations and the inheritance rights of land transactions, the family could become a communal entity for production, an accumulative family community, and a profit-oriented community.[54] With the opportunities for accumulating wealth that officials had in traditional Chinese society, the goal of the family profit-oriented community was directed toward the pursuit of education and official positions. This involved nurturing outstanding members within the family to enter schools, pass examinations, and obtain official appointments. After assuming official positions, these individuals would also strive to increase the wealth of their family and promote the appointment of other family members to official positions.[55] The cohesion of the family relied on ancestor worship. The patriarch held the highest authority, and each member had to accept the leadership of the patriarch. The patriarch typically presided over ancestral worship, wedding and funeral ceremonies within the clan, and exercises the power of judgment in resolving disputes and lawsuits within the lineage. Family property was collectively owned by the members, while the clan possessed communal property such as ancestral temples, community land, and schools. Each family had obligations to contribute to labor and fulfill other duties.[56]

In China, villages, unlike cities, had both the legal and practical status and the capacity of local self-governing bodies. Families living in the same area formed a village community (township) based on geographical relationships, which was an autonomous body united by common customs and moral norms. In political terms, a township was the basic administrative unit of a country, and it was under the jurisdiction of the higher-level county administration. Apart from paying taxes, it was a self-sufficient natural economy and a self-disciplined social organization based on tradition.[57]

3. Non-autonomous Cities and the Pursuit of Substantive Justice through the Law

Unlike in the West, cities in China and other Eastern countries lacked political autonomy. In ancient China, there were neither city-states like those in ancient Western civilizations nor urban laws similar to medieval Western cities. This was because ancient Chinese cities did not possess political privileges as independent entities. They lacked a citizen class armed for self-defense, as well as political organizations and autonomous groups formed by citizens.[58] On the surface, China also had craft guilds similar to the merchant guilds of England, such as the Shanxi merchants. These guilds wielded significant power in controlling urban economic life. However, the most significant and crucial difference is that, even at that time, cities in England had charters that guaranteed their freedom, while such situations were never seen in China.[59] China lacked the unique development of various institutions facilitated by the emerging bourgeois class in Western medieval cities.

The nature of the property system determined the character of legal principles, which differed from the formal law in the West. We read, "In an ethically oriented property system, the pursuit is always for substantive justice rather than formal legalities."[60] Private law provisions were minimal, individual freedom rights were not guaranteed, and there was no separation between the administrative and judicial branches. In a manner aligned with the property system, officials personally employed servants at their own expense. This gentry administration exhibited a character that was anti-formalistic and patriarchal in nature. The laws in China were more of a codification of ethical norms, referred to as substantive ethical law, rather than a formal law that guaranteed the development of a capitalist economy.

4. Analysis of Institutions before the Emergence of Capitalism

Weber believed that the reasons rationalized capitalism failed to emerge in China were quite complex when viewed from an institutional perspective. The combination of a property-based state and the integration of monetary salaries led to the reinforcement of a mentality among the ruling class that focused solely on maintaining vested interests and existing economic conditions. This resulted in societal stagnation, the perpetuation of traditionalism, and a lack of social development. The monopolization of power by the property system stifled the rationalization of administrative operations, fiscal management, and economic policies. The nature of the family-based profit-sharing community was that of exploitative capitalism, which ran counter to the rationality of a business community. Family solidarity exerted a strong resistance to the elimination and discipline of free labor in capitalism. The extensive kinship organization hindered individual independence and personal development. The organization of family and village autonomy prevented central power from penetrating the border areas and grassroots levels to establish an effective political and legal order. Cities lacked political and military autonomy and unity in community organization. However, the fiscal and legal background on which rational capitalism development relies was solidified on the basis of such autonomy and unity. The entire legal system lacked formal laws and rational judicial procedures that could ensure the operation of a capitalist economy. Substantive ethical laws were only suitable for the interests of hereditary monarchs and the needs of kinship organizations.

Further, the imperial unity enabled the free movement and circulation of population and resources across vast territories without political barriers. While replacing the hostility and strife between feudal states with unity and peace, this also meant that there was no longer competitive pressure to drive improvement in bureaucratic and economic organizations through rational means. As the emperor and his officials took control of religious functions, it weakened the position of the clergy class, which could have acted as a counterbalance to secular authority. This resulted in a situation in which there was no clergy class or independent religious force capable of bringing about significant transformations in the socio-economic order to facilitate the development of capitalism. Weber points out that the continuous land reforms driven by the state in China over the past two thousand years resulted in the fragmentation of the land into numerous small plots, which prevented the emergence of large-scale, rational agricultural operations in China, and it hindered technological progress.

It is important to note that while Weber highlighted the obstacles to capitalism in Chinese society in terms of its institutions, he also listed many conditions within the Chinese institutional framework that were conducive to the emergence of capitalism. Because the theme of this chapter is understanding Liang Shuming's cultural views, the favorable institutional conditions listed by Weber will not be reiterated here.

5. Cultural Reasons for the Non-emergence of Capitalism

According to Weber, the factors of the system were not the determining reasons for capitalism not emerging in China, because the traditional Chinese social system had both aspects that were conducive to capitalism and aspects that were not. He believed "many of the conditions in China that may or inevitably hinder capitalism also exist in the West," and "the conditions often regarded as obstacles to the development of Western capitalism do not exist in China, which has a history of thousands of years. For example, the shackles of feudalism, manorial lordship, and certain guild systems are absent in China. Furthermore, the significant barriers to trade, such as monopolies, which are characteristic of the West, are not pronounced in China as well." But the fact remains that "the various external conditions favorable for the establishment of capitalism that China possesses are not sufficient to bring it about."[61] We are certainly aware that the conclusion Weber aimed to reach had already been established beforehand in his research on world economic history. Indeed, in his view, mentality was a powerful factor that strongly hindered the development of capitalism in non-Western societies.

Weber believed that the Confucian ethic provided a different psychological environment for Chinese society compared to the favorable mentality provided by the Protestant ethic for the development of capitalism. The main difference between them was that, although both belonged to rationalistic ethics, the Protestant ethic exhibited a tremendous intense tensional opposition to the secular world, viewing the world as irrational and believing in the rational subjugation, domination, and transformation of the world. By contrast, Confucian ethics aimed to reduce the tension with this world to an absolute minimum and advocated a traditionalist adaptation to the order and customs of this world.

VII. Comparison between Liang Shuming and Max Weber's Views on Chinese Culture

Based on the above, it can be seen that Liang's *Essence of Chinese Culture* is similar to *The Religion of China: Confucianism and Taoism* and fits neatly into the field of cultural sociology. The only difference lies in the specific topics they address. A comparison of the research of the two scholars reveals, first, that *Essence of Chinese Culture* places great emphasis on social structure. Liang asserts that "the social structure of a particular time and place constitutes the backbone of the entire culture of that time and place." This distinguishes his approach from his earlier work, *Eastern and Western Cultures and Their Philosophies*. Weber emphasizes the sociological foundation and provides numerous analyses of the institutions related to the emergence of capitalism. Both scholars devote considerable attention to the analysis of social structure. The difference lies in Liang's focus on the overall transformation of Chinese society and culture, while Weber's focus is primarily on the historical process of the emergence of capitalism. Therefore, Liang's perspective appears more encompassing because he aims to address the overall response of Chinese culture to modernization and the position of Chinese culture in world cultural history.

In addition, while both scholars emphasize the analysis of social structure, they also place great importance on the role of religious culture. Liang explicitly points out that Chinese customs and rituals are not determined by the economy; rather, economic development or stagnation is influenced by customs and rituals. Weber's analysis of the emergence of capitalism also emphasizes the almost decisive role of religious ethics in the economic development of capitalism. Liang considers religion to be the ultimate reason for the different development directions of Chinese and Western cultures and societies, and in comparison, his argument is that with the rise of a new belief, a new social organization follows, carrying a more universal perspective on history.

Both scholars agree that traditional Chinese society was not conducive to the emergence of capitalism. However, Liang believed that the direct reason China could not generate capitalism lay in its ethically based social organization. Weber, on the other hand, argues that this direct reason was more related to the spiritual temperament and mentality than to social institutions. In Liang's view, the role of religion, culture, and ethics in the absence of capitalism in China carries a sense of historical destiny. Confucian thought led China to embark on a path that could never enter capitalism.

Further, Liang approaches Chinese society as an organic whole, whereas Weber focuses on dissecting various Chinese institutions from the perspective of the emergence of capitalism. This leads to a difference in their structural analysis of Chinese society. Weber places more emphasis on institutional factors related to the emergence of capitalism, such as currency, cities, guilds, law, taxation, and bureaucracy. Liang, on the other hand, places more emphasis on factors such as family, social classes, the state, and society. With Liang's personal experiences and practical involvement in rural development, he has a specific understanding of traditional social life. Further, his thorough assimilation of the achievements of Chinese anthropologists, psychologists, and sociologists enables him to provide a more comprehensive, accurate description of Chinese society.

On specific issues, Liang believed that China was a society with a strong ethical foundation centered around family life. Weber also highlights the importance of family-based religion in Chinese society and the ethical orientation of the system of family property. Both scholars held the same view regarding village autonomy, and both agreed that the social and cultural aspects of ancient China were similar to those of the West. Both also believed that Confucian culture has a peaceful character.

Finally, Liang and Weber had different perspectives on certain aspects. One of the major differences between them was that Weber emphasized the forms of the state, such as patrimonial states and bureaucratic states based on family property, while Liang focused more on social forms, such as ethical societies and class societies. Liang fundamentally believed that China was not a state or does not resemble a state, but saw China instead as a society that integrated the concept of the state within it.

VIII. Concluding Remarks: National Character and Orientation of Life

During the May Fourth Movement in China, there were extensive discussions among Chinese scholars regarding national character and the transformation of national character. In modern academic discussions, psychology and social psychologists have conducted numerous studies on personality, which are often related to discussions on national character. Anthropologists, too, have shown particular interest in describing the psychological characteristics of groups. In *Essence of Chinese Culture*, Liang Shuming draws upon the cultural and academic discussions that took place beginning with the May Fourth Movement. He utilized the advantages and disadvantages of national character as supporting evidence for his arguments. He points out that sometimes, the distinction between advantages and disadvantages is not clear cut, and the unique aspects of national character are largely shaped by cultural influences within the ethnic group.[62] He specifically cites the works of Pan Guangdan and Zhuang Zexuan, particularly utilizing the discussions on Chinese national character found in Zhuang's collection of Western and Japanese perspectives on China. These discussions include anthropological perspectives that were influenced by imperialism and colonialism. However, their observations and conclusions often hold objective value. After synthesizing various opinions, Liang categorizes Chinese national character into ten points:

(1) Selfishness and self-interest
(2) Diligence and thrift
(3) Politeness and etiquette
(4) Peaceful and weak-willed
(5) Contentment and self-satisfaction
(6) Conservatism and adherence to traditions
(7) Carelessness and lack of attention to detail
(8) Perseverance and cruelty
(9) Tenacity and resilience
(10) Maturity and wisdom[63]

He agreed that these ten points are characteristics of Chinese national character and believed that they are largely shaped by social structure and the demands of the times. For example, diligence and thrift are the result of occupational differentiation; politeness is a product of an ethics-oriented society, while being peaceful and weak is connected to the lack of group conflict. Weakness, in this context, is attributed to the early awakening of reason and the decrease in instinctual behavior, among other factors.

The distinctive feature of Weber's analysis of Protestant ethics is the emphasis on practical ethical principles rather than doctrine, and is thus often related closely to social life in his discussions. In the book *The Religion of China: Confucianism and Taoism*, Weber's focus is on the analysis of sociological foundations and orthodox culture, which leads to a deviation in his analysis of Confucian ethics compared to his approach in analyzing Protestant ethics. However, Weber still gives considerable attention to the non-doctrinal aspects of Confucian culture and frequently discusses the issue of Chinese national character, which he refers to as a life orientation. From the scattered discussions found in the latter half of *The Religion of China: Confucianism and Taoism*, Weber's understanding of the Chinese life orientation can be summarized as follows:

(1) A worldly spiritual inclination, emphasizing blessings and longevity in this life[64]
(2) Possesses a strong desire for profit and a long-standing tradition of high development in this regard[65]
(3) Meticulous in financial matters and contented and modest disposition[66]
(4) Diligence and work ethic, which have always been regarded as unparalleled[67]
(5) The virtue of unimaginable frugality[68]
(6) Alert self-control, introspection, and caution, suppressing indulgence and excessive passion[69]
(7) Emphasis on outward demeanor and the dignity of forms, placing importance on saving face[70]
(8) Adherence to established norms and customs[71]
(9) A character inclined towards pacifism[72]
(10) Pragmatism[73]
(11) Tendency toward extreme dishonesty, but with a particular emphasis on loyalty and trustworthiness among major traders[74]
(12) Lack of empathy[75]
(13) Mutual distrust among individuals[76]

As Weber himself stated, the material he utilized, like other sociologists of his time, primarily came from the accounts of missionaries. At the same time, Weber did not systematically organize or categorize these materials, and his use of them was relatively scattered in his discussions. However, from the observations made in his descriptions, it can be seen that the first six points synthesized by Liang are already encompassed within Weber's understanding.

In terms of conceptualization, Weber's use of life orientation refers to the attitude toward life that emerges under certain cultural temperaments. It may be preferable to Liang's use of national character in this context. However, neither Weber nor Liang distinguished between those aspects rooted in tradition and belonging to cultural patterns and those that are merely linked to specific social systems and particular cultural environments. In Feng Youlan's terminology, what belongs to cultural patterns and cultural traditions can be referred to as nature, while what is influenced solely by specific social systems and environments can be referred to as habit. The former is long-standing and stable, while the latter is subject to change.[77] Of course, if the concept of ethnicity or national character refers only to the behavior and psychological orientations of people in a specific contemporary context and is subject to change, then such a concept can still be applicable.

From the perspective of their academic positions, Liang uses national character as evidence to support his views on the social structure and cultural trajectory of China, while Weber sees the attitude toward life as a concrete manifestation of a Confucian ethical orientation. Since the 1960s, social science research on Chinese behavior and psychology has achieved significant concrete results. In the research on the issue of modernization, the approach initiated by Weber, which emphasizes the cultural orientation of society, is closely linked to the study of cultural patterns and behavior. All of these aspects ultimately need to be grounded in the cultural habits of individuals. In this regard, the observations of Liang and Weber still hold certain relevance and can be a source of inspiration.

Notes

1. Wang Zhangyu, *Chronology of Liang Shuming* (Taipei: Dongda Books, 1992), 308.
2. Guy Alitto also believed that by the late 1940s, "Liang Shuming's analytical focus shifted from philosophy to sociology and history," and "the second expression of his cultural theory can be called 'Chinese-Western Culture and Its Society.'" See *The Last Confucian*, 182.
3. Liang Shuming, *Essence of Chinese Culture* (Taipei, Liren Publishing, 1982), 3.
4. Ibid.
5. Feng Youlan, "A New Treatise on Practical Affairs," in *Complete Works of Sansongtang*, vol. 4, 256.
6. *Essence of Chinese Culture*, 36.
7. Ibid., 45.
8. Ibid., 49.
9. Ibid., 80.
10. Ibid., 70.
11. Ibid., 52.
12. Ibid., 51.
13. Ibid., 53.
14. Ibid.
15. Ibid., 56.
16. Ibid., 59.
17. Ibid., 62.

18. Ibid., 65.
19. Ibid., 80.
20. Ibid., 81.
21. Ibid.
22. Ibid., 66.
23. Ibid.
24. Ibid., 143.
25. Ibid., 150.
26. Ibid., 152.
27. Ibid., 156.
28. Ibid., 159.
29. Ibid., 158.
30. Ibid., 171.
31. Ibid., 224.
32. Ibid., 175.
33. Ibid., 197.
34. Ibid., 198.
35. Ibid., 42.
36. Ibid., 79.
37. Ibid., 177.
38. Ibid., 96.
39. Ibid., 89.
40. Ibid., 115.
41. Ibid., 118.
42. Ibid., 128.
43. Ibid., 125.
44. Ibid., 119.
45. Ibid., 246–247.
46. Max Weber, *The Religion of China: Confucianism and Taoism,* trans. Jian Huimei (Taiwan: Yuanliu Publishing Company, 1989), 115.
47. Ibid., 117–121.
48. Ibid., 124.
49. Ibid., 125.
50. Ibid., 333.
51. Ibid., 107.
52. Ibid., 121.
53. *The Religion of China: Confucianism and Taoism,* 153.
54. Ibid., 150.
55. Ibid., 150–151.
56. Ibid., 153.
57. Ibid., 156–159.
58. Ibid., 77.
59. Ibid., 79.

60. Ibid., 166.
61. *The Religion of China: Confucianism and Taoism.*
62. *Essence of Chinese Culture*, 22.
63. Ibid., 23–24.
64. *The Religion of China: Confucianism and Taoism*, 209, 295.
65. Ibid., 127.
66. Ibid., 309.
67. Ibid., 127.
68. Ibid., 297.
69. Ibid., 221.
70. Ibid., 311.
71. Ibid., 298.
72. Ibid., 234.
73. Ibid., 298.
74. Ibid., 299.
75. Ibid., 298.
76. Ibid., 299.
77. Feng Youlan, *Complete Works of Sansongtang*, vol. 4, 319.

CHAPTER 8

Liang Shuming's *Human Nature and Human Life*: An Exploration of the Theory of the Human Nature

In 1921, Liang Shuming published his renowned work *Eastern and Western Cultures and Their Philosophies,* which proved to be an important contribution during the later stage of the New Culture Movement. However, given the prevailing simplistic cultural thinking during that time and the profound, complex nature of the book, it was not properly understood for many years. In evaluating Liang's work in terms of its impartial attitude and fair discussion, the primary endorsement came from He Lin, who said, "Although he puts effort into comparing the similarities and differences between Eastern and Western cultural orientations, he has one significant strength, which is that he does not limit himself to the narrow debate of the superiority or inferiority of Chinese and Western cultures. Rather, he emphasizes that Chinese people should fully embrace Western science and democracy, considering them as universal elements that are indispensable in human life. Without mincing words, he subtly implies that the Eastern attitude toward life is deeper and more profound than the Western pursuit of progress and competition... This, without a doubt, can be seen as a testament to his skillful, well-rounded argumentation."[1]

After the publication of *Eastern and Western Cultures and Their Philosophies* in 1924, Liang himself soon became aware of significant shortcomings in the book. He resolved to write a book titled *Human Nature and Human Life* to make corrections and further develop his ideas. His dissatisfaction with *Eastern and Western Cultures and Their Philosophies* did not stem from the controversial notion of Eastern and Western cultures, but rather from the issues related to human life and human psychology. After completing *Human Nature and Human Life* in 1975, he wrote a "Preface to the Completed Book," in which he mentioned that "in 1921, I foolishly published a draft of the lecture series titled *Eastern and Western Cultures and Their Philosophies,* in which I highly praised Confucian and Mencian thought. In 1923, I gave a lecture on Confucian Philosophy at the Department of Philosophy at Peking University, in which I expounded on Confucian ethical thought, drawing on my own understanding of human psychology. Such exposition was initially used in *Eastern and Western Cultures and Their Philosophies*, and there were indeed significant shortcomings. Now, these shortcomings are being corrected. The main focus of the corrections lies in distinguishing between human life (human psychology) and animal life (animal psychology)."[2]

Liang delivered three lectures titled "Human Nature and Human Life" in 1926, 1927, and 1934, but he only began writing this book in 1960. One-third of the book was completed by 1966, but it was interrupted due to the "Cultural Revolution." He resumed working on it in 1970, and the entire book was finally completed in 1975. *Human Nature and Human Life* was a work that Liang aspired to write in his early years and was completed in his later years after more than a decade of dedicated effort. The philosophical viewpoints presented in it were the culmination of his deep, thoughtful reflections accumulated over several decades.[3] If we consider *Eastern and Western Cultures and Their Philosophies* as representative of his early years, it can be categorized as a study that combines philosophy and culture in terms of its content. *Essence of Chinese Culture* can be considered one of his representative works in the middle period, and it focuses more on the study of ancient Chinese social structure and value orientations. *Human Nature and Human Life* is then representative of Liang's later years, and it focuses on the natural foundation and fundamental characteristics of human psychology.[4] This book can be considered a phenomenology of the human spirit written by a Chinese modern philosopher. The process of writing this book indicates that the issue of human psychology was a fundamental concern for Liang throughout his life.

I. Psychology and Ethics

Liang placed great importance on psychology, providing a clear explanation for his emphasis on this field. It is worth noting that his writings often express his thoughts directly, and they can be lengthy, but coherent. The only possible way to provide readers with a comprehensive understanding of his stance is to faithfully record what he said.

In the preface to the eighth edition of *Eastern and Western Cultures and Their Philosophies* in 1929, Liang states, "After the publication of this book in the autumn of the 10th year of the Republic of China (1921), I soon regretted several passages. Therefore, when the book reached its third edition in the 11th year (1922), I wrote a special preface to make a declaration. Later on, I had even more regrets, not just about recognizing errors in certain parts, but realizing that there was a fundamental problem with my approach. As a result, in the spring of the 15th year (1926), I sent a letter to The Commercial Press requesting the discontinuation of further editions and printing of the book." In describing these "fundamental problems," he writes, "In general, there are probably two fundamental points. The first is that the psychological interpretations used at that time to explain Confucianism were incorrect. The second is that there was a lack of proper methodology in interpreting Confucian teachings, or it could be said that the methodology used was flawed." He goes on to explain the importance of psychology, stating, "Every ethical school or ethical thinker must have psychology as the foundation on which they build their theories. All of my ethical ideas and assertions stem from my understanding of human psychology. In this book, when discussing Confucianism, I particularly enjoyed using the language of psychology at the time to explain it. However, looking back now, I realize that most of it was incorrect. Indeed, at that time, the understanding of human psychology within Confucianism was not clear, and I haphazardly used contemporary psychology as a basis without considering the fundamental incompatibility between the two. As for the various schools of psychology I referenced, they each have different approaches and perspectives, and it was a mistake to try to merge them into a unified explanation, an error within the error. It was only after twelve years that I began to realize this. I understood that it was not about criticizing contemporary psychology, but rather about elucidating the Confucian perspective on human psychology in order to discuss Confucian ideas on human life. From the thirteenth to the fifteenth year (1924–1926), my understanding gradually deepened. Consequently, I decided to discontinue the publication of that book and began planning to write *Human Nature and Human Life* instead."[5]

In fact, he had already expressed this idea in detail in 1926. Although *Human Nature and Human Life* was completed in 1975, Liang had written "Preface to *Human Nature and Human Life*" as early as 1926. In this preface, he states:

> Why did *Human Nature and Human Life* come into existence? Why did I want to talk about psychology? We should know that every ethical school or ethical thinker has their own psychology as its foundation. It can be said that their ethics is built upon their view of human psychology. Confucianism is a major ethical school. Many of the statements made by Confucius are ethical in nature. This is quite evident. Therefore, Confucius must have had his own understanding of human psychology, and all of the statements he made, whether implicitly or explicitly, were either directly or indirectly related to that understanding. That is certain. If we cannot discover Confucius's understanding of psychology, then talking about Confucius would be meaningless. Indeed, the ancients have passed away. There is no way to engage in conversation with the deceased. What we have access to are only a few words and phrases that have been passed down to us through the surviving written records. Those words and phrases had specific meanings and references at the time they were uttered, but by the time they reached us, they had become mere symbols. If we are unable to investigate their intended meanings and instead speak about them in a vague, ambiguous manner, it is nothing more than playing with terminology and deducing symbols. The true essence and understanding ultimately remain elusive... If you cannot uncover Confucius's psychology, there is no need to discuss Confucius's ethics. Furthermore, to determine the validity of the principles advocated by Confucius, it is necessary to examine the soundness of his psychological

> understanding... If you cannot compare and examine Confucius's psychology with modern psychology, there is no need to discuss the application of Confucian principles. But these two perspectives of psychology are clearly incompatible... So, if you cannot refute modern psychology and establish Confucius's psychology, there is no need to engage in comparison or examination.[6]

In his view, any ethical ideology must be based on and rooted in a certain psychology. Without understanding the Confucian psychology that serves as the foundation for Confucian ethics, one cannot truly comprehend Confucian ethics and Confucian thought. From this perspective, the purpose of writing *Human Nature and Human Life* is to elucidate the foundation of Confucian thought, which is the Confucian perspective on human nature. Based on Liang's statements and considering the trajectory of his thought, his Confucianism can be characterized as a modern Confucian philosophy that emphasizes psychological interpretation. The development of modern Confucian thought is fundamentally guided by the approach of psychology. This differs significantly from Xiong Shili's approach, with its development of modern Confucian thought with a focus on cosmology, which can be better characterized as a modern Confucian philosophy that emphasizes the construction of cosmology.

So, is Liang's "psychology" the same as the psychology classified in academic disciplines in modern times? Or does the psychology he talks about belong to the field of psychology, but represent a distinct school of thought different from existing ones? Is his Confucian psychology the same or different from the concept of heart-mind nature found in the Confucian philosophy of the late imperial period? Can we say that his psychology is a form of the study of the mind? These questions will be addressed in this chapter.

II. Instinct and Reason

Liang regarded the human mind as the fundamental essence of being human. He stated that "when it comes to human beings, one cannot separate them from the human mind" and "the reason one is a human lies solely in this mind." He further stated, "To speak of a person, one must perceive it through the mind; to speak of the mind, one must perceive it through people. People and the mind are inseparable; the mind and people are always interconnected."[7]

Liang's definition of the human mind has two main characteristics. First, he emphasized the unity of the mind and life. He said, "The human mind, in essence, is nothing other than a manifestation of life that emerged from primitive organisms. It has evolved over countless ages and eventually culminated in this magnificent display. The fact that humans have mental activities is similar to other organisms displaying signs of life. Although there may be variations in quality, it is ultimately just one phenomenon. It should be said that the mind and life are synonymous."[8] It is evident that when Liang discusses the mind, he places great importance on life. He views the mind as a manifestation of life in the universe and emphasizes that the mind cannot be understood apart from the phenomenon of life in the natural world as a whole. Therefore, he also stated, "When speaking of the human mind, it encompasses the entirety of human life's capacity for activity."[9] Secondly, he defined the human mind as specifically referring to a higher level of psychology beyond instinct. He writes, "When we speak of the mind, we refer to that aspect of human life that emerges when it transcends the confines of bodily instincts, namely, what we call reason and rationality."[10] He continues, "What is the mind? The mind is not a single entity; its meaning lies in the concept of being a master or ruler. Master refers to being in control or taking initiative, while ruler refers to exercising governance. In relation to things, we speak of governance, and in relation to oneself, we speak of taking initiative."[11] In this context, the governance of things refers to reason, while the concept of taking initiative encompasses rationality as well.

Liang's approach to discussing the human mind also has a fundamental characteristic. He believes that conventional psychology "generally focuses on individual life" and "does not adequately consider the development of the human mind in the context of human social history."[12] Liang's approach, however, is different. The reason *Human Nature and Human Life* took such a long time to be completed was because he aimed to discuss its development and characteristics through the lens of biological evolution and the development of human society. This required substantial knowledge preparation. *Human Nature and Human Life* is divided into two parts: "Psychology" and "Ethics." The former discusses the human mind by examining the origin and development of human life, highlighting the actual existence of the human mind, while the latter discusses human life by focusing on the human mind, elucidating the ideals that one should strive for in practical life based on the reality of human nature. Based on Liang's earlier description, it is evident that the psychology section forms the main part of the book, and the main theme of this section is to describe how life develops from instinct to reason and further evolves from reason to rationality.

It is helpful to first examine his discussion of the relationship between instinct and reason. Liang believed that "in order to elucidate the human mind, it is necessary to discuss the issue of reason and instinct." To address this issue, he extensively studied books on evolutionary theory, biology, anatomy, neuroscience, and psychology. He writes:

> In the evolution of the animal kingdom, there are indeed two distinct pathways: instinct and reason. The apparent planning seen in insects and fish is a result of natural evolution. Although it may resemble deep thought and deliberation, it is not conscious, but rather a development guided by instinct, leading to remarkable achievements. The other pathway leads to the development of reason, which is followed by vertebrate animals. However, it is only with the emergence of humans that this pathway reaches its highest level, characterized by consciousness and proficiency in planning... Indeed, reason and instinct are two distinct tendencies of life activity. They complement and counterbalance each other, existing in a reciprocal relationship rather than being separate from one another.[13]

He further states:

> Speaking from the biological realm, we observe two major divisions: plants and animals. Plants are autotrophic organisms that obtain nutrients from a fixed location without mobility, while animals are heterotrophic organisms that constantly move and seek plants or other animals as food. The two factions share the same origin, differing only in their approach to seeking a livelihood. Speaking from the animal kingdom, we can also observe two major factions, with their differences also lying in their methods of survival. Arthropods, represented by bees and ants, follow their instincts. Vertebrate animals, on the other hand, tend to lean towards rationality, with humans being the ones believed to have achieved it. Other higher animals are considered to have fallen short in this regard.[14]

Liang believed that there are two types of life activities in animals: one is following instincts, and the other tends toward rationality. If we consider the process of evolution, we can say that rationality is a tendency that goes against instincts. Instincts are innate, while rationality is a later development. Although both originate from the same source, they are opposite yet inseparable.[15] Liang believed that among the category of animals tending toward rationality, true development and realization can only be achieved in humans. The rationality that arises after instincts, through long-term evolutionary processes, undergoes quantitative changes that eventually result in qualitative changes. This becomes the fundamental characteristic that distinguishes human life from animal life. Liang states:

> Rationality, in relation to instincts, is initially just a matter of different tendencies in methods of living. However, when the inclination to go against instinct develops and ultimately undergoes a sudden change, it transforms into a fundamentally different nature of human life. This goes beyond mere differences in methods of living and becomes a fundamental distinction in the essence of human existence. As a result of this fundamental change, humans achieve rationality, which other animals generally do not attain.[16]

Rationality is considered a tendency that goes against instincts because, from the perspective of the coexistence and interplay of rationality and instincts in the process of life evolution, "instincts are specialized abilities that are innate and serve specific purposes or intentions in life, while rationality, on the contrary, tends to have a broad, more general application. Although their tendencies are opposite, they originate from the same source and are inseparable. As biological life evolves toward rationality, its instincts may fade, relax, or weaken. This process of gradual decline or transformation signifies intelligence, which refers to the natural, non-deliberate aspect of life redirecting its specialized pathways toward more general, more useful applications."[17] Indeed, it can be said that with each step of development, rationality comes at the cost of simultaneously weakening instincts.

To illustrate the notion that rationality is counter to instincts, Liang used human rationality as the representative of rationality and animal-like instincts as the representative of instincts. He concretized the relative opposition between rationality and instincts into the following points:

> Instinctual activities are closely tied to physiological functions and closely connected to the body. In contrast, rational activities are not primarily focused on the body; they are more detached from it and primarily related to the brain.
>
> Instinct is the innate capacity (or tendency) for individual life, inherited through race, that cannot be removed from an individual's life and cannot be acquired during their lifetime. Therefore, instinctive behavior does not rely on experience. As instincts weaken in higher animals and rationality emerges, they become influenced by the experiences of their environment. Life experiences, which are acquired after birth, play a crucial role in shaping their behavior through learning and conditioning.
>
> Instinct involves immediate knowledge and action, where knowledge and action are unified. Its perceptual activities are closely tied to specific environmental stimuli and objects. This is true for animal life. Humans, at times, may exhibit a gap between knowledge and action, and when this gap is significant, there is a distance between what one knows and what one actually does. Human perceptual activities have indeed surpassed mere responses to specific environments. Humans have the capacity to engage in knowledge for the sake of knowledge itself. Knowledge becomes an independent activity, separate from immediate environmental stimuli. This is evident in the pursuit of scientific knowledge and all forms of academic disciplines.
>
> It can be said that the knowledge obtained through instincts is concrete and tangible, while the knowledge obtained through rationality is more abstract and conceptual in nature.
>
> The knowledge derived from instincts can be seen as direct and conclusive for life activities. On the other hand, the knowledge derived from rationality can be viewed as indirect and provisional for life activities. Instincts perceive and comprehend limited, specific aspects, while rationality perceives and comprehends the broader, universal aspects of everything, transcending limitations.[18]

Liang points out, "One key point is that it brings about an attitude of observing things in a detached manner in our lives (referred to as 'being detached from knowledge in action, knowing for the sake of knowing'). To observe things in a detached manner is to adopt an objective perspective."[19] He believed that this kind of detached observation embodies the highest development of rationality going against instincts. It represents the "fundamental change" in human life.

Liang believed that all living beings revolve around two major life issues: individual survival and the propagation of the species. To address these two fundamental issues, lower animals rely on instincts as a means, while higher animals can utilize rationality. Liang believed that rationality is fully developed in humans and that rationality is inherently the method for addressing these two major life issues. However, once human rationality is formed, its activities gradually distance themselves from the two major life issues. He writes, "The manifestation of the emergence of rationality in higher animals lies in the development of their brains. The development of the brain corresponds to the development of intelligence. Their life's emphasis shifts from action to knowledge, as their interests extend beyond the two major issues. Lower animals are limited in their interests, and their knowledge and actions are confined to the two major issues. The instinct of exploration in higher animals is closely linked to their defensive instincts, and their departure from the two major issues may not be as far-reaching. If we consider the curiosity of primates such as apes and chimpanzees, it appears to be a departure from the two major issues. As for humans, their desire for knowledge and their wide-ranging interests that extend to various fields can be considered a significant departure from the two major issues."[20] Human rational activities can extend beyond direct associations with survival issues and encompass a wide range of diverse developments.

He cites science and philosophy as examples to illustrate how rational activities extend beyond survival issues, saying, "The desire for knowledge encompasses everything unrelated to the two major issues, and scientists and philosophers are known to be consumed by it, neglecting sleep and meals. The boundless expansion of these interests arises from the development of the inclination of rationality going against instincts. In the instinctual life of animals, their interests and emotions are strongly connected to specific relevant things, while they are indifferent to things beyond those specific contexts... Rationality, on the other hand, gradually loosens its ties to specific relationships and eventually breaks free from them."[21] He believed that this was a significant development, wherein humans acquired life characteristics that are fundamentally different from all other animals. He writes:

> At this stage of life's development, humans are fundamentally different from all other existing beings. Existing beings are trapped in instinctual living, where their entire lives become a means and tool for addressing the two major issues, akin to mechanical instruments. In this process, they lose their essential life nature and inevitably create a separation from the grand life of the universe. Only humans, inheriting the trends of biological evolution, transcend the confines of the two major issues and continue to manifest their essential life nature. They have been persistently advancing and have become the pinnacle of the grand life of the universe.[22]

Liang regarded the development of human rationality as a natural trend in biological evolution, but he did not overlook the significance of human productive practice and social activities in the development of human rationality. In this regard, he specifically emphasized the significant influence of labor and language on human sensory perception, cognition, and mental faculties.[23] Indeed, his discourse on this aspect is relatively brief, and he does not provide exceptional insights, making it unnecessary to elaborate on this topic here.

III. Ability to Be Calm and Self-Awareness

It is helpful here to explore Liang's understanding of the "fundamental characteristics of human nature." He begins his book with a discussion of the concepts of initiative, flexibility, and planning through the lens of *On Protracted War.* He considers these three qualities to be somewhat related to rationality, but he does not believe that they are the most suitable for explaining the fundamental characteristics of the human mind. In his view, these qualities can be summarized under the concept of quietude, which he consistently uses when discussing the human mind. He states, "I believe that the fundamental characteristic of the human mind lies in its ability to be quiet."[24] According to his explanation, the ability of the mind to be quiet refers to having a calm mind and maintaining inner tranquility. This statement is quite unique. He states, "When it comes to the source of the mind's ability to be calm, is there anything that can be said about it? Indeed, this distinction between vertebrate and non-vertebrate animals in the process of biological evolution has led to the emergence of rational living and its subsequent development."[25] In the process of evolution, the divergence between vertebrate and non-vertebrate animals has led to the development of rationality, and the development of human rationality has culminated in the formation of a mind capable of being calm. According to this explanation, the concept of a quiet mind is indeed a way of describing the characteristics of human rationality or another way of referring to human rationality.

The human intellectual activity of "knowing apart from doing, and knowing for the sake of knowing," Liang believes, is precisely the manifestation of the ability to be calm. He points out that reason frees itself from the immediacy of two major problems, and its interests are extensive, saying, "It is not confined to limited relationships but can embrace boundless possibilities, focusing on this or that. Interest can arise in anything, precisely because it is also possible to lack interest in anything or even have no interest in certain things. When interest does not arise, it is referred to as the ability of this mind to remain quiet. Indeed, it is precisely because of its quietude that it can be active."[26] He goes on, "Animals are inherently meant to be active; they do not seek stillness. However, stillness develops from within the activity itself. Instinct is eager for action after knowing and is thus biased toward activity. On the other hand, reason emphasizes knowing before action, and is thus biased toward stillness. The development of reason, some may say, is not due to anything aside from the reduction of the body's organs' approximate mechanical reactions to specific things, and the expansion of the brain's mental functions. Its nature is one of hesitant deliberation before action. Amid hesitation, there exists a certain degree of calmness. With further extension and development, it ultimately leads to pure tranquility."[27]

He further points out:

> How can humans break through the limitations of the two major problems? This is achieved by using reason to counter instincts, as these two major problems are firmly rooted in various instincts. Instinctive activities are always accompanied by their corresponding emotional impulses... However, all emotional impulses can be obstacles

> to reason. Reason must always operate with the elimination of emotional impulses. Put differently, it requires a tranquil state of mind to be fully effective. Consequently, with each advancement of reason, a portion of emotional impulse is removed, leading to a state of tranquility. Simultaneously, it brings about a partial liberation from the two major problems. Continuing this development, from quantitative changes to qualitative changes, human life undergoes a fundamental transformation, thereby breaking through the limitations of the two major problems.[28]

Indeed, it means that instincts give rise to emotional impulses, and reason, in opposition to instincts, must eliminate emotional impulses to fulfill its function effectively. Quietude means not being moved by instincts and not being swayed by emotional impulses.

Liang also believed that using reason to seek quietude to explain the nature of the mind is not as clear as using self-awareness. He says:

> The human mind, through the tendency of reason to seek quietude, unexpectedly transcends the limitations of the two major problems, no longer entangled by them... Self-awareness and calmness of the mind are inseparable. Only when there is self-awareness deep within can it be called the calmness of the mind, and it is only through this calmness of the mind that self-awareness arises. However, by emphasizing self-awareness now, compared to merely mentioning the calmness of the mind, its relationship to knowledge and planning becomes even more evident.[29]

In defining self-awareness, Liang says, "Self-awareness resides within one's own mind, not directed toward the external world, whereas consciousness is directed toward the external world. In other words, self-awareness is an inward awareness of one's own thoughts and feelings, while consciousness is the awareness of external objects and events."[30] He further says, "Self-awareness is present in every aspect of human mental activity, although it may vary in its clarity, strength, obscurity, or manifestation. It is by no means fixed. In other words, self-awareness exists in all mental processes, but its intensity and visibility can vary from person to person and from situation to situation... Human sensations and perceptions arise from the cognitive functions related to their environment, while self-awareness resides solely within one's own mind and is not directed toward the external world. It is extremely pure and generally serves no other purpose apart from subtle internal awareness. However, all outward activities of the human mind are in some way supported by this self-awareness."[31] He also mentions, "In general, the mind has a tendency to be outwardly oriented, leaning toward external distractions, and in doing so, self-awareness loses its clarity... When the mind is restless and drawn toward external influences, self-awareness diminishes."[32] He continues, "In summary, for humans who have progressed from being driven by instincts to being guided by reason, there is a considerable flexibility between quietude and restlessness. Often, the variation lies in whether individuals operate with self-awareness or without self-awareness in these states of quietude or restlessness. Indeed, for beings in the realm of life that can be observed to be deeply entangled in instincts and unable to extricate themselves, there is no room for self-awareness. To further clarify, it is clear that animal life lacks self-awareness, while human life has entered the domain of self-awareness. However, in real-life situations, there are times when the self-awareness in one's life seems to be obscured and inactive, which happens quite frequently. Although it is common, such occurrences indicate a state of negligence and lethargy rather than the norm for proper self-awareness. Moreover, even though its effect may be obscured and not evident at that moment, the power of self-awareness remains ever present and does not truly vanish."[33] So, he says that merely stating "the essence of being human lies in mind" is not enough; it should also be said that "the essence of the mind lies in self-awareness."[34]

The essential manifestation of the heart's self-awareness is the power to seek truth without calculating gains and losses. Liang states:

> The pursuit of truth and the distinction between good and evil exist within the spontaneous self-awareness of the human mind. It is the foundation upon which our knowledge and learning can be firmly established… The pursuit of truth and the recognition of falsehood occur naturally as an inherent power within the human mind during its engagement with the external world. For example, when we calculate numbers, we must seek their correctness. If there is any ambiguity or uncertainty, we lack confidence. In such cases, we will recalculate repeatedly until it becomes clear and error-free, and only then will we feel content. This is not driven by considerations of personal gains or losses. For example, when calculating the profits and losses in production and business, we do not let our preferences for gains or aversions to losses influence us. Instead, we solely seek truth in the numbers. This consideration, disregarding personal gains or losses and distinguishing between right and wrong, is what is referred to as the conscience. The conscience is clearly present within our self-awareness… If one is swayed even slightly by personal gains or losses, for example, being eager for quick success, unable to distinguish between right and wrong, and speaking without careful consideration, then one cannot become a true scientist. They cannot achieve true science.[35]

This kind of rationality that seeks truth without considering personal gains or losses is also what Liang refers to as the calmness of non-action or non-doing calmness. His statement means that "rationality must reach the level of calmness in non-action, and only then can it be fully utilized."[36] This idea is closely connected to what he mentioned earlier about the tranquility of the mind.

If we consider the development from instinct to rationality discussed earlier, Liang's narrative does not differ significantly from psychology. However, in this section, when he talks about the quietude of the mind and self-awareness, his discussion has already surpassed the scope of psychology. He considers the calmness of the mind a characteristic of rationality. The association of quietude with being unaffected by personal gains or losses allows him to derive the concept of rationality. As a result, calmness of the mind becomes an important intermediary concept in his philosophical psychology.

IV. Rationality and Selfless Emotions

Non-doing calmness holds significant importance within Liang's theoretical framework, as it is the concept from which he logically derives the core idea of his philosophy, rationality. It is useful here to examine his discourse on this matter.

The previous section discussed rationality, which enables humans to seek truth without considering personal gains or losses. This represents a significant breakthrough in human psychology. According to Liang, there has also been a similar breakthrough in the functioning of the entire human emotional and volitional aspects. He believed that the human emotional and volitional realm could be simply summarized into two major directions: good and evil. The previous section discussed how humans seek truth and distinguish between good and evil in the realm of knowledge activities. This pursuit of truth and distinction between good and evil is naturally inherent in the human mind and is not influenced by the concerns of daily life, gains, or losses. Liang believed that humans' rational capacity can be understood by examining the biological activities of life. Higher animals all have preferences and choices based on good and evil, and the expressions of good and evil in biological life directly stem from the two major life issues of survival and reproduction. The beneficial aspects are considered as gains or benefits, while the opposite is regarded as harmful or losses. Those associated with gains are seen as good, while those related to losses are seen as evil. He notes:

> In general, animals instinctively determine whether something is good or evil. Humans have evolved to the stage of rationality, and their rational faculties have surpassed direct relevance to survival issues. Therefore, their evaluations of good and evil are not solely based on instinct and the two major life issues. The same applies to emotions and volition. The good and evil in human emotions and volition generally do arise, either directly or indirectly, from the gains and losses related to the two major life issues. However, they are not limited to just this aspect; there are also factors that go beyond these considerations. Beyond the calculations of gains and losses, there are moments when humans may have thoughts or considerations that go beyond these material concerns and are more focused on higher ideals or values. Thought or consideration toward higher ideals means the inclination toward higher aspirations or ideals, and it implies that human life is an ongoing pursuit of flexibility and freedom. No external gains or losses can overpower the vitality of life's aspiration for freedom. In the early stages of the development of rationality, it initially evolved as a new means to seek survival and livelihood. Therefore, from the perspective of pursuing survival and livelihood, it is natural for us to constantly consider gains and losses. However, the development of rationality has transcended the

constraints of the two major life issues. Despite constantly focusing on dealing with and solving problems, it is not bound by any particular issue and can operate independently. Indeed, not being bound by any particular issue means that rationality can act calmly and independently, not easily swayed by any gains or losses, and can make decisions with composure and autonomy."[37]

The initial development of rationality transcended is entangled by gains and losses, achieving a leap beyond the constraints of the two major life issues. Similarly, the development of human emotions and volition also includes the attainment of higher thoughts, which means transcending survival issues and pursuing freedom without being bound by gains and losses.

It can be said that rationality can reach a state of non-action calmness, as can emotions and volition. Liang points out, "All visible emotions and volition in animals are accompanied by their instincts. Once human life has been liberated from instinct, emotions and volition no longer need to be directly associated with instinct. However, in general, it is often difficult to completely dissociate emotions and volition from instincts, especially when it comes to bodily functions and responses. Each instinct is a means or method designed to address the two major life issues, and each involves some form of action or response. Therefore, all emotions that are associated with instincts also involve some form of action or response, driven by gains and losses (related to survival and livelihood). Whether it is for individuals or for the entire species, if they are overly focused on self-preservation and confined to a narrow scope, their emotions can be considered selfish emotions."[38] Animal emotions are based on instincts and involve action or response. On the other hand, human emotions can transcend instincts and reach a state of non-action calmness.

Animal life is constrained by the organism's instincts and becomes a mechanistic tool for addressing the two major life issues. When humans liberate themselves from animal-like instincts, they experience sudden enlightenment and a clear path toward the complete integration with the vast life of the universe, and their life activities focus on continuously striving for flexibility and freedom, not necessarily driven by more actions, because they are no longer mere mechanistic tools for the two major life issues, although they still require some resources for survival and reproduction. In the primitive stage, emotions accompany instincts and are constantly influenced by gains and losses, just as the development of rationality requires attaining the state of non-action calmness before it is fully utilized. Gradually, this transformation results in the emergence of selfless emotion.

In the process of human evolution and social development, rationality evolves from being a means of seeking livelihood to reaching a state of non-action calmness. Correspondingly, emotions evolve from being instinct-driven to developing into selfless emotions. Therefore, Liang states, "Indeed, rationality must reach the state of non-action calmness to be fully utilized; it is from this point that selfless emotions emerge. This constitutes rationality itself."[39]

Selfless emotions are emotions that are free from actions driven by gains and losses. They are feelings that arise independently of any considerations of personal interests, and they are considered tendencies that arise later in opposition to instincts. Selfless emotions and non-action calmness may both be forms of non-action and counter to instincts, but they are not the same. The key difference lies in the fact that the use of rationality is characterized by non-action calmness, whereas the use of emotions (selfless emotions) is non-action, but not necessarily calm.

Selfless emotions are the essence of rationality. Liang says, "This emotion, in its nature and manner, does not belong to instincts, but is precisely what I referred to as selfless emotions in the previous context. The reason rationality is rational lies precisely in this aspect as well."[40] Liang's concept of rationality differs from the general concept found in Western philosophy. If we say that in his philosophy, reason refers to the intellectual aspect of human beings, including the ability to reason and think logically, then rationality refers to the emotional and volitional aspect of humans, where emotions are free from the influence of gains and losses and act independently of instincts. He thus says, "I have introduced the term selfless emotions to represent the emotional and volitional aspects of the human mind that is liberated from animal-like instincts, in addition to the concept of rationality, which represents the intellectual aspect. Reason tends toward calmness to observe things, and its emphasis lies solely on acquiring knowledge. The proposal of rationality is meant to represent the emotional and volitional aspects of the human mind. With both reason and rationality presented together, how could one be missing?"[41]

Reason and rationality are thus different. The role of reason is to seek knowledge, while rationality is described as the virtue of purity, greatness, brightness, and justice within the human heart, and it manifests as moral sentiments or emotions. Reason is the heart that seeks truth, while rationality is the heart that desires goodness and kindness.[42] Liang says:

> Reason is the marvelous application of the human mind, while rationality is the virtue of the human heart. The latter represents the essence, and the former represents its application. Though essence and application are inseparable, it is necessary to distinguish them to better understand the human mind.
>
> Reason observes things calmly, and what it acquires can be called physics, as it is devoid of even the slightest trace of emotions. On the other hand, rationality revolves around the center of selflessness, where judgments are made without self-deception regarding one's preferences or aversions. What it acquires can be called emotional reasoning or moral sentiment... Indeed, all emotional reasoning is evident in emotional sentiment, and it may appear to be dynamic rather than calm. However, it is not impulsive; it is a kind of emotion that maintains clarity and self-awareness.[43]

Rationality is indeed the moral conscience of a person, and its ethical significance will be discussed in detail later.

This is Liang's exposition on psychology, specifically the development of human psychology, which he intends to elucidate in detail. It serves as the foundation for a developmental history of psychology that he provides for Confucian thought. There are three main concepts in his psychological system: instincts, rationality, and selfless emotions. His entire theory aims to explain the natural historical process of human evolution and development, wherein humans progress from instincts to reason, and finally, to rationality. This development is seen as a fundamental aspect of human psychology in his philosophical framework. He says, "The emergence of humanity, which is synonymous with the appearance of the human mind, has its origins in biological evolution, but it is not merely an extension or amplification of animal instincts... From the perspective of the history of biological evolution, it was simply a matter of following the path of rationality. Through cumulative changes, it eventually led to a qualitative transformation, resulting in the emergence of the virtue of rationality. Indeed, it is in this aspect that humans are distinguished from other beings. In the secular world, people often only see the superiority of human reason and consider it to be the defining characteristic of humanity. However, they fail to recognize that rationality represents the essence, while reason is the application. The essence is the fundamental aspect, while the application is secondary. Therefore, it may not be accurate to consider rationality alone as the defining characteristic of humanity; rationality plays an equally significant role."[44] Comparing this with the previous statement, one can interpret it as follows: in Liang's thought, fundamentally speaking, the quietude of the mind and self-awareness are not the most fundamental characteristics of humanity; rather, rationality is the most fundamental characteristic of humanity.[45]

V. Life's Inherent Nature and Cosmic Life

According to Liang's perspective, in the long river of history, the emergence of reason and rationality was closely connected to what he refers to as life's inherent nature. In his discourse on the human psychological development from instincts to rationality, he continuously emphasizes the dominant role of life's inherent nature in this process. Life's inherent nature is a philosophical concept, and in his discourse, it has completely shed any semblance of psychological interpretation.

Life's inherent nature is primarily characterized by initiative. He says, "Mind is synonymous with life, and it is not wrong to say that everything that contains life has a mind. The consistent, unchanging aspect that is evident throughout is the initiative found in the human mind."[46] This initiative is inherent in life itself, and its source lies in life. Therefore, it can be said that "initiative is not something separate from life; it is the dynamic, vital, powerful aspect of life itself."[47] This initiative, as manifested in humans, he also refers to as a self-aware initiative.

In his view, being proactive implies constantly progressing and moving forward. He observes, "All living beings' lives are characterized by continuous growth, with each present moment following the next; every single present moment possesses initiative. This proactive aspect of the human mind is even more apparent in its development and expansion. It is evident in the efforts, struggles, and applications made by humans, where each subsequent effort builds upon the previous one, continuously creating something new and unceasing... Starting anew and continuously starting anew, it is precisely what is meant by new and unceasing in this context."[48] He emphasizes that "Life's inherent nature can be described as an endless upward striving, continuously renewing itself without knowing the reason behind it. It permeates the entire history of biological evolution for countless millions of years, right up until the emergence of humans. Furthermore, it continues throughout the history of human social development up until the present day, and it will continue to develop and strive forward, continuously renewing itself."[49]

The characteristic of life's inherent nature lies in the pursuit of freedom. He writes, "The continuous innovation and evolution in the biological world are ample evidence that life's inherent nature is not confined to the two major issues of survival and reproduction. Life's inherent nature is an endless upward striving; it is about seeking to expand the vitality of life, seeking greater and greater flexibility, and striving for more and more freedom... Only humans represent this inherent nature of life."[50] Freedom is the liberation from the limitations of the two major life issues, and this attainment of freedom is rooted in the demands of life's inherent nature. He points out that the development of reason initially serves as an alternative path in seeking solutions to the two major life issues, but during its development, it unexpectedly goes beyond the scope of these two major issues. He says, "Is it not that life's inherent nature is relentlessly seeking greater flexibility and freedom, and that it cannot be contained? Not only is the development of reason a result of life's inherent nature, but also the manifestation of rationality in human behavior is due to the expression of life's inherent nature."[51]

According to Liang's thought, "The nature of life exists in all things but is concealed within the instinctive activities of animals. Reason and rationality are liberated from instinct, and the essence of life (that is, the nature of life) is revealed, no longer obscured."[52] The nature of life is liberated from the concealment of instinct, and this is truly realized only in humans.

In Liang's thought, the nature of life is not confined to individual organisms or humans alone, but is interconnected with the universal life of the cosmos. He says:

> The nature of cosmic life, which strives for freedom, seeks initiative, and constantly progresses upward, is now only visible in humans. Those who say doing for no particular purpose imply that, besides striving for freedom and seeking initiative, there is also another aspect of action.[53]

It can be seen that striving for freedom and progressing upward is not only the nature of human life but also the nature of cosmic life. Universal life is indeed a philosophical concept related to ontology. In fact, at the beginning of the book, he writes, "My book discusses the human mind, starting from knowledge and leading to super-knowledge and anti-knowledge, namely from science to metaphysics, and from the human mind that influences practical life to a universal ontology. This is a preview for the readers."[54] The concept of the nature of universal life and Liang's preference for using the concept of universal life both fall within the realm of universal ontology.

The term universal life refers to the idea that the entire universe's life is interconnected as one entity. He states, "In the world of living beings, there are countless variations and forms, but they all originate from one source. Indeed, it seems that while individual lives may appear separate, they are inseparable in essence. When referring to the universal life, it means that life permeates throughout the entire universe, forming one interconnected entity."[55] Each individual entity possesses its own life, while the life of all things, in reality, forms an inseparable, interconnected, and interrelated totality, which is known as the universal life of the cosmos. Indeed, the concept of the nature of life is not only evident in humans but also represents the essence of the universal life. This is the essence of universal ontology. In this context, one can observe traces of his early influence of Bergsonian philosophy.

According to Liang's view, the essence of life is obscured within the instinctive activities of animals, which means that life is separated from the universal life of the cosmos in these instinctive activities. He says, "Life has evolved to this point, and humans are fundamentally different from all existing species. Existing species are trapped in instinctive living, and their entire life becomes a means and a mechanical tool for addressing two major issues. In doing so, they lose their essential nature of life and inevitably become separated from the universal life of the cosmos. Only humans, on the other hand, inherit the situation of biological evolution but are not confined to the two major issues. They continue to promote the essence of life and have been advancing steadfastly, standing proudly as the pinnacle of the universal life of the cosmos."[56] Eliminating separation from the universal life of the cosmos leads to achieving harmony and communion with the universal life.

Universal life itself is interconnected as one entity, and the nature of universal life also seeks this interconnectedness. Therefore, it is crucial for each category and each individual to recognize the unity of all things and manifest the essence of life that seeks interconnectedness. Liang says:

> To understand life, one must first recognize its unbounded nature... The essence of life seeks connection, not separation, and in reality, everything is inherently interconnected as one whole, not divided into two. Our life is directly connected with the universe, and both space and time are infinite. The ancient concept of the unity of all things in heaven and earth originates from their intimate understanding and direct experience of this interconnectedness.[57]

The life of all things in the universe is originally interconnected as one, but due to the limitations imposed by their nature and physical bodies, their inherent nature of seeking interconnectedness cannot manifest fully. They become isolated and unable to express this interconnectedness, which is the state of separation. Only the human spirit can transcend the limitations of instinctive mechanisms and fully embody the essence of life. Therefore, Liang says:

> All living beings rely on their physical bodies for existence, but existing species adhere to fixed patterns of life tied to their bodies. As a result, their life appears to be isolated and confined within these patterns, with only a rare few being able to breathe in harmony with the vast universe. Humans, on the other hand, are different. While their bodies serve as the means of living, they are like a house with open doors and windows, allowing

> air to flow freely without hindrance between heaven and earth. Although humans may not always realize the vastness and interconnectedness that surrounds them, and they sometimes get entangled in intricate details without knowing how to break free, their nature remains open and unrestricted, never imprisoned. Selfless emotions, when expressed, reveal the greatness of life's interconnectedness, where there are no barriers or separations.[58]

In terms of manifesting the essence of life, reason and rationality play different roles. The point of interconnectedness is to avoid dividing things into separate boundaries and instead see them as one interconnected entity. Indeed, the function of reason often involves division. Liang says, "From their adeptness at dividing through reason, people tend to separate themselves spatially and temporally, viewing everything as if it is irrelevant to them."[59] Rationality and reason are different, and rationality can intimately perceive the unity of all things.

From the above analysis, it can be seen that the main points of Liang's notions of the nature of life and universal ontology are two-fold. The first point is to strive for progress. He says, "Our consciousness is always engaged in external activities based on the needs of life, constantly calculating gains and losses. However, at the same time, our internal self-awareness lies in pure, vivid perception, with no intention of action. At times, we may act in accordance with our inner self-awareness, disregarding gains and losses and letting our hearts govern our actions. During these moments, even in our interactions with others, we do not calculate personal gains. This unbounded, unrestricted state of mind, which is not limited or separated from universal life, can be rightly called conscience or innate goodness. It is a manifestation of the upward progress of universal life, and the human heart is the greatest revelation of the essence of life precisely because of this."[60] Its manifestation in the human heart should be reflected in the realm of rational will, and its striving upward means that it is continuously seeking freedom.

The second point is interconnectedness as one entity. Interconnectedness has two meanings for humans. First, it refers to being in unity with others, signifying the connection between individuals and others, and all things. Since rationality primarily pertains to the emotional aspect, interconnectedness represents the emotional aspect of rationality. This is distinct from the emphasis on willpower in striving for progress. Liang says, "Between individuals, when viewed from the perspective of the physical body, there may be divisions and separations, but when viewed from the heart, even if there are divisions, there are no separations... Human life is inherently in unity with all things, and its emotions can reach every aspect of existence. In every place where pain and discomfort are felt, it is experienced as a part of oneself; there is no need to limit it to the mere physical body. It is precisely because of the unbounded nature of the human heart that pain, itchiness, likes, and dislikes are shared, related, and interconnected."[61] Indeed, this idea is fully consistent with the Confucian teachings of the Song and Ming dynasties, which emphasize the unity of the benevolent person with all things in heaven and earth and the interconnectedness of all people and things, reflecting the ethical significance of interconnectedness in Confucian teaching.

Interconnectedness also refers to being in unity with the undifferentiated, which indicates the connection between the individual and the universal ontology. Liang says, "Yangming's poem praising innate knowledge says, 'No sound, no smell, only knowing the moment; this is the foundation of the universe, encompassing all things.' The foundation of the universe, as implied, refers to universal ontology. Universal ontology is undivided and limitless, while the human body possesses duality. The beauty lies in the crystal clear mind's ability to transcend duality and reach the limitless. The self-awareness of silence and inaction is the radiance it emits, where the one is all, and all is one—the universal ontology is this very essence. The function of the human heart is commonly visible, while its essence is invisible, and this essence is indeed the universal ontology. Although the human body may be limited, the human heart is boundless."[62] This represents the essence of interconnectedness in its ontological sense.

From the statement, "The one is all, and all is one—the universal ontology is this very essence," it can be inferred that Liang believed that the self-awareness of the human heart is the universal ontology. The essence of the human heart is the universal ontology, which constitutes a form of ontology. Indeed, this form of ontology considers the spirit and the essence of life as the universal ontology. It shares similarities with the ideas of Xiong Shili and Ma Yifu, who regarded the mind as the basis of ontology. One could say that Liang's perspective of the essence of life aligns quite closely with the modern School of Mind philosophy.

VI. "Human Nature Is Inherently Good" and "Human Nature Is Inherently Clear and Bright"

The concepts of universal ontology and the essence of life in Liang's thought have been discussed. It is useful here to examine his views on human nature. In his preface, he mentions that the volume is a treatise on human nature, and although the main framework of the book *Human Nature and Human Life* revolves around the analysis of instinct, reason, and rationality, one can also understand his thoughts on human psychology from the perspective of human nature.

In broad terms, human nature is what distinguishes humans from other animals and is common to all humans; it is the characteristic of humanity. Indeed, there are many characteristics that define humanity. In the context of human nature, Liang refers to the psychological inclinations or tendencies of human beings. But psychological inclinations are not singular. The term psychological inclinations includes aspects such as logical reasoning with analogous metaphors in thought, finding beauty in certain colors, and developing preferences for particular tastes. It also encompasses the shared experiences and emotions that individuals may have in common.

Liang affirms that humans have a common human nature, which cannot be obscured by class distinctions. His reasoning is based on the premise that "living beings with similar physical bodies must possess similar functions, and when it comes to humans, the correlation between body and mind is inseparable. Indeed, even among people from different eras, races, and classes, if their physical aspects share basic similarities, it is reasonable to expect that they would also share fundamental psychological inclinations."[63] This argument is based on the premise that if humans have a similar physical body, then they must also share basic similarities in their psychological foundation, psychological functions, psychological qualities, and psychological inclinations. Liang's definition of human nature is: "By emotion, I refer to human emotions and will; and the inherent inclinations or tendencies that emotions and will always possess, I call them nature."[64]

The specific aspects of his understanding of what human nature encompasses include:

> Human nature is not as passive and inert as blank paper. If we compare it to the fierceness of a tiger, the timidity of a mouse, or the stupidity of a pig, I would still say that human nature is inherently good. Or, in other words, one could say that the nature of humans is clear and bright, and there is nothing that cannot be achieved.[65]

Liang opposes the idea that human nature is merely like blank paper, because if human nature were only like blank paper, it would be entirely passive and without any capacity for action or influence. Liang advocates the view that human nature is inherently good, but he does so in the context of comparing it to the fierceness of a tiger, the timidity of a mouse, or the stupidity of a pig. It is only through comparisons with other animals that we may understand human nature.

Liang attached great importance to the influence of nurture and environment on human nature. He believed that human nature is shaped by the influences of nurture and environment. The term nurture here does not only refer to the period after an individual's birth, but also includes the continuous development of physical constitution, temperament, and intelligence throughout the evolutionary process since the divergence of humans and apes. He believed that there are three levels of human nature that are influenced by nurture, and at each level, the impact of nurture is different.

The first level refers to the traits that human beings have acquired through millions of years of evolution. This character has become a common trait of all human beings, regardless of their geographic location, and is characterized by self-awareness and agency. Liang refers to this first level of human nature as the fundamental human character.

The second level is characterized as influenced and shaped by the lives of people from different times, places, and diverse groups. This level refers to the cultural and ethnic aspects of human nature, which are molded and influenced by the interactions and experiences with various cultures and societies throughout different periods and locations. People from different ethnic and cultural backgrounds may have slightly different ethnic characteristics. Liang refers to this second level as the second human character or the second level of human nature.

The third level is built upon the foundation of the first and second levels of human nature. It is influenced by the social environment and is more susceptible to change. In comparison, the second level of human nature, although also influenced by nurture, is relatively more resistant to change. The third level of human nature is relatively shallow and more easily influenced and changed. Liang considers class character to fall within this third level, indicating that it refers to the social aspects of human nature.

These three levels of character all constitute the connotation of human nature. However, Liang did not explicitly state that human nature is the combination of these three character levels. It is evident that the three levels of character in human nature are acquired through nurture, but he considers whether there is anything innate in the human heart. He states, "So, is there no such thing as the innate? This is also not the case. The innate refers to the essence of universal life or the universal ontology."[66] He affirms that human nature consists of the three levels of character shaped by nurture, but he also acknowledges the existence of an innate aspect in human nature, which is the essence of life and universal ontology.

From the previous discussion, it becomes evident that Liang did not support the idea of human nature as a blank slate. Indeed, if universal life is manifested in human life, and if universal ontology is synonymous with the essence of life, which is characterized by upward progress and interconnectedness without separation, then it follows that the psychological inclinations of humans cannot be detached from these principles. If we consider human life the highest expression of universal life and view rationality as the embodiment and manifestation of the essence of life, then human nature is inevitably intertwined with rationality and self-awareness, which are closely connected to the essence of life.

On the other hand, since real human nature encompasses the three levels of character discussed earlier, it is evident that human nature is not a blank slate. Why is human nature considered good then? In fact, the first level of character is not acquired from external influences during the evolutionary process. Instead, it is an expression of human life overcoming the limitations of the organism in the course of evolution. It is distinct from the second and third levels of character, which are subject to change. The first level of character progresses only forward and does not regress, making it an essential characteristic of human nature. Liang states:

> As for human nature, it refers to the tendency of human emotions. How this tendency unfolds is not necessarily fixed, but rather more likely to occur in certain ways or to a greater extent. In fact, human beings can also possess evil, which often arises from self-imposed limitations and barriers that hinder understanding. Those who understand and empathize with others perceive a shared connection, while those who isolate themselves view emotions as separate and confined. Affirming that evil arises from isolation and goodness stems from empathy, it is evident that the inherent nature of universal life, represented by humanity, is continually evolving toward connectivity and progress. Given this clear observation, what reason is there to doubt the theory of inherent human goodness?[67]

If human nature is merely a reflection of life's inherent nature, then it is indeed a fixed characteristic and cannot be described as being more likely to occur in certain ways or to a greater extent. For Liang, human nature is a comprehensive reality, comprising a combination of life's inherent nature and the first, second, and third levels. While life's inherent nature plays a dominant role, it interacts with other factors, resulting in human behavior being manifested as tendencies and greater possibilities. However, life's inherent nature is ultimately dominant. In this sense, the concepts of striving upward and unity undoubtedly belong to the realm of goodness. He goes on to say:

> As mentioned earlier, human nature is inherently clear and bright. This means that humans are liberated from being purely driven by instincts, and their inclinations are not fixed like those of other animals. Instead, they are like blank white paper, easily influenced and shaped. However, this adaptability is not a passive characteristic; it is a result of their rich, transformative life, allowing them to actively respond and adapt to their living environment... The premise of human nature being inherently good and clear lies in the conscious activities of the human heart and mind.[68]

In saying that human nature is inherently good, it corresponds to the rationality of the human heart. And when we say human nature is clear and bright, it corresponds to the reason of the human mind. Clear and bright refers to the reason unrestricted by limited relationships, and thus its potential relationships are boundless and immeasurable. It can focus on this or that, without being confined by finite connections. Interest can arise in anything precisely because the potential exists for not having a fixed interest in anything, and even some interests may not develop. Those who lack interest are said to possess a mind capable of quietude. Precisely because of this quietude, they are able to act. The difference between human reason and that of animals lies in the fact that human activities have already surpassed the direct constraints of survival, while animals are constantly confined to the issue of survival. Human reason can take an interest in any issue beyond survival and be influenced by these matters. Human goodness refers to the rational aspect of human nature, while human clarity refers to the intellectual aspect of human nature, and human self-awareness encompasses both of these qualities.

In *Eastern and Western Cultures and Their Philosophies,* Liang uses Peter Kropotkin's dichotomy of human psychology, which divides it into two parts, instinct and reason, to explain the psychological theory of Confucianism, and he considers moral sense as a social instinct, believing that it follows from the social instincts of animals. During this period, Liang emphasized that instincts and their corresponding emotional impulses are the sources of human behavior.[69] He attributed the moral sense to instincts as well. Later, after years of careful observation, contemplation, and self-reflection, he finally realized the inadequacy of the two-part division of instincts and reason. Instead, he embraced Bertrand Russell's three-part division, which includes instincts, reason, and spirituality in harmonious balance. The term spirituality, according to Russell, centers around selfless emotions and serves as the source of religion and morality within society. Liang believed that spirituality had a sense of mystery,[70] so he chose to express it using the term rationality while incorporating significant developments from Chinese culture into the concept. Here, he places the moral sense within the realm of rationality. It is evident that regardless of the changes in the structure of his psychological philosophy, the moral sense and its corresponding categories always maintain a dominant position.

From the perspective of Liang's ideas about human nature, his purpose is to provide a psychological foundation for Confucian moral and ethical thought. His system of psychology, in fact, is more of a philosophy as a whole, distinct from the scientific sense of psychology. This psychological theory's basic thread is derived from some reflections on psychology in modern Western philosophy, and concepts like instinct, reason, and rationality are all ideas from modern Western philosophy and psychology. From these ideas, Liang developed the basic concepts and theoretical structure of his philosophical psychology. His ontological concept of the cosmic life force also draws inspiration from the school of Henri Bergson, a figure in Western modern philosophy. Indeed, from his early work on human nature and human life to his later completion of the text *Human Nature and Human Life*, there are several aspects related to ancient Chinese philosophy (including Buddhism), including discussions on the mastery of the heart, the essence and function of the heart, and the dynamics of the heart which clearly have connections to ancient Chinese philosophy. This interaction with ancient Chinese thought in his ideas can sometimes lead to confusion and conflation of his thoughts with ancient philosophy if not carefully distinguished. For example, if one interprets Liang's theory of human nature using the categories of ancient Chinese philosophy, it can lead to the impression that instinct corresponds to emotions, reason to heart, and rationality corresponds to nature. The three-part division of instinct, reason, and rationality can be likened to the three-part division of heart-mind, nature, and emotions in Neo-Confucianism. The statement, "The body of rationality is the essence of the heart, and the function of reason is the use of the heart" can be seen as being akin to the Neo-Confucian idea of the relationship between essence, function, and heart-mind. According to this interpretation, his ideas indeed bear resemblance to the heart-mind theory of Song-Ming Neo-Confucianism, though such an interpretation might not necessarily align with Liang's actual thoughts. The most evident difference is that when Liang talks about rationality, it is not the same as the unrevealed nature discussed in Song-Ming Neo-Confucianism, but rather the already manifested aspect, a psychological category related to emotions and sentiments. When Liang refers to rationality as the essence of the heart, he is not talking about an internal, profound, unrevealed essence, but rather the aspect that governs and dominates the mind.

Liang claimed that his theory of human nature is a scientific psychology, but in reality, it remains a form of spiritual philosophy that incorporates elements from physiology, psychology, and scientific theories. Its purpose is to provide historical and psychological support for Confucian ethics. In this sense, its function aligns with the heart-mind theory of Song-Ming Neo-Confucianism. In his system, there are several unclear, contradictory aspects that remain unresolved. The most significant tension lies between rationality and reason. According to Liang, reason must eliminate emotions to fulfill its purpose, while rationality operates in the opposite manner. Rationality cannot be separated from emotions. Indeed, given this perspective, how rationality and reason can coexist is a valid question. While Liang himself may not perceive any conflict between the two, the issue remains present in his system. Furthermore, when he refers to reason, he is actually referring to cognitive rationality, while what he calls rationality pertains to moral sentiment. He suggests that the human heart has moral sentiments as its essence and uses cognitive rationality as its function, emphasizing the role of passionate emotions. This viewpoint, as a Confucian assertion, forms a distinctive doctrine, but whether it reflects an accurate representation of human psychological development remains uncertain. This relates to his fundamental methodological assumption: to prove the rationality of an ideal, one must demonstrate its accordance with reality. He stated that his work *Human Nature and Human Life* is divided into two parts: the first part deals with psychology, where he points out the factual aspects of human nature, and the second part focuses on ethics, using the facts about human nature to clarify what is morally appropriate in life. These expressions fully reflect his idea that "an ideal must conform to reality" and "once you understand what the human heart is like, you will know how to navigate the path of life."[71] In reality, all ideals serve as guiding principles for reality rather than mere confirmation of existing facts. Liang's departure from Confucian ideals is not problematic per se, but his attempt to use the history of human psychological development as the factual basis for Confucian ethics leads him to inadvertently emphasize a particular aspect of reality, portraying moral sentiments as the core of human nature, and blurring the distinction between what is and what should be. His belief in proving ideals through reality was a guiding principle throughout his life. While it supported him in completing his work on psychology in his later years, the actual value of the psychological part may not be particularly high. His more significant contributions perhaps lie in the ethical aspect. However, a detailed discussion on this topic would require a separate chapter.

Notes

1. He Lin, *Contemporary Chinese Philosophy* (Zongqing Publishing Company, 1978), 12.
2. *Complete Works of Liang Shuming*, vol. 3, 758.
3. In 1958, Liang stated, "The year I turned sixty, I told the chairman, Perhaps I'll live another ten years. In that period, the one thing I must do is write the book *Human Nature and Human Life*, which I've wanted to write for decades but have not yet done." See *Complete Works of Liang Shuming*, vol. 7, 55. In 1965, he remarked, "*Human Nature and Human Life* must be written. For forty years, not a day has passed that I haven't thought about it. I've begun writing it and hope to complete about a third of it this year." (ibid, p. 137)
4. Liang said, "Before *Eastern and Western Cultures and Their Philosophies* was completed, I was very enthusiastic, completely unaware of its shortcomings. After the book was published, I felt an emptiness inside me, and gradually the problems became more apparent. I regretted the hasty publication and even halted its printing for a period. Later, when it was reprinted, I added a preface declaring that the book's indiscriminate use of contemporary psychology to interpret Confucianism was erroneous. During the academic year of 1923-24, I taught Confucian Philosophy at Peking University, aiming to correct the mistakes in the original book, but that remained in oral, not written, form. The seventh chapter of *Essence of Chinese Culture*, published in 1949, roughly represents my later understanding, but it lacks detail. Now, in this section, I will recount my latest understanding of human nature." See Chapter Seven, Section Two of *Human Nature and Human Life, Complete Works of Liang Shuming*, vol. 3, 598–599.

5. "Eastern and Western Cultures and Their Philosophies," in *Complete Works of Liang Shuming*, vol., 1, 324, "Preface to the Eighth Edition."
6. "Human Nature and Human Life," in *Complete Works of Liang Shuming*, vol. 1, 326–327, "Preface."
7. *Complete Works of Liang Shuming*, vol. 3, 527.
8. Ibid., 540.
9. Ibid., 536.
10. Ibid., 528.
11. Ibid., 539.
12. Ibid., 539.
13. Ibid., 558.
14. Ibid., 561.
15. Ibid.
16. Ibid., 562.
17. Ibid., 563.
18. Ibid., 562–565.
19. Ibid., 565.
20. Ibid., 568.
21. Ibid., 568.
22. Ibid., 570.
23. Ibid., 610–613.
24. Ibid., 559.
25. Ibid., 560.
26. Ibid., 568.
27. Ibid., 569.
28. Ibid., 570.
29. Ibid., 575.
30. Ibid., 577.
31. Ibid., 576.
32. Ibid.
33. Ibid., 577.
34. Ibid., 582.
35. Ibid., 578–579.
36. *Essence of Chinese Culture*, 125.
37. *Complete Works of Liang Shuming*, vol. 3, 580.
38. Ibid., 581.
39. Ibid., 125.
40. Ibid., 600. A character is missing from the original. It has been replaced here for clarity.
41. Ibid., 600.
42. The concept of the heart seeking truth and goodness is found in *Essence of Chinese Culture*, Chapter 7, in *Complete Works of Liang Shuming*, vol. 3, 125.
43. *Complete Works of Liang Shuming*, vol. 3, 603.
44. Ibid., 606.

45. *Essence of Chinese Culture* states, "The general characteristic of humanity is reason. This is true, but I want to add that the general characteristic of humanity is rationality." (Ibid, 123.)
46. *Complete Works of Liang Shuming*, vol. 3, 540.
47. Ibid., 543.
48. Ibid., 542–543.
49. Ibid., 544.
50. Ibid., 569.
51. Ibid., 606.
52. Ibid., 528, 606.
53. Ibid., 605.
54. Ibid., 539.
55. Ibid., 571.
56. Ibid., 570.
57. Ibid., 572.
58. Ibid., 605.
59. Ibid., 573.
60. Ibid., 640.
61. Ibid., 604.
62. Ibid., 656.
63. Ibid., 534.
64. Ibid., 659.
65. Ibid., 536.
66. Ibid., 660.
67. *Complete Works of Liang Shuming*, vol. 6, 661.
68. *Complete Works of Liang Shuming*, vol. 3, 661.
69. Ibid., 590–595.
70. Ibid., 599–603.
71. Ibid., 529, 678.

CHAPTER 9

Liang Shuming's Views on Confucian Ethics

In the conclusion of my paper discussing Liang Shuming's later work *Human Nature and Human Life* (1975), Chapter Eight of this book, I stated, "His belief in proving ideals through reality was a guiding principle throughout his life. While it supported him in completing his work on psychology in his later years, the actual value of the psychological part may not be particularly high. His more significant contributions perhaps lie in the ethical aspect."[1] This chapter presents a narrative and discussion of his ethical ideas, observing the response of Confucian tradition to modern ethical concerns. It concludes by briefly discussing his ethical philosophy that prioritizes the Other.

I

After the section on the theory of human nature in *Human Nature and Human Life*, Liang transitions into what he refers to as a theory of human life. In his theory of human life, he continues to adhere to the Three Fundamental Issues of Human Life that he proposed earlier in his career: (1) the question of humans' relationship with the external world, (2) the question of humans' relationship with each other, and (3) the question of humans' relationship with their own lives. He stated, "The idea of these three fundamental issues of human life was conceived by me over fifty years ago as a fundamental concept in the theoretical framework of my earlier work *Eastern and Western Cultures and Their Philosophies*. From today's perspective, I see that there are many errors in this book, and what can be retained from it is quite minimal. However, this fundamental concept remains a difficult, enduring theory. Hence, in the subsequent work, *The Final Awakening of the Chinese National Self-Salvation Movement*, there is further elaboration, and the writing in this later work is more appropriate and clearer than in the initial one."[2] Liang here indicates the developmental thread of his ideas regarding the three fundamental issues of human life, though he does not provide a detailed explanation at this point.

He then points out the moral practice of human life, saying, "Human life has both an individual aspect and a collective aspect, and the practice of life must be discussed separately. The previous chapter mainly focused on the individual aspect, discussing the true essence of morality as conscious self-improvement, aligning one's actions with one's heart. This chapter will elaborate on the moral principles within human collective (social) life, emphasizing the importance of fulfilling ethical relationships, which can be encompassed by the term fulfilling relationships."[3] Liang's idea implies that morality pertains to the conscious self-improvement and elevation of the individual's heart, while ethics pertains to fulfilling one's obligations in human relationships and social responsibilities. In other words, this perspective considers morality as a subjective inner state and ethics as objective human relationships. This understanding closely aligns with Hegel's views on morality and ethics.[4]

Regarding ethics, Liang says in Chapter Eighteen of *Human Nature and Human Life*:

> Due to their developed reason, humans possess a special richness in emotions (a realm beyond that of animals). Emotions primarily arise in the interplay among people (although humans also share emotional connections with the cosmos and all things). The term ethical relationships refers precisely to this interplay of emotions among individuals. Ethical refers to the pairing of individuals who are related to each other in life, whether through prolonged companionship or momentary encounters. In this interconnected life, the mutual affection between individuals is what constitutes ethics. How does this work? It is through caring for one another. To further clarify, it means that one should regard each other as important, value the other person as much as oneself, and not neglect the other while solely focusing on oneself.[5]

Liang's introduction of emotion into the discussion of ethics is noteworthy. Here, emotion does not refer to simple feelings like joy, anger, sorrow, or desire for romantic love. Instead, it pertains to a caring, affectionate sentiment between individuals, similar to the warmth found among family members. For Liang, in essence, ethics refers to the relationship between two parties, where ethics represents the two sides of interpersonal relationships, and rationality signifies the mutual emotional resonance and reasoning between these two sides. It is evident that his concept of ethics aligns with Mencius' idea of human relationships, and his notion of rationality is consistent with intrinsic reasoning rather than an externally imposed rule. He emphasizes positive moral emotions between individuals as the foundation and principle of ethical relationships. If this kind of affection or ethics were to be expressed as a concept, it would be encapsulated in the idea of valuing the other person as important. It should be noted that the notion of valuing the other person as important represents Liang's sociological observation of Chinese culture, and it serves as a principled demand that transcends all relative social-ethical relationships. However, this does not mean that valuing the other person as important necessitates a reciprocal expectation for the other person to also prioritize oneself. Therefore, in the context of an ideal society, the expectation is for each relative ethical relationship (such as parent-child, husband-wife, etc.) to embody the principle of valuing one another as important; on an individual level, the ethical principle is simply to value the other person as important.

Starting from the distinction between the physical and the mental aspects, Liang believed that valuing the other person as important arises from a person's heart or inner being. If one starts from the physical aspect, they will be concerned primarily with themselves. Only those who possess a mindset of keeping others in mind can transcend the limitations of self and truly hold others in their hearts. Taking it a step further, individuals who keep others in mind not only hold others in their hearts, but to a considerable extent, they may even forget themselves for the sake of the other person. He states, "Isn't it often the case with mothers and their infants? All these various considerations, big or small, that take into account the feelings of the other party, are collectively referred to as ethical relationships. Affection can also be referred to as an emotional bond, with the bond representing obligation. When individuals fulfill their various ethical obligations within society, they make significant contributions to the community."[6] This is what constitutes morality. This mind-body perspective can be seen as an inheritance of Mencius' ideology, and his concept of the heart undoubtedly goes beyond the realm of the mere sensual self in moral consciousness. He regards ethics as a state of mind, which aligns with the teachings of traditional Neo-Confucianism.

II

Based on the outline provided by Liang, it is possible to trace the development and evolution of his ethical viewpoint. As early as the early 1920s, in his work *Eastern and Western Cultures and Their Philosophies,* he had already demonstrated his emphasis on moral emotions. He stated that filial piety and sibling respect are truly the only important points advocated by Confucianism. This was his main point; he simply wanted people to lead a life rich in emotions. Naturally, he wanted people to start from the place where emotions originate.[7]

He further explains that Westerners have a sense of self, while the Chinese do not focus on the self. In the relationship between mother and son, the mother's emotion seems to exist for the son and not for herself. In the son's relationship with the mother, his emotions seem to exist for the mother and not for himself. Between siblings, friends, and companions, one can disregard oneself and willingly subordinate one's own interests to serve others. He does not distinguish the boundaries between the self and others, and he disregards notions of rights and obligations. The teachings of filial piety, sibling respect, and courteousness everywhere emphasize fostering emotions and selflessness.[8]

In his view, the Chinese approach to interpersonal relationships tends to mirror the way family relationships function, much like the relationships between mother and son, or between siblings. This attitude involves yielding oneself to accommodate others and prioritizing emotions without the self. He later incorporated this understanding of the Chinese cultural attitude and inclination in handling interpersonal relationships as the essence of ethics.

Indeed, in *Eastern and Western Cultures and Their Philosophies*, Liang did not explicitly emphasize the formulation of the Three Fundamental Issues of Human Life as he later did in *Human Nature and Human Life*, where he articulated the notions of humanity's relationship with the external world, humanity's relationship with each other, and humanity's relationship with their own lives. In his positive discussion of the three fundamental issues of human life in the third chapter, Liang emphasizes these issues as confronting a "satisfiable" material world, an "indefinitely satisfiable" subjective world, and an "absolutely unsatisfiable" world of causality,[9] or three directions of "striving forward," "maintaining harmony within," and "looking backward."[10] However, in the later part of this book, he addresses this matter, saying:

> The initial problem of humanity is the pursuit of survival... all aspects of clothing, food, shelter, and various material needs must be obtained from the natural world. Therefore, at this stage, the attitude should be one of striving forward. For humanity, the transition will occur from an era focused on the relationship with material things to an era focused on the relationship between individuals—the era of the second type of subjective issue mentioned earlier. The attitude of conquering nature cannot be applied to interactions between people.[11]

He does mention "the issue of humanity's relationship with material things" and "the issue of humanity's relationship with each other," but does not explicitly encompass the third issue as "the issue of humanity's relationship with oneself."

As Liang himself stated, it is in his book *The Final Awakening of the Chinese National Self-Salvation Movement* that he presents the three fundamental issues in a clearer, more appropriate manner. *The Final Awakening of the Chinese National Self-Salvation Movement*, published in 1933, contains his writings from 1930 to 1932. It is also referred to as *Essays on Village Governance*. The most significant piece in the volume is the titular essay. Liang later emphasized the significance of this book in his writings. Indeed, many of the important arguments found in his work *Essence of Chinese Culture* from the late 1940s had already taken shape in *The Final Awakening of the Chinese National Self-Salvation Movement*. This includes focusing on the social system structure and observing two major characteristics of China: the enduring, unchanging society and the near absence of religious life, among others.

In this article, he states:

> There are three distinct problems In human life and three distinct aspects in the attitudes held by people living their lives. Consequently, human culture undergoes three different phases: the first problem pertains to humanity's relationship with things, the second

problem involves humanity's relationship with people, and the third problem concerns humanity's relationship with oneself.[12]

The article, published in 1930, explicitly presents the three fundamental issues of *Eastern and Western Cultures and Their Philosophies* as humans' relationship with things, humans' relationship with people, and humans' relationship with themselves. In fact, his formulation of the three fundamental issues and the three directions implies a certain contradiction: if the three approaches, methods, or attitudes (a, b, c) for solving problems correspond to three distinct issues (A, B, C) rather than representing three different attitudes toward the same issue, then it would not be appropriate to abstractly classify any particular attitude as early or late, as we can only state that a culture's dominant inclination is shaped by the primary issues it faces. Alternatively, we can acknowledge that within a certain culture, an inappropriate attitude (such as b) was applied to solve a particular issue (such as A), which could be seen as a misuse of attitude b for solving problem A. In this context, the notion of early or late is not relevant.

III

Returning to the question of ethics, Liang proposes in this article that ethics pertains to the relationships between individuals in life (or more accurately, the attitudes toward these relationships). Therefore, ethical issues do not belong to the first fundamental problem of human life; instead, they fall under the category of the second issue. Resolving ethical issues, then, requires the second type of attitude toward life. It cannot be solely about moving forward, nor can it involve forceful conquest. Ethical relationships should ideally be based on the foundation of familial bonds. He further adds, "The second attitude involves frequently turning one's attention back to oneself, reflecting upon oneself, doing one's utmost within one's capabilities, and seeking harmony and understanding between oneself and the other party."[13] He goes on, "At this moment, all we can do is to reflect upon ourselves and do our utmost within our capabilities. The improvement of ethical relationships fundamentally depends on both parties doing their respective parts. However, this idea of doing one's part can only be proclaimed by a third party; the parties involved are only allowed to question themselves about whether they have fulfilled their obligations. This self-inquiry is the first step on an endless journey, which is why it is widely acknowledged that only self-criticism is allowed, not criticizing others."[14] It is evident that he firmly emphasizes using family and kinship as the prototype of ethics, with the attitude of individuals within the family forming the foundation of ethical principles. In the context of belonging to the second direction, he clearly believes that the attitude for solving ethical issues should involve reflecting upon oneself and doing one's utmost within one's capabilities, which means demanding from oneself rather than from others.

He concludes:

> Ethical relationships originate in the family and then extend to social and national life: the relationships between ruler and subject and between official and citizen can be likened to that of parents and children; relationships like employer and employee, master and apprentice, as well as friendships and peers in society, can be compared to that of siblings or parent and child. In ethics, each party has its own obligations to fulfill. Ethical relationships signify a sense of duty; it is as if an individual does not exist for themselves, but only for others.[15]

In fact, Liang's concept of ethical relationships largely refers to interpersonal relationships within a familial context. In this context, the idea of valuing the other person as important becomes quite evident. These ideas are reiterated in another of his later articles titled "The First Untranslatable Road in Our Politics."

Liang's important essays written between 1932 and 1936 were compiled into his third book titled *The Theory of Rural Construction*. In his "Outline of Rural Construction," written in 1933, he states:

> To clarify the importance of rural construction for the reconstruction of organizational structures and the establishment of new governance principles, it is necessary to first discuss the organizational structures of traditional Chinese society and its concept of governance. In the past, the West emphasized individual interaction with the church, and recently, individual interaction with the state. Especially in modern times, individualism has prevailed, leading to the formation of a society centered around the individual. However, as the shortcomings of this approach became apparent, there was an attempt to reverse course and transform it into a society centered around the community. In ancient China, society did not resemble either of these two models but was rather centered around ethics. Human life is inherently bound by relationships, which are the bonds of kinship, and life unfolds within the realm of interactions between individuals, which constitutes ethics. The feelings of warmth and connection arise from the bonds of kinship, and this extends to all kinds of relationships where natural emotions exist. Where there is emotional rapport, obligations naturally arise. Fathers should show kindness, sons should demonstrate filial piety, brothers should be friends, younger siblings should show respect, and even in the relationships of spouses and friends, as well as all other kinds of interactions, mutual obligations naturally emerge. Ethical relationships signify a sense of obligation where an individual's existence seems to revolve not around oneself but rather around existing for and with others. In contrast, in recent times, Westerners have often exhibited a self-centered attitude, where everything is seen from the perspective of individualism, and actions are often motivated by a focus on rights and entitlements.[16]

In the context of Liang Shuming, individualism refers to the fundamental attitude of using individual rights to address ethical issues, with its embodiment being the capitalist societies of

Europe and America since modern times. Social orientation refers to the fundamental attitude of using collectivism to address ethical issues, with its manifestation being the socialist society represented by the Soviet Union. On the other hand, ethical orientation represents the attitude of dealing with ethical issues in traditional Chinese society and culture. This attitude is based on the development of relationships within the hierarchy and the sense of obligation to exist for one another. He specifically points out that the individual orientation is expressed through the concept of rights, while the ethical orientation is entirely different, rooted in the concept of obligations.

In his practice of rural governance in North China, Liang gradually realized and incorporated the concept of respect to express this ethic of existing for one another. This was because, through social practice, he came to understand that the familial attitudes of kinship ethics cannot be directly applied to communities beyond the family. Community ethics must transform kinship into a more universally meaningful respect. This also reveals his attempt at a certain modern transformation of traditional ethics. In his essay "Interpretation of Village and Township Learning" in 1934, he explained that village and township learning refers to rural organizations. These organizations, on the one hand, fully embody the spirit of modern Western progressive groups, and on the other hand, they completely incorporate the two major characteristics of Chinese culture: ethical idealism and the aspiration for personal advancement. These two characteristics, as he later mentioned in *Human Nature and Human Life*, refer to ethical idealism and moral spirit. He states:

> The essence of ethical idealism is to respect the other person, as if one does not exist, which is precisely the opposite of the individual orientation that starts from oneself. The Western debate over individual and social orientations can be entirely resolved within the ethical orientation of Chinese people. Neither the concept of individual orientation nor of social orientation is effective. It should be that Party A respects Party B, and Party B respects Party A. It cannot be stated as, "You should respect me, and I don't respect you." Groups should respect individuals, and individuals should also respect groups. Our arrangement is exactly the opposite of the Western principle of checks and balances. This arrangement stems from ethical idealism.[17]

As a result, Liang summarized the previously mentioned Chinese ethical attitude as ethical idealism, and he attributed the essence of this ethical idealism to respecting the other person, as if one does not exist. He believed that the Western debate about individual or social orientation appeared one-sided from the perspective of Chinese ethical idealism, as both sides failed to emphasize the importance of respecting the other party. Following his ethical idealism, if all parties respect each other as if they don't exist themselves, mutual respect between the parties can be achieved. At this point, he realized that ethical relationships encompass more than just the interpersonal dynamics of the traditional Five Relationships or the individual-to-individual relationships that extend beyond the family in modern society. Ethical relationships also encompass the interactions between individuals and groups. The stance and essence of ethical idealism lay in respecting the other party in all ethical relationships. This statement already encompasses the transformative creation of familial ethics.

Regarding this matter, in another article from 1934, he points out:

> Chinese ethics originate from interpersonal relationships and emotions. Therefore, it does not revolve around the self but rather places emphasis on the other person. If one were to center themselves, it would contradict the essence of ethics. When ethics prioritize the other person, relationships between individuals can achieve a seamless, closely integrated state… In ancient China, there was the concept of the Five Relationships, and now we can add another: the relationship between groups and individuals, where mutual respect and mutual obligations are paramount.[18]

It is evident that from 1930 to 1934, the idea of summarizing the essence of the Chinese ethical spirit as prioritizing the other person and considering this spirit as the core of "ethics" gradually took shape in Liang's thought.

IV

The root of this Chinese ethical thought, in Liang's view, is the ethics advocated by Confucius. When he speaks of Chinese ethics or ethics, he is referring to Confucian ethics. However, his understanding of Confucian ethics is different from that of typical Confucian scholars, as well as from typical religious researchers. He does not summarize the discussions in the classics, but instead, he arrives at a modern interpretation based on his own experiences in Chinese social and cultural life, as well as observations of village governance practices. His approach is akin to that of sociologists and anthropologists, and this aspect is worth noting in terms of his perspective and methodology. This is also why he was able to write works of social science, such as *Essence of Chinese Culture*, which rival Weber's theory of Chinese religion in significance.[19] Liang's grasp of the spiritual essence of Confucian ethical culture and his emphasis on distinguishing between the Confucian ethical spirit and the modern Western ethical spirit provide a path that is rarely explored in contemporary moral philosophy or ethics. Instead, it is more closely associated with the realms of cultural philosophy and comparative culture. This is consistent with his early focus on Eastern and Western cultures and their philosophies.

In the book *The Final Awakening of China's National Self-Salvation Movement*, he points out:

> China's possession of ethics seems to be strongly attributed to Confucius, and this ethics has been the central backbone of the cultural and social system for thousands of years, undergoing little major change… If Chinese people are to experience contentment and happiness, as Russell mentioned, it is also solely through the bestowal of this ethics.[20]

> Because China has embraced the second attitude toward life, it no longer requires religion. In the absence of a major religion, what can provide solace and inspiration for the lives of the people in a society, and what can sustain and guide them? My answer is that what they rely on is the ideological, scholarly, and ritual system represented by Confucian thought, learning, and cultural practices, which correspond to the second attitude toward life.[21]
>
> Chinese people have deeply embraced the second attitude toward life, transcending regional differences and persisting for thousands of years without significant change. Intellectuals and talented individuals have all directed their pursuits and careers toward this path of learning and cultural practices, much like how in India, individuals delve into the third attitude toward life, dedicating their intelligence and abilities to religious pursuits. Confucius serves as the great guide, opening the door and illuminating the path, which subsequent generations have continued to follow without exhausting its wisdom and utility. As a result, once embarked on this path, one finds it difficult to deviate from it.[22]
>
> In both the nation and society, there is a strong emphasis on the family unit, and emotions and relationships are highly valued. Everything that China refers to as principles or rituals is essentially an expression of these emotions and relationships. In China, despite its vast geographical expanse, diverse regional customs, numerous dialects, and challenges in communication, the ability to maintain a unified culture is rooted in a shared, nurtured central spiritual core within the collective consciousness of the nation… In other societies, this central spiritual core would likely manifest as a major religion, but in China, it is centered around the ethical teachings advocated by Confucius.[23]

Liang held that the life attitude embodied in the concept of Chinese ethics was established and inspired by Confucius. Confucius's ideas play a decisive role in shaping this perspective, according to his perspective. The correct attitude to address the second question of life is the ethical attitude found in China, and the representative of the second attitude toward life is the thought and culture of Confucius and his school, which is also known as Confucianism. And the characteristic of Confucian thought is precisely the attitude of addressing ethical issues. He notes, "Confucius's teachings consistently point to self-examination and self-improvement, urging individuals to look inward and apply effort to their selves… Chinese people, through Confucius's teachings, have exhibited a remarkable distinction in society, making morality more prevalent than religion."[24]

Though they discuss ethics in general terms, Liang's theories actually refer to Confucian ethics, the ethical attitude of Confucianism towards human relationships. In other words, his discussions of ethical relationships, ethical principles, and ethical foundations are essentially referring to Confucian ethics. Therefore, the emphasis on prioritizing the other party should be seen as his unique understanding, development, interpretation, and expression of Confucian ethics.

This sort of expression of Confucian ethics belongs more to the appreciation and articulation of the spiritual essence of Confucian ethical culture, or a comparative approach to the similarities and differences between Eastern and Western ethics. It may not delve into a specific study of the virtues, principles, ideals, and norms of Confucian ethics, but this does not diminish the depth of its understanding. While this discourse certainly occurs within the framework of East-West cultural comparison, the understanding and development of Confucian ethics it presents do hold significant importance that cannot be overlooked.

V

In the same way that Liang discusses in *Eastern and Western Cultures and Their Philosophies* the Chinese attitude of yielding oneself to accommodate others when dealing with the traditional Five Relationships, he continued to use similar expressions in the 1930s to convey the spirit of Confucian ethics. For instance:

> Ethical relationships envelop the Chinese people, giving them a sense of having nowhere to escape within the realm of heaven and earth. How to navigate these various relationships well is indeed the primary concern of their lives... Self-accountability becomes a universally acknowledged and undeniable principle for the Chinese people, and yielding to others becomes a habitual practice in their daily lives... In ethics, an individual seems to exist not solely for themselves but as if they exist for others, thereby rejecting the prevailing self-centeredness that individuals often exhibit.[25]

Naturally, when observing actual social behavior, it is not that all Chinese people consistently embody self-accountability and yield to others. However, we need not question Liang on this point. In fact, the significance of his statement lies in the fact that regardless of whether Chinese people can consistently adhere to it in their actions, the general attitude is that they naturally consider self-accountability and yielding to others as fundamental principles. They do not ideologically or morally believe that asserting oneself is the right course of action. Indeed, it is precisely in this aspect that traditional Chinese ethics differs from modern Western self-centeredness.

Naturally, in Liang's view, in terms of actual behavior, compared to Westerners, Chinese people tend to exhibit more of an approach of yielding to others. In the 1936 work "The Problem of China's Social Structure," he emphasizes the characteristics of China's social structure and specifically discusses the comparison between China and the West. He states:

> The essence of ethics refers to a relationship of camaraderie and obligation, wherein individuals are required to respect, care for, and mutually assume responsibilities for one another. In essence, ethics implies sacrificing oneself for the sake of the other...

> Both parties must possess the spirit of self-sacrifice and consideration for each other, prioritizing the other party equally. Chinese people always prioritize others, while Westerners tend to prioritize themselves, placing the individual at the center of their considerations… Within the context of respecting and prioritizing others, there is an element of the spirit of yielding, while the Western emphasis on individualism and self-centeredness embodies a spirit of striving… In China, ethics originated from the significance of family life, where ethics originally referred to the relationships within the family. However, Chinese ethics extend beyond the family to encompass all relationships in society and imbue them with ethical values.[26]

Liang believed that the attitudes of the East and West toward interpersonal relationships are completely opposite. Westerners emphasize the self as primary, emphasizing a spirit of striving, while Chinese people prioritize others, emphasizing a spirit of yielding. While this comparison between Eastern and Western cultures has indeed continued since the New Culture Movement, Liang did not merely limit himself to simplistic comparisons. His discussions evolved in a more profound direction from the perspective of ethics, showcasing a deeper exploration than in his earlier works.

As mentioned earlier, the idea of summarizing the ethical spirit of Chinese culture as prioritizing others gradually took shape in Liang's thinking during the early to mid-1930s. Furthermore, concepts like considering rationality as a moral sentiment and asserting that the essence of the Chinese national spirit is human rationality were emphasized in his later work, *Essence of Chinese Culture*. These ideas also took shape and solidified his thinking during the early to mid-1930s, though they might not have been fully systematized at that time.

In his 1935 article "Where Lies the Distinctive Feature of Chinese Culture," Liang touched upon the core idea later presented in *Essence of Chinese Culture*. He highlighted that the distinctive feature of Chinese culture lies in the early development of human rationality.[27] He further elaborated on two aspects of this rationality's manifestation, noting that the first aspect is the ethical foundation. He writes, "In ancient Chinese society, the emphasis was neither on individualism nor on collectivism, but on an ethical foundation… The social relationships among Chinese people are ethical relationships, where individuals have emotional bonds and obligations within their interconnectedness, and they prioritize each other."[28] The second aspect is upward aspiration in life. Liang believed that Chinese people differ from Indians and Westerners. They neither embrace asceticism and view life as sinful, nor do they base their lives solely on desires and the pursuit of material happiness. Chinese people affirm life and actively pursue the rightness of life, striving for the rationality of life and embodying the spirit of upward aspiration.[29] While Liang does not explicitly define what upward aspiration in life means here, it is reasonable to assume that he is referring to the pursuit of a moral and ethical way of life. It can thus be said that during the early to mid-1930s, his practical experiences in rural reconstruction sparked a series of significant insights into China's social structure and ethics. These insights were later refined and culminated in his work *Essence of Chinese Culture* in the late 1940s. He himself has stated that

Essence of Chinese Culture is a continuation of his work on *Theory of Rural Reconstruction*, with the former expounding on and elaborating on the ancient characteristics of Chinese society as presented in the latter.[30] In fact, his theoretical work also carries a characteristic of constructing Chinese culture.

The ethical ideas that Liang developed in the early to mid-1930s, which is his modern interpretation of the Confucian ethical spirit, can be summarized as a form of ethics that is non-individualistic, non-self-centered, and not based on a rights-centric perspective. Liang succinctly encapsulated this ethical attitude as prioritizing others, which is quite evident. Now we must ask, why did he choose to use ethical foundation, instead of the more popular term family-centered, when referring to this attitude that he often emphasized as emerging from the significance of family life to generate ethics?

Regarding this matter, Liang himself provides a clear answer in *Essence of Chinese Culture*. He first emphasizes the practical significance of the family in Chinese social organization, acknowledging the high regard Chinese people have for family ethics. He highlights the importance of family life as a distinguishing factor between China and the West. At the same time, he states:

> However, is Chinese society consistently family-centered? No, it is not always the case… The term family-centered is inappropriate and insufficient to explain it. Only in a patrilineal society can it be called a family-based society, as explained by Edward Jenks in *A History of Politics*. China, however, has already transitioned away from a patriarchal society… At this juncture, it is necessary to use the term ethical foundation to elucidate the relationships within Chinese society and address the central issue. If one were to say family-centered, it would not only be narrow in scope but also biased toward one aspect.[31]

Liang believed that the ancient Chinese cultural concept of one world, one family, and brotherhood under the heavens surpassed the confines of a patriarchal or family-based society. He asserts, "If it were merely a family-centered, patriarchal system, how could it be compatible with China's vast spatial expansion and enduring longevity over time?"[32] Since Chinese culture is imbued with such expansive consciousness, it is inappropriate to label Chinese ethics as family-centered. The characteristic of Chinese culture is that "Chinese people extend and develop family relationships, organizing society through ethics."[33] In other words, Chinese society is structured using the ethics derived from family relationships. Therefore, "Ethics places primary emphasis on the family," and "ethics originates in the family, but extends beyond the family." In fact, Liang's mention of ethical relationships clearly refers to the relationships within clans and quasi-clans. His concept of an ethical society also refers to a society in which all social relationships are organized along familial lines,[34] treating and handling all interpersonal relationships as familial relationships.

Liang's understanding of Confucian ethics and Chinese culture is indeed insightful. However, in modern society, the traditional ethics that he describes as originating in the family and their modern interpretation may raise questions about their applicability to interpersonal relationships in a modern society primarily centered around industry and commerce. His cultural confidence in that era stems from his optimism about the prospects of socialism and his pessimism about the contradictions within capitalism. Certainly, while the global situation after the end of the Cold War has challenged the previous optimism toward planned socialism, it does not render ethical critiques of capitalism devoid of value. However, after the end of the Cold War, the rationalized market economy has been widely acknowledged as a fundamental element and framework of modernity. Alongside the market economy, modern ethical values have emerged, characterized by "Western individualism, wherein the individual is placed at the center and a spirit of competition prevails."[35] Therefore, when facing the reality of the converging development of modern market economies across both sides of the Taiwan Strait and in the broader region, we might wonder: if Liang Shuming were still alive today, and if his summarized Confucian ethical spirit were indeed accurate, how would he and this ethical spirit address their divergences with modernity? How would they confront the challenges posed by modernity? Would it still be necessary to shape a distinct form of modernity? Alternatively, how could a broader form of rationality be established to guide and constrain modernity?

VI

Because modern ethical values are often based on rights, it is helpful here to delve into Liang's analysis of rights and obligations.

In *The Final Awakening of the Chinese National Self-Salvation Movement*, after discussing the characteristics of Chinese ethics, such as introspection and doing one's best, Liang proposes:

> Everyone knows that democracy is the term used by Westerners to describe the struggles of the people oppressed by those in power. The concepts of equality and freedom arise from individuals' pursuits of their inherent rights and their unwillingness to compromise, resulting in a balance and mutual recognition that prevents encroachment upon one another. But how can one imagine that the life attitude cultivated through thousands of years of ethical living and the nurtured national character would suddenly adopt such concepts?[36]

This implies that the pursuit of individual nature and the struggle for individual rights are the fundamental life attitudes of Westerners, and the pursuit of other values, such as equality and freedom, is based on the quest for individual nature and the fight for individual rights. The Western emphasis on seeking individual rights is a response to the excessive oppression of individuals by medieval Western collectives, leading to resistance. Liang believed that the greatest distinction between China and the West lay in their differing attitudes toward the individual-centric approach, and this divergence was rooted in their respective historical and cultural backgrounds. He writes:

> In every aspect, we can observe that in the West, there appears to be an individual-centric perspective, placing oneself at the forefront, whereas in China, there seems to be a concept rooted in ethics, namely respect for others. This notion of respecting others implies that in mutual relationships, one party prioritizes the other... It's quite clear that an individual-centric perspective emphasizes rights, while an approach based on respecting others emphasizes obligations. Both of these perspectives likely have their own origins.[37]

He states in another essay, "What gives rise to the existence of the West before legal systems is its individualism and concept of rights. However, the greatest fact in China is ethics, where everything exists within ethical relationships, and its significance is primarily focused on non-individual and obligatory matters."[38] He continues, "From ethics, and among Chinese individuals, there is no natural emergence of the concept of relative opposition and equality of rights. Through the deduction of ethical relationships, between the Chinese government and its people, there is no formation of a situation with relative opposition."[39] He believed that the West's emphasis on self-centeredness led to the creation of oppressive, exploitative practices and institutions against others. On the other hand, Chinese interpersonal relations prioritize self-restraint and accommodation, with a focus on harmonization in their systems. As a result, "The concept of letting go became a significant aspect of the Chinese spirit, contrasting with the competitive spirit of striving that emerged from the West's first attitude."[40]

Liang points out that within the duality of individualism and the concept of rights, the concept of rights is based on individualism. Therefore, individualism is the fundamental aspect of the Western life attitude. (Liang's reference to the "West" pertains specifically to modern times and is not a generalization spanning all historical periods, but rather for convenience of expression.) He further states:

> The West is oriented around individualism, while China is rooted in an ethical standpoint. For instance, when Westerners host a gathering, they take the main seat while guests sit on either side, placing themselves at the center. In contrast, in any situation, Chinese people prioritize the importance of the other party. The Western concept of rights emanates from an individualistic perspective. It advocates for one's own share, and in discussions of local autonomy, each citizen has a rightful portion. China is a society rooted in ethics, starting from an obligation-based perspective. The concept of obligation binds individuals together in a continuous chain of connections. In China, if one were to approach things from a perspective of rights, it would lead to even greater disarray and constant disputes, without the concept of cohesion.[41]

Liang's statements are not merely historical descriptions of cultural differences between the East and the West. In fact, they imply his dissatisfaction with individualism and prioritizing rights, from the perspective of traditional Chinese Confucian values. Furthermore, in the context of the 1930s, Liang believed that the introduction of Western individualism and the subsequent emphasis on rights would lead to increased conflicts among Chinese people, preventing the formation of cohesive unity and undermining the stability and integration of the nation.

Liang believed that all ethics are based on a certain psychology, and therefore, any ethical orientation must be rooted in a particular psychological priority. Therefore, when connected with psychology, an individualistic perspective is linked to a focus on desires, where individuals only see themselves within their desires and overlook the presence of others. An ethics-centered perspective, on the other hand, is linked to a focus on interpersonal relationships, where individuals consider the other person within their emotions and may forget about themselves. He states:

> Though both desires and emotions are common to humans, they are conflicting and incompatible. From the familial bonds of kinship arises the notion of obligation—a notion that is not in opposition to the concept of rights. In the West, rights and obligations are treated in parallel. For instance, if you owe me money, you have an obligation to repay the debt, and I have the right to demand repayment. In China, the concept of obligation is based on one's own recognition rather than being forcefully demanded by others. It is a subjective understanding rather than an externally imposed requirement from others.[42]

It is evident that the term obligation used by Liang carries a specific meaning. His notion of obligation refers to an attitude within ethical relationships, rather than the conventional sense of obligation that is treated in opposition to rights. Instead, it leans more toward a sense of dedicated responsibility or commitment. His usage of terms like emotion, ethics, and obligation indeed holds specific meanings that require careful attention in our reading and understanding of his works. It is evident that although he did not delve deeply into ethical discussions, he did provide clear explanations within the framework of comparing Eastern and Western cultures regarding the differences between the rights-obligations ethical orientations. He expressed a distinct non-rights-oriented ethical stance in his writings.

Liang later made a clearer declaration of this point:

> The Chinese term for rights is a relatively recent import over the past fifty years, translated from the English word. Examining its original meaning, we see that it signifies legitimate and reasonable, which is consistent with our basic values. However, there is a fundamental difference, namely that it does not stem from the recognition of others or the general consensus of a third party, but rather, it is asserted by oneself. For example, children benefiting from the education and provision of their parents, who would argue that it is not appropriate? However, if children were to say to their parents, "This is my right. You should support me. You need to provide me with the expenses for my education," it would greatly go against the Chinese way of thinking. If parents were to say to their children, "I should support you as you grow up," or "I should provide you

> with expenses for your education," it would be more in line with the Chinese way of thinking. In other words, it is equally inappropriate for parents to assert their rights over their children... In summary, fulfilling one's own obligations comes first, while rights await recognition from the other party, rather than being self-asserted. This is the guiding principle of Chinese ethical society. And in fulfilling their respective obligations, rights naturally come into play, without omission or delay; the reality remains unchanged, while the spirit undergoes a transformation.[43]

In fact, Liang attached great importance to political rights and never generally opposed the concept of rights. Therefore, the reasonableness of his proposition lies in the perspective of Chinese culture. The demand for rights should not serve as the fundamental principle for all human social relations. Instead, it is more suitable for individual-state relations, rather than general interpersonal ethical relationships. In other words, rights should belong to the realm of political science rather than being a fundamental concept of ethics. Therefore, when it comes to the question of how Confucianism deals with rights, Liang endorsed the demands for political and social rights, as well as economic and property rights. However, in the context of general interpersonal relationships, it can be said that he opposed using individualism and a rights-based perspective as the fundamental attitude toward life. In essence, this can also be seen as a rejection of individualism and liberalism as the fundamental attitude and ethical principles of life. What Liang advocated is a Confucian attitude, which can be viewed as a modern Confucian perspective on the ethics of rights.

Liang's summarization of Confucian ethics as a prioritization of others that is neither individualistic nor rights-oriented holds valuable insights for discussions on global ethics. It signifies that a comprehensive understanding of ethical principles from various religious or cultural traditions does not necessarily have to be extracted solely from ancient scriptures, but can also be achieved through the synthesis and grasp of contemporary philosophers within these traditions.

Regarding the issue of human rights, Liang addressed it to some extent in his attention to the emphasis on people's rights and responsibilities in the constitutions of various European countries after the First World War. Initially, individuals hoped that the state would refrain from interference, but now they wish for it to take an active role. As a result, many countries' new constitutions (represented by the 1919 German Constitution) not only specify the passive rights of the people but also include provisions for active rights, such as the right to survival, the right to work, and the right to education. Another shift is the resurgence of social-centered thinking, where the state adopts an interventionist approach and emphasizes the obligations of the people. Thus, new constitutions also add provisions stating that the appropriate use of property is an obligation of the people, as is receiving an education and engaging in work. Even activities like participating in elections and voting become obligations of the people, which the state may enforce. These two shifts clearly stem from a common trend, namely the increasing significance of the nation-state as an entity.[44]

It is evident that on one hand, Liang approved of the addition of people's rights, such as the right to survival and the right to work, to the constitution, beyond the traditional political and social rights. At the same time, he interpreted this constitutional change as a shift from a passive view of the state, where people initially did not want state intervention, to an active view, where people expect the state to take proactive responsibility. As a result of demanding increased relative duties from the state, there was a corresponding increase in the state's demands for obligations from the people. From these instances, it seems that Liang held an approving attitude toward these new changes in the relationship between rights and obligations. In other words, his concern for the people's right to survival and his acknowledgment of state rights appear to be connected to his Confucian socialist ideas, rather than aligning closely with the classical liberal perspective on rights. His ideas can be observed in various ways in contemporary Chinese political culture, indicating the widespread influence of Confucian values.

Conclusion

Since modernity emerged in the Western world in recent centuries, its construction has been consistently met with questioning and criticism. Following the two world wars, this questioning and criticism intensified even further. Reflections on technological rationalization, alienation of human nature, and the shrinking of value rationality have become the focal points of criticisms of modernity. Certainly, postmodernity represents both an intensification and extension of modernity, even as it is a questioning and critique of previous understandings of it. Since the time of Levinas, the philosophical development of postmodernity has increasingly emphasized the issue of the Other. The concept of the Other was introduced as a response to the modern notion of subjectivity, and some scholars even argue that the development of the Other is one of the most significant contributions of postmodernity.

The modern concept of subjectivity was founded by the French philosopher René Descartes, while the postmodern concept of the Other was established by French philosophers such as Emmanuel Levinas, Gilles Deleuze, and Jacques Derrida. Levinas believed that only by acknowledging the Other could ethics exist, and it is through appealing to an absolute Other that ethics finds its ultimate foundation. Ethics is the primary philosophy. Deleuze pointed out that the Other encompasses other possible worlds, the face of the other person, and the words of the other person. In his later works, Derrida built upon Levinas's ideas and also asserted that the essence of ethics lies in the generous and unconditional gift to the Other, without seeking reciprocity. Treating others with selflessness and without expecting anything in return, as emphasized in this perspective, is significantly distinct from the mutual subjectivity of respect and exchange.[45]

From this perspective, Liang Shuming's ethical view of placing the other as important, or the Confucian ethics as expounded by him, indeed possesses a distinct significance compared to the emphasized subjectivity and the concept of mutual subjectivity. It represents an ethics characterized by prioritizing the Other. In this ethics, not only is the recognition of the Other emphasized, but also the emphasis is placed on the sentiments of, obligations to, and respect toward the Other. This form of respect is not based on a sense of exchange, but rather on the principles of selflessness, self-sacrifice, and a sense of putting the other as more important, as if one were disregarding oneself. In the context of the significance attributed to the concept of the Other, Liang's ethical philosophy holds important relevance.

Notes

1. Chen Lai, *The Pursuit of Modern Chinese Philosophy* (People's Publishing House, 2001), 275.
2. *Complete Works of Liang Shuming*, vol. 3, 716–717.
3. Ibid., 726.
4. Charles Taylor, *Hegel and Modern Society* (Taiwan: Linking Publishing Company, 1990), 132–133.
5. *Complete Works of Liang Shuming*, vol. 3, 726.
6. Ibid., 727.
7. *Complete Works of Liang Shuming*, vol. 1, 467.
8. Ibid., 479.
9. Ibid., 439.
10. Ibid., 382.
11. Ibid., 494.
12. *Complete Works of Liang Shuming*, vol. 5, 74.
13. Ibid.
14. Ibid., 88–89.
15. Ibid., 94.
16. Ibid., 370.
17. Ibid., 440.
18. "Some Thoughts," in *Complete Works of Liang Shuming*, vol. 5, 537.
19. Of course, classical Confucian classics also have discussions on this aspect, especially in the *Book of Rites*, such as "The rites begin with self-humiliation and end with honoring others," and, "A gentleman values others and belittles himself," as well as the concepts of respect and humility. Liang's formulation can also be seen as a modern expression of the ethics of reciprocity.
20. *Complete Works of Liang Shuming*, vol. 5, 86.
21. Ibid., 75.
22. Ibid., 84–85.
23. Ibid., 587.
24. Ibid., 79.
25. "Did China Have Rural Autonomy in the Past?" in *Complete Works of Liang Shuming*, vol. 5, 588.
26. Ibid., 854–855.
27. Ibid., 697.
28. Ibid., 706.
29. Ibid., 707.
30. *Complete Works of Liang Shuming*, vol. 3, 4.

31. Ibid., 81.
32. Ibid., 82.
33. *Complete Works of Liang Shuming*, vol. 3, 82.
34. *The Pursuit of Modern Chinese Philosophy*, 49.
35. Wan Junren points out, borrowing Sandel's words, that modern moral ethics is based on the morality of rights. Starting from the essence of rights as the demands of individual subjects on society, it can be deduced that the moral values of individual self-centeredness or personal opinions. Wan Junren, *Ethical Discourse of Modernity* (Heilongjiang People's Publishing House, 2002), 135.
36. *Complete Works of Liang Shuming*, vol. 5, 89.
37. Ibid., 902.
38. Ibid., 160.
39. Ibid., 160.
40. Ibid., 94.
41. Ibid., 536.
42. Ibid., 903.
43. *Essence of Chinese Culture*, vol. 3 of *Complete Works of Liang Shuming*, 93.
44. *Complete Works of Liang Shuming*, vol. 3, 89.
45. Shen Qingsong, *Comparison, Extrapolation, and Dialogue* (Wunan Cultural Enterprise, 2002), 11–12.

CHAPTER 10

Self-Cultivation and Progress in Liang Shuming's Thought

As previously pointed out, Confucian philosophy in the 20th century occupied a significant position in the domain of modern philosophy. As a philosophical tradition, it was not in decline, but rather remained relatively active throughout the 20th century. However, this does not change the awkward position Confucianism held in the socio-cultural aspects of modern China.[1] This chapter discusses how the prominent Neo-Confucian masters of the 20th century made significant new developments in philosophy and theory within the context of ancient Confucianism, even while making fewer contributions to the traditional practice of cultivating the heart and mind. What is meant here is not the attention and explanation given to the practice of Confucianism in ancient times, such as the work of Song-Ming Confucianism—though this naturally does constitute an important part of the interpretations and writings of contemporary Neo-Confucian scholars—but instead refers to the fact that as modern Confucian scholars, their own cultivation, statements of self-recognition, observations of others' cultivation, and practical guidance are not as prominent as in Song-Ming Confucianism. Lu Jiuyuan writes, "Learning has its clear explanation and its practical application," and, "In general, clear explanation and inner nurturing are two important aspects."[2] From this perspective, even someone like Liang Shuming, who displayed rigorous self-cultivation among contemporary Neo-Confucian scholars, still tended to prioritize "clear explanation" over "inner nurturing." To fully grasp this point, a deeper analysis is required. This chapter focuses on Liang as a case study to provide some analysis and exploration of this matter.

I

Liang placed significant emphasis on self-cultivation, as is evident primarily in his use of self-cultivation to comprehend and define Eastern scholarship, allowing him to grasp and elucidate the distinctive academic traits of Confucianism and Buddhism. For instance, in his discourse on the interconnectedness of Confucian and Buddhist teachings, he compares the schools, saying:

> The two schools present differing perspectives, yet the subject matter they discuss pertains to the same discipline of self-cultivation in their lives. Their studies do not belong to natural sciences or social sciences, nor are they the philosophical pursuit of wisdom as seen in ancient Western philosophy. They also differ from literature and the like, but both are forms of learning that involve one's own internal efforts at self-improvement and advancement in life.[3]

Liang believed that ancient Eastern traditions like Confucianism and Buddhism were studies of life cultivation. He referred to life as the manifestation of cosmic evolution in human beings, while the term cultivation carries two meanings. First, it refers to an inward focus, directing effort towards one's inner self, and second, it signifies elevation, aiming to elevate one's life condition. The concept of cultivation entails applying effort to one's inner self, thereby facilitating an elevation of both the inner being and the entirety of one's life.

From this perspective, it is evident that Liang had his own viewpoint regarding the classification of Eastern and Western scholarship. He believed that ancient and modern Eastern and Western scholarship could be categorized into four types: (1) science and technology, (2) philosophical thought, (3) literature and the arts, and (4) self-cultivation and refinement, or cultivation.[4]

In his view, various ancient Chinese academic traditions, including Confucianism, do not fall under the categories of natural science and technology, literature and the arts, or even philosophy and social sciences. He specifically points out that the various ancient Chinese academic traditions, such as Confucianism, are often now classified as philosophy, which is not an appropriate categorization. According to Liang, the academic traditions of ancient China should be categorized under the fourth type, self-cultivation and refinement.

The term "self-cultivation and refinement," as explained by Liang,

> specifically refers to the kind of scholarship that involves an individual's conscious and autonomous self-improvement in their physical and mental life. It encompasses a transformation and elevation of the entire existence. This form of scholarship includes knowledge and ideas, primarily directed inward for self-awareness, and serves to guide one's physical and mental life. Because this type of scholarship differs greatly from dealing with external matters, it is thus named self-cultivation, refinement, or enlightenment.[5]

Turning inward is in contrast to focusing outward. Generally, people tend to direct their attention outward, so turning inward is often referred to as introspection. The effort made when looking inward involves self-reflection and observance, hence the term self-cultivation and refinement. These efforts also involve self-awareness, thus the reference to enlightenment. The scholarship of self-cultivation and refinement pertains to guiding the physical and mental life of individuals. This practice of cultivating one's physical and mental existence corresponds to what is known as the spiritual aspect within the Christian religious tradition.[6] In his perspective, Confucianism, Buddhism, and Daoism can all be considered academic disciplines that involve transforming and elevating one's own life.[7] Liang wrote *An Overview of Eastern Scholarship*, in which the earlier draft also discusses this concept. He says:

> The common characteristics of Eastern scholarship are essentially those of the fourth category, the scholarship of self-cultivation and refinement. These characteristics can be summarized in three aspects: (1) The focus of mental effort is directed inward, not outward. (2) Scholars have a sincere, compelling aspiration. (3) Learning should be based on personal realization rather than mere words.[8]

While slightly different from the previous three mentioned, these three points share a consistent underlying spirit. Directing mental effort inward is equivalent to introspection, personal realization over mere words equates to enlightenment, and sincere aspiration finds its roots in Buddhist vows, later transformed into refinement. This illustrates that the old draft and the finalized version remain consistent in discussing the fundamental characteristics of self-cultivation and refinement.

This interpretation of Confucian scholarship places self-cultivation at its core. It is helpful here to examine the relationship between philosophy and this form of self-cultivation.

While Confucianism indeed involves reflection within its practice, implying the presence of philosophy, it is primarily a byproduct of practical living. It is best not to view it primarily through the lens of theoretical thought. For instance, concepts like benevolence and Heaven's will, as discussed by Confucius, should not be explained casually. Explanation is necessary, but it should not be done hastily or presumptuously. When teaching students, it is important to guide them to introspect, practice, silently comprehend, and avoid idle talk. Through this approach, they may achieve some understanding.[9]

Treating the profound self-cultivation of Confucianism—the teachings of Confucius and Mencius—as mere philosophical discourse without putting it into practice is a mockery.[10] This statement suggests that there is indeed philosophical contemplation within Confucianism. However, philosophical thought is just one component of Confucianism, not its primary focus. The philosophy found in Confucianism stems from reflecting on its practical aspects and is a byproduct of the practical application of Confucian teachings. Confucianism is thus fundamentally practical, and studying it involves primarily adhering to its teachings, practicing introspection, and silent comprehension. It is not mainly about explaining concepts, analyzing theories, or proving arguments.

II

Liang regarded both Confucianism and Buddhism as disciplines of self-cultivation, which is where the two align. But it is only by understanding the point of differentiation between the two that can one comprehend his advocacy of the spiritual essence of Confucianism. He had a clear perspective on this matter, believing that human life manifests two extremes or poles. One is the higher pole, which lies in the aspect of humans far surpassing animals, giving rise to boundless potential for development and allowing for the manifestation of a profoundly great, noble life. This life is bright and splendid, harmoniously aligned with the cosmos, flowing together with heaven and earth, and finding joy within it. The other is the lower pole, which not only refers to those who resemble animals in their everyday lives but also encompasses those who are debased, wicked, treacherous, and malicious, far removed from the characteristics of animals. In practice, it is gloomy and sordid, a boundless sea of suffering from which one cannot extricate themselves.[11] Liang believed that the distinctive feature of Confucianism lay in recognizing and fully harnessing the higher pole of human life, and a Confucian who embodies this essence harmonizes their life with the cosmos and finds joy within it. The pursuit of Confucian learning entails deeply comprehending the immense potential of human life and applying one's intellectual and mindful efforts to realize it, striving to embody one's true nature through action and not letting go of what nature (the universe) has endowed upon us.[12]

Liang frequently employs the phrase "fulfilling form and exhausting nature" to describe Confucian learning. According to Liang, this concept refers to fully realizing the higher pole of human life and embodying it to the fullest extent. In contrast, he believes that Buddhism is founded upon the perspective that all sentient beings experience suffering. Buddhist teachings recognize the lower pole of human life, grasping that the suffering in life arises from attachment and desire and seeking liberation from this suffering. The study of Buddhism involves breaking dualistic attachments and severing dualistic desires, freeing oneself from the constraints of current existence. On the one hand, all phenomena in the world are seen as empty, and on the other hand, one realizes that the universe is unified and indivisible.[13]

Liang discusses the differences between Confucianism and Buddhism not only in terms of their distinct understandings and attitudes toward life, but also emphasizes the disparities in their practices and methods of cultivation. The divergence in the practices and methods of cultivation, as Liang explains, revolves around the concept of ego-clinging or self-attachment. This serves as the focal point for his analysis.

Starting from the perspective of Buddhism, he observes that all sentient beings' activities are rooted in self-attachment. Internally, there is attachment to self, and externally, there is grasping for objects. The act of grasping and the objects of grasping constitute dualistic attachment and dualistic desire. The attachment to self and the attachment to phenomena are referred to as dualistic attachments.[14]

The attachment to self has two levels: the inherent innate self-attachment, primarily present in the seventh consciousness (manas-vijnana), which constantly revolves and clings, and the discernment of consciousness, known as discriminative self-attachment. The latter type of attachment exists on the sixth consciousness (mental consciousness) and is intermittent. Only through deep practice of Prajnaparamita (the Perfection of Wisdom) can the attachment to self be eradicated.[15]

The attachment to self has two levels. The self-attachment at the level of the sixth consciousness (mental consciousness) is called discriminative self-attachment, and relatively speaking, it is shallower. On the other hand, the self-attachment at the level of the seventh consciousness (manas-vijnana) is referred to as innate self-attachment. This type of attachment is inherent from birth and represents a deeper level of self-attachment. Liang holds that merely removing the self-attachment at the level of the sixth consciousness is not enough to fundamentally resolve the issue. It is necessary to eliminate self-attachment at the level of the seventh consciousness in order to achieve true liberation, and such elimination can only be achieved through the practice of the Six Paramitas (Six Perfections). He points out that from this perspective, Buddhism aims to break the innate self-attachment, while Confucianism does not focus on breaking the innate self-attachment. This fundamental difference in their cultivation practices is what sets the two traditions apart.

As previously discussed, both traditions involve a form of learning that focuses on self-cultivation and inner improvement within the realm of human life. However, in their practices of self-cultivation, Confucianism is devoted to upholding proper human relationships, emphasizing filial piety, fraternal love, kindness, and harmony. Confucians strive to engage wholeheartedly in worldly affairs without neglect. On the other hand, Buddhists focus on cultivating inner stillness, distancing themselves from human relationships, and abstaining from various worldly matters. The root of this difference is that, in Buddhism, it is necessary to engage in profound yogic practices (deep Prajnaparamita) to fundamentally eliminate dualistic attachments and achieve liberation from the constraints of current existence. Such practices are not conducive to the approach of solely seeking stillness, distancing oneself from human relationships, and abstaining from worldly matters. The Confucian concept of the Four No's suggests that they emphasize avoiding extremes and attachments. They appear to focus on preventing excessive attachment to discriminative consciousness, or at least minimizing such attachments. In daily life, Confucians live much like ordinary people. They engage in pursuits and activities as they naturally arise without significant alteration, because the innate self-attachment is allowed to follow its natural course without attempting to break it.[16]

The Confucian philosophical system originally did not have this distinction between the two levels of self-attachment, which meant that the question of breaking or not breaking innate self-attachment was not a concern within Confucian thought. However, according to Liang's view, Confucianism addresses a shallower level of self-attachment, and there is a lack of awareness within Confucianism regarding the deeper level of self-attachment. On the other hand, he also recognizes that while Confucianism may not explicitly address innate self-attachment as Buddhism does, it has the potential to prevent this innate self-attachment from becoming an obstacle. Within Confucian practice, where the mind is regarded as the master of form, one can transcend innate self-attachment and achieve a state of unity with all things, connecting with the universe itself. In this context, self-attachment becomes the foundation of the Confucian greater self, rather than an impediment to the activities of human life. He states:

> Not breaking the innate self-attachment, yet not allowing it to hinder is because there is a way to transcend it. In this way, the mind is not enslaved by form… And this mind becomes one with all things, harmoniously united with the universe. Although the universe is vast, it can be interconnected without obstruction… Regarding this innate self-attachment, it is observed to serve as a foundational condition for life activities, yet it has never been an obstruction. Isn't this perfectly clear?
>
> Buddhism aims for Buddhahood, while Confucianism aims for self-realization or self-actualization, which can also be described as harmonizing with the world or, in common parlance, becoming a true human. Being a true human entails surpassing innate self-attachment without necessarily needing to eliminate it. This fundamental difference between Confucianism and Buddhism lies precisely in this aspect.[17]

The notion of not being obstructed primarily refers to various worldly activities. In this context, for Confucianism, as long as the self-attachment at the level of the sixth consciousness is overcome and a state of no-self is reached at the level of consciousness, the pursuit of sagehood and virtuous endeavors within Confucianism can be fulfilled. However, if one aims to break free from the cycle of reincarnation, achieve complete liberation from life, and eradicate self-attachment at its root, then it is necessary to renounce worldly pursuits, engage in the practice of the Six Paramitas, and fundamentally eliminate the innate self-attachment. He goes on to say, "The great delusion of sentient beings lies in the innate self-attachment deeply concealed between the seventh and eighth consciousness. However, common people often mistakenly believe that the absence of self-consciousness in the sixth consciousness implies no-self, which is inadequate."[18]

These perspectives, presented by Liang from the standpoint of Buddhism, do not necessarily require complete agreement, though his perspective on the issue of no-self can be considered for reference. However, Confucian cultivation is not solely focused on the concept of no-self. This comparison with Buddhism is presented in a negative light and does not fully capture the depth and richness of Confucian practices. Positively speaking, as Liang himself stated, the highest realm for a Confucian is to be "bright and splendid, harmoniously aligned with the cosmos, and finding joy within it," and for the benevolent person, to perceive "heaven, earth, and all things as one entity." This embodies the pinnacle of Confucian ideals.

Regarding the worldly nature of Confucian cultivation practices, Liang has a clear understanding. He points out that Confucians are devoted to upholding proper human relationships, emphasizing filial piety, fraternal love, kindness, and harmony. They wholeheartedly engage in various worldly matters without neglect. In this context, he says, "Therefore, Confucian cultivation does not involve abstaining from worldly affairs; rather, the crucial effort lies in seeking refinement through daily human activities and life experiences. Only by being cautious and attentive in every moment, without straying from the realm of current reality, can one fully realize one's potential through practical application. It is through diligent learning and continuous effort that one can achieve higher levels of attainment."[19]

This emphasizes both the Confucian practice of proper human relationships and individual self-cultivation. Confucianism underscores the idea that personal cultivation should not be divorced from everyday human interactions. All efforts at self-improvement must be honed through practical engagement in various aspects of life. In this context, fulfilling form refers to making every effort in daily affairs, while exhausting nature signifies elevating one's state of being and fulfilling one's innate potential. The phrase "being cautious and meticulous in every moment" reflects his emphasis on the characteristics of self-cultivation, which will be further discussed in subsequent sections.

III

While Confucianism places significant emphasis on social harmony, human relationships, and individual self-cultivation, it also encompasses higher spiritual aspirations beyond these practical aspects. Confucianism also seeks higher moral and ethical principles, the cultivation of virtues, and the realization of a harmonious relationship between individuals, society, and the universe. Chapter Two of his *An Overview of Eastern Scholarship* is a specialized discussion on the learning of Confucianists and the Confucian school, which explores Confucius' self-identification as a learner and discusses the characteristics of Confucian studies and the realm of Confucius himself.

> What kind of learning is the school of Confucius? This can be discerned from Confucius's own words in the *Analects*, which illustrate the progression of his learning and development. He says, "At fifteen, I set my heart on learning. At thirty, I established my stand. At forty, I had no more doubts. At fifty, I knew the decrees of Heaven. At sixty, my ear was an obedient organ for the reception of truth. At seventy, I could follow what my heart desired, without transgressing what was right." To understand what Confucius dedicated his life to, one should look beyond the passage starting with, "At fifteen, I set my heart on learning." However, when it is mentioned that "at thirty, I established my stand," what exactly was established is not explicitly made clear. Continuing further, "At forty, I had no more doubts" suggests a state of being free from confusion and uncertainty, although the specific content remains unclear. When he says, "At fifty, I knew the decrees of Heaven," what does the term "decrees of Heaven" actually refer to? Certainly, it suggests a further advancement in his studies, but the specific nature of this advancement and how

> it occurred remains elusive. In "At sixty, my ear was an obedient organ for the reception of truth," the phrase "ear was an obedient organ" is somewhat difficult to interpret. And in "At seventy, I could follow what my heart desired, without transgressing what was right," while the literal meaning might seem easier to understand compared to "ear was an obedient organ," the higher realm of this statement and its actual implications remain beyond our grasp.[20]

Liang discussed the meaning of this passage many times, demonstrating his deep admiration for Confucius's level of scholarly attainment. From his perspective, "At fifteen, setting the heart on learning" refers to setting the heart's aspiration on learning; "At thirty, I established my stand," though not fully clear, could refer to establishing a firm foundation for his pursuits; "At forty, I had no more doubts" indicates a mind free from confusion; "At fifty, I knew the decrees of Heaven" signifies a higher spiritual understanding; "At sixty, my ear was an obedient organ" might be hard to grasp, yet it represents a higher realm of spiritual progress; and finally, "At seventy, I could follow what my heart desired, without transgressing what was right" signifies a level of self-mastery beyond our current comprehension. In essence, while Liang admired Confucius's scholarly and spiritual achievements, the exact nature and depth of each stage remain beyond our complete understanding. Therefore, when Confucius describes his learning journey, he is essentially referring to the progression of his spiritual state with the heart as the foundation, representing the process of his lifelong self-cultivation and inner improvement. He says:

> Even though we, as outsiders, may not fully comprehend the systematic progression of Confucius's lifelong pursuit of learning, it is evident that his scholarship is not about acquiring knowledge of external matters or engaging in philosophical speculations. Instead, it is a form of learning rooted in his personal life, a constant striving to improve and elevate himself. This type of learning could be aptly referred to as the study of practical life experiences.[21]

Confucianism's pursuit is not of academic knowledge or abstract philosophical speculation, but rather a continuous effort to achieve spiritual advancement within the context of life. It aims to attain a higher state of being within one's own existence, or as Liang puts it, "Striving to reach a higher realm in one's personal life."[22] While he avoids directly stating the specific nature of the realm Confucius reached at the age of seventy, he does provide some insights into this Confucian state. In essence, it involves the concept of "all things being interconnected in the universe" and "attaining the oneness of cosmic life" (detailed later).

However, attaining a higher spiritual realm requires translating it into practical effort. Only through practice is such attainment possible. In this sense, Liang often summarizes Confucianism as the study of practical implementation and fully realizing one's potential through practice. He says:

> The school of Confucius originally embodies the human pursuit of fully realizing one's potential through practice. After all, human intentions and aspirations are manifested through visible actions and behavior. It is indeed inevitable, but the manifestation of the human heart through the human body is a possibility rather than an absolute certainty. To fulfill one's potential means to fully realize what is possible according to one's nature. Striving for progress and turning possibilities into realities is what I refer to as the study of life's practical experiences... This learning necessitates active practice. Therefore, later Confucian scholar Wang Yangming emphasized the unity of knowledge and action, asserting that true knowledge cannot be considered without corresponding action. Therefore, the question arises: what should one actively practice? This doesn't necessarily need to be asked of others; it should be personally introspected and acted upon according to what one should do in the given time and place.[23]

The concept of fully realizing one's potential involves embodying it in one's daily life, while fulfilling one's nature requires manifesting the higher developmental possibilities of a person. Both require dedicated practice and effort in action.

Liang placed significant emphasis on the practice of self-examination in solitude. He believed that this sort of self-examination is a continuation of the Confucian lineage and tradition of self-cultivation that has been advocated since the time of Confucius.

> The Confucian practice of self-cultivation encompasses all aspects of life, and self-examination in solitude is the quintessential practice within it. As our lives are inherently connected with the universe, the practice of self-examination in solitude encompasses everything within it. In this way, it becomes an integral, essential part of our existence.[24]

Confucius introduced the principle of self-cultivation, which has been a consistent goal within Confucianism. Self-examination in solitude is the practice that embodies this principle. When it is practiced to its fullest extent, it can lead to the realization of the unity between oneself and the universe, encompassing all things. Indeed, from the inherent nature of human life, it is interconnected with the universe and all things. However, obscured by habitual desires and ego, one cannot truly connect with everything. Therefore, only through dedicated practice of self-examination in solitude to its fullest extent can one attain unity with all things. This practice leads to a return to one's inherent nature and the restoration of the original state of being.

> The term self-examination in solitude does not appear in the *Analects*. However, the behaviors of Yanzi and Zengzi, who were diligent and cautious, likely align with the essence of this practice. *The Doctrine of the Mean* and *The Great Learning* were written later, and the term self-examination in solitude likely emerged as a later concept... It was Yanzi who first grasped its essence, and Zengzi followed suit. Later, Mencius contributed significantly to this study. Although his writings do not explicitly mention self-

> examination in solitude, they do emphasize self-cultivation and personal improvement. Self-cultivation and personal improvement both refer to the cultivation of one's character and self-improvement, and they indeed reflect the transmission of this scholarly tradition.[25]

Certainly, while personal improvement is explicitly mentioned in the *Analects*, self-examination in solitude is not directly mentioned. However, according to Liang's view, Yanzi's ability to control his anger and not hold grudges, as well as Zengzi's unwavering dedication, could be considered embodiments of it. Similarly, Mencius continued the tradition of self-cultivation, as exemplified by his use of the term self-improvement while inheriting Confucius's teachings. Indeed, the practice of self-examination in solitude was not only consistent within early Confucianism but also aligned with the tradition passed down from Confucius. In this sense, Liang's emphasis on it resonates with the emphasis it receives within later Confucian schools, such as the teachings of scholars like Liu Jishan in the Song and Ming dynasties.[26] It is worth noting that Liang's emphasis on self-cultivation and self-examination in solitude not only provides an interpretation of Confucian teachings but also reflects his own distinctive approach to personal self-improvement.

The Great Learning and *The Doctrine of the Mean* are considered highly significant texts in this study precisely because they elucidate the practice of self-examination in solitude and guide individuals within the Confucian tradition in a straightforward manner, tracing the lineage of Confucian teachings. Solitude refers to a place where one knows something that others do not, an individual's unique knowledge or insight. It signifies the self-awareness inherent within a person's mind. The initial sprouting of thought within us is something only we are aware of; others cannot perceive it. Only through delving deeper into calmness and quietude can our understanding become clearer and more illuminated.[27]

Liang's interpretation of innate self-awareness is similar to Zhu Xi's, where self-awareness means a domain of knowledge that one knows and others do not. However, Liang modernized this concept with his own explanation, placing significant emphasis on self-awareness, which is consistently highlighted in his philosophy. He viewed innate self-awareness as a form of self-awareness in the human heart. Furthermore, he pointed out that the self-awareness of innate self-awareness in the human heart is most clear in stillness. As we know, in his work *Human Nature and Human Life*, Liang particularly emphasizes the ability to be still of the human mind. Stillness means not being swayed by instincts, not being influenced by emotional impulses, and not being driven by self-interest. It represents the characteristics of reason and rationality.[28]

> In the *Analects*, the phrase used can be understood as cultivating oneself with reverence. However, in other classical texts like *Mencius*, *The Great Learning*, and *The Doctrine of the Mean*, the term personal improvement is often interchangeably written as self-cultivation, conveying a similar meaning. For instance, in *Mencius*, you can find the phrase, "The conduct of a noble person consists in self-cultivation, and the whole world

> will be at peace." While there might be slight differences in wording, the meaning remains essentially the same. Indeed, this statement in *Mencius* encapsulates the essence of the whole of *The Great Learning*. The term self-cultivation appears repeatedly in *Mencius*, *The Great Learning*, and *The Doctrine of the Mean*, underscoring its significance in this line of thought. It is evident that self-cultivation is a commonly used term within this philosophical tradition. Self-cultivation implies focusing on oneself, bringing one's mind close to inner matters, concentrating one's thoughts on the present, and thus dealing with external matters with mindfulness at every moment. When not explicitly mentioning self-examination in solitude, the concept of guarding against solitude is inherent. In the past, scholars who pursued this field of study were not within my reach. Among those I have come across, Mr. Wu Yongbo from Panyu, Guangdong, is someone who truly excelled in this learning.[29]

Liang pointed out that the concept of personal improvement in the *Analects*, as mentioned in *The Great Learning*, *The Doctrine of the Mean*, and *Mencius*, refers to the idea of self-cultivation, and the meaning is entirely consistent. Thus, self-cultivation has become a core term in the Confucian teachings of Confucius and Mencius. He also advocates that self-cultivation encompasses self-examination in solitude. The introduction of the concept of self-examination in solitude makes the effort of self-cultivation more focused and succinct.

He provides a clear explanation for the significance of diligence in life:

> Our conscious self-awareness of our own agency represents the inner aspect. Why then do we still need the pursuit of knowledge and effort? While the inherent self-awareness within the human heart is a natural aspect of life, it often wavers in its presence. Achieving a focused mind in the present moment and aligning with external circumstances is no simple task. This is because the mind is often preoccupied with bodily needs (such as food and desires) and various ingrained habits, causing it to always be outwardly focused and seeking. As a result, those who pursue this path should strive to introspectively acknowledge this self-awareness. They must constantly be vigilant against losing it, thus ensuring a better chance of success.[30]

Liang goes on to say that while individuals possess an innate self-awareness, the demands of everyday life often cause this self-awareness to fluctuate. Therefore, it is necessary to practice vigilance and solitude, as without such practice, self-awareness can easily diminish. With these practices in place, a person's focus can be centered on the present inner self, leading to constant introspective recognition and the prevention of loss.

From the above, it is evident that Liang's concept of self-examination in solitude refers to the practice of focusing one's mind on the present moment when not engaged with external matters, and introspectively acknowledging one's innate self-awareness. Engaging with external matters should also be accompanied by continuous self-awareness, and one should always be cautious not to lose this self-awareness, being vigilant against its lapse. It can be said that this understanding of diligence aligns with Zhu Xi's teachings on cultivation, introspection, vigilance, and self-examination in solitude. Liang's discourse on diligence is more relatable to contemporary individuals.

The degree of emphasis on self-introspection became a major point of contention between Liang Shuming and Xiong Shili. This difference is particularly evident in Liang's criticisms of Xiong. He writes, "The discourses considered philosophical in ancient Eastern texts emerged from the practice of introspection by individuals of the past... To delve into this topic, one must also engage in a process of cultivating practical experiences and knowledge before further elaboration."[31]

This viewpoint suggests that the discussions found in ancient Confucian texts are based on the insights gained from introspection. Therefore, for contemporary individuals to truly understand, analyze, and expand upon these ideas, they must first engage in a process of personal cultivation and experiential practice. Otherwise, any discussion is merely empty and unfounded. This brings him to say, "In Eastern philosophical traditions, every school of thought emerges from the genuine practice of introspection. Departing from this authentic practice and discussing their philosophical theories results in empty, unfounded talk. It is of utmost importance to avoid straying from this genuine practice."[32]

These remarks were directed at Xiong Shili, suggesting that he lacked genuine introspective practice and that many of his theoretical discussions lacked a foundation in self-awareness. Liang explicitly criticized Xiong for not engaging in personal cultivation and practical verification, but instead being enamored with intellectual tricks and theoretical maneuvers.[33] He believed that Xiong's approach was a result of his departure from the practical tradition of self-cultivation within Confucianism. In Liang's view, Xiong chose to pursue the path of a philosopher rather than adhere to the tradition of self-cultivation. He says:

> Mr. Xiong's significant failure lies in his strong inclination toward philosophy, which leads him down the path of a thinker and theorist. As a result, he ventures outward rather than diligently focusing on self-cultivation. Had he earnestly engaged in introspective practice, following the Confucian path of nurturing one's nature through practical efforts, his achievements could have been remarkably different from what they are today. His personal character and influence on Chinese society and even humanity as a whole could have been different as well.[34]

In this context, Liang is essentially criticizing Xiong for not diligently practicing introspection, not fully realizing his innate potential, and not making an effort to transform his personal character. Instead, he emphasizes Xiong's strong inclination toward philosophical theories, which, in Liang's view, limited his achievements and influence. Liang's assertion regarding Xiong's deficiencies may not be definitively proven on a factual level, and therefore, we refrain from making conclusive judgments. Instead, we should focus on understanding Liang's perspective on philosophy and practice through his criticisms.

IV

In Liang's writings throughout his life, although he possessed a proud, individualistic personality, he often engaged in self-reflection and self-critique of his words and actions. His introspection was marked by sincerity and is clearly evident. In this regard, he was indeed quite capable of introspection and self-examination. Apart from what his writings convey, his endeavors in personal cultivation are also discernible between the lines. Even after reaching his eighties, he continued to talk about his own cultivation of beliefs.

> As seen from the above (i.e., the belief in embracing the course of destiny), I believed in fully accepting all fortune and misfortune, honor and disgrace, gain and loss without doubt, surprise, blame, or resentment. However, for this belief to be sustained, there must be certain prerequisites in daily life, such as the admonition to "proceed with caution as if on the edge of an abyss and tread carefully as if on thin ice." This meaning becomes even clearer especially after being convinced by Wu Yongbo's teachings on introspection and guarding against solitude. However, due to my inherent generosity and audacity, I found it difficult to practice. Now I realize that even if my conscience is rarely visible, it is not enough to simply talk about "being cautious where unseen and fearing where unheard." Instead, it requires restraining and solemnizing one's heart, maintaining the attitude of caution as if on the edge of an abyss and treading carefully as if on thin ice, which is essential in everyday life. This is a newfound realization.[35]

The belief in "fully accepting all fortune and misfortune, honor and disgrace, gain and loss without doubt, surprise, blame, or resentment" signifies a certain attitude toward life, a spiritual state. By stating that he held this belief, Liang indicates that he had attained this state of mind in his later years. According to his words, attaining such a state requires the groundwork of daily practice, and this state is a natural outcome of such practice. This prerequisite and practice are embodied in "restraining and solemnizing one's heart, maintaining the attitude of caution as if on the edge of an abyss and treading carefully as if on thin ice." I agree that the notion of restraining and solemnizing the heart aligns closely with Zhu Xi's concept of reverence as a practice. The attitude of "proceeding with caution as if on the edge of an abyss, and treading carefully as if on thin ice" resonates with his practice of self-cultivation in solitude, which is essentially the same as the earlier notion of being cautious and meticulous in every moment. By consistently practicing this vigilant self-discipline in daily life, one can naturally attain the spiritual state of not blaming heaven or resenting others. Liang doesn't specifically address here whether one should continue practicing vigilance and self-examination in solitude after attaining such a spiritual state. However, based on my understanding, he likely advocated that even after achieving this state, one should still engage in the practice of vigilance and self-examination in solitude. Although he remains in favor of the Confucian tradition's belief in inherent goodness, he places significant importance on the influence of habits, inclinations, and the physical body. Therefore, he might find it difficult to believe that this spiritual state can be easily achieved through short-term effort. On the contrary, from his perspective, attaining such a state requires prolonged, consistent practice. Moreover, it is difficult to determine at which stage or level one might no longer need the practice of vigilance and self-examination in solitude, as that would be the realm of a sage.

The essay "Deep Sighs over the Inability to Overcome Habitual Practices," written by Liang in his seventies, most clearly expresses his emphasis on self-cultivation. It also demonstrates that apart from the practice of vigilance and self-examination in solitude, he paid attention to cultivating practices influenced by Buddhist teachings. As he stated, "When right thoughts lack strength, idle, extraneous thoughts abound. However, the reason for the lack of strength in the right thoughts is the insufficiency of aspiration and compassion, and compassion is the foundation of everything." He explicitly states, "My compassion and aspiration are genuine," and, "Thus, with an aspirational mind, I wish to share what I understand with others," adding, "The wisdom known to the ancients of the East is not understood by people today. If there is anyone capable of making it understood, can it be someone other than me today?"[36] This compassion and aspiration are not only about setting an intention to awaken oneself and then awaken others; they are also about making a vow in the practice of self-cultivation. He wrote a "Declaration" around the 1960s to 1970s, in which he expresses sentiments such as "I wholeheartedly confess and repent," "Now, I feel deeply ashamed of everything," "I pledge and vow not to create further," and, "Moment by moment, I only aspire to manifest my true nature." This illustrates his earnestness in making vows for self-cultivation.[37] He also mentions, "In the practice of self-cultivation, one should start with cultivating the great compassion and the view of equanimity. Whenever habitual tendencies arise, apply the practice of compassionate contemplation to illuminate them." The view of emptiness in Prajnaparamita is synonymous with the view of equality. Equality means not discriminating or harboring feelings of attachment or aversion, and from there, the true inherent nature can be manifested."[38] To begin with compassionate contemplation and then observe things with an attitude of equality is the kind of Buddhist practice he sought to implement. He also mentions:

> Sentient beings are ensnared and enveloped by the karma of beginningless habits and tendencies, unable to break free. However, this kind of entanglement is illusory and unreal. The path to liberation is characterized by a single flavor of equanimity. Reduce karma and habits without harboring aversion or impatience. Be consistent without straining, diligent without rushing, and serene without neglect. From this narrow crevice of equanimity, gradually loosen the grip. Other methods all tend to increase it.[39]

In order to overcome the entanglements of habits, Liang also introduced the threefold practice of "consistency without force, diligence without haste, and serenity without neglect." From these aspects, it is evident that he paid significant attention to personal cultivation. The ultimate goal of this cultivation is to allow the true heart and inherent nature to manifest, which is what he understood as the transformation of consciousness into wisdom.

Liang practiced quietude in his earlier years. In his later years, he recalled his conversations with Lin Zaiping, stating, "Master [Lin] also paid attention to Buddhist scriptures and often engaged in silent meditation to clarify the mind. I practiced quietude too, but my progress was limited compared to Master Lin's."[40] The term practiced quietude here refers to the practice of seated meditation. Although Liang mentions that he had limited progress in his practice of quietude, he still intermittently engaged in this practice later on. For his speech during the 1958 Political Consultative Conference's rectification group meeting, he requested leave and didn't attend the conference because he wanted to "reserve more time for writing and practicing quietude."[41] He calmly explained, "I initially learned the practice of quietude due to illness. I mentioned it in my previous leave request. Later, I shifted to practicing in the Buddhist tradition, which is one of the six paramitas, cultivating it to break the two attachments of self and phenomena."[42] He goes on, "In the Buddhist practice of the six paramitas, the fifth paramita is meditation, which aims to eliminate the attachment to self. In this practice, one seeks to enter a state of focused concentration and tranquility, observing a stillness that is illuminating, and an illumination that is still."[43] In his later years, Liang also wrote an essay titled "On Stillness," in which he analyzed the similarities and differences in the practices of stillness among Confucianism, Buddhism, and Daoism.[44]

However, it appears that he did not delve very deeply into the practice of stillness. In his work *An Overview of Eastern Scholarship*, written in 1975, he mentions, "Yoga is indeed meditation, one of the six paramitas. Practicing the six paramitas, one returns from meditative concentration to introspection and obtains all aspects of life. This is explained as a pointer for those engaged in this study." And, "I have not engaged in this practical cultivation..."[45] This indicates that while he was attentive to practicing quietude, he wasn't a scholar primarily focused on meditation. His main emphasis remained on vigilance, caution, and solitary reflection.

Returning to the initial topic mentioned in this text, modern Confucian scholars tend to discuss their personal experiences and insights about cultivation less frequently compared to scholars from the Song and Ming dynasties. The emphasis in modern times leans more toward explicit exposition rather than internal nurturing. In contrast, the explicit exposition among Confucian scholars in the Song and Ming dynasties often centered around practical cultivation, whereas in modern Confucianism, explicit exposition is not primarily focused on the practice of cultivation. Certainly, during the Song and Ming dynasties, explicit exposition by Confucian scholars was not limited to discussions about inner cultivation, but also encompassed a wide range of philosophical principles and concepts. In modern Confucianism, the explicit exposition of philosophy tends to be more prominent.

Although Liang firmly asserted that Confucianism is the study of self-cultivation, he also acknowledged that the natural progression of philosophical contemplation within Confucianism has its rational basis. He writes:

> Since the Song and Ming dynasties, Confucian scholars have extensively discussed topics such as heart-mind, human nature, and the innate goodness of human nature to the fundamental heart-mind and essential nature. All these discussions have led to the categorization of Confucianism as a study of innate principles. In the West, what is known as philosophy seems to resemble these discussions, but they were not originally present in the teachings of Confucius and his school. On the one hand, this development of scholarship involves the natural progression from specific facts to abstract generalizations. On the other hand, for those engaged in the practice of self-cultivation, the inclination to explore and contemplate these abstract concepts is an inherent tendency.[46]

Liang saw that since the Song and Ming dynasties, Confucianism had engaged in numerous theoretical discussions on concepts and issues related to human nature, life, destiny, and the heavens. It also explored ideas related to ontology. With these philosophical discussions, Confucianism had been referred to as the study of the principles of human nature. However, such discussions did not occur during the time of Confucius and his school. Liang proposed that the difference between early Confucianism and the Confucianism of the Song and Ming dynasties arose from the inevitable progression of academic development from concrete facts to philosophical abstractions. The emphasis of Confucianism on self-cultivation and nurturing naturally led to explorations of its origins and foundations. From this perspective, it can be seen that Liang did acknowledge the positive significance of philosophical thinking within Confucianism.

Clearly, while Confucianism places self-cultivation as its main theme, it has also consistently emphasized practical application in the world. Therefore, the cultivation of oneself and the governance of others cannot be neglected. After the Song Dynasty, Confucianism faced the challenge posed by Buddhism. It had to vigorously develop its practices of cultivating the heart-mind and philosophical theories, thereby giving rise to a discourse that differed from that of pre-Qin Confucianism. In modern times, the greatest challenge that Confucianism has faced is the challenge posed by Western philosophy and religion. As a result, in the 20th century, Neo-Confucian scholars started with historical interpretation and emphasized the development of philosophical theories. This progression was quite natural. In fact, since the Warring States period, Confucianism has already been a rich tradition, encompassing not only the cultivation of the self but also the study aspect, which predominantly involves the transmission and study of the Six Classics. It is not solely focused on the practice of self-cultivation. The study of classical texts after the Han Dynasty held great importance in various Confucian schools throughout different periods, especially during the Han and Tang dynasties. The continuity of scholarly traditions played a crucial role in these eras of Confucianism. After the Song Dynasty, Confucian scholars of the Neo-Confucian school dedicated a significant portion of their writings to the interpretation of classical texts and the explication of philosophical theories, in response to the inherent necessity of theoretical development within Confucianism. In modern society, individuals are inevitably engaged in some form of occupation, and it is not feasible to dedicate all or most of their time to self-cultivation. In fact, during the Song and Ming dynasties, Confucian scholars also had to participate in government service, facing the same reality. Therefore, being a Confucian does not depend on whether one dedicates the majority of their time to self-cultivation. Confucian self-cultivation is not a solitary pursuit detached from the world, but an ethical practice integrated within the context of everyday life. Wang Yangming expressed the idea that "knowledge and understanding are achieved through practical matters," and that engaging with the affairs of government is a genuine way to practice. He emphasized that apart from the trivialities of daily life, there is no other way to attain true moral understanding. Acting in accordance with nature, handling practical affairs, and writing books all stem from the ethical principles of Confucianism. When engaging with the world, practical matters, and writing, one should not go against one's moral understanding and should maintain introspection. This embodies the cautious practice of "not departing from the investigation of things," which is the life practice of Confucian scholars. As Liang pointed out, the distinction between Confucian scholars and Buddhist practitioners lies in the fact that Buddhists must dedicate themselves entirely to spiritual cultivation, whereas Confucian scholars must strive to fulfill their responsibilities in worldly affairs without negligence.

Regarding the social and political concerns of Confucian scholars and their practical engagement in society, Liang is one of the most prominent representatives of practical spirit and action in modern Confucianism. This is well-known to anyone with even a basic understanding of 20th-century Chinese history. His social activities were rooted in his Confucian thought. He once said, "The terms inner sage and outer king are found in the *Zhuangzi*. Some people might call Confucianism the school of inner sage and outer king, but I dare not say whether this is appropriate or not. As I understand it, regardless of the era or the society in which a Confucian scholar lives, they must maintain a positive attitude toward people's lives and public affairs. This fundamental difference from Buddhism and Daoism is consistent throughout time and circumstances. He always tends toward progress, and this stems from his pursuit of benevolence. This is also consistent, but beyond this, there doesn't seem to be any fixed rules."[47] This indicates that while the spiritual essence of Confucianism places emphasis on inner cultivation, it remains connected to the world of affairs. Not only does it stay engaged with practical matters, but its spiritual essence naturally leads to a proactive social and political attitude and practice, fostering societal transformation and political reform.

There are still aspects of this topic that have not been fully explored in this discussion. Due to time constraints, a thorough examination is not possible here. Hopefully, there will be an opportunity for further study and discussion in the future. Furthermore, in this preliminary text, initially titled "Liang Shuming's Discourse on the Study of Self-Cultivation," it later became apparent that the term discourse on self-cultivation might not be appropriate, as those who discuss the study of self-cultivation might not necessarily possess the actual cultivation and practical experience of it themselves. The conjunction *and* in the title of this chapter is more inclusive and can convey Liang's personal cultivation and progress. Therefore, the title has been revised to better convey this intention and provide clarity to the readers.

October 26, 2007

Notes

1. Chen Lai, "The Dilemma of Modern Chinese Culture and Confucianism," in *Tradition and Modernity: Perspectives of Humanism* (Peking University Press, 2006), 84.
2. "Correspondence with Zhao Ran Dao," vol. 12, "Correspondence with Peng Zishou," vol. 7 of *Collected Works of Lu Jiuyuan*.
3. "Comparison of Confucianism and Buddhism," in *Complete Works of Liang Shuming*, vol. 7 (Shandong People's Publishing House, 1992), 153.
4. "An Overview of Eastern Scholarship," in *Complete Works of Liang Shuming*, vol. 7, 365.
5. Ibid., 367.
6. For understanding of "Confucian Spirituality," see Julia Ching, "What Is Confucian Spirituality," in *Confucianism*, ed. Irene Ebered (Macmillan, 1986).
7. See Liang Shuming's statement, "Both Daoism and Buddhism can be regarded as studies for transforming ones' own life." *Complete Works of Liang Shuming*, vol. 7, 363.
8. "An Overview of Eastern Scholarship" (Unfinished old manuscript), in *Complete Works of Liang Shuming*, vol. 7, 386.
9. "Confucianism and the School of Confucius as Studies in Understanding Human Life," in *Complete Works of Liang Shuming*, vol. 7, 498.
10. "The Essence of Confucian Studies," in *Complete Works of Liang Shuming*, vol. 7, 500.
11. "Comparison of Confucianism and Buddhism," in *Complete Works of Liang Shuming*, vol. 7, 155.
12. Ibid.
13. Ibid., 157.
14. Ibid.
15. Ibid., 157–158.
16. Ibid., 159.
17. Ibid., 159.
18. "Re-reading Mr. Ma Yifu's Miscellaneous Writings," in *Complete Works of Liang Shuming*, vol. 7, 847.
19. "Comparison of Confucianism and Buddhism," in *Complete Works of Liang Shuming*, vol. 7, 160.
20. "An Overview of Eastern Scholarship," in *Complete Works of Liang Shuming*, vol. 7, 329.
21. Ibid., 330.
22. Ibid., 333.
23. Ibid.
24. "On the Contributions of Huian Zhu Xi in Confucian Studies and the Gaps in His Theoretical Thinking," in *Complete Works of Liang Shuming*, vol. 7, 465.
25. "An Overview of Eastern Scholarship," in *Complete Works of Liang Shuming*, vol. 7, 335.

26. Naturally, here it is only about emphasizing the importance of self-examination in solitude, not suggesting that Liang Shuming and Liu Jishan share the same self-examination in solitude.
27. "An Overview of Eastern Scholarship," in *Complete Works of Liang Shuming*, vol. 7, 335.
28. Chen Lai, "Liang Shuming's Theory of the Mind in *Human Nature and Human Life*," in *The Quest of Modern Chinese Philosophy* (People's Publishing House, 2001), 255–259.
29. "An Overview of Eastern Scholarship," in *Complete Works of Liang Shuming*, vol. 7, 358.
30. Ibid., 361.
31. "Records of Reading at Mianren Study: Post-Reading of Xiong's Various Books," in *Complete Works of Liang Shuming*, vol. 7, 757.
32. Ibid., 759.
33. "Records of Reading at Mianren Study: Post-Reading of Xiong's Various Books," in *Complete Works of Liang Shuming*, vol. 7, 756.
34. Ibid., 758.
35. "On the Joy of Knowing Destiny," in *Complete Works of Liang Shuming*, vol. 7, 497. From this, it can be observed that Liang's practice had a lineage, as he considered himself a disciple of Wu Yongbo, indicating the continuity of their teachings.
36. "Deep Sighs over the Inability to Overcome Habitual Practices," in *Complete Works of Liang Shuming*, vol. 7, 499.
37. "Declaration," in *Complete Works of Liang Shuming*, vol. 7, 227.
38. "Deep Sighs over the Inability to Overcome Habitual Practices," in *Complete Works of Liang Shuming*, vol. 7, 499.
39. Ibid.
40. "In Memory of Mr. Lin Zaiping," in *Complete Works of Liang Shuming*, vol. 7, 569.
41. "Speech at a Small Group Meeting after Exchanging Ideas with the Party," in *Complete Works of Liang Shuming*, vol. 7, 57.
42. Ibid.
43. "An Overview of Eastern Scholarship," in *Complete Works of Liang Shuming*, vol. 7, 357.
44. The essay "On Stillness" has not yet been published. I've received guidance from Mr. Liang Peikuan, son of Mr. Liang Shuming, and express sincere gratitude.
45. "An Overview of Eastern Scholarship," in *Complete Works of Liang Shuming*, vol. 7, 353.
46. "Comparison of Confucianism and Buddhism," in *Complete Works of Liang Shuming*, vol. 7, 161.
47. "An Overview of Eastern Scholarship" (Unfinished old manuscript), in *Complete Works of Liang Shuming*, vol. 7, 390–391.

CHAPTER 11

Liang Shuming and Esoteric Buddhism

In 2007, through Liang Peikuan, son of Liang Shuming, it was revealed that in his later years, Liang Shuming had written an unpublished essay titled "On Stillness," in which he analyzes the similarities and differences in the practices of cultivating stillness among Confucianism, Buddhism, and Daoism. In light of this, I revisited his writings and gained new insights into his experiences with cultivating stillness over time. Though his personal experiences in cultivation, particularly his involvement in the practice of esoteric Buddhism, have rarely been mentioned by earlier scholars, they offer a valuable example for analyzing the spiritual cultivation and practical efforts of modern Confucian scholars. This chapter will discuss and analyze his experiences in practicing esoteric Buddhism, especially the esoteric aspects.

I

In the diary section of Volume 8 of *Complete Works of Liang Shuming*, a note under the entry for the year 1947 reads:

> This is an excerpt from the author's posthumous papers, discussing the issue of cultivating stillness. Because it is presented in a daily chronological format, it has been included in the diary section.[1]

This diary section contains entries spanning six days from February to April of 1947, documenting Mr. Liang's experiences before and after his first attempt at cultivating stillness.

The following is the record of his practice of stillness from this diary section:

> In February, Mr. Shili came from Wutong Bridge to Mianren Academy and stayed briefly for about a month. During a conversation, he told me that making vows and experiencing the body are the most crucial matters in our lives. This should serve as a significant reminder for the present. If we lack both of these aspects throughout our lives, we will only fall lower, and our lives will not surpass each other. Therefore, I often think about them and cannot forget them.[2]

In late 1946, Liang left Nanjing and returned to Beibei after withdrawing from the peace talks between the Nationalist and Communist parties. At that time, both Mianren Middle School and Mianren Academy in Chongqing were facing significant challenges. After the victory of the Anti-Japanese War, Xiong Shili returned to Sichuan from Hubei in the early summer of 1946 and spent his days in the Huanghai Chemical Industry Research Society founded by Sun Yingchuan. An attached department of philosophy research was specifically established to accommodate Xiong, and the address of the Huanghai Society was in Wutong Bridge, in Leshan.[3] In early 1947, Xiong came from Wutong Bridge to Beibei in Chongqing, where he visited Liang's Mianren Academy, visiting this old friend who had withdrawn from the political current in hopes that he would redirect his effort toward academia. Xiong's focus on spiritual subjects and ultimate concerns had a thought-provoking effect on Liang, who had just withdrawn from political affairs.

After Xiong left Mianren Academy, influenced by his visit, Liang embarked on a pursuit of new intellectual horizons. At the end of February, he visited the Han Chinese esoteric master Nenghai, who was then in Chongqing.

> On the 29th, along with Dong Ming, I paid a visit to Master Nenghai at No. 13 Jialing Xin Cun. Humbly seeking guidance, the master fist asked about my age, and I replied that I was fifty-five years old. The master said, "Within each day, there should be a period of practicing tranquility." I respected this instruction. I also asked about the method of practice. The master replied that one could choose any method, and there was no need to be rigid.[4]

When Liang met Master Nenghai and sought his guidance, the master seemed to understand his inclination toward worldly activities. Therefore, he did not delve deeply into Buddhist teachings, but simply advised him to practice tranquility each day. The master indicated that there were various methods for practicing tranquility and that he should not confine himself to a single approach. This indicates that Master Nenghai didn't specifically recommend Buddhist practices like esoteric meditation to Liang. Accompanying Liang on this visit was Dong Ming, who was quite knowledgeable about Buddhism and had been practicing it for a long time.[5]

The advice from Master Nenghai resonated with Liang, prompting him to begin seeking a teacher for the practice of tranquility. By the end of March, he had decided to learn tranquility from Mr. Jiang, who had thirty years of experience in meditative practice.

On the afternoon of the 31st, Liang and Dong visited Jiang Zizhai in the laboratory of the 24th Porcelain Factory in Ciqikou. They listened to his account of more than thirty years of meditative practice and were deeply impressed by his achievements. During their conversation, they found resonance with things that Liang had observed in the past and also gained new insights. Their discussions about nurturing aspirations and experiencing the body greatly inspired them, particularly resonating with their hearts and evoking both joy and sorrow. Therefore, Liang made the decision to learn tranquility from Jiang.[6]

Jiang worked in a laboratory in Chongqing, and it seems he might not have been a scholar in the humanities. He could have been a lay practitioner, but this is uncertain. The account of his achievements in meditative practice deeply impressed Liang, and their conversation was highly resonant. The origin and lineage of Jiang's meditation method are not clear, but in any case, Liang decided to study quietude following his approach.

There are three remaining entries in the April meditation diary. One of them is:

> On the 2nd, I stayed at the upper floor of Te Garden. Before dawn, I thought that practicing tranquility should be done in the latter part of the night, so I decided to attempt it upon waking. Furthermore, I considered that each night before sleeping, one should purify the mind, so that there are fewer scattered thoughts in dreams, leading to peaceful sleep and better mental clarity upon waking.[7]

This entry is about practicing tranquility on the upper floor of Te Garden at Shangqing Temple in Chongqing, where the Democratic League was established.[8] The diary mentions "attempting it upon waking," indicating that this meditation practice was just beginning. It also appears that the method of tranquility that Jiang Zizhai taught him involved practicing during the latter part of the night.

The second entry is:

> On the 8th, despite not forgetting for several days, I still haven't managed to settle into the practice. Today, I sat down around four o'clock, but I haven't yet found a comfortable position for my hands and feet. During the practice, I noticed two things. First, it is essential to clarify one's motivation. If the motivation is unclear or improper, one definitely shouldn't proceed. Second, it is crucial to differentiate the nature of "experiencing the body." This concept has Confucian aspects and hints of Buddhist origins. The former is the starting point, and the latter is the destination. Following self-reflection and contemplation, when I initiate thoughts, my mind is directed upward, toward departure from delusion. This is the path that has evolved from the biological world leading to humans, always tending toward stillness, stillness, stillness... and returning to non-delusion. Continuing: a heart that seeks stillness is not yet still; as long as there is delusion, there will be no way out of it. The nature of Confucian practice and Buddhist practice is not separate; they belong to two different stages.[9]

From the 2nd to the 8th, although Liang often desired to practice tranquility, he hadn't been able to establish the practice. This delay was likely due to the numerous affairs related to the management of Mianren Academy. On the morning of the 8th, he got up at four o'clock to meditate, but he didn't have any positive experiences or achievements in his meditation that day. This was mainly because he had many thoughts arising and was not conscious of them. During his meditation, he first aimed to clarify the motivation for practicing tranquility, believing that without a clear motivation, one should not practice. Next, he attempted to differentiate between the concept of "experiencing the body" that Xiong had mentioned, seeking to distinguish the differences between Confucian and Buddhist perspectives. Regarding motivation, he recognized that it should involve aiming upward and departing from delusion, essentially pursuing stillness and returning to non-delusion. This perspective on seeking stillness aligned with his longstanding view that stillness is a characteristic of human nature. Regarding "experiencing the body," he believed that the concept of "experiencing the body" in Confucianism and Buddhism was consistent, yet they belonged to two different stages. Although he did not explicitly explain the nature of these two stages, based on his consistent thinking, it seems he considered Confucian experiencing the body as the initial stage, while Buddhist experiencing the body represented the ultimate stage.

From the fact that Xiong had recently mentioned "experiencing the body," it can be inferred that Liang was aspiring to a Confucian understanding of that notion at this time. It can be inferred that the Buddhist understanding of experiencing the body would be a matter for later. From this, one can also deduce the distinction between Confucianism and Buddhism. The meditation method he was practicing, then, belonged to the Buddhist tradition of meditation. Given the nature of his consciousness, which primarily involved thinking and introspection, and considering his inclination toward Confucian experiencing the body, it is understandable that he was not experiencing any noticeable results in his meditation practice. However, in terms of understanding, his statement that "a heart that seeks stillness is not yet still; as long as there is delusion, there will be no way out of it" reflects a correct perspective. He believed that one should not approach meditation with the intention of achieving stillness, which is a valid viewpoint.

The third entry is:

> On the 18th, for several days, I've been in a state of confusion, and despite attempting to sit down, I haven't been able to achieve any focus. Today, I had an insight: all the Buddhas are naturally present now, with no separation from me; not deceiving oneself is fundamental and the starting point; not deceiving oneself is stillness, and apart from this, there is no true stillness.[10]

From the 8th to the 18th, although Liang attempted to meditate in the morning, he felt that he had not been able to achieve any focus, which is what he meant by achieving focus or gaining insight. By the 18th, he had an insight that not deceiving oneself is stillness, and apart from this, there is no true stillness. This seems to be interpreting stillness using the perspective of the "Sincerity" chapter of *The Great Learning*. It is as if he is substituting the practice of sincerity for the practice of stillness, which essentially diminishes the independent significance of stillness as a practice.

While this perspective is reminiscent of Wang Yangming's teachings, it indicates that Liang's meditation practice during this period did not yield genuine results in terms of the practice of tranquility itself. Ultimately, he only arrived at the principle of not deceiving oneself through sincerity. His attempt to approach meditation from a Buddhist perspective seemed to lead him back to Confucianism.

From the perspective of the origin of this meditation practice, it can be inferred that after Xiong's visit, Liang immediately sought to learn tranquility from a teacher. Additionally, his conversation with Jiang inspired him in terms of making aspirations and experiencing the body. Based on this, it is reasonable to assume that this meditation practice was not solely about calming and nourishing the mind, but it also had the purpose of nurturing aspirations and experiencing the body. This motivation became an important aspect of this particular period of meditation practice, distinguishing it from his practice two years later.

II

Two years passed after the meditation practice in the spring and summer of 1947, and in 1949, Liang once again engaged in meditation. However, in this instance, although the starting point was meditation, the scope of his practice had actually transcended mere meditation.

Complete Works of Liang Shuming contains a letter to Yan Shenfu, written in 1984, which mentions the events of 1949 as follows:

> Mr. Shenfu,
>
> Recently, I received a letter inquiring about the situations of Mr. Liu Zhongmai and Mr. Hou Yishi. I regret to admit that I haven't heard of Mr. Liu's name before. I have heard Mr. Hou's name in the past, though at present, the details of his life story have also faded from my memory, becoming rather unclear. In the summer and autumn of 1949, Gongga Rinpoche visited Beibei in Chongqing and stayed at the park. I was introduced to him by a friend and had the privilege of receiving teachings on the Inconceivable Great Seal and receiving empowerment. At that moment, it was as if I had tasted ambrosia, an experience unlike any other. Since my youth, I had a strong interest in Buddhism (not guided by anyone but arising spontaneously). I harbored the thought of becoming a monk and entering the monastic life until the age of 29, when I eventually abandoned that idea and got married. Nevertheless, I consistently aspired to not abandon sentient

> beings and not remain in Nirvana. I had dedicated a decade to rural movements, and I was also active during the invasion by the Japanese forces, involving myself in national affairs. Regarding the Buddhist precepts, meditation, and wisdom, I only upheld the small precept of not consuming meat, while I couldn't claim any significant practice. Without engaging in cultivation, at the present age of 91, I don't recite Amitabha Buddha's name, but I recite the name of Avalokiteshvara. Not cultivating Pure Land practice, my motivation remains centered on the aspiration to relieve suffering and provide assistance during times of difficulty. Cultivating concentration leads to the unfolding of wisdom. Regrettably, in my earlier years, I couldn't fully attain concentration. During middle age, there were moments of entering it, but now, in old age, it's difficult to gather my thoughts and achieve deep concentration. As for your kind letter and manuscripts, I can only read them, but I am unable to offer any comments. This is the truth, not an attempt to evade the matter. I can only express my gratitude for your understanding and indulgence.
>
> Respectfully offering my regards,
> Liang Shuming[11]

This was written by Liang Shuming in his later years. Considering the context before and after this passage, it seems to be a response to inquiries regarding his meditation and concentration practice. The questioner might have assumed that Liang had engaged in such practices, and in his response, he talks about his experiences with meditation and concentration in 1949. In this passage, he candidly mentions his past engagement with esoteric Buddhism's practices, a topic not covered elsewhere in *The Complete Works.* This indeed constitutes a rare and valuable piece of literature.

Since the matter of his engagement with esoteric Buddhist practices occurred in 1949, it is helpful to look at his diary entries from that year. In the beginning of the 1949 section of *The Complete Works* diary, there is a commentary written by Liang himself in his later years:

> This passage, based on my recollection, should be from the diary entries of a certain year when I, along with my friends Luo Yingzhong and Cao Mufan, and also Mr. and Mrs. Xie Wuliang, were engaged in meditation and concentration on the mountaintop of Mount Jinyun.
>
> Shuming, 1983[12]

Luo Yingzhong is also known as Luo Yong. In *The Complete Works,* there is a footnote on this page that reads, "The author practiced meditation during the summer of 1949 in a cottage near Jinyun Temple on Mount Jinyun, Beibei Hot Springs, Chongqing. At that time, Luo Yingzhong was a professor and head of the Chinese Department at Mianren College of Letters and Science and was formerly a professor at Southwest Associated University. Cao Mufan was a faculty member of the same college."[13] Mianren Academy was located near the foot of Mount Jinyun, which is situated by the Jialing River amid picturesque scenery. Jinyun Temple, an ancient temple dating back to the Southern Dynasties, was located there as well. It is worth noting that this area was also where Master Taixu (1889–1947) established the Han-Tibetan Buddhist Academy, which suggests that it was a suitable location for engaging in meditation and concentration. The footnote mentioning meditation in a cottage might not be accurate. Subsequent references suggest that Liang also practiced meditation in Buddhist temples.

The commentary provided by Liang here referring to the summer of 1949 in Chongqing's Jinyunshan for meditation and retreat seems to be connected with what is mentioned in the letter to Yan Shenfu, where it is stated that "Gongga Rinpoche visited Beibei in Chongqing and stayed at the park. I was introduced to him by a friend and had the privilege of receiving teachings on the Inconceivable Great Seal and receiving empowerment." Furthermore, referring to the diary entry of August 19, 1949, which will be quoted later, where it states, "From the day I took refuge in my guru, I had previously examined the matter myself," it is evident that Liang took refuge with Gongga Rinpoche and thus engaged in the practice of Tibetan Buddhism during the summer of 1949.[14] This portion of the diary not only confirms that Liang diligently practiced the Great Seal of Tantra after receiving the empowerment, but also provides detailed accounts of the practice process.

However, Liang's commentary in 1983 regarding this portion of the diary also suggests that he might have viewed the practice of Tibetan Buddhism as a form of "meditation in retreat." It is interesting to note that Liang's two episodes of meditation in the 1940s were both connected to Tibetan Buddhist masters of the Vajrayana tradition. Liang's meditation practice in 1947 was guided by the instructions of Mater Nenghai, who was a prominent figure in propagating Vajrayana Buddhism in China before and after the Second Sino-Japanese War. During the 1930s and 1940s, Master Nenghai was active in Sichuan, spreading Buddhist teachings. It was under Master Nenghai's guidance that Liang was advised to engage in meditation,[15] and Liang continued to maintain a connection with him. According to the diary entry on August 14, 1956, Liang "met Master Nenghai in the park yesterday. His concern for me is deep and genuine. He urged me to visit him and suggested setting a date to visit with Mr. Xian."[16] On August 25 of the same year, Liang's diary entry reads, "After a meal, I visited Mr. Xian, and together we went to see Master Nenghai. The discussion went on for some time, and we even stayed for lunch. The master gave us many instructions and gave me a list of books to read alongside the article 'Key Points for Practice.' He also instructed me to borrow books from Tang Mufeng. It seems that the master has passed on teachings deeply rooted in the tradition of Master Tsongkhapa."[17] Master Nenghai's "practice" corresponds to Liang's concept of "cultivating quietude" or "practicing meditation." Master Nenghai even provided Liang with a written document titled "Key Points for Practice," suggesting that Liang's interactions with Buddhist teachers were indeed centered around the practice of meditation.[18]

III

It is helpful to look at the diary of this meditation practice, from August 4 to September 11, 1949, spanning nearly forty days. The diary entries are consistent and plentiful, showing his dedicated effort during this period of meditation. It is evident that he approached this meditation practice with great seriousness, a significant departure from his practice two years prior. This period for meditation also happened to coincide with him completing *Essence of Chinese Culture* and waiting to proofread the manuscript, which meant that his writing and spiritual practice did not conflict significantly during this time.

> (August) 4th (10th day of the 7th lunar month). The study of Buddhism must be pursued by those with great greed, great caution, and great foolishness in order to attain enlightenment and achieve great things. Not using the thinking mind, but also not stopping conceptual thinking. All life forces are manifestations of this substance, so great afflictions are in fact great enlightenment. Arrange daily lessons and recite the Hundred Syllable Mantra and Dhāraṇī for Protecting the Dharma. Use sleep to recover from fatigue and replenish the energy for spiritual practice.[19]

On this day, he set up a schedule for daily practice and began his spiritual cultivation. The Hundred Syllable Mantra and the Dhāraṇī for Protecting the Dharmas are practices from tantric Buddhism. The Hundred Syllable Mantra is also known as the Vajrasattva Purification Mantra, and its primary function is to purify and dissolve karmic obstacles, allowing for a clear, tranquil mind for meditation. The term Vijrasattva encompasses the meanings of vajra, courageous, and sentient beings, which is translated as "vajra courageous heart" in Tibetan. The phrase symbolizes the unshakable bodhicitta and the profound principle of enlightenment within afflictions. This diary entry proves that from the very beginning, this retreat for meditation was focused on practicing the methods of tantric Buddhism. It is clear that immediately after receiving the empowerment and teachings from the Gongga Rinpoche, Liang began to put into practice the teachings he had received. Furthermore, even though "not using the thinking mind, yet also not stopping conceptual thinking" is mentioned here, the entire process of practice demonstrates that Liang engaged in considerable thinking, which likely played a significant role in the effectiveness of his meditation practice.

> August 5 (7th day of the 7th lunar month). Began practicing the daily schedule involving the Four Dharmas. Wrote a letter to Lu Ziying. In the afternoon, attempted to practice the Mahamudra seal. Newspaper reported local peace in Changsha.[20]

The Four Dharmas is an essential practice in Vajrayana Buddhism. The term Dharmas refers to the foundational practices of cultivation. In the practice of Vajrayana Buddhism, the ultimate goal of cultivation is to attain Buddhahood. To achieve Buddhahood, one must first purify the accumulated karmic obscurations from countless lifetimes of cyclic existence and accumulate the necessary conditions and resources. The various Dharma practices are fundamental methods for engaging in confession, purification, and the accumulation of positive conditions. They serve as both preparatory practices before engaging in significant cultivation and as methods that must be consistently practiced throughout one's lifetime, even up to the point of attaining Buddhahood. The explanations of the Four Dharmas vary slightly among different schools, but generally they involve: Taking Refuge Practice (visualization and contemplation on the objects of refuge), Prostration Practice (complete prostration to the ground as an act of reverence), Vajrasattva Practice (chanting the hundred-syllable mantra of Vajrasattva), and Guru Yoga Practice (reciting prayers and visualizing the guru with complete devotion and faith). The Hundred Syllable Mantra belongs to the Vajrasattva practice and serves the purpose of purifying negative karma and obscurations. Both prostration and mantra recitation should be repeated numerous times, often exceeding hundreds or even thousands of repetitions. The term Great Seal mentioned in the diary likely refers to the Great Hand Seal practice in Vajrayana Buddhism.

> August 6 (12th day of 7th lunar month). "The spirit is uplifted, the energy is grounded, and the mind does not cling to outer experiences, but is focused on the inner emptiness." The practitioner knew the intention but didn't attain actual realization. The practice followed the prescribed routine and yielded some preliminary results. Tried seated meditation in the Buddha hall, with the indoor environment being more conducive for the practice. Feeling drowsy in the mind without being able to fall asleep, lacking the mental clarity necessary for meditation. If departing from attachments is seeing the King, if being free from dispersion is cultivating the King, if not seeking is practicing the King, if without abiding is realizing the fruit, then beyond the realm of conditioned phenomena, the mind's essence is revealed. The path of no abode is the path to Buddhahood, and enlightenment without cultivation or conditions—these are all concepts I acknowledge and believe in, yet they remain aspirations rather than immediate attainments. For the past two days, entering the practice of the Great Seal has proven difficult. During the afternoon, I persistently reiterate the Four Dharmas. The Great Seal seems unattainable with effort, whereas the application of effort is more suitable in the context of the Four Dharmas.[21]

The mind does not dwell on phenomena but resides within the mind itself, resembling Master Jinul's True Mind Suppresses Delusion Method. The three elements of spirit, energy, and mind might represent teachings from the transmission of the Great Seal practice. The Buddha Hall of Jinyun Temple is a suitable place for meditation, better than a regular dwelling. Historically, Confucian scholars during the Song and Ming dynasties practiced meditation in temples, similar to Liang's retreat in the Buddhist temple. There seems to be common ground in this regard. Liang acknowledged that the practice of the Great Seal was challenging to master and that it lacked tangible effectiveness. The four characteristics of the Mahamudra Seal in esoteric Buddhism are solidity, purity, liberation, and completeness. The Great Seal is a fundamental practice in esoteric Buddhism and is considered a supreme, profound teaching. It encompasses the aspects of realization, cultivation, and practice. In terms of realization, it signifies the understanding of one's Buddha nature. Practice involves purifying defilements and manifesting purity. In general training, one receives appropriate empowerment, transmission of teachings, and instructions from a spiritual teacher. Afterward, the practice of the Four Dharmas is undertaken: taking refuge, generating the bodhicitta, engaging in prostrations, visualization of Vajrasattva, and guru yoga. Specialized training includes the Six Yogas and other advanced practices. Practice represents the highest state, characterized by purity and effortlessness, where one acts effortlessly and naturally. In Vajrayana Buddhism, particularly in the Kagyu, Nyingma, and Sakya traditions, practitioners aim to maintain non-dual awareness and reveal the luminous nature of the mind within an open, spacious state. This approach to practice shares similarities with the Chan tradition of silent illumination meditation in Chinese Buddhism.

The phrases, "If departing from attachments is seeing the King, if being free from dispersion is cultivating the King, if not seeking is practicing the King," are from the *Verse of the Great Seal of the Ganges*, which is associated with the Mahamudra practice. Gongga Rinpoche composed the *Explanation of the Great Seal of the Ganges* in 1938, providing detailed commentary on the verse. It is likely that Liang was familiar with this commentary as part of his study and practice of Mahamudra.[22] This indicates that the Venerable Gongga Rinpoche specifically transmitted the *Verse of the Great Seal* of *the Ganges* to Liang. However, in his initial attempts, Liang found the practice of the Great Seal to be challenging to enter. He speculated that the issue might lie in not exerting enough effort in the Four Dharmas. Therefore, he decided to focus on applying effort in these preliminary practices first.

> August 7 (13th day of the 7th lunar month). It is necessary to detach oneself from the tendency of worldly existence with its grasping, delusion, and pursuit. This pursuit is connected to the entanglement of one's life with dualistic perceptions. The Buddha is one who has awakened, transcending the limitations of ordinary life and encompassing all things. It is a unity without duality, which leads to a clear, unobstructed realization, where stillness and movement are naturally in harmony. The human body is best suited for the practice of Buddhist teachings when it has already transcended duality and progressed to non-duality. This transcendence goes beyond inherent intellectual and rational reasoning, and it is precisely where one liberates oneself from the pursuits of grasping and delusion. The immediate awareness of the feeling is just one example of this. However, what we possess today is already a form of consciousness, rather than mere sensation. In practicing the Great Seal (Mahamudra), it seems necessary to begin by grasping onto sensation. Grasping sensation requires starting with a state of relaxed, open-minded tranquility, which helps to detach from the impulse of constant pursuit. Normally, I find myself unable to fall asleep due to even the tiniest unresolved matters.

> This inability to let go is a manifestation of the mentality of pursuit. Although outwardly, it seems like I am at ease, in reality, it is not. Now, in practicing the Great Seal, there is one obstacle that lies here.[23]

This entry still revolves around the practice of the Great Seal, with self-reflection on the obstacles encountered during its practice. However, the preceding extensive passage consists of Liang's own concise perspective on life. He emphasizes that human life should transcend the state of pursuit and be ensnared by desires, moving toward a state of unity with all things, free from duality. This transition involves overcoming inherent instincts, leading to a realm of rationality. These ideas about the unity of life and the understanding of the evolution of instincts, reason, and rationality form the fundamental tone of Liang's philosophy of life. He elaborates on these concepts in his various works, both before and after this diary entry. His book from late in life, *Human Nature and Human Life,* provides the most comprehensive exposition of these ideas. From this self-reflection, Liang realized that his own problem lay in his inability to let go of things and be at ease with them. This inability to release attachment to external matters was a manifestation of his being caught up in worldly pursuits. His challenge was to transcend this tendency and not be hindered by it in his practice of the Great Seal. According to Liang's initial experiences in practicing the Great Seal, he believed that before delving into the practice, one should first establish a sense of openness and tranquility within oneself, rather than merely understanding it on an intellectual level. This state of spaciousness is often used by Gongga Rinpoche when transmitting the concept of the state of spontaneous liberation in the practice of the Great Seal.

> August 8 (14th day of the 7th lunar month), Monday. Yesterday, I consulted Cao Mufan about this diary, and today, we briefly discussed his experiences. My intention is to cultivate the Vajra Yogini practice, and Cao agrees with this suggestion. Copied the translation of the Hundred Syllable Mantra in Chinese[24] and read summaries of the teachings from *Explanation of the Four Systems of Tantra.*[25] Had a fair amount of sleep, but after sleeping, the mind didn't feel refreshed, and there was a sense of fatigue, which is puzzling. Getting more accustomed to the practice of the Four Dharmas, but still finding it difficult to enter into the practice of the Great Seal.[26]

While practicing, Liang exchanged diary entries and insights with Cao and Luo, hoping for mutual inspiration. On this day, Liang not only engaged in recitation, but also copied the translated text of the Hundred Syllable Mantra, while also studying the teachings of Gongga Rinpoche's Brief *Explanation of the Four Systems of Tantra.* Liang felt that his practice of the Four Dharmas was becoming more familiar on this day, but he continued to struggle with entering the practice of the Great Seal. Therefore, he brought up the idea of practicing the Vajra Yogini method. The Vajra Yogini practice in Tibetan Buddhism is known to eliminate afflictions and cognitive obstacles and to harmonize energies and channels. It is likely that this method was also transmitted to him by his guru. He mentioned that his practice of the Four Dharmas was gradually becoming more familiar, indicating that there was progress in the initial stages of his practice.

> August 9 (15th day of the 7th lunar month), Tuesday. In last night's dream, various behaviors such as killing, stealing, and sexual misconduct were revealed, reflecting the deep-rooted habitual tendencies accumulated over countless lifetimes. Midnight, wanted to start the Vajrasattva purification practice to cleanse impurities and obscurations, but due to insufficient lamp oil, it couldn't be carried out. Morning, practiced the Four Dharmas with doubled warmth. Also, it's the Zhongyuan Festival for ancestral worship.[27]

It is not stated what happened during the daytime of this day, but in a dream, various actions related to killing, stealing, and sexual misconduct were revealed, which Liang attributed to deeply ingrained habitual tendencies from countless lifetimes. This prompted him to reflect deeply and recognize the need for purification. He attempted to practice the Vajrasattva purification practice during the middle of the night but was unable to do so. The practice involves two main aspects: visualizing the Vajrasattva Bodhisattva and reciting mantras like the Hundred Syllable Mantra. This practice is a crucial part of the Four Dharmas. Liang began his practice by reciting the Hundred Syllable Mantra from the start on the 4th of the month. His note about feeling a stronger sense of connection suggests that his practice had started to yield positive results.

> August 10 (16th day of the 7th lunar month), Wednesday. Through the night, dreams were filled with thoughts of fame and fortune, as well as self-preservation. Copied notes on the meditation technique of Vajra Yogini. Received five letters from Kuang Er and replied immediately. Among them were letters to Liu, Sun and others. Due to the tasks of copying and other matters, the practice of the Great Seal was not pursued. The regular Four Dharmas practices were carried out as usual.
>
> August 11 (17th day of the 7th lunar month), Thursday. "With a single thought, everything is real; with a single thought, nothing is real." Today, the practice of the Four Dharmas felt more genuine. I began practicing the Vajra Yogini for the first time and created a seventeen-syllable mantra diagram.
>
> August 12 (18th day of the 7th lunar month), Friday. My greatest ailment lies in not being able to feel clear and at ease within my heart. As a result, each thought is not grounded, and every day, my mind is divided in two directions, far from the path. I have always been aware of this, but today, during my practice, I felt the most profound realization of it. Practiced the Four Dharmas and the Vajra Yogini. Wrote a letter to Miao Ziyong. The weather is hot and dry. Practiced the first four forms of the Twelve Dharmas of Bodhidharma.
>
> August 13 (19th day of the 7th lunar month), Saturday. Practiced the Four Dharmas and the Vajra Yogini as usual. While reciting the Vajra Yogini mantra, couldn't quite

grasp the essential points of the mantra wheel's rotation. Rainfall, not heavy. Reading Nagarjuna's "Bodhicitta Treatise" brought great delight; started copying it.

August 14 (20th day of the 7th lunar month), Sunday. Clear and pleasantly cool day. The clear, pristine sky uplifts the spirit. Nearly dreamless night, yet afflicted by the malady of the restless mind; others might think I'm likely to achieve ease in meditation, but in reality, it's quite the opposite. Still struggling with the rotation of the syllable mantra of the Vajra Yogini practice. Continued copying the text of "Bodhicitta Treatise."[28]

On the 8th, Liang planned to practice Vajra Yogini, a suggestion welcomed by Cao Mufan. He began preparations from the 10th, copying notes from others who had practiced this method. On the 11th, he started his attempt at the practice. The practice of Vajra Yogini within the Kargyu tradition belongs to the Great Seal of Emptiness and Bliss lineage. Therefore, the formless Great Seal that Gongga Rinpoche transmitted to Liang may likely have been a part of the Great Seal of Emptiness and Bliss teachings, which is one of the three main lineages of Great Seal teachings within Tibetan Buddhism. This practice requires receiving empowerment, engaging in the Four Dharmas, developing a correct view through listening and contemplation, practicing Vajra Yogini, cultivating the practice of "entering the rough fire," and ultimately realizing the Great Seal, which is the pinnacle of the practice. From the diary entries, it is evident that from the 11th to the 14th day, he focused on practicing the Vajra Yogini method along with the Four Dharmas. However, he found it challenging to grasp the rotation of the Vajra Yogini mantra wheel, indicating that he encountered difficulties in mastering this aspect of the practice. The practice of Vajra Yogini in Tibetan Buddhism involves visualization. In this visualization, Vajra Yogini is imagined to have a moon disc on her body, with mantras arranged on the disc. This arrangement of mantras is referred to as the mantra wheel, and practitioners visualize it rotating while reciting the mantras. The rotation of the mantra wheel is believed to help clear and open the subtle energy channels, and it is considered part of the preliminary stages of the Vajra Yogini practice within the context of the broader teachings of the Great Seal. Indeed, it seems that Liang encountered some difficulties in the practice of rotating the mantra wheel. He Liang had a habit of reading books, so when he faced challenges in his meditation practice, he turned to reading Nagarjuna's "Bodhicitta Treatise" and then proceeded to copy its contents. This act of copying appears to have stemmed from his genuine interest in the scriptural texts rather than being solely aimed at eliminating distractions. Indeed, this sets Liang apart from his fellow practitioners, Luo and Cao.

August 15 (21st day of the 7th lunar month), Monday. During the night, there were still many disturbing dreams, leading to fatigue upon waking. The fatigue is expected to dissipate after some time. Excerpts from the essential parts of "Bodhicitta Treatise" and "Annotations on the Forest of Esotericism" were summarized. Suddenly realized that if the ailment of my mind's inability to rest is countered, the ailment grows worse; it should be left as it is without trying to control it, and only then can it become quiet; this "leaving

> it" requires a profound trust, then non-distraction arises by itself; this is the practice of the Great Seal. Seeking truth outside of delusion only increases delusion; recognizing that delusion doesn't depart from truth, delusion itself becomes unapparent. Reflecting on the principle that the five aggregates are not the self. Wu Hanji arrived; Wu Yuseng did not take up the position as the abbot of Baisha Monastery, but instead recommended Xiong Dongming and wrote a letter to urge his appointment. Reread the *Universal Virtue's Practices and Vows.* Stomach discomfort, reducing the practice session.[29]

Three days earlier, in the diary entry from the 12th, Liang's self-examination revealed, "My greatest ailment lies in not being able to feel clear and at ease within my heart." In the previous and this day's entries, he refers to this ailment as "the inability of the mind to be at leisure." One of its manifestations is long-term insomnia. Liang believed that he could not use a method of "counteracting" to treat his "mind's inability to be at leisure," but rather, he should approach it by allowing it to naturally unfold. Therefore, he needed to have immense trust in the approach of "leaving it." This aligns with the essence of the Great Seal practice of "abiding in the state of spontaneity."

> August 16 (22nd day of the 7th lunar month), Tuesday. Last night's dreams seemed to be somewhat reduced, and my stomach also improved slightly. Earlier, I mentioned that to study Buddhism, one must transcend the tendency of the pursuit of worldly life. Today, I realized that the root cause of this pursuit lies in discriminative calculations. As long as the mind that calculates discriminatively remains, the pursuit will not cease. In recent days, I've come to understand the principle of "not eliminating delusions and not seeking the truth." Normally, being unable to maintain an equanimous mind means being unable to be objective, veiling one's clarity. This not only hinders my ability to study Buddhism but also impacts my interactions with the world. Mufan's diligence is truly admirable, while I remain rather slow-witted. I wonder if age has something to do with it. Entering the sixth decade of life, it seems difficult to change the habits of the mind. I attempted to transition from practicing the Vajra Yogini method into the Great Seal practice, but I couldn't quite grasp it. I received a letter from Zhang Dongsun.[30]

"Not eliminating delusions and not seeking the truth" is a line from the *Song of Enlightenment.* The issue raised on the 7th about transcending greed, delusion, and chasing after desires is once again mentioned in this day's diary entry, reflecting on how this pursuit arises from a mind preoccupied with discrimination and calculation. This topic seems to be a recurring theme, suggesting that true realization has not yet been achieved. The understanding of the *Song of Enlightenment* still revolves around the concept of letting things take their natural course. Perhaps his thoughts were too entangled, as both the practice of the Vajra Yogini and the Great Seal seemed to yield no results.

> August 17 (23rd day of the 7th lunar month), Wednesday. The sky showed signs of cloudy, rainy weather, but it did not rain. During the night, my dreams were more leisurely, resembling a stroll by West Lake or watching a play. However, as soon as sleep set in, dreams emerged; there was always some form of dreaming, unable to achieve a state of dreamlessness. Those who practice the Dharma often use the metaphor of an infant or a nursing baby. An infant lacks cognitive understanding and exists purely in the present moment of sensory experience. Everything is returned to the infant; most of their experience is immediate perception. This can be considered a gateway to entering the path of the Dharma. First, eliminate conceptual attachments, and then proceed to eradicate attachment to dualistic conceptions. In the midst of the practice of the Four Dharmass, when reciting the phrase "with this, one can achieve great compassion and transform into a responsive incarnation," I suddenly realized the concept of attaining Buddhahood in Tantric Buddhism. Although I hold this belief, I lack a personal aspiration to achieve Buddhahood myself. My intention in undertaking this practice is primarily to refine and illuminate the mind. While the essence of becoming a Buddha lies in illuminating the mind, I wonder whether my practice lacks the determination and self-confidence required for achieving Buddhahood, making the progress less effective. I am unsure if this assessment is accurate or not.[31]

The esoteric sect advocates the concept of attaining Buddhahood in this body. Its meaning is twofold: one is to achieve Buddhahood in this lifetime, and the other is to attain Buddhahood in this physical body. Here, Liang raises an important question: when practicing the methods of esoteric Buddhism or practicing other Buddhist meditation techniques, is it necessary to take the practitioner's aspiration to become a Buddha as a prerequisite? Liang believed in the principle of attaining Buddhahood in this body in esoteric Buddhism, and he recited the phrase, "With this, I can become a Buddha or a Bodhisattva." However, he himself did not have the aspiration to attain Buddhahood in this body. His current practice of esoteric Buddhism was solely for the purpose of calming and nourishing his mind, aiming to overcome his ailment of a restless mind. He reflects on the inadequacies in his spiritual cultivation and suspects that his lack of aspiration to become a Buddha is the fundamental reason for it. In fact, practicing esoteric methods or other Buddhist practices does not necessarily require the explicit aspiration to become a Buddha in order for the practice to be effective. What esoteric Buddhism emphasizes is the use of a pure, clear mind in cultivation, which is the key factor.[32] Liang's characteristic is his tendency to engage in extensive contemplation, even though his contemplation is rational. This trait is attributed to his "habitual way of thinking at the age of nearly sixty."

> August 18 (24th day of the 7th lunar month), Thursday. During my morning meditation session, there seemed to be a state of "no thought" in the Great Seal practice, which is unprecedented in my previous experiences. Medicine was delivered from the junior

> high school. I handed over the corrected manuscript of chapters thirteen and fourteen and wrote a letter to Zhu Shaoyun, discussing matters related to Luo's elevation. The medication's effects seem to be limited, and my studies have slightly weakened, with a persistent lack of focus. I heard that there's a withdrawal of defenses in Fuzhou.[33]

This "no thought" refers to the no thought within the context of the Great Seal's practice of bliss, clarity, and no thought. Bliss, clarity, and no thought are three types of sensory experiences that arise during the process of practicing the Great Seal. Liang personally perceived that the state he achieved in his practice on this day was unprecedented, indicating progress in his spiritual practice. The "corrected manuscript of chapters thirteen and fourteen" refers to the proofreading of the book *Essence of Chinese Culture*.

> August 19 (25th day of the 7th lunar month), Friday. Silently observing, embracing the simplest in Yingzhong is most straightforward; following Mufan closely is also quite similar. Apart from studying Buddhism, there is nothing else to do. However, for me, it's not the same. From the day I took refuge in my guru, I had previously examined the matter myself: among all teachings, the teachings of Buddhism are the most supreme. How could I doubt that? However, considering the development of human culture, the present need is for Chinese culture rather than the timing for the teachings of Buddhism. At the same time, I am keenly aware of my responsibility regarding the current issue of nation-building in China and the transformation of world culture. There is no one else who can fulfill this role, and in my heart, I can say that nothing else matters apart from this. Those who take refuge feel that their wisdom is insufficient, and afflictions are still abundant. They seek to understand their own minds so that they have the capacity to handle tasks without becoming overwhelmed. However, due to an inability to detach from worldly matters, spiritual practice becomes challenging. Yet, upon careful reflection, what is meant by "letting go" is more about finding balance rather than completely abandoning responsibilities. Finding balance is in accordance with Buddhist teachings, while complete abandonment is not. This principle applies not only to the compassionate heart but also to the Great Seal's doctrine of "not making distinctions and choices." When my guru bestowed the formless Great Seal upon me, he also advised me not to hold onto things too tightly. This essence has remained consistent. Both Buddhist teachings and worldly matters coexist here; to follow their path without losing oneself might not be considered impure. If progress in spiritual practice is not achieved, it is necessary to further seek the cause.[34]

This continues the reflection from the 17th regarding the presence or absence of the aspiration to attain Buddhahood and the reasons for engaging in spiritual practice. According to Liang's statement here, when he took refuge in Gongga Rinpoche, he had a moment of introspection. First, he consistently believed that Buddhism was the supreme teaching, so his act of taking refuge was not deceptive to himself or others. However, he also recognized that in the current context of human culture, there was a need for Chinese culture rather than Buddhism. The value of Chinese culture was something only he could explain; there was no one else in the world capable of doing so. Therefore, he felt an immense responsibility toward the world and humanity. He could not forsake worldly matters for his refuge; worldly matters were his primary concern at the moment. And, the reason for his refuge was to reduce and eliminate afflictions, and to clarify and nurture his mind, in order to engage in tasks and responsibilities. This would be accomplished by maintaining a better mental and psychological state for handling worldly matters. He speculated that his inability to make progress in his spiritual practice was due to his inability to let go of worldly matters. However, he also acknowledged that he genuinely could not detach himself from worldly affairs, which led to the inner contradiction he faced. According to his own account, his lack of effectiveness in his esoteric practice stemmed primarily from an excessive Confucian inclination toward engagement with the world.

In this context, it is also mentioned that when Gongga Rinpoche transmitted the formless Great Seal, he specifically advised Liang to grasp the principle of "not holding onto things too tightly." Liang wholeheartedly accepted and upheld this approach.

> August 20 (26th day of the 7th lunar lunar month), Saturday. After the morning meditation session, I had a conversation with someone from the U.S. embassy. Ziying had called yesterday to arrange the meeting, most likely to discuss past matters related to the Democratic League. Chaojie and Fuyuan have returned to the mountain; their tasks have been accomplished. There was rain from last night until the morning, and it continued until around two o'clock in the afternoon. The practice of the Great Seal still hasn't yielded results. Chen Yucheng sent a lengthy letter.[35]

This day's practice of the Great Seal had not yet yielded results. The mention of tasks being accomplished likely refers to matters related to something involving Mianren Academy.

> August 21 (27th day of the 7th lunar month), Sunday. The recitation of the Vajra Yogini mantra was not flexible, and entering the practice of the Great Seal through visualization and calming the mind also did not bring about effectiveness. Nighttime dreams have not diminished, and the mind remains unclear. Li Dongsheng called. Ziying came to the mountain for a discussion. Xie Yan brought Sun's letter to visit. Introduced them to Ziyin. Yasan sent a letter but refused to come up the mountain; should ask again. The practice is being hindered.[36]

Liang continued the practice of the Vajra Yogini mantra. The mantra wheel could now rotate, but not smoothly. The attempt to transition into the practice of the Great Seal through visualization and calming the mind also had not yielded results. Numerous miscellaneous matters were affecting the practice. The previous entries leading up to this day had not mentioned the term visualization, which is crucial in esoteric practices, though the specific methods of visualization are not explained here.

> August 22 (28th day of the 7th lunar month), Monday. Rainfall, tranquility undisturbed. The sky is increasingly cool and pleasant. Practice continued without interruption. However, during meditation, while distractions have been somewhat subdued, it is uncertain whether this is equivalent to the state of "no thought." Mastery of the Vajra Yogini practice is still not proficient. Wrote letters to Deng Shaoqin, Jiang Dongzhi, and Ma Qiufan. Read the *Diamond Sutra*.[37]

During meditation, the restless thoughts subsided, and there was progress in the practice. However, he remained uncertain whether this corresponded to the stage of "no thought" in the Great Seal practice. He acknowledged that he was still not proficient in the Vajra Yogini practice. It appeared that his attempts with the Vajra Yogini practice had consistently been less effective. He read the *Diamond Sutra* again, probably aiming to understand the similarities and differences between the "no thought" practice of the Diamond Sutra and the formless meditation practice in esoteric Buddhism.

> August 23 (29th day of the 7th lunar month), Tuesday. Rain continued, alleviating the dryness. Rain stopped in the afternoon. Slight stomachache. Listened to Yingzhong's conversation, which made me feel vigilant. Practice remains consistent.[38]

The practice was the same as usual, with the primary focus still on practicing the Great Seal method.

> August 24 (1st day of the lunar leap month), Wednesday. After the morning meditation, Hou Ziwen came to discuss various matters related to the institute. Tang Shunyao, Luo Chonggao, Yu Changmao, and others also came to visit. Wrote a letter to Lü Zongheng. Received a letter from Gu Xiwu in Hong Kong, and Gu Mengxu eagerly awaits a conversation with me. Again, I preferred not to move around. Sent my diary to Yingzhong to read, and he also informed me about the situation after coming to the mountain and provided guidance. Rain started at four in the afternoon. There was an interruption in practice.[39]

Luo Yong and Liang exchanged their experiences in spiritual practice. According to Liang, Luo had a simple, focused mind, with no other concerns outside of studying Buddhism. This single-mindedness allowed him to make relatively quick progress. Thus, Luo could provide Liang with insights and experiences from his practice.

> August 25 (2nd day of the lunar leap month), Thursday. The nighttime temperature was very low. Replied another letter to Zhang Dongsun, which I asked Gu to forward. The two phrases "inherent purity" and "original Buddha" touched me deeply and brought tears to my eyes. Today, my concentration wasn't particularly good, and there was an interruption in practice.[40]

These two days were a bit occupied with external matters, causing his mind to scatter, so he did not engage in his practice. The phrases "inherent purity" and "original Buddha" touched him deeply, indicating that he had a profound emotional resonance with Buddhist teachings and principles; otherwise, tears would not have come forth in response.

> August 26 (3rd day of the lunar leap month), Friday. After the morning meditation, Yasan came to discuss matters related to the institute and the farm. Wrote a letter to Deng Ziqin. Replied to a letter from Chai Dongsheng. Took a slightly longer nap in the afternoon, resulting in an interruption in practice. Discussed my views on achieving Buddhahood with Yingzhong and Mufan. My practice remains consistent, but there hasn't been any progress.[41]

Liang resumed his practice in the evening, likely focusing on the Great Seal, but felt no advancement. Considering his discussion with Luo and Cao about their views on achieving Buddhahood, it seems that his attention might have still been divided between the aspiration to achieve Buddhahood and the effectiveness of his practice. His thoughts seemed to be predominantly intellectual, which might explain the slower progress in his spiritual practice.

IV

> August 27 (4th day of the lunar leap month), Saturday. After Yasan left, I suddenly realized that Chaojie's absence in the new farm plan was odd. I wrote a letter to Yasan inquiring about it and also wrote a letter to Chaojie. The rotation of the Vajra Yogini mantra wheel seems to be stiff. For several consecutive days, the practice of the Great Seal has been following the instruction of "mind focused on the eyes, eyes focused on emptiness," avoiding looking at any object.[42]

According to Nan Huaijin, he learned from Gongga Rinpoche that the essence of the transmission of the Great Seal practice was encapsulated in the instruction of "mind focused on the eyes, eyes focused on emptiness," which he considered as the foremost essence.[43] Liang's adherence to the instruction he mentioned here is consistent with Gongga Rinpoche's teaching. The practice of "mind focused on the eyes, eyes focused on emptiness" is a key method he emphasized in his current practice. As for his statement about the Vajra Yogini mantra wheel feeling stiff in rotation, it could be due to the interruptions in his practice over the previous week, though it also suggests that during the previous two days, the rotation of the Vajra Yogini mantra wheel had been flowing smoothly.

> August 28 (5th day of the lunar leap month), Sunday. After the morning meditation, Songtian and Yucheng came to the mountain. Discussed matters related to the farm with Sangtian. Wrote a letter to Zhou Taixuan and asked Zuofu to deliver it to Hong Kong; later heard that Zuofu had already left. Received a letter from Liang Zhonghua and replied. Heard about the withdrawal of defenses in Lanzhou.[44]

On this day, there is no record of practice, but there might have been changes in current events that influenced it. Liang had been concerned about politics for the previous twenty years, and the changes in the current situation undoubtedly had an impact on him.

> August 29 (6th day of the lunar leap month), Monday. I feel that there are only the demands of all living beings, yet I do not perceive any of my own demands. My eyes are focused only on the empty space about four finger widths in front of my nose, without looking at anything else. This is quite challenging, especially when gazing without any movement. Furthermore, to achieve the gaze without movement, one must exert effort. However, if one stares forcefully at an empty space, that very space is bound to transform into an object once again. It is necessary to let go of intense visual focus on the empty space and, instead, gaze without effort, as if not looking at anything, then after a long while, the thoughts will cease, and one can eventually enter emptiness. Regrettably, I have not yet been able to accomplish this. The bliss, clarity, and thoughtlessness must certainly begin with thoughtlessness. Songtian has sent someone to deliver the draft of the fourteenth chapter. Today, the mind and spirit are relatively refreshed. All living beings possess a mind, and the mind is the faculty of understanding and consciousness. This faculty exists even in plants (albeit in a weak, subtle manner), is more pronounced and stronger in animals, and is most pronounced and strongest in humans. The concept of consciousness in Yogacara philosophy refers to this, while consciousness related to the senses, sensations, thoughts, and actions points to another aspect of consciousness. The notion that the mind is Buddha is present here, and the clarity of bliss, clarity, and non-thought is also present here. Generally, all our understanding contains an element of clarity. Unfortunately, this clarity is often mixed with the impurities of habitual tendencies, and its scope is confined to a very small extent. Thoughtlessness is precisely the means to quiet the momentum of these habitual tendencies and to break through limitations. Bliss essentially resides in a state of natural ease, contentment, and self-sufficiency. Therefore, the three qualities of bliss, clarity, and non-thought are interconnected and signify a

> glimpse into the realization of Buddhahood. During the afternoon introspection, many shortcomings arose. There were gaps in my practice. I will read the *Combined Sources for the Five Lamps.*[45]

The first half of this day's diary entry still records the practice of contemplating the emptiness. Gongga Rinpoche emphasized *The Three Incisive Precepts* with particular emphasis on gazing into emptiness. According to the teachings of Gongga Rinpoche in the book *Exegesis on the Profound Techniques of the Three Incisive Precepts,* the condensed essence mantra is, "The mind focuses on the eyes, the eyes focus on emptiness. This is the essence of all essential points."[46] In the book *Essential Instructions on Guiding the Very Quintessential Heart Essence of Great Perfection,* transmitted by Gongga Rinpoche, the method of gazing into emptiness with the eye faculty involves fixing the gaze on the empty, tranquil space while maintaining awareness that clarity is also present within the preceding emptiness. Gazing into emptiness is established at a distance of sixteen finger widths, with a width as broad as an ox yoke, as a quantitative measure.[47] The practice of observing internal emptiness further builds upon this foundation of gazing into external emptiness. Liang found this method of contemplating emptiness challenging after his practice, indicating that it was not easy for him to enter into this state. Bliss, clarity, and non-thought constitute the experiential aspect of the Great Seal. Liang perceived bliss as a state of ease and contentment, clarity as unobstructed understanding, and non-thought as the tranquility within emptiness. These three qualities are interconnected, with non-thought as the foundation. By attaining non-thought, one can quiet the hindrance of habitual clarity and consequently achieve the freedom of bliss. These interpretations seem to reflect one's personal perspectives and innovations in terms of theory. Additionally, the reference to Chapter Thirteen and Chapter Fourteen in the diary entry from the 18th day and the current diary entry likely pertain to the proofs of *Essentials of Chinese Culture,* indicating that even within the practice of stillness, the mind can be quite diverse in its distractions.

Liang believed that all living beings possess a mind, which serves as a faculty of understanding. In the case of humans, this faculty of understanding becomes precious through clarity. His discourse appears to integrate multiple dimensions: this clarity of understanding is both reflective of the esoteric clarity of tantric Buddhism and the bright virtue of clarity of mind from *The Great Learning.* It also resonates with Mencius' concept of the clear awareness of an innate moral sense. However, human clarity of understanding is often obscured by impurities of habitual tendencies, making it challenging to break through and manifest clearly. Indeed, this framework of interpretation does not align strictly with Buddhist teachings; rather, it aligns more closely with Confucian thought. It represents Liang's personal understanding of the clarity of consciousness within life, reflecting a perspective that integrates elements from both Confucianism and his own insights into the nature of consciousness. Certainly, by intertwining these concepts and linking the notion of non-thought within the context of the Great Seal, Liang appears to exhibit an inclination toward amalgamating the Confucian philosophy of life with Buddhist teachings.

> August 30 (7th day of the lunar leap month), Tuesday. People in the world prioritize external matters over internal ones, focusing on the significant aspects of things while considering themselves insignificant. The sages of old have already spoken of this. In reality, the multitude of sentient beings sinking into the cycle of life and death is all due to this. Compared to animals, only humans can still lift their heads up and look forward. It is not necessarily fixed like this, so there is hope. Confucianism holds that there is inherent brightness and integrity in the human heart, surpassing all things. This is where confidence lies, and it is firmly believed without doubt. Indeed, if one's thoughts are consistent without deviations, then being born or not being born into life and death can also be of no concern. Regrettably, the influence of various ingrained habits and tendencies is exceedingly strong, and there is nothing reliable to depend upon. In fact, the tendency to prioritize the external over the internal persists. This is why in Buddhism, it is necessary to eliminate the roots of attachment to discrimination and attachment to existence. By actualizing the true nature and the Dharma body, the distinctions between internal and external, self and others, vanish, and only then are problems dissolved. My stomach has been consistently unwell, affecting the efficacy of the Vajra Yogini mantra. Took another round of anti-inflammatory pills. I wrote a letter to Xu Shuren. The osmanthus flowers are in full bloom in front of the temple.[48]

The temple where the flowers were blooming must be the Jinyun Temple. Despite practicing the Vajra Yogini mantra, there had been no progress. In addition, Confucianism and Buddhism were the lifelong topics that Liang had expounded upon. He always believed that Buddhism addresses the issue of life and death in a way that Confucianism has not and cannot. However, he also affirmed that Confucianism recognizes the inherent positive brightness within the human heart and can demonstrate its virtues. He maintained his trust and confidence in Confucianism's belief in the inherent brightness of the human heart.

> August 31 (8th day of the lunar leap month), Wednesday. Upon careful reading of the *Platform Sutra of the Sixth Patriarch,* I have gained significant insights (despite having read it multiple times in my earlier years). Its teachings align perfectly with the concept of the Great Seal, and though I have heard these teachings before, they are no longer mere novelty. In my present state, my understanding has taken a significant turn, freeing me from constant distractions. My midday nap was deep, yet dreams still persisted. There was a slight deficiency in my studies.

Rereading the *Platform Sutra of the Sixth Patriarch,* he felt its alignment with the teachings of the Great Seal practice. Liang's sentiments about this should indeed be relatable. Although this wasn't his first time reading the *Platform Sutra,* he still found it beneficial for his practice, bringing a sense of tranquility to his mind and freeing him from constant distractions. This could be said to be the result of the combination of theory and practice.

The above is the practice diary for August, and the following is the practice diary for September:

> (September) 1 (9th day of the lunar leap month), Thursday. When one's actions conform to worldly conventions and are guided by habitual tendencies, one continues to revolve in the cycle of life and death. However, through self-awareness arising from a single thought, the distractions of the world are put to rest. Abiding in the genuine heart, there is no duality in stillness and movement. This is referred to as the inherent Buddha. Derived this insight from reading the *Platform Sutra of the Sixth Patriarch*. For several days, my practice of the Vajra Yogini mantra has been somewhat lax. Today, I resumed the practice of the mantra, but the rotation of the mantra wheel was difficult to establish. Ziying still could not come to the mountain due to a phone call; we rescheduled for Sunday. There are only two ways in which ordinary people live their lives: rushing through days in haste or passing the time in leisure. If practitioners of Buddhism fall into either of these two categories, it's quite a ridiculous matter (even Confucian scholars do not fall into this). Wan and Wang both came to the mountain. I read the *Record of the Transmission of the Lamp*.[49]

The main ideas he derived from reading the *Platform Sutra* can be considered quite succinct and concise. It is evident that his understanding of Buddhism was actually quite accurate. Liang's distinctive feature lay in his emphasis on theoretical reasoning. He used theory to guide practice and believed he had gained insights. However, in reality, these insights did not contribute to actual spiritual practice. Not only did they fail to assist, but they might have even hindered his practice. His practice of the Vajra Yogini mantra was not very smooth, missing a few days of practice in the course. Surprisingly, on this day, there was considerable regression, and the rotation of the mantra wheel had become difficult. As the practice was not progressing well, he turned to reading the *Record of the Transmission of the Lamp*.

> September 2 (10th day of the lunar leap month), Friday. I read Master Sengcan's *Inscription of Faith*, repeatedly self-examining and studying without end—not necessarily achieving understanding, but the sentiment was unstoppable. After ten o'clock at night, I had already fallen asleep. Suddenly, Ziying sent a telegram informing me of the massive fire in Chongqing. The disaster is extremely severe, and prayers for its cessation are sought. It is currently scorching at noon, and the wind will soon rise. The fire is being fueled by the wind, making it even more intense. I read volumes 28, 29, and 30 of the *Record of the Transmission of the Lamp*.[50]

Reading the *Inscription of Faith* and studying the *Record of the Transmission of the Lamp* were both attempts to seek the methods and teachings of ancient practitioners in order to learn from them. However, even if some understanding was gained, it remained at the level of theory, and it may not necessarily have contributed to actual meditative practice. From here, it can be observed that Liang's approach to practicing esoteric Buddhism was not exclusive; he always resorted to methods from exoteric Buddhism to engage with it. This not only resulted in his lack of progress in his practice, but also accounted for his inability to delve deeply into the practice.

> September 3 (11th day of the lunar leap month), Saturday. It's drizzling and cool. Ziying sent another telegram describing the dire situation of the fire disaster. He is planning to lead his subordinates to Chongqing for relief efforts. I wrote letters to reassure Lei Renbai and Wen Deyang. Zhao and Hu came to the mountain. Practice remains quite inadequate.[51]
>
> September 4 (12th day of the lunar leap month), Sunday. In the morning, there was a light rain, and it cleared up in the afternoon. Starting today, I switched to performing the Four Dharmas practice after breakfast and the Great Seal after waking up in the morning. Upon waking up, I no longer felt the twisting sensation in my heart that I had previously. Ziying called and won't be coming up to the mountain anymore.[52]

On August 31, Liang mentioned that the practice of the mind had greatly turned around. On September 4, he felt that the practice of the mind was still present. He practiced the Great Seal after waking up in the morning, and later engaged in the Four Dharmas practice. It seems that there hasn't been any noticeable effectiveness in either of these practices.

> September 5 (13th day of the lunar leap month), Monday. In the past, I was fixated on the idea of concentrating the mind on the eyes, and the eyes on emptiness, striving to stabilize my gaze on the realm of emptiness. However, I found it difficult to maintain focus. The instruction to gaze at the space in front of the nose and then turn the attention back to observe the mind also posed challenges. Now, I suddenly realize that gazing at the emptiness and gazing at the mind are essentially the same thing. The notion of turning back is perhaps unnecessary. Moreover, by observing the mind, there is no need to intentionally stabilize the gaze on the realm of emptiness; the gaze will naturally stabilize. Additionally, through observing the mind, it is also easier to attain a state of thoughtlessness when the mind becomes empty and devoid of arising thoughts. Received a report from Yu Changmao about the affairs of the farm on the mountain. Responded to Yasan and Ziwun's letters. Also wrote a letter to Xu Nülun, inquiring about the safety of the Lei family. Luming Bookstore sent advertisements. After a discussion with everyone, it was agreed that we would descend the mountain on the 20th of the lunar calendar.[53]

Before this, practicing the Great Seal involved the instruction to concentrate the mind on the eyes, and the eyes on the mind, focusing the gaze on the realm of emptiness. There was also an emphasis on gazing at the space in front of the nose and turning back to observe the mind. Liang found both of these practices to be quite challenging. On the day when the decision to end the retreat and descend the mountain was made, he inevitably had some commentary on the practice of the Great Seal. It seems he was starting to lose firm belief in it. His remarks, such as indicating that fixating on the realm of emptiness while gazing or the notion of turning back were unnecessary, and even suggesting that there was no need to intentionally stabilize the gaze on the emptiness, all indicate his disappointment with this round of practicing the Great Seal.

V

> September 6 (14th day of the lunar leap month), Tuesday. It rained. I had a dream last night that felt like the initial days here. Even during the nap in the afternoon, my mind remained unsettled. I sigh at Mr. Wu's ability to casually nap for fifteen minutes, something I find unattainable. In the *Recorded Sayings of Guifeng*, it says, "To verify whether one is at ease or not at ease at the moment of death, just observe whether the ordinary mind is free or not free while engaged in worldly matters." Observing from the sidelines, it is undoubtedly true that Mr. Wu finds great satisfaction in his deep cultivation. Although Confucianism and Buddhism are different, they share a common thread in this regard. I heard there have been changes in Kunming, and the airlift has been suspended. My stomach has been consistently unsettled, which is quite strange. The practice of the Vajra Yogini mantra has been temporarily halted.[54]
>
> September 7 (15th day of the lunar leap month), Wednesday. The weather is cloudy with rain. I wrote a letter to Ziying, informing him of the date we will descend the mountain, and I also entrusted him to pass on a letter to Zuofu (attached with the draft of the 14th chapter). I also wrote to inform Peikuan that he should find time to come to the mountain, to discuss matters related to relocating.

Liang sighed that Wu Yongbo was a pure Confucian, yet his sense of ease and freedom in both mind and action was akin to that of Buddhism. The lack of significant progress in this current practice seemed to evoke his thoughts about Confucian learning. In the matter of cultivating and illuminating the mind, he seemed to feel that there was no distinction of superiority between Confucianism and Buddhism. This might be one reason he could not wholeheartedly commit to exclusively practicing esoteric methods.

> September 8 (16th day of the lunar leap month), Thursday. I was awake almost the entire night, with a short nap just before dawn. I felt extremely fatigued. Amidst the tossing and turning, a deep realization of everything being nothing but the mind emerged. In my humble understanding of taking refuge in a teacher, the initial motivation stemmed from a strong sense of discomfort and suffering, which primarily revolved around insomnia. Experiencing severe insomnia before descending the mountain seems to signify the failure of the one-month mountain retreat. In the morning, I did not practice the Great

> Seal, only the Four Dharmas. After breakfast, I attempted to take a short nap, but it remained elusive, though my mind rested for about half an hour. Strangely, I did not feel as tired or sleepy as anticipated. Furthermore, there was no clear reason for this bout of insomnia. While reading selected quotations from the *Yongzheng Imperial Selection*, I sighed at the unattainability of its content.

Liang openly admits that his commitment to esoteric practice this time was motivated solely by the desire to alleviate his discomfort and suffering. However, the fact that he experienced severe insomnia on the day before descending the mountain seems to symbolize the failure of this round of practice. Nevertheless, he still persisted in practicing the Four Dharmas rather than giving up.

> September 9 (17th day of the lunar leap month), Friday. The weather cleared up in the afternoon. The situation in Yunnan seems to be easing. Mufan and Daohong descended the mountain. Sleep and appetite appear to be better today. Received a reply from Liangyong. Reading the news, Lei Renbai is safe. Also received a response from Shuren. Peiying came to the mountain. Received a letter from Shili. Additionally, my wife received a letter from Ms. Chen, which provided insights into the ideological trends in Wuhan and Beiping. Studies were slightly relaxed. Heard that Daohong's relapse of illness is related to his old ailment in the chest.[55]

The studies were slightly relaxed, but practice was still maintained, likely focusing mainly on the Four Dharmas.

> September 10 (18th day of the lunar leap month), Saturday. The weather was clear and delightful, with rising temperatures. Yao Mingshan came to bid farewell as he was returning to the north. Yingzhong and his wife spoke highly of Peikuan's virtuous disposition. Yingzhong seems to believe that my continuous exertion outside is the cause of my ailment (he mentioned this a few days ago). I'm not unaware of my own condition either. This probably encompasses two aspects. On the one hand, there's a strong inclination toward the path, yet the diligent efforts I engage in might not align with my real needs, and also, I might feel that my movements are cumbersome and heavy, which is one layer of the situation. In addition, I might have gained some understanding of the realm of Prajnaparamita, Madhyamaka, and even the principles of the Great Seal. However, it is regrettable that I am preoccupied with worldly considerations in the midst of seeking a livelihood. I am constantly moving back and forth externally, and the more I am absorbed in these considerations, the more distant I become from realizing the truth. This is another layer of the situation. Perhaps these two aspects are closely related and cannot be separated. Knowing the issue and not being able to let go—if I were to let go, it would mean fully relinquishing everything, but it is like having heavy hands. Moreover,

> I cannot truly let go from within myself. (Thinking that letting go would be beneficial is still not letting go. Or thinking that letting go means being completely perfect, but being unwilling to let go.) Unable to let go and continuously bringing it up, I am still inevitably caught up in worldly considerations. Because action requires some level of consideration, knowing the issue yet not being able to let go tends to be something like this. So, what conclusion can be drawn? It seems that the only way forward is to reduce excessive contemplation and calculations, and instead proceed in a simple, straightforward manner. Stick to the current routine and curriculum without aiming for results. Whenever there is a breakthrough, consider it a success, and if not, just continue the practice without being attached to outcomes.[56]

This is his summary of this retreat's practice. Luo Yong believed that the lack of effectiveness in Liang's practice at this time was due to his lack of focus, as he could not seem to detach his attention from external matters. This was why he was unable to see the results of his practice. Liang reflected on himself, acknowledging that his aspiration toward the path was sincere, but he struggled to grasp the essentials. More importantly, he realized that he often indulged in contemplation and calculations, which obstructed the direct realization of truth. In essence, he had been overly engaged in intellectual analysis, while he should have actually abandoned conceptual thinking and focused solely on the practical aspect of the practice. Indeed, even though he had gained some understanding of the principles behind the Great Seal on an intellectual level, he had struggled to dive deep into the practice itself.

> September 11 (19th day of the lunar leap month), Sunday. After the morning practice session, I went down the mountain as scheduled to meet Zuofu. I entrusted him with various letters and gave him some books to pass on to Gu and Zhou. Workers from the institution came to move our luggage, getting prepared for the descent from the mountain tomorrow.[57]

With the conclusion of this retreat, Liang ended his several years of non-political life in Chongqing. He was invited to return to Beijing and reenter political life. Whether he continued practicing the Four Dharmas or other methods after descending the mountain is not known.

The first generation of modern Neo-Confucian masters, such as Xiong Shili, Ma Yifu, and Liang Shuming, all had deep connections with Buddhism. Although Xiong criticized Buddhist teachings, he continued to recite the death-rebirth mantra frequently before his passing.[58] This demonstrates the intricate relationship they had with Buddhism, which cannot be explained in a few words. The reason we pay attention to Liang's engagement with esoteric practices is not primarily to inquire about his relationship with Buddhism. Rather, it stems from our interest in his cultivation efforts, aiming to highlight the fact that there were individuals who truly emphasized spiritual practice among the first generation of modern Neo-Confucian scholars. In fact, Liang's lifelong practice encompassed various aspects; meditative practices were just one facet of his overall endeavors. However, his documented meditative practice, as a case study of the spiritual dimension within modern Neo-Confucianism, can provide some insights into understanding the contemplative practices of Confucian scholars in the Song and Ming dynasties. This is also a reason for our attention to this particular case.

Even for individuals who, like Liang, held Buddhism as their ultimate concern, their engagement in esoteric meditation was primarily functional. It was not about using these practices as a means to attain Buddhahood in this life; their purpose was not to achieve Buddhahood, but rather to utilize these practices as tools to alleviate mental afflictions and pursue inner tranquility. From this, it can be inferred that in ancient times, Confucian scholars who interacted with Buddhists and practiced meditation within temples did not necessarily have to abandon their Confucian societal concerns and value positions.

In addition, transcending the hustle and bustle of worldly pursuits and entering a realm of spacious tranquility is a shared spiritual pursuit among Confucianism, Buddhism, and Daoism. Liang's engagement in meditative practice aligns with this aim. Spirituality encompasses various aspects and is not limited to the cultivation of moral character alone. The pursuit of inner freedom and ease is not only about overcoming the troubles of life but also represents a positive, ultimate aspiration toward understanding the human mind and human existence.

Further, Liang's example illustrates that not all practitioners of meditation need to attain profound realization. Even if a practitioner has philosophical commitments, it does not necessarily lead to a direct experiential realization of those philosophical principles. In terms of inner disposition, even though one might engage in meditation to varying degrees, it does not necessarily result in a profound internal experience. This is particularly true for those who are accustomed to rational thinking.

The extent of effectiveness in meditation and whether one has experiential insights can potentially influence a person's understanding of their entire spiritual practice and their choice of personal cultivation methods. Liang later emphasized virtues like caution, fear, and solitude in his discussions on Confucian cultivation, advocating for self-awareness in reflection and constant vigilance to prevent faults. This might align with aspects of Zhu Xi's teachings, and it could be related to his experiences in meditation.

Finally, Liang's experience highlights that his attempt at esoteric practice during this period was not particularly successful. A significant reason for this might be how Confucianism and Buddhism were situated within his life and consciousness, creating a unique internal issue for him. He says, "The foundation of my thoughts is both Confucianism and Buddhism,"[59] and further expresses, "In terms of thought, I'm inclined toward Buddhism; in terms of life, I'm aligned with Confucianism." He consistently believed that for him, Confucianism and Buddhism were not conflicting forces. However, during his meditative practice, it seems unclear whether his ultimate concern lay more with worldly engagement or with transcending the world. The balance between his concern for the world and his spiritual aspirations remains ambiguous.

The significance and reconciliation of these two aspects remain a question that Liang left us. He consistently acknowledged his fundamental alignment with Buddhism in his thinking, as seen in his affirmation of Buddhist worldviews like the notion that life is neither continuous nor permanent and that all phenomena are devoid of self. At the same time, he emphasized the Mahayana Bodhisattva path of not forsaking sentient beings and not abiding in Nirvana, which aligns with his Confucian-like commitment to an engaged compassion for the world. This is why his lifestyle is akin to Confucianism. However, how does someone who believes in the Buddhist worldview automatically become Confucian when they engage in worldly affairs? Does merely engaging in worldly matters make someone fully Confucian? Clearly, it doesn't. Liang's beliefs in life extolled the positive aspects of human nature, praised ethical values in the human realm, and elaborated on and promoted the values of Chinese culture. These are not things that can be simply embraced through mere worldly engagement. According to his perspective, his worldview of the cycle of life and death did not directly manifest in the practical aspects of his life. It appears largely disconnected from his practical existence. In his view, his actions in real life were not guided by his life-and-death worldview. Instead, his practical life and actions were founded on inner values rooted in a Confucian understanding of human nature and human existence. The promotion of Chinese culture and Confucian values seemed to be of paramount importance to him, dominating his practical concerns with the sentiment in the phrase, "Among myriad things, this is the greatest." As a result, within his inner self, a distinct cultural-psychological structure was formed. On the human level, encompassing politics, society, culture, and ethics, he embraced Confucian values and Chinese culture. Simultaneously, in matters of belief about life, death, and religious experiences, he leaned toward Buddhism. This might appear similar on the surface to Daniel Bell's notion of non-monolithic cultural identity structure. However, for Liang, this was not merely a superficial juxtaposition. Instead, it reveals his personal and distinct dualistic ultimate concern. Because he rarely discussed his inner beliefs about life and death, his life was mostly characterized by Confucian actions, convictions, values, and personality traits in many instances.

(The initial draft was written at Zhongyang University on November 1, 2008.)

Notes

1. *Complete Works of Liang Shuming*, vol. 8 (Shandong People's Publishing House, 1993), 420–421.
2. Ibid., 420.
3. Guo Qiyong, "Three Letters and One Article of Xiong Shili and Liang Shuming's Lost Letters."
4. *Complete Works of Liang Shumnig*, vol. 8, 420.
5. Dongming, also known as Xiong Dongming, graduated from Yenching University and once studied Buddhism at The Chinese Inner Studies Institute. He also had association with Master Taixu.
6. *Complete Works of Liang Shuming*, vol. 8, 421.
7. Ibid.
8. The area around Shangqing Temple was the place most frequented by political figures during the period of the Nationalist government. "Te," "Fan," "Gui," and "Zhou" were places where well-known individuals lived and engaged in political activities. During this period, Zhang Lan, one of the founders of the

Democratic League, lived in Te Garden, where many famous democratic figures gathered, earning it the title "Home of Democracy." The Chinese Democratic League was founded in Te Garden, with Liang Shuming being one of the initiators. Liang later mentioned that during his time in Chongqing, he often stayed in the garden (Liang Shuming's letter to Chen Zhongyu on December 30, 1976. *Complete Works of Liang Shuming*, vol. 8, 106).

9. *Complete Works of Liang Shuming*, vol. 8, 421.
10. Ibid.
11. Ibid., 308.
12. Ibid., 421.
13. Cao Mufan (1912–1993), also known as Chi'an, was from Luzhou, Sichuan. He was a professor in the Chinese Department of Southwest Normal University. He graduated from Jinling University early in his career and studied Buddhist and Neo-Confucian philosophy under Xiong Shili at the Chinese Philosophy Research Institute in Wutong Bridge, Leshan, Sichuan, from 1946 to 1947. From 1947 to 1950, he served as an associate professor in the Chinese Department of Beibei Mianren College (founded by Liang Shuming). After 1953, he became the deputy director of the library at Southwest Normal College (later renamed Southwest Normal University) and a professor in the Chinese Department and the Institute of Chinese Language and Literature. According to his diary, only Luo and Cao were mentioned, seemingly without Xie Wuliang and his wife.
14. Gongga Rinpoche (1893–1957) visited mainland China twice in the 1930s and 1940s. Over a period of more than eight years, he traveled to and fro between Sichuan, Yunnan, Hubei and Hunan, Jiangsu, Jiangxi, Beijing, Shanghai, Shaanxi, and Jiangxi, attracting tens of thousands of followers, including many high-ranking officials of the Kuomintang.
15. Master Nenghai (1886–1966) served as the vice chairman of the Southwest Military and Political Committee and the vice chairman of the Chinese Revolutionary Committee of the Kuomintang after 1949. He was also the vice chairman of the Chinese Buddhist Association.
16. *Complete Works of Liang Shuming*, vol. 8, 584.
17. Ibid., 586.
18. Mr. Xian, also known as Xian Ying (style name Tesheng), was the original owner of Te Garden. See the diary entry for May 27–28, 1950, *Complete Works of Liang Shuming*, vol. 8, 433.
19. *Complete Works of Liang Shuming*, vol. 8, 422.
20. Ibid., 422.
21. Ibid., 422.
22. This book is also known as *The Direct Discourse no Gonga Rinpoches' Ganges Mahamudra*, as mentioned in *The Essential Explanation of Mahamudra Yoga in the Great Seal: Khenpo Kartse Rinpoche's Lecture Collection* (New Wenfeng Publishing Company, 1993), 73–95.
23. *Complete Works of Liang Shuming*, vol. 8, 422.
24. Hundred Syllable Mantra was originally in Tibetan. There are several translations, but it's unknown which one Liang Shuming used. It means "transmitted by Gongga." Chen Jianmin has translated hymn of Hundred Syllable Mantra that may be referred to:
    Hail the great Vajrasattva's secret vow,
    Suddenly manifesting its own pure nature,
    In the position of the Vajra heart Buddha,
    Making me firmly abide,

Manifesting my true essential nature,
Granting me supreme joy,
Manifesting my vast essential nature,
Allowing me to follow my greedy essential nature,
Granting me all accomplishments,
Allowing me to accomplish al endeavors,
Granting my mind complete great courage,
Allowing me to generate the great uses of the five wisdoms.
The great one who has gone to bliss, all Buddhas,
Do not abandon the Vajra essence of me,
Allowing me to dwell in the Vajra nature,
Having a complete great vow heart,
Regarding the ultimate essence of Dharma as unborn,
Generating the joy of empty wisdom, hum,
Subjugating all demonic adversaries, phat.

25. Refers to Gongga Rinpoche's *Brief Explanation of the Four Systems of Tantra*, originally titled *Introduction to the Four Systems.*
26. *Complete Works of Liang Shuming*, vol. 8, 422.
27. Ibid., 423.
28. All the above references are found in *Complete Works of Liang Shuming*, vol. 8, 423.
29. *Complete Works of Liang Shuming*, vol. 8, 423.
30. Ibid.
31. Ibid., 424.
32. "The Essential Explanation of Mahamudra Yoga," in *The Great Seal: Khenpo Kartse Rinpoche's Lecture Collection*, 64.
33. *Complete Works of Liang Shuming*, vol. 8, 424.
34. Ibid.
35. Ibid.
36. Ibid., 425.
37. Ibid.
38. Ibid.
39. Ibid.
40. Ibid.
41. Ibid.
42. Ibid.
43. Nan Huaijin wrote a preface to the combined edition of *Ganges Mahamudra* and *The Three Incisive Precepts.* The full text reads, "Tracing back to the Yuan Dynasty, when Emperor Kublai Khan's tutor, Master Phags-pa, disseminated and translated the Tibetan Esoteric Buddhism, the *Great Seal Mahayana Tantra*, initially, the state of Mahayana Esotericism within the country fluctuated and changed. With the establishment of the Republic of China, the teachings of Tibetan Esotericism resurged once again. The trend of practicing Esoteric Mahayana became popular, especially regarding the Great Seal Mahayana as the highest practice without cultivation or certification. *The Three Incisive Precepts* is considered the ultimate practice of the Great Seal Mahayana. Those who obtain it are said to have attained the great path of enlightenment,

exclusively in this practice. However, those profound in Esoteric Mahayana also consider the *Great Seal* and *The Three Incisive Precepts* akin to the Mind Seal of Zen Buddhism. It is said that when Bodhidharma, the Great Master, passed the Mind Seal, he later transmitted it to Tibet, thus forming the Great Seal Mahayana. I have heard this and have doubts. When I was in Sichuan and Xikang, I once asked the confirmation of this matter from the Gongga Rinpoche, and he also said it was passed down like this. After practicing this method myself, comparing it with the essential points of Zen Buddhism, I realized that although they are similar, they are quite different from the Mind Seal transmitted by Bodhidharma. It is not to be confused in discussion. The Mind Seal of Zen Buddhism is essentially the gateless gate, if expressed in words, it is already not true. How can there be methods to transmit or practices to cultivate? If there are, they are only superficially similar to the gradual cultivation of Zen Buddhism, ultimately realizing the instantaneous enlightenment beyond words and concepts. Following this path of practice, accumulating merits through eons, one can also ascend to the position of a saint. If one desires to break through the peak of Pilu, abandoning all traces without hiding, there is still much to be done. Moreover, taking the sudden cessation of thought as the practice method, without demonstrating that the nature of the mind is inherently pure and complete, it is unclear about the superiority of the whirlwinds subside, and the mountains and rivers flow ceaselessly. It claims bliss, clarity, and non-thought as the ultimate of Buddhist teachings, without elucidating what constitutes bliss, clarity, and non-thought, leaving much unexplained. It regards focusing the mind on the eyes, the eyes on emptiness as the essence of the three essentials, without clarifying the subtlety of 'no law in front of the eyes, the intention is in front of the eyes, not what the eyes see, not what the ears and eyes perceive.' Few can transcend attachment to practices. Now, encountering the fortuitous opportunity to compile these two practices together, I do not hesitate to elaborate on their profound meanings and append them as prefaces, even if it means dragging my eyebrows on the ground."

44. *Complete Works of Liang Shuming*, vol. 8, 425.
45. Ibid., 426.
46. "Exegesis on the Profound Techniques of the Three Incisive Precepts," in *The Mahamudra Yoga of The Great Seal* (New Wenfeng Publishing Company in 1993), 72.
47. Qiu Ling, *Ten Lectures on the Essentials of Tibetan Esotericism.*
48. *Complete Works of Liang Shuming*, vol. 8, 426.
49. Ibid.
50. Ibid., 427.
51. Ibid.
52. Ibid.
53. Ibid.
54. Ibid.
55. Ibid.
56. Ibid., 428.
57. Ibid.
58. "Liang Shuming's Letter to Tian Muzhou," in *Complete Works of Liang Shuming*, vol. 8, 183–184.
59. *Complete Works of Liang Shuming*, vol. 8, 1137.

CHAPTER 12

Metaphysics in Feng Youlan's *New Neo-Confucianism*

Though Feng Youlan's system of New Neo-Confucianism is quite clear, this chapter aims to further elaborate on and review some basic concepts of the metaphysics of New Neo-Confucianism, so as to gain a deeper understanding of the pros and cons of its philosophical framework. A simple comparison will also be made between the study of metaphysics in New Neo-Confucianism and the theory of principles and vital energy in traditional Neo-Confucianism, to highlight the similarities and differences between the two and deepen our understanding of both theories.

I. Reality and Truth

Three fundamental concepts are introduced at the beginning of *New Neo-Confucianism*, namely "objects in reality," reality, and truth. The first question that naturally arises is the distinction between objects in reality and reality. According to *New Neo-Confucianism*, "objects in reality" refers to things that have a factual basis, while reality refers to all things that actually exist.[1] However, this definition is not entirely clear. It does not specify whether "objects in reality" refers to a specific or any existing entity, or if it encompasses every entity that exists. If it includes all entities that exist, what, then, is the difference between objects in reality and reality? Moreover, this definition does not clarify whether reality pertains to the existence of everything or the entirety of existence. In other words, it does not clarify whether reality is a categorial (universal) or collective concept.

This does not mean that Feng's thoughts are unclear; rather, some expressions in the formulation of his New Neo-Confucianism require further clarification and refinement. According to the way of New Neo-Confucianism, in the proposition, *this is a dog*, "this" is the object in reality, while "dog" is the reality. Considering Feng's methods and the logic in "New Neo-Confucianism," it can be said that "objects in reality" is a concept of "something specific," which is an "individual." On the other hand, the issue with "reality" is slightly more complex.

Chinese terms tend to have multiple conceptual meanings, potentially referring to any one of a certain category of things, the entirety of that category, or abstract attributes of that category. They can thus function as both categorial and collective terms, as well as specific identifiers (as suggested by Gongsun Long). In relation to specific entities, reality is a categorial term, a universal concept. It is established to differentiate between individual entities and categories, and is used to refer to different categories of existing entities. In comparison with the underlying truth, reality is a collective term that refers to the world of affairs, similar to the concept of actual existence.

Another concept that requires clarification is truth. The word *ji*, which appears in *zhenji*, the term translated here as "truth," also carries the meaning of existence in Chinese philosophy. *New Neo-Confucianism* states, "Truth refers to everything that can be regarded present, and can be referred to as fundamental nature. Reality refers to all things that actually exist, and can be termed nature."[2] The contrast between the concepts of truth and reality shows that truth can be true but not real. Though not real and not actually existing, it is still a kind of presence, one with no real presence. As expressed later in *A New Understanding of Words*, it is "present, yet non-existent." According to the thought of *New Neo-Confucianism*, truth is a presence, which includes real presence and potential presence. Real presence refers to the real world, while potential presence pertains to a logical world. New Neo-Confucianism argues that it is insufficient to acknowledge real presence; one must also recognize the potential presence that exists beyond real presence, as mentioned in new realism. Yet, truth often narrowly refers to potential presence, or pure truth. In this sense, the distinction between pure truth and real presence differs from that between presence and actual existence in Hegel's philosophy. In the latter system, presence is an abstraction of real presence, while in New Neo-Confucianism, the true presence that is differentiated from real presence is established for the logical world in the first place, akin to Plato's realm of ideas.

As the meaning of truth broadly encompasses reality and sometimes narrowly refers to pure truth, misunderstandings may inadvertently be created when the same term is used in different contexts. If truth only refers to pure truth, or the world of principles, it cannot encompass the world of things (if we disregard the ambiguous expressions used in traditional Neo-Confucianism). In fact, there is no need for the broad concept of truth. Another issue is that if truth refers to the existence of principles, then since principles lie within the truth for things that do not yet exist, do the principles lie within things when the things come into being? If so, can these principles be considered as part of the truth? This question is one of the main concerns in this chapter.

II. Presence and Being

The establishment of the three concepts of objects in reality, reality, and truth was originally intended to explain that any object will always belong to a certain category, and that the commonality of the objects in that category can exist independently of these specific objects. Therefore, a world of principles exists beyond the real world. However, due to the ambiguity of various concepts mentioned above, *A New Treatise on the Nature of Dao* does not emphasize the three concepts mentioned above. Instead, it organizes the thoughts expressed by these three concepts into the first among four sets of propositions.

There are two lines in this set of propositions, the first being, "Every object must be a certain kind of object." This is an individual-as-general judgment, such as, "This is a dog," which corresponds to objects in reality encompassing the reality in *New Neo-Confucianism*. The second states, "For there to be a certain kind of object, there must be a reason that makes the object that kind of object," whereby the reason for being a particular kind of object is a principle. This corresponds to the notion that reality encompasses the truth in *New Neo-Confucianism*.

These two propositions in New Neo-Confucianism have actually assumed the positions of new realism and Platonism, because if objects in reality are nothing more than the reality created in accordance with the principles of truth, then objects in reality would be near identical copies of principles. From this standpoint, the existence of the real world naturally implies the existence of the reasons upon which the real world is based. This is just like the image we see in the mirror, where there is bound to be a real person being reflected. However, in terms of existence, the implicational relationship in New Neo-Confucianism is not as clear-cut as the relationship between a real person and the mirror image.

It is worth asking whether the propositions, "Every object must be a certain kind of object," and, "For there to be a certain kind of object, there must be a reason that makes the object that kind of object," are propositions about existence or understanding. In other words, are these relationships built in the world in our thoughts, or are these relationships that exist objectively? From the perspective of understanding, when I make a categorical judgment, "This is a dog," about an individual animal before me, I am already aware of the existence of dogs. I did not learn about their existence after making the judgment. If I were encountering a dog for the first time, I might not be able to make a categorial judgment about it, and would not know if there are many other similar things that exist and belong to the same category. The phrases "the procedure of thinking" and "generalization comes after analysis"[3] in the *New Neo-Confucianism* are actually not appropriate. The proposition, "This is a square object," is not just an analytical proposition, as it presupposes the generalization of the category of square objects. As seen above, when judgments like, "This is a dog," are made based on understanding, the existence of the category of dogs and the knowledge of its existence are already implied. However, from the perspective of existence, the existence of one thing does not necessarily imply that there are other similar things in the world. It may not even imply the existence of all other things. Being is a judgment of understanding, and presence is deduced from being. This is a logic of understanding, and thus, the phrase "must be a certain kind of object" is only meaningful in the aspect of understanding.

Therefore, when we say an object is square, we regard it as square according to the principles of being square. This is a statement of understanding, not existence. For the proposition, "For there to be a certain kind of object, there must be a reason that makes the object that kind of object," it is acceptable for a category of things to have common properties. The proposition in New Neo-Confucianism not only affirms that a category of things has common properties, but also intends to affirm that the common properties of these things are independent of the actual entities. In other words, the main purpose of this proposition is to affirm the truth.

When we say, "This is square," it is evident that we recognize that "this" conforms to "the reason a square is a square" (i.e., the principles of being square). Since "this" is called a square as it conforms to the principles of being square, the principles of being square precede the judgment of "this." In the words of the *New Neo-Confucianism*, this relationship is expressed as, "Every object that is a square... is so as it adheres to the reasons for being square."[4] However, such a proposition in New Neo-Confucianism has clearly been existentialized. According to this statement, there is first a world of principles, which contains the principles of being square. The square object in reality is considered a square object in reality because it adheres to the principles of being square in this world of principles.

New Neo-Confucianism has clearly transformed discussions on understanding to that of existence. One may thus easily mistake what comes first logically and grammatically for what exists first and independently. In the proposition, "For there to be a certain kind of object, there must be a reason that makes the object that kind of object," the presence of a certain object not only refers to its existential presence, but also its real presence. In such a statement, presence in the context of the reason for the object to be that kind of object may be understood as an existential, real presence. Later in *A New Understanding of Words,* though the proposition, "for there to be... there must be" is changed to, "a certain kind of object is a certain kind of object, because there must be something that makes it so,"[5] New Neo-Confucianism retains its fundamental thought process of conflating questions on understanding with questions on existence.

III. Principles and Characteristics

A prominent issue in the system of New Neo-Confucianism is the issue of principle and its existence. In New Neo-Confucianism, the text *New Neo-Confucianism* takes squares as an example, saying, "Every square object must have its reason for being square, and it should adhere to the reasons that make a square a square. The reason this square is a square is that all square objects adhere to, which makes them square. This is the principle of being square."[6] What is reason? What is the reason a square is a square, a mountain is a mountain, and water is water? In traditional Neo-Confucianism, the word reason is also used to express principles, but the reason why is a concept of basis when static, and a concept of rules when dynamic. It refers to both the deep and subtle principles inherent in objects, as well as the inner principles of things in motion.

The difference between Feng's philosophy and that of Song Dynasty's Neo-Confucian scholars is that, on the one hand, reason is a categorial specification, as seen in Feng's later saying, "The reason that defines a category of things is the commonality of that category, and that includes the specifications that are common across that category of things."[7] In the period of New Neo-Confucianism, although Feng did not make a clear statement about this, it is clear that the principles in his thought mainly refer to the commonality of forms, which differs from their definition in traditional Neo-Confucianism. On the other hand, principles in traditional Neo-Confucianism are deemed inherent in vital energy or things, while New Neo-Confucianism does not affirm this point.

According to New Neo-Confucianism, principles are objective, not subjective. Therefore, principles can exist without real examples, but they, themselves, are real, not unreal, which also explains why principles are present. However, the concept of presence of principles does not refer to physical presence or physical being. In New Neo-Confucianism, principles are believed to be a potential presence that transcends time and space, instead of an object that actually exists in a certain time and space. Only things that exist in a certain time and space are considered physically present. As New Neo-Confucianism opposes the physical presence and physical being of principles, it also rejects the traditional philosophical notions that there are principles on things and principles in things. It argues that if the presence is a physical one, then the things said about principles on things or in things would be incorrect. The same goes for things encompassing principles. *New Neo-Confucianism* states, "When saying that things encompass or have principles or supreme ultimate, the use of "encompass" and "have" easily leads to misunderstandings that principles or the supreme ultimate can exist as individual entities within or on things. In line with our thought, a category of things should adhere to one set of principles. Things can conform to principles but not encompass them. Principles can set the rules for things but not be within them."[8] This, then, leads to the question: Are there principles on things? Are there principles in things?

Traditional Neo-Confucianism posits that where there is an object, there must be rules, and that there must be a principle for every object. In saying that there must be rules and principles, traditional Neo-Confucianism refers to the existence in things. Similarly, New Neo-Confucianism asserts that where there is an object, there must be rules, and that there must be principles that define a category of things. However, the use of "must be" in New Neo-Confucianism refers to existence in the world of principles. In other words, with reference to an entity that has a real presence, there must be a corresponding principle of that entity in the world of principles with a potential presence. As for whether there are principles within objects, it is not clear in New Neo-Confucianism. In this aspect, it not only differs from traditional Neo-Confucianism, but also distinguishes itself from Platonism, because in Plato's or Aristotle's philosophies, specific entities are a combination of form and matter, meaning that the forms are integrated into objects.

Although Feng advocates that "principles are an abstract presence, but one cannot ask where they are present" in *New Dialogue*, some statements in New Neo-Confucianism appear confusing. For instance, in discussing the relationship between things and principles, it is said in *A New Treatise on the Nature of Dao* that Mount Tai is a mountain because it must adhere to "the reason that makes a mountain a mountain. The reason a mountain is a mountain and not something else is that the mountain has a reason for being a mountain. The reason water is water and not something else is because water has a reason for being water."[9] The reason a mountain is a mountain is the principle of a mountain, while the reason water is water is the principle of water. According to these statements, it can be said that a mountain has the principle of a mountain, and water has the principle of water. Feng also says that the principle of a mountain is not unique to a particular mountain; other mountains may be different from this one but they also encompass the principle of a mountain. In line with this thought, Mount A encompasses the principle of a mountain, and Mount B likewise encompasses the principle of a mountain. The principle of a mountain is shared by mountains like A and B. For us, the implication of this saying in *A New Treatise on the Nature of Dao* is not just "where there is a mountain, there is the principle of a mountain," but also "there is the principle of a mountain within the mountain." This is inconsistent with the notion that things can only conform to principles but not encompass them in the *New Neo-Confucianism*.

According to the original logic in New Neo-Confucianism, the world of things and the world of principles are two completely separate realms. It is also stated in *A New Treatise on the Nature of Dao* that the presence of a mountain is a real presence that exists in a particular time and space, while the presence of principles is a true presence, which exists potentially and transcends time and space.[10] True presence does not encompass things within it. In line with this logic, the statement "a mountain encompasses the principle of a mountain," does not hold, because if a mountain has principles, the principles become a real presence. We know that traditional Neo-Confucianism acknowledges the presence of principles of objects, but according to New Neo-Confucianism, the truth with potential presence does not encompass principles of objects. In traditional Neo-Confucianism, while principles are metaphysical, they can exist within things. However, according to New Neo-Confucianism, one of the fundamental meanings of metaphysics is that it cannot exist in a particular time and space, or within things. Principles can only be adhered to by things and cannot exist in them.

However, New Neo-Confucianism acknowledges that things have characteristics. Feng says that "anything that conforms to a certain principle and becomes a certain kind of thing realizes a certain principle and has a certain characteristic. Principles are realized in things in the form of characteristics."[11] In other words, although it cannot be said that things have principles, the idea that things have characteristics is valid. Therefore, it can be said that all square objects have square characteristics, and all white objects have white characteristics.

According to Jin Yuelin's (1895–1984) philosophy, the possibility (equivalent to Feng's principle of truth) realized in things is also known as commonality. Thus, it can be said that there are principles on things because things are a combination of possibility and capability. In New

Neo-Confucianism, while it can be said that principles are realized in things in the form of characteristics, it is not the case that the principle of truth becomes the characteristic of an object after combining it with substance. The term realization here does not mean that the principle of truth descends onto an object; rather, it means that a real object is formed in accordance with that principle of truth. Only in this sense can it be said that the followed is realized in the follower. Therefore, regarding commonality, what Jin Yuelin describes is concretely integrated into things, while Feng's interpretation is laid out abstractly in truth. In his later years, Feng also recognized this difference between Jin Yuelin's and his concept of commonality, whereby one is abstract and the other concrete. Certainly, due to variations in quality, followers tend not to conform perfectly, so the real characteristics and the original principle of truth are not exactly the same. But this is another issue.

New Neo-Confucianism not only acknowledges that things have characteristics, but also recognizes order in things. For instance, it states that "Zhu Xi says, 'If *yin*, *yang*, and the five elements do not lose their order, that is principle.' This regards order as principle. While order can be called principle, abstract order does not equate to specific order in concrete things. Rather, it refers to the reason order is considered order, or the reason a certain order is a certain order."[12] According to traditional Neo-Confucianism, the characteristics and order in Feng's philosophy are all considered principles. However, in New Neo-Confucianism, characteristics and order are not considered principles; principles are something else that is referenced upon, on a level above characteristics and order. Characteristics and order are mere instances derived from the principles in truth.

In accordance with the above, New Neo-Confucianism can be said to also acknowledge that things encompass some form of principles that are akin to real attributes and order. However, in the language of traditional Neo-Confucianism, such real principles of things are merely temperament characteristics and temperament principles, not inherent characteristics or principles of heaven and earth. In traditional Neo-Confucianism, it is also said that inherent characteristics are found in things, but they transform into temperament characteristics due to their mixture with temperament. As for New Neo-Confucianism, inherent characteristics or inherent principles only exist in the higher realm of truth, not as entities intrinsic to things. It can be said that inherent characteristics and temperament characteristics are two separate realms.

On the other hand, New Neo-Confucianism uses the term "reference" in place of "inherit" in traditional Neo-Confucianism. While traditional Neo-Confucianism also distinguishes between goodness inherited and characteristics accomplished, concrete principles of heaven and earth can be inherited to endow objects with principles. Zhu Xi says, "Goodness inherited marks the beginning of the circulation of heavenly principles, while characteristics accomplished suggests that each of these principles has settled somewhere."[13] In this sense, Feng can also repeat this idea. New Neo-Confucianism acknowledges that only the inherited are principles, while the accomplished are characteristics. However, the characteristics in New Neo-Confucianism are not formed in such a way that the principles of goodness inherited are settled in things, so it avoids saying that things have principles.

In view of this reasoning, another issue that arises with Feng's consideration of principle as a commonality is that if things have both characteristics and order, what principles do these things follow to become what they are? A category of things needs to conform to the pure forms in truth (as in the case of squares) to be what they are, while the order of real things in motion also depends on the reason for order in reality. This point is not exactly the same as the concept of one object adhering to various principles in *New Neo-Confucianism*. The concept of one object adhering to various principles suggests that for a cat to be a cat, it not only adheres to the principles of a cat, but also the principles of an animal, a living thing, and so on. This notion has many loopholes. On the contrary, what is being discussed here is that the forms and motion of objects must follow different principles separately. In this regard, as analyzed in the previous section, the flaw in New Neo-Confucianism still lies in conflating understanding with existence. While analytical thinking can break down a particular object into many specifications, a specific object is a unity of diversity after all. It is neither possible nor feasible to adhere to countless principles to constitute a specific object.

IV. *Qi* and "Qi"

The concept of *qi* (vital energy) in New Neo-Confucianism is also noteworthy. Just as Feng's concept of principles is closer to the form and commonality in Greek philosophy than the principles in Neo-Confucian, the *qi* in Feng's thought is undoubtedly closer to the concept of substance in Aristotle's philosophy, though it still adopts traditional philosophical categories. Feng himself emphasizes that "what is called 'substance in Plato's and Aristotle's philosophies is similar to the *qi* in the New Neo-Confucianism."[14] Therefore, the *qi* in New Neo-Confucianism is significantly different from the *qi* in traditional Neo-Confucianism.

According to New Neo-Confucianism, after abstracting characteristics from objects until nothing else can be abstracted, one obtains the absolute substance, which can be referred to as the "*qi* of true essence," or simply, *qi*. *New Neo-Confucianism* emphasizes that *qi* not only lacks materiality, but also all characteristics. However, if *qi* is "devoid of all characteristics after abstraction," it becomes a Hegelian concept of pure presence. It is not appropriate for *A New Treatise on the Nature of Dao* to describe the principle of truth as akin to the concept of presence in Western philosophy to begin with. Aligning the concept of *qi* to pure presence is, again, not appropriate, because *qi* is not a pure presence. It is defined by at least one logic, "That on which objects in reality are based to become what they are." The distinction between principle and appearance in *qi* in the forms of that which is based on and adhered to is a fundamental rule of *qi*. The lack of rules for *qi* and substance only pertains to its formless regulative nature. Acknowledging the rule that *qi* has a basis of dependence does not equate to considering *qi* as an object in reality, just as principles are not objects in reality even though they have rules.

New Neo-Confucianism emphasizes that such *qi* is not an object in reality, or anything real or the truth, but is merely a logical concept. However, all logical propositions should be considered the truth. If the proposition, "where there is an object, there must be a basis on which the object depends on to become what it is," is true, it should be part of the truth. Consequently, the basis of dependence itself should also be part of the truth. Feng has always emphasized that truth is objective, while logical concepts are subjective. From the metaphysical viewpoint of New Neo-Confucianism, if principle is an objective reality, while *qi* is a logical concept without objectivity, there will be an imbalance between the two. *New Neo-Confucianism* says, "In our system, *qi* is a concept based on logic. What it refers to is neither a principle nor an object in reality. An object in reality is what *qi* becomes by adhering to principles."[15] How a logical concept depends on objective principles to become an object in reality is perplexing. Feng also says that, "A concrete object must have two dependencies, one which it adheres to, and the other which it is based on. That which the object adheres to is the principle, while that which it is based on is *qi*."[16] If this *qi* on which the object is based is the *qi* of true essence, how can it adhere to principles or settle in individuals? If this *qi* is a real *qi*, then it already possesses characteristics formed in adherence to principles and cannot be depended on like principles.

New Neo-Confucianism distinguishes between the two concepts of *qi*, one being the *qi* with actual presence, and the other a logical concept. The *qi*, which is a logical concept, lacks characteristics, while the *qi* with actual presence "at least possesses the characteristic of existence."[17] However, the *qi* with actual presence must have adhered to the reasons that make it *qi* (or the principles of *qi*) to become *qi*. Consequently, there is a reason that makes *qi* what it is (as in the case of a square) in the realm of truth, and a *qi* with actual presence in reality. The *qi*, whch is a logical concept, then becomes a third party. This can be somewhat confusing. According to *A New Treatise on the Nature of Dao*, *qi* is merely a potential existence. However, principles can also be said to be something that has the potential of being realized. How these two possibilities are distinguished is also worth considering.

If there is *qi* in reality, then, like Feng, we need to affirm that *qi* must at least have the characteristic of existence, and also that there is the reason for *qi* to be *qi* in the realm of truth. Just as there is a square in the realm of truth to explain why a square is a square, there should also be *qi* in the realm of truth to explain why *qi* is *qi*. This *qi* is common across all *qi* in reality; it is the template to which all *qi* in reality adhere. However, New Neo-Confucianism does not affirm this *qi* and does not clarify the distinction between this *qi* and the *qi* of true essence.

According to the methodology in New Neo-Confucianism, rational analysis gives rise to the concepts of principles and *qi*, while rational summary results in the concepts of totality and the Dao body. Although all four fundamental concepts are obtained through logical analysis, principles are not a logical concept, while *qi*, Dao body, and totality are. Principle is abstract, while *qi* and totality are not. Comparing principle and *qi* in particular, one is real while the other is not, but both are derived from rational analysis. This is theoretically imperfect. Ideally, principle should also be a logical concept, not an independent entity. If Feng does not advocate for the theory of objectivity in new realism, this system may be more complete, as it would be a logically consistent system. However, logical consistency does not necessarily prove that a system is true.

V. Substance and Function

In terms of metaphysics, New Neo-Confucianism is considered a completely new metaphysics. At the same time, it continues the discourse of Neo-Confucianism. In this sense, "completely new" does not imply a lack of continuity from traditional philosophy. From the "History of Great Philosophy" to *A New Treatise on the Nature of Dao,* Feng consistently proclaims that he has inherited Chinese philosophical traditions. Interpreting the metaphysics of Chinese traditional philosophy or the Neo-Confucian doctrine of the Cheng-Zhu school of thought using the theory of universals and particulars may not yield a correct understanding, but as an interpretation, it has its legitimacy. Feng subjectively believes that the metaphysics in the Cheng-Zhu school of thought addresses the issue of universals and particulars precisely, and his discussion of New Neo-Confucianism from the perspective of universals and particulars does indeed bear resemblance to traditional Neo-Confucianism. Thus, both the "History of Great Philosophy" and *A New Treatise on the Nature of Dao* are successful in the interpretation of the history of philosophy.

Feng uses the expression "old wine in new bottles" to illustrate the way his philosophy is connected to tradition. It is not uncommon for post-May Fourth Movement modern Chinese philosophers to selectively utilize concepts from classical philosophy. In this regard, Feng's notion of old wine in new bottles is not surprising. What is remarkable is that he not only completely filled the classical old bottles with all his new wine, but that his collection of old bottles covers almost all the important categories of Chinese classical philosophy. This not only demonstrates the vitality of classical philosophy in new interpretations, but also Feng's remarkable ability to integrate old knowledge with new insights. Zhu Guangqian once exclaimed, "In the hands of Feng, the scattered sand of ancient Chinese philosophy turns into a high-rise building, complete with doors and windows, like a well-organized system. It is a miracle."[18] In this respect, no modern philosopher has yet been able to surpass Feng.

As Feng repeatedly emphasizes, since New Neo-Confucianism does not follow, but rather continues the Cheng-Zhu school of thought, it is only natural that his usage of each category differs (significantly, or even completely) from early Confucian scholars. Examining the thought of Neo-Confucian scholars, one will notice that their use of principles, characteristics, supreme ultimate, Dao, metaphysics, and physics also differ from early Confucian scholars. The criticism of New Neo-Confucianism being not in line with early Confucian thought is not justified. In fact, the development of Neo-Confucian in the Song and Ming dynasties integrated many elements from Buddhism. Thus, Feng's incorporation of new realism in the development of New Neo-Confucianism is perfectly legitimate. New Neo-Confucianism employs logical analysis as its fundamental method, adopts new realism as its fundamental stance, and draws on the criticisms of metaphysics by new logic. Its clear awareness of philosophical issues, profound self-awareness of methods, and the clarity and coherence of its concepts and structures give it its indisputable modern character.

In terms of the fundamental orientation of metaphysics, where do the differences between New Neo-Confucianism and traditional Neo-Confucianism lie? I believe the core issue is found in its advocacy of the unity or separation of substance and function.

A major difference between Neo-Confucianism and New Neo-Confucianism lies in the former's acknowledgment of the presence of principle within *qi*, and principle within things. Zhu Xi states, "It is believed to exist before the absence of objects but that does not preclude its existence in the presence of objects; it is believed to extend beyond *yin* and *yang*, but that does not preclude its movement within *yin* and *yang*; it is believed to permeate entirety and exist everywhere with no form, no sound, and no smell."[19]

Cheng Yichuan emphasizes the unity of substance and function, saying, "All substances originate from a single source, unified without separation." This represents the fundamental stance of Neo-Confucianism on the ontological and phenomena realms. Consequently, even though Zhu Xi advocated for the existence of principles before the emergence of *qi*, he also recognized that principles lie within *yin* and *yang*, and within physical entities as profound and subtle principles. On the other hand, Feng's thought posits that principles exist only in the realm of truth and not reality or real entities. Such a Platonic type of principles can only serve as the original form upon which real entities adhere, and it is unable to provide the inherent laws that dictate the motion of the entities. This differs from the Neo-Confucian thought that emphasizes the idea that principles are inseparable from and are intricately intertwined with *qi*, being the reason for the circulation of *qi*. While Neo-Confucianism considers the principles of objects and order as principles or *qi* rather than fundamental principles, the principles of *qi* are still a form of manifestation of fundamental principles within the realm of *qi*. On the other hand, in New Neo-Confucianism, fundamental principles and the characteristics of *qi* are two separate realms, a stance that traditional Neo-Confucianism views as a dichotomy between substance and function.

Because the concepts of substance and function represent people's analysis and grasp of different aspects of things, the separation of substance and function in thought distinguishes between abstract and concrete, essence and phenomenon, and general and individual, thus deepening theoretical thinking. However, the separation of substance and function in thought does not imply an ontological separation, and a logical sequence does not equate to a factual separation. The substance and function that are distinguished and separated in thought actually originate from a single source and are a unity that cannot be divided in existence. Cheng Hao says, "Whatever metaphysical is Dao, whatever physical is tools. It must be said this way: tools are also Dao, and Dao is also tools."[20] The distinction between the concepts of abstract and concrete must be said this way, but the two are not ontologically distinct. In his later years, Feng had a clear understanding of this. He says, "Principles and phenomena, connotation and extension, are unified to begin with. It is only through human thought analysis that their differences and oppositions become apparent. This is a matter of understanding, and not about existence. In terms of existence, there is no issue about order or hierarchy to begin with. The reason such issues exist is because the questions about understanding and existence have been mixed up."[21]

Traditional Neo-Confucianism emphasizes the unity of substance and function, which reflects the wisdom of ancient philosophers, but there is a lack of logical development and conceptual analysis. New Neo-Confucianism divides substance and function, providing a detailed analysis and demonstrating rigor from logical training. Yet, the question of understanding is often confused with the question of existence. The unity of substance and function in traditional thought should complement and integrate with the modern idea of the separation of substance and function. Perhaps this should be a point to note when we reflect on the metaphysics of New Neo-Confucianism.

Critiquing a theory of metaphysics is much easier than constructing one. In fact, there is yet to be a theory of metaphysics that is free from criticism. When it comes to theories of metaphysics, we should bear in mind the familiar admonition: it is more important to raise good questions than to provide correct answers. While the critique in this chapter is based on Feng's self-reflection in his later years, I must acknowledge that not all questions posed by New Neo-Confucianism can be deemed to have correct answers. In this sense, the Neo-Confucianism continues to stimulate our philosophical thinking today.

Notes

1. *Complete Works of Sansongtang*, vol. 4, 11.
2. Ibid., 11.
3. Ibid., 24.
4. Ibid., 32.
5. *Complete Works of Sansongtang*, vol. 5, 224–225.
6. *Complete Works of Sansongtang*, vol. 4, 32.
7. *Sansongtang: An Account of My Life*, 235.
8. *Complete Works of Sansontang*, vol. 4, 43.
9. *Complete Works of Sansongtang*, vol. 5, 149.
10. Ibid.
11. *Complete Works of Sansongtang*, vol. 4, 32.
12. *Complete Works of Sansongtang*, vol. 5, 146.
13. *Getting to Know Master Zhu Xi*, vol. 74.
14. *Complete Works of Sansongtang*, vol. 5, 229.
15. *Complete Works of Sansongtang*, vol. 4, 49.
16. Ibid., 54.
17. Ibid.
18. *Complete Works of Sansongtang*, vol. 5, 509.
19. *Collected Works of Zhu Xi: Reply to Lu Zijing*.
20. *Posthumous Writings*, vol. 1.
21. *Sansongtang: An Account of My Life*, 240.

CHAPTER 13

Feng Youlan's Cultural Views in *A New Treatise on Practical Affairs*

I. Culture and Philosophy

Most students of Feng Youlan's academic thought focus on its pure philosophical aspects, and that is not without reason. Even Feng himself says in the preface of *A New Understanding of Words*, "The pure philosophical foundation of the New Neo-Confucianism must form the backbones of *New Neo-Confucianism, New Origins of Humanity, A New Treatise on the Nature of Dao*, and this book (*A New Understanding of Words*)."[1] Although Feng specifically mentions "pure philosophy," it seems that he is looking beyond philosophy. In the preface of *New Origins of Humanity*, he emphasizes, "While this book was written after *A New Treatise on Practical Affairs* and *A New Treatise on the Way of Life*, it is actually a continuation of *New Neo-Confucianism*. It is recommended that readers read this first."[2]

I asked Feng in his later years which of the "Six Books of Zhenyuan" was the most important, and his answer then matched the four works listed in the preface of *A New Understanding of Words*. This shows that Feng himself had a higher regard for pure philosophical systems such as *New Neo-Confucianism* and *New Origins of Humanity*. In comparison, he only made a brief mention of his thoughts in *A New Treatise on Practical Affairs* in less than five hundred words under the header of "Political and Social Thought" in the fourth section of the 79th chapter of *On Feng Youlan's Philosophy*, Volume Seven of his last work *A New History of Chinese Philosophy*. He also evaluates the viewpoint of *A New Treatise on Practical Affairs* as, "Subjectively, it supports China's modernization, but its actual impact is not entirely satisfactory," and "its social impact is not satisfactory."[3]

However, the focus of this chapter is to understand the worries that Chinese intellectuals from the early 20th century had and the choices they made regarding Chinese and Western cultural thought, using Feng Youlan as a case study. The thought presented in *A New Treatise on Practical Affairs* is particularly relevant. In fact, what *A New Treatise on Practical Affairs* discusses is precisely the core issue that was present in the May Fourth Movement, the cultural debates in the 1930s, and the cultural discussions in the 1980s—the issue of culture. In particular, the arguments about the conflict between Chinese and Western cultures and their resolutions are especially relevant to modern scholars. The cultural issue discussed in *A New Treatise on Practical Affairs* and such is far beyond what political and social thought can encompass.

Moreover, in his address at the ceremony where he was awarded an honorary Doctor of Letters by Columbia University in 1982, Feng said:

> I live in an era where many cultural conflicts exist. The questions I need to answer are: how to make sense of the nature of such conflicts, how to deal with and resolve them appropriately, and how to adapt myself to such conflicts."[4]

In 1983, he also wrote in the preface of *Collected Works of Sansongtang* that:

> For over sixty years, since embarking on Chinese philosophical studies as a student at Peking University in 1915, I have written several books and numerous articles. Generally speaking, the issues I discuss revolve around Eastern and Western cultural issues centered on the history of philosophy. I was born in an era when cultures were in conflict and at loggerheads. How to make sense of these conflicts, how to resolve them, and how I should navigate them are the types of questions I have been addressing and answering.[5]

Sansongtang: An Account of My Life (hereinafter referred to as *An Account of My Life*), published in 1984, recounts Feng's cultural experiences beginning in his youth, stating, "This is a contradiction between two cultures, a contradiction which runs through modern and contemporary Chinese history. At that time, some people did not acknowledge this as a contradiction between past and present, or the old and the new, but rather one between the East and the West, or China and other countries. Eastern and Western cultures differ precisely because their fundamental ideas are different. Their fundamental ideas are their philosophies. Sima Qian says, 'Scholars who are eager to learn and who contemplate deeply will understand the meaning.' Liang Shuming is considered such a scholar, eager to learn and contemplate, as he discusses the meaning of Eastern and Western cultures. He gave a lecture on Eastern and Western cultures and their philosophies, which sparked widespread interest at that time. It did not matter whether his conclusions were correct; what was important was that he touched on a topic close to the hearts of many. This was something that the general populace had strong feelings for, though they differed in their understanding and interpretation of the conflicts. At that time, there was a multitude of opinions, many of which only reflected the conflicts. Explanations and reviews of the conflicts were few and far between. In 1919, I was awarded a public scholarship to study abroad. I arrived in the United States in winter that year and began my graduate studies in the Department of Philosophy at Columbia University the following year. I went there with this question in my mind."[6] Feng points out that in the sixty-odd years since then, while his philosophical activities varied with the times, and "the objects of study also differed, all of them aligned with the question above and are aimed at providing a comprehensive answer to that question."[7] This suggests that grasping the conflicts between Eastern and Western cultures, whether as context or clue, is crucial for understanding Feng's academic endeavors.

In his acceptance speech delivered at Columbia University, Feng provided a concise review and summary of his thoughts on understanding the conflicts between Chinese and Western cultures, saying:

> When I first entered the United States, it was during the late stages of the May Fourth Movement in China. The movement marked the climax of different cultural conflicts at that time. I came here with this issue in mind, and began to study those conflicts seriously. To answer these questions, my thinking evolved through three stages. In the first stage, I explained cultural differences using geographical regions, that is, cultural differences stem from differences in the East and the West. In the second stage, I explained cultural differences by historical eras, that is, that cultural differences stem from differences between the past and present. In the third stage, I explained cultural differences by social development, that is, that cultural differences are a reflection of different societal types.[8]

According to the explanation in *An Account of My Life*, the paper titled "Why China Has No Science," published in 1922, represents the viewpoint of the first stage. *A Comparative Study of Philosophies of Life*, published in 1924, broke away from the East-versus-West notion, but did not offer a new explanation. The book *A History of Chinese Philosophy*, published in the early 1930s, contains new implicit explanations, but is not clear. It was only during Feng's visit to Europe between 1933 and 1934 that he made a definitive shift toward a new explanation, whereby "the difference between Eastern and Western cultures is essentially the difference between the medieval and modern times."[9] This reflects the viewpoint of the second stage. *A New Treatise on Practical Affairs*, published in 1940, proposes that the difference between medieval and modern times is actually a difference in societal types, marking the third stage. Feng clearly articulated the different views he bore on the conflicts between Eastern and Western cultures and divided them into three distinct stages. Since the mid-1980s, his cultural viewpoint of "regarding East and West as ancient and modern" has been widely recognized in academic circles.

One of the objectives of the analysis in this chapter is to trace and organize the actual development and complexities of Feng's cultural views in historical sequence. One will find that the actual development of his thought is far more complex than what he recounted in his later years. Additionally, the chapter will examine how Feng's cultural views address the issues of tradition and nationalism in relation to modernization. Through this analysis, it will become clear that it is insufficient to interpret Feng's cultural views as a discourse of "ancient versus modern," and this will serve as a reference for contemporary cultural discussion.

II. From East versus West to Ancient versus Modern

In the year after Feng Youlan arrived in the United States, he had a conversation about Eastern and Western cultures with Tagore, the renowned Indian philosopher. The second question posed by Feng to Tagore during the conversation was, "Lately, I've had a question in my mind, which is whether the difference between Eastern and Western civilizations is a difference of degree or a difference of kind." Tagore's reply was, "I can answer this question. It is a difference of kind. In the West, the purpose of life is activity, whereas the purpose of life in the East is realization."[10] The difference of kind refers to the difference between Eastern and Western cultures. The difference in degree refers to the difference in the level of social development, or later expressed as the difference between ancient and modern times. It can be seen that shortly after he arrived in the US, Feng already had doubts about the argument in the New Culture Movement in which the differences between the East and the West were seen as a difference of kind. Tagore told him without hesitation that the difference between the two cultures is a difference between the East and the West (not between ancient and modern times).

Not long after the conversation with Tagore, Feng presented the paper titled "Why China Has No Science" at a philosophy discussion forum at Columbia University. The paper, later published in the April 1922 issue of *The International Journal of Ethics*, states frankly:

> If we compare Chinese history with the history of Europe of a few centuries ago, say before the Renaissance, we find that, although they are of different kinds, they are nevertheless on the same level. But now China is still old, while the western countries are new. What keeps China back? It is a natural question.[11]

The opening paragraph suggests that Feng believed there indeed exists a difference of kind between Eastern and Western cultures, but the Eastern and Western cultures of different kinds were at the same developmental level before the Renaissance. Yet, in modern times, the difference between Eastern and Western cultures not only involves a difference of kind, but also a difference in level of development. Using a more recent expression, Feng says that the differences between Eastern and Western cultures in modern times encompass both the distinction between the East and the West and the difference between ancient and modern times. He was not concerned about what the differences between the East and the West were, but rather why there emerged differences between ancient and modern times later, and specifically why China did not develop to the level of modern Western civilization. Because the essence of modern times, as he understood it, was science, he narrowed his research to understand the reasons China failed to develop science.

Feng says, "It is beyond question that geography, climate, and economic conditions are very important factors in making history, but we must bear in mind that they are conditions that make history possible, not that make history actual. They are the indispensable settings of a drama, but not its cause."[12] He concludes that "China has no science, because according to her own standard of value, she does not need any,"[13] and that "China does not have modern science, because Chinese philosophers believe that it is in our own mind, not in the external world, that we can seek for happiness and truth."[14] In fact, China developed much technology, but "in Europe, technology developed was for knowing and controlling matter, while in China, it developed for knowing and controlling the mind."[15] Since the beginning of time, thinking of Chinese civilization had been "to devote all energy and strength to... directly seeking goodness and happiness within the mind."[16] In other words, the values of Chinese culture prevented China from developing to the levels of the modern era through the possession of science as Western civilizations did.

Although Feng's perspective during this period leaned toward East-West differences, it did not specifically mean explaining cultural differences using geographical regions, as it appeared in Feng's address. Rather, it aligned with the prevailing view of the May Fourth Movement, whereby "Eastern and Western cultures differ because their fundamental ideas are different. Their fundamental ideas are their philosophies (referring to values)."[17] However, Feng's main objective was not to provide a general explanation for the difference of kind between Eastern and Western cultures with such a concept, but to explain the reasons that resulted in the difference in levels between Eastern and Western cultures. Feng was of the opinion that the differences in the core values between Eastern and Western cultures had existed since the beginning of civilization, but they remained purely a difference of kind for a long time. It was only in modern times that it evolved into a difference in standards and levels.

More interestingly, he concluded at the end of his address, "Speaking in abstract, general terms is always risky. But I will still say here, that the West is outward-looking, while the East is inward-looking. The West emphasizes what we have, while the East emphasizes what we are. How to reconcile these two to achieve happiness for the body and the mind remains a difficult question. Regardless, perhaps the Chinese' perspective of life is wrong, but the Chinese experience will not be a failure. If humanity becomes increasingly wise and seeks inner peace and happiness, they will turn to China's wisdom and be dutifully rewarded."[18] Such an approach that provides a positive affirmation of the value of Chinese culture beyond utilitarian judgments through envisioning its future societal significance was commonplace among the cultural reflections of Chinese intellectuals throughout the 20th century.

In early 1922, Feng wrote an article titled "On Comparing China and the West," in which he expresses weariness with abstract discussions of national characteristics of Chinese and Western cultures. He points out that Chinese culture is merely the aggregate of China's history, arts, and philosophy. Nothing else can be called Chinese culture apart from these, just as Beijing is the aggregate of places like Xidan, Dongdan, and Qianmen, and there is nothing else that can be singularly called Beijing. In this sense, discussing Chinese culture requires many experts to conduct in-depth research over a very long period of time. Discussing the superiority and inferiority of Chinese and Western cultures in abstract terms is futile, as the argument could sway either way, which would not solve the problem. On the other hand, he points out that Chinese culture is not something made, but something in the making. We, as living Chinese, are its makers and are responsible for its quality.[19] This perspective is consistent with recent discussions in cultural discourse that emphasize the distinction between traditional cultures and cultural traditions, and it aligns with the viewpoint on the openness of tradition in the dimension of time. This discussion suggests that even in the early 1920s, Feng's cultural perspective was not as simplistic as commonly understood, and that his cultural thought had a fairly broad scope.

In the summer of 1923, Feng defended his doctoral thesis titled "A Comparative Study of Life Ideals." He included a discussion section at the end of each chapter, in which he expounded on the comparison between Eastern and Western philosophies. For instance, he finds Yang Zhu's hedonism closely aligned with Cyrenaicism and fundamentally similar to Epicureanism.[20] He observes similarities between Stoicism and Confucianism,[21] and he notes many similarities between the philosophy of Marcus Aurelius and Confucianism.[22] He also argues that Aristotle's Doctrine of the Mean resonates with Confucianism's notion of moderation, and so on.[23]

Feng later reflected on his thesis, saying, "In 1922, I submitted a paper to the Philosophy discussion forum… In this paper, I argued that the difference in culture is the difference between the East and the West. This was actually a popular belief at that time. However, as I delved deeper into the history of philosophy, I found this belief to be inaccurate. I discovered that things traditionally considered Eastern philosophy also existed in Western philosophical history, and vice versa. I found that humans have the same nature and face the same existential questions. This perspective later became the main theme of my doctoral thesis."[24] "At that time, I believed that my perspective was unique and had its own characteristic, which was breaking the so-called East-West boundary. I believed then that the opposition between inward and outward perspectives was not the opposition between the East and the West. Human thought is the same, regardless of East or West."[25]

Indeed, as Feng himself remarked, the completion of his doctoral thesis marked a significant change in his early cultural views. The notion highlighted in the paper "Why China Has No Science" regarding the historical dissimilarity between Chinese and Western cultures, as well as the idea that the West is outward-looking while the East is inward-looking, were all abandoned in the doctoral thesis. Feng's understanding had shifted from the differences between the East and the West to the similarities between them, at least on the surface level. This difference between seeking similarities and seeking differences also constitutes the different courses later taken by Feng and Liang Shuming in their cultural theories.

It is clear that Feng benefited from a deep understanding of Western culture, especially ancient Western culture, to have broken the previous boundaries that classified Eastern and Western cultures as different kinds and to have negated the notion of East as inward-looking and West as outward-looking, instead subscribing to the belief that human nature is the same, with both Eastern and Western cultures having their own inward and outward tendencies. Clearly, Feng was no longer convinced by the explanation of kind, which means that his thought logically became dominated by the explanation of degree. In 1924, Feng's doctoral thesis was published in English by The Commercial Press, with the Chinese "Preface" stating, "In recent years, the so-called cultural problem has become perhaps the most popular topic. Since the New Culture Movement, we often hear or come across the terms culture, civilization, and Eastern and Western cultures in writing, as well as discussions about them. We are born in this era of integration between Europe and Asia, having experiences that many of our predecessors did not have and seeing things that many of our predecessors did not see. These can be roughly divided into two categories: one being what we originally possess, and the other being what has come anew from the West. They are quite different, and often more contradictory and conflicting. Therefore, it is natural that we compare, criticize, and evaluate them."[26] In the section "East and West" in the "Preface," he writes:

> Liang Shuming believes that each ethnic group has its own cultural characteristics due to the different paths taken, while Hu Shih believes that the style of resolution adopted by individual ethnic groups during specific time periods differ, and these define the cultural characteristics of the ethnic groups in those time periods. Hu's view is more appropriate on this topic. In fact, what Liang and ordinary people now refer to as Western culture is not truly Western culture but modern Western culture. The thoughts of ancient Greece and Rome, in fact, share many similarities with Confucian thought... What is known as the spirit of striving forward, or what I term as progressivism in my book, is actually a product of modern Western culture, and should not be labeled as merely Western culture... In my book, I deliberately break the so-called East-West boundaries, but I present ten ideal ways of life, each represented by a philosophical system, and compare and study them equally.[27]

This clearly indicates that Feng had already realized that what was commonly referred to as Western culture was only modern Western culture, and thus, the distinction between the East and the West should be understood as the difference between China and modern Western culture. He opposed Liang's explanation of kinds (directions), and instead leaned toward an explanation based on eras. In this line of thought, the difference between Eastern and Western cultures stems from cultural styles in different eras. Therefore, it is not true that the publication of *A Comparative Study of Life Ideals* merely "rejected the popular explanation for conflicting cultures," and did not "present a new explanation to replace it," until *A History of Chinese Philosophy*, published in the 1930s, made "an implicit remark that the difference between Eastern and Western cultures is actually the difference between ancient and modern times."[28] It should be said that Feng was already quite close to the new interpretation of the East and West as ancient and modern by the mid-1920s.

It is also worth noting the relationship between Feng's cultural views and Liang Shuming. Yin Ding attributes Feng's attention to culture in the early days to Liang's influence. He says, "Feng was deeply interested in the questions and insights raised by Liang. He was also puzzled by the differences and conflicts between Eastern and Western cultures and sought a rational explanation himself. Many years after leaving Peking University, Feng still remembered how he was drawn to the insights shared by Liang during his time as a student at Peking University, and he began to delve into the differences between Eastern and Western cultures and their origins."[29] Furthermore, "the question posed by Liang continued to bother Feng when the latter graduated from Peking University, and he brought this question with him when he studied in the United States, hoping to find a rational explanation."[30]

Yin Ding was misled by the incomplete recount recorded in *An Account of My Life*. The debate on Eastern and Western cultures in the New Culture Movement actually began as early as the founding of *La Jeunesse* magazine in 1915, and both Feng Youlan and Liang Shuming's attention to cultural issues was influenced by this movement. Feng moved to the United States in 1919, while Liang delivered his lecture series "Eastern and Western Cultures and Their Philosophies" in 1920. Records of the lecture series were only published in Peking University's *The University Daily* from October 1920, and compiled into a book that was published in 1921,[31] but Feng could not have attended Liang's lectures during his time at Peking University.

Feng mentioned in the article "Conversation with Tagore," published in December 1920, "I saw Liang Shuming's lectures 'Eastern and Western Cultures and Their Philosophies' published in *The University Daily*, which arrived two days ago. Unfortunately, only the preface was published, not the full text."[32] This proves that Feng's understanding of the issue of Eastern and Western cultures was actually influenced by prominent figures like Chen Duxiu. The topic was widely discussed at that time. Since Liang's lecture series "Eastern and Western Cultures and Their Philosophies" was conducted a year after Feng arrived in the United States, Feng could not have traveled to the United States specifically to seek answers to Liang's questions. Moreover, after Feng returned to China, it became increasingly clear that his cultural views were developing in a different direction from Liang's.

This shows that Feng had begun doubting the prevailing single explanation of kinds for cultures as early as 1920, leaning toward a degree sort of explanation. By 1922, he had already combined these two explanations, and in his thesis completed in 1923, he had broken away from the East-West notion, largely abandoning the explanation of kinds. The English and Mandarin versions of his doctoral thesis were published between 1924 and 1926, in which he not only rejects the East-West construct, but also introduces the concept of ancient and modern, indicating that the overall trend of his cultural views in the early 1920s was shifting from East and West to ancient and modern, and by the mid-1920s, this transition was essentially complete. Through the lens of modern history, Feng's cultural views during this period may not have been originally proposed by him, but were indeed the result of his own arduous exploration and deep thought, which laid the foundation for the subsequent development of his cultural views.

III. Types and Individuals

In *An Account of My Life*, Chapter Five, "The Thirties," quotes the article "History and Philosophy from the Qin and Han Dynasties," which was published in 1935. Feng remarks:

> I quoted most of this article because it perfectly summarizes the theoretical conclusions I drew from my observations and experiences in Europe in 1933 and 1934. It marks a

turning point in my thinking, where I realized that the distinction between the East and the West is nothing more than the difference between ancient and modern times.[33]

He also said when commenting on *A New Treatise on Practical Affairs* in Chapter Six, "The Forties":

> I developed an interest in the East-West cultural issue during the May Fourth Movement. Later, I gradually realized that it was not a matter of East versus West, but one of ancient versus modern times. What is commonly regarded as the distinction between the East and the West is essentially just the difference between ancient and modern times. My work in the 20s, *A Comparative Study of Life Ideals*, touches upon this issue. What I set out to explain in publishing that book is to demonstrate that the philosophies of life held by various schools are present in the philosophical histories of countries around the world. It is difficult to say which philosophies are uniquely Western and which are uniquely Eastern. In the 1930s, I took a vacation to Europe and saw the relics from Europe's feudal era, which broadened my perspectives. It dawned on me that modern Europe is the transformed and developed form of Europe in the feudal era, while the United States is an extension and developed form of Europe. Europe's feudal era bears many similarities with ancient China. As for what people commonly refer to as Western culture, it is, in fact, modern culture. What is termed Westernization should be referred to as modernization instead.[34]

In line with the above, we know that Feng's viewpoint that "what people commonly refer to as Western culture, is in fact modern culture" was already proposed in the mid-1920s. His trip to Europe in the 1930s not only solidified his understanding of this viewpoint, but also led him to develop the concept of modernization. From the late 1920s to the early 1930s, his research was entirely focused on the academic field of the history of Chinese philosophy. This enabled him to complete the groundbreaking work *A History of Chinese Philosophy*, and even form the historical method of explaining antiquity, which is different from believing antiquity and doubting antiquity.[35] This interrupted his thoughts on the conflict between Eastern and Western cultures after the 1920s. In this regard, the significance of his trip to Europe in the 1930s was that it brought his attention back to the issue of Chinese versus Western cultures and led to the formation of the cultural perspective of modernization, later detailed in *A New Treatise on Practical Affairs*, after the movement to restore the status of Chinese traditional culture in the mid-1930s.

Feng's statement that the "History and Philosophy from the Qin and Han Dynasties," published in September 1935, "marks a turning point in my thinking, where I realized that the distinction between the East and the West is nothing more than the difference between ancient and modern times." The article does not discuss the issue of East versus West or ancient versus modern times. The analyses of history and social structure presented in the article, which were influenced by the materialist concept of history, will be discussed in the final section of this chapter when discussing the issue of substance and function. What is noteworthy, however, is the article "General Trends of Modern National Movements in China," published in August 1936. In it, one can clearly observe the development of Feng's cultural perspective following his return from Europe and stimulated by the debates on the status of culture.

The article reads, "In today's world, all economically advanced nations have become urbanites, while those economically backward have become rural dwellers. In other words, economically backward nations have become colonies of economically advanced ones."[36] This viewpoint forms the basis for the main theme of his third chapter, "Distinguishing between Urban and Rural," in his later work *A New Treatise on Practical Affairs*. The article further states, "The Industrial Revolution can be said to be the most fundamental among all revolutions in the modern world. It has completely changed all systems built on the foundation of old economies. Someone said that the result of the Industrial Revolution was that 'the countryside is now reliant on the city' and 'the East is now reliant on the West.' I think this statement is very accurate. Without the Industrial Revolution, Easterners would become rural dwellers. This is a fundamental idea. By looking at history through the lens of this fundamental idea, everything makes sense."[37] The observation he references was made by Karl Marx, and the "fundamental idea" refers to the materialistic concept of history. Feng did not interpret the inevitable demise of the bourgeoisie from *The Communist Manifesto*, but rather the way out for backward countries, which is the historical view of the evolution theory. He notes:

> The world today is an industrialized world, and civilization today is an industrial civilization. To achieve freedom and equality, the Chinese nation must industrialize… For a nation to seek freedom and equality, it must inevitably become an industrialized nation to be truly free and equal. Otherwise, everything is a façade.
>
> Our Chinese civilization was an agrarian one. Many Chinese or foreigners often comment that the Chinese have many characteristics, such as being "leisurely," which can be interpreted as "lazy" in the negative sense or "enjoying life" in the positive sense. This is just a characteristic of an agrarian culture, not of any particular ethnic group.[38]

Once Feng became deeply influenced by the historical view that "the economy wields the ultimate, most decisive power"[39] on his visit to Europe, he no longer used the spiritual and cultural lens to make sense of the conflicts between Chinese and Western cultures. Instead, he turned to categories that focus on social and economic types, like industrial civilization and agrarian culture, to explain cultural issues. In line with this approach, the way a society's economy is built is then regarded as the foundation of each historical era and a fundamental element that determines the characteristics of its civilization. In other words, the respective characteristics and differences between Chinese culture and modern Western culture can be explained based on agrarian and industrial civilizations. Such a methodological shift cannot be solely explained by the idea that the difference between Eastern and Western cultures is actually the difference between ancient and modern times. The concept of ancient versus modern can actually presuppose or imply changes in the societal type with the progress of time, but simply the notion of ancient and modern alone cannot identify the unique traits that distinguish modern from ancient. This article states that the basis for Feng's cultural views has shifted from a period of time to societal types, with an emphasis on understanding how the economy is built. Consequently, he views the Industrial Revolution as the key to modernization, shifting his focus from culture (in a narrow sense) to economy when understanding the complete picture of the conflict between Chinese and Western cultures, and clearly stating that industrialization is the fundamental path that will lead the Chinese nation to freedom and equality. This train of thought is reflected in his later work, *A New Treatise on Practical Affairs*, which explains the book's subtitle, "China's Path to Freedom." In this sense, the significance of Feng's trip to Europe or the transformation it brought to his thought is not in the change from East versus West to ancient versus modern, but rather in the understanding of the difference between ancient and modern through the perspective of societal types. In this sense, the influence of the materialist conception of history was key.

Alongside the materialist conception of history, Feng was also influenced by the new realism school, which was put forth by philosophers such as William Pepperell Montague in the late 1920s. This is reflected not only in the metaphysics and discussion on ethics in the *New Discussions*,[40] but also in his cultural analyses. As for the debate between complete Westernization and restoration of culture, Feng points out that if the Chinese were to follow the logic of complete Westernization, everyone should convert to Christianity, wear suits, and stop eating steamed buns. However, proponents of complete Westernization did not necessarily advocate such measures, and therefore, it only amounts to some form of partial Westernization. Among proponents of partial Westernization, different people advocated different parts. Even proponents for the restoration of Chinese culture do not necessarily demand that everything from the past should be preserved. Instead, they advocate preserving what should be preserved and discarding what should be discarded. From Feng's perspective, these debates are ambiguous either in their logic (as in the case of "complete") or the standards they uphold. In the same article cited above, Feng points out that it is necessary to distinguish between cultural individuals and cultural types when discussing cultural issues. For instance, when we speak of a university, that is a type, whereas Tsinghua University is an individual. Taking the same lens to analyze Western culture, if the focus is placed on Western cultural "individuals," we would not be able to distinguish which elements are relevant and which are not. Feng believes that only by viewing Western culture as a cultural type can one determine what is relevant and worth learning, and what is not.

In January 1937, Feng discussed cultural issues at the Third Annual Meeting of the Chinese Association of Philosophy, in which he emphasized the use of logic to resolve the debate. He stated:

> If one takes a logical approach to these debates, most of them can be easily resolved. Logically, there is a distinction between individuals and types. An individual can represent many types; for example, Confucius can represent someone from the Spring

> and Autumn Period, a Shandong native, someone who has lived past the age of seventy, a sage, and so on. When an individual learns the ways of another, he is studying a certain type or several types represented by the latter. For example, someone wants to learn the ways of Confucius, but in reality, he or she wants to learn the ways of a sage, which Confucius represents. An individual cannot be learned. The term the West is an individual, and in the cultural aspect, it represents many types, such as Christian culture, scientific culture, industrial culture, and so on. When we say we are learning the ways of the West, we are actually learning a particular cultural type or several cultural types that it represents, such as the scientific culture or industrial culture. Aspects of Chinese culture that do not conflict with these need not be changed.[41]

This idea of distinguishing between types and individuals is the main theme of the first chapter, "Distinguishing Universals and Particulars," in *A New Treatise on Practical Affairs*, which shows that Feng had made his stand clear on the explanation of Chinese and Western cultures. The types and individuals here are referred to as universals and particulars in "Distinguishing Universals and Particulars,"[42] and the logic mentioned here refers not only to formal logic, but also to the logical analysis method represented by Bertrand Russell. This is also the basic methodology in *New Neo-Confucianism*.

New Neo-Confucianism was written during the fall and winter periods of 1937, lithography printed in Mencius in 1938, and officially published by The Commercial Press in 1939. The twelve chapters in *A New Treatise on Practical Affairs* were written and published in the magazine *New Trends* in Kunming from 1938 to April of the following year, and then published by The Commercial Press in 1940. Both the Preface of *New Neo-Confucianism* and the Preface of *A New Treatise on Practical Affairs* discuss the "utility" of *New Neo-Confucianism*.[43] The casual reader might mistake this for a self-justification by Feng and not buy into the claims of the usefulness of the New Neo-Confucianism methodology and the relationship between *New Neo-Confucianism* and *A New Treatise on Practical Affairs*, as put forth by Feng. However, it is evident from the article from the Annual Meeting of the Chinese Association of Philosophy in January 1937, cited above, that the methodology of "Distinguishing Universals and Particulars" in *A New Treatise on Practical Affairs* was already established before the publication of *New Neo-Confucianism*.

"Distinguishing Universals and Particulars" is manifested metaphysically in the form of the discussion about the reasons for the existence of a category of things and things of its kind, and in the Chinese version of the discussion of universals and particulars in new realism. As a methodology in cultural theory, "Distinguishing Universals and Particulars" is manifested in the form of the distinction between "viewing culture from the perspective of types" and "viewing culture from the perspective of specifics."[44] Therefore, it is not wrong to say that the cultural analysis in *A New Treatise on Practical Affairs* is an application of the philosophical method in *New Neo-Confucianism*. In fact, the articles "General Trends of Modern National Movements in China" and "From the Chinese Association of Philosophy to the Utility of Philosophy," published in August 1936 and January 1937, outline the later work *A New Treatise on Practical Affairs*.

In *A New Treatise on Practical Affairs,* the arguments of these two pre-war articles are elaborated in detail, with the first being "Distinguishing Universals and Particulars." Universals refer to types, while particulars refer to specifics and individuals. Feng advocates viewing Western culture from the perspective of types, instead of specifics (individual), and he believes that the terms Chinese culture and Western culture are a reflection of viewing culture through the lens of individuals, while the terms capitalist culture and socialist culture reflect viewing culture through the lens of types. He observes that most people have been viewing Western culture through the lens of specifics since the early days of the Republic of China, as "they often comment, 'the Chinese are as such, while the Westerners are as such,' as if the Chinese are as such just because they are Chinese, and the Westerners are as such just because they are Westerners. They seem to not be aware, or at least not have paid attention to the fact that the Chinese are as such because the Chinese culture adheres to a certain type of culture in some aspects, while the Westerners are as such because the Western culture adheres to a certain type of culture in some aspects."[45] He held the opinion that any culture that is of the same type as Chinese culture would definitely possess characteristics similar to Chinese culture. The distinctive characteristics and relative weakness of the Chinese people or Chinese culture, as well as the distinctive characteristics and relative prosperity of Western culture, all stem from their different cultural types. In line with this thought, if one were to say that Chinese culture has any ailments, such ailments are determined by the cultural type it belongs to.

In understanding the differences between Chinese and Western cultural types, the most intuitive way is to understand the differences between ancient and modern times. Feng is supportive of this proposition, noting, "What people generally term Western culture actually refers to modern or contemporary culture. The reason Western culture is considered superior is not because it is Western, but because it is modern or contemporary." He says, "Some say Western culture is a culture of automobiles, while Chinese culture is one of rickshaws. However, automobiles are not inherently Western. The presence or absence of automobiles is explained by the difference in times, not a matter of Chinese versus Western. The difference between China and the West in most people's minds is largely the difference between ancient and modern times." And, "The reason we always get the short end of the stick is not because our culture is Chinese, but because our culture is medieval."

Only by confirming the type by which to identify Western culture can we grasp the essence of learning the ways of Western culture. If we view Western culture as a specific individual, we would not be able to distinguish its predominant characteristics and incidental features. Only by regarding Western culture as a type of culture, such as modern or contemporary culture, can we grasp its modern elements and avoid complete Westernization. Therefore, the problem that the Chinese culture faces is "merely to change our cultural type to another type, not change our specific culture to another specific one."[46] If we view Einstein as a specific individual, there are many aspects that define him as Einstein, such as his appearance, personality, hobbies, and his identity as a Jew. However, if we view him as a physicist, studying him would not mean studying all the different characteristics that make him a unique individual, but rather learning his scientific methods. Similarly, complete Westernization is not necessary, and also not possible. When the Chinese learn the ways of the West, it is not about adopting its specific culture (including traits like blond hair, blue eyes, and Christian faith). Rather, it is about transforming Chinese culture to the same type as contemporary Western culture, which is to modernize or contemporize.

Inspired by Marx, Feng makes a further distinction between ancient and modern times based on economic types and the way economies are built. He points out that Chinese culture has always emphasized the distinction between barbarians and Chinese, which is essentially a difference between rural and urban areas if viewed through a cultural lens. Having been urbanites for thousands of years, the Chinese unexpectedly became rural dwellers toward the end of the Qing Dynasty. The intelligence, wealth, and power of Westerners are not attributed to their Western identity, but to their status as urbanites. Similarly, the ignorance, poverty, and weakness of the Chinese are not inherent to their Chinese identity, but rather because they have reduced to rural dwellers. Westerners successfully qualified as modern urbanites because there was a significant transformation in their economy, which was the Industrial Revolution. Again, Feng quotes Marx's observation that the Industrial Revolution made the countryside dependent on the city, and the East dependent on the West, which indicates Marx's influence on his historical views.[47]

Following Marx's historical view, the distinctions between ancient and modern and city and countryside are still too abstract to truly grasp the types of culture to which Chinese and Western cultures belong. Feng further points out that Chinese culture, which has stayed stagnant as ancient and is considered countryside relative to the West, is a culture of a family-based economy when considering the societal type. Western culture, which progressed to modern after the Industrial Revolution and is considered urban relative to the East, is a culture of a society-based economy.[48] The Industrial Revolution transformed the method by which the economy was built from a family-based structure to a society-based one, and in so doing, changed the system of the economy. This transformation led to changes in people's entire way of life, social organizations, and the standards of social ethics.[49] The industrial revolution and industrialization were the imminent and fundamental way for the Chinese culture or China as a nation to achieve freedom and equality among the world's nations.

A New Treatise on Practical Affairs offers a comprehensive elaboration of Feng's modern cultural view after the mid-1930s, distinguishing between universals and particulars, ancient and modern, and urban and rural, as well as through the discussion of the concept of family and nation. His cultural view in the 1930s emphasized the immediate practice of culture more than the ultimate explanation of history. For instance, he criticized Liang Shuming's historical explanation in the 1920s, saying that drawing parallels between East versus West and ancient versus modern could not sufficiently explain how the West had progressed to modern times, while the East remained in ancient times. However, by the 1930s, he no longer pursued a single ultimate explanation for history, but instead focused on learning the practical aspects of the West. Objectively, this shift also marked a turning point in the cultural debates in the 1930s.

"Distinguishing between Universals and Particulars" emphasizes the need for Western culture as a cultural type and focuses on the methods for learning from the West. Learning the ways of the West should not be mixed up with the explanations for China remaining in ancient times and the West progressing to modern times. Marx's emphasis on the mode of production for a material life and his explanation on the Industrial Revolution and economy building on a capitalist society led Feng to make a complete shift toward understanding the foundation and characteristics of modern culture from the perspective of industrialization, whereby an economy is built on a society-based structure. Compared to the transition from East versus West to ancient versus modern in the 1920s, this change in his thinking in the 1930s not only reflects the influence of the materialist concept of history, but also new cultural consciousness and national consciousness of industrial revolution for salvation among intellectuals in the same era during China's industrialization (such consciousness would not fundamentally reject a particular path of industrialization).

IV. Modernization and Nationalization

In the decade or so before the Marco Polo Bridge Incident,* Feng Youlan's central focus in his cultural view was Eastern and Western cultures and their conflict. It is worth noting that issues of tradition and nationalism within modernization were not part of his cultural view during that period. He instead focused on Chinese culture's transition from an agrarian (ancient) to an industrial (modern) one. It can be said that his cultural view was completely modern-oriented up till 1937. Although he was against complete Westernization, his advocacy for industrialization can be read as a form of Westernization of the economy, which did not cause any tension between tradition and modernization, not because there is a seamless integration of the two, but rather, the issues on tradition and national culture had yet to make an entrance, while the issue on cultural identity was non-existent. This is also where his view significantly differs from the prevailing cultural conservatism before and after the May Fourth Movement, as well as the thoughts of early Neo-Confucian philosophers like Ma Yifu, Liang Shuming, and Xiong Shili. Feng Youlan later remarked that "on cultural issues, Liang's purpose is fundamentally different from mine. He sets out to seek differences, while I aim to seek commonalities. His focus is on the comparison between China and the West, while mine is on ancient versus modern."[50] Actually, Liang's pursuit of differences stems from his emphasis on cultural identity, whereas Feng's modern-oriented cultural view that seeks commonalities, while bearing significant positive implications, overlooks cultural identity and nationalism in culture.

Feng's thoughts changed significantly after the War of Resistance against Japanese Aggression in 1937. After February 1939, the latter half of *A New Treatise on Practical Affairs,* which was

---

* Also known as Lugou Bridge Incident or the July 7 Incident, which occurred in 1937 and marked the beginning of an all-out War of Resistance against Japanese Aggression.

published in the magazine *New Trends*, was mostly related to national culture as an individual.[51] Originally, taking the simplistic view of the theory of evolution, it was logical for traditional Chinese culture as a whole to be negated since it needed to progress from an ancient agrarian culture to a modern industrialized one. However, after 1939, Feng highlighted that it was necessary to view Chinese culture not only from the perspective of a cultural type, but also as an individual culture. The philosophy of *New Neo-Confucianism* emphasizes universals, and the distinctions between ancient and modern, urban and rural, and family and nation in the first half of *A New Treatise on Practical Affairs* highlight the analyses of cultural types, not individual cultures. They focus on the modernization of Chinese culture, and not the treatment of cultural heritage, historical traditions, and ethnic groups. The different orientations of the two parts of *A New Treatise on Practical Affairs* thus reflect the complex relationship between modernization and nationalization during the war.

According to the perspective in the latter half of *A New Treatise on Practical Affairs*, it can be said that from the perspective of types, to call Einstein a scientist is to focus on the reasons that make him a scientist; his other characteristics are irrelevant in this view. From the perspective of individuals, Einstein is a whole person, and all his characteristics are indispensable qualities of him as a person. Attributes such as his appearance, personality, and hobbies may have nothing to do with him as a member of the scientist category, but they are important qualities that make Einstein who he is and distinguish him from others. In this sense, individuals become significant.

Types is a category of cognition, rather than of existing entities. On the other hand, individuals may be classified under different categories, which is relative, but their existence is absolute. People live in countries built on ethnic groups, and cultures develop from these entities. Many characteristics of a national culture may not be significant from the perspective of cultural types, but are important from the point of view of cultural identity or the nation's survival. This is especially so in times of national crisis, where a national culture is the only one that can inspire national enthusiasm and morality and motivate people to engage in the fight for national liberation. In order to ensure the survival of the nation as an individual, Feng started strongly emphasizing the differences between different nations' cultures. These differences are what distinguish one nation from another, allowing each of them to exist independently as distinct entities. It is thus clear that the issue of national identity cannot be overlooked in the midst of modernization, just as Britain and Germany in the Second World War could not resolve the real national identity issues despite belonging to the same type of industrialized culture with economies built on a society-based structure.

On the stance that emphasizes individuality, Feng proposes several distinctions about affirming cultural nationality.

First, national culture should be divided into two parts: one shares similarities with other nations but exhibits differences to some extent (such as horse-drawn carriages in China and trains in the West), while the other exhibits differences in type and pattern rather than simply in degree (such as Chinese style versus Western style architecture). For the former, efforts should be made to uplift those at the lower level to a higher level, and this should not be limited to functional objects, but also include the full range of industrialization in material production. As for the latter, the question of whether to modernize does not exist, as in the case of Chinese cuisine, clothing, and architecture.[52]

The second is the distinction between the terms "of" and "based." When referring to the modernization of clothing and architecture, one is referring to their form. While improvements in fabrics and building materials may not constitute Westernization, they can be modernized. In Feng's words, the unchanging forms refer to the styles and patterns of a nation's existence. Among these patterns, he particularly emphasizes art and literature, pointing out that the terms British industry and British science merely denote the industry of the British and the science of the British, that is, those that exist in Britain and are owned by the British people. On the other hand, British literature is British-based literature. "Of" means that something exists within the scope of the national state, while "based" is used to denote something that is unique and inherent to the nation. Literature and art are things based on, not of, a nation. These styles and patterns created on the basis of the nations are crucial to them, because "if these things only differ in their patterns, every nation can adhere to its own traditions, but that is not enough to preserve a nation's uniqueness."[53] In other words, that is "innovation without losing its essence."

The third is a distinction between expression and matter. He notes, "The production methods, economic system, and social system of a society constitute its matter, while its art, literature, and so forth, constitute its expression." Taking architecture as an example, the building materials are the matter, while the architectural style is its expression. Feng points out that "from the perspective of matter, expression is not a primary element. But from the viewpoint of an entity, a society, or a nation, expression is an important foundation." The expression of a nation is what it relies on for emotional exchanges in life. Only when a nation produces its own literature and art can it fully appreciate and derive pleasure from them. Since each nation can only find joy in the patterns it produces, "it is vital that each nation cherishes its own literature and art. This is not because a nation needs to distinguish itself, but because its life is deemed fully enriched, fulfilling, and enjoyable only when it is immersed in its own literature and art." Moreover, "cherish" here does not mean treating one's cultural patterns with a conservative attitude, nor does it mean treating them like relics, as advocates of the Quintessence of Chinese Culture in the early days of the Republic of China did. Rather, it means "to treat something as a living entity, nurturing and cultivating it to grow and develop."[54]

In *A New Treatise on Practical Affairs*, the emphasis on cultural styles and patterns specifically refers to art and literature, while intentionally omitting philosophy. If expression is closely related to the realm of spiritual civilization, how does philosophy relate to the foundation of a nation? If patterns and styles need not be modernized, what about philosophy? Feng focused on these questions after the war began. In the early stages of the war, he wrote an article titled "On National Philosophy,"[55] in which he points out that people often speak of German philosophy and American philosophy, but seldom mention German chemistry and American chemistry. Even if someone mentions German chemistry or American chemistry, he or she refers to them as the chemistry of Germany or chemistry of America, not German-based chemistry or American-based chemistry, "because there is only one chemistry; we cannot add adjectives like German-based or American based to it. On the other hand, when we talk about German philosophy or British philosophy, we say German-based philosophy and British-based philosophy, as with literature. This means that adjectives like German-based or British-based can be added to philosophy and literature. Overall, it shows that national distinction may exist for philosophy or literature, but not science." In Feng's view, philosophy, like literature, is built on the basis of the nation, but it is different from literature. In certain ways, philosophy is closer to science than literature. Literature is written in national languages, each with its own unique grammar, which gives rise to specific techniques that display its uniqueness and beauty, making it easy to understand the national attribute of literature. Although scientific principles are also expressed in different national languages, "the specific grammar of a language has nothing to do with the principles of science; there is no specific relationship and no relevance. Scientific principles are common and universal, and so is science." Literature does not pursue objective universal principles, and "one can only say if it is good or bad; there is no right or wrong."

Feng was of the opinion that while philosophy is also influenced by national languages and grammar, it differs from literature. He says, "The objective of philosophy lies in seeking universal and common principles. We need to adhere to this standard when critiquing philosophical thoughts. If we depart from this standard, the philosophies of different nations, like their languages, will have no right or wrong." Thus, "philosophy contains universal and common principles, or at least seeks to achieve such principles. These principles also need to be expressed in the languages of different nations, but there is no specific relationship and no relevance between national languages and their principles. In this respect, philosophy is the same as science, or at least it should be so."[56]

Feng regards philosophy as part of science, to a large extent. There is no distinction between Eastern and Western philosophy, and the questions they seek to address belong to the same series or system. However, Eastern philosophy may discuss only a part of this series or system, and the discussions may be unclear. Like many scholars in the modern era, Feng seems to regard Western philosophy as the paradigm of philosophy, just as Western natural science is seen as the paradigm of science. This perspective did not change until the 1940s.

It is precisely because philosophy possesses attributes that lie between literature and science that philosophy bears the dual tasks of modernization and nationalization. The last section of the chapter "On Jin Yuelin" in Volume Seven of *A New History of Chinese Philosophy* specifically discusses the issue of modernization and nationalization. Feng observes that the metaphysics in *On Dao* is Chinese philosophy (i.e., Chinese-based philosophy), not philosophy in China (i.e., philosophy of China), while *Theory of Knowledge* and *Logic* is "theory of knowledge and logic in China," not "China's theory of knowledge and logic."[57] Indeed, Jin Yuelin himself has also said that logic is similar to mathematics and the natural sciences, in that people can study it from an external perspective in a calm state. Metaphysics, on the other hand, involves human emotions, desires, and the mind. Good metaphysics can move the heart, bring joy, and cultivate character.[58]

The chapter "On Feng Youlan" in Volume Seven of *A New History of Chinese Philosophy* says, "China needs to modernize, and so does philosophy. Modernized Chinese philosophy does not mean creating a brand-new Chinese philosophy out of thin air. That is impossible. A new modernized Chinese philosophy can only be achieved by analyzing traditional Chinese philosophical concepts on the basis of the research outcomes of modern logic, so as to clarify any seemingly vague concepts."[59] It goes on, "New Neo-Confucianism uses the research outcomes of modern logic to elaborate on important questions in Neo-Confucianism. This is beneficial to the modernization of Chinese philosophy."[60] This perspective maintains that both Chinese and Western philosophies pursue the same universality of principles. Chinese philosophy differs from Western philosophy not in the questions asked, but in the lack of clarity of the questions pursued as compared to Western philosophy. To modernize philosophy is to utilize logical analysis to clarify what Chinese philosophy has not made clear.

Since philosophy needs to be modernized, it is helpful to consider the significance of nationalizing it. Feng points out in "On National Philosophy":

> A nation's philosophy is built upon the nation's appearance, not its content. We believe that national philosophy is built upon the nation not only because it belongs to that nation, but also because it follows the historical development of that nation's philosophy and is expressed in that nation's language. We may call these distinctions superficial or external based. However, these so-called appearance and external aspects pertain to philosophy. In national terms, these distinctions significantly contribute to the spiritual unity and emotional fulfilment of the nation, making philosophy an integral part of a nation's spiritual life.[61]
>
> What is discussed here is precisely the thought on cultural individuality emphasized in the latter part of *A New Treatise on Practical Affairs*. From the perspective of cultural individuality, the various superficial and external (formal) aspects of a nation's culture may not be important, but they constitute the intrinsic quality of a nation's spiritual life and are important for its development and fulfillment.

It was natural that Feng's discussion reflected a nationalist stance given the context of that time. However, while the issue of tradition is seen here in the form of nationalism, it is not supported by a thorough elaboration of cultural theory. In fact, Chinese culture, whether in its various forms of conscious activities or its traditional values, spirit, and realms, cannot be fully affirmed through a type-individual analysis, nor can it be fully reflected through national unity in spirit and emotional fulfillment. There are indeed similarities between Eastern and Western philosophy, and *New Neo-Confucianism* is a successful example of old wine in new bottles. However, the works *New Origins of Humanity* and *A New Treatise on the Nature of Dao*, published in the 1940s, cannot be seen as clarifying Chinese conceptual issues through Western logical analysis. In fact, the concept of the cosmic realm discussed in *New Origins of Humanity*, the notion of upholding high morality while keeping to the golden mean found in *A New Treatise on the Nature of Dao*, and the method of negation presented in *A New Understanding of Words* are all imbued with the spirit of Chinese philosophy. Such a spirit is neither the appearance of a national spirit formed by the use of a national language nor something that the Western philosophical model encompasses.

Finally, we will here discuss the issue of moral tradition in spiritual civilization. I have mentioned that Feng's cultural perspective in the early days is modern oriented, as it developed from a focus on East versus West to ancient versus modern. When, then, did his cultural perspective start to incorporate affirmation of traditional Chinese culture, and can this affirmation be accommodated in the pure philosophical system of the New Neo-Confucianism?

As early as 1927, Feng remarked in his essay "Social Ethics in China" that the loyalty displayed in past eras, exemplified by loyal officials, filial children, and faithful wives, was dedicated to the concept of the ruler or husband. Such a spirit resided in the conceptual world of Plato rather than in specific individuals in the concrete world.[62] It is also stated in *New Discussions* that an official would sacrifice himself out of loyalty to a specific ruler, so he would not question whether the ruler is worth his sacrifice. Such sacrifice completely stems from his loyalty to his title, to the principle, and to the universal ruler.[63] Similarly, in the 1950s, Feng raised the issue of abstract inheritance, in which he attempted to elicit certain affirmations of tradition by uplifting particulars to universals and from individuals to commonplace, giving particular emphasis to morality.

According to the system of New Neo-Confucianism, an object becomes a member of a category based on the principles of that category, which include principles of common categories. For example, a cat is a member of the category of cats based on the principles of cats, and the principles of cats include the principles of animals, and so on. As such, a cat adheres to the principles of cats to become a cat, and it also adheres to the principles of animals to become an animal.[64] Therefore, "when an object adheres to one principle, it can also adhere to multiple principles, and in fact, it must adhere to multiple principles."[65] In line with this logic, regardless of the type to which an individual culture belongs, it should contain the principles of that societal type and also the principles of a society. While being a "culture whose economy is built on a family-based structure," Chinese culture also contains principles applicable to general society and life, which make it a concrete universal. From this perspective, there should be some unchanging elements in Chinese culture.

However, in reality, Feng did not receive affirmation of traditional moral culture from the new realism school. The affirmation mainly stemmed from his own moral identification and choices. Yin Ding believed this affirmation is closely related to his mother's moral model.[66] In his first article in *New Discussions* in 1932, he clearly asserts that "there is no new or old when it comes to morals."[67] He observes that a human society must have its principles, and people must organize their societies in accordance with these principles. To build a sound organization, there must be conditions that members of the organization must adhere to, and some of these are morals, such as benevolence and loyalty. Without these basic conditions, there would be no sound human organizations.

In his final article in *New Discussions,* he points out, "There are many political and social organizations, and each has its own type... Above these various types, there is a general type of societal organization. The principles contained therein are common to all the societal types. If these principles are realized, they constitute the common morals of all the social organizations."[68] He maintains his belief that "some morals come with the society. As long as a society exists, those morals will exist. Without them, society cannot be built, and even if they are built temporarily, they are bound to collapse eventually. Some morals follow certain societal types and are only required in such societies. Outside of such societies, these morals are not needed. I call the former constant morals, and the latter variable morals."[69] It is on the basis of these constant morals and variable morals that Feng proposed a clear moral conservatism very early on in his work (as early as the publication of *New Discussions*), reaffirming basic traditional morals.

The war and the experiences drawn from it showed that traditional morals were the main pillar of spiritual support for the unity of the Chinese people during the War of Resistance against Japanese Aggression. In the final article in *A New Treatise on Practical Affairs* titled "In Praise of China," Feng insisted on the Five Constant Values: benevolence, righteousness, propriety, wisdom, and sincerity. He says, "These are constant, fundamental morals, regardless of old or new, past or present, Chinese or foreign."[70] He follows with the conclusion, "We are advocating a modernized foundation, but basic morals are indifferent to modernization. Some people often confuse certain social systems with basic morals, which is very wrong. Certain social systems are variable, but basic morals are constant. The issue of modernization or not exists for variables, but not for constants."[71] It is also based on this stance that Feng gave his affirmation to "Chinese substance with Western function" during the late Qing Dynasty.

V. Substance and Function in Cultural Theory

In *An Account of My Life,* there is mention of *A New Treatise on Practical Affairs,* and it concludes with the following remark, "As *A New Treatise on Practical Affairs* highlights the importance of developing productivity, it seems to endorse the proposition of learning the Chinese way as the substance and the Western way for the function advocated by the Westernization Movement during the late Qing Dynasty. However, this is not the case. I advocate the inseparability of substance and function. Every substance will lead to a corresponding function, and every function will tell us what the substance is. If we were to apply the categories of substance and function in Chinese philosophy, I believe that in a social context, economic foundations like productivity will be the substance, while superstructures such as politics and culture will be the function. When substance changes, the function will change accordingly. It does not mean that human effort is not required. Human effort is required, but humans will put in their efforts accordingly."[72] Feng's thoughts regarding the economic base as substance and superstructure as function and the inseparability of substance and function originated in the 1930s, when he was inspired by Marx's thinking during his trip to Europe.[73]

In September 1935, Feng pointed out in "History and Philosophy from the Qin and Han Dynasties" that "according to the materialist concept of history, when the economic system of a society undergoes changes, other aspects of the system will definitely change accordingly,"[74] and that "all social and political systems are built upon the economic system. For every type of economic system, there will be a corresponding social and political system. In other words, for every type of material civilization, there will be a corresponding spiritual civilization. They are all interconnected."[75] Furthermore, he says, "Many people comment that the extended family system is not reasonable [note: 'not' is added to express the meaning in line with the context], finding people of the past foolish. However, if we consider the extended family system together with the agrarian economic society, we will see that the establishment of the extended family system was not without reason. Furthermore, considering each stage of historical evolution, each set of economic, social, and political systems has its historical mission. For instance, the historical mission of a capitalist society was to centralize and socialize all endeavors, in preparation for a socialist society. When the capitalist society achieved success, that was when it should and must step down."[76] It is evident that Feng was deeply influenced by Marx's thoughts. The view that economic, social, and political systems are interconnected with spiritual cultivation later translates to the monistic principle of substance and function, where there is a corresponding function for every substance.

It was with this view that Feng expounded his own perspective on substance and function in his 1936 article "General Trends of Modern National Movements in China," distinguishing it from those advocated by the late Qing Westernization Movement and intellectuals of the May Fourth Movement. On explaining his view that "industrialization is the fundamental way for the Chinese nation to achieve freedom and equality," he points out:

> Our perspective seems to be aligned with those of Zeng Guofan, Li Hongzhang, and Zhang Zhidong from the late Qing Dynasty. All of them advocated for railways, machinery, and factories. Zhang Zhidong established many new-era factories in Wuchang, and the Guangzhou–Wuchang Railway, which is about to be completed, was initiated by him as well. The political changes at that time were necessary, and if they had succeeded, we would have been on par with Japan. Later, during the May Fourth Movement, some people felt that we should learn beyond the Western material civilization and ought to begin with the spiritual civilization. And so, the winds changed, and focus was placed on scientific theories, philosophy, and literature. Since our current proposition is similar to those from the late Qing Dynasty, did the efforts from the May Fourth Movement go to waste? No. Although our proposition seems largely similar to those from the late Qing Dynasty, they are actually different. They had only advocated for material civilization, but believed that that the Chinese spiritual cultivation was superior, which explains the proposition of "learning the Chinese way as the substance and the Western way as the function." During the May Fourth Movement, the prevailing thought was that the West not only had material civilization, but also a superior spiritual civilization. Moreover,

> spiritual civilization was recognized as the fundamental, which was where people should begin. The industrialization we are proposing now encompasses both material and spiritual civilizations, with spiritual civilization as the foundation. If a particular material civilization is achieved, its corresponding spiritual civilization will follow naturally.[77]

The Westernization Movement only pursued modernized material civilization, but not modernized spiritual civilization. Feng opposed this, feeling that it was a case of a divergence between substance and function. On the other hand, intellectuals during the May Fourth Movement advocated regarding spiritual civilization as fundamental and prioritized spiritual civilization. Feng also disagreed with this approach, feeling that it was reversing the order of substance and function.[78] Feng was of the opinion that material civilization should come first. With material civilization in place, spiritual civilization would naturally follow. He felt that his perspective was an amalgamation of the for and against propositions put forth by the previous two factions.[79] When writing the article "The Purpose of Fighting the War and Principles of Nation Building," he continued to highlight that China must grasp the elements of a modern nation in order to transform into one. He remarks, "After the opium war, people from the late Qing Dynasty under the rules of Emperors Xianfeng and Tongzhi believed that the key elements of a modernized nation were warships and cannons. Those under the rules of Emperors Guangxu and Xuantong believed that the key elements were having a parliament and a constitution. Later, during the early days of the Republic of China, the prevailing opinion was the need for Mr. De (democracy) and Mr. Sai (science). Now we know, the key element to a modernized nation is industrialization. With industrialization, warships and cannons will naturally be produced. With social industrialization, people's lifestyles will change; Mr. De will naturally be embraced, and Mr. Sai will be promoted… This is the truth, a truth that China only came to realize in the past decade."[80]

However, Feng's thought did not alwasys adhere to the monistic view of interconnectedness, as he claimed in *An Account of My Life*. There were changes in his views before and after the war. As mentioned above, the latter half of *A New Treatise on Practical Affairs* highlights that some aspects of traditional culture are indifferent to modernization and need not be changed, as seen in the statement, "Basic morals are indifferent to modernization." The views on substance and function mentioned at the end of *A New Treatise on Practical Affairs* are also different from Feng's views before the war. We read:

> Speaking of this, we feel that the late Qing scholars' proposition of "learning the Chinese way as the substance and the Western way as the function" is on one hand very superficial, but on the other, still valid. For instance, the idea of "learning the Chinese way as the substance and the Western way as the function" could mean that we can study the Four Books and Five Classics as the substance and use firearms as the function. This statement would be absolutely inconsistent and superficial. Studying the Four Books and Five Classics would not lead to an understanding of the use of firearms. People in

> the early days of the Republic of China criticized such an idea as a divergence between substance and function. But if we say that the morals that build a society are inherent to the Chinese and what needs to be added now are Western knowledge, technology, and industry, this statement would make sense. This is what we mean in *A New Treatise on Practical Affairs*... The late Qing scholars did not have such clarity on the fundamentals. They did feel that some things in China need not be changed, but they could not discern and articulate what these were exactly.[81]

We will now turn to the structure and changes of Feng's cultural views in the 1940s, from the perspective of Chinese versus Western and substance versus function. In the mid-1930s, Feng internalized Marx's historical analysis and believed that modern urban industrial civilization was essentially socialized mass production. He also subscribed to Marx's structural analysis of an economic base—superstructure and economic determinism, advocating for the economic system as the foundation, which would determine the political structure, with the economic, social, and political systems in turn determining ideological culture. Using the substance-function framework to express this proposition, the economy would be the substance and culture would be the function, with substance determining function, which demonstrates the monism of the substance and function theory. Such a substance-function view, when seen from the perspective of a historical-social structural analysis, is influenced by the materialist concept of history, but from a cultural analysis standpoint, it highlights types and degrees. Overall, it is a theory of the evolution from history to culture. There exists a decisive relationship between substance and function, which is both causal and structural.

During the war, while focusing on nationalism and emphasizing individuality, Feng proposed another analytical model, consisting of matter and expression. By matter, he means the economic and social political systems. In this sense, the extension of matter and its purpose as a basis are the same as substance. Expression is used to refer to literature, art, and other forms and styles. The concept of expression tends to be formal, especially in the forms of various ethnic activities. He also points out that matter should be modernized and needs changing, while expression is indifferent to modernization and can remain constant. Therefore, the relationship between matter and expression is different from that of substance and function. A definitive relationship also does not exist for the former pair. The model of matter and expression was not used by Feng to replace the historical and cultural perspectives of substance-function completely, as expression is merely a subset of function. In fact, Feng did not abandon the view of interconnectedness during the war. Compared with the substance-function model, which is used to demonstrate a modern cultural perspective, the matter-expression model is used to highlight national characteristics, which makes Feng's cultural views more comprehensive than before. When put together in Feng's cultural view, it can be said that the substance-function model is primary, while the matter-expression model is secondary.

For a historical and cultural entity in the midst of change, on the macro level, the substance-function model where social existence determines social consciousness is still relevant. However, the materialist concept of history, according to Marx's thought, cannot rightly determine the continuity of cultural traditions during social transformations, which is why Feng has attempted to supplement it with the national cultural stance with the matter-expression model. Culture presents itself as two parts in different states, in response to changes in the mode of economy building. One part is changeable, such as artifacts, technology, science, variable morals, philosophies requiring modernization, and social lifestyles. These aspects are subject to change or modernization along with the modernization of the mode of economy building. In terms of the differences between Chinese and Western cultures, the old things in these aspects only differ from modern Western culture in degree. Another part of culture is constant, which includes indigenous literature, art, immutable morals, nationalized philosophical discourse, and architectural forms. These are indifferent to modernization. Some of them differ from Western culture in terms of type, and need not be modernized, while some represent cultural values that transcend time and geography, such as basic morals. In this way, Feng can affirm Chinese-based literary forms, aesthetic tastes, moral principles, and philosophical spirit while on the path to modernization.

Feng's cultural views in the 1940s cannot be easily summarized as Chinese substance with Western function or Western substance with Chinese function. For instance, regarding the concept of matter and expression, equating matter to substance and expression to function would make Feng's matter-expression model a type of Western substance with Chinese function. Certainly, the Western aspect here is industrialization, which refers to modern economic and political systems, and ethnic literary and artistic forms, but expression is only a part of what is generally referred to as spiritual civilization, which is not equivalent to the general understanding of function. Moreover, there is no definitive relationship between matter and expression that can be interpreted literally, so simply categorizing the matter-expression model as substance-function often distorts the relationship between matter and expression. Furthermore, "The Purpose of Fighting the War and Principles of Nation Building" makes it clear that Feng Youlan still maintained a macroscopic view of the substance-function monism when he proposed the matter-expression model.

The debates on substance and function in modern times are partly caused by the myriad usage of this concept in Chinese philosophy. In Chinese philosophy, there are two basic applications for substance and function. In the first type of application, substance is similar to the concept of a concrete entity, while function refers to the action or function derived from the concrete entity. In the second type of application, substance refers to something internally profound, while function denotes the external actions and display of the substance. When Feng criticized the Westernization advocates in the late Qing Dynasty for diverging substance and function, and the intellectuals during the May Fourth Movement for reversing the order of substance and function, he was taking the social existence primarily built on the economic system as the substance, which is to adopt the first application. When Feng sympathetically affirmed the notion of Chinese substance with Western function by the late Qing scholars, he was taking basic moral principles as the substance, which is to adopt the second application.

Because of the different applications of substance and function in various arguments, it is impossible to distinguish the substantive positions of the proponents of substance and function solely based on the notion of substance-function. While the applications of matter, expression, and Eastern spirit with Western knowledge do not address as wide a range of issues as that of substance-function, they address issues more clearly and are less prone to confusion and misunderstanding. Moreover, in the discourse of matter versus expression or spirit versus knowledge, there is no implication that one aspect is prioritized over another, as seen in the discourse for substance versus function.

In conclusion, contrary to Feng's general statement about the evolution of his cultural views in *An Account of My Life*, this chapter argues that his cultural views that are centered on East versus West and ancient versus modern, and later developed and modified, can be analyzed in four stages. The first, in the 1920s, included a transition that was made from the discussion of cultural conflicts between the East and West to ancient and modern. Second, in the 1930s, he grasped the difference in societal types between ancient and modern societies through the degree of socialization of economic production. Overall, he displayed the substance-function cultural view of modernization (industrialization) which was inspired by Marx's view on historical philosophy. Third, during the 1940s, his attention shifted toward the issues of nationalization during the process of cultural modernization. He affirmed the national character of cultural forms through the matter and expression model. As a result, the framework and characteristics of his cultural views could not be reduced to a Chinese-Western substance and function model, and this formed the early mature form of his cultural views. Finally, after the 1950s, unlike the emphasis on a new mandate in the 1940s, questions on the cultural significance of the old nation, referring to cultural continuity and cultural identity, became prominent. From the cultural perspective, the rewriting of Chinese philosophical history is supported by a combination of historical materialism and historical dialectics. This affirms the inevitably and rationality of viewing the past as an element of the present in the development of culture and history. The discussion in this chapter follows the development of Feng's cultural views up to the 1940s. Hopefully, there will be further opportunities to look into the development beyond the 1950s.

Notes

1. *Complete Works of Sansongtang*, vol. 5, 163.
2. *Complete Works of Sansongtang*, vol. 4, 511.
3. *A New History of Chinese Philosophy*, vol. 7, 176.
4. *Selected Works of Feng Youlan*, 2.
5. "Preface," in *Collected Works of Sansongtang*, 2.
6. *Sansongtang: An Account of My Life*, 191.
7. Ibid., 191–192.
8. *Selected Works of Feng Youlan*, 3.
9. Ibid.

10. *Collected Works of Sansongtang,* 12.
11. *Collected Works of Sansongtang,* 23. (Note: This article was published in April 1922. It was submitted to the Philosophy discussion forum in Fall 1921. Refer to "To Liang Shuming" written on March 4, 1922).
12. *Collected Works of Sansongtang,* 24.
13. Ibid.
14. *Sansongtang: An Account of My Life,* 192.
15. *Collected Works of Sansongtang,* 39.
16. Ibid.
17. *Sansongtangs: An Account of My Life,* 188.
18. *Collected Works of Sansongtang,* 42.
19. Ibid., 44–47.
20. *Complete Works of Sansongtang,* vol. 1, 415.
21. Ibid., 416.
22. Ibid., 471.
23. Ibid., 484.
24. *Selected Works of Feng Youlan,* 3.
25. *Sansongtang: An Account of My Life,* 193.
26. *Complete Works of Sansongtang,* vol. 1, 575.
27. Ibid., 580. Phrases such as "The attitude of striving forward is actually a product of modern Western culture," should be added to Chapter Seven "Epilogue" of *A Comparative Study of Life Ideals.*
28. *Selected Works of Feng Youlan,* 3.
29. Yin Ding, *Feng Youlan* (Taipei: The Grand East Book Co., Ltd., 1991), 19.
30. Ibid., 20.
31. Wang Zongyu, *A Chronology of Liang Shuming.*
32. *Collected Works of Sansongtang,* 11. (Note: The footer of this document is signed "Written in New York, December of the seventh year of the Republic of China." "Seven" should be corrected to "nine.")
33. *Sansongtang: An Account of My Life,* 229.
34. Ibid., 243–244.
35. Ibid., 211.
36. *Collected Works of Sansongtang,* 387.
37. Ibid.
38. *Sansongtang: An Account of My Life,* 389–390.
39. Ibid., 388.
40. The idea that the principles of airplanes existed before the invention of airplanes, and the unchanging characteristic of morals was already proposed in *New Discussions.*
41. "From the Chinese Association of Philosophy to the Utility of Philosophy" published in *Shen Bao* on January 24, 1937. *Complete Works of Sansongtang,* vol. 5, 359.
42. *Complete Works of Sansongtang,* vol. 4, 217.
43. In the preface of *New Neo-Confucianism,* it is stated, "Although this book may seem impractical, there are many practical problems today whose solutions are closely related to the discussions made in this book." The preface of *A New Treatise on Practical Affairs* also quotes this statement.
44. *Complete Works of Sansongtang,* vol. 4, 218–220.
45. Ibid., 222.

46. Ibid., 225–228.
47. Ibid., 244.
48. Ibid., 252.
49. Ibid., 259.
50. *Complete Works of Sansongtang*, vol. 5, 450.
51. Referring to Chapters 8–12 in *A New Treatise on Practical Affairs*.
52. *Complete Works of Sansongtang*, vol. 4, 304–305.
53. Ibid.
54. Ibid., 306–310.
55. "On National Philosophy" is part of the *Nandu Collection*. The chronology in Yin Ding's *Feng Youlan* states that this article was written in 1937, but the basis for this is unknown. The article is also part of Volume 5 of the *Complete Works of Sansongtang*, in which there is a line that says, "Refer to the preface of *New Neo-Confucianism* for a detailed discussion of this point." This suggests that the article was written after the completion of *New Neo-Confucianism*, presumably in the early days of the war.
56. *Complete Works of Sansongtang*, vol. 5, 306–308.
57. *A New History of Chinese Philosophy*, vol. 7, 162–163.
58. Jin Yuelin, *On Dao* (The Commercial Press, 1985), 3, 16.
59. *A New History of Chinese Philosophy*, vol. 7, 166.
60. Ibid., 176.
61. *Complete Works of Sansongtang*, vol. 5, 309.
62. *Collected Works of Sansongtang*, 88.
63. Ibid., 248.
64. *Complete Works of Sansongtang*, vol. 4, 44.
65. Ibid.
66. Yin Ding, *Feng Youlan*, 11–12.
67. *Complete Works of Sansongtang*, vol. 5, 278.
68. Ibid., 303–304.
69. *Complete Works of Sansongtang*, vol. 1, 279.
70. *Complete Works of Sansongtang*, vol. 4, 359.
71. Ibid., 364.
72. *Sansongtang: An Account of My Life*, 245–246.
73. Feng Youlan made a remark at the International Congress on Philosophy in Prague in 1934 about "only adopting Marx's theory of human nature, and not his theory of materialism." *Contemporary Chinese Philosophy* and *Collected Works of Sansongtang*, 288.
74. *Collected Works of Sansongtang*, 346.
75. Ibid., 347.
76. Ibid., 348.
77. Ibid., 392–393.
78. *Complete Works of Sansongtang*, vol. 4, 248.
79. *Collected Works of Sansongtang*, 392–393.
80. *Complete Works of Sansongtang*, vol. 5, 432.
81. *Complete Works of Sansongtang*, vol. 4, 364.

CHAPTER 14

Feng Youlan's Philosophy of Life in *A New Treatise on the Way of Life*

Different interpretations arise from different theoretical perspectives formed by historical and cultural contexts of different eras, and different individuals reading the same historical text will also have different interpretations. From this perspective, when it comes to the issue of understanding, it is important to be attentive to acquiring new perspectives that could activate the theoretical significance of the text. Clearly, the comprehension and understanding of the meaning of a philosopher's work cannot be solely constrained by the philosopher's self-expression. For example, when Feng Youlan was alive, I once asked him, "Which of the "Six Books of Zhenyuan" is the most important?" At that time, he did not mention *A New Treatise on Practical Affairs* and *A New Treatise on the Way of Life*. Further, he says in the preface to *Sansongtang* and the seventh volume of *A New History of Chinese Philosophy* that he believed these two books had little value. However, in the early 1990s, when I was studying *A New Treatise on Practical Affairs,* I discovered that the book discusses the most prominent issues related to Sino-Western cultural matters and the relationship between culture and modernization since the mid-1980s, which led me to form a very different understanding of its contemporary relevance and importance than Feng's own views.[1] Based on this experience, I hope to find a similar perspective in understanding *A New Treatise on the Way of Life*. In this chapter, I attempt to incorporate its discourse into the ethical transformations of modernity in order to reevaluate its significance.

I

Over the past two decades, China's transition from a socialist planned economy to a socialist market economy has allowed us to discover through direct experience that in a modern society based on a market economy, success is the most popular value orientation among young people, while nobility becomes a relic of past cultural symbols. The ancient Confucian ideal of sages and virtuous individuals, as well as the moral pursuits during revolutionary times, have gradually faded and declined.[2] In fact, this is the prevailing trend in the moral and spiritual life of the post-"Cultural Revolution" era. Certainly, in the early stages of the post-"Cultural Revolution" era, the emergence of this trend was primarily a reaction to the deep revulsion people felt toward the excessive revolutionary environment of the "Cultural Revolution." However, as developments unfolded, it became intertwined with the growth of the market economy. In this process of social and cultural development, the assertion of the individual self and the pursuit of personal interests have increasingly gained prominence, echoing the establishment of economic reforms and the socialist market economy, and they have become a part of the construction of modernity in China.

The unfolding of modernity in China did not begin until the 1980s, though China's modernization process had already undergone initial developments in the first three decades of the 20th century. The shift in cultural ideas toward a departure from the traditional and an embrace of the contemporary[3] was also advanced in the New Culture Movement during this time. Despite the focus on overcoming political fragmentation and chaos in the transition from the Revolution of 1911 to the end of the Northern Expedition, with science and democracy at the core of the cultural movement, attention also gradually turned toward how to rebuild one's morality and life direction in a modern society.[4] Entering the 1930s, the pace of modernization accelerated, and awareness of issues surrounding modernization began to rise in cultural discourse. All of these developments inevitably had an impact on the ethical and philosophical reflections of intellectuals regarding human life. At the same time, Chinese culture had a long-standing tradition of moral thought, and though the New Culture Movement challenged traditional social norms and customs, it did not entirely resolve the question of tradition versus modernity in the realm of ethics and morality. In the later stages of the New Culture Movement, the voices of cultural radicalism diminished, and there was a growing recognition of the significance of traditional morality in modern society, laying the foundation for a more reasoned discussion of this issue.[5]

In the 1920s, Feng published *A Certain View of Life* (1924) and *Philosophy of Life* (1926), and in the 1930s, he delivered several lectures on issues related to life. It can be said that this philosophy of life was a consistent focus of his attention throughout his career. *Philosophy of Life* was indeed included as a high school textbook at the time, while the chapters of *A New Treatise on the Way of Life* were first published in various issues of *Middle School Students* magazine in late 1939 and early 1940. If we consider the former as a passive choice for high school students, the latter can be seen as intentionally written with a young audience in mind. Guiding the lives and cultivation of young people became the underlying theme of *A New Treatise on the Way of Life*, even though it can also be seen as an application of the philosophy of *New Confucianism* within its framework, and it represents a new interpretation of the moral teachings of traditional Confucianism in the context of modern life.

From the mid-1910s to the mid-1930s, significant socio-economic changes centered around modern industrialization took place in China. The modern industrial sector began to grow rapidly (even though it remained a relatively small part of the overall economy), urban social organizations and structures underwent drastic transformations, and a large population of educated young people emerged as a result of a new style of education. Social life in large and medium cities had already departed from traditional norms during this period.[6] All of these changes led to a growing awareness of modernity or industrialization among scholars in the 1930s. The debates and discussions about modernization in China that emerged in 1933 were a significant milestone in this regard.[7] As discussed before, Feng Youlan's early cultural perspective, represented by the first half of *A New Treatise on Practical Affairs*, is indeed a modern cultural perspective in which traditional and nationalistic issues are entirely absent.[8] In line with this cultural perspective, his *A New Treatise on the Way of Life*, written around the same time, also clearly carries this meaning.[9] It presents ethical teachings aimed at interpreting traditional virtues in a way that suits individual life in the modern secular society of the post-sage era. We can refer to this as the pursuit of life after the sages, where individuals navigate their moral journey in a post-traditional context.[10]

The distinctive feature of this modern philosophy of life is that, compared to traditional teachings, the most prominent aspect of *A New Treatise on the Way of Life* is its emphasis on non-moralistic ways of life. Ethics typically categorizes the concept of morality into three general distinctions: moral, immoral, and non-moral. Moral and immoral are opposites, while non-moral refers to something that is morally neutral or lies outside the realm of morality, though non-moral does not imply that it is unrelated to life. In comparison to traditional life teachings, what stands out in *A New Treatise on the Way of Life* are precisely the exhortations related to non-moral aspects of life.

Why is it called the "Way of Life"? What is new about the "New Treatise"? Feng did not provide a detailed explanation in the text. In my interpretation, the phrase emphasizes the importance of adopting appropriate, suitable behavior in one's life rather than focusing solely on inner cultivation, a starting point different from the perspective of Song-Ming Confucian philosophers. Feng provides a clear explanation regarding what is new. First, he states that "the way of life must not violate the fundamental principles of morality,"[11] and, "The method of learning by Neo-Confucian scholars of the Song and Ming is entirely moral, while the ways of living we speak of, though not violating moral principles, can be non-moral."[12] It is evident that while the first point is crucial, it is not the primary distinguishing feature that makes the treatise new. The second point is the one that truly sets it apart as something novel.

He points out:

> In many of the "teachings about morality and advocacy of righteousness" by those in the past, we can see that what was taught can be divided into three categories. The first category is the moral principles required by any society, such as benevolence, righteousness, propriety, wisdom, and society. The second is the moral principles required by a specific society, such as loyalty and filial piety. The third is ways of living that do not violate moral principles, such as diligence and frugality. Saying that these things do not violate moral principles means that, while they do not necessarily actively conform to moral principles, they do not actively violate them either. Those things that actively conform to moral principles are moral, those that violate moral principles are immoral, and those that do not actively conform to moral principles but also do not actively violate them are non-moral. Expressed in these terms, these ways of living, while not violating moral principles, are not necessarily moral. Saying that they are not necessarily moral does not mean that they are immoral, but rather, non-moral.[13]

In other words, from today's perspective, past teachings about morality and righteousness contain three types of principles. The first is the universal moral principles, which are needed by all societies of all ages. The second is the special moral principles that are needed by specific societies. And the third is some life behaviors that are of a non-moral nature, but which are beneficial to an individual's success.[14]

He goes on to say, "The Confucian scholars of the Song and Ming dynasties believed that every action and thought of a person must either be moral or immoral, but I believe that human behavior or thoughts do not necessarily have to be categorized as moral or immoral. The way of life we discuss can, in some aspects, extend beyond the realm of morality."[15]

Neo-Confucian scholars emphasize a stark contrast and tension between moral and immoral thought, believing that human thought is either in accordance with the principles of heaven or driven by human desires. This perspective leaves little room for morally neutral thoughts and emotions and effectively categorizes many morally neutral thoughts and emotions as part of human desires. A significant characteristic of modern social ethics is the liberation of many morally neutral thoughts and behaviors from the Neo-Confucian framework of either this or that, reducing the intrusion of excessive moral judgment into people's lives. Feng's perspective certainly includes criticism of Song-Ming Neo-Confucianism, but its significance goes beyond that. Its primary aim is not merely to liberate the desires of life from the strict control imposed by Confucianism, but rather to emphasize the significance of non-moral life teachings, specifically the methods of life.

Of course, this does not mean that *A New Treatise on the Way of Life* does not discuss moral methods of life. For instance, Feng still views loyalty and forgiveness as "methods for practicing morality" on the one hand, while he also regards loyalty and forgiveness as a common "approach to dealing with people and things."[16] This latter point, which emphasizes life methods not as means to practice morality but as general and common approaches to interacting with people and things, is a key focus and feature of *A New Treatise on the Way of Life*. Thus, the perspective presented in this chapter does not suggest that Feng only discusses non-moral life teachings. Instead, it highlights that while promoting moral life teachings, he also values non-moral life teachings, which form a distinctive feature of the book.

This distinction lies in the difference between moral and non-moral, or in other words, between moral and rational. Feng states, "The life methods we discuss emphasize both the moral activities of individuals and their rational activities."[17] He believed that the statement, "Man is a rational animal," is correct. However, it can be further analyzed as "what sets humans apart from animals is their moral rationality and their practical rationality. Moral rationality allows them to engage in moral activities, while practical rationality enables them to engage in practical activities."[18] It should be noted that moral rationality's object is moral rules, while practical rationality's object is the laws of existence, and there is indeed a distinction between the two. Non-moral life teachings are largely based on social experience and constitute worldly wisdom[19] formed through practical rationality. Non-moral life teachings aim to guide people toward wiser paths in life.

The concept of the reason humans differ from animals originally pertained to the essence and nature of human beings, and the full realization of this essence and nature is what the ancients considered the sage as an ideal personality. Feng points out:

> While Daoist scholars of the Song and Ming dynasties emphasized the moral aspect when they spoke of humans being different from animals, we, when we speak of humans being different from animals, not only emphasize the moral aspect but also focus on the rational aspect of humans. The Daoist scholars of the Song and Ming dynasties believed that the ultimate realization of a person was to be entirely moral. In contrast, what we refer to as the ultimate realization of a person encompasses both the moral and rational aspects of their being.[20]

In this way, the view of human nature in *A New Treatise on the Way of Life* breaks away from the traditional understanding of humans solely through their moral nature, instead advocating understanding humans through their rational nature as well. Human nature is reflected not only in its moral aspect, but also in its rational aspect, encompassing both dimensions. Regarding the question of what it means to be human, Feng believed that "if a person acts in accordance with what makes a human, what distinguishes humans from animals, then they are being human."[21] The sage is someone who has already fully achieved what it means to be human in their way of being, and, "If a person has reached a level of being human that can be considered complete, they can be called a human sage, and a human sage is a sage."[22] Because there are two aspects of rationality, moral rationality and practical rationality, the realization of human nature must also progress and improve in both aspects. He states, "Regardless of which aspect of rationality we talk about, humans possess rationality, but are not entirely rational. However, being entirely rational is the highest standard for humanity," and, "So, individuals must consciously and diligently strive to move in this direction."[23] Being human, then, requires reaching the highest standard not only in morality, but also in rationality.

This characteristic is also fully expressed in his emphasis on rules. He states, "All people live, and their lives must to some extent follow a certain set of rules, just as all people think, and their thoughts must to some extent follow a certain set of rules."[24] He believes that the rules governing human thought are the laws of logic, and these rules are not imposed by humans but are inherent, the natural laws of thought. The rules governing human life are the methods of life, and human life also has its inherent rules. The natural laws of human social life require a corresponding field of study, which is the study of life methods. In terms of philosophical conceptual usage, rules originally referred to a concept of natural necessity, requiring individuals to adhere to the natural necessity of reality. Laws and moral rules, on the other hand, are artificially established normative regulations, not limited to the empirical experiences of social life. Just as Neo-Confucianism encapsulates both the normative and the causal under the concept of principle, Feng's New Neo-Confucianism also refers to both moral rules and life rules as rules.[25]

Because this book's distinctive feature is its emphasis on non-moral life teachings, it is called *A New Treatise on the Way of Life.* Correspondingly, Feng equates life methods with life rules, referring to the methods of life adopted to conform to the rules of life. His emphasis on rules is deliberate and meaningful.[26] Rules are used in the context of moral life, so we commonly use the term moral rules, while rules often refer to the summary of life experiences outside the realm of morality. His emphasis on life rules, while related to his metaphysical New Neo-Confucianism, is even more related to the emphasis of *A New Treatise on the Way of Life* on non-moral aspects of life. Moral rules are about how people should behave, while life rules are about how people should act to achieve their interests and avoid harm. In its approach, this book transforms the norms of moral teachings into the laws of experiential discourse or embeds moral rules within experiential discourse. In traditional Chinese culture, there are many such examples, as seen in texts like the *Laozi* and the *Book of Changes,* which contain numerous experiential teachings emphasizing the success and failure of human life, many of which can be said to reflect the laws of social life. Confucian culture also contains many such elements. Especially in secular Confucian culture, which is the practical form of Confucian thought and values as applied to family, society, and interpersonal interactions, practices like family instructions and family rules are influenced by Confucian values but also manifest in the form of experiential teachings.

II

Here, I will turn to specific content from *A New Treatise on the Way of Life* to illustrate Feng's approach in this book, where he simultaneously emphasizes moral and non-moral aspects through a dual focus. Among the ten chapters of this book, one part discusses the traditional moral virtues (such as loyalty, benevolence, moderation, and sincerity) in the context of both moral and non-moral modern applications, while another discusses the traditional non-moral virtues (such as diligence, non-action, and modesty) and their significance in modern life. I will outline several noteworthy points.

1. Loyalty and Benevolence

In the second chapter of *A New Treatise on the Way of Life,* titled "The Practice of Loyalty and Benevolence," Feng discusses loyalty and benevolence, saying, "According to our interpretation, loyalty and benevolence are, on the one hand, methods for practicing morality and, on the other, ordinary methods for interacting with others and dealing with the world."[27]

He then discusses the way Confucius and Mencius preached the path of loyalty and benevolence, which is described as "considering loyalty and benevolence as methods for practicing morality."[28] Loyalty and benevolence, in this context, refer to "treating others as oneself" and "extending one's self-consideration to others." According to Feng, "Treating others as oneself means that when you do something for others, you must do it as if you were doing it for yourself. Only then can it be considered to be treating others as oneself. When a person does something for themselves, they do it with their utmost effort and dedication. If they do something for others, they should do it with the same level of effort and dedication as if they were doing it for themselves. This is what it means to treat others as oneself." And "So, loyalty means treating others as you would want to be treated. We can say that if you treat others as you wish to be treated, that is loyalty. If you refrain from doing to others what you would not want done to yourself, that is benevolence."[29] He goes on, "When a person can understand the desires or aversions of others based on their own desires or aversions, it is called 'the ability to draw analogies from one's own situation.'"[30] And, "The benefits of the path of loyalty and benevolence are that those who follow it find the standard for their behavior within their own hearts, without needing to seek it from outside sources."[31] While the idea of treating others as you would treat yourself has ancient origins, Feng's interpretation of loyalty and benevolence, especially his explanation of loyalty as "treating others as you would treat yourself, can indeed be seen as an enriching contribution to traditional Confucianism. The emphasis on treating others as you would treat yourself adds depth and nuance to the concept of loyalty in Confucian ethics.

Continuing, Feng states, "Now, let us consider the path of loyalty and benevolence as an ordinary method for interacting with others and dealing with the world." In this context, he shifts the focus away from moral behavior and toward non-moral ways of living. He goes on to say, "In our daily lives, there are many situations where we may not know how we should to act."[32] This concept of "should" is not framed from a moral perspective but rather from what we might call a social or interpersonal perspective. In this context, social or interpersonal considerations serve as the starting point for non-moral ways of living based on loyalty and benevolence. As an example, Feng states, "When someone comes to see me in ordinary circumstances, I must look back at them. When someone gives me a gift in ordinary circumstances, I must reciprocate, which is a matter of social etiquette." He adds, "To accept without giving in return is not proper. If we treat these interactions purely as rituals of giving and receiving, it can create a sense of hollowness and insincerity." And, "But if I go to see someone, and that person does not come to see me, or if I give a gift and receive nothing in return, or if I invite them for a meal and they do not reciprocate, and this person is not my teacher or my superior, in ordinary circumstances, I would feel a sense of displeasure." He goes on, "So, we can understand that if we treat others in this way, they would also feel displeased. Following the principle of do not do to others what you would not want to be done to yourself, we do not need to study rituals, but we naturally understand that to accept without giving in return is not appropriate."[33] Therefore, in the context of non-moral loyalty and benevolence, one's actions should align with social conventions. Feng suggests that if a person has done something for someone else and is unsure whether it conforms to social expectations, they only need to ask themselves how they would feel if someone else did the same thing for them. He says, "If he feels happy about it, then this action is in line with social expectations. If he believes he would feel unhappy about it, then this action is against social expectations."[34] He provides an example related to saying good things about others, saying, "People generally like to hear good things about themselves; this is a fact. To say good things about someone in a way that pleases their ears is a manifestation of the path of loyalty and benevolence. It conforms to social expectations… These words have made the recipient happy without harming anyone else. Therefore, saying these good things is in line with the path of loyalty and benevolence; it is in accordance with social expectations," yet, "if saying good things goes beyond a certain limit, the listener may suffer as a result."[35] This is the most evident example of a non-moral but not immoral way of life, and it is a method of navigating life to avoid harm and seek success.

In the chapter "Practicing Loyalty and Kindness," Feng also extensively discusses how to practice the way of loyalty and kindness in various complex situations and its principles. As this goes beyond the scope of the current discussion, we will not delve into it here.

2. Non-action

The second section of this book, titled "Non-action," uses the term *wuwei* (无为) to refer to acting without action. Feng points out that there are two forms of acting without action. One is moral, as described by Confucianism, and the other is non-moral, as described by Daoism.

He said, "Confucianism's attitude toward 'wei' is not 'non-action' but 'non-doing yet doing.' If one does something because it is beneficial or meritorious to oneself, then this action is doing something. Benefit or merit is the reason for doing something. If one does something because it should be done, then this action is non-doing yet doing. Non-doing yet doing is different from non-action, but if a person can engage in non-doing yet doing, they can also attain a form of non-action. The concept of non-action, as discussed by the Daoist scholars of the Song and Ming dynasties, belongs to this category of non-doing yet doing."[36] He also points out that from the Confucian perspective, "An individual should only consider whether a task should be done, without taking into account their personal gain or loss, and without worrying about the possible success or failure of the task. This is what is meant by non-doing yet doing."

He continues, "What Daoism refers to as acting in accordance with one's nature, or non-doing, is in fact a form of non-doing yet doing, but Daoism emphasizes it in terms of one's interests. By contrast, Confucians, like the Daoist scholars of the Song and Ming dynasties, refer to non-doing yet doing, emphasizing it in terms of ethics." And, "We discuss non-doing yet doing from both perspectives, one from the standpoint of interests and the other from the standpoint of ethics."[37]

Doing things out of interest means following one's natural inclinations without pretense or utilitarian motives. For example, "Chess enthusiasts play chess for the sake of playing chess, and theater enthusiasts sing on stage for the love of it. They don't necessarily aspire to become grandmasters or famous actors, but engage in these activities purely out of interest. Their chess playing or acting is non-doing yet doing. Even though they may put in hard work and dedication to chess or acting, they only feel the joy of it and not the hardship. Therefore, it is also considered non-doing. Anyone who can truly follow their interests in this way experiences the same."[38]

Through the discussion above, Feng affirms the non-utilitarian life attitudes and approaches to action found in both Confucianism and Daoism.

3. The Doctrine of the Mean

Regarding the original meaning of the mean in Confucianism, Feng believes, "The mean means neither excessive nor deficient, that is, the idea of being just right or appropriate... When it comes to doing things appropriately, it can be discussed from two perspectives: one from the ethical perspective and the other from the perspective of gain and loss." From the ethical perspective, the idea of doing things appropriately means that certain actions must be carried out in such a way that the doer can achieve the highest degree of moral fulfillment. From the perspective of gain and loss, doing things appropriately means that certain actions must be performed in a manner that allows the doer to obtain the maximum benefit in their pursuits. It can be seen that even though both involve a must, the meanings of these two types of musts are different. Feng holds that in Confucianism, the concept of the mean is discussed from an ethical perspective, whereas in Daoism, it is discussed from the perspective of gain and loss. He says, "Confucianism talks about using the mean to avoid excess or deficiency in actions, which is related to the ethical aspect of the mean. Daoism speaks of guarding the center, which means in all things, one should avoid extremes, extravagance, and excess, and this relates to the aspect of gain and loss in the mean."[39]

He not only distinguished between the moral and non-moral interpretations but also made distinctions within these two interpretations, as when discussing the concept of the mean further in the context of Confucianism, he notes, "Chengzi said, 'The mean is the right path (Dao) for all under heaven.' The word Dao used here might have a special meaning, but we can also interpret it as a path. For any matter, there is a middle path that one can follow, a path that is accessible to everyone, so it can be called the right path, and it can also be called the main road. Those who do not follow this main road but prefer to take a side path are referred to in the Doctrine of the Mean as 'seeking obscurity and acting strangely,' and 'seeking peril and hoping for luck.' While some may indeed take these side paths, and there may be occasional advantages to doing so, walking the side path also generally entails specific inconveniences."[40] From an ethical perspective, the right path under heaven is the universally applicable moral principle, which is to treat others as one would like to be treated, following the principle of "do not do unto others what you would not have them do unto you."

From a non-moral perspective, it is also the same. Feng pointed out, "The above discussion primarily focuses on the ethical aspect of mean. From the perspective of utility, any method that can lead to the most successful outcome in a certain matter is also the most common method. For example, if someone wants to become wealthy, the most common method is to vigorously engage in industry or commerce..." This is the great path, which is the same as the main road mentioned earlier. This is something that everyone knows and can follow. If someone finds this main road too circuitous or the method too clumsy and seeks an alternative shortcut or a clever method, then that can be considered "seeking peril and hoping for luck."[41] Indeed, Feng not only distinguished between moral and non-moral interpretations but also provided a comprehensive explanation of their significance in teaching about life, both from an ethical and utilitarian perspective.

4. Moderation

Feng believed that "in traditional Chinese thought, humility is a life attitude rooted in deep philosophical principles. Some of these philosophical principles can be found in the teachings of *Laozi* and the *Book of Changes*." From his perspective, many of the teachings in *Laozi* and the *Book of Changes* focus on non-moral aspects, and discussions about humility are one example of this focus on non-morall values.

He notes, "Laozi had a profound understanding of life. He observed life and discovered many principles or truths. He referred to these principles and truths as 'the constant' or 'the way.' He believed that if people understood these constants and followed them in their actions, they could gain benefits and avoid harm. If one does not understand these constants and acts recklessly, they will face failure and harm. He says, 'Understanding the constant is enlightenment, while not understanding the constant leads to reckless actions and misfortune.'" It is clear that this perspective, in which a lack of humility leads to failure and harm, is discussed from a utilitarian point of view rather than an ethical one. In other words, this teaching about humility is also emphasized in a non-moral sense, focusing on practical lessons and consequences rather than solely on moral values.

Feng believed that this analytical approach, which evaluates the success and failure of things based on their practical consequences, is quite similar to a scientific perspective and can be considered morally neutral. He stated, "In this regard, Laozi exhibits a scientific spirit... Many of his teachings are morally neutral. In this respect, he is similar to typical scientists. The principles that scientists put forth are morally neutral. Some people may apply these scientific principles to ethical actions, while others may use the same principles for unethical purposes. However, in these matters, scientists are not responsible, nor can they be held responsible. In some ways, Laozi likewise only expounds upon the principles he has discovered; he is not responsible for how people choose to apply these principles, nor can he be held responsible. For example, Laozi says, 'To contract what is expanded, one must first expand it,' but he does not dictate specific actions or their moral implications."[42]

The concept of keeping to the middle and being modest can apply to objective circumstances as well as subjective psychology. Feng explains, "If you want to ensure that the development of something does not reach its extreme, the best method is to include elements that are close to its opposite within it. For example, in a capitalist society that has developed to a certain extent, if you want to maintain its system, the best approach is to implement some policies that are close to socialism within that society."[43] This applies not only to societal contexts but also to individuals. He says, "If a person wants their career or knowledge to continue developing and progressing, they must always have a sense of caution and fear. If a person consistently maintains a sense of caution and fear… it is akin to keeping a mindset that is close to being satisfied with one's achievements. So, regardless of how successful or progressive his career is, it is not at its extreme, allowing it to continue to develop and progress… This mindset of caution and fear in a person, when manifested in their attitude, is what we call humility."[44]

Impetuousness or emptiness pertains to a person's psychological state, while humility refers to the outward expression of this psychological state. The reason for its external expression is that humility can help regulate a person's relationships with others. Feng states, "This discussion pertains to individuals and their careers. When it comes to relationships between people, humility is also a way of interacting with others. People often have feelings of envy. If I excel in my career or knowledge, others may unconsciously harbor feelings of jealousy. If I further accentuate my superiority and show arrogance, it will only intensify their jealousy and provoke their resentment. Being excessive in either humility or arrogance can lead to negative consequences."[45] He acknowledges, "The benefits of humility that we discussed earlier and the drawbacks of arrogance are also discussed from a utilitarian perspective."[46] On the other hand, a person can possess a certain knowledge or cultivation, and those who have this knowledge or cultivation can be naturally humble without consciously seeking it, and naturally avoid arrogance without conscious effort. From a utilitarian perspective, this is discussed in a non-moral sense.

A New Treatise on the Way of Life advocated that young people should be humble, diligent, focused, honest, motivated, and full of vitality in their conduct as individuals. In their actions, they should make decisions based on reason and consider the feelings of others, and the principle "do not do unto others what you would not have them do unto you" was also emphasized. In their actions, they should not be overly hasty for quick gains, should strive to act without attachment, should meticulously plan and execute their tasks, should follow the right path and avoid relying on clever tricks, should practice tolerance, should let go of past matters, and should harmonize their emotions with the world around them while letting go of the ego, all of which are valuable and beneficial things for young people to learn. Many of these principles are morally neutral and can be applied to various aspects of life. They emphasize qualities like humility, diligence, patience, and ethical behavior, which are valuable for personal growth and building positive relationships with others.

The task of this chapter is not to provide a comprehensive overview of the content of *A New Treatise on the Way of Life*, so we will not delve further into it here. What we want to point out is that, on the surface, the moral way of life discussed in *A New Treatise on the Way of Life* appears to be influenced by Confucianism, while the non-moral way of life is more aligned with Daoism. However, one should not simply view this book as a cultural hybrid that combines elements of both Confucianism and Daoism. In fact, these non-moral ways of life have also been accommodated within the broader Confucian cultural context throughout history. In terms of its intended readership, *A New Treatise on the Way of Life* shares similarities in nature with popular Confucian works of the Ming and Qing dynasties, such as educational texts for the masses, and thus, it likely contains elements that are morally neutral and utilitarian. What we should also recognize is the contemporary social context that underlies this focus on non-moral ways of life. It is within this context that Feng attempts to present a life philosophy that adapts to individuals, especially young people, in modern society. It can also be said that he recognized the significance of non-moral ways of life in modern existence, and thus, he sought to harness the extensive philosophical resources within Chinese culture to address this aspect of contemporary life.

III

As mentioned earlier, the term "way of life" focuses on appropriate or suitable behavior in one's life. Here, appropriate and suitable means that these behaviors contribute to an individual's success in society. In his later years, Feng reflected on this in the preface to *An Account of My Life*, saying:

> Before the War of Resistance against Japanese Aggression, the Enlightened Bookstore published a magazine called *Middle School Students*, which featured articles on youth cultivation and similar topics. While I was still in Nanyue, they invited me to contribute articles, but I did not write anything at that time. After I arrived in Kunming, I wrote a few articles that were serialized in the magazine. Later, these articles were compiled into a book titled *A New Treatise on the Way of Life*. At that time, I thought that this kind of article was traditionally called family teachings, but in a society that emphasizes the collective, the readership has expanded, so it was worldly teachings. Now, it seems that this book mainly discusses some practical ways of dealing with the world. It may not have much philosophical significance, and the level of wisdom is not particularly high. It is simply a path to success for people in the realm of pragmatism, and there is nothing particularly memorable about it.[47]

From the terms youth cultivation and family teachings, it can be inferred that the initial purpose of writing this book was likely to instruct young people on how to conduct themselves and manage their affairs. However, the actual content of the book predominantly focuses on how to conduct oneself in order to achieve success as a person. In other words, this book discusses how a person should conduct themselves, behave, and interact in order to achieve success in society. The focus on success falls into the realm of utilitarianism, which has been historically distinct from orthodox Confucianism, which often strictly differentiates between achievement and virtue. The distinctive feature of Feng's book, according to his own words, is that it combines achievement and principle, meaning it integrates personal success with the principles or rules of social life, combining personal utilitarianism with moral conduct. Moral rules emphasize acting without acting, while practical advice pertains to acting to achieve. Moral rules stress that one should act in a certain way, following moral principles, even if it means personal sacrifice. Practical advice, on the other hand, informs people how to act in order to navigate life smoothly and attain success.

Even earlier than the preface to *An Account of My Life*, during his period of self-criticism in the 1950s, Feng made statements such as, "In the book *A New Treatise on the Way of Life*, the discussion of methods of cultivation is primarily focused on the individual and begins from an individual perspective. In contrast, when it comes to the new philosophy, regardless of the topic, it is discussed from a collective standpoint and begins with the masses. This represents a significant difference between old philosophy and new philosophy."[48]

He points out that traditional philosophy, with its emphasis on seeking sagehood and virtuousness, while not divorced from social activities, primarily aimed at self-improvement and self-fulfillment. In contrast, the new philosophy (referring to the proletarian philosophy advocated after 1949) advocated serving the people in all aspects, with no room for any motivation stemming from personal interests or self-benefit. He writes, "If a person constantly thinks about becoming a saint, he is still thinking about himself. To constantly think about oneself is to be unable to forget oneself. Song-Ming Neo-Confucian philosophers often regarded those who aim to become a Buddha in Buddhism as selfish." And, "Proletarian philosophy is the philosophy of the proletarian society. In such a society, there is no private property, and therefore, there is no individualism. A person not only does not desire to become rich and powerful but also does not aspire to become a saint."[49] This means that even the desire to become a saint still carries a motivation for oneself and does not represent selflessness. This also means that *A New Treatise on the Way of Life* still retains or pursues a form of individualism. However, the individualism that Feng mentions is not the egoism that contemporary socialist culture negates, but rather the individualism as discussed in Western social culture since modern times.

Here we find one of his more significant self-descriptions:

> Back when I was young, I greatly enjoyed reading *The Autobiography of Benjamin Franklin*, in which he describes how he went from being a poor child to becoming a successful, world-renowned figure. Of course, his success was not achieved through harmful or selfish means, and it was also related to the progress of American society. We cannot deny that he was a patriot with democratic ideals, but the primary driving force behind his activities was bourgeois individualism... What I promote in *A New Treatise on the Way of Life* is, in fact, this way of life. While I frequently reference the life methods advocated by Chinese feudal philosophers and quote their sayings, there is a fundamental difference between me and them in one aspect. I wrote, "What the Song-Ming Neo-Confucian

> philosophers call the way of learning is entirely based on morality, but the way of life we discuss, while not violating the rules of morality, may not necessarily be moral. Saying it is not moral does not mean it is immoral; rather, it is non-moral." In other words, the way of life I discuss, and a significant part of what I seek to achieve, is to strive for personal success within the boundaries of not violating morality. This is undeniably a life philosophy rooted in bourgeois individualism... The ultimate goal of *A New Treatise on the Way of Life* is personal success.[50]

This is a crucial point, meaning that the book focuses on and aims to address the significant question of how to pursue personal success without violating morality. It explores how an entrepreneurial spirit of seeking success can coexist with morality. This has significance not only for the worldview of the young people in the 1930s, who were experiencing the first wave of modernization in China, but also for today's society undergoing the transition from a socialist planned economy to a socialist market economy, as it holds practical relevance. This is why Feng emphasizes the fundamental reason for his life lessons in the non-moral aspect in the book. However, during his self-critical period, he did not acknowledge the positive aspects of this book, namely that while it affirms individual pursuit of success, it also undoubtedly has a positive social function in guiding the lives of young people and promoting socially beneficial behavior under market economic conditions.

While these reflections come from Feng's period of self-criticism, I believe that when we remove labels like bourgeois and excessive self-criticism, many of his original ideas are still valuable and hold significant worth. In the study of his works, I have always advocated not viewing those texts with a self-critical and introspective tone as insincere or perfunctory. On the factual level, those descriptions not only do not deviate from the truth, but they also often provide a more vivid picture due to their proximity to the New Neo-Confucianism period. For example, even during this period of self-criticism, he not only did not avoid it, but still affirmed the connection between Franklin's individualism and the progress of American society. He even stated that *A New Treatise on the Way of Life* discusses a Franklin-style way of life. We know that Max Weber highly valued Franklin's work ethic and considered the Protestant ethic of diligence and a sense of vocation as the spirit of modern capitalism. Feng's use of the term "individualism" here can be seen, to some extent, as the ethical spirit of modern society that Weber recognized.

Max Weber, in the second chapter of *The Protestant Ethic and the Spirit of Capitalism*, titled "The Spirit of Capitalism," extensively quotes Franklin's advice to young people, such as, "Remember, time is money," and, "Remember, credit is money." Such passages highlight the alignment between Franklin's teachings and the spirit of capitalism that Weber analyzed. In addition to diligence and hard work, Weber emphasizes the importance of punctuality and adherence to the principles of fairness in interactions with others, which he finds to be highly beneficial for young people in establishing themselves in society.[51] He regards these sayings as ethical maxims and sees them as reflecting a spirit of modern capitalism.[52] Weber points out, "All of Franklin's moral ideas have a utilitarian character. Honesty is useful because it brings about reputation, and punctuality, diligence, and thrift are all useful, and are thus virtues."[53] These ideas share some similarities with the content of *A New Treatise on the Way of Life*, even though what Feng discusses, compared to Franklin, is more extensive in terms of personal conduct and actions.

While Franklin's statements can be taken to the extreme, leading to the conclusion that external appearance is more important than inner virtues, Weber also points out that Franklin himself still valued the cultivation of inner character and virtues. Nevertheless, Weber points out that "the kind of thinking manifested in the quotations from Franklin which we have cited, although it had already been entirely accepted by a whole nation, would have been rejected in ancient or medieval city-states ... In fact, all social groups which have so far failed to adapt to the modern capitalist environment even today, and with very few exceptions, react in this way."[54] If we translate Weber's focus on economic ethics or work ethics into the language of general ethics, it can be said that what Weber saw in Franklin was the transition from traditional non-utilitarian ethics to modern utilitarianism, a modern societal attitude and spirit. This also indicates that thought with utilitarian aspects was rejected by orthodox thinking in ancient times. Therefore, as Weber points out, both Franklin and Feng's *A New Treatise on the Way of Life* are morally neutral pieces of advice containing utilitarian shades representing a transition in ethical concepts from ancient times to modernity.[55] The ethical characteristics of *A New Treatise on the Way of Life*, which adapt to the changing times, are consistent with the cultural perspective of modernization in the first half of *A New Treatise on Practical Affairs*, in which Feng hopes to provide behavioral ethics suitable for the modernization process. It is an ethics that adapts to modern society and the structure of a market economy, aiming to serve the majority of people.

IV

We can easily observe that the emphasis of *A New Treatise on the Way of Life* is on conduct, as seen in the titles of various sections: "The Practice of Loyalty and Benevolence," "The Doctrine of the Mean," "The Act of Non-action," "The Practice of Maintaining Moderation," and "The Pursuit of Harmony." These titles reveal that the focus of this book is on behavior rather than virtue,[56] which differs from the traditional Confucian emphasis on the cultivation of inner virtues and is also distinct from the later focus on the heart (state of mind or spiritual cultivation) in *New Origins of Humanity*. Because of this, Feng explicitly states that this approach to life is not a method of cultivation. He says, "What we have described is a way of living, and all people in their lives must to some extent follow it." He specifically points out that this way of living is preparation for someone who wants to become capable of doing things, in other words, a method for acquiring the ability to act. He notes, "As for cultivation methods, they may vary depending on a person's worldview. However, the way of living that we are discussing here does not vary with different people's worldviews because the way of living we are discussing is a way of life, and all people in their lives must use it,"[57] so many parts of this book seem to emphasize the technical sense of life lessons rather than normative sense, and, of course, the technical aspect is the object of reason. Of course, because *A New Treatise on the Way of Life* emphasizes non-moral teachings, highlighting the arts of handling affairs and living, it places significant emphasis on technical guidance in interpersonal relationships and self-management. Therefore, it is not a comprehensive treatise on moral ethics, but its guidance for the youth in their lives holds important significance that should not be underestimated.

If we use the perspective of *New Origins of Humanity* and Feng's statements after 1949, *A New Treatise on the Way of Life,* while discussing moral behavior, is actually treating morally upright behavior as a means to achieve individual success and benefit. Therefore, their behavior is in accordance with morality, but it does not emanate from a moral state of mind.[58] In other words, the behaviors advocated in *A New Treatise on the Way of Life* are not only morally neutral, meaning they are moral behaviors, but they are also viewed from the perspective of being beneficial for one's success.[59] In *New Origins of Humanity,* Feng states, "All altruistic actions can be regarded as a method for benefiting oneself. Throughout history, in various cultures, including our *A New Treatise on the Way of Life,* although they all preach morality and speak of benevolence and righteousness, most of them use moral values and benevolence as a means to seek personal benefit." This is a clear admission made by Feng himself. He also points out that it is not just ancient proverbs and sayings, but also many passages in classical texts that contain similar teachings, such as "In *Laozi,* there are many passages that present morally upright behavior as a means of seeking advantage and avoiding harm." For example, he says, "'Is it not because he is without self-interest that he is able to accomplish his own interests?' And, 'It is because he does not contend that no one in the world can contend with him.' Being selfless and non-contentious is a morally upright behavior, but Laozi presents it as a method of seeking personal advantage."[60] Because this book's perspective is focused on behavior, its advocated approach to dealing with the world seems to belong more to the realm of effectiveness rather than goodness.

It should be noted that while *A New Treatise on the Way of Life* contains many philosophical explanations, in terms of its nature and function, it shares similarities with ancient popular ethical literature. It is not a discussion of the cultivation practices of elite Confucian scholars, but rather offers behavioral guidance for ordinary members of society, which is why it exhibits the characteristics mentioned above. So, in *New Origins of Humanity,* completed two years after the publication of *A New Treatise on the Way of Life,* the discussion of the worldview shifted away from the focus of the latter. Feng later reminisced about it, stating:

> I can further mention that *A New Treatise on the Way of Life* is essentially a popular book, and the way of life it discusses is intended for the general populace. The worldview of Neo-Confucianism is not limited to just this perspective. Within the framework of Neo-Confucianism, a noble purpose of life is presented, which is to hope for sages and hope for the virtuous. *A New Treatise on the Way of Life* discusses a relatively basic worldview and way of life, while *New Origins of Humanity* presents a more advanced worldview and approach to life.[61]

> The worldview and way of life discussed in *A New Treatise on the Way of Life* represent individuals in a utilitarian realm, as discussed in *New Origins of Humanity*. In *New Origins of Humanity*, I also acknowledge that this realm is not particularly elevated, and I believe that the higher realm is what is referred to as the moral state of mind.[62]

It is evident that the difference between *A New Treatise on the Way of Life* and *New Origins of Humanity* primarily lies in their target audience. As has been discussed here, Feng emphasized in *A New Treatise on Practical Affairs* a way of life suitable for ordinary people, which, in terms of spiritual elevation, falls within a relatively utilitarian realm; and in *New Origins of Humanity*, he moves away from the utilitarian realm and presents a more advanced worldview and way of life, aligning with the moral state of traditional sages and virtuous individuals, even transcending it. In this sense, *New Origins of Humanity* can be seen not as a negation of *A New Treatise on the Way of Life* but as an evolution or development of the ideas presented in it. Indeed, from another perspective, for Feng, these two books, even if they do not create contradictions, do exhibit significant differences, reflecting the profound contradictions in the evolution of social ethics from tradition to modernity. In short, he both recognized the changing trends in modern social ethics and sought to make an ethical adjustment, as seen in *A New Treatise on the Way of Life*, while also wishing to preserve the ideals of ancient life, as reflected in *New Origins of Humanity*. Concerning *A New Treatise on the Way of Life*, one of the key questions it addresses is how to deal with the ethics of individualism. The concept of the utilitarian realm also needs to be understood in the context of the issue of individualism in ethics to fully grasp its modern significance. Here, individualism does not refer to individualism in contrast to collectivism, nor does it solely pertain to a focus on rights and claims. Instead, it refers to a form of individualistic lifestyle that is alienated from virtue ethics. This kind of individualism is morally neutral, distinct from unethical selfishness.

Indeed, while the moral state is considered higher than the utilitarian realm, the term "relatively basic worldview" that Feng used here clearly reflects the zeitgeist of the early 1950s, a post-war period in which there was a significant unanalytical rejection of individualism. From a modern perspective, individuals encouraged in *A New Treatise on the Way of Life* to "be human," even if not reaching the level of a sage, already embody a positive life rarely found in modern society, and their positive significance should be fully acknowledged. Just as negative freedom differs from positive freedom, negative freedom still holds its important significance. In this sense, *A New Treatise on the Way of Life* leans more toward negative freedom, emphasizing how to avoid moral violations, while *New Origins of Humanity* further develops positive freedom, focusing on how to progress from the moral state of mind to transcendental or super-moral states.[63] Certainly, in *New Origins of Humanity*, Feng appears to have found what he considered a better solution, and in this sense, *A New Treatise on the Way of Life* may not have held ultimate significance for him personally. However, when placed within the context of the evolving ethics of modern Chinese society, the issues addressed in *A New Treatise on the Way of Life* are indeed worth considering, particularly regarding how traditional Confucian ideals of character adapt to contemporary society. For people in modern society, philosophers cannot merely propose the highest spiritual states that only a few can attain. They must provide reasonable, achievable ways of life that can guide the majority of individuals in their contemporary existence. *A New Treatise on the Way of Life* indeed offers behavioral guidance targeted at the majority of modern individuals. Its nature is distinct from *New Origins of Humanity* and holds a more practical function in terms of contemporary social ethics. If an unethical way of dealing with the world is elevated to a value system, it is also a part of the healthy life concept that modern people need, which means not singing moral high notes, but still providing life with appropriate guidance. In this sense, the ethical significance of the *A New Treatise on the Way of Life* cannot be ignored. It is precisely in this sense that "*A New Treatise on the Way of Life* addresses the fundamental laws of human behavior in modern society, seeking the transition from ancient sage ethics to modern, individual-based moral life."[64]

As mentioned at the beginning of this chapter, the pursuit of success has become the dominant value orientation among today's youth. However, the integration of success and one's ethical conduct, along with the pursuit of legitimate or correct means to achieve success while maintaining good behavior to prevent falling into immorality, is precisely the behavior guidance needed in this era. From this perspective, *A New Treatise on the Way of Life* holds significance. Particularly, it suggests that beyond virtue, it is not necessarily about sensual extravagance. In the post-sage era, the idea that life methods must not violate moral principles remains an important subject in life. Beyond laws and ethics, morally neutral life lessons are also greatly needed by modern individuals. In fact, *A New Treatise on the Way of Life* does not advocate the value of success, but aims to find suitable ways to provide young people with the right guidance for life after demystifying the traditional ideals of the sages. As for the more positive aspects of Feng Youlan's thoughts on life and value ideals, they are fully developed in *New Origins of Humanity*, which will be discussed further later.

Notes

1. Chen Lai, "A Discussion on Feng Youlan's Cultural Perspectives," *The Scholar* 4, 1993.
2. In terms of ideology, I consider Mainland China from 1948 to 1976 as part of the revolutionary era. Furthermore, success here refers to individual career and personal development.
3. Borrowed from the phrase "departure from Asia and entry into Europe," used in Japan's Meiji era, to represent the cultural perspective of the Westernization faction in New Culture Movement.
4. In fact, from the early Republic of China period to the May Fourth Movement, this moral concern has been continuous.
5. The ethnical revolution during the May Fourth era had the slogan of overthrowing the Confucian family system, but the focus was always on the family, gender relations, specifically the individual's liberation from traditional family constraints, and women's pursuit of freedom in love, and marital autonomy. Therefore, the May Fourth period did not delve into other aspects of modern ethnical transformation.
6. Rozman, ed., *The Modernization of China* (Jiangsu People's Publishing House, 1998).
7. Luo Rongqu, ed., *From Westernization to Modernization* (Peking University Press, 1997), 221.

8. Chen Lai, *In Search of Modern Chinese Philosophy* (People's Publishing House, 2001), 90–91.
9. Most chapters of *A New Treatise on the Way of Life* were first published in *Middle School Students* magazine from October 1939 to March 1940. *A New Treatise on Practical Affairs* was published in May 1940, and *A New Treatise on the Way of Life* was published in July 1940.
10. Although Feng did not deny the concept of "sage" in *New Neo-Confucianism, A New Treatise on the Way of Life* and *New Origins of Humanity,* the significance of *A New Treatise on the Way of Life* must be understood in the context of the pursuit of modern human life after the sage.
11. "A New Treatise on the Way of Life," in *Complete Works of Sansongtang,* vol. 4, 373.
12. *Complete Works of Sansongtang,* vol. 4, 374.
13. Ibid.
14. In this sense, it means that within the lesson of speaking of morality, talking about righteousness, there can be some non-moral life principles. Therefore, here speaking of morality and talking about righteousness is actually a broad lesson on life.
15. *Complete Works of Sansongtang,* vol. 4, 375.
16. Ibid., 400.
17. Ibid., 389.
18. Ibid., 387.
19. The term worldly wisdom comes from Weber, distinguishing it from ethical ideas.
20. *Complete Works of Sansongtang,* vol. 4, 389.
21. Ibid., 384.
22. Ibid., 385.
23. Ibid., 389.
24. Ibid., 371.
25. Feng had already distinguished between the natural way and the conventional way in the final part "A New Theory of Life" in *Philosophy of Life,* but considered normative rules to be objective and not subject to individual subjectivity, a viewpoint seemingly influenced by new realism. *Complete Works of Sansongtang,* vol. 2 (2001), 217.
26. Whether it's laws or rules, Feng Youlan's emphasis here inevitably brings to mind the concept of "moral rules" different from "virtue ethics." Shi Yuankang, *From Chinese Culture to Modernity* (Dongda Books, 1998), 107.
27. *Complete Works of Sansongtang,* vol. 4, 394.
28. Ibid., 400.
29. Ibid., 396.
30. Ibid., 398.
31. Ibid., 399.
32. Ibid., 400.
33. Ibid., 401.
34. Ibid,
35. Ibid., 404.
36. Ibid., 413.
37. Ibid., 414.
38. Ibid., 419.
39. Ibid., 429.

40. Ibid., 437.
41. Ibid., 438.
42. Ibid., 444.
43. Ibid., 445.
44. Ibid., 446.
45. Ibid., 447.
46. Ibid., 448.
47. *Complete Works of Sansongtang*, vol. 1, 221.
48. *Complete Works of Sansongtang*, vol. 14, 927.
49. Ibid., 929.
50. Ibid., 980–981.
51. *The Protestant Ethic and the Spirit of Capitalism* (Sanlian Bookstore, 1987), 33–35.
52. It should be noted that Weber's "spirit of capitalism" refers to "the influence of certain religious ideas on the development of an economic spirit or rather, a social spirit, of an economic system." *The Protestant Ethic and the Spirit of Capitalism*, 16.
53. *The Protestant Ethic and the Spirit of Capitalism*, 36.
54. Ibid., 39.
55. Feng Youlan's attitude may or may not have been influenced by Dewey, but at least the discourse of "respect for reason" is close to Dewey's. Dewey's *Individualism Old and New* is quite similar to Feng Youlan's thought.
56. If *A New Treatise on the Way of Life* is about action, then *New Origins of Humanity* is about mindset.
57. *Complete Works of Sansongtang*, vol. 4, 381.
58. Chen Zhanguo pointed out that Feng believed in *New Neo-Confucianism* that moral behavior is behavior that conforms to moral laws, emphasizing the objective principles of morality; *New Origins of Humanity* believes that behavior motivated by morality is moral behavior, emphasizing the subjective principles of morality; the two seem contradictory, but in reality, Feng wanted to combine utilitarianism and moral self-discipline. Chen Zhangou, *A Study of Feng Youlan's Philosophical Thought* (Peking University Press, 1999), 181.
59. In fact, what is referred to here as "from non-moral aspects" often means adopting morally sound behavior for personal success.
60. *Complete Works of Sansongtang*, vol. 4, 593.
61. *Complete Works of Sansongtang*, vol. 14, 984.
62. Ibid., 986.
63. The concepts of negative freedom and positive freedom are different from those of both Kant and Berlin.
64. Please see my *From Zhenyuan Period to the New Mandate of the Old State: Written on the Occasion of the Publication of Feng Youlan's Complete Works*. In fact, from the mid-Qing Dynasty on, thought and culture no longer featured the ideal of he sage prominently, and this traditional ideal continued to decline after the May Fourth Movement, a process of what might be called "desanctification." However, the absence of the ideal of the sage does not mean that virtue ethics cannot be established. The key point in the modern progression of Chinese ethics is how virtue ethics can be maintained after desanctification. Further, the realization of virtue ethics after desanctification is closely related to the conditions of politics and education that enable the establishment of moral authority, not just the changes in politics and education associated with desanctification.

CHAPTER 15

Mysticism in the Philosophy of Feng Youlan

It is generally accepted that Feng Youlan's philosophy is a form of new realism and rationalism, and this assertion is largely accurate. However, this can sometimes lead to the overlooking of the mystical elements within his philosophy. He himself once said, "My past philosophical thoughts ultimately boil down to mysticism." In fact, among Chinese philosophers of the 20th century, Feng was one of the earliest to give attention to the issue of mysticism. His understanding and attitude toward mysticism were influenced by pragmatism, and the mystical elements in his own thought were largely derived from the mysticism found in ancient Chinese philosophy. This unique combination allowed him to have a distinctive grasp of ancient Chinese philosophical tradition. On the other hand, mysticism was also incorporated into the new rationalism, becoming an integral part of that entire philosophical framework. Feng affirmed mysticism within ancient Chinese philosophy as a significant contribution that could enhance and advance world philosophy. In light of this, the issue of mysticism is a significant aspect that should receive special attention in the study of his philosophy. This chapter offers a historical examination of how the understanding of mysticism evolved and developed in Feng's thought, as well as the role it played within his philosophical system, enabling us to understand that in his philosophy, alongside the pursuit of logical clarity and analysis, there is another consistent cornerstone that runs through his work. It should be noted that this chapter extensively quotes materials from Feng's academic self-narratives and retrospective accounts of his thought development written in the 1950s. In my view, these narratives, despite any political biases or labels that may have been imposed on him, are generally reliable when it comes to factual accounts of his personal intellectual development.

I. Religious Experience

According to the perspective of comparative religion, mysticism is closely related to mystical experience, which refers to a special state of consciousness achieved by individuals through certain psychological control methods (practice). Its fundamental characteristic is the experience of oneness, which can be divided into two types: internal and external. Outward-oriented practitioners in this state of sensation perceive a sense of unity with all things, while inward-oriented practitioners perceive a self-awareness that transcends time and space, encompassing the entirety of existence. All mystical experiences involve the disappearance of the subject-object boundary and all distinctions, accompanied by an indescribable sense of excitement, joy, and sublimity.

In the summer of 1920, Feng wrote an essay titled "Bergson's Philosophical Method," in which he introduced and critiqued Bergson's philosophy of intuition. He pointed out that Bergson's philosophy is fundamentally rooted in instinctive intuition rather than intellectual analysis. He says, "True intuition is a form of intellectual sympathy. Through this sympathy, we place ourselves within the object, seeking unity with that object, and ultimately reaching the inexpressible. This kind of experience is something that everyone possesses to some extent."[1] In the conclusion of the article, he says, "Let me say a few more words to conclude. I've argued that intuition comes after analysis. Advocates of intuition only oppose making analysis the ultimate, but they do not oppose analysis itself. If one thinks that advocating intuition means rejecting analysis altogether, that would be a serious mistake."[2] From this passage, it can be seen that the experience described by Feng as "unity with the object, ultimately reaching the inexpressible" is indeed a mystical experience. However, at that time, he neither used the term mysticism nor paid special attention to it. During this time, he placed more emphasis on the significance of reason.

In the mid-1920s, Feng published a booklet titled *A Certain View of Life* (1924). He later said, "In *A Certain View of Life*, I emphasized the importance of reason and opposed Liang Shuming's so-called intuition ... I thought I had already moved away from the influence of Bergson. I consider myself similar to new realism, emphasizing logic and reason."[3] He elsewhere acknowledges, "This pamphlet, on the surface advocating for rationality and opposing the mysticism of intuition, actually reserves a space for mysticism."[4] It appears that he is here referring to "Preface to the Theory of the Gains and Losses of Heaven and Man," included as an appendix in *A Certain View of Life*. He later repeated this perspective in *A History of Chinese Philosophy*. *A Certain View of Life* was incorporated into *Philosophy of Life* in 1926 as the theoretical part, while *A Comparative Study of Life Ideals* was included as the historical part of *Philosophy of Life*. While the concluding part of *Philosophy of Life*, which serves as the historical section, may not explicitly mention the concept of mysticism, it contains discussions and ideas that are closely related to mysticism. In the chapter "On Daoism," Feng points out that Daoist cultivation advocates a return to the state of infancy and a union with heaven and earth. He says, "Even though infants engage in activities without knowledge, this kind of experience without knowledge is known as pure experience. In moments of pure experience, in relation to what is being experienced, the person experiences it only perceives it as 'such' (what William James referred to as 'that'), without knowing it as 'what' (to borrow the term from James). William James's concept of pure experience indeed refers to the face value of experience, where one perceives things as they are without the addition of language or conceptual distinctions. This idea bears resemblance to the Buddhist concept of pratyakṣa or direct perception. Additionally, Zhuangzi's notion of the experience possessed by the true person aligns with this idea."[5] While William James wrote extensively on religious experiences, including mystical experiences, Feng Youlan, despite having read James's works, may not have paid specific attention to the concept of mysticism. This is evident in his discussion of Guo Xiang's idea of "from pure experience to the mystical unity of self and others" when he states, "This statement has no mystical significance whatsoever."[6] This differs significantly from his later interpretation of mysticism as a philosophy that acknowledges the mystical unity of all things and believes that Guo Xiang held mystical ideas.

In Chapter Thirteen of *Philosophy of Life*, when discussing religious experience, he says:

> In addition, there is what is called religious experience. In such experience, the person feels as if he or she is awakening from a great dream, perceiving this world as truly illusory, with another higher reality beyond it. They also feel the individual self merging with the whole (the entirety of the universe), and the distinction between self and other, both inner and outer, ceases to exist. Those who acknowledge such experiences as true and seek to explain them often start with the assumption of an idealistic or panpsychic cosmology. We believe that one can acknowledge the truth of these experiences without necessarily assuming such cosmological hypotheses. Philosophies like those of Zhuangzi and Spinoza appear to share a similar perspective on this matter ... In order to have a religious experience, one must first transcend the self-view, reaching a state of no-self. When one reaches a state of no-self, the individual has already merged with the universe. Once merged with the universe, their perspective on observing things can be considered to have reached a higher level. Therefore, at that moment, one can truly perceive all things as illusory and the totality of the universe as the sole reality.[7]

He further states, "If we do not accept the assumption of an idealistic or panpsychic cosmology, how can we acknowledge the individual's ability to merge with the universe? Answer: What is meant by 'merge' is a matter discussed in epistemology, not in ontology. Speaking from an epistemological perspective, if a person truly feels in harmony with the whole, then they are indeed in harmony with the whole. As for families, society, and the nation, if we also feel their unity rather than their differences, then we perceive them as a unity. If one person, in relation to the universe, only feels the sameness and not the differences, then wouldn't all things be considered as their individual self, and wouldn't their individual self be considered as merging with the universe? This is what is meant by "the perfect person has no self"—the ultimate state of not making distinctions. The fact that some individuals have such experiences is undeniable. Those who have these experiences perceive within them the highest truth and the greatest happiness, and this is also a fact."[8] The religious experience mentioned here undoubtedly refers to mystical experiences. However, Feng clearly avoids using the term mysticism, possibly to avoid potential misunderstandings or misinterpretations associated with the concept of Daoism at that time in Chinese culture and philosophy. In Chapter Thirteen, he references William James's *The Varieties of Religious Experience* (which includes a chapter specifically discussing mysticism), saying, "We indeed acknowledge the lowly origin of these experiences, but we must still recognize their high value. We do not take it as the path to seek truth, but we should also take it as the path to seek happiness. In other words, we do not seek the truth within it, but we should seek the good within it."[9] This suggests that Feng believed that while mysticism may not be a philosophical method, it can serve as a path for spiritual life in the pursuit of ideals and happiness.

II. All Things Are One

In his *Philosophy of Life*, Feng Youlan mentions pure experience and religious experience, but his awareness of the issues is influenced by the May Fourth Movement and Liang Shuming's cultural perspective. He only considers the realm of unity of all things as a "loss of the Way," as the opposite of progressivism, only connecting it to the negation or affirmation of the self to understand the philosophy of life, without delving into it from a broader perspective of philosophy and spiritual life. In 1927, he published an important essay titled "Mysticism in Chinese Philosophy." The opening words of this work are as follows:

> The term mysticism has various meanings. In this article, when I refer to mysticism, I specifically mean a philosophical perspective that acknowledges the existence of a state known as the unity of all things. In this state, the individual becomes one with the whole, and concepts like subjectivity, objectivity, distinctions between self and other, and inner and outer cease to exist. Many philosophers commonly associate this mysticism with idealism and cosmology. While this is a common view among philosophical scholars, mysticism does not necessarily have to be linked to idealism or cosmology.[10]

Here, Feng not only explicitly affirms the realm of the unity of all things as the mystical realm, but his description and definition of mysticism are also entirely consistent with the statements in *Philosophy of Life* regarding religious experience. This change in perspective may indeed be related to his process of translating the *Zhuangzi* into English in 1926. It is worth noting that he defines mysticism as a realm of philosophy rather than religious experience.

In this article, Feng points out that in Chinese philosophy, both Confucianism and Daoism consider the mystical realm as the highest state and mystical experience as the ultimate achievement of personal cultivation. Specifically, Daoism tends toward materialism in its cosmology, while Confucianism tends toward idealism in its cosmological views. The Daoist approach to attaining the highest state involves eliminating all distinctions in epistemology, aiming to reach the state in which "heaven and earth are born together with me, and all things are one with me." On the other hand, the Confucian approach to achieving the highest state involves self-restraint and selflessness in ethics, with the goal of realizing the state of "returning to the inherent unity of heaven, earth, and all things."[11] Regarding Daoism, in the second section of this article, Feng points out that Daoism opposes knowledge based on intellectual distinctions and emphasizes pure knowledge. He then repeats a passage from *Philosophy of Life* about William James' discussion of pure experience, but what is different from the description in *Philosophy of Life* is that here, he discusses pure experience in the context of mystical experience and the realm of the unity of all things. Therefore, he interprets the passage from the *Zhuangzi · Great and Most Honored Master* that talks about external things and seeing alone as, "Since 'external' encompasses everything, what is seen is only the oneness in its entirety. This is what is meant by seeing alone. Within this complete unity, all distinctions between past and present or life and death cease to exist."[12] Regarding Confucianism, he points out, "Confucius never explicitly spoke of the realm of the unity of all things; his concept of benevolence may simply be a form of morality without mystical significance. It is only in *The Doctrine of the Mean* and the writings of Mencius that the mystical aspect of Confucianism becomes fully apparent."[13] He points out that when Mencius talks about "all things being prepared in me," it implies that all things are one with him. Mencius' concept of the "vastness of mind" refers to the spiritual state of the individual in this highest realm. He further indicates that what the Song and Ming Dynasty philosophers discuss "is essentially the same mysticism mentioned above, but they may have added more detailed reasoning to their methodical practice."[14] In the final section of this article, the eighth section, he makes the following assessment of Song and Ming Dynasty philosophy:

> In an overall view of the statements from Cheng-Zhu and Wang Yangming, all of these philosophers believed that 1) heaven, earth, and all things are originally one, but 2) due to human selfishness, the inherent unity gives rise to distinctions and the duality of self and other, and 3) we must cultivate ourselves by eliminating selfishness to return to the state of unity with heaven, earth, and all things. Zhu Hui'an (Zhu Xi) and Wang Yangming were prominent figures in the two major schools of Song-Ming philosophy, and their views were remarkably similar in essence. In summary, the philosophers of the Song and Ming dynasties all regarded the mystical realm as the highest state and achieving this state as the ultimate goal of personal cultivation.[15]

He also points out that while Zhu Xi's attempt to thoroughly understand all things in the world is commendable, using this method as a means to reach the mystical realm is not evident. Seeking the mystical realm through intellectual knowledge is, in fact, moving in the opposite direction. In the chapter on Mencius in the first volume of his 1931 book *A History of Chinese Philosophy*, he incorporates all the key points of this article to illustrate Mencius' mystical tendencies.[16]

In the same year, Feng also published an article titled "The Philosophy of Guo Xiang." Unlike his discussion of Guo Xiang in *Philosophy of Life*, in this essay, he affirms that Guo Xiang's ideal personality is mystical.[17] He states, "When we read Spinoza's *Ethics*, we initially perceive his philosophy as realism, but by the end, his realism is overshadowed by mystical philosophy. He is able to reconcile realism with mysticism. And the same is true of Guo Xiang's philosophy. I believe this is one of their merits ... Daoist philosophies like that of Guo Xiang, although they contain mysticism, are not in conflict with science."[18] He no longer avoids the concept of mysticism and, to some extent, finds it quite convenient and useful.

From this, it can be seen that from the mid-1920s to the late 1920s, it appears that Feng had gained a comprehensive understanding of both Western and ancient Chinese mysticism in philosophy, and his research on ancient Chinese mysticism can be considered pioneering during that period. He affirmed the value of mysticism and believed that one can attain a mystical state of life without necessarily subscribing to idealism. In his description of mystical experience, we can already see, either implicitly or explicitly, the foundational and initial germ of the concepts of the Great Whole and the realm of heaven and earth later discussed in *New Neo-Confucianism* and *New Origins of Humanity*.

III. Intuition and the Unknowable

In the introduction of the first volume of his 1931 book *A History of Chinese Philosophy*, when discussing philosophical methods, Feng writes, "All that is called intuition, sudden insight, mystical experience, and the like, although of very high value, need not be mixed into the methods of philosophy. Whether it is science or philosophy, the way to write or speak about principles must always be expressed with a rigorous intellectual attitude. No author or speaker is an exception, so even in the highest realm of Buddhist thought, though it is said to be unspeakable, it still depends on realization. However, what is unspeakable is not philosophy. Philosophy is the expression of principles with a rigorous attitude. So, while we can attain a kind of mystical experience through intuition as a method, we cannot attain philosophy through intuition as a method. Therefore, we acknowledge the value of intuition and the like but do not recognize them as methods of philosophy."[19] Indeed, this passage originally appeared in the appendix titled "Preface to the Theory of the Gains and Losses of Heaven and Man" in *A Certain View of Life*. In Feng's view, philosophy is solely a rational discourse, and therefore, intuition and mystical experiences are not philosophy and not methods of philosophy. But at the same time, he acknowledges that intuition and mystical experiences hold significant value. It appears that he believes philosophy is a rational method for seeking truth, while mysticism is a special path for achieving goodness.[20] Thirty years later, in his retrospective work *A Forty-Year Retrospective*, he writes, "Looking at this passage, it seems I never escaped the influence of Bergson. I wasn't fundamentally opposed to intuition, sudden insight, and mystical experiences. I still recognized their high value. However, I believed they were not a philosophical method."[21] And he continues, "Although I value reason, in practice,

I have actually defined a scope for the activities of reason, limiting them to the realm of discourse, which is close to Kant's agnosticism. This is an attempt to restrict the scope of application of the scientific method so that it can coexist peacefully with mysticism."[22] In *A History of Chinese Philosophy*, he not only reiterated his understanding of mysticism as presented in the appendix to the chapter on Mencius but also repeated his previous citations of William James's discussion of pure experience in the chapter on Zhuangzi. This made the discussion of mysticism a distinctive feature of the book within the context of Chinese philosophy history. Feng later states, "In *A History of Chinese Philosophy*, I superficially said that I should have a sympathetic understanding of various schools of thought, but in reality, what I truly sympathize with is objective idealism and mysticism," and, "Gongsun Long and Zhu Xi are both representative figures of objective idealism, and they are both individuals I have particularly recognized and praised. Similarly, Mencius and Zhuangzi are representatives of mysticism, and I also particularly commend them. I believe they each indicate two distinct methods for reaching the mystical realm."[23]

Feng later admitted that *A History of Chinese Philosophy* and, even earlier, *Philosophy of Life*, show signs of the influence of pragmatism, which he attributed to agnosticism and mysticism. As early as in *A New Theory of Life*, he believed, "The pragmatist view asserts that science can only comprehend one aspect of the world. Science is nothing but the product of human reason, yet the universe has multiple aspects. Apart from reason, there must be other faculties that humans use to approach the essence of the universe... by what is called the consciousness of ethics and intuition, as faculties that can directly approach the essence of the universe."[24] This implies that pragmatism sees rational-based scientific knowledge as limited and suggests that intuition and mysticism are ways to approach the essence of the universe beyond reason. Feng often quoted James in his early works, which is one of the indications of his influence by pragmatism. He acknowledges that during the period of *Philosophy of Life*, his thinking was entirely pragmatic. He says, "In *A Certain View of Life*, I entirely adopted the ethical views and theory of truth of pragmatism."[25] Due to the influence of pragmatism and its empiricism, he writes in *Philosophy of Life*, "Our experience is the basis of all our knowledge; apart from this, we have no other way to acquire knowledge."[26] He viewed human knowledge as "assumptions that harmonize various experiences." He later summarizes his position in *Philosophy of Life* by saying, "In terms of a worldview, I adopt the position of new realism, and in terms of epistemology, I adopt the position of pragmatism."[27] And, "I used to believe in pragmatism, and later I believed in new realism."[28]

In *A History of Chinese Philosophy*, Feng makes a distinction between objective history and subjective history. He holds that the former refers to past events themselves, while the latter refers to accounts written by historians. Historians cannot write a history that perfectly aligns with the true historical events as they occurred. He said, "As Max Nordau noted, objective truth in relation to the writer of history is, as Kant said, the thing in itself is to human knowledge. Written history can never perfectly align with actual history."[29] He later acknowledged in his self-critique that this interpretation of historical agnosticism was influenced by pragmatism. He stated, "I advocate new realism, but I also do not completely reject pragmatism... Idealistic philosophy inherently tends toward agnosticism." He explained that because he wanted to maintain a connection with pragmatism, there was a stronger presence of agnosticism in his past philosophical thinking. Agnosticism leaves something unknowable precisely to reserve a forbidden area for religion and open a door for mysticism. He says, "My past philosophical thinking ultimately boils down to mysticism."[30] In *A History of Chinese Philosophy,* he proposes that a genuine philosophical system must have a consistent goal, which is the philosopher's insight that serves as the foundation of the entire system, from which this extensive system is developed. Later on, in his self-critique titled "Self-Criticism of My Past Work in the History of Philosophy," he mentions, "I cited the words of one of the founders of pragmatism, James, who said that 'philosophers each have their insight (vision), and they use it as the fundamental idea to apply it to various aspects.' The term insight, as used by James, was originally a religious term. Religious individuals sometimes have a kind of vision and believe they possess a special ability to communicate with God, thereby having knowledge that ordinary people cannot have. James used this term to mystify philosophy, and I used this term and mystified philosophy in *A History of Chinese Philosophy.*"[31] In fact, the description of James's insight can be traced back to the introduction to *Philosophy of Life.* The mystical insight mentioned here and the visions of religious individuals undoubtedly encompass elements of mysticism.

IV. Realm of Heaven and Earth

Before the period of *A History of Chinese Philosophy,* Feng only treated mysticism as a typological concept in the history of philosophy, and the influence of mysticism on his own philosophy had not yet manifested. It is helpful here to examine the mysticism in his thought during the "New Neo-Confucianism" period (1937–1945) and its changes.

According to Feng himself, during the writing of *A History of Chinese Philosophy,* he was still in the process of transitioning from pragmatism to new realism, which entails the belief in an independent objective existence beyond human consciousness, although that existence is unknowable.[32] However, during the New Neo-Confucianism period, his philosophy based on the insight of mysticism underwent further development. Using his later self-critique terminology, he notes, "Later in *New Neo-Confucianism,* I extended this mystical thought further… In *New Neo-Confucianism,* I referred to this world of reason as the 'book without words.' I said that the book without words, some can read it, some cannot. Those who can read the book without words experience a certain spiritual state during their reading, as if they feel they have transcended experience and themselves. This kind of experience is undoubtedly akin to the religious-style mystical experience."[33] He also states, "The *New Origins of Humanity* elaborated on the mystical thoughts I expressed in *A History of Chinese Philosophy,* describing attaining heaven, rejoicing in heaven, and being in harmony with heaven as the happiest state for human beings."[34] Feng himself says, "In summary, the realm theory is the central idea of New Neo-Confucianism."[35] And the realm theory within the New Neo-Confucianism is the primary part of the entire system related to mysticism.

In the realm theory, the concept most closely related to mysticism is the realm of heaven and earth. In summary, the main characteristic of the realm of heaven and earth is being identical with the whole, and the "whole is unspeakable, incomprehensible, and beyond understanding." The realm that is identical with the whole transcends all distinctions and is characterized by chaos.[36] Because in the realm of heaven and earth, a person is identical with the whole, the distinction between "me" and "not me" no longer exists. Therefore, one feels that "all things are prepared within me."[37] The realm of heaven and earth includes four stages: knowing heaven, serving heaven, rejoicing in heaven, and being in harmony with heaven. When a person becomes consciously aware that they are not only a part of society but also a part of the universe or the whole, this is called knowing heaven. Those who know heaven view their actions as a conscious fulfillment of their duty to the universe, and this is called serving heaven. Those who serve heaven find a transcendent meaning in their actions and things, leading to a sense of joy, as the ancients said, "The happiness of Confucius and Yan Hui."* This joy is called rejoicing in heaven. The highest stage of the realm of heaven and earth is being in harmony with heaven. Feng Youlan states:

> In the realm of heaven and earth, the highest achievement for a person is not only to realize that they are a part of the whole but also to be identical with the whole. As Zhuangzi said, "Heaven and earth are the one thing from which all things come. To understand this unity and be the same as it means that life and death, end and beginning, are like day and night, and there is no way to escape from them. How much more so when one attains what is between loss and gain, misfortune and fortune?" To understand this unity and be the same as it means being identical with the whole. When a person is identical with the whole, the distinction between "me" and "not me" no longer exists for them. The Daoists say, "Merge with things." Merge means the merging of the distinction between me and all things. The Confucianists say, "All things are prepared within me." The whole is the entirety of all things, and I am identical with the whole, so "all things are prepared within me." Such a realm is what we call being in harmony with heaven ... The whole is beyond comprehension, and the realm of being in harmony with the whole is also beyond comprehension. The realm of realizing the true nature of Buddhism and the realm of attaining the Dao in Daoism, according to their descriptions, are all beyond comprehension. The highest realm in Confucianism, though not explicitly stated, is also beyond comprehension.[38]

* This term means the happiness and contentment of Confucius (551–479 BC) and Yan Hui (a disciple of Confucius, 521–481 BC). It is a mental outlook admired and advocated by Confucian scholars, especially by Song and Ming Neo-Confucianists. Most people do not want to be put up with poverty, but poor material conditions cannot keep Confucius and Yan Hui from maintaining a happy state of mind. It embodies inner joy and happiness obtained from transcending material desires and the profound understanding and quest for principles of heaven and ethical principles.

Comparing the way *Philosophy of Life* discusses religious experience with the presentation in "Mysticism in Chinese Philosophy" and what is said about the realm of heaven and earth in *New Origins of Humanity*, it is undeniable that the concept of the realm of heaven and earth in the latter work is undoubtedly based on mysticism. The definition of the realm of heaven and earth aligns perfectly with the definition of mysticism, according to Feng Youlan. Indeed, he explicitly affirms that "the realm of being in harmony with heaven is essentially what we call mysticism." He goes on to say, "In the realm of being in harmony with heaven, a person is identical with the whole. The whole is beyond comprehension and also not an object of understanding. All the experiences that a person has in the realm of being in harmony with heaven are commonly referred to as mystical experiences. Mystical experiences are somewhat akin to pure experiences. Daoists often mix these two, but in reality, they are quite different. Mystical experiences are beyond understanding, and their incomprehensibility surpasses comprehension, while pure experiences are without understanding, and their lack of understanding falls short of comprehension."[39] Here, Feng describes pure experience as a natural realm, which differs from his earlier views.

However, the realm of heaven and earth does not quite exclusively refer to mystical experiences. Strictly speaking, mystical experiences are momentary and brief, while a realm represents a relatively long-lasting, stable level of awareness. Experiences and realms are thus distinct. What is more important to note is that mystical experiences are obtained through introspective intuition, while the realm of heaven and earth, as emphasized by Feng, is built on the foundation of rational understanding, specifically "knowing heaven" or "knowing the Way." From the perspective of New Neo-Confucianism, a person must have an understanding and knowledge of principles, reality, commonalities, and the whole in order to reach the state of being in harmony with heaven advocated by New Neo-Confucianism. Among these concepts, principle and vital energy are the ideas derived from rational analysis of things, while the whole is the concept obtained by rational synthesis of things.[40] Feng states, "The concepts of principle and vital energy can enable people to wander at the beginning of things. The concepts of Dao (the Way) and the whole can enable people to wander in the fullness of existence. These concepts can help people to know heaven, serve heaven, delight in heaven, and ultimately attain the state of being one with heaven."[41] If a person can view things from the perspective of principle and the whole, all things will present themselves with a new meaning, and this new meaning will bring about a new state of being, which is the state of heaven and earth.[42] He writes, "The concepts of the principle of the universe or the whole, the world of principles, as well as the concept of Daoist philosophy, are all philosophical concepts. When a person possesses these philosophical concepts, they can come to know heaven. Knowing heaven allows them to serve heaven, find joy in heaven, and ultimately reach the state of being in harmony with heaven."[43] Therefore, even though the concepts of the whole and the state of being in harmony with heaven are unimaginable, they still need to be reached through rational contemplation. He writes:

> But the unimaginable must still be reached through imagination, and the incomprehensible must still be reached through comprehension. Through imagination, one

> then knows that it is unimaginable. Through comprehension, one then knows that it is incomprehensible. The unimaginable is also the unspeakable, yet if one wishes to communicate it to others, one must use words. However, after speaking, one must then say that it is the unspeakable. Many philosophical works are attempts to reason about the unimaginable and speak about the unspeakable. Scholars must go through reasoning to reach the unimaginable and go through comprehension to reach the incomprehensible. The unimaginable and the incomprehensible are the highest attainments of reasoning and understanding. Philosophical mysticism represents the ultimate achievement of reasoning and understanding, and it is not opposed to them.[44]

These statements indicate that, on the one hand, Feng firmly adhered to a philosophical method rooted in rational analysis and synthesis, while, on the other hand, he saw the highest spiritual realm achieved through philosophy as a realm of mysticism. For him, the highest mystical realm could only be reached through rational philosophical analysis. The ultimate realm of the unspeakable, in which one is self-identical with the totality, could only be achieved through intellectual reflection and rational understanding. Philosophical rational analysis and synthesis could only fulfill their fundamental purpose when aimed at achieving the highest realm of unity with heaven and earth. His understanding of the relationship between rational methods and mystical realms, as well as his earlier emphasis on the relationship between analysis and intuition when discussing Bergson, shows remarkable consistency. However, in his earlier years, he had not yet established a more active connection between the two. On the other hand, while both mystical aspects of realms and mystical experiences (phenomenological) can be considered epistemological discussions and do not necessarily involve commitments to ontology, the difference lies in the fact that experiences can be fleeting and passive, whereas realms represent a stable attitude of awareness. The mysticism of experiences is rooted in pure intuition, whereas the mysticism of realms emphasizes the need for a foundation in rational analysis to reach the realm of heaven and earth. This distinction marks the difference between religious mysticism and philosophical mysticism.

V. Negative Method

In 1948, Feng wrote an article entitled "Chinese Philosophy and a Future World Philosophy" for A Symposium on Oriental Philosophy column of the American journal *Philosophical Review*. In this article, he emphasized the significance of mysticism as philosophy rather than religious experience in terms of methodology and worldview.

When comparing Western and Chinese metaphysics, he highlighted two main Western traditions—the Platonic tradition and the Kantian tradition, and two main Chinese traditions—the Confucian tradition and the Daoist tradition, in particular, comparing the philosophies of Kant and Daoism. In his view, Kantian philosophy distinguishes between the knowable and the unknowable. According to Kant, what humans can know are phenomena, while things in themselves, which are unknowable, exist beyond human knowledge. He believed that between the knowable and the unknowable, there is a boundary that reason cannot surpass, and it remains on this side of the boundary. Furthermore, he argued that Daoism also distinguishes between the knowable and the unknowable, but Daoism crosses this boundary. However, Daoism does not use reason to cross this boundary; Rather, it negates reason. Through silence, Daoism crosses the boundary to reach the other shore, attaining the realm of chaos.[45] Feng referred to this method in Daoism as the negative method of metaphysics. The negative method refers to describing things on the other side of the boundary that reason cannot describe by using language to say what they are not rather than what they are. Feng says, "Here, we obtain true mysticism. From the perspectives of Daoism and Zen Buddhism, Western philosophy, although it contains elements of mysticism, is still not mystical enough. Western mystic philosophers often talk about God and the unity of humans with God. However, since God is all-knowing and all-powerful, in essence, it is still a rational concept. As long as humans hold onto one or more rational concepts, they remain on this side of the boundary."[46] In other words, a person can only cross the boundary and reach the other side by completely negating all rational concepts, including God. Feng also proposed:

> Over the past twenty years, my colleagues and I have been working hard to introduce the methods of logical analysis into Chinese philosophy, making Chinese philosophy more rationalistic. In my view, the philosophy of the future world must be more rationalistic than traditional Chinese philosophy and more mystical than traditional Western philosophy. Only the unity of rationalism and mysticism can create a philosophy that corresponds to the entire future world.[47]

Just as He Lin once distinguished between intuition as experience and intuition as a method,[48] in the late 1940s, Feng's thought on mysticism can be distinguished as mysticism as state and mysticism as a method. The challenges posed by the Vienna Circle's methods in the 1940s led him to emphasize methodological issues during this period. When he talked about future philosophy being more mystical than traditional Western philosophy, he was referring to the mysticism of the method, especially the negative method. In this article, he discusses the issue of an ideal life, pointing out that Indian philosophy advocates that when a person reaches the inexpressible and incomprehensible state, they become one with absolute reality. In Spinoza's philosophy, the unity of the individual with the universe is described as love for God's intellect. All of these are aspects of mysticism. Feng admits that what he refers to as the realm of heaven and earth is also of a mystical nature.

At the same time, he also insisted on the significance of philosophical reason. He says, "The realm of heaven and earth must be seen as a philosophical realm because without gaining some understanding of the universe through philosophy, it is impossible to reach the realm of heaven and earth."[49] The mystical realm of identity "must be accomplished by negating reason because only by negating reason can a person achieve identity with that which cannot be an object of reason or rationality. But this unity is, in fact, the love of reason because the negation of reason itself is an activity of reason."[50] Therefore, he believed that "in order to eliminate reason, it is necessary to fully employ reason. The reason true mysticism must be preceded by genuine rationalism and negative methods must be combined with positive methods is that the truth lies in this very combination."[51]

Indeed, there are reasons to consider this article as an elaboration of the last chapter of *A Short History of Chinese Philosophy,* which was written in 1947 and published in 1948, titled "Chinese Philosophy in the Modern World." In this chapter, Feng points out that positive methods attempt to make distinctions and tell us what their objects are, while negative methods attempt to eliminate distinctions and tell us what their objects are not. He acknowledged that the methods used in his book *New Neo-Confucianism* were entirely positive analytic methods. After completing *New Neo-Confucianism,* he began to realize the importance of negative methods as well.[52] He stated, "Now, if someone were to ask me to define philosophy, especially metaphysics, I would answer in a paradoxical way: philosophy, especially metaphysics, is a kind of knowledge that, in its development, ultimately becomes knowledge of the unknown. If that is indeed the case, we cannot do without negative methods."[53] The negative method is essentially the method of mysticism, and knowledge of the unknown refers to mysticism as the endpoint. Philosophy aims to use the negative method to reach the destination of knowledge of the unknown. According to Feng, the ultimate development of philosophy is to reach a form of mysticism. These ideas can indeed be compared to the later developments in the thought of philosophers like Martin Heidegger.

From a methodological perspective, philosophy begins with experience, but the development of metaphysics leads it to ultimately reach something beyond experience, beyond description, something that is mysterious and transcendent. That which cannot be sensed and cannot be thought of is beyond reason, and one must use the method of negation to reach it. This negational method possesses the nature of mysticism. Feng says:

> A complete metaphysical system should begin with positive methods and end with negative methods. If it does not conclude with negative methods, it cannot reach the ultimate pinnacle of philosophy. However, if it does not begin with positive methods, it lacks the clear thinking that constitutes the essence of philosophy. Mysticism is not the opposite of clear thinking, nor is it beneath clear thinking. It is better to say that it lies outside clear thinking. It is not against reason; it is beyond reason.[54]

Philosophy must commence with rational activity, employ rational methods to understand the common and the whole, employ rational methods to expound the unknowable east and west of the boundary line, and ultimately transcend the limits of reason using negative methods to reach the summit of the realm of the unknown. The realm of the unknown, which is the pinnacle of philosophy, is the realm that is self-identical with the whole. Therefore:

> In philosophy, all great metaphysical systems, whether they adopt a positive or negative method, invariably adorn themselves with the mysticism label. The negative method, in essence, is a method of mysticism. However, even in the works of philosophers like Plato, Aristotle, and Spinoza, where the positive method is employed skillfully, their systems still have a mystical quality at their zenith. Philosophers, whether in Plato's *Republic* recognizing the Idea of the Good and becoming one with it, or in Aristotle's *Metaphysics* perceiving the thought thinking itself as God and becoming one with it, or in Spinoza's *Ethics* viewing all things sub specie aeternitatis (from the eternal viewpoint) and experiencing the intellectual love of God, in these moments, what else can they do but be in silent contemplation?[55]

It is evident that Feng's statement in his later self-critique, "My past philosophical thought ultimately boils down to mysticism," aligns with his philosophical thinking in the 1940s.

In Western culture, from Neoplatonism to medieval Christian theology, Christian mysticism based on the concept of God is not uncommon.[56] In addition to religious mysticism, secular forms of mysticism emerged, often referred to as naturalistic mysticism, after the Renaissance. In the history of philosophy, cosmic mysticism, represented by Spinoza's metaphysical philosophy, is one such example. In the 19th century, Arthur Schopenhauer was influenced by Indian philosophy, which led to the development of mysticism. In the Chinese philosophical tradition, there has historically been a blurred line between religion and philosophy, and transcending belief does not occupy an important position. Therefore, mysticism in Chinese philosophy has been a continuous, integral aspect of the tradition. However, traditional mysticism developed entirely within the Neo-Confucianism system and was in complete opposition to rationalism.[57]

In summary, Feng's understanding of mysticism encompasses three levels: mystical experience, mystical realms, and mystical methods. His philosophy is essentially a system that combines rationalism with mysticism, and this mysticism not only led him to acknowledge the negative method of metaphysics but also affirmed the realm of self-identity with the whole as the goal of philosophy and the highest spiritual state for humans. What distinguishes his mysticism from a more general mysticism is his consistent emphasis on a mysticism that serves as a philosophical realm, rather than being purely a religious experience. He consistently emphasizes that reason and the analysis and synthesis of reason are the fundamental philosophical methods and the necessary path to reach the highest spiritual realm. He also emphasizes the complementary relationship between logical analysis and negative methods. Although in the systematic expression, mysticism may be defined as the ultimate pinnacle, rationalism should not be regarded as subordinate to it. In Feng's system, both rationalism and mysticism carry equal weight and are indispensable. This remains consistent in his later work, such as *A New History of Chinese Philosophy*. More prominently, his understanding of mysticism is not merely a fleeting psychological state but a philosophically conceptualized spiritual realm. Pursuiting this spiritual realm, as Feng stated, represents the ultimate aspiration in traditional Chinese Confucian and Daoist philosophy. For him, the true function of philosophy is to address human existential needs and provide a spiritual realm that brings inner peace and purpose to human life. Indeed, this understanding of philosophy offers valuable insights, especially in the context of the modern-day tension between philosophy and religion, as well as the struggle to find meaning and purpose in a rapidly changing world.

Notes

1. *Collected Works of Sansongtang*, 7.
2. Ibid., 10.
3. *Complete Works of Sansongtang*, vol. 14, 184–85.
4. Ibid., 168.
5. *Complete Works of Sansongtang*, vol. 1, 370.
6. Ibid., 372
7. Ibid., 536.
8. Ibid.
9. Ibid., 537.
10. *Collected Works of Sansongtang*, 49.
11. Ibid., 49–50.
12. Ibid., 52.
13. Ibid., 54.
14. Ibid., 56.
15. Ibid., 58.
16. Ibid., 178.
17. Ibid., 80.
18. Ibid.
19. *A History of Chinese Philosophy*, vol. 1, 5.
20. He also stated in *Philosophy of Life* that the goal of philosophy is to seek goodness, while the goal of science is to seek truth. *Complete Works of Sansongtang*, vol. 1, 352.
21. *Complete Works of Sansongtang*, vol. 14, 185.
22. Ibid., 144.
23. Ibid., 113.
24. *Complete Works of Sansongtang*, vol. 1, 509.
25. *Complete Works of Sansongtang*, vol. 14, 178.
26. *Complete Works of Sansongtang*, vol. 1, 523.
27. *Complete Works of Sansongtang*, vol. 14, 97.
28. Ibid., 123.
29. *A History of Chinese Philosophy*, 19.
30. *Complete Works of Sansongtang*, vol. 14, 95.
31. Ibid., 101.
32. Ibid., 187.
33. Ibid., 101–103.
34. Ibid., 114.

35. Ibid., 223.
36. *Complete Works of Sansongtang*, vol. 4, 558.
37. Ibid., 632.
38. Ibid., 632–35.
39. Ibid., 517.
40. *Complete Works of Sansongtang*, vol. 5, 155.
41. Ibid., 159.
42. *Complete Works of Sansongtang*, vol. 4, 625.
43. Ibid., 627.
44. Ibid., 635.
45. *Complete Works of Sansongtang*, vol. 11, 515–516.
46. Ibid., 517.
47. Ibid.
48. He Lin, "The Methodology of Song Confucians," in *An Explanation of Modern Idealism* (Chongqing Independent Press, 1942), 92.
49. *Complete Works of Sansongtang*, vol. 11, 519.
50. Ibid., 520.
51. Ibid., 521.
52. *A Short History of Chinese Philosophy*, 387.
53. Ibid.
54. Ibid., 394.
55. Ibid., 393–394.
56. Zhao Dunhua, *1,500 Years of Christian Philosophy* (People's Publishing House, 1994), 195, 281, 356.
57. "Mysticism in the Tradition of the Study of the Mind," in *The Realm of Being and Non-being* (People's Publishing House, 1991).

CHAPTER 16

Feng Youlan on Emotion and Non-emotion in Chinese Philosophy

In Feng Youlan's understanding of Chinese philosophy, the source of emotions and the approach to dealing with emotions is a significant issue. His insights into this question are not only a crucial avenue for him to grasp the essence of Chinese philosophical thought but also influence the development of his own philosophical ideas. The discussion in this chapter is a dedicated study of this particular issue.

I. The Art of Life

On March 2, 1935, Feng Youlan delivered a lecture at Tsinghua University titled "The Art of Life," organized by the Tsinghua Youth Association as part of a university discussion forum. The content of the lecture was published in the *Beiping Morning News* the following day.

According to Feng's own explanation, "the art of life" here refers to "the assumption that life is about seeking happiness. So, how to attain happiness is what the art of life is all about."[1]

According to this statement, "the art of life" refers to "the method of seeking happiness in life." Feng believed that modern schools prioritize knowledge input, so the question of the art of life is rarely discussed in such schools, but it was a topic that ancient Chinese scholars discussed extensively. The examples he listed of ancient scholars, such as "The rigid conduct of the past Daoist scholars was nothing more than seeking happiness," and "Confucius in the *Analects* saying, 'Enjoyment should not be joyless; we do not know when old age will come,' and 'With coarse rice to eat, with water to drink… the joys of life do not change, he did not alter his joy,' all show that they discussed the art of life."[2] According to what is mentioned here, he believed that Confucius' "enjoyment" and the various cultivation methods pursued by Daoist scholars to attain such enjoyment all fall under the category of seeking happiness.

From this, it can be seen that what Feng truly focused on was not the conventional notion of happiness. Some people consider wealth and fame as happiness, and others view high rank and titles as happiness, while some may see the salvation of all people as happiness. However, all of these are external forms of happiness, and the joy they bring is also external in nature. What Feng refers to as happiness is actually related to inner happiness; the joy he spoke of is the joy of one's spiritual state.

In Feng's view, the key to attaining inner happiness and joy lies in the method of dealing with emotions. If people can correctly manage their own emotions, they can achieve inner happiness and joy. The lecture titled "The Art of Life" focused entirely on the issue of emotions. He says:

> The art of life is vast, but today, I will only discuss one aspect, which is the method of dealing with emotions. Emotions include joy, anger, sorrow, and happiness. While the entire issue of happiness is not solely dependent on emotions, joy and anger have a significant impact on life. For example, in the historical novel *Romance of the Three Kingdoms,* Zhou Yu became extremely angry and died from it; in *General Yue Fei,* when Niü Gao captured Jin Wuzhu, he angered Jin to death, which also delighted himself to death. All of these are the effects of emotions. I will discuss how we deal with them today.[3]

It can be seen that Feng was concerned with how to regulate one's personal emotions of joy, anger, sorrow, and happiness to achieve a sense of inner happiness. In his lecture, he specifically emphasized Zhuangzi's understanding of the origin and function of emotions, saying:

> Zhuangzi said that the reason people have emotions is because their knowledge is not sufficient. If one has abundant knowledge, then there will not be any emotions. For instance, on a windy day, it may be inconvenient for people to go outside, but adults generally do not experience any emotional turmoil in such situations. However, children who cannot go outside may become very angry and curse the weather as terrible. This is because children do not have as much knowledge as adults, so they are more prone to emotional distress. The ethical philosophy of Spinoza, a Western philosopher, states that emotions are a form of bondage for humans, and if people have complete knowledge, they can break free from this bondage.
>
> In the main chapter on nurturing life in *Zhuangzi,* there are many discussions on this topic. It mentions that when Laozi died, many people were very sorrowful. *Zhuangzi* describes this as "escaping from heaven and turning away from emotions," which is what the ancients referred to as the punishment of "escaping from heaven." They lacked complete knowledge about the nature of life, and they did not understand that death is the result of life. Therefore, they experienced the "punishment of escaping from heaven," which is sorrow.

> Zhuangzi understood this principle very well. When his wife passed away, he famously responded by beating a drum and singing. Hui Shi once criticized him for this, to which Zhuangzi replied, "At first, I was indeed grieved in my heart. But then I thought about it: originally, there was no Mrs. Zhuang in the world. Suddenly, there was Mrs. Zhuang, and now, suddenly, there is no Mrs. Zhuang again. It is just like the cycle of the seasons. There is nothing to be sad about." Zhuangzi's perspective demonstrates his ability to reconcile his emotions with his understanding of the nature of life.[4]

According to this perspective, Feng's focus on emotional phenomena primarily pertains to negative, detrimental emotional states. He uses Zhuangzi's words to suggest that when people fail to adapt to the natural changes in understanding the world and life, it is akin to "escaping from heaven." Consequently, individuals who suffer from these negative emotional states due to their detachment from natural changes are experiencing the "punishment of escaping from heaven." On the other hand, he notes that the emergence of emotions is caused by ignorance, and there are two types of knowledge. One is knowledge about nature, such as meteorology, and the other is knowledge about life and death, which essentially refers to a philosophical understanding. Without these two types of knowledge, people will be bound and tormented by their emotions, unable to find liberation.

Feng observes that the primary reason people cannot free themselves from the bondage of emotions is not solely because they cannot prevent emotions from arising. Instead, it is mainly because the mind becomes entangled with external objects after emotions have arisen and cannot easily detach itself from them. He says:

> Wang Bi* and others argue that people should "respond to things without being entangled by them." They believe that emotions are a natural reflection and cannot be entirely avoided, but it is sufficient as long as one does not become entangled with external objects. In *Zhuangzi*, there is a passage that says, "The sage uses his mind like a mirror: going after nothing, welcoming nothing, responding but not storing. In this way, he can triumph over things without harming himself." The idea of the mirror not harming is based on the concept of not becoming entangled with external objects. However, Zhuangzi primarily focused on using reason to transform emotions without elaborating extensively on this point. It was during the Song Dynasty that Confucian scholars developed and expanded on this concept. Cheng Hao's *Book of Fixed Nature* states, "The constant of heaven and earth is that they universally embrace all things without having a self. The constant of the sage is that their emotions harmonize with all things without having emotions. Therefore, a noble person should be broad and impartial, accepting things as they come and conforming to them." The Song Confucian scholars elaborated on this concept,

* Wang Bi (226–249), courtesy name Fusi, was a Chinese philosopher and politician of the state of Cao Wei in the Three Kingdoms period of China.

> often citing examples like Yan Hui's "not taking offense" and "not shifting blame." Being able to reach such a state means that one can be broad and impartial, accepting things as they come and conforming to them. For instance, if someone gets into an argument with their spouse and gets so angry that they even break a teacup, it is because they were unable to be broad and impartial, accepting things as they come. Wang Yangming said, "The seven emotions should not have anything to grasp onto." Grasping here means becoming entangled, or in other words, the seven emotions should not become sources of entanglement. When discussing the passage from the *Great Learning*, "When the mind is troubled, one cannot be at ease; when the mind is angry, one cannot be upright," the emphasis is on the word 所 (*suo*, "having" or "having something"). When the mind is troubled or angered, it implies that there is an object or something external causing this entanglement, which leads to suffering. For example, when we see someone slapping another person, we might feel angry in the moment, but once the incident passes, it is over. If someone were to slap me, that would be a different situation. Not only would I feel anger toward them at that moment, but I might continue to hold onto that anger whenever I think about it. This is because my mind has become entangled, and I cannot be broad and impartial. The presence of the self, the I, prevents me from treating the situation with the same equanimity as if someone else were slapped.[5]

Feng notes that Zhuangzi's philosophy tends toward a perspective that is close to non-emotion, while the views of Wang Bi and the Song Confucian scholars are not advocating for the complete absence of emotions. Wang Bi and the Song Confucian scholars both recognized that human emotions are a natural reflection and cannot be entirely avoided. Therefore, what people should strive for is not a state of complete emotionlessness or the elimination of all emotions, but rather ensuring that the seven emotions do not become sources of entanglement and suffering with external objects.

Feng concluded his lecture by pointing out that the fundamental reason the seven emotions become sources of entanglement with external objects is the presence of the self, the I. The existence of the self is the root cause of the mind becoming entangled and the inability to be broad and impartial. Feng writes:

> Whether or not a person becomes entangled with external objects depends entirely on the presence or absence of the self, the I. In contemporary terms, this can be described as the presence or absence of an objective attitude. Being broad and impartial indeed has significant implications for one's happiness in life and for achieving success in one's endeavors … If one cannot be broad and impartial and the self is always present, it often leads to anxiety, fear, and constant worry, which can result in unfavorable outcomes … Therefore, being broad and impartial, selfless, and free from ego, while it may not sound particularly exciting when discussed in the context of Daoist philosophy, is indeed relevant to one's happiness in life.[6]

This suggests that one of the significant factors determining happiness in life is the ability to achieve a state of selflessness. It is only through selflessness that one can be broad and impartial, not become entangled with external objects, and avoid suffering and harm from external entanglements. In other words, individuals should have emotions but be devoid of ego or allow their emotions to harmonize with external circumstances without ego. Therefore, the crucial aspect is not a lack of emotions, but rather a lack of ego.

II. Unity of Movement and Stillness

It is useful here to backtrack and trace the context and trajectory of this issue in the development of Feng's academic thought. As early as in the second chapter, the second section of *Philosophy of Life*, "What Is Happiness," he pointed out that according to Zhuangzi, "Everything has its own way and virtue, meaning that everything has its natural disposition. If one follows the natural disposition of everything, then happiness is immediate."[7] The term natural used here is in contrast to artificial. The artificial involves imitation of the natural and the alteration of what is natural. The realm of the artificial leads to the loss of the happiness enjoyed in the natural realm. In the fifth chapter, the third section of the book, titled "Yang Zhu's Art of Life," we read, "The way Yang Zhu believed in pursuing happiness is that … we should simply speak and act according to our own inclinations, without regard for social praise or criticism … Yang Zhu placed great emphasis on physical pleasure, and perhaps this is because among all forms of happiness, physical pleasure is the easiest to attain. By choosing the most immediate form of happiness, one can avoid suffering and pain."[8] These discussions are from his early explorations of the art of life and the path to happiness.

In the later published *A New Theory of Life*, in the fifth section titled "The Art of Life," Feng proposes that what Confucianism teaches as "understanding one's fate" is a form of the art of life. To understand the art of life, one must first comprehend what is good. Good is divided into two kinds: intrinsic goodness and instrumental goodness. Intrinsic goodness refers to things that are desirable in themselves, and their value lies within the things themselves. Instrumental goodness refers to things that do not have intrinsic value on their own, but they serve as means to achieve intrinsic goodness. Feng holds that intrinsic goodness often requires the use of instrumental goodness to attain them. However, instrumental goodness is often dry and tasteless, which can lead to suffering in life. If people can subjectively perceive instrumental goodness as having intrinsic goodness, much of their disappointment and suffering can be alleviated.

Feng further notes that when ancient Chinese people spoke of "doing without doing," it was because doing has intrinsic goodness within it; doing without doing means that doing has intrinsic goodness. Those who approach their actions with a playful attitude do so with the belief that there is intrinsic goodness in doing, rather than simply treating play as a means to an end. Therefore, if we perceive most of the means in our lives as having intrinsic goodness, we can attain a state in which "a noble person finds contentment in everything he does," thus significantly reducing suffering in life. Feng refers to this as "a method for resolving the problems of life."[9] From this, it can be seen that even before Feng's *A New Theory of Life*, when discussing the art of living, he had already considered the alleviation of subjective despair and suffering as an important method for seeking happiness.

The period from 1926 to 1927 was a time of significant advancement in Feng's understanding of the spirit of Chinese philosophy. In 1926, while teaching at Yenching University, he wrote an article titled "Contributions of Chinese Philosophy," which was published in the July 1926 issue of the Japanese magazine *Kaizo*. In this article, he argues that Chinese philosophy often provides more detailed, comprehensive discussions on certain topics compared to Western philosophy, such as the exploration of the concept of the unity of motion and stillness. His article primarily focuses on elaborating on the concept of the unity of motion and stillness in ancient Chinese thought.

He notes that since the time of pre-Qin Confucianism and Daoism, Chinese philosophers have all regarded the unity of motion and stillness as the highest state of human existence. For instance, the *Xici* text states, "Quiet and motionless, it is sensitive and thus understands the causes of all happenings in the world." Mencius speaks of the "unmoving heart," and Zhuangzi mentions, "The use of a perfect man's mind is like a mirror—it does not hold on, it does not oppose, and it responds but does not retain. Therefore, he can triumph over things without injury."

Following the Han Dynasty, Daoist philosophy thrived during the Wei and Jin periods, while Confucian thought experienced a revival during the Song and Ming dynasties. Neo-Confucianism and the School of Principle significantly developed the ideal of the unity of motion and stillness and studied its practical methods.[10] In this article, Feng discusses Guo Xiang's thoughts, which are presented in his commentary on the *Zhuangzi*. He interprets Guo Xiang's statements of *Commentary on Zhuangzi*, such as, "Sincerity should not be with the heart, and the principle itself is profound and mysterious," "Being sufficient as the master of things and in accordance with the time without limit," and "With a mind without intention, the profound response occurs; it only follows from feeling," as conveying the same idea as Zhuangzi's notion that the use of a perfect man's mind is like a mirror. He also points out that among the philosophers of the Song and Yuan dynasties, there were many who emphasized the idea of the unity of motion and stillness. For example, he mentions Cheng Hao, who, in his *Book of Fixed Nature*, expressed the notion that "what is called 'fixed' includes both motion and stillness, without directing, without internal and external … the constant state of the sage is to let their feelings harmonize with all things, yet remain without feeling." Additionally, he highlights the thought of Wang Yangming, who states, "With things, we see forms, and yet the bright mirror is never tainted. This is what is meant by harmonizing one's feelings with all things, yet having no feelings." These statements all contribute to the discussion of the state of the unity of motion and stillness. In contrast to the previous section, it can be understood that the state of unity of motion and stillness mentioned here is indeed equivalent to the method of dealing with emotions that was discussed earlier.

Feng points out, "As for the method to attain this state, there is no other way except to control emotions and the self through knowledge. According to modern psychology, emotions are the underpinning of psychological activity, and what we call sorrow and joy are all emotions. To control emotions with knowledge is not to forcefully suppress them from outside."[11] Feng suggests that if we have a thorough understanding and substantial knowledge of the things that trigger emotions, then emotions naturally diminish. He believes that controlling emotions with knowledge aligns with Wang Bi's statement "to let emotions follow reason" (from the *Response to Xun Rong's Letter*) and corresponds to Guo Xiang's idea that those with emotions should use reason to dispel them. He says, "If one cannot control emotions with knowledge, it is what Zhuangzi referred to as 'escaping from heaven and turning away from emotions, forgetting one's origins.' If one tries to escape from heaven and turn away from emotions, it will inevitably result in 'the punishment of escaping from heaven,' that is, suffering. However, if one possesses knowledge that can control emotions and understands that life is about timing and death is about following, then one can live in harmony with the timing and follow the natural course. Sorrow and joy will not be able to enter. Being able to transcend sorrow and joy allows one to attain true happiness. Transcending sorrow and joy is akin to being liberated from the torment of hanging upside down."[12] It is evident that here, the term knowledge does not refer to ordinary knowledge but signifies a philosophical understanding. Indeed, during this period, Feng essentially used the concept of controlling emotions with knowledge to explain the issue of dealing with emotions.

Feng notes that individuals who can control their emotions with knowledge are not necessarily devoid of emotions. As Wang Bi argued, "Sages are more spiritual than ordinary people, and they share the same emotions as ordinary people ... When the emotions of the five elements are shared, one cannot be without sorrow and joy in response to things. However, the emotions of sages allow them to respond to things without being burdened by them." When people encounter things that trigger emotions, they naturally generate feelings, "but immediately use knowledge to control them, making them dissipate. In this way, emotions do not cling to one's heart, and we will not become attached." Feng references Cheng Hao's statement, "When angry, quickly forget anger and contemplate the right and wrong of the situation," and also cites Wang Yangming, who said, "Sages have no goodness or wickedness, only the absence of doing good and the absence of doing evil, unmoved by external influences." He believes that if one can achieve a state where "feelings harmonize with all things without being influenced by emotions," then "in this way, emotions in the heart are like clouds in the vast sky—they exist but do no harm."[13]

Feng points out that the reason people cannot harmonize their feelings with all things without being influenced by emotions is because of the existence of the self. When there is a sense of self, individuals often harbor worries about the future and regrets about the past. This is what Cheng Hao referred to as "selfish and calculating intelligence." If one understands that the self fundamentally does not exist and merges the self with the universe, one can forget both internal and external distinctions, achieving a state of impartiality where all worries, regrets, personal desires, calculations, and plans cease to exist. Reaching this state, one does not dwell on any changes, and this is what is meant by the unity of motion and stillness. Feng observes that "the philosophers of the Song and Ming dynasties paid the most selfless attention to this point." It can be said that his understanding and appreciation of Song-Ming Neo-Confucianism were indeed based on his understanding of Daoism and metaphysics, particularly in the context of emotional issues.

III. Methods for Dealing with Emotions

In the second volume of *A History of Chinese Philosophy*, published in 1934, Feng Youlan explicitly introduced his thoughts on methods for dealing with emotions. When discussing metaphysics, he writes:

> The study of Zhuangzi emphasized the transformation of emotions through reason, which is described as "being at ease in the moment and following the natural course, so that sorrow and joy cannot enter." He Yan* believed that a sage has no joy, anger, sorrow, or happiness, which approximately corresponds to what is said in *Zhuangzi*. Wang Bi initially endorsed this idea, saying, "Let emotions follow reason." When Yan Yuan passed away, Confucius wept bitterly. However, someone who is at ease in the moment and follows the natural course observes from a perspective of reason. They understand that death is a natural outcome of life, so the emotions of grief and sorrow naturally do not arise. This is what is meant by transforming emotions through reason. However, as humans possess emotions, these emotions are also a part of their natural disposition. Because of this natural disposition, they "cannot be without sorrow and joy in response to things." However, in the case of sages, even though they have emotions, they "respond to things without being burdened by them." Zhuangzi says, "The use of a perfect man's mind is like a mirror—it does not hold on, it does not oppose, and it responds but does not retain. Therefore, he can triumph over things without injury" (from *Ying Di Wang* in *Zhuangzi*). "Triumph over things without injury" is equivalent to "responding to things without being burdened by them." However, Zhuangzi's approach to dealing with emotions does not necessarily employ this method. On the other hand, Wang Bi expanded the application of this philosophy and used it to deal with emotions. Subsequently, the methods employed by later Confucian scholars, especially those of the Song Dynasty, for handling emotions align with this approach.[14]

Regarding Cheng Yi and Cheng Hao, in the section discussing the mutual generation and dissolution of *yin* and *yang*, good and evil, we read:

> Zhuangzi says, "The use of a perfect man's mind is like a mirror—it does not hold on, it does not oppose, and it responds but does not retain. Therefore, he can triumph over

* He Yan (c. 195–249), courtesy name Pingshu, was a Chinese philosopher and politician of the state of Cao Wei in the Three Kingdoms period of China.

> things without injury." Daoist philosophers also assert that our use of the mind should be like this. However, in Daoism, what the mind should respond to does not include emotions. The Daoist method for dealing with emotions is indeed to transform them through reason. Those who can transform emotions through reason are themselves free from emotions. Daoist philosophers assert that emotions can exist, but when we experience emotions, we should consider them as something external to the self. Even when sages encounter things that can be pleasing or anger-inducing, they may experience feelings of joy or anger, but these are not their own emotions. Instead, they arise from the nature of the things themselves, which can be either pleasing or anger-inducing. Because of this, when the event has passed, the emotional feelings of joy or anger in sages also disappear. This is why Yan Hui was able to avoid holding onto anger. Ordinary individuals, on the other hand, harbor their anger, so even when the source of anger is gone, they still have feelings of anger. They become angry even when they encounter something that should not provoke anger. This is what is meant by holding onto anger or transferring anger. The idea that "the constant state of sages is to let their feelings harmonize with all things without being influenced by emotions," aligns with Shao Yong's idea of "taking pleasure in things as they are and feeling sadness for things as they are," which expresses a similar idea.[15]

In the chapter discussing Wang Yangming, the sixth section is titled "The Origin of Evil," Feng quotes Wang's *Record of Instructions for Practice*, saying, "The seven emotions follow their natural flow, all of them are the function of the innate knowledge. One should not distinguish between good and evil, but one should not become attached to them." He also cites another passage from Wang, saying, "Anger and annoyance are natural emotions; how can the human heart be without them? It is just that one should not become attached to them. When ordinary people become angry or annoyed and attach even a fraction of their own intention, they become excessively angry, losing the state of impartiality. If there is any anger or annoyance, they cannot maintain their correctness. In ordinary cases of anger and annoyance, one should just let things follow their course, without holding onto any personal intention. By doing so, the mind and body become impartial and attain their inherent correctness." Feng proceeds to explain:

> Therefore, one should not become attached to the seven emotions, as "attaching even a fraction of their own intention will lead to excessive anger, not the state of impartiality." The *Platform Sutra of the Sixth Patriarch* states, "When the former thought clings to an object, it leads to affliction; when the latter thought clings to an object, it leads to enlightenment." When there is anger or annoyance, it is a form of clinging to an object. "The joy of sages is based on what is appropriate for joy; the anger of sages is based on what is appropriate for anger." This means that they do not possess joy or anger in the sense of having a personal intention to be joyful or angry. The heart of a sage is like a clear mirror, "impartial and all-encompassing, responding to things as they come." When there

is a reason to be joyful, they are joyful; when there is a reason to be angry, they are angry. However, their fundamental nature remains empty and clear. They have no attachment or clinging to the things that cause joy or anger, and therefore, they are not burdened by them.[16]

In the seventh section, titled "Unity of Motion and Stillness," after quoting Wang's saying, "See forms with things, yet the bright mirror remains untainted," Feng points out, "If one can achieve this, even though they may be active all day long, their mind remains as if inactive, and this is what is meant by the unity of motion and stillness. Unity of motion and stillness is true stillness, absolute stillness; the idea that motion is settled, and stillness is also settled is true settledness, absolute settledness. This is in line with Cheng Hao's *Book of Fixed Nature* as well."[17]

IV. Balancing Emotion and Reason

After completing *A History of Chinese Philosophy,* Feng used the phrase "unity of motion and stillness" less frequently and instead employed expressions like "dealing with emotions" or "handling emotions" more often. In later years, especially after 1950, he incorporated this concept into discussions about spiritual realms. However, during the "Six Books of Zhenyuan" period, the discussion of this method for dealing with emotions was not found in *New Origins of Humanity,* which focused on spiritual realms, but rather in *A New Treatise on the Way of Life,* which dealt with approaches to life.

In fact, this is not surprising because, in Feng's own words, the content of *A New Treatise on the Way of Life* focuses on life methods or what he called "the art of living." At the same time, it is possible to speculate that *A New Treatise on the Way of Life* came before *New Origins of Humanity* in his writing process. When he was writing *A New Treatise on the Way of Life,* Feng may not have yet fully realized that the method for dealing with emotions is one aspect of spiritual realms.

In the sixth section of *A New Treatise on the Way of Life,* titled "Balancing Emotion and Reason," Feng provides a comprehensive discussion of the issue of dealing with emotions. When discussing the Daoist concept of transforming emotions through reason, he points out, "What is referred to as emotion here is what we now call feelings. What is referred to as reason has a more complex meaning; sometimes, it refers to the underlying principles manifested in emotions or circumstances discussed earlier; sometimes, it refers to knowledge or understanding of these principles; and sometimes, it refers to our cognitive abilities to have such knowledge or understanding, which we call reason or intellect."[18]

He begins by describing the Daoist perspective on this issue. Daoists believe that emotions arise when individuals lack understanding of things. For example, if a child stumbles and falls because of a stone on the ground, they may become very angry and scold the stone. This is because the child lacks sufficient understanding of the object (the stone), leading to the emergence of emotions. Even though adults have a greater understanding of things compared to children, their understanding can still be partial, which is why they may not always be free from emotions. Only when one has a complete, comprehensive understanding of the universe and things can one be completely free from emotions. Daoism thus advocates a state of being free from emotions. However, this lack of emotions does not mean being like dry wood or a lifeless rock; rather, it means that one's emotions are transformed in accordance with reason, i.e., emotions are transformed through reason. These teachings align with the lectures given in 1935. Feng further quotes a passage from the *Shishuo Xinyu* that says, "most enlightened people are not burdened by emotions and remain unaffected; the lowest people are troubled by the world and have no time for emotions; those who are bound by emotions are just people like us." He points out that the lack of emotions in dry wood or lifeless rocks is incapable of emotions, while the emotionlessness of Daoist sages is not burdened by emotions and remain unaffected. Daoists believe that when one understands the principles behind things, they do not generate emotional responses to events, allowing them to remain unaffected by external circumstances. Being unaffected by external circumstances is what it means to see through certain things. When you see through them, you can maintain composure because being unable to maintain composure in the face of emotions is when emotions momentarily overpower you. Understanding the principles behind things allows one to be more tolerant because within such understanding, we do not develop excessive attachment to things that go in our favor, nor do we harbor intense resentment toward things that go against us. When one can see through all things, one can achieve complete emotionlessness. In the "De Chong Fu" chapter of *Zhuangzi*, we read, "Sages have the form of a person but lack the emotions of a person." What is meant by lacking emotions is that they do not internally harm themselves through likes and dislikes. When one harms onself internally due to one's likes and dislikes, it is referred to as a punishment or burden. However, being unaffected by external circumstances does not mean not doing anything; it means engaging in actions without generating emotional responses. Daoist sages are therefore considered individuals entirely free from emotions. Feng notes that while this Daoist ideal may be an unattainable ideal, "If a person can eliminate useless emotions, they can reduce many burdens and accomplish many things."[19] He has a sympathetic understanding of this Daoist ideal of life.

Feng continues by explaining that Neo-Confucianism differs from early Daoism in its perspective. Neo-Confucianism believes that "sages are not devoid of emotions, but are individuals who have emotions without being burdened by them. Daoism regards having emotions as a burden and being free from emotions as being unburdened. Wang Bi views being burdened by emotions when one has them as a burden and being unburdened by emotions when one has them as not being burdened."[20] Similarly, Song and Ming Dynasty Confucian scholars also advocated that sages have emotions without being burdened by them. While their expressions may not be directly borrowed from Wang Bi, the essence is the same. What Cheng Hao meant by "harmonizing emotions with all things without having emotions" does not refer to Daoist emotionlessness. Rather, it means "having emotions without a strong sense of self (ego)."[21] Feng specifically cites examples from Wang's philosophy to illustrate the idea of aligning with things. He says:

> Wang Yangming, in his *Record of Instructions for Practice*, says, "It is just letting things follow their course, without holding onto any personal intention. The mind and body become impartial, attaining their inherent correctness. For example, when you go out and witness people fighting, it is not that you do not get angry inwardly, but even though you get angry, your heart remains impartial, without stirring up the slightest bit of agitation." And, "Today, even if you get angry at someone, it can be like this, and then it is correct." Yangming's example is excellent. If I see someone unjustifiably slap another person, I would naturally feel anger at their arrogance and bullying. However, this anger does not contain a sense of self and is devoid of personal intentions. Therefore, my mind remains impartial and untroubled, and this anger is a result of letting things follow their course, and these emotions are in harmony with all things, just as Cheng Hao described. When we say "having emotions without a strong sense of self," this is precisely what we mean. Such anger is easily dispelled and transient. There may be anger when witnessing a certain event, but once that event passes, the mind returns to a state of calmness. It is like having passing clouds in the sky—even though there might be fleeting clouds, the sky remains vast and empty. This is what is meant by "harmonizing emotions with all things without being burdened by emotions."[22]

As in his lectures in 1935, Feng here continues to adopt Wang's approach, using vivid examples of seeing someone slap another person and being slapped by someone else to help people understand this principle. Feng also points out that Daoists aim to transform emotions through reason to achieve emotionlessness, while Song-Ming Confucian scholars do not seek emotionlessness but advocate having emotions without a strong sense of self. This is why Song-Ming Confucianism benefits from the Daoist approach of transforming emotions through reason without encountering the difficulties associated with the Daoist view of emotional transformation.

In the 1940s, Feng taught first-year students at National Southwest Associated University to read *A New Treatise on the Way of Life* and *New Origins of Humanity.* His teaching method involved having students read the texts and then posing questions for group discussions. Through these class discussions, certain topics were brought to public attention. As a result, in 1944, Feng published an article titled "On Emotions" to respond to criticisms from Li Wenxiang and Hu Sheng regarding *A New Treatise on the Way of Life.* He clarified, "In the chapter 'Harmonizing Emotions and Reason' in *A New Treatise on the Way of Life*, my suggestion is to 'have emotions without being burdened by emotions,' not to 'have no emotions.'" He further explained, "My exhortation is to 'have emotions without a strong sense of self,' where to 'have emotions without a strong sense of self' distinguishes between public and private matters ... Having emotions with a strong sense of self pertains to individual likes, dislikes, joys, and sorrows, which are private matters, while having emotions without a strong sense of self pertains to having likes, dislikes, joys, and sorrows for the sake of one's country, society, righteousness, and humanity, which are public matters."

In 1947, Feng went to the United States to teach, and in 1948, he published *A Short History of Chinese Philosophy*. In the chapter on Zhuangzi, while discussing relative happiness, he reiterates the ideas from the 1930s. In the chapter on Wei-Jin Neo-Confucianism, he refers to the concept of sages forgetting emotions as the Principal Emotional School. Most importantly, in Chapter Twenty-Four, titled "New Confucianism: The Beginning of Two Schools," Feng dedicated a section to "Methods of Handling Emotions." In this section, he summarized his discourse on dealing with emotions that he had presented after completing *A Short History of Chinese Philosophy*.

V. Emotion and Non-emotion

Among other issues worth exploring in Feng's discourse are three questions he himself raised regarding the discussion of emotional issues in Chinese philosophy: 1) Is complete non-emotion a desirable and attainable goal? 2) Is complete non-emotion possible? and, 3) What are the differences between Song-Ming Daoism and pre-Qin Daoism in their discussions of this concept?

Regarding the first point, Feng believed that when Daoism speaks of complete non-emotion, it refers to the state of "forgetting emotions," which corresponds to the psychological state of contentment as described by Zhuangzi. According to Cheng Xuanying's* commentary, the term contentment, when broken down into its constituent parts in Chinese, means tranquility and joy. This joy is different from the relative pleasure in contrast to suffering. It is not the turbulent kind of joy, but a calm joy, and this calm, joyful non-emotion is considered good and desirable. This perspective differs from earlier interpretations in which Feng considered Daoism as an emotionless school. According to this interpretation of forgetting emotions, Daoism pursues a state of tranquility and contentment, which, although emotionless, contains a sense of joy. Consequently, it becomes challenging to distinguish this perspective from the joy emphasized in Song-Ming Daosim.

Regarding the second point, Feng believed that from Wang Bi's perspective, complete non-emotion is not possible. Therefore, Wang Bi later advocated for the idea of having emotions without being burdened by them. On the third point, Feng believed that the early Daoist philosophers of the pre-Qin period advocated for complete non-emotion, while Song-Ming Daoist philosophers did not endorse complete non-emotion. They did not consider it desirable or possible to achieve such a state. Therefore, Daoist philosophers shared similarities with Wang Bi, while differing from the early Daoist thinkers of the pre-Qin period. The issue with Feng's argument lies in the fact that in this interpretation, it becomes challenging to distinguish between the spiritual realms of metaphysics and Daoism.

---

* Cheng Xuanying, courtesy name Zishi, was an outstanding Taoist scholar and Taoist theorist during the Tang Dynasty. He is mainly known for his commentaries to the *Tao Te Ching* and the *Zhuangzi*.

Feng's discussion of Daoist thought is insightful, just as his analysis of Neo-Confucianism is insightful. However, when he advocates for the concept of "no feelings and no burdens" in Chinese philosophy, a significant challenge arises. The key issue is that while presenting these ideas in the history of Chinese philosophy, Feng appears to be biased toward sympathy and admiration for the "no feelings and no burdens" perspective. The interpretation of the "no feelings and no burdens" perspective not only fails to distinguish between Daoism, mysticism, and Neo-Confucianism, but it also highlights a significant issue. This perspective largely views emotions as primarily negative emotions (disappointment, anger, suffering). So, the question arises: how should one handle those great, positive emotions? In fact, in "Harmonizing Emotions and Reason" of *A New Treatise on the Way of Life*, Feng notes that some people like strong emotions, while others believe that human emotions can enrich life and that tranquility is too monotonous. At that time, Hu Sheng asked Feng, "Why can't we have deep, profound emotions like 'worrying about the world's worries first and enjoying the world's joys later' or 'a loyal minister in danger sheds tears, and a wicked son falls from grace'?"[23] In response, Feng simply replied, "As for the emotions of worrying and rejoicing for the world, it is precisely 'having emotions without a self.' If there were a self, one would certainly rejoice in the world's joys first and worry about the world's sorrows later."[24] However, what Feng meant by "having emotions without a self" emphasized the absence of self rather than the emphasis on having emotions. His mention of having emotions was simply to emphasize the necessity of not lacking emotions, and it did not imply advocating the active utilization of emotions. Clearly, in this context, Feng was only discussing the aspect of the absence of the small self and did not address the presence of the greater self, leaning toward the absence aspect without giving due consideration to the presence aspect. Therefore, he did not provide an explanation of how to approach positive emotions. In *New Origins of Humanity*, although there is a discussion of the selflessness and the presence of the greater self, it does not mention the states of consciousness as described in *Book of Fixed Nature*.

Because Feng did not include methods from metaphysics and Daoism for managing emotions as a dimension of human life in his discussion of states of consciousness in *New Origins of Humanity*, he faced criticism from Xiong Shili. Feng responded to Xiong's criticism in his book, saying:

> What Xiong describes as "the realm without attributes" is equivalent to what *New Origins of Humanity* refers to as the "same heaven realm." In Xiong's discussion of the "realm without attributes," *New Origins of Humanity* also mentions that "in the same heaven realm, humans possess knowledge yet also lack knowledge." Xiong talks about the "true sovereign," and *New Origins of Humanity* similarly states that "in the realm of heaven and earth, humans are without a self yet also have a self." In the realm of heaven and earth, individuals consciously perceive that their self is the ruler of the universe. Xiong's statement about "not clinging to things and never having grasped" aligns with what *New Origins of Humanity* expresses when it mentions that in the realm of heaven and earth, individuals "act yet do not act." If we carefully examine these passages, it is possible to

> see a convergence in our respective viewpoints, and there are indeed many similarities between our ideas in this regard.[25]

What Xiong Shili described as the "realm without attributes" and "not clinging to things and never having grasped" is indeed consistent with the concepts discussed earlier by Cheng Hao and Wang Yangming, such as "responding to things as they come," "harmonizing emotions with all things without having emotions," and "not attaching to a single thought." It appears that Feng did not explicitly address these points in *New Origins of Humanity.*

Feng's early studies, particularly his research on Daoism and metaphysics (primarily Zhuangzi and Guo Xiang), allowed him to approach the issue of spiritual states from two main angles. One was mysticism, with the theme of the unity of all things at its core, and the other was the management of emotions, with the concept of having emotions without a self as its central idea. His understanding of Song-Ming Daoism was also influenced by these perspectives.

Ten years ago, I published *The Realm of Existence and Non-existence: The Philosophy of Wang Yangming's Spirit,* thinking that I had made significant contributions. Upon recently re-reading the works of Feng Youlan, I have come to realize that many questions were already raised by him years ago, and the issue of "managing emotions" is one of them. Therefore, I have presented Feng's arguments as stated above to highlight the depth of his insights and the significance of his contributions.

Notes

1. *Complete Works of Sansongtang,* vol. 13, 123.
2. Ibid.
3. Ibid., 123.
4. Ibid., 724.
5. Ibid., 725.
6. Ibid., 725.
7. *Complete Works of Sansongtang,* vol. 1, 365.
8. Ibid., 409.
9. Ibid., 569.
10. *Complete Works of Sansongtang,* vol. 11, 81.
11. Ibid., 82.
12. Ibid., 83.
13. Ibid., 84.
14. *A History of Chinese Philosophy,* vol. 2, 607.
15. Ibid., 890.
16. Ibid., 963.
17. Ibid., 966.
18. *Complete Works of Sansongtang,* vol. 4, 454.
19. Ibid., 457.

20. Ibid., 464.
21. Ibid.
22. Ibid., 465.
23. *Complete Works of Sansongtang*, vol. 5, 447.
24. Ibid., 448.
25. *Complete Works of Sansongtang*, vol. 14, 34.

CHAPTER 17

Feng Youlan's Ethics of Realm in *New Origins of Humanity*

Among Feng Youlan's "Six Books of Zhenyuan," the book *New Origins of Humanity* has garnered the most attention. Its main theme revolves around four types of realms, the term Feng uses in this book to refer to the realms of human life. In his later years, he emphasized that the realms he mentioned are essentially spiritual realms. From the perspective of the history of ethics, Western ethics has traditionally not focused on the issue of human spiritual realms or states of consciousness. While there have been individual philosophers in Western philosophical history who have discussed philosophical, spiritual stages related to realms, such as Søren Kierkegaard's aesthetic stage, ethical stage, and religious stage, which can be seen as related to realms, Western philosophy as a whole has not generally considered the issue of states as a part of ethics. Instead, it has primarily been addressed within the context of religious philosophy. Feng's "Six Books of Zhenyuan" began with the construction of the new realism in *New Neo-Confucianism* and concluded with the doctrine of realms in *New Origins of Humanity.* This entire system is grounded in the tradition of Chinese philosophy and has made significant contributions to modern Chinese philosophy.

The discussion of realms of human life also falls under the domain of philosophical inquiry into the nature of human existence. The concept of a philosophy of life has become less commonly discussed in recent times, and it appears that a philosophy of life is no longer considered a distinct or separate field within philosophy. In ancient philosophy, from Aristotle to the Stoics, the study of human life was considered a part of ethics, and discussions related to a philosophy of life were often subsumed under the broader discussions of ancient ethics. However, in modern ethics, the explicit focus on a philosophy of life as a separate subfield has diminished, and it is less commonly discussed in contemporary ethical discourse. In early 20th century China, though, the situation was somewhat different. During that time, the philosophy of life received significant attention, and scholars like Feng Youlan placed a particular emphasis on it. It was, in fact, the topic of Feng's doctoral dissertation in the United States. In his early work, *Philosophy of Life,* he points out that philosophy encompasses three major parts: metaphysics, epistemology, and philosophy of life. The purpose of a philosophy of life is to seek the principles or wisdom regarding human life, and ethics is considered a part of a philosophy of life.

Since the 1990s, many scholars have discussed Feng's return to Neo-Confucianism in his later years. It is worth noting that his late career intellectual development did not lead to a complete return to Neo-Confucianism, especially in the realm of metaphysics. While he did emphasize the fundamental importance of the concepts of the common and the particular (shared and distinct characteristics) in the history of philosophy in his later years, he also incorporated elements of Hegelian and Marxist philosophical thinking about concrete universals. This led to a reconfiguration of his philosophical understanding of the common and the particular and a transformation of the metaphysics within Neo-Confucianism. Indeed, it can be argued that his return to the core of Neo-Confucianism in his later years was primarily centered around his ideas concerning spiritual realms or states of consciousness. One could even say that spiritual realms remained a consistent, fundamental aspect of his thought from his early work to his later years, as is evident in the fact that even when he engaged in a critical reevaluation of his Neo-Confucian system in the 1950s, one of the most perplexing issues for him was the criticism of his doctrine of spiritual realms.[1] Furthermore, in his later years, he not only did not change his doctrine of realms but also deepened his understanding of it in *New Origins of Humanity.*[2]

I. The Beginning of the Doctrine of Realms

New Origins of Humanity is the fourth work of Feng's "Six Books of Zhenyuan." He himself notes that although this book was written after *A New Treatise on Practical Affairs* and *A New Treatise on the Way of Life,* it is actually a continuation of *New Neo-Confucianism,* and readers should first examine that work. This means that although *New Origins of Humanity* was written after *New Neo-Confucianism, A New Treatise on Practical Affairs,* and *A New Treatise on the Way of Life,* its basic ideas had already begun to be introduced in *New Neo-Confucianism.*

In his book *New Neo-Confucianism,* in the last chapter titled "Sage," Feng made a distinction between talented individuals and sages. Talented individuals are those who possess talent and learning, while sages are those who possess complete virtue. He writes:

> The aforementioned psychological state can also be described as a spiritual realm. Those who reach this realm as talented individuals seem to feel that they have transcended experience and themselves. Those who reach this realm are still themselves but have transcended themselves. Although this realm is a form of experience, it has already transcended all ordinary everyday experiences. This kind of spiritual realm exists within

> what is called the realm of the sage. Talented individuals can only reach this realm for a brief moment during their creative process. Talented individuals, while they can enter the realm of the sage, cannot reside there permanently. Although they can experience a certain state within the realm of the sage, they cannot attain the complete realm of the sage. Those who can consistently dwell within the realm of the sage and possess the complete realm of the sage are sages.[3]

Here, the concept of a spiritual realm is introduced, specifically emphasizing that the realm of a sage is one that is beyond experience and beyond oneself. Talented individuals can only occasionally reach this realm within their creative domain, while sages can consistently and continuously reside in this realm.

New Neo-Confucianism also proposes that we should view all things from the perspective of the heavens in order to gain a certain understanding of them. It says:

> Understanding the heavens allows one to view all things from the perspective of the heavens. When you view all things from the perspective of the heavens, you can see that various kinds of things all conform to their own principles. Each principle represents the ultimate goodness, and those who conform to these principles are considered followers of goodness. *The Doctrine of the Mean* says, "All things are nourished together without their injuring one another. The courses of the seasons, and of the sun and moon, are pursued without any collision among them. The smaller energies are like river currents; the greater energies are seen in mighty transformations. It is this which makes heaven and earth so great." This passage reflects the perspective of viewing all things from the standpoint of the heavens. Those who perceive things as harmful to each other are looking at them from the standpoint of one particular thing. If we consider the tiny bacteria that can cause illness from a human perspective, we might say that they harm people. However, when viewed from the perspective of the heavens, these microorganisms are not intentionally causing harm to humans; they are simply seeking to carry out their own existence. When we view things from the perspective of the heavens, we can develop a kind of sympathetic understanding of them.[4]
>
> In social life, the most societal aspect of human behavior is moral conduct. We can have two perspectives on moral conduct: one from the viewpoint of society and the other from the viewpoint of the heavens. When viewed from the societal perspective, moral conduct by individuals is seen as fulfilling their responsibility as a part of society. When viewed from the perspective of the heavens, human moral conduct is considered the fulfillment of their responsibility as a part of the universe, that is, the fulfillment of the Way of Humanity. If viewed from this perspective, human acts of moral conduct are akin to serving heaven. The *Western Inscription* by Zhang Zai emphasizes the way of serving one's parents as a means of serving heaven[5] and adopts the perspective of serving heaven to view human moral conduct.

> When viewing things from the perspective of heaven, there is a compassionate understanding of all things. Within this concept of transcending oneself, the compassion for things continues to expand, eventually reaching what the Neo-Confucian scholars of the Song and Ming dynasties called the realm of the unity of all things. Neo-Confucian scholars referred to this realm as benevolence.[6]
>
> In the state of transcending oneself, one perceives no separation or boundaries between oneself and the greater whole. The self becomes indistinguishable from the greater whole, and the greater whole becomes one with the self. This is what is meant by being in perfect harmony with all things, and it corresponds to the concept of great benevolence mentioned earlier.[7]

The state of transcending oneself and merging with the greater whole, as described here, corresponds to the concept of the realm of heaven and earth mentioned in *New Origins of Humanity*. This suggests that while the concept of the realm of heaven and earth may not have been explicitly introduced in *New Neo-Confucianism*, it was implicitly addressed within the philosophy. In fact, the realm of heaven and earth is a key and innovative aspect of Feng's theory of realms. The primary significance of the four realms theory is not just to distinguish between the utilitarian realm and the moral realm, but to introduce the concept that above the moral realm, there exists the realm of heaven and earth.

It should be noted that this concept is closely related to Feng's understanding of Daoism. In the following section, "The Chaos of Daoism," he states:

> In regarding all things without making distinctions, without making judgments, without speaking, all distinctions, as far as we are concerned, cease to exist. What we perceive is simply the great whole, completely unified and undifferentiated. The statement, "Departing from form, departing from wisdom, and merging with the great unity" (from *Zhuangzi · Great and Most Honored Master*), describes this state. The terms profound unity and chaotic unity both refer to this state. Those who can attain this state are what we call true individuals or perfected individuals.[8]

Feng further points out:

> People who follow Daoism often compare themselves to infants, as infants are only capable of sensing but not thinking. This view is fundamentally mistaken. The essential difference between the state of attainment in Daoist cultivation and the inherent state of animals lies in the presence or absence of self-awareness. The ultimate individuals in Daoism, when they reach the state of being aware of the complete and undifferentiated whole, are aware of their own awareness of the complete and undifferentiated whole. In contrast, animals, although they exist within the complete and undifferentiated whole, do

> not have this awareness, or they may not be aware of their own awareness. The distinction between having self-awareness and lacking self-awareness is significant.[9]
>
> Using Daoist methods, we can also attain a state beyond ourselves. The passage from *Zhuangzi*, specifically the "Interactions with the Spirit of Heaven and Earth" mentioned in the "Heaven and Earth" chapter, describes this state.[10]

The state of attainment described in Daoist cultivation methods aligns with what is referred to as the realm of heaven and earth in *New Origins of Humanity.* This perspective on such a realm is in line with Feng's own efforts, starting from his earlier work, *A Certain View of Life*, to "reserve a territory for mysticism." Understanding the Daoist realm played a significant role as a foundational concept for his exploration of mysticism and metaphysical philosophy.

In the earlier work, *Philosophy of Life*, in the second chapter titled "The Romantic Daoists," specifically in the seventh section titled "The Unity of All Things," Feng stated, "If it is so, then all things and I are blended together and become one. The use of the term 'blended together' here is marvelous, for this 'becoming one' is achieved by blending without differentiation." What Guo Xiang referred to as "blending with things" aligns with this understanding. At this state, one can "ride the regularity of heaven and earth and govern the distinctions of the six breaths to roam endlessly." This statement lacks any sense of mysticism, as it is a natural consequence of harmonizing with the way of all things.[11] After 1927, Feng no longer considered the concept of the unity of all things to be distinct from mysticism. Instead, he believed that the unity of all things itself constituted mysticism. He stated, "In short, all the philosophers of the Song and Ming dynasties regarded a realm characterized by a kind of mysticism as the highest state."[12] During this period, his essay "The Primary Contributions of Chinese Philosophy" also explicitly emphasized the importance of the concept of realm in Chinese philosophy.

Later in *New Origins of Humanity*, he mentioned, "In Chapter Seven, I will discuss the realm of being of the same nature as heaven. In the realm of being of the same nature as heaven, individuals are in harmony with the great whole. The great whole is unimaginable and beyond comprehension. All the experiences that individuals have in the realm of being of the same nature as heaven are commonly referred to as mystical experiences."[13]

It can be said that Feng's understanding of mystical realms guided him to formulate the theory of the four realms based on the mystical realm and formed the foundation of his fundamental understanding of the philosophical function.

Regarding his theory of realms, he once reflected after the establishment of the People's Republic of China, saying:

> In the preface to *A Comparative Study of Life Ideals*, I mentioned that the role of philosophy is to establish an ideal life as a standard to guide and critique actual life. Therefore, philosophy is synonymous with the ideal of life. My perspective on philosophy has not changed significantly over time, but the way I express it has evolved. In later discussions,

> I often emphasized that philosophy may not provide individuals with concrete, practical knowledge, but it can elevate one's realm or state of being.
>
> In *New Neo-Confucianism*, the discourse begins with the concept of the limitless and the supreme ultimate, and in the final chapter, it discusses the sage. It suggests that the reason a sage is considered a sage does not primarily lie in possessing an abundance of practical knowledge, but rather in having a profoundly elevated spiritual state or realm. Subsequently, there is *New Origins of Humanity*, which specifically delves into the concept of realms, and *A New Treatise on the Nature of Dao*, which introduces the idea of being "extremely brilliant while following the Doctrine of the Mean," providing historical foundations for the theory of realms presented in *New Origins of Humanity*. In summary, the theory of realms is indeed at the core of New Neo-Confucianism's philosophical thought.[14]

New Origins of Humanity discusses the concept of realms primarily in the context of an individual's spiritual and mental state, focusing more on the inner world, consciousness, and the spiritual aspect rather than behavior. This emphasis on the inner realm is distinct from many Western ethical theories, which often prioritize external actions and behaviors. Indeed, the emphasis on the inner world, consciousness, and spiritual states is a distinctive feature of ancient Chinese philosophical thought. Within the three major traditions of ancient Chinese thought—Buddhism, Daoism, and Confucianism—there is a shared pursuit of different forms of spiritual and mental realms. Buddhism seeks enlightenment and liberation through awakening to a particular state of consciousness, Daoism seeks a state of spiritual freedom, and Confucianism, especially in the Song and Ming dynasties, aims for the attainment of sagehood and excellence, which are also forms of elevated spiritual realms. Throughout Chinese history, these three traditions have emphasized the cultivation of certain spiritual states through various practices and disciplines. The theory of realms presented in *New Origins of Humanity* builds upon the foundation laid in *New Neo-Confucianism* and reflects Feng's evolving understanding of Chinese philosophy. It indeed differs from the concept of realms he discussed in earlier works like *Philosophy of Life*.

While *New Origins of Humanity* primarily focuses on concepts related to life and spiritual realms that are distinct from Western ethics, it does touch upon utilitarian realms, which can be compared to Western utilitarian ethical theories advocated by thinkers like Jeremy Bentham and John Stuart Mill. So, while it is distinct in its primary focus on spiritual and mental realms, there are elements within the text that can be related to Western ethical thought, particularly in terms of utilitarianism. In *New Origins of Humanity*, the discussion of the moral realm is influenced by Kantian ethics, particularly in terms of the ethics of intention or the ethics of good will. However, it is important to note that the chapters related to the natural realm and the realm of heaven and earth do not have direct parallels in Western ethics. The realm of heaven and earth, with its mystical aspects, does not fit within the framework of Western ethics but aligns more with themes found in religious studies and mysticism. Indeed, the concept of the natural realm in *New*

Origins of Humanity is more closely related to Chinese Daoist philosophy rather than Western naturalism or naturalistic ethics.

II. Meaning and Understanding

At the beginning of *New Origins of Humanity*, Feng raises the question of meaning, saying:

> The meaning of a thing arises only when there is someone who understands it. Without someone who understands it, a thing may have properties, potential, and so on, but it lacks meaning. We can say that the meaning of a thing arises from a person's understanding of that thing. Since people have varying levels of understanding about a thing, the thing has different meanings for them.[15]

This implies that the nature of things is objective, inherent in the things themselves, or one could say, it exists within the things, and meaning is the result of a person's understanding of things, which is essentially a form of cognition. This kind of cognition does not refer to scientific knowledge about things but rather the understanding of the significance of things for people. Things can also be something in which people are actively engaged, not just static external objects.

Feng then proceeds to raise the question of understanding and consciousness, saying:

> To understand is to comprehend, as we have discussed in the previous text. Consciousness is self-awareness. When a person does something and understands how it is done, that is understanding, and that is comprehension. When they are doing something and are aware that they are doing it, that is self-awareness, or consciousness. If you were to ask, "What kind of thing is a person?" you could say, "A person is something with understanding and consciousness, or something with a higher degree of understanding and consciousness." If you were to ask, "What is life?" you could say, "Life is a form of existence with understanding and consciousness, or a form of existence with a higher degree of understanding and consciousness." This is what sets humans apart from animals and distinguishes human life from the lives of other animals.[16]

Feng distinguishes between understanding and consciousness, noting that understanding is comprehension, and consciousness is self-awareness. When combined, they are referred to as understanding and consciousness. Understanding involves comprehending meaning, while consciousness is a state of awareness, the subject's self-awareness of their actions. Expanding on this, we can view understanding and consciousness as states of the mind. As Feng suggests, "The reason people can have understanding and consciousness is that people have a mind. People have a mind, and the elements of the mind … in the terminology commonly used by Chinese philosophers, are referred to as knowledge, perception, and spiritual clarity."[17] When examined through the lenses of self-awareness and spiritual clarity, understanding and consciousness clearly possess rational connotations.

According to Feng's philosophy, strictly speaking, various realms are distinct levels of self-awareness in consciousness. Therefore, it can be said that realms refer to states of the mind. This is indeed different from the meaning of realms as discussed in ancient Buddhist traditions, particularly in the context of the Huayan school, where realms refer to the phenomenal aspects of reality. The concept of understanding and consciousness was not explicitly introduced in *New Neo-Confucianism* but was developed and emphasized by Feng in *New Origins of Humanity* as a foundational element of the theory of realms.

> Any action that can be called a moral action must also be an action with understanding and consciousness. Actions without understanding and consciousness, even if they align with moral principles, are not strictly considered moral actions.[18]
>
> The relationship between ruler and subject is an action with understanding and consciousness. When engaging in such behavior, one can clearly understand what their actions entail and is also self-aware that they are engaged in such behavior. By contrast, the hierarchical structure among bees and ants represents behavior without understanding and consciousness. Actions without understanding and consciousness cannot be considered moral. For instance, in the case of ants going to war, each ant acts for its colony, often selflessly. At first glance, there may not seem to be much difference between people organizing armies and fighting for their countries with great dedication and ants going to war selflessly. However, human warfare involves actions with understanding and consciousness. Advancing in the midst of gunfire and danger is something humans do with clear self-awareness and understanding. Soldiers who act selflessly and bravely, even risking their lives, can indeed exhibit moral behavior, and understanding and consciousness are essential prerequisites for this. In the case of ants going to war, while they may act selflessly, their behavior is instinctual and lacks understanding and consciousness. Therefore, strictly speaking, their behavior cannot be considered moral.[19]

Understanding and consciousness serve as the sole criterion for evaluating realms. The concept of realms is used to determine the nature and degree of understanding and consciousness. As mentioned, behavior that aligns with morality but lacks inner moral understanding and consciousness cannot be termed as moral behavior. A more detailed explanation of this is provided in the subsequent discussion on moral realms. When viewed in the context of understanding and consciousness relative to instinct, it should be noted that understanding and consciousness, as forms of self-awareness, belong to the realm of reason rather than instinct or immediate intuition.

> Some things do not necessarily have a mind, but all things have characteristics or nature. The nature of a certain category of things distinguishes it from other categories of things. Human nature, for instance, is what makes humans distinct from animals. Things without

> a mind or understanding do have their nature, but they are not aware of it themselves. Humans, on the other hand, have understanding and consciousness, which not only allow them to understand the nature of other things but also, when their understanding and consciousness are fully developed, enable them to be self-aware of their own nature and what makes them human, distinguishing them from animals. The full development of the mind's understanding and spiritual clarity is referred to as completing the heart. When the heart is fully developed, one understands their nature. As Mencius said, "He who fully completes his heart knows his nature. Knowing his nature, he knows heaven." Regarding knowledge of heaven, there is a more detailed discussion in Chapter Seven, but for now, it is important to note that when people understand their nature, they strive to fully actualize this nature. To fully realize one's nature is to complete one's nature. As mentioned earlier, what distinguishes humans from animals is their higher level of understanding and spiritual clarity. Having a higher level of understanding and spiritual clarity is part of human nature. Therefore, when a person's understanding and spiritual clarity develop to the point of understanding their nature, it signifies a higher level of self-awareness, as mentioned in the previous chapter. Because understanding one's nature is essentially self-awareness of understanding and spiritual clarity, it can also be seen as self-understanding through consciousness. As a person's understanding and spiritual clarity develop further, their nature becomes more fully realized. Therefore, completing the heart is synonymous with completing one's nature.[20]

This concept involves the notion of nature. The nature of a thing is its intrinsic essence, its inherent characteristics that define its essence, and it is the distinguishing characteristic that sets it apart from other types of things. Human nature is what makes a human distinct from animals. Things possess nature but cannot be self-aware of their nature, and of course, they lack consciousness. Humans, however, have a heart with understanding and spiritual clarity, which enables them to be self-aware of their nature. When humans develop their understanding and spiritual clarity, it is called completing the heart, and when they make efforts to fully realize their nature, it is called completing their nature. Human beings possess understanding and spiritual clarity, which entails self-awareness. Self-awareness of understanding and spiritual clarity is referred to as knowing one's nature. Understanding and spiritual clarity enable people to have self-awareness, and knowing one's nature represents self-awareness and understanding at a higher level, often referred to as a higher level of consciousness. However, it appears that in this context, Feng considers humans to have two aspects of nature: one related to self-awareness and spiritual clarity, as indicated by the statement "having a higher level of understanding and spiritual clarity is part of human nature," and the other being the nature that distinguishes humans from other beings. He does not seem to differentiate between self-awareness of understanding and spiritual clarity and self-awareness of the nature that makes humans distinct from other creatures; instead, he regards both as knowing one's nature. The relationship between completing the heart, knowing one's nature, and completing one's nature can be understood as follows: completing the heart is the prerequisite; when you have fully developed your heart, you can come to know and understand your nature. Once you understand your nature, you can strive to fully realize it, which is completing your nature. In other words, completing your nature enables knowing your nature, and knowing your nature leads to the pursuit of completing it.

> Humans not only have understanding and consciousness but can also understand what understanding and consciousness are and be self-aware of their understanding and consciousness. For example, as we discuss understanding and consciousness now, we understand what understanding and consciousness are, and while discussing understanding and consciousness, we are also self-aware of our own understanding and consciousness. When philosophers like Guishan* and Zhu Xi discuss knowledge and understanding, they are also engaging in self-awareness of their own understanding and consciousness. This represents a higher level of understanding and consciousness, which is not possessed by everyone.
>
> To strive for the completion of one's heart and nature, a person needs to develop the understanding and spiritual clarity of their heart. To seek the development of understanding and spiritual clarity, one must cultivate understanding and consciousness and strive for a higher level of it, as discussed in the previous chapter. As mentioned, having understanding and consciousness is akin to enlightenment, while lacking understanding and consciousness is akin to ignorance. However, if one only has understanding and consciousness without a higher level of understanding consciousness, their enlightenment is still within the realm of ignorance, similar to a person dreaming within a dream.[21]

According to this perspective, being self-aware of one's understanding and consciousness represents a higher level of understanding and consciousness that is not easily attainable by everyone. Feng Youlan does not explicitly provide a detailed explanation in *New Origins of Humanity* regarding why he introduces the concept of being self-aware of one's understanding and consciousness or how it leads to a higher level of understanding and consciousness. The concept of self-awareness of one's understanding and consciousness can indeed be seen as a form of reflection on understanding and consciousness and represents a philosophical comprehension of understanding and consciousness. During this period, Feng may not have explicitly articulated the idea that philosophy is the reflection of the spirit.

> Many people suggest that by striving to fulfill one's heart and nature, individuals can attain a certain state or level of happiness. Daoist philosophers, for example, often advise people to seek happiness in simplicity and contentment, as reflected in the saying, "Seek happiness in the simplicity of life; what else do you need to be happy?" Wang

* Yang Shi (1053–1135) was a Chinese historian and scholar of the Song Dynasty, also known as Guishan.

> Gen composed a song about learning and music, which says, "Joy comes from delight in learning, and learning comes from the delight in joy. Without joy, there is no learning, and without learning, there is no joy." Learning here refers to the study of sages and sages' teachings, and joy refers to the delight derived from the wisdom of sages. Wholeheartedly dedicating oneself to both learning and living in accordance with one's true nature can lead to a specific state of being. In this state, people can experience a unique kind of happiness, which is what will be discussed in the next chapter. Within this state of being, individuals can indeed find a form of joy, and this is something that we acknowledge.[22]

Based on the Confucian concept of seeking joy in studying the wisdom of Confucius and Yan Hui in Song-Ming Neo-Confucianism, Feng provided a new explanation in his theory of realms. He acknowledged that attaining a high realm can bring a certain kind of happiness to people. However, he also pointed out that pursuing happiness as the sole objective is a lower level of realms and not the essence of the study of sages. He writes:

> It can be said that those who seek joy in the wisdom of Confucius and Yan Hui pursue a kind of happiness that differs in nature from the happiness sought by ordinary people. There are higher and lower levels of happiness, which cannot be equated or compared in the same way. In this regard, we discuss the differences in the nature of happiness in more detail in Chapter Five. Even if there are differences in the nature of happiness, those who seek happiness are typically seeking "my own" happiness. Those who aim to seek their own happiness, regardless of the noble nature of the happiness they seek, are operating within the framework of what will be discussed in the next chapter as the utilitarian realm. The utilitarian realm is not the highest level of realms; those who have not reached the highest realm cannot be said to have fully achieved fulfilling both heart and nature. A sage does not pursue their own happiness as their goal. Of course, within their realm, they experience a profound sense of joy. However, this kind of happiness arises naturally within the sage's realm, and it is not something they actively seek. When a person reaches this state of being, they naturally experience this kind of happiness. However, if they exclusively seek this kind of happiness as their goal, they will never be able to attain this state.[23]

Feng believed that states of being are subjective states, and the pursuit of personal happiness, regardless of how noble that happiness may be, falls under the category of utilitarian realm. The happiness that comes from the state of a sage is not pursued by the sage but comes naturally. Therefore, it can be seen that understanding and consciousness not only involve rationality, but also encompass one's attitude towards life. For instance, the state of seeking the happiness of Confucius and Yan Hui represents a higher level of spirituality than mere rationality.

III. Overview of the Four Realms

On this basis, Feng proposed four realms, from low to high, stating:

> Realms have highs and lows. The distinction between high and low is based on the amount of understanding and consciousness a person needs to reach a certain realm. Those requiring greater understanding and consciousness have higher realms, and those requiring less understanding and consciousness have lower realms. The natural realm requires the least understanding and consciousness, making it the lowest. The utilitarian realm is higher than the natural realm, but lower than the moral realm. The moral realm is higher than the utilitarian realm, but lower than the realm of heaven and earth. The realm of heaven and earth requires the most profound understanding and consciousness, thus making it the highest realm. At this level of understanding, human insight has developed to its highest degree. Those who attain this realm are called sages.[24]

The differentiation of human realms into high and low is the fundamental viewpoint of *New Origins of Humanity.* The height of these realms depends on the degree of understanding and consciousness, with realms requiring more understanding and consciousness being higher than those requiring less. The four realms are ranked from lowest to highest, the lowest being the natural realm, higher than the natural realm is the utilitarian realm, higher than the utilitarian realm is the moral realm, and the highest realm is the realm of heaven and earth.

Among the four realms, the first one is the natural realm. He explains:

> The characteristic of the natural realm is that people in it act in accordance with their innate talents or acquired abilities. . . . What we mean by acting in accordance with talents is essentially what is commonly referred to as following one's nature. In the previous chapter, we referred to logical nature as nature and biological nature as talent. What is commonly referred to as following one's nature corresponds to a person's biological nature. We do not use the term "nature"; instead, we use "following one's talent." As for following one's talent, it can refer to an individual's personal habits or the customs of a society. In this realm, individuals act in accordance with their talents, doing what they must do and stopping where they must stop, or they act in accordance with their habits, acting according to established practice. Regardless of whether they act in accordance with their talents or habits, they do not have a clear understanding of the nature of their actions. This means that the things they do lack a clear meaning for them. In this respect, their realm appears to be a state of chaos. However, it does not mean that they have no understanding of anything, nor does it mean that everything has no clear meaning for them. Therefore, their realm seems to be only like a state of chaos.[25]

To follow one's talent is to follow one's inherent nature, and to follow one's habit is to follow one's accustomed ways. Feng's explanation here seems to have some contradictions. On one hand, his definition of the natural realm implies a state of chaos, where nothing is clear and nothing is understood. On the other hand, he also says that people in the natural realm are not without understanding of anything, and not everything is without clear meaning for them. He goes on to say,

> "People with this kind of realm are not limited to those in so-called primitive societies. Even in the most industrialized societies today, there are many people with this kind of realm. While they may not be engaged in 'working from sunrise to sunset,' 'digging wells for water,' or 'cultivating fields for food,' they are still 'unaware and unknowing, following the ways of the world.'"[26]

From a perspective that seeks to unify history and logic, the lowest realm should theoretically belong to people in primitive societies. However, because he also mentions that individuals in the natural realm are "not without understanding of anything, and not everything is without clear meaning for them," he suggests that people in the natural realm are not limited to those in primitive societies. In fact, there are many individuals in highly industrialized societies today who also belong to this kind of realm. In this regard, he seems to equate the realm of people in primitive societies with that of most individuals in modern societies, considering them all to be in the natural realm. This interpretation may indeed have some issues, and it is worth further analysis, as discussed later.

The second is the utilitarian realm, which he describes as:

> The characteristic of the utilitarian realm is that people in this realm act for profit. What is meant by for profit is acting for one's own benefit. The behavior of all animals is for their own benefit. However, most animal behaviors, even though they are for their own benefit, are driven by instinct rather than conscious planning. In the natural realm, people also engage in actions for their own benefit, but they do not have a clear understanding of themselves and benefit. They are not aware of having such behavior, nor do they understand why they behave in this way. In the utilitarian realm, people have a clear understanding of themselves and benefit. They understand their actions and how they work. They are aware of having such behavior. Their actions may involve seeking to increase their own wealth, develop their own career, or enhance their own honor. When engaged in such behaviors, they understand what these actions entail and are conscious of having such behaviors.[27]

In this explanation, people in the natural realm seem to act on instinct, much like animals, without conscious planning. The utilitarian realm involves people consciously pursuing fame and profit. In reality, people are not entirely unaware of their pursuit of fame or profit. Because Feng described the utilitarian realm as the pursuit of one's own interests, it could be viewed as the self-interest realm or private interest realm. In his subsequent definition, the utilitarian realm represents not only the pursuit of self-interest but also a certain understanding of individual and societal relationships, namely that individuals and society are in opposition. This falls within the realm of individualism. It may not be necessary to place the understanding of individual and societal relationships within the utilitarian realm, as it might create a sense of disconnection. Values and realms should indeed be distinguished from one another.

The third is the moral realm. Feng describes it as:

> The characteristic of the moral realm is that a person's behavior in this realm is righteous conduct. Righteousness and self-interest are both opposed and complementary. When one's actions seek personal gain, it is an action for personal gain. When one's actions seek the benefit of society, it is righteous conduct.
>
> In this realm, individuals have a realization of human nature. They understand that human nature encompasses elements of society, social systems, and the moral and political rules within them. They perceive these as mechanisms for sanctioning individuals. In the realm of utilitarianism, most people tend to believe that society and the individual are in opposition. Regarding individuals, society is often seen as a "necessary evil." People are aware that society can be oppressive to the individual, but in order to preserve their own existence, they cannot do without it. In the moral realm, people understand that one must consider the whole in dealing with others in order to develop according to their nature. Society and the individual are not necessarily in opposition. The notion of individuals existing independently outside of society is a speculative concept held by some philosophers.
>
> Not only must people exist within society, but they must also be within society to achieve completeness. Society is a whole, and individuals are a part of that whole. When a part is separated from the whole, it ceases to be a true part. The systems, moral principles, and political rules within society are not necessarily oppressive to individuals. These elements are part of the principles that make individuals human and are expected within the human condition. Individuals must exist within the systems, political forms, and moral rules of society in order to develop what they have acquired as part of the essence of being human.[28]

It is evident that Feng's description of the characteristics of the moral realm has two key points. One is that the actor subjectively and consciously practices righteousness, which means acting in accordance with moral values and seeking the benefit of society. The other point is that the actor can correctly understand the relationship between the individual and society. They know that a part cannot exist separately from the whole, that an individual cannot exist independently of the societal whole, and that individuals must develop and thrive within society.

The fourth is the realm of heaven and earth, of which he says:

> The characteristic of the realm of heaven and earth is that, in this state, a person's behavior is serving the greater good or serving the heavens. In this state of the realm of heaven and earth, individuals understand not only the entirety of society, but also the totality of the universe. It is only when one comprehends the full scope of the universe that they can fully develop what they have acquired as part of the essence of being human and realize their true nature. In this realm, individuals possess a higher level of complete awareness. This means that they have fully understood their own nature because they have come to know the heavens. They understand the heavens, and therefore, they know that humans are not only a part of the whole of society but also a part of the whole of the universe. Not only should individuals contribute to society, but they should also contribute to the universe.[29]

The characteristics of the realm of heaven and earth also have two key points. One is that the actor subjectively serves the greater good or serves the heavens, viewing issues from the perspective of the universe. The other is that, based on an understanding of the relationship between the individual and society as a whole, they can also comprehend the relationship between the individual and the entirety of the universe. Individuals can truly achieve the fullest understanding of their own nature when they attain a comprehensive understanding of the entirety of the universe.

Feng emphasizes that behavior and realms are distinct, with realms being delineated not by external actions but by internal understanding and consciousness. He writes:

> Among these four realms, the distinction between the utilitarian realm and the natural realm, as well as the distinction between them and the moral realm, is the most easily discernible. The distinction between the moral realm and the realm of heaven and earth, as well as the distinction between the natural realm and the moral realm and the realm of heaven and earth, may not be as readily apparent. This is because, at times, when one lacks a sense of self, it may appear as if there is no self or a larger self. The concept of no self can sometimes appear as if it is synonymous with a greater no self. The natural realm and the realm of heaven and earth may also seem somewhat chaotic. While there is clarity in distinguishing between the moral realm and the realm of heaven and earth, the differentiation between the natural realm and the realm of heaven and earth is often less clear in the perspective of Daoism. The Confucian perspective often provides clarity in distinguishing between the natural realm and the moral realm. However, they may have difficulty in differentiating between the moral realm and the realm of heaven and earth.[30]

According to Feng's later statement, the natural realm is the original chaos, and the realm of heaven and earth is the chaos that comes afterward. However, for Confucianism, the highest realm is the unity of heaven and humanity or the unity of all things, not chaos. For Confucianism, especially for Neo-Confucian scholars, the distinction between the moral realm and the realm of unity with all things is clear. Ultimately, Feng suggests that a person's realm of being is not the same as what they do. He says, "Although one exists within the realm of heaven and earth, the things one does are also the same as what ordinary people do in their daily lives." He goes on, "People in different realms of being can do the same things, and even when they do the same things, the meaning of those same things can be vastly different for them. These various differences in meaning constitute their different realms of being."[31] This illustrates that the differences in a person's realm of being cannot be reflected solely in their actions. People in different realms of being may engage in similar actions. Therefore, the distinctions in a person's realm of being are not observed through their behavior, but rather through their inner selves. This differs from the focus on behavior in modern ethics. Feng's theory of realms emphasizes the division between the mind and its thoughts, as well as the division between the mind and its actions. It places the mind at the forefront and follows a form of idealism (though it should be noted that this form of idealism is different from the usual understanding of idealism), rather than focusing primarily on external actions or utilitarianism. The evaluation of a person is based on their realm of mind rather than their actions. This is determined by the core ideas of *New Origins of Humanity*. We believe that if the system could move toward unity of mind and actions, it would represent a further development in philosophy.

IV. Reflection on the Natural Realm

Here, I will offer some thoughts on Feng's four realms of being, with the aim of further advancing the analysis of the philosophy of realms of being based on his theory. I will start with the natural realm. Feng says:

> In the previous chapter, we mentioned that in the natural environment, people's behavior is in accordance with their talents or habits. This is often the case for primitive people in their way of life. Children and foolish individuals also often behave in this manner. So, the realm of children and foolish individuals is also often in line with the natural environment. Because primitive people, children, and foolish individuals often exist in a natural realm, when we speak of the natural environment, we often use their realms as examples. In Daoism, when discussing the situations of people during the time of the Yellow Emperor and Shen Nong, they often mention infants, babies, and foolish individuals. When talking about these types of people, the focus is not on the individuals themselves, but on the realms they represent within the context of common situations.[32]

According to what is said here, the typical natural realm refers to the realm of primitive people, children, and foolish individuals. Such a realm should have the lowest level of consciousness, almost close to none.

The individuals mentioned, "with little knowledge and few desires" and "neither clinging nor observing," have realms that seem to resemble chaos.

The pre-Qin Daoist concept of "pure and simple" or "unadorned" sometimes refers to the life of people in primitive societies and at other times to the individual's state resembling chaos. They aim to encourage people to return to simplicity and embrace the unadorned.[33]

The pre-Qin Daoists praised chaos ... They praised simplicity; they praised the lives of people in primitive societies, infants, and foolish individuals. In our terms, they praised the natural realm.[34]

This lowest level of understanding and consciousness is characterized by limited knowledge or ignorance, a lack of attachment and observation, simplicity, and chaos. On the other hand, Feng also uses the terms "in accordance with talent" and "in accordance with habit" to describe the natural realm. It should be noted that these are two different states of consciousness with distinct qualities. If we say that the natural realm is a realm of understanding and consciousness close to that of ignorant individuals or children, then it may not be necessary to consider such a realm as one of the spiritual realms in life, because discussions about realms of being are often aimed at elevating the spiritual realms of ordinary individuals, and Feng's description of the natural realm of ignorant individuals and children is indeed lower than that of ordinary individuals. Considering it as the lowest realm only has logical significance and may not have practical relevance in the context of enhancing one's spiritual realm. Especially when referring to this realm of ignorance and childlikeness as the natural realm, it may not be entirely appropriate. In its direct sense, "natural" should indeed refer to ordinary people, and another meaning of "natural" should be the natural attitude towards life, which Daoists praised. Feng's statements could potentially lead to a misunderstanding, where Daoism's natural attitude toward life is conflated with the realm of ignorance and childlikeness. This would be inappropriate because Daoism's natural attitude toward life is already a form of transcendent naturalness, meaning it goes beyond one's immediate, mundane reality.

In the realm of unity with the heavens, the realm appears to resemble the natural realm. Daoism may not always make a clear distinction in this regard."[35]

While the realms of primitive people, children, and foolish individuals often align with the natural realm, not all instances of the natural realm necessarily involve these specific types of individuals. In any society, among people of any age, and with varying levels of intelligence, including those determined by intelligence tests, their realms can potentially be considered as the natural realm. For example, in American society, which is highly industrialized, there are individuals who, following legal and cultural norms, live their lives routinely. They pay taxes, work in factories, receive wages, and may be considered as "not knowing the working of heaven, but aware of the power of the emperor." These

> individuals are not necessarily children and may not all have low intelligence. They live in a highly modernized environment, yet their realm can still be considered a natural realm.[36]

The majority of people in modern American society who follow legal norms and pay taxes should not be equated with the lowest realms resembling primitive people, fools, or children. In fact, even primitive people have a survival instinct. In history, even in the most secluded rural settings, people have a consciousness of providing for themselves and their families, which indicates a level of purposeful awareness. The idea of making a living and providing for one's family is a common utilitarian mindset among ordinary people in China, and it shows that utilitarian consciousness is not inherently negative or devoid of awareness. Even in traditional societies, ordinary farmers often have a strong sense of filial piety and are influenced by the moral and cultural values of their society. It is unlikely that their lives are completely devoid of awareness or guided solely by a state of chaos. In modern society, this is even more apparent. Modern society's workers are not only influenced by social culture but may also have class consciousness. Any culture transcends the natural state. So, apart from individuals with severe cognitive impairments and infants younger than a year old, there are no people who are not influenced by social culture. Such individuals are unlikely to be completely devoid of self-awareness, and their ream is not likely to align with Feng's concept of the natural realm. He writes:

> Mencius said, "To act with benevolence and righteousness is not to act benevolently and righteously." Acting with benevolence and righteousness certainly involves acting in accordance with benevolence and righteousness, but it is not just about acting in accordance with them. When one acts in accordance with benevolence and righteousness, the individual not only acts in alignment with these principles, but also has an understanding of benevolence and righteousness and is aware that they are acting in accordance with them. This is acting in accordance with benevolence and righteousness with awareness. Acting in accordance with benevolence and righteousness with awareness is called acting benevolently and righteously. If someone acts in accordance with benevolence and righteousness but has no understanding of them and is not aware that they are acting in accordance with these principles, then even though they act in accordance with benevolence and righteousness, it cannot be said that they are acting benevolently and righteously. Instead, it can be described as acting through benevolence and righteousness. No one's behavior can be entirely devoid of benevolence and righteousness. This means that the actions of all individuals align with benevolence and righteousness to some extent. However, for some individuals, their alignment with benevolence and righteousness is merely a matter of following their natural inclinations or learned habits, so they are merely acting through benevolence and righteousness rather than truly acting benevolently and righteously. This is what is meant by, "The people can be made to follow, but they cannot be made to understand." In other words, most people

> adhere to morality without fully understanding it. When it comes to following without understanding, their realm can also be considered as the natural realm.[37]

Feng's interpretation in this context appears to have reversed Mencius' words.[38] In fact, what Mencius meant by acting with benevolence and righteousness is different from the "following" mentioned in the *Analects*. Mencius was referring to actively and consciously acting in accordance with the inner drive of benevolence and righteousness, whereas acting benevolently and righteously implies acting without conscious awareness but in alignment with benevolence and righteousness. The distinction made by Feng, namely between conscious adherence and unconscious adherence, is indeed valid. However, unconsciously following moral rules should refer to many who involuntarily adhere to moral rules, reluctantly conforming to ethical principles through selective behavior. The state of such individuals is by no means a natural state. Even individuals with the highest intelligence can have a realm that is considered a natural realm.[39]

Tang Junyi's *Nine Realms of Life* discusses realms that encompass a synthesis of cognition, morality, and religious realms, while Feng excludes the conscious realm of intellectual activity and focuses solely on the understanding of life. Consequently, individuals with the highest intelligence may be assigned to the lowest realm. This clearly has its irrational aspects and must involve certain issues. We believe that individuals with the highest intelligence cannot possibly have the same lowest level of the spiritual realm as fools or children. Feng writes:

> In the previous passage, we stated, "Regardless of who they are, their behavior must conform to moral laws to some extent, but they may only do so without knowing it. Some people are what we call 'born with innate goodness.' Many biographies, inscriptions, and tombstones of individuals describe them as 'naturally filial and friendly,' or, 'innately filial and friendly.'" For some individuals, these words may indeed be mere compliments, but it cannot be said that in reality there are absolutely no such people. For example, as Han Feizi stated, "self-straightening arrows" and "self-circularizing wood," although rare, cannot be claimed to be completely nonexistent. Such individuals naturally follow their innate inclinations, which align well with certain moral principles, and in some cases, may even exceed the standards set by those moral principles. While this is the case, these individuals may not necessarily understand the significance of certain moral principles, nor are they consciously aware that their behavior conforms to or even surpasses certain moral standards. We refer to this type of behavior as spontaneous adherence to moral standards. In and of itself, this behavior is a natural product. Regarding the realm or state of those who exhibit such behavior in this aspect, their realm is a natural realm.[40]

With a naturally sincere, spontaneous adherence to moral principles, in Feng's classification, they are also considered to belong to the natural realm, which is seen as the lowest realm, similar to children and fools. This, however, may be deemed unreasonable. In reality, while children and fools may not have highly developed intellects, their self-preservation instincts are quite direct, and not all of their behavior naturally conforms to moral rules. Indeed, individuals with a sincere, virtuous disposition do not need to exert conscious effort to have their behavior naturally conform to moral standards. In terms of not requiring conscious cultivation, it can be considered natural and unforced. However, this realm of being is distinct from that of children and fools. Feng observes:

> Moral behavior, as well as achievements in art, scholarship, and accomplishments in various fields, strictly speaking, all stem from the creativity of the mind. Great achievements in art, scholarship, and accomplishments in other fields are not solely dependent on the author's natural talents. The author's realm may indeed be a natural one, but their creative activities cannot be solely the product of nature. Authors rely on their interests to create, and during the creative process, they may not be consciously aware of their genius or the value of their creations. They can have many great creations, but they may not consciously perceive their creations as such or be aware of their greatness. From this perspective, their creativity is natural, as it flows effortlessly without self-awareness.[41]

This also means that individuals in the natural realm can achieve significant success in various aspects, such as art, scholarship, and even morality. Conversely, individuals with great achievements in areas like art and scholarship may belong to the lowest realm, and even those who excel in moral behavior may be in the natural realm; the notion that authors create based on their interests being considered a natural realm can indeed make the concept of a natural realm seem ambiguous. In reality, even if most authors of great works are not consciously aware of their greatness during the creative process, it does not necessarily mean that their spiritual realm is equivalent to the lowest realms, such as those of fools or children. Feng categorizes all activities that are not aimed at astonishing fame as belonging to this natural realm. He says, "Those who intend to say astonishing things to gain fame belong to the utilitarian realm. Those who follow their interests and have no intention of saying astonishing things belong to the natural realm."[42] The unintentional nature described here can indeed align with a Daoist-like attitude, and it is not necessarily the same level of consciousness as that of fools or children, but a state of being that requires further analysis and differentiation.

V. A Reflection on the Utilitarian Realm

> This section discusses the utilitarian realm, which is centered around individuals pursuing their own interests and happiness as their primary objective. It focuses on behaviors by which people act with the intention of benefiting themselves or seeking personal happiness.[43]
>
> We are stating that the behavior of most people, or the behavior of the majority of ordinary individuals, is primarily driven by the pursuit of their own interests. When people

> engage in actions with the aim of seeking personal benefit, their realm is considered to be within the utilitarian realm.[44]

The concept of realms is indeed distinct from behavior, but it appears that Feng often unconsciously combines the two. This suggests that, in his view, the discussion of one's realm cannot be entirely separated from their behavior.

As described above, it is believed that the introduction of the realms of children and fools into the philosophy of life might not hold much significance. Realms should ideally pertain to ordinary individuals. The utilitarian realm, then, is considered the realm of ordinary people, in other words, the lowest realm for human beings. Feng also acknowledges that "the behavior of most ordinary people is aimed at their own interests. The realm of most ordinary people is the utilitarian realm."[45] Within the utilitarian realm, there are two distinct categories. One involves individuals who pursue their self-interest without harming others, and they exhibit a degree of self-restraint. The other category consists of those who seek personal gain at the expense of others and lack any form of self-restraint. The latter is undoubtedly a lower realm compared to the former. This point is only mentioned in Feng's book as a distinction between heroes and villains and is not explicitly differentiated in a general sense.

Due to the presence of utilitarianism in Western ethics, Feng occasionally uses Western utilitarian philosophy as a reference when discussing the utilitarian realm. He observes:

> So, individuals in the utilitarian realm are all motivated by self-interest and are considered selfish. Bentham believed that all human actions are driven by the pursuit of pleasure or the avoidance of pain. Bentham argued, "Nature has placed mankind under the governance of two sovereign masters, pain and pleasure. It is for them alone to point out what we ought to do, as well as determine what we shall do." In Bentham's *Introduction to the Principles of Morals and Legislation,* avoiding pain can also be seen as seeking pleasure. Therefore, Bentham can be simplified to say that the purpose of human behavior is to seek pleasure. It can also be said that nature subjects humanity to the rule of a single supreme authority, which is happiness.[46]

Feng's reference to Bentham's ideas when discussing the realm of utility is evidently because Bentham is a representative figure of utilitarianism in Western ethics. However, in Western ethics from modern to contemporary times, the term utilitarianism does not refer solely to actions pursued for individual self-interest, but rather emphasizes the promotion of overall happiness for all. Utilitarianism has historically encompassed elements of hedonism, dating back to ancient Greece, which is perhaps why Feng defines the utilitarian realm as the realm in which individuals seek their own self-interest or happiness.

Another representative of utilitarianism in modern Western ethics, is John Stuart Mill. It appears that Feng also references Mill's ideas, particularly those related to happiness. He says:

> Mill states, "If a person has experienced both higher and lower pleasures, they would undoubtedly choose to die as Socrates rather than live as a fool. The happiness of dying as Socrates and the happiness of living as a fool are of fundamentally different natures. As mentioned in the previous text, happiness is considered incomparable. Even if it were comparable, one could still ask: why would a person be willing to die as Socrates but not willing to live as a fool?"[47]

Bentham indeed proposed that there are various kinds of happiness, including fourteen simple pleasures and twelve simple pains, as well as complex forms of happiness and suffering. Mill, on the other hand, shifted the focus away from mere happiness as the ultimate goal of life and introduced the broader concept of well-being as the foundation. It appears that Feng utilizes Western utilitarian ethics for his own purposes and does not strictly adhere to the original meaning and definition of the term utilitarian realm. Instead, he selectively borrows useful elements, such as hedonism, as supplementary explanations. His concept of the utilitarian realm may thus differ from traditional utilitarian ethics, which is not surprising, given that he adapts these ideas to his own framework and purposes.

> If individuals in the universe are solely focused on getting by in life, then those within the utilitarian realm can manage to get by and even have some surplus. If all individuals in the world do not surpass the utilitarian realm, humanity can still maintain its existence and its superior position over other forms of life. Humanity has the potential to be the pinnacle of creation, to "seize the opportunities of nature," and to "dominate all things," as envisioned in Daoism and achieved by modern individuals. As long as everyone genuinely understands where their own interests lie, then even if everyone pursues their own interests, it is possible to "coexist and nurture without harm to one another" and "walk together without conflicting." Not only that, but people can also "divide labor and cooperate," mutually assist each other, organize complex societies, and create a brilliant culture.[48]
>
> As long as individuals genuinely understand where their own interests lie, then they can organize complex societies and create a brilliant culture. The realm of such individuals is the realm of utility. In fact, the majority of people are within the utilitarian realm. Our present society is primarily organized by individuals of this kind, and much of our current culture has also been created by individuals within the utilitarian realm.[49]

If people were to only exist within the utilitarian realm, where they seek their own self-interest, it would allow them to sustain their lives, maintain humanity's superiority over other species, engage in division of labor, cooperate, and create a splendid culture. From the perspective of human culture, one might ask why humans should still pursue higher realms. Feng even notes that the majority of human culture throughout history has been created by individuals in the utilitarian realm. (This pertains to what he refers to as "splendid culture." I believe his reference might encompass cultural activities such as Greek mythology, sculpture, and the organization of city-states. Human endeavors cannot stop here, and the pursuit of human spirit cannot be confined to this. There must be a spiritual culture, a moral culture.) Clearly, focusing solely on the aspect of human culture creation is insufficient to argue for the necessity of higher spiritual realms. This also suggests that Feng's book may not provide sufficient evidence for the need to elevate one's realm.

> All altruistic actions can be seen as a form of self-interest. Throughout history and across cultures, many proverbs, sayings, and moral codes, including texts like *A New Treatise on the Way of Life*, often emphasize morality and benevolence, but they often present moral and benevolent conduct as a means to seek one's own benefit. In the *Tao Te Ching*, there are numerous passages that depict morally upright behavior as a way to pursue gain and avoid harm. For example, phrases like, "Is it not because he has no selfishness that he is able to accomplish his own selfish ends?" and, "The sage does not contend, and therefore, no one can contend with him," from the *Tao Te Ching* depict selflessness and non-contention as morally upright behaviors, but Laozi presents them as methods to pursue one's own benefit.[50]
>
> The perspectives of happiness theorists or utilitarians, when viewed as practical guidance for navigating life, can indeed have their utility. However, when considered as a moral philosophy, they may not hold up universally.[51]

Feng holds that *A New Treatise on the Way of Life*, happiness theory, and utilitarianism can serve as practical strategies for navigating life. However, he categorizes these strategies within the utilitarian realm rather than the moral realm. Their actions can align with morality, but they are not inherently moral, and their starting point is to benefit the individual. Feng states that their actions are morally acceptable, but not moral actions, and they do not belong to the moral realm. This aspect will be further discussed in the section on the moral realm. What is of interest, from Feng's perspective, is that individuals in the utilitarian realm may view the moral teachings of ancient sages and altruistic actions observed in others as a means to pursue their own interests. The most direct way to do this is to regard these teachings and actions as methods for navigating life, such as using loyalty, forgiveness, benevolence, and righteousness as practical strategies for living, rather than as ways to achieve moral excellence. In other words, for individuals in the utilitarian realm, engaging in behaviors associated with loyalty, forgiveness, benevolence, and righteousness may be driven by a desire for personal gain, such as gaining the applause or approval of others, and so those in this realm may engage in morally acceptable behavior not for the sake of morality itself, but for their own benefit.

> While those in the utilitarian realm, may exhibit morally acceptable behavior as a means to pursue their own benefit, if one believes that moral behavior is nothing more than this, it indicates a partial understanding of ethics. According to this perspective, people who

> engage in morally upright actions are merely performing morally acceptable behaviors rather than truly moral behaviors. Their realm is that of utility rather than morality.[52]

From a subjective perspective, since these moral actions are motivated by self-interest, they are naturally considered utilitarian. In ethics, scholars in the tradition of Kant argue that actions motivated by utility, even if they align with morality, cannot be considered moral actions. The issue here is that realms are a subjective concept entirely based on the subjective world, while behavior is not solely subjective. Why should the nature of all behaviors be determined based on their subjective motives? Why is Kant's position specifically singled out here? Feng had not previously elaborated on this point.

Feng's discussion of the utilitarian realm is particularly noteworthy for his arguments concerning talented individuals and heroes. He states:

> Individuals who excel in knowledge and possess significant expertise are referred to as talented individuals. They may have extensive knowledge or achieve great work, but they often do not possess very high realms. Those who achieve great success in their endeavors are referred to as heroes. They may have significant accomplishments in their careers, but they also often do not have very high realms. Heroes are distinct from what is referred to as villains or unscrupulous heroes. The realms of heroes and unscrupulous heroes are both within the utilitarian realm. Individuals in the utilitarian realm may exhibit behavior that is not necessarily immoral; it may even align with morality, but it cannot be considered moral behavior. Their behavior may not necessarily be immoral, but it can also be immoral. When they achieve their self-interested goals through immoral actions, they are referred to as unscrupulous heroes. Unscrupulous heroes achieve their self-interested goals through actions that are not necessarily immoral but may harm others. Heroes, on the other hand, achieve their self-interested goals without causing harm to others, or even by benefiting others. Many of the great heroes in history have achieved remarkable accomplishments that are both self-serving and beneficial to others. In terms of their positive impact on others, their actions and their legacy deserve admiration from future generations. However, in terms of their self-serving motivations, their achievements are not the result of moral behavior, and their realm is that of utility.[53]

Talented individuals excel in cultural and creative pursuits, while heroes achieve great feats in their careers and accomplishments. However, these accomplishments pertain to external deeds, while the realm is concerned with the heart or inner motives. Therefore, according to *New Origins of Humanity*, individuals with significant achievements in cultural creation and career accomplishments may not necessarily belong to high realms inwardly. The assessment of realms is based on their subjective world and is not determined by whether their external actions and accomplishments benefit others. Feng's understanding of heroes appears to focus on individuals in the utilitarian realm who have significant achievements, but it may not fully account for the possibility of heroes who possess both achievements and high realms. Further refinement of his analysis in this regard may be necessary. Therefore, when he states that "the realms of heroes and unscrupulous heroes are both within the utilitarian realm," he is essentially characterizing heroes as those who achieve great deeds and accomplishments for their self-benefit without causing harm to others, while unscrupulous heroes achieve similar feats for self-benefit, but at the expense of others. Both heroes and unscrupulous heroes are motivated by self-interest, and therefore, they both fall within the utilitarian realm. In ethical terms, the actions of heroes are considered morally upright, while the actions of unscrupulous heroes are seen as immoral or contrary to morality. Both cases illustrate that moral behavior should not be motivated by self-interest but should stem from the intrinsic value of morality itself.

Feng's distinction between heroes and unscrupulous heroes highlights an important differentiation within the utilitarian realm, as we previously discussed. It underscores that there are two variations within the utilitarian realm: one that involves self-benefit without causing harm to others and another that involves self-benefit at the expense of others. These two types of individuals indeed have significant differences. Those who pursue self-benefit without causing harm to others are not necessarily heroes, but their actions can align completely with the requirements of *A New Treatise on the Way of Life* and be regarded as commendable by modern society. Those who pursue self-benefit without causing harm and who also benefit others are even more highly esteemed in modern society, while individuals who pursue self-benefit at the expense of others and their actions are indeed generally looked down upon by society. Categorizing these two types of people together under the umbrella of the utilitarian realm may not be appropriate in practice. This underscores a limitation of the idealistic theory of realms, particularly in its capacity to comprehensively assess and evaluate individuals. Feng's analysis revolves around the specific categories of heroes and unscrupulous heroes, without necessarily considering these distinctions as crucial subtypes within the utilitarian realm. He says:

> Regardless of the field of knowledge or art, as long as it can be a legitimate field of study or art, it generally benefits humanity. However, those who excel in knowledge or engage in creative pursuits may do so with the aim of personal gain. If their motivation is primarily self-interest, then their realm falls within the utilitarian realm.[54]

The same applies to individuals with talent. Even if their motivation is self-interest, they can achieve great success in fields such as art and literature, ultimately benefiting others. While individuals with talent can have significant cultural accomplishments that benefit others, their motivation is often driven by personal gain, and they thus fall in the utilitarian realm. From this perspective, those with talent and heroes can be seen as sharing a similar category.

Feng's emphasis on the issue of heroes and talented individuals is clearly related to the discussion in Song-Ming Neo-Confucianism regarding the achievements of heroes. During the

Southern Song Dynasty, scholars like Zhu Xi and Chen Liang* engaged in a famous debate on this topic. Feng states:

> We must distinguish between the realm of talented individuals and heroes and their achievements. These two should not be conflated. Whether it is a work of art or a political accomplishment, if it is deemed great, its greatness is judged based on its own standards, and it does not necessarily correlate with the level of the author's realm.[55]
>
> In the past, scholars in the realm of Daoism might have held a bias that the realms of talented individuals and heroes are inherently low, and therefore, their achievements are not worth considering.[56]
>
> Hence, the belief that talented individuals and heroes can achieve greatness in their accomplishments also implies that their realms of existence must be high. This is another common bias among people. The realms of existence that talented individuals and heroes commonly belong to may not necessarily be very high. Still, their achievements can be great, and may even benefit society and humanity. Furthermore, their conduct often embodies a sense of aesthetic value and can be appreciated and admired when viewed as part of nature.[57]
>
> In this realm, people's actions can vary widely, but their ultimate goal is always their own benefit. They may not necessarily adopt a purely self-centered approach like Yang Zhu. They can actively strive for goals, and they might even be willing to sacrifice themselves, but their ultimate motivation remains their own benefit. Indeed, their actions can also benefit others and bring great advantages. For example, the accomplishments and deeds of emperors like Qin Shi Huang and Emperor Wu of Han can be seen as having a positive impact on the world and benefiting future generations, but their motivation for pursuing these achievements was primarily for their own benefit. Even though they are considered exceptional heroes in history, their underlying mindset was within the utilitarian realm.[58]

Evaluating historical or contemporary figures should consider more than just their personal spiritual mindset. Their actions, achievements, and impact on society also play crucial roles in assessing their contributions and character. What Feng is talking about here, as summarized by Chen Fuliang† in the context of Zhu Xi's viewpoint, is that "achievements do not necessarily require virtue." The evaluation of the moral character of significant historical figures should not be the sole criterion, but rather, a comprehensive assessment of their contributions to human culture and history should be considered. It is evident that the concept of realm, as presented

* Chen Liang (1143–1194) was a Chinese politician, philosopher, and lyricist of the Southern Song Dynasty.

† Chen Fuliang (1137–1203) was a famous scholar, politician, thinker, and educator of the Southern Song Dynasty.

in *New Origins of Humanity*, cannot serve as a comprehensive system for evaluating individuals. Of course, the concept was not originally designed for evaluating individuals, but because Feng often mentions historical figures like Qin Shi Huang and Emperor Wu of Han, it might give the impression that his concept is too narrow for evaluating historical figures comprehensively and might not provide a reasonable framework for such evaluations.

Feng goes on to point out the differences between heroes, talented individuals, and sages, saying:

> Heroes and talented individuals are not in the same category as sages. Heroes and talented individuals belong to the utilitarian realm, while sages belong to the realm of heaven and earth or the moral realm. This is not to say that sages cannot achieve great feats like heroes or create significant works like talented individuals. Sages can also achieve all the great things of talented individuals and heroes, but talented individuals and heroes cannot have the same level of spiritual enlightenment as sages.[59]

Heroes and talented individuals belong to the utilitarian realm, virtuous individuals belong to the moral realm, and sages belong to the realm of the universe and nature. While Feng may not have explicitly categorized them in this way, his logic appears to suggest such a classification. The concept of heroes inherently involves the idea of achieving great deeds, while the concept of sages or virtuous individuals does not necessarily focus on achievements, but rather on the highest level of personal character and moral development. While the concept of sages or virtuous individuals may not inherently focus on external achievements, it is possible for them to have significant accomplishments similar to those of heroes and talented individuals.

Feng also asserts that heroes and talented individuals can be people of a natural disposition. He writes:

> People of such disposition are not limited to only being able to do low-value tasks. In the realm of scholarship and art, they can be creators, and in the realm of moral deeds and achievements, they can do things that "astound heaven and move spirits." Often, they are also those who "act where they cannot help but act and stop where they cannot help but stop," and "nobody knows how they do it, yet they do it." The state of mind of such individuals is also a natural realm.[60]
>
> However, in the conduct of talented individuals and heroes, this aspect often involves a kind of "mysterious, spontaneous intuition," where they act without conscious intention. For example, Xiang Yu's refusal to return to the west of the Yangtze River was not a deliberate display of stubbornness, but rather because he could not bear to see "my parents and elders feeling sorry for me and making me their king." From this perspective, the state of mind of talented individuals and heroes when they exhibit such behavior is a natural realm. Their actions are admirable and praiseworthy, but they are done "for the sake of others" rather than "for the sake of themselves."[61]

The natural realm is the lowest level of realms. Due to Feng's complete separation and even division of the heart and conduct, as well as disposition and behavior, there appear to be irrational aspects in his *New Origins of Humanity.* In this context, individuals who achieve groundbreaking accomplishments in scholarship, achievements, morality, and art, as well as talented individuals and heroes, can still be considered people of the lowest realm. This indicates that his theory must have its limitations. The issues involved in this theory align with the debates between Zhu Xi and Chen Liang in certain respects.

VI. Reflection on the Moral Realm

> The social relationships between people are called human relationships. In ancient times, it was said that there were five basic human relationships: ruler and subject, father and son, husband and wife, brothers, and friends. These are also considered human relationships. When we refer to human relationships here, however, we need not limit the discussion to these five, which are the fundamental human relationships within the context of the family. When we talk about human relationships here, we are referring to any kind of human relationship within any type of society.[62]
>
> What one should do in these relationships varies depending on their roles.[63]
>
> Fulfilling one's roles and responsibilities in these relationships constitutes moral behavior. All moral actions are related to fulfilling these roles and responsibilities to the best of one's ability.[64]

Ethics refers to ethical or moral relationships, and fulfilling ethics means completing one's ethical obligations. Ethics and morality are distinct concepts: ethics is objective, while morality is subjective. Based on Feng's understanding of morality, we cannot abstractly claim that fulfilling ethical obligations is equivalent to moral behavior, because fulfilling ethical obligations may only align with moral behavior. True moral behavior is when one's actions are driven by a subjective desire to fulfill ethical obligations. Feng states:

> In the utilitarian realm, people's actions are driven by self-interest, seeking their own benefit. In the moral realm, people's actions are guided by doing what is right. Those who act for their own benefit are focused on seeking their own advantage through their actions. On the other hand, those who act morally adhere to the principle of "what ought to be," disregarding the potential consequences for their own interests in their actions.[65]

Here, the distinction between moral and non-moral behavior, as well as between the realms of morality and utility, is made based on the motivation of righteousness and the motivation of self-interest. In this context, the motivation of self-interest refers to individual desires for personal gain. Indeed, following Feng's earlier statement, self-interest or benefit can also refer to the benefit of society, and seeking the benefit of society can be considered an act of righteousness. Whether seeking the benefit of society falls under the category of "what ought to be" is a matter that requires further analysis and discussion. Feng writes:

> For example, consider two soldiers, both charging into the heat of battle. One soldier does so with the motivation of receiving rewards from superiors or gaining recognition from comrades. The other believes that this is simply fulfilling the duty of a soldier and does it without any ulterior motives. The actions of these two soldiers may appear the same on the surface, but there are significant differences in their underlying motivations. The first soldier's actions are primarily driven by personal gain or self-interest, and some might still consider it moral behavior due to the outcome (fulfilling their duty as a soldier). But generally, people also believe that the actions of the second person have a higher moral value compared to the actions of the first, because actions done without any ulterior motives are more in line with the principles of morality. If actions carried out without any ulterior motives are more in line with the principles of morality, then actions undertaken with ulterior motives are essentially contrary to the principles of morality. Actions taken with ulterior motives, while they may be in accordance with morality to some extent, are not truly moral actions.[66]

What is meant here by having ulterior motives is actions motivated by individual self-interest. Emphasizing acting without ulterior motives is a tradition in Neo-Confucian moral philosophy that has been prominent since the Song Dynasty. In the context of Song-Ming Neo-Confucianism, acting without ulterior motives means that actions are carried out without any personal utility or self-interest as the primary motivation. Feng goes on:

> Some individuals mistakenly believe that anyone who opposes the doctrine of happiness does not value happiness. They might also assume that anyone who values happiness must be a proponent of happiness theory. Similarly, some may think that anyone who prioritizes righteousness does not care about any form of gain, and conversely, anyone who prioritizes gain does not care about righteousness. These assumptions are indeed incorrect, and they stem from a muddled way of thinking. In ethical philosophy, there is a distinction between the object of one's intentions and the goodness of those intentions. For example, when a person enjoys food and drinks with their parents, their action is an expression of filial piety. In this type of behavior, food and drink are the objects of their intentions (what they are enjoying), and filial piety is the goodness of their intentions (the virtue they are demonstrating). Food and drink are not filial piety itself, but in this context, filial piety can be expressed through them. Similarly, when someone teaches others about filial piety, their action can be seen as an expression of loyalty. In this type

> of behavior, filial piety is the object of their intentions (what they are teaching), and loyalty is the goodness of their intentions (the virtue they are demonstrating). Filial piety is not loyalty itself, but in this context, loyalty can be expressed through teaching about filial piety. If we make such distinctions, then seeking the benefit of others would be considered righteousness. In this type of behavior, the benefit of others is the object of one's intentions (what they are seeking), and righteousness is the goodness of their intentions (the virtue they are demonstrating). These two forms of goodness do not exist on the same level.[67]
>
> When King Hui of Liang talked about "benefit," he was primarily concerned with how to benefit himself and his own state. He asked, "What is in it for the country?" but the country was his own. When Mencius talked about benefits, he was more focused on how to benefit the people and society as a whole. Indeed, what he discussed as benefit was the object of his intentions (what he aimed to achieve) rather than the goodness of his intentions themselves. The true goodness of his intentions was rooted in concepts like benevolence and righteousness. So, when he spoke of how to benefit the people, it was not merely about discussing self-interest but about practicing benevolence and righteousness in his actions.[68]

According to this perspective, there is a distinction between intention and the object of intention. Intention represents one's subjective motivation or motive, while the object of intention is the external form through which the intention is expressed. Therefore, goodness can also be divided into the goodness of intention and the goodness of the object of intention. The goodness of intention relates to one's subjective motivation, while the goodness of the object of intention pertains to the form of behavior through which the intention is manifested. Righteousness is a moral concept and represents an understanding of morality, making it an aspect of intention and a moral realm. According to Feng's earlier statement, seeking the benefit of others can be considered righteousness when discussing one's intentions or mindset. However, it might not be accurate to say that seeking the benefit of others is inherently righteous, because behavior can be in accordance with righteousness but not necessarily equivalent to it. Here, Feng affirms that seeking the benefit of others is the goodness of intention. However, intention is a realm, whereas the object of intention is not a subjective world and thus not a realm. The intention of righteousness constitutes the realm, while the act of seeking the benefit of others is behavior, not a realm. Feng states that the behavior of seeking the benefit of others is righteousness and represents a logical inconsistency. He says:

> If there are those who engage in such behavior, it is purely because their emotions related to pain and pleasure are at play. Their realm is the natural realm. While their actions may be in accordance with moral principles, they are not truly moral in essence. If there are those who engage in such behavior, there is indeed a moral value in such actions. The intention

> behind these actions, aimed at realizing this value, makes these intentions virtuous. Thus, their actions are considered moral, and their realm is a moral realm. If, in the process of realizing this value and virtuous intention, one's heart is devoid of emotions related to the pain and pleasure of others, and they act in such a way merely because it is the right thing to do, then their actions can be considered righteous actions. If they also have emotions related to the pain and pleasure of others while acting, then their actions can be considered benevolent actions. Benevolent actions may appear similar to the actions of ordinary people in the natural realm as mentioned earlier, but they are indeed different because they are actions that realize moral values within the realm of consciousness. In the history of Western philosophy, Immanuel Kant made a clear distinction between morally acceptable actions in the natural realm of humanity and morally virtuous actions in the moral realm. However, his concept of moral actions pertains primarily to righteous actions and not benevolent actions. Moral actions can be further divided into two types: righteous actions and benevolent actions, a distinction that Kant does not seem to have emphasized.[69]

Unlike classical Confucianism, which teaches that emotions related to the pain and pleasure of others are the origin of benevolent emotions and that actions stemming from these emotions are benevolent actions, Feng contends that this realm is not a moral realm but rather a natural realm. This perspective views the starting point of benevolence, as affirmed by classical Confucianism, as the lowest level akin to that of simple-minded individuals or children. This is a viewpoint that we cannot endorse and may suggest that Feng has been heavily influenced by Kant. Feng also believes that only when actions originate from moral awareness, coupled with emotional factors related to the pain and pleasure of others, can they be considered moral actions, and only then can their realm be characterized as the moral realm of benevolence. The absence of these emotional factors, with actions originating solely from moral awareness, represents a general moral realm. This emphasis on benevolence and the distinction between Kant's perspective on righteousness and benevolence is indeed a viewpoint worthy of consideration. However, in this context, the relationship between the moral realm and moral actions is not clearly explained. According to Feng's logic, moral actions should correspond to the moral realm, meaning that there is a moral realm of benevolence that leads to benevolent moral actions, and a moral realm of righteousness that leads to righteous moral actions. It should not be directly about moral actions themselves. Furthermore, Feng's concept of the moral realm does not seem to clarify the significance of conscience and where actions arising from conscience fit within this framework. He writes:

> Strictly speaking, moral actions are only those that are carried out with an awareness of moral values. Therefore, the realm of those who engage in moral actions cannot be the natural realm. Artistic works are the outcomes of artistic activities, and these outcomes

> possess artistic value. However, the artistic activity itself does not necessarily need to have artistic value. In contrast, the moral value of moral actions is inherent in the actions themselves. If the action itself is not carried out for the sake of morality, then the action can only be morally permissible but not morally virtuous. A person can engage in artistic activities based on their interests or natural inclinations. However, strictly speaking, a person cannot engage in morally virtuous actions solely based on their interests or natural inclinations. Such actions can be in accordance with moral principles but may not be morally virtuous. People who engage in such actions are guided by morality but may not necessarily exhibit virtuous behavior.[70]

The statement "moral value is inherent in the action itself" is not in line with Feng's philosophical framework. Strictly, according to his thought, actions themselves may not inherently distinguish between moral and immoral. Rather, the distinction should come from the inner motives of the individual. Therefore, the value of moral actions lies not in the actions themselves but in the motives behind them. Feng's emphasis on motives aligns with a Kantian perspective. He writes:

> Kant indeed shares a similar perspective with the idea that genuinely moral actions are those that conform to the commands of reason. If actions arise from natural inclinations and are done out of necessity rather than free moral choice, then while these actions may be morally permissible, they can only be referred to as lawful actions and not as moral actions. For example, one person witnesses a child falling into a well and, prompted by spontaneous compassion, follows this feeling and rushes to rescue the child. Another person, due to a personal vendetta against the child's parents, chooses not to help and watches from a distance. From the outward appearance of the two individuals' actions, it may seem that the first person's action is morally good while the second person's action is morally wrong. However, when we consider the motives behind their actions, the motive of the second person is indeed unethical. Still, the motive of the first person is not necessarily morally virtuous either. Therefore, the action of the first person, while morally permissible, can be described as lawful but may not necessarily be categorized as morally virtuous. The actions described earlier, which are based on spontaneous and emotionally driven responses, do not necessarily involve conscious obedience to the commands of reason. Therefore, while these actions may align with certain moral principles, they may not be considered morally virtuous actions in the sense of conscious adherence to moral duty. In Kantian terms, these actions could be described as merely lawful. In more general terms, they could be considered as aligning with moral principles.[71]

This reflects Kant's formalistic perspective, which differs from traditional Confucianism. In traditional Confucianism, the act of seeing a child about to fall into a well and being moved by compassion to rescue them would be fully affirmed and considered virtuous. Indeed, according to Kant and Feng's perspectives, such an action might not be considered a moral action or part of the moral realm, but rather falls within the realm of nature, potentially even lower than the utilitarian realm. It is clear that Feng's understanding of the moral realm aligns with Kant's but differs from traditional Confucianism. He says:

> It can be argued that this perspective appears to be overly formalistic. If we define moral actions as those that must involve an awareness of moral values and actions done for the sake of morality to be considered moral actions, then spontaneously aligning with moral principles may indeed not be classified as moral actions.[72]
>
> In this context, we can argue that a person who generally performs morally right actions may not necessarily reside in the moral realm. If their morally right actions are a result of innate disposition or habit rather than conscious moral deliberation, then their realm could be considered the natural realm. If a person performs morally right actions with the hope of gaining fame, fortune, or respect, then their realm could be considered the utilitarian realm. To truly inhabit the moral realm, one must act morally based on a genuine understanding of morality and act accordingly to that understanding. This understanding requires a deep, conscientious intellectual effort to truly grasp. We should not assume that the moral realm does not require a significant level of moral awareness just because simple-minded individuals from a small village can also perform morally right actions. A genuine, comprehensive understanding of morality typically demands a more significant level of moral awareness and intellectual engagement. Indeed, individuals who may not possess advanced intellectual capacities can still perform morally right actions, but it does not necessarily mean that they reside within the moral realm.[73]

Feng asserts that the moral realm requires a significant level of moral awareness, but moral actions themselves may not demand such a high level of moral understanding. Being able to perform morally right actions does not necessarily mean one fully resides within the moral realm. If Feng exaggerates the gap between the moral realm and moral actions, it could lead to undervaluing the significance of moral actions. On the other hand, the capacity for compassion and empathy is an expression of human nature and moral character. It is not the lowest realm of human existence. Conversely, motives driven solely by selfish desires, even if they are obscured by one's true human nature, cannot necessarily be considered a higher realm of expression than actions rooted in unobscured human nature. It is evident that Feng was significantly influenced by Kantian formalistic ethics in this regard. Furthermore, if simple-minded individuals from the village are able to perform moral actions without selfish intentions, as described in the context of Mencius's philosophy, where their "original hearts" remain uncorrupted, then this state should indeed be considered higher than the realm of utilitarian motives. It would not be appropriate to view it as lower than the realm of selfish interests.

VII. Reflections on the Realm of Heaven and Earth

> Mystical experience is similar to pure experience. Daoists often conflate these two, but they are actually quite different. Mystical experience is incomprehensible, and its incomprehensibility surpasses comprehension. Pure experience is uncomprehensible, and its lack of comprehension is inferior to comprehension."[74]

He here emphasizes that in order to approach problems from a heaven perspective, one should base one's understanding on heaven. Understanding heaven means grasping the concepts of the universe, the entirety, and the Daoist nature in philosophy. With this understanding of heaven, one can then act in accordance with heaven and find joy in it, ultimately reaching a state of harmony with heaven. The realm of harmony with heaven is synonymous with the realm of heaven and earth. Feng says:

> Religion inspires faith in people, while philosophy fosters knowledge. The principles mentioned earlier, such as the understanding of the universe, the entirety, the world of reason, and the concept of the Daoist nature, all fall under the realm of philosophical concepts. When a person possesses these philosophical concepts, they can come to understand heaven. With this understanding of heaven, one can then act in accordance with heaven, find joy in it, and ultimately reach a state of harmony with heaven. This concept of heaven refers to the universe or the entirety.[75]

Religion is about having faith in heaven, while philosophy is about acquiring knowledge of it. The faith in heaven within religion can also lead to a transcendent moral realm. However, *New Origins of Humanity* emphasizes reaching a transcendent moral realm through the knowledge of heaven in philosophy. This transcendent moral realm, as Feng calls it, is referred to as the realm of heaven and earth. He writes:

> The celestial individual occupies a certain position in society, and this position for them is equivalent to a celestial position. Within society, they assume a certain role, and this role is akin to a celestial role for them. The actions they should take while occupying a specific position and role in society are essentially the same as what an ordinary person should do when in that position and role. However, their actions hold a deeper significance related to acting in accordance with heaven. So, when ordinary people perform the tasks they should in society, they are essentially fulfilling their human duties and responsibilities. On the other hand, when heavenly individuals carry out the same tasks in society, even though these actions align with fulfilling human duties and responsibilities, they also encompass fulfilling heaven duties and responsibilities.[76]

Those who possess knowledge of heaven not only find new meaning in the actions they undertake, but also perceive a different significance in the things they encounter.[77]

Different individuals can indeed perform the same actions, but their understanding of these actions varies, leading to different meanings attached to the same task. As a result, each person's state or realm is different. Feng's theory of realms is grounded in the perspective of the mind, which allows his explanations to coherently support his ideas. He emphasizes the significance of a person's actions both in terms of their impact on society and their broader implications for the universe or heaven. Understanding the meaning of one's actions solely within the context of society is seen as fulfilling one's human duties and responsibilities, while grasping the meaning of one's actions in the context of the universe or heaven realm is considered as fulfilling heaven duties and responsibilities. Feng says:

> Those who perceive such meanings within things experience a certain kind of joy. This joy, which arises from understanding and aligning with these meanings in the world, is referred to as finding joy in heaven.[78]
>
> In the realm of heaven and earth, the highest achievement for a person is not only to understand that they are a part of the entirety but also to become one with the entirety itself. Zhuangzi says, "Heaven and earth are the one thing from which all things are. When one attains unity with this one thing, then life and death, beginning and end, are like day and night, and there is no place one can slip away to. How much more so when one attains what intervenes between misfortune and blessing?" Attaining unity with the one thing and becoming one with the entirety implies a state where the distinction between self and non-self ceases to exist. Daoism says, "Merge with things." To merge means to eliminate the distinction between the self and all things. Confucianism says, "All things are complete within me." The whole encompasses all things, and when the self becomes one with the entirety, it results in the realization that "everything is included within me." This realm of being, which is often referred to as "harmony with heaven," cannot be achieved by the practical achievements of people in the utilitarian realm, nor by the fulfillment of ethical duties in the moral realm. Those who attain this state of consciousness not only participate in the harmony of heaven and earth but become one with heaven and earth itself. Achieving this state is considered the highest level of accomplishment within the realm of heaven and earth. It can also be said that a person truly enters into the realm of heaven and earth only when they attain this state of consciousness. Understanding heaven, acting in accordance with heaven, and finding joy in heaven are all preparations leading to the attainment of this elevated state of being.[79]

Feng's definition of the realm of heaven and earth as being one with the whole underscores the concept of harmony with heaven. To be one with the whole, to be one with heaven, and to merge the shared and the individual into a single unity all represent a heightened state of consciousness and spiritual awareness. Feng observes:

> Understanding the whole may seem as though one is perceiving it from outside, seeing only the whole without recognizing its individual parts. However, when one understands that the whole is beyond comprehension, they also come to understand that they themselves exist within the whole. This awareness of being within the whole while perceiving only the whole and not its individual parts leads to the realization that one is in harmony with the whole. Becoming one with the whole is not a physical transformation, but a state of consciousness. Even though one's physical body and mind are just a part of the whole, in the realm of consciousness, one can achieve a sense of unity with the whole. This state of being is primarily a spiritual and mental state rather than a physical change.[80]

The concept of the realm of heaven and earth as presented in *New Origins of Humanity* does indeed bear resemblance to the principles of mysticism. The definition of the realm of heaven and earth aligns closely with the definition of mysticism, according to Feng. Therefore, he explicitly affirms that the state of harmony with heaven is essentially a form of mysticism.[81]

The key characteristic of the realm of heaven and earth is becoming one with the entirety. The entirety is described as something beyond description, thought, or comprehension. In this state of being one with the entirety, the realm transcends all distinctions and boundaries, entering into a realm of profound unity and transcendence that is often described as beyond ordinary understanding. In the realm of heaven and earth, where individuals become one with the entirety, the distinction between self and non-self disappears, leading to the profound feeling that everything is included within oneself. This realm of heaven and earth encompasses four stages: knowing heaven, serving heaven, rejoicing in heaven, and being in harmony with heaven. If a person becomes self-aware and understands that they are not only a part of society but also a part of the universe or the entirety, this is referred to as knowing heaven. When someone who knows heaven views their actions as a conscious fulfillment of their duties to the universe, this is described as serving heaven. Those who serving heaven find a transcendent moral significance in their actions and interactions with the world, resulting in a sense of joy. This joy, often described in ancient texts as the happiness of Confucius and Yan Hui, is referred to as rejoicing in heaven within the framework of the realm of heaven and earth. The highest stage within this realm is achieving harmony with heaven, which is known as harmony with heaven.

Because Feng did not include the spiritual realms of Buddhism in his theory of realms in *New Origins of Humanity*, he faced questioning from Xiong Shili. Shortly after the publication of *New Origins of Humanity*, Xiong Shili wrote a letter in which he raised some criticisms and concerns regarding Feng's theory of realms. Feng wrote in letter to Xiong's letter:

> What Xiong describes as "the realm without attributes" is equivalent to what *New Origins of Humanity* refers to as the "same heaven realm." In Xiong's discussion of the "realm without attributes," *New Origins of Humanity* also mentions that "in the same heaven realm, humans possess knowledge yet also lack knowledge." Xiong talks about the "true sovereign," and *New Origins of Humanity* similarly states that "in the realm of heaven

> and earth, humans are without a self yet also have a self." In the realm of heaven and earth, individuals consciously perceive that their self is the ruler of the universe. Xiong's statement about "not clinging to things and never having grasped" aligns with what *New Origins of Humanity* expresses when it mentions that in the realm of heaven and earth, individuals "act yet do not act." If we carefully examine these passages, it is possible to see a convergence in our respective viewpoints, and there are indeed many similarities between our ideas in this regard.[82]

What Xiong Shili described as the "realm without attributes" and "not clinging to things and never having grasped" is indeed consistent with the concepts discussed earlier by Cheng Hao and Wang Yangming, such as "responding to things as they come," "harmonizing emotions with all things without having emotions," and "not attaching to a single thought." It appears that Feng did not explicitly address these points in *New Origins of Humanity*, indicating that his theory of realms does not fully incorporate Buddhist realm theories.

Not only did Feng's system not encompass the realms of Buddhism, but it also did not fully incorporate the spiritual realms of Daoism. He primarily incorporates the mystical aspect of Daoist realms under the concept of harmony with heaven, but does not explicitly express the Daoist idea of the natural realm in his system. Feng's concept of the natural realm differs from the Daoist reverence for a natural way of life. The Daoist natural realm was indeed absorbed into the Neo-Confucian philosophy of the Song and Ming dynasties, with notable figures like Chen Baisha embodying this incorporation. This elevated, non-utilitarian natural realm is fundamentally different from the lowest realm described by Feng, which he likened to that of a foolish person or a child, representing a more advanced and enlightened state of being.

VIII. Refinement of the Realm of Heaven and Earth

Hegel points out that morality involves the mind, and it concerns individual conscience, motives, purposes, intentions, and other inner consciousness. It is the subjective world of consciousness, an inner, subjective world. He says, "In morality, the will returns to its own subjectivity." The will is an inner state, while family, nation, and society are objective systems. If morality becomes objective and concrete, it becomes social ethics. However, Hegel fails to point out that morality involves the subjective world of consciousness, but moral consciousness is just a part of the subjective world of consciousness. The subjective world of consciousness is much broader than moral consciousness and encompasses various forms of consciousness, including non-moral and super-moral aspects. Feng's theory of realms precisely addresses this inclusive nature of the diverse levels of consciousness.

Realms are subjective, so how do people perceive and judge someone's spiritual realm? In reality, it is not that difficult. Words are the expression of the heart, and actions are the form of the heart. When it comes to a person's spiritual state, individuals can observe their words and actions to gain insight into their inner world. Moreover, this understanding can lead to consensus, indicating its objectivity. Therefore, a person's spiritual realm, at whatever level it may be, is not something only known to themselves but can be known and understood by others, despite the exceptions where someone may conceal their true state.

A New Treatise on the Way of Life can be seen as a form of virtue ethics, but it tends to emphasize non-moral virtues. On the other hand, *New Origins of Humanity* reduces non-moral virtues to the level of utilitarianism. *New Origins of Humanity* acknowledges that non-moral motives can lead to morally acceptable actions. However, since it is rooted in the spiritual realm as a subjective world, the foundation of the evaluative system changes. Therefore, the conclusions about non-moral motives may differ from those of a traditional moral framework. *New Origins of Humanity* is not a type of virtue ethics but can be categorized as a form of ethics related to states of consciousness or spiritual states, often referred to as ethics of states of consciousness.

Feng advocates the theory of realms rather than focusing on virtue ethics, likely because he was influenced by Daoist thought in his early years. This influence may have played a significant role in shaping his philosophical thinking and served as a path dependency in his intellectual development. The emphasis on virtue ethics in pre-Qin Confucianism and the focus on states of consciousness in Daoism influenced his philosophical outlook. His later concepts, such as the natural realm and the realm of heaven and earth, are directly related to his understanding of Daoism, which had a significant impact on him in the 1920s. Considering the emphasis on revolutionary consciousness in the 1950s, it may be argued that the concept of realm is more suitable for explaining the changes in people's mindset during that era compared to virtue ethics. It is important to note, though, that neither Feng's theory of realms nor Feng Qi's theory of virtue was as prevalent and influential as the concept of revolutionary consciousness during that time.

In broad terms, compared to *A New Treatise on the Way of Life*, *New Origins of Humanity* is quite different. Both books fall within the realm of ethics, with the former discussing methods for living and the latter focusing on the states of consciousness or spiritual realms that define one's life. The main distinction lies in the fact that *A New Treatise on the Way of Life* primarily discusses action, while *New Origins of Humanity* primarily discusses mind or the inner world of consciousness. Modern Western ethics often focuses on moral behavior and moral character, while *A New Treatise on the Way of Life* places its emphasis on non-moral virtues, and *New Origins of Humanity* explores states of consciousness beyond morality. These approaches differ significantly from the mainstream of Western ethics. Realms or spiritual states have been a focal point in ancient Chinese ethics, whereas modern Western moral philosophy shifted its emphasis, often placing less importance on the pursuit of sublime spiritual realms, instead focusing more on moral character at best.

Not only has modern Western ethics not emphasized spiritual realms as a significant focal point, but also many works in the history of modern Chinese ethics, influenced by the West, have not highlighted this aspect. For example, in *A Study of Chinese Ethical Thought*, Zhang Danian discusses the doctrine of effort but does not touch upon the theory of realms. Recent research in Chinese philosophy has focused on theories of skill and craftsmanship, but it has not particularly highlighted the theory of realms. In fact, as I clearly pointed out in *The Realm of Existence and Non-existence,* the fundamental issues in Song-Ming Confucianism encompass ontology, the doctrine of effort, and the theory of realms, and these three aspects are inseparable. Of course, in Song-Ming Neo-Confucianism, the concept of ontology refers to the ontological nature of the mind-heart, which differs from the typical notion of ontology as discussed in general philosophical discourse.

In ancient Confucian philosophy, apart from the ideas presented by Mencius, the ethical theories of pre-Qin and Han Dynasty Confucianism mainly emphasized virtue ethics and did not particularly highlight the concept of the mind-heart. It was during the Song and Ming dynasties that Neo-Confucianism prominently emphasized the concept of the mind-heart. Pre-Qin Daoism had already placed significant emphasis on the concept of the mind-heart, and this influence can be seen in the thought of philosophers like Xunzi. However, during the Qin and Han dynasties, mainstream Confucianism continued to primarily focus on virtue ethics rather than a detailed exploration of the concept of the mind-heart. Western ethics has not considered the issue of the mind as a central concern in ethics; instead, it has consistently revolved around moral behavior and action.

If we consider the moral realm as the core concept, it can be said that *New Origins of Humanity,* while centered around the moral realm, also focuses on the natural and utilitarian realms beneath the moral realm. This approach aims to elevate natural and utilitarian realms to higher levels of the moral realm. On the other hand, it also pays attention to stages of higher understanding and consciousness beyond the moral realm, namely, the realm of heaven and earth. In this sense, *New Origins of Humanity* presents a form of ethics centered on realms. This is how Feng sees it. In ancient times, both Daoism and Confucianism had their own ways of aspiring to the realm of heaven and earth. What sets Feng's New Neo-Confucianism apart from ancient Confucianism and Daoism is his assertion that achieving the realm of heaven and earth should be based on philosophical rationality as a method rather than relying on spiritual cultivation.

It is worth asking whether the main purpose of introducing the theory of realms was to address the evaluation of individuals or to propose a goal for spiritual elevation. If one were to argue that the theory of realms is merely an evaluative system for individuals, it could be said that its criteria are overly narrow and may not adequately assess the overall contributions and significance of historical figures. This is a common source of dissatisfaction when reading *New Origins of Humanity.* It should be noted that the system of *New Origins of Humanity* is not intended for evaluating individuals and does not assume the role of assessing historical figures, in order to avoid confusion among readers. However, as a philosophy of life that guides realms and is dedicated to the development of the spirit, the theory of states of consciousness indeed holds significant importance. It should be noted that the introduction of this theory is not primarily aimed at establishing a foundation for evaluating individuals, but rather at elevating spiritual realms.

Within Chinese culture, the evaluation of individuals is not always solely based on historical assessments or behavioral judgments. It often delves directly into the human heart and the inner states of consciousness in real-life contexts. Statements such as, "This person is too utilitarian," "This person is too self-centered," "This person is not that great," "This person is too insincere," and "This person is solely focused on personal advancement," indeed suggest that "this person" lacks outstanding moral character and does not reach the moral and ethical states associated with being a virtuous person. These are common evaluative expressions used in Chinese culture in everyday life.

It is important to note that individuals described using such expressions are not necessarily committing moral wrongs or engaging in unethical behavior. This highlights that in Chinese culture, the evaluation of individuals places significant importance on the human heart and the states of consciousness. People's assessments of character are not solely based on their actions, but also on their inner qualities and states of consciousness. Saying, "This person is insincere," implies a lack of genuine virtue, with virtue being considered on a specific level. Saying, "This person is not that great," suggests a lower level of moral and ethical realms, with realms being evaluated on a more general level. It is evident that the theory of realms shares some similarities with virtue ethics, but also exhibits distinctions between the two approaches.

When a person makes the pursuit of utility their fundamental goal, such individuals may have lower realms, but this does not necessarily mean that they commit moral wrongs or engage in unethical behavior in their daily lives. It can be said that individuals who prioritize utility over higher realms are more prone to committing moral wrongs, especially in critical moments. In practical life, we observe that some individuals, despite having lower realms, do not necessarily commit moral wrongs.

It can be said that such individuals have become commonplace in modern society, and their realms are even rationalized as what Max Weber referred to as the "spirit of capitalism." This distinction could indeed be considered a fundamental difference between classical and modern personalities, or between aristocratic and common personalities. For modern individuals, can we still expect higher realms beyond lawful behavior? In other words, can we still propose moral and super-moral realms beyond lawful behavior? In this era, individuals who embody the moral realm of a cultured individual are quite rare. Does it still make sense to strive for super-moral realms? *A New Treatise on the Way of Life* requires that human behavior be in accordance with moral rules, while *New Origins of Humanity* demands that human behavior be based on moral principles. It also suggests that individuals can attain higher realms, namely, the realm of heaven and earth, which is "beyond" the moral realm. In today's context, does this still hold significance?

It can be argued that the significance of moral and super-moral realms should be affirmed. Pursuing spiritual realms beyond utilitarianism and lawful behavior is an intrinsic requirement of human nature and spirit. Internally, individuals often find themselves unsatisfied with the utilitarian realm limited to lawful behavior, and the inherent human quest for higher realms in terms of character exceeds the common standard in modern society. This reflects the collective pursuit and ideal of personal development that humanity has accumulated over thousands of years of existence. The pursuit of excellence in one's endeavors and the quest for spiritual transcendence need not be in conflict. For instance, when a writer strives to produce their best novel, it is not driven by utilitarianism or personal desires but rather a reasonable aspiration for the flourishing and development of one's life.

Bernard Williams remarked, "Our deepest ethical convictions often resemble more the ethical thought of ancient Greece than the moral systems of the later Enlightenment," and, "modern ethics and contemporary moral philosophy have transformed the ancient ethical question of 'How should I live?' into 'What moral rules should people obey?'"[83] It can be argued that Feng's *New Origins of Humanity* and his theory of realms are more aligned with the thinking of ancient ethics, because modern moral philosophy has largely sidelined questions of life's meaning and states of consciousness, often becoming constrained by the spirit of "capitalism." I believe that the ethics of the realm continues to hold significant relevance in contemporary society and is worth further development.

The ethics of realm was established by Feng, and as a form of ethics, it should indeed be further refined and diversified. More scholars should be conducting research and contributing to the development of this field. Here, I would like to briefly propose some improvements and modifications to Feng's theory of states of consciousness in light of contemporary life. Building upon his concept of states of consciousness as a framework for life, the first modification is to eliminate what he referred to as the natural realm. Instead, we can consider the utilitarian realm of the majority of ordinary individuals as the lowest level of realms. Within this category, we can further distinguish between several sub-levels, including self-serving at the expense of others, self-serving with a strong heart but without harming others, and having a self-serving disposition without being overly forceful. In contemporary society, it is important to be tolerant and appreciative of the generally reasonable utilitarian states of consciousness. Secondly, we can introduce the concept of a non-utilitarian realm as the second level of consciousness, which can also be divided into several sub-levels. This includes the Confucian moral realm, the Daoist natural realm, and the Buddhist formless realm. These higher realms serve as remedies for the utilitarian realm and contribute to the transformation of one's spiritual realm of being. Then, we can introduce the concept of an ultimate caring realm as the third level of realms. This can also be subdivided into several layers, including a realm of social ideals, a realm of oneness with all things, and a realm encompassing various Eastern and Western religious traditions throughout history. These higher realms represent more elevated spiritual realms. When referring to "higher" in this context, we do not necessarily mean the difficulty of achieving these states of consciousness at the individual level. It also implies the potential for these states to have a broad influence on society and the capacity for significant transformative effects. As a result, in our modified framework, there are three levels, comprising a total of nine realms.

This framework takes the utilitarian realm of ordinary individuals as the lowest level. Above the utilitarian realm, the moral realm negates utilitarianism, the natural realm diminishes utilitarianism, and the formless realm eliminates utilitarianism. These states represent inherent spiritual systems within Chinese culture aimed at countering utilitarian inclinations of the heart. The ultimate caring realm, as mentioned here, encompasses beliefs from religions beyond Confucianism, Buddhism, and Daoism, particularly Western religions. It also includes other political and societal beliefs, such as the belief in Communism. The distinctive feature of faith is its ability to swiftly transform the mundane, utilitarian realm of life and elevate the believer's spiritual realm, resulting in a profound renewal. This renewal brings forth a new sense of life purpose and a completely fresh perspective on life. Feng's book *New Origins of Humanity* does not explicitly mention this faith-based realm, and his reflections on *New Origins of Humanity* after 1949 appear to have overlooked this aspect. In hindsight, he could have adjusted the theory of realms in *New Origins of Humanity* to accommodate the significant spiritual changes brought about by the early stages of the People's Republic of China and the revolutionary fervor among young people, including incorporating a realm related to revolutionary faith. While a revolutionary realm may differ from moral and religious realms, and a specific revolutionary realm may not necessarily be enduring like certain religious faith realms, it can still have a similarly significant impact on transforming and reshaping individuals' states of consciousness. It seems that Feng remained steadfast in explaining new realities using the old framework and missed opportunities for improvements or adaptations to his previous theories.

October 6, 2015

With this text, we commemorate the 120th anniversary of Mr. Feng Youlan's birthday.

Notes

1. In Feng Youlan's *Forty Years of Retrospect*, there is a section titled "Questioning and Inquiring," in which he expresses some confusion regarding the criticism of the "theory of realms" in *New Origins of Humanity*. *Complete Works of Sansongtang*, vol. 14 (Henan People's Publishing House, 2000), 1066.
2. This mainly refers to the understanding of the "Great Unity" in *New Origins of Humanity*, as discussed in the preface to *Sansongtang*.
3. *Collected Works of Feng Youlan*, vol. 4 (Changchun Publishing House, 2008), 137.
4. Ibid., 139.
5. Ibid., 140.
6. Ibid., 141.
7. Ibid., 142.
8. Ibid., 142.
9. Ibid., 143.
10. Ibid.
11. "Philosophy of Life," in *Complete Works of Sansongtang*, vol. 1, 3rd ed. (Zhonghua Book Company, 2014), 36.
12. "Mysticism in Chinese Philosophy," in *Collected Works of Sansongtang*, 58.
13. *Collected Works of Feng Youlan*, vol. 5 (Changchun Publishing House, 2008), 7.
14. *Complete Works of Sansongtang*, vol. 14 (Henan People's Publishing House, 2000), 1051.
15. *Collected Works of Feng Youlan*, vol. 5, 5.
16. Ibid., 9.
17. Ibid., 14.
18. Ibid., 18.

19. *Collected Works of Feng Youlan,* vol. 5, 18.
20. Ibid., 19.
21. Ibid., 20.
22. Ibid., 23.
23. Ibid.
24. Ibid., 30.
25. Ibid., 28.
26. Ibid., 29.
27. Ibid.
28. Ibid.
29. Ibid., 30.
30. Ibid., 34.
31. Ibid., 35.
32. Ibid., 37.
33. Ibid., 38.
34. Ibid.
35. Ibid., 40.
36. Ibid., 43.
37. Ibid., 31.
38. Xiong Shili pointed this out in a letter to Feng.
39. *Collected Works of Feng Youlan,* vol. 5, 43.
40. Ibid., 44.
41. Ibid., 45.
42. Ibid., 45.
43. Ibid., 50.
44. Ibid., 53
45. Ibid., 49.
46. Ibid., 50.
47. Ibid., 51.
48. Ibid., 53.
49. Ibid., 55.
50. Ibid.
51. Ibid., 56.
52. Ibid.
53. Ibid., 56–57.
54. Ibid., 57.
55. Ibid.
56. Ibid., 58.
57. Ibid., 59.
58. Ibid., 29.
59. Ibid., 57.
60. Ibid., 29.
61. Ibid., 59.

62. *Collected Works of Feng Youlan*, vol. 5, 63.
63. Ibid., 64.
64. Ibid.
65. Ibid.
66. Ibid., 65.
67. Ibid., 66.
68. Ibid.
69. Ibid., 68.
70. Ibid., 45.
71. Ibid., 45.
72. Ibid., 46.
73. Ibid., 32.
74. Ibid., 7.
75. Ibid., 77.
76. Ibid., 78.
77. Ibid., 79.
78. Ibid., 80.
79. Ibid., 80–81.
80. Ibid., 81.
81. Ibid., 82.
82. "Letter to Xiong Shili," in *Complete Works of Sansongtang*, vol. 14, 34.
83. Bernard Williams, *Moral Luck*, trans. Xu Xiangdong (Shanghai Translation Publishing House, 2007), 10, 15.

Afterword to the *Collected Works of Chen Lai* in the *Boya Yinghua* Series

I am grateful for the compilation of my academic works, previously published as the *Collected Academic Works of Chen Lai* in twelve volumes by the Sanlian Bookstore. There is no need to express my gratitude further. Currently, the copyright for this collection by Sanlian Bookstore is about to expire, and Peking University Press has expressed interest in publishing a hardcover edition of my works in the *Boya Yinghua* series. This news has taken me by surprise, and I am extremely pleased.

I served at Peking University for thirty years, and starting in 2004, the university entrusted me with the responsibility of overseeing the work of the publishing house. As a result, I have formed a unique bond with Peking University Press. Even after I moved to Tsinghua University in 2009, I continued to collaborate with Peking University Press and published books such as *Confucius and the Modern World, Beijing · Confucianism · University, From the World of Thought to the World of History*, and others. In the past two years, *The Realm of Existence and Non-existence* and *Interpretation and Reconstruction* were also published as hardcover editions in the *Boya Yinghua* series by Peking University Press and received a warm welcome from readers. The publication of this hardcover edition of my collected works holds special significance for me, as it reflects the friendship and warmth extended to an old friend by Peking University Press, and I am deeply touched by this gesture.

Now, Peking University Press plans to publish my other works, in addition to *The Realm of Existence and Non-existence* and *Interpretation and Reconstruction*, as part of the *Boya Yinghua* series. There are some changes in the collection of works published by Peking University Press compared to the Sanlian edition. *The Ancient Religion and Ethics: The Roots of Confucian Thought* published in this series is an expanded edition with an additional chapter. *The World of Ancient Thought and Culture: Religion, Ethics, and Social Thought in the Spring and Autumn Period* includes a commentary by Yu Dunkang. *The World of Zhu Xi's Learning* is based on the Zhu Xi section of *Research on the History of Modern Chinese Thought* and includes recent papers on Zhu Xi that have been combined into one volume. *Modern Confucian Philosophy* is an expanded and revised edition of *The Quest for Modern Chinese Philosophy*. *Research on Early Modern East Asian Confucianism* is an expanded edition of *Nine Essays on East Asian Confucianism*. The other books, such as *Research on Bamboo and Silk Texts: The Five Elements and Bamboo Slips, Research on Zhu Xi's Philosophy, Chronological Verification of Zhu Xi's Correspondence* (revised edition), *The Realm of Existence and Non-existence: The Philosophy of Wang Yangming's Spirit, Interpretation and Reconstruction: The Philosophical Spirit of Wang Chongshan, Neo-Confucianism in the Song Dynasty, A Course in the History of Philosophy in the Song, Yuan, and Ming Dynasties*, and *Tradition and Modernity: The Horizon of Humanism*, remain unchanged.

I sincerely thank Zhang Fengzhu and other leaders of the publishing house, as well as friends like Tian Wei and the editors, for giving me the honor of presenting my collected works published by Peking University Press to the readers.

Chen Lai
May 26, 2016

Index

A

absorption of substance into function, 30
agnosticism, 315–16
ālayavijñāna (eighth consciousness), 83–86, 202
"all matters within the universe are part of the duty of one's nature," 75–76. *See also* "nothing beyond oneself"
arising, ceasing dharma, 19. *See also* non-arising, non-ceasing dharma
attaining wisdom, 49–50, 52
Awakening of Faith in the Mahāyāna, 81–87, 89, 92

B

Bentham, Jeremy, 346, 361–62
Bergson, Henri, 4, 30, 113, 117, 173, 310, 314, 319
bi (闢), 28–29, 42–44, 54. *See also qian*
Book of Changes (*I Ching*), 4, 17–18, 21–23, 27, 44–45, 53, 65–66, 77, 80, 294, 298

C

Cao Mufan, 222–23, 227, 229
change, 11, 14, 23, 29–30, 59, 64–68, 79, 81–82, 86, 100, 107, 110, 120, 123, 140, 148, 156–57, 170–71, 184–85, 193, 197, 230, 266, 271, 273, 275, 278, 281–85, 312, 325, 342, 376
Chan school, 73, 82–84, 92
Characteristics school, 86
Cheng-Zhu school, 22, 58, 73, 258
  Cheng Hao, 79, 259, 327, 330–32, 334–36, 339, 377
  Cheng Yi, 21–22, 59–60, 69, 79, 332
  Zhu Xi, 22, 50, 53–54, 61–62, 69, 206, 208–9, 244, 255, 259, 313, 315, 350, 366, 368, 386
circumstance(s), 14, 78, 82–84, 86, 88–89, 91, 107–8, 133, 207, 213, 295–96, 299, 329, 334–35
Confucianism, 1–4, 9, 11–13, 17–18, 20, 46, 53–55, 57, 61, 70, 73, 90, 92, 111, 127–28, 130, 144, 147, 153–54, 172, 179, 185, 192, 197–206, 208, 211–13, 217, 220–21, 237–38, 241, 244–45, 266, 291–92, 295–97, 300–301, 312–13, 317, 329–30, 336–37, 346, 355, 371–73, 375, 378–79, 381, 385–86
Confucius, 11, 20, 25, 27–28, 36, 58, 66, 99, 114, 117–18, 136, 138–40, 153–54, 184–85, 199, 203–7, 212, 271–72, 295, 313, 317, 325–26, 332, 351, 376, 385
consciousness, 4, 7–8, 13, 29, 36–41, 44, 46, 48–49, 80, 82–86, 88–92, 102–3, 131–32, 136, 155, 160, 168, 179, 185, 188, 201–2, 211, 220, 226, 236–37, 244, 275, 284, 310, 315–16, 338, 341–42, 346–52, 355–58, 360, 371, 375–82

constancy, 64–68, 79–82, 85
corvée system, 141
cosmology, 1, 3–6, 8, 10–12, 14, 35–36, 43–44, 46, 69, 154, 311–12

D

Daoism, 2–3, 48, 52, 73, 199, 211, 213, 217, 244, 296–97, 300, 310, 312–13, 317, 319–20, 330, 332–33, 335, 337–39, 344, 346, 355–57, 362, 366, 375, 377–79, 381
Duke of Zhou, 139–40

E

Easternization, 100–101, 117–18
emotionlessness, 328, 335–36
empirical investigation, 46–47
Emptiness school, 19, 23. *See also* Existence school
epistemology, 6–7, 14, 40, 42, 53–54, 311, 313, 315, 342
eternalism, 65–66, 79–80
ethical cultivation, 46–47
Existence school, 19
experiencing the body, 218–21

F

faxiang (dharma character), 18–19
faxing (dharma nature), 18–19
Feng Youlan, 91–92, 115, 129, 138, 148, 249, 261–62, 264, 268, 275, 279, 285, 289, 291, 306, 309, 311–12, 317–18, 325, 332, 339, 341–42, 350, 382
- art of life, 325–26, 329
- four realms, 344–45, 352, 355–56
  - moral realm, 344, 346, 352, 354–55, 363, 367–68, 370–71, 373–75, 379–81
  - natural realm, 318, 329, 346, 352–53, 355–60, 367–68, 370–71, 373, 377–78, 381
  - realm of heaven and earth, 186, 314, 317–20, 338, 344–46, 352, 354–56, 367, 374–80
  - utilitarian realm, 305, 344, 351–55, 360–68, 373, 375, 380–82
- matter-expression model, 284–85
- "no feelings and no burdens," 338
- objects in reality, 249–51, 256
- principles on things, 253–54
- "this is a dog," 250–51
- "this is square," 252
- understanding and consciousness, 236, 347–52, 355, 357, 379
- works
  - *Comparative Study of Life Ideals, A*, 266–67, 269, 310, 345
  - *History of Chinese Philosophy, A*, 263, 267, 269, 310, 313–16, 332, 334
  - *New Discussions*, 271, 280–81
  - *New Neo-Confucianism*, 249–61, 272, 276, 279–80, 294, 302, 314, 316, 318, 321, 341–44, 346, 348, 379
  - *New Origins of Humanity*, 261, 279, 303–6, 314, 316, 318, 334, 336, 338–39, 341–42, 344–48, 350, 352, 356, 364, 367–68, 374, 376–82
  - *New Treatise on Practical Affairs, A*, 261–63, 269–77, 279, 281, 283–84, 289, 291, 303, 305, 342
  - *New Treatise on the Nature of Dao, A*, 251, 254, 256–58, 261, 279, 346
  - *New Treatise on the Way of Life, A*, 261, 289–95, 299–306, 334, 336, 338, 342, 363, 365, 378, 380
  - *Philosophy of Life*, 289–90, 310–16, 318, 329, 342, 345–46
  - *Sansongtang: An Account of My Life*, 262

Four Dharmas, 224–29, 240, 242–43
"function beginning from substance," 63–64, 68–69. *See also* "function returning to substance"
"function returning to substance," 63–64, 68–69
fundamentalism, 13

G

Gongga Rinpoche, 221, 223–24, 226–27, 229, 232–33, 235, 237
Great Function, 28–30, 42, 69
Great Seal, 221, 223, 225–35, 237–38, 240–43

H

habitual mind, 36–39, 41–42, 46, 53
habituation, 36–42, 44
Hegel, Georg Wilhelm Friedrich, 14, 63, 178, 250, 377
Huayan school, 63, 66, 73, 82–85, 89, 92, 348

Huineng, 83–84, 92
- *Platform Sutra of the Sixth Patriarch, The*, 84, 92, 238–39, 333

Hundred Syllable Mantra, 224–25, 227–28

I

ice-water metaphor, 27
idealism, 15, 43, 73, 81–82, 86, 90, 183–84, 312, 314–15, 356
Industrial Revolution, 106, 129, 270–71, 274–75
inherent source(s), 27, 29–30
innate clarity, 39
interconnectedness, 66, 167–69, 171, 187, 198, 283–84
internal transcendence, 92–93
intuition, 46–47, 49, 310, 314–15, 318–20, 348, 367

J

James, William, 311–13, 315–16
Jiang Zizhai, 219

K

Kant, Immanuel, 14, 315, 319–20, 364, 371–73
karma, 38, 84, 210, 225
kun, 30, 42, 44–45, 59

L

La Jeunesse (*New Youth*), 97, 101, 268
Liang Qichao, 70, 113–14
Liang Shuming, 1–5, 8–13, 58, 73, 93, 97–98, 100–101, 103, 112, 114–15, 117, 120–22, 127, 129, 144, 146, 151, 177, 182, 189, 193, 197, 208, 213, 217, 221–22, 243, 262, 266–68, 274–75, 310, 312
- cultural pluralism, 118, 122
- ethics-oriented society, 130, 132–34, 137–39, 147
- *Human Nature and Human Life*, 151–55, 169, 173–74, 177–78, 180, 183, 206, 227
- Three Directions Theory, 105, 107
- Three Fundamental Issues of Human Life, 177, 180
- works
  - *Eastern and Western Cultures and Their Philosophies*, 97–99, 114, 120–21, 127, 145, 151–52, 172, 177, 179–81, 186, 268
  - *Essence of Chinese Culture*, 127–28, 144, 146, 152, 180, 184, 187–88, 224, 232
  - *Final Awakening of the Chinese National Self-Salvation Movement, The* (*Essays on Village Governance*), 177, 180, 189
  - *Overview of Eastern Scholarship, An*, 199, 203, 211

li (principles), 22, 44, 58–62, 77
love of wisdom, 2, 10
Lu-Wang school, 41, 50, 53
- Lu Jiuyuan, 62, 73–74, 86, 92, 197
- Wang Yangming, 24–25, 41–42, 49–51, 53–54, 61–62, 73, 86, 92, 205, 213, 221, 313, 328, 330–31, 333, 336, 339, 377, 386

M

Mahayana Buddhism, 17–19, 23
Marx, Karl, 14, 112, 270, 274–75, 281–82, 284–86
Master Nenghai, 218, 223
materiality, 28–29, 40, 256. *See also* spirituality
May Fourth Movement, 31, 35, 94, 97, 112, 122–23, 146, 258, 262–63, 265, 269, 275, 282–83, 285, 312
Ma Yifu, 1, 3, 11–13, 57–64, 67–70, 73–74, 76–77, 79, 81, 84, 86, 92–93, 169, 243, 275
- "all vital energy makes principles, and all principles make vital energy," 67, 69
- theory of mind and matter, 53, 73–74, 76, 81–82, 86, 90
- theory of principles and vital energy, 60–61, 73, 79, 249

Mencius, 5, 36–37, 41, 66–67, 78, 136, 138, 178–79, 199, 205–7, 237, 272, 295, 313, 315, 330, 349, 358–59, 370, 373, 379
metaphysics, 7, 10, 14, 27, 166, 249, 254, 258–60, 271, 278, 319–22, 332, 337–39, 342
Mianren Academy, 218, 220, 223, 233
mingji, 41–42
multiculturalism, 13–14, 99, 119
myriad dharmas, 23, 25–26, 77
mysticism, 309–2, 338–39, 345–46, 376

N

Nature school, 86

Neo-Confucianism, 1–2, 22, 35–36, 38, 48, 52, 54–55, 58–61, 64–65, 69, 73, 92, 173, 179, 244, 249–61, 272, 276, 279–80, 292, 294, 302, 304, 314, 316, 318, 321–22, 330–31, 335, 337–38, 341–44, 346, 348, 351, 365, 369, 379, 386
New Culture Movement, 97–98, 100, 107, 112, 114–15, 122–23, 151, 187, 264, 266, 268, 290
new realism, 250–51, 257–58, 271–72, 280, 309–10, 315–16, 341
nihilism, 64–66, 79–80. *See also* eternalism
non-arising, non-ceasing dharma, 19
"nothing beyond oneself," 76
"nothing beyond the mind," 74–75, 77–79, 81, 86, 90

O

ocean-waves metaphor, 27
On Change, 17, 23, 28–30, 35
"one mind with two doors," 81, 83–84
ontology, 1, 3–8, 10–11, 14, 21, 27, 30, 47, 54, 61, 64, 69, 81, 90, 93, 166–69, 171, 212, 311, 319, 379
original mind, 11, 36–37, 41–44, 46–47, 53. *See also* habitual mind
Ouyang Jingwu, 3, 10

P

patrimonial system, 141. *See also* property system
"personal experience apart from words," 8, 10
Platonism, 251, 253
pragmatism, 147, 300, 309, 315–16
primary cause, 20
property system, 143
pure experience, 310–13, 315, 318, 374

Q

qian, 29–30, 42–45, 54, 59, 65. *See also kun*
qi (vital energy), 22, 44, 58–62, 68, 77–78, 84, 256–57, 259. *See also li* (principles)

R

rational speculation, 2
reason and rationality, 139, 155, 164–66, 168, 206
residual force(s), 37–39, 41
"Reversal is the movement of the Way," 45
righteousness, 12, 44, 57, 281, 292, 304, 336, 354, 358–59, 363, 368–71

S

School of Mind, 51, 53, 61, 73, 76, 92–94, 169
science and democracy, 101, 103–5, 111, 116–17, 121–22, 137, 151, 290
seeds, 19, 38–41
self-attachment, 200–202
self-awareness, 8, 160–61, 164–65, 168–72, 198–99, 206–8, 239, 244, 258, 310, 344–45, 347–50, 358, 360
self-cultivation, 5–12, 46, 53, 197–201, 203–10, 212–14
self-examination, 185, 205–10, 230
selfless emotions, 163–64, 172
self-reflection, 8, 12, 47, 49–50, 172, 199, 209, 219, 227, 260
simplicity, 64–67, 79–80, 350, 357
Six Arts, 13–14
sixth consciousness, 8, 13, 201–2
social structure, 127, 129–30, 132, 134–35, 138, 144–45, 147–48, 152, 186–87, 269
Spinoza, Baruch, 30–31, 311, 314, 320, 322, 326
spirituality, 28–29, 172, 351
substance and function, 1, 4, 17–28, 30–31, 35–36, 42–44, 53, 63–69, 93, 259–60, 270, 281–86
  "function is substance," 24–25, 27, 30, 65, 69
  non-duality of, 18–19, 21–24, 26, 35, 53, 66
  "substance is function," 24–25, 27, 30, 65, 69
  theory of, 19, 21, 23, 31, 35–36, 42–44, 63–67, 69
  unity of, 4, 17–18, 21–26, 28, 30, 43, 259–60

T

Tagore, 115, 264, 268
taiji (supreme ultimate), 22, 59–60, 62, 77

U

unity of
  motion and stillness, 330–31, 334
  principles and vital energy, 66–67
  wisdom and knowledge, 48, 51–54
universal life, 43–44, 166–68, 171

V

Vajra Yogini, 227–30, 233–36, 238–39, 241

W

Wang Bi, 327–28, 331–32, 335, 337
Weber, Max, 51, 127, 130, 140–48, 184, 302–3, 380
  Religion of China: Confucianism and Taoism, The, 127–28, 144, 147
Westernization, 97, 99–101, 103–8, 111, 114, 117, 120, 269, 271, 273–75, 277, 281–83, 285

X

xi (翕), 28–29, 42–43. *See also kun*
Xiong Shili, 1–15, 17–20, 22–23, 25, 28–31, 35–36, 39, 41, 51, 58, 63, 69, 73, 86, 91–92, 154, 169, 208, 218, 243, 275, 338–39, 376–77
  onto-cosmology, 2
  theory of *mingxin*, 35–36, 43, 46, 48, 51, 53
  works
    New Treatise on Consciousness-Only, A, 8, 17, 35–36, 48, 86, 88
    Treatise on Substance and Function, A, 17, 21, 26, 30, 35–36

Y

yang, 5, 22, 60, 64, 77, 255, 259, 332. *See also yin*
yin, 5, 22, 60, 64, 77, 255, 259, 332
Yogācāra school, 19, 53, 83–84, 86

Z

Zhang Dongsun, 6–7, 10, 230, 235
zhenru (suchness), 18–19
Zhuangzi, 213, 312–13, 326–27, 330, 332, 335, 344–45

ABOUT THE AUTHOR

Born in 1952, Chen Lai serves as Dean of the Tsinghua Academy of Chinese Learning, Deputy Director of the Academic Committee of Tsinghua University, and Professor of the Department of Philosophy of Tsinghua University, while also serving as President of China Philosophy History Association, Librarian of the Central Museum of Literature and History, member of the Social Sciences Committee of the Ministry of Education, Chairman of the Zhuzi Society, and Vice Chairman of the International Confucian Association, among other roles.